NEW!

7th edition

BABY

BARGAINS

S E C R E T S

to saving 20% to 50% on
baby furniture, equipment,
clothes, toys, maternity wear
and much, much more!

Denise & Alan Fields
Authors of the Best-Seller
Bridal Bargains

Copyright Page and Carbon-Neutral Credits

Saxophone, lead guitar and breast-feeding by Denise Fields
Drums, rhythm guitar and father stuff by Alan Fields
Congas on "Grandparents" by
Max & Helen Coopwood, Howard & Patti Fields
Cover/interior design and keyboard solo by Epicenter Creative
Screaming guitar solos on "(Let's Go) Perego" by Charles & Arthur Troy
Additional guitar work on "Diaper Changing Blues" by Todd Snider
Backing vocals on "(She's Got A) LATCH Car Seat" by Ric Ocasek
Band photography by Moses Street

*This book was written to the music of Barenaked Ladies,
which probably explains a lot.*

To order this book, call 1-800-888-0385. Or send $17.95 plus $3 shipping to Windsor Peak Press, 436 Pine Street, Boulder, CO 80302. Questions or comments? Please call the authors at (303) 442-8792. Or fax them a note at (303) 442-3744. Or write to them at the above address in Boulder, Colorado. E-mail the authors at authors@babybargains.com.

Learn more about this book online at www.BabyBargains.com

Distributed to the book trade by National Book Network, 800-462-6420.

Library Cataloging in Publication Data

Fields, Denise
Fields, Alan
    Baby Bargains: Secrets to saving 20% to 50% on baby furniture, equipment, clothes, toys maternity wear and much, much more/ Denise & Alan Fields
    608 pages.
    Includes index.
    ISBN 978-1-889392-25-7
    1. Child Care—Handbooks, manuals, etc. 2. Infants' supplies—Purchasing—United States, Canada, Directories. 3. Children's paraphernalia—Purchasing—Handbooks, manuals. 4. Product Safety—Handbooks, manuals. 5. Consumer education.
    649'.122'0296—dc20. 2008.

We miss you Dee Dee.

Version 7.1

CONTENTS

Chapter 1

"IT'S GOING TO CHANGE YOUR LIFE"

Chapter 2

NURSERY NECESSITIES: CRIBS, DRESSERS & MORE

Chapter 3

BABY BEDDING & DECOR

Chapter 4

THE REALITY LAYETTE: LITTLE CLOTHES FOR LITTLE PRICES

Chapter 5

MATERNITY/NURSING CLOTHES

Chapter 6

FEEDING: BREASTFEEDING, BOTTLES, HIGH CHAIRS

Chapter 7

AROUND THE HOUSE: MONITORS, DIAPER PAILS, SAFETY & MORE

Chapter 8

CAR SEATS

Chapter 9

STROLLERS, DIAPER BAGS, CARRIERS AND OTHER TO GO GEAR

Chapter 10

CHILD CARE: OPTIONS, COSTS & MORE

Chapter 11

CONCLUSION: WHAT DOES IT ALL MEAN?

ICONS

 **Getting Started**

 **Money-Saving Secrets**

 **Sources**

 **Best Buys**

 **Parents In Cyberspace**

 **The Name Game**

 **What Are You Buying?**

 **Do it By Mail**

 **Safe & Sound**

 **Email from the Real World**

 **Smart Shopper**

 **More Money Buys You . . .**

 **Wastes of Money**

 **Bottom Line**

CHAPTER 1

CHANGE YOUR LIFE!

"It's Going to Change Your Life!"

Inside this chapter

That had to be the silliest comment we heard while we were pregnant with our first baby. Believe it or not, we even heard this refrain more often than "Are you having a boy or a girl?" and "I'm sorry. Your insurance doesn't cover that." For the friends and relatives of first-time parents out there, we'd like to point out that this is a pretty silly thing to say. Of course, we knew that a baby was going to change our lives. What we didn't realize was how much a baby was going to change our pocketbook.

Oh sure, we knew that we'd have to buy triple our weight in diapers and be subjected to dangerously high levels of the Wiggles. What we didn't expect was the endless pitches for cribs, gear, toys, clothing and other items parents are required to purchase by FEDERAL BABY LAW.

We quickly learned that having a baby is like popping on the Juvenile Amusement Park Ride from Consumer Hell. Once that egg is fertilized, you're whisked off to the Pirates of the Crib ride. Then it's on to marvel at the little elves in StrollerLand, imploring you to buy brands with names you can't pronounce. Finally, you take a trip to Magic Car Seat Mountain, where the confusion is so real, it's scary.

Consider us your tour guides—the Yogi Bear to your Boo Boo Bear, the Fred to your Ethel, the . . . well, you get the idea. Before we enter BabyLand, let's take a look at the Four Truths That No One Tells You About Buying Stuff For Baby.

The Four Truths That No One Tells You About Buying Stuff for Baby

1 **BABIES DON'T CARE IF THEY'RE WEARING DESIGNER CLOTHES OR SLEEPING ON DESIGNER SHEETS.** Let's be realistic. Babies just want to be comfortable. They can't even distinguish between the liberals and conservatives on "Meet the Press," so how would they ever be able to tell the difference between Baby Gucci crib bedding and another less famous brand that's just as comfortable, but 70% less expensive? Our focus is on making your baby happy—at a price that won't break the bank.

2 **YOUR BABY'S SAFETY IS MUCH MORE IMPORTANT THAN YOUR CONVENIENCE.** Here are the scary facts: 59,800 babies per year are injured (and 61 deaths are caused) by juvenile products, according to government estimates. Each chapter of this book has a section called "Safe & Sound," which arms you with in-depth advice on keeping your baby out of trouble. We'll tell you which products we think are dangerous and how to safely use other potentially hazardous products.

3 **MURPHY'S LAW OF BABY TOYS SAYS YOUR BABY'S HAPPINESS WITH A TOY IS INVERSELY RELATED TO THE TOY'S PRICE.** Buy a $200 shiny new wagon with anti-lock brakes, and odds are baby just wants to play with the box it came in. In recognition of this reality, we've included "wastes of money" in each chapter that will steer you away from frivolous items.

4 **IT'S GOING TO COST MORE THAN YOU THINK.** Whatever amount of money you budget for your baby, get ready to spend more. Here's a breakdown of the average costs of bringing a baby into the world today:

The Average Cost of Having a Baby

(based on industry estimates for a child from birth to age one)

Crib, mattress, dresser, rocker	$1600
Bedding / Decor	$315
Baby Clothes	$525
Disposable Diapers	$630
Maternity/Nursing Clothes	$1260
Nursery items, high chair, toys	$425
Baby Food / Formula	$950
Stroller, Car Seats, Carrier	$425
Miscellaneous	$525

TOTAL **$6,655**

The above figures are based on buying name brand products at regular retail prices. We surveyed over 1000 parents to arrive at these estimates.

Bedding/Decor includes not only bedding items but also lamps, wallpaper, and so on for your baby's nursery. Baby Food/Formula assumes you'd breastfeed for the first six months and then feed baby jarred baby food ($425) and formula ($525) until age one. If you plan to bottle-feed instead of breastfeed, add another $525 on to that figure. (Of course, the goal is to breastfeed your baby as long as possible—one year is a good target.)

Sure, you do get an automatic tax write-off for that bundle of joy, but that only amounts to about $3200 this year (plus you also get an additional $1000 child care tax credit, depending on your income). But those tax goodies won't nearly offset the actual cost of raising a child. And as you probably realize, our cost chart is missing some expensive "extras" . . . like medical bills, childcare, saving for college and more. Here's an overview of what can add to the tab:

◆ ***Medical/adoption bills.*** Yes, for most couples, conceiving a child is free (although some may argue about that). But not everyone is that lucky—fertility treatments for the estimated 10% to 15% of couples who can't conceive naturally can run $10,000 to $20,000 a try (although there are less expensive treatments out there as well). Only a handful of states require health insurance policies to cover infertility—hence, the vast majority of couples who face this challenge do so without insurance and must pay those costs out of pocket. Or if their insurance covers infertility, it may just pay for the infertility diagnosis but not treatments. Bottom line: it is not uncommon for couples to spend upwards of $40,000 on infertility treatments (again, check with your doctor for less expensive alternatives).

Besides the normal prenatal visits to the doctor, the biggest medical bill is for the birth—about $7090 for a "normal" delivery at a hospital. The same study (Expenditures on Children by Families, 2005 annual report by the US Dept. of Agriculture) pegs the cost of a Caesarean at $11,450. Medical bills for first year routine check-ups and immunizations can cost $2500 or more. Yes, insurance typically picks up most of those costs, but there are many children (15% of the total births this year) that are born without any coverage. So, if you have insurance, count yourself among the lucky.

Couples who adopt a baby typically face fees and expenses that range from $5,000 to $40,000. Check out a great website, www.costs.adoption.com, for cost details for all types of adoptions. There is a $10,000 federal tax credit that offsets some adoption expenses—check with your tax preparer for details (see IRS publication 968, "Tax Benefits for Adoption"). One bargain for parents who are considering an overseas adoption: some airlines now offer adopting parents a break on airfares. Several airlines offer 50% or more discounts off full coach fares (the fares adopting parents have to use, as most adoptions are done on short notice). The baby's one-way fare back home is also discounted. Always ask your airline if they have an adoption fare deal.

◆ **Child Care.** According to the Department of Agriculture, the average cost of childcare for a three to five-year old child is $1970 per year. But those costs seemed low to us—our research on child care costs (detailed in chapter 10 later in this book) revealed family daycare runs $6000 to $15,000 and center care can cost up to $13,000 per year. What about a nanny? Most run $10,000 to $20,000 in average cities, but that depends on whether they are live-in or not. In high cost cities like New York or San Francisco, childcare costs for families can top $30,000 a year.

◆ **Housing.** Those neighborhoods with the best schools aren't cheap. The government estimates the average middle-class family with one child will spend an extra $63,000 on shelter until the child is 18. The average annual cost of housing one child is $2770 to $5960, according to government estimates.

◆ **Transportation.** Yes, a brand new minivan today tops $25,000 and some models approach $40,000. All those trips to daycare (and later, the mall) add up—the government says average parents will spend $32,580 to transport a child to all those required activities until the age of 18.

◆ **And more.** Additional expenses that parents face include health care (the government says even the average, healthy child can rack up $14,460 in medical bills for the first 18 years), clothing (if you think baby clothes are pricey, check out the $9870 bill the average kid racks up in clothes and education (private school, anyone?).

The bottom line. If you're still with us, let's see what the government says is the GRAND TOTAL of expenses to raise a baby to age 18. Are you sitting down? Try $190,980. And that's for middle class Americans. More affluent parents spend $279,450. Yes, there are economies of scale if you add more children—but there's a limit to the savings. On average, each additional child costs just 24% less than a single child.

But wait! The government leaves two critical costs out of its equation: saving for college and lost wages from a parent who stays at home. Let's look at both:

◆ **College.** Price college tuition lately? Even if you forget about Harvard, the cost of attending a state school today is staggering. And with college costs expected to continue to rise in the future, you'll have to put away $375 each month for baby's college fund if you start at birth to pay for the average state school's four-year program (tuition plus room and board). Wait longer to get started and the costs rise rapidly. T Rowe Price (troweprice.com) has an excellent free "college planner" feature on their web site that lets you compare savings plans for public versus private schools. Fidelity also has a college cost calculator that is easy to use (fidelity.com; go to Retirement & Guidance and then College).

◆ **Lost wages.** Having a baby is a financial double-whammy— not only are your expenses rising, but your income drops. Why? At least one parent will have to take off time to care for the baby. Yes, lost wages could be a short six-week maternity leave . . . or the next 18 years for a stay-at-home parent.

Hence, when you add in saving for college and lost wages for a stay-at-home parent for 18 years, the cost of raising an average middle class child to age 18 will run $1,589,793. Amazing, eh?

(Source: the above numbers are from the 2005 "Expenditures on Children by Families" by the US Dept of Agriculture.

Reality Check: Does it Really Cost that Much to Have a Baby?

Now that we've thoroughly scared you enough to inquire whether the stork accepts returns, we should point out that children do NOT have to cost that much. Even if we focus just on the first year, you don't have to spend $6655 on baby gear. And that's what this book is all about: how to save money and still buy the best. Follow all the tips in this book, and we estimate the first year will cost you $4038. Yes, that's a savings of over $2600!

Now, at this point, you might be saying "That's impossible! I suppose you'll recommend buying all the cheap stuff, from polyester clothes to no-name cribs." On the contrary, we'll show you how to get *quality* name brands and safe products at discount prices. Most importantly, you will learn how to not WASTE your money on dubious gear. And much more. Yes, we've got the maximum number of bargains allowed by federal law.

A word on bargain shopping: when interviewing hundreds of parents for this book, we realized bargain seekers fall into two frugal camps. There's the "do-it-yourself" crowd and the "quality at a discount" group. As the name implies, "do-it-yourselfers" are resourceful folks who like to take second-hand products and refurbish them. Others use creative tricks to make homemade versions of baby care items like baby wipes and diaper rash cream.

While that's all well and good, we fall more into the second camp of bargain hunters, the "quality at a discount" group. We love discovering a hidden factory outlet that sells goods at 50% off. Or finding a designer stroller on Craigslist at 75% off its original retail. We also realize savvy parents save money by not *wasting* it on inferior goods or useless items.

While we hope that *Baby Bargains* pleases both groups of bargain hunters, the main focus of this book is not on do-it-yourself projects. Books like the *Tightwad Gazette* (check your local library for a copy) do a much better job on this subject. Our main emphasis will be on discount web sites, catalogs, outlet stores, brand reviews and identifying best buys for the dollar.

What? There's No Advertising in This Book?

Yes, it's true. This book contains zero percent advertising. We have never taken any money to recommend a product or company and never will. We make our sole living off the sales of this and other books. Our publisher, Windsor Peak Press, also derives its sole

The 7 Commandments of Baby Bargains

Yes, we've come down the mountain to share with you our SEVEN commandments of *Baby Bargains*—the keys to saving every parent should know. Let's review:

1 **SAFETY IS JOB ONE.** As a parent, your baby's safety is paramount. We never compromise safety for a bargain—that's why hand-me-down cribs or used car seats are not a good idea.

2 **FOCUS ON THE BASICS.** Baby stores are so overwhelming, with a blizzard of baby products. Key on the basics: setting up a safe place for baby to sleep (the nursery) and safe transport (car seats). Many items like high chairs, toys, and so on are not needed immediately.

3 **WEED OUT THE FLUFF.** Our advice: take an experienced mom with you when you register. A mom with one or two kids can help you separate out needed items from the fluff!

4 **TWO WORDS: FREE MONEY.** As a parent, you NEVER pass up free money! From tax deductions to tax credits, being a parent means freebies. And don't overlook your employer:

income from the sale of this book and our other publications. ***No company recommended in this book paid any consideration or was charged any fee to be mentioned.*** (In fact, some companies probably would offer us money to leave them *out* of the book, given our comments about their products or services).

As consumer advocates, we believe this "no ads" policy helps to ensure objectivity. The opinions in the book are just that—ours and those of the parents we interviewed.

We also are parents of two kids. We figure if we actually are recommending these products to you, we should have some real world experience with them. (That said, we should disclose that our sons have filed union grievances with our company over testing of certain jarred baby foods and that litigation is ongoing.)

Of course, given the sheer volume of baby stuff, there's no way we can test everything personally. To solve that dilemma, we rely on reader feedback to help us figure out which are the best products to recommend. We receive over 100 emails a day from parents; this helps us spot overall trends on which brands/products parents love.

take advantage of benefits like dependent care accounts—using PRE-TAX dollars to pay for child care will save you HUNDREDS if not THOUSANDS of dollars.

5 **MORE FREEBIES.** Many companies throw swag at new parents, hoping they will become future customers. We keep an updated freebie list on our web site—get free diapers, bottles, supplies and more. Go to BabyBargains.com, click on message boards and then go to the Bargain Alert forum to find the pinned Freebie List.

6 **SHOP AT STORES THAT DO NOT HAVE "BABY" IN THEIR NAME.** Costco for diapers? Pet web sites for safety gates? Regular furniture stores for rockers and dressers? IKEA for high chairs? Yes! Yes! Yes! You can save 30% or more by not buying items at baby stores.

7 **ONLINE SHOPPING SAVVY.** Let's face it: as a new mom and dad, you probably won't have much time to hit the mall. The web is a savior—but how do you master the deals? One smart tip: ALWAYS use coupon codes for discounts or FREE shipping before you order. We keep a list (updated daily!) of the best coupon codes on our Bargain Alert Forum on our free message boards (BabyBargains.com).

What you need, when

Yes, buying for baby can seem overwhelming, but there is a silver lining: you don't need ALL this stuff immediately when baby is born. Let's look at what items you need quickly and what you can wait on. This chart indicates usage of certain items for the first 12 months of baby's life:

	MONTHS OF USE				
ITEM	**BIRTH**	**3**	**6**	**9**	**12+**
Nursery Necessities					
Cradle/bassinet					
Crib/Mattress					
Dresser					
Glider Rocker					
Bedding: Cradle					
Bedding: Crib					
Clothing					
Caps/Hats					
Blanket Sleepers					
Layette Gowns					
Booties					
All other layette					
Around the House					
Baby Monitor					
Baby Food (solid)					
High Chairs					
Places to Go					
Infant Car Seat					
Convertible Car Seat*					
Carriage Stroller					
Umbrella Stroller					
Front Carrier					
Backpack Carrier					
Safety items					

*You can use a convertible car seat starting immediately with that first ride home from the hospital. However, it is our recommendation that you use an infant car seat for the first six months or so, then, when baby grows out of it, buy the convertible car seat.

And which ones they want to destroy with a rocket launcher.

Finally, we enlist readers to test new products for us, evaluating items on how they work in the real world. One bad review from one parent doesn't necessarily mean we won't recommend a product; but we'll then combine these tests with other parent feedback to get an overall picture. (If you'd like to volunteer to be a product tester, sign up for our free e-newsletter on our web site BabyBargains.com. Also check the message boards on our site for postings about product tests).

What about prices of baby products? Trying to stay on top of this is similar to nailing Jell-O to a wall. Yet, we still try. As much as we can confirm, the prices quoted in this book were accurate as of the date of publication. Of course, prices and product features can change at any time. Inflation and other factors may affect the actual prices you discover in shopping for your baby. While the publisher makes every effort to ensure their accuracy, errors and omissions may exist. That's why we update this book with every new printing—make sure you are using the most recent version (go to BabyBargains.com and click on Which Version?).

Our door is always open—we want to hear your opinions. Email us at authors@BabyBargains.com or call us at (303) 442-8792 to ask a question, report a mistake, or just give us your thoughts. Finally, you can write to us at "Baby Bargains," 436 Pine Street, Suite 700, Boulder, CO 80302.

What about the phone numbers listed in this book? We list contact numbers for manufacturers so you can find a local dealer near you that carries the product (or request a catalog, if available). Unless otherwise noted, these manufacturers do NOT sell directly to the public.

So, Who Are You Guys Anyway?

Why do a book on saving money on baby products? Don't new parents throw caution to the wind when buying for their baby, spending whatever it takes to ensure their baby's safety and comfort?

Ha! When our first son was born, we quickly realized how darn expensive this guy was. Sure, as a new parent, you know you've got to buy a car seat, crib, clothes and diapers . . . but have you walked into one of those baby "superstores" lately? It's a blizzard of baby stuff, with a bewildering array of "must have" gear, gadgets and gizmos, all claiming to be the best thing for parents since sliced bread.

Becoming a parent in this day and age is both a blessing and curse. The good news: parents today have many more choices for baby products than past generations. The *bad* news: parents today have many more choices for baby products than past generations.

Our mission: make sense of this stuff, with an eye on cutting costs. As consumer advocates, we've been down this road before. We researched bargains and uncovered scams in the wedding business when we wrote *Bridal Bargains*. Then we penned an exposé on new homebuilders in *Your New House*.

Yet, we found the baby business to be perilous in different ways—instead of outright fraud or scam artists, we've instead discovered some highly questionable products that don't live up to their hype—and others that are outright dangerous. We were surprised to learn how most juvenile items face little (or no) government scrutiny, leaving parents to sort out true usefulness and safety from sales hype. In addition, in recent years new "discount" baby product web sites have failed to live up to their own promises of prompt delivery and customer service.

So, we've gone on a quest to find the best baby products, at prices that won't send you to the poor house. Sure, we've sampled many of these items first hand. But this book is much more than our experiences—we interviewed over 1000 new parents to learn their experiences with products. Our message boards have over 15,000 members, buzzing with all sorts of product feedback and advice. We also attend juvenile product trade shows to quiz manufacturers and retailers on what's hot and what's not. The insights from retailers are especially helpful, since these folks are on the front lines, seeing which items unhappy parents return.

Our focus is on safety and durability: which items stand up to real world conditions and which don't. Interestingly, we found many products for baby are sold strictly on price . . . and sometimes a great "bargain" broke, fell apart or shrunk after a few uses. Hence, you'll note some of our top recommendations aren't always the lowest in price. To be sensitive to those on really tight budgets, we try to identify "good, better and best" bets in different price ranges.

First Time Parent 101

As a first-time parent, it's easy to get confused by all the jargon in the world of parenting books. But since you've never had a baby before, you may wonder how we define basic terms like "newborn," "infant," "toddler," "sleep deprivation" and so on. So, here's a quick primer:

◆ **Newborn.** As you'd expect, these are very young bambinos just recently born. Most folks define a newborn as a baby under four weeks or so in age.

◆ **Infant/baby.** We generally refer to children under age two as babies or infants.

◆ **Toddler.** For purposes of our books, we define a toddler as a child who is age two to five. As the name implies, these are young children who are just learning to walk. Okay, obviously most babies do this before age two. Some books define "toddler hood" as age 18 months to three years. "Toddler" clothes are typically for children age one to three. Confused yet? The point: there isn't one single definition of "toddler." We use it to describe the slew of products for older children (booster car seats, potty seats, etc).

◆ **Sleep deprivation.** See "newborn."

We get questions: the Top 5 Questions & Answers

From the home office here in Boulder, CO, here are the top five questions we get asked here at *Baby Bargains*:

1 **DO YOU HAVE A BOOK FOR OLDER CHILDREN? WHAT OTHER PARENTING BOOKS DO YOU PUBLISH?** In the past, we focused *Baby Bargains* on products for babies age birth to two. For this edition of *Baby Bargains*, we have added content from our other book (*Toddler Bargains*) that covers such topics as booster car seats, hook-on chairs and kitchen-table boosters. The rest of our *Toddler Bargains* book (including a round-up of potty chairs and all-terrain double strollers) is now available as an e-book from our web page (BabyBargains.com).

Yes, we do have two other parenting books: *Baby 411* and *Toddler 411*. Co-authored by an award-winning pediatrician, these books cover topics such as sleep, nutrition, growth and more. See the back of this book for details.

2 **HOW DO I KNOW IF I HAVE THE CURRENT EDITION?** We strive to keep *Baby Bargains* as up-to-date as possible. As such, we update it periodically with new editions. But if you just borrowed this book from a friend, how do you know how old it is? First, look at the copyright page. There at the bottom you will see a version number (such as 7.0). The first number (the 7 in this case) means you have the 7th edition. The second number indicates the printing—every time we reprint the book, we make minor corrections, additions and changes. Version 7.0 is the initial printing of the 7th edition, version 7.1 is the first reprint of the 7th edition and so on.

So, how can you tell if your book is current or woefully out-of-date? Go to our web page at www.BabyBargains.com and click on "Which version?"—this shows the most current version. (One clue: look at the book's cover. We note the edition number on each cover. And we change the color of the cover with each edition). We update this book every two years (roughly). About 30% to 40% of the content will change with each edition. Bottom line: if you pick up a copy of this book that is one or two editions old, you will notice a significant number of changes.

3 WHAT IF I SEE A NEW PRODUCT IN STORES? HOW CAN I FIND INFO ON THAT? First, make sure you have the latest edition of *Baby Bargains* (see previous question). If you can't find that product in our latest book, go to our web page at BabyBargains.com. There you will find a treasure trove of information. First, check out our blog, which tracks the latest news on baby gear. Second, search the "Message Boards" section to see if other readers have tried out the product and reported to us on their experiences. Finally, click on "Reviews" to read parent-penned reviews of baby products. Of course, you can email us with a question as well (see the How to Contact Us page at the back of this book). Be sure to sign up for our free e-newsletter to get the latest news on our book, web page, product recalls and more. All this can be done from BabyBargains.com. (A note on our privacy policy: we NEVER sell reader email addresses or other personal info).

Even though we have a treasure trove of FREE stuff on our web page, please note that we do not post the entire text of Baby Bargains online (hey, we have to make a living somehow). If a friend gives you a ten year-old edition of this book, you can't go online and just download all the changes/updates for free. We appreciate your purchase of the most recent edition of this book.

4 I AM LOOKING FOR A SPECIFIC PRODUCT BUT I DON'T KNOW WHERE TO START! HELP! Yep, this book is 600+ pages long and we realize it can be a bit intimidating. But you have a friend in the Index—flip to the back of the book to look up just about anything. You can look up items by category, brand name and more.

If that doesn't work, try the Table of Contents. We sort the book into major topic areas (strollers, car seats, etc). In some chapters, we have "also known as" boxes that help you decode brand names that might be associated with other companies (for example, Eddie Bauer car seats are made by Cosco).

Don't forget the handy Telephone/Web Site Directory in the back of the book as well. You can pop to any company's web page to find more details about a product we review in *Baby Bargains*.

5 WHY DO YOU SOMETIMES RECOMMEND A MORE EXPENSIVE PRODUCT THAN A CHEAPER OPTION? Yes, this is a book about bargains, but sometimes we will pick a slightly more expensive item in a category if we believe it is superior in quality or safety. Sometimes it makes sense to invest in better-quality products that

Baby Bargains versus *Consumer Reports*

First off, let us say right here and now that we are BIG fans of *Consumer Reports* (CR) magazine. The magazine (and now web site) are the gold standard of consumer journalism.

That said, we often get deluged with email from readers when CR reviews and rates a baby product category. Many folks ask us why we at *Baby Bargains* sometimes come to different conclusions than *Consumer Reports*.

First, understand that we have different research methods. *Consumer Reports* often lab tests products to make sure they are safe and durable. At *Baby Bargains*, we rely on parent/reader feedback to make our recommendations. Yes, we do hands-on inspections of products and meet with manufacturers at trade shows to demo the latest gear, but the reader feedback loop is our secret sauce.

Not surprisingly, most of the time we actually agree with *Consumer Reports*. In recent articles on strollers in CR and in our book, we both picked the same three of four brands as best. Yet, sometimes there are differences—we might pick a model as a "best bet" that CR thinks is only a second runner-up. And vice versa. We suppose you can chalk up the differences in ratings to different research methods.

Another issue: out of date reports. We love CR, but sometimes they are WAY behind when it comes to reviewing baby products. Since they don't focus on baby products, it can be YEARS between reports for certain categories. Models and brands change very quickly in this industry. Trying to compare a five year old report in a CR back issue with a current edition of this book isn't very helpful.

Of course, we don't take everything *Consumer Reports* says as the gospel truth. They (like us) make mistakes; we always try to verify results if CR determines a product is unsafe. In cases where we differ with CR, we'll point that out in our book and on our web site.

will last through more than one child. And don't forget about the hassle of replacing a cheap product that breaks in six months.

To be sure, however, we recognize that many folks are on tight budgets. To help, we offer "Good, Better, Best" product suggestions that are typically sorted by price (good is most affordable, best is usually more expensive). Don't torture yourself if you can't afford the "best" in every category; a "good" product will be just as, well, good.

Another note: remember that our brand reviews cover many options in a category, not just the cheapest. Don't be dismayed if we give an expensive brand an "A" rating—such ratings are often based on quality, construction, innovation and more. Yes, we will try to identify the best values in a category as well.

Why does our advice sometimes conflict with other publications like *Consumer Reports*? See the box on the previous page for more on this.

Let's Go Shopping!

Now that all the formal introductions are done, let's move on to the good stuff. As your tour guides to BabyLand, we'd like to remind you of one key rule: the Baby Biz is just that—Business.

The juvenile products industry is a $7.3 BILLION DOLLAR business. While all those baby stores may want to help you, they are first and foremost in business to make a profit. As a consumer, you should arm yourself with the knowledge necessary to make smart decisions. If you do, you won't be taken for a ride.

What's New in This Edition?

So, what's new in this 7th edition of *Baby Bargains*? First, we have added over a dozen new crib brand reviews—many of these newcomers are part of the modernist nursery trend, featuring high style (and high prices).

What's the best (and most affordable) knock-off of the Bugaboo stroller? We've got the scoop in our new feature, *Bugaboo Smackdown*. This handy comparison chart rates and reviews the best Bugaboo imitators. Also new in strollers: reviews of ten new stroller brands, including the latest European imports such as Mutsy and Quinny.

For car seats, we have added a big new section on boosters—you'll find in-depth advice and reviews/ratings of the top picks. We also cover new car seats that use a five-point harness up to 65 pounds.

We've crowned a new winner in the carrier section . . . plus we have the low-down on new hip carriers, Asian-inspired wraps and more. For the kitchen, we have added reviews of booster seats and hook-on chairs. And cloth diaper fans will note an expanded and updated section with the latest brands and picks.

Of course, we've kept the features you love about *Baby Bargains*, including those nifty comparison charts that sum up our picks and our ever-popular baby registry at-a-glance (Appendix B).

Don't forget to check out our expanded online offerings, including an updated blog, message boards and bonus material. Plus: read reviews of baby products posted by our readers.

So, buckle your seat belts and secure all loose items like sunglasses and your sanity. We're off to Baby Gear Land.

CHAPTER 2

Nursery Necessities: Cribs, Dressers & More

Inside this chapter

H ow can you save 20% to 50% off cribs, dressers, and other furniture for your baby's room? In this chapter, you'll learn these secrets, plus discover smart shopper tips that help clarify all those confusing crib options and features. Then, you'll learn which juvenile furniture has safety problems and where to go online to find the latest recall info. Next, we'll rate and review over three dozen top brands of cribs, focusing on quality and value. Finally, you'll learn which crib mattress is best, how to get a deal on a dresser, and several more items to consider for your baby's room.

Getting Started: When Do You Need This Stuff?

So, you want to buy a crib for Junior? And, what the heck, why not some other furniture, like a dresser to store all those baby gifts and a changing table for, well, you know. Just pop down to the store, pick out the colors, and set a delivery date, right?

Not so fast, o' new parental one. Once you get to that baby store, you'll discover that most don't have all those nice cribs and furniture *in stock*. No, that would be too easy, wouldn't it? You will quickly learn that you have to *special order* much of that booty.

To be fair, we should note that in-stock items vary from shop to shop. Some (especially the larger chain stores) may stock a fair number of cribs. Yet Murphy's Law says the last in-stock Futura Crib with that special chartreuse trim was just sold five minutes ago. And while stores may stock a good number of cribs, dressers are another story—these bulky items almost always must be special-ordered.

Most baby specialty stores told us it takes four to six weeks to order most nursery furniture. And here's an unpleasant surprise: other imported brands can take 12 or even 16 weeks to arrive. Or longer. It's hard to believe that it takes so long for companies to ship a simple crib or dresser—we're not talking space shuttle parts here. The way it's going, you'll soon have to order the crib *before* you conceive.

Obviously, this policy is more for the benefit of the retailer than the consumer. Most baby stores are small operations—stocking up on cribs, dressers and the like means an expensive investment in inventory and storage space. That's understandable, but it makes the nursery furniture shopping process more daunting for consumers. Why you can't get a crib in a week or less is one of the mysteries of modern juvenile product retailing that will have to be left to future generations to solve. What if you don't have that much time? There are a couple of solutions: some stores sell floor models and others actually keep a limited number of styles in stock. Discounters also stock cribs—the only downside is that while the price is low, often so is the quality.

Here's an alternate idea submitted by a reader: don't buy the crib until *after* the baby is born. The infant can sleep in a bassinet or cradle for the first few weeks or even months, and you can get the furniture later. (This may also be an option for the superstitious who don't want to buy all this stuff until the baby is actually born.) The downside to waiting? The last thing you'll want to do with your newborn infant is go furniture shopping. There will be many other activities (such as sleep deprivation experiments) to occupy your time.

So, when should you make a decision on the crib and other furniture for the baby's room? We recommend you place your order in the fifth or sixth month of your pregnancy. That should leave plenty of time for delivery. (The exception: if your heart is set on a furniture brand with long lead times, you may have to order in your fourth month to ensure arrival before Junior is born).

First-time parent question: so, how long will baby use a crib? Answer: it depends (and you thought we always had the answer). Seriously, most babies can use a crib for two or three years. Yes, some babies are out of the crib by 18 months, while others may be pushing four. One key factor: when does baby learn they can climb out of the crib? Once that happens, the crib days are numbered, as you can understand. Of course, there may be other factors that push baby out of a crib—if you are planning to have a second child and want the crib for the new baby, it may be time to transition to a "big boy/girl" bed. We discuss more about the transition out of a crib in our other books, *Toddler Bargains* (an ebook available for download*)* and *Toddler 411*. See the back of this book for more info.

Cribs: Sources to Find

This year, more than one million households plan to buy infant/nursery furniture, according to a survey by *Kids Today*. That translates into $1.5 billion in sales of infant furniture—yes, this is big business. In their quest for the right nursery, parents have five basic sources for finding a crib, each with its own advantages and drawbacks:

BABY SPECIALTY STORES. Baby specialty stores are pretty self-explanatory—shops that specialize in the retailing of baby furniture, strollers, and accessories. Some also sell clothing, car seats, swings, and so on. Independents come in all sizes: some are small boutiques; others are as large as a chain superstore. A good number of indie retailers have joined together in "buying groups" to get volume discounts on items from suppliers—these groups include Baby Furniture Plus (babyfurnitureplus.com), Baby News (BabyNewsStores.com), NINFRA (ninfra. com) and USA Baby (USAbaby.com). Another good resource to find a specialty store near you is AllBabyAndChildStores.com.

Like other independent stores, many baby specialty shops have been hard hit by the expansion of national chains like Babies R Us. Yet, those that have survived do so by emphasizing service and products you can't find at the chains. Of course, quality of service can vary widely from store to store . . . but just having a breathing human to ask a question of is a nice plus.

The problems with specialty stores? Consumers complain the stores only carry expensive brands. One parent told us the only baby specialty store in her town doesn't carry any cribs under $500. We understand the dilemma faced by mom and pop retailers—in order provide all that service, they have to make a certain profit margin on furniture and other products. And that margin is easier to get on high-end goods. That's all well and good, but failing to carry products in entry-level price points only drives parents to the chains.

Another gripe with some indie stores: some shops can be downright hostile to you if they think you are "price-shopping" them. A reader said she found this out when comparing high-end nursery furniture in her town. "When I asked to price cribs and dressers at two baby stores, I met with resistance and hostility. At one store, I was asked if I was a 'spy' for their competition! The store managers at both baby stores I visited said they didn't want people to comparison shop them on price, yet both advertise they will 'meet or beat' the competition's prices."

Crazy as it sounds, the only way to write down prices at some stores is to have a friend distract the sales help (Hey, look over there! A naked basketball team crossing the street!).

The bottom line: despite the hassles, if you have a locally owned baby store in your town, give them a shot. Don't assume chains always have lower prices and better selection.

2 THE CHAINS. There are two types of chains that sell baby products: specialty chains like Babies R Us who focus on juvenile products and discounters like Wal-Mart, Target, and K-Mart that have small baby departments. We'll discuss each in-depth later in this chapter. The selection at chains can vary widely—some carry more premium brands, but most concentrate on mass-market names to appeal to price-conscious shoppers. Service? Fuggedaboutit—often, you'll be lucky to find someone to help you check out, much less answer questions.

3 DEPARTMENT STORES. A few department stores still have baby departments that carry clothing and some gear; most furniture and nursery items are relegated to department store catalogs. Prices aren't typically as low as the discounters, but occasional sales sometimes bring bargains.

4 ONLINE. Long before the web, companies tried to sell furniture via mail order, albeit with mixed results. Perhaps the best example is JCPenney (jcpenney.com), whose catalog and web site specializes in affordable cribs and dressers. Despite the challenge of shipping bulky items like dressers, web sites and specialty retailers are still piling into online nursery niche. We'll discuss the options and caveats more in depth later in this chapter.

Even if you decide to order your entire nursery online, there are several roadblocks. Given the weight and bulk of cribs and dressers, only a few (mostly lower-end) brands are typically sold online. Shipping charges can be exorbitant—and that assumes you can get items shipped at all (most sites don't ship to furniture Hawaii, Alaska, Canada or military addresses). With shipping, you then have the issue of shipping damage, delays and worse. Given the limitations of the web as it is today, it is more realistic to use online sites buy accessories (lamps, rockers, décor) for your nursery than an entire furniture suite.

5 REGULAR FURNITURE STORES. You don't have to go to a "baby store" to buy juvenile furniture. Many regular furniture stores sell name-brand cribs, dressers and other nursery items. Since these stores have frequent sales, you may be able to get a better price than at a juvenile specialty store. On the other hand, the salespeople may not be as knowledgeable about brand and safety issues.

Parents in Cyberspace: What's on the Web?

As with everything else online, the growth in web sites that sell nursery furniture has been nothing short of amazing. Despite the limits and logistical headaches (see the above discussion), there are no shortage of sites who will ship you a crib, dresser, glider rocker and other nursery items.

Here's a quick run-down of what you can do online:

◆ **Research.** Sites like Amazon and BabiesRUs.com have user reviews of furniture and other nursery items. On our web site (BabyBargains.com, click on Reviews), we let readers rate and review over 40 brands of nursery furniture.

Once you focus on a brand that meets your budget, most manufacturers have web sites with online catalogs (see the brand reviews later in this chapter for web site info).

Of course, you can also use message boards on our site and other parenting web sites to post a query about nursery furniture, read others experiences/ideas and more.

◆ **Buy.** The online sellers of nursery furniture fall into two camps: discounters/specialty whose massive web sites have a baby/kids area and pure e-tailers who specialize in baby gear.

In the first category, huge discounters like **Wal-Mart** and **Target** have been greatly expanding their online baby offerings in recent years. When you go to Wal-Mart or Target's web sites, you'll notice a wide range of nursery items and gear, much of which is only sold online. Some sites (notably Wal-Mart) are even experimenting with in-store pickup.

Specialty retailers have also been muscling into the online baby biz: the best known is **Pottery Barn Kids**, but you can find cribs on sites ranging from **Room & Board** to **Design Within Reach**. Of course, big baby retailers **Babies R Us** and **Baby Depot** also sell nursery furniture online, albeit with a more limited selection than what you'd see in their stores.

The biggest e-tailers in the baby biz include **Amazon** (who recently parted ways with partner Babies R Us), **BabyStyle.com**, **BabyUniverse.com** and **BabySuperMarket.com**. To find current parent experiences with each site, do a quick search on our web site message boards (BabyBargains.com). In general, we found most of the baby e-tailers did a decent job when it comes to customer service.

What Are You Buying?

Ok, let's break this down. Outfitting a nursery usually means buying three basic furniture items: a crib, dresser (which doubles as a place to change baby's diaper) and rocker. Here's a quick discussion of each.

◆ **Crib.** Crib prices start at $100 for an inexpensive crib at a discounter like Wal-Mart. The mid-range for cribs is probably best typified by what you see at chains stores such as Babies R Us and Baby Depot—most of their cribs are in the $200 to $400 range. Specialty stores and catalogs tend to carry upper-end cribs that run $400 to $700. And what about the top end? We'd be remiss not to mention the modern-design cribs, which run $1000 to $1500.

Surprise! The vast majority of cribs don't come with mattresses; those are sold separately ($60 to $200). Bedding is also extra ($50 to $500). We'll discuss mattresses later in this chapter; bedding gets its own entire chapter (Chapter 3).

◆ **Dresser.** Most nurseries need a place to store clothes, diapers, supplies and so on. Known in the baby biz as case pieces (because they are, uh, a case), dressers range from simple ready-to-assemble four-drawer chests to elaborate armoires (and their smaller cousins, chiffarobes).

Now, there is no federal law that says you MUST buy a dresser or armoire that exactly matches the finish of your crib. Some folks simply re-purpose a dresser from another room to baby's nursery— or pick up a dresser second-hand or at a discount from a regular furniture store. That's fine, of course.

But . . . we realize the lure of that shiny new dresser that matches your crib convinces many new parents to pony up the bucks. So here are some general price guidelines: a ready-to-assemble dresser from IKEA or a discount store runs $170 to $200.

Now, if you'd like to have something fancier (and already assembled), prices for dressers range from $200 to $300 at Wal-Mart to $400 to $500 at Babies R Us. Step into a specialty store and you'll find plenty of fancy dressers, armoires and chiffarobes . . . for $500 to $1000 and higher.

Most dressers also double as a place to change baby—some have tops specifically designed for that purpose. These changer tops remove after baby is done with the diapers (usually right before college). So most parents today do not need to buy a separate changing table.

◆ **Rocker.** A place to sit and nurse baby is an important part of any nursery's function—so the next question is . . . where to sit? Again, you can re-purpose a rocker from grandma's house or pick up one secondhand. If you have the room, a small loveseat or over-sized chair is a workable solution for nursing baby.

Brand new "glider-rockers" run the gamut from wooden chairs with thin pads to fully upholstered models. And the price range reflects this: you can spend as little as $100 to $200 for a rocker from Target or Wal-Mart . . . as much as $900 for a tricked out leather model from a specialty store. Most folks probably buy a basic model from chain stores like Toys R Us for $200 to $400. Yes, ottomans are a nice extra—but cost $100 to $300 more.

Glider rockers get their own section later in this chapter.

The Grand Total. As you can see, the bare-bones budget for a nursery would be $450 (simple crib, mattress, dresser and rocker). The mid-range would run about $800 . . . and on the designer end, you could blow $2000 to $3000 easy on a nursery.

And these figures are BEFORE you get to any of the other décor items: bedding, lamps, paint, artwork, curtains, etc.

 *More Money Buys You . . .*

Here's a little secret expensive crib makers don't want you to hear: ALL new cribs (no matter what price) sold in the U.S. or Canada must meet federal safety standards. Yes, the governments of both the U.S. and Canada strictly regulate crib safety and features—that's one reason why most cribs have the same basic design, no matter the brand or price. So, whether you buy a $100 crib special at K-Mart or a $1500 wrought iron crib at a posh specialty boutique, either way you get a crib that meets federal safety requirements.

Now, that said, when you spend more money, there are some perks. The higher the price tag of the crib (generally), the fancier the design (thicker corner posts, designer colors, etc.). And more expensive cribs tend to have quieter drop-sides (cheap cribs can be noisy when you raise or lower the side rail). Another perk when you spend more: pricey cribs are likely to convert into a twin or double bed. Lower-price cribs are just, well, cribs.

Some extras have dubious value, however—take the under-crib storage drawer. Often seen on cribs that run $300 or more, this feature appeals to parents who have a storage crunch in their home (you can put blankets, extra clothes in the drawer). The problem? The drawer usually doesn't have a top. So, anything inside will be a dust magnet.

Ok, so now you know the typical prices of nursery furniture . . . and what more money really buys you. How do you decide what is best for your baby's nursery? See the following box for our Three Golden Rules of Buying Nursery Furniture.

Three Golden Rules of Buying Nursery Furniture

◆ **Don't fall in love with a finish**—think about your needs first. Here's a common first time parent mistake: rushing out to a local baby store and ogling that fancy cognac finish on a chiffarobe. Instead, think about what you really NEED. Start with the size of your baby's nursery—most secondary bedrooms in a typical suburban home are 10 x12 (some are smaller). That barely leaves room for a crib, dresser and rocker. Don't let a baby store sell you on a dresser PLUS an armoire when you don't have room. For urban apartment dwellers, space is critical. Closets need to be tricked out to provide maximum storage. Expect furniture to do double duty.

◆ **Three words: set a budget.** Don't waste your time falling in love with a designer look if you haven't done the math. As you saw from the discussion on the last few pages, a three-piece nursery set (crib, dresser, rocker) runs anywhere from $450 . . . up to $3000. Pick a budget and stick with it. Then read the brand reviews later in this chapter—you'll quickly realize which ones are in your budget and which aren't! Again, it pays to think outside the box: can you re-purpose a dresser from another room? Get a hand-me-down rocker from friend or off Craigslist?

◆ **Decide on nursery style.** There are two theories of nursery design: either a baby's room should look, well, babyish . . . or it should be more adult-looking, able to adapt as the child grows. Neither is right or wrong. If you subscribe to the baby-theme, then go with a simple (non-convertible) crib and dresser that will be later swapped out for a twin bed and computer desk/hutch. If you prefer the other path, then buy a convertible crib (which converts to a full size bed) and dresser that can do double duty. Some brands have dressers that are first a changing area for diapers . . . and then convert to a computer area complete with pull out keyboard drawer.

Safe & Sound

Here's a fact to keep you up at night: cribs are the third-biggest cause of injuries and deaths among all nursery products. In the latest year for which statistics are available, 9800 injuries and 21 deaths were blamed on cribs alone.

Now, before you get all excited, let's point out that old cribs cause the vast majority of crib-related injuries. Surprisingly, these old cribs may not be as old as you think—some models from the 1970s and early 1980s have caused many injuries and deaths. (Safety standards for cribs were first enacted in 1973 then again in 1976; these rules were revised in 1982 and again in 1999). All *new* cribs sold in the United States must meet the current safety standards designed to prevent injuries. In fact, the annual death rate for cribs (21) is dramatically below that in the 1970's, when nearly 200 children died each year from crib hazards.

These facts bring us to our biggest safety tip on cribs:

♦ ***Don't buy a used or old crib.*** Let's put that into bold caps: **DON'T BUY A USED OR OLD CRIB.** And don't take a hand-me-down from a well-meaning friend or relative. Why? Because old cribs can be death traps—spindles that are too far apart, cutouts in the headboard, and other hazards that could entrap your baby. Decorative trim (like turned posts) that looks great on adult beds are a major no-no for cribs—they present a strangulation hazard. (Note: cribs with TALL posts are fine; it is the shorter posts that are prohibited—see the graphic on the next page).

Other old cribs have lead paint, a dangerous peril for a teething baby. Another hazard to hand-me-down cribs (regardless of age): missing parts and directions. It only takes one missing screw or bolt to make an otherwise safe crib into a danger. Without directions, you can incorrectly assemble the crib and create additional safety hazards. So, even if your friend wants to give/sell you a recent model crib, you could still have problems if parts or directions are missing.

It may seem somewhat ironic that a book on baby bargains would advise you to go out and spend your hard-earned money on a new crib. True, we find great bargains on Craigslist and second-hand stores. However, you have to draw the line at your baby's safety. Certain items are great deals second-hand—toys and clothes come to mind. However, cribs (and, as you'll read later, car seats) are no-no's, no matter how tempting the bargains. And second hand stores have a spotty record when it comes to selling safe products. A recent report from the CPSC said that a whopping two-thirds of all U.S. thrift/second-hand stores sell baby products that have been recalled, banned or do not meet current safety standards (specifically 12% of stores stocked old cribs). Amazingly, federal law does not prohibit the sale of cribs (or other dangerous products like jackets with drawstring hoods, recalled playpens or car seats) at second-hand stores.

Readers of the first edition of this book wondered why we did not put in tips for evaluating old or hand-me-down cribs. The reason is simple: it's hard to tell whether an old crib is dangerous just by looking at it. Cribs don't always have "freshness dates"—some manufacturers don't stamp the date of manufacture on their cribs. Was the crib made before or after the current safety standards went into effect in 1999? Often, you can't tell.

Today's safety regulations are so specific (like the allowable width for spindles) that you just can't judge a crib's safety with a cursory examination. Cribs made before the 1970's might contain lead paint, which is difficult to detect unless you get the crib tested. Another problem: if the brand name is rubbed off, it will be hard to tell if the crib has been involved in a recall. Obtaining replacement parts is also difficult for a no-name crib. Another important point: in 1999, new rules for cribs went into effect that mandated slat attachment strength (in the 1990's, several crib models were recalled because the slats fell out).

What about floor model cribs? Is it safe to buy a crib that has been used as a floor sample in a baby store? Yes—as long as it is in good working condition, has no missing/broken parts, etc. Floor model cribs CAN take a tremendous amount of abuse from parents, who shake

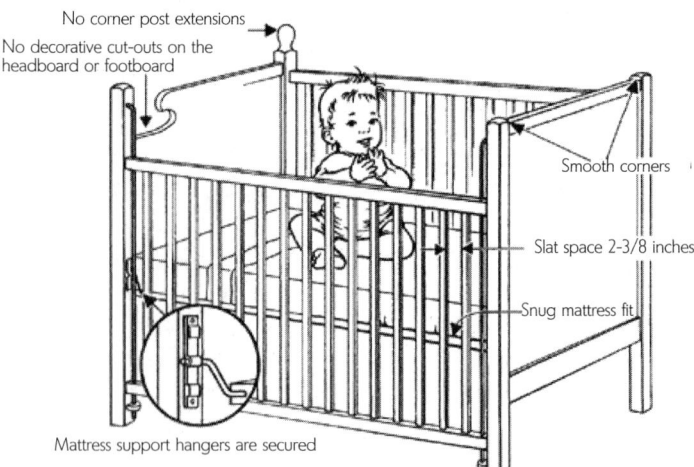

Older cribs typically have many hazards. Here's a graphic of what is dangerous. Note: all new cribs sold today are required by law to NOT have any of these features.

them to check stability and so on. As a result, the bolts that hold the crib together can loosen. Obviously, that can be fixed (just have the store tighten the bolts) . . . and as a result, we think floor model cribs are fine. That isn't what we mean by avoiding a "used" crib!

What if a relative insists you should use the "family heirloom" crib? We've spoken to dozens of parents who felt pressured into using an old crib by a well-meaning relative. There's a simple answer: don't do it. As a parent, you sometimes have to make unpopular decisions that are best for your child's safety. This is just the beginning.

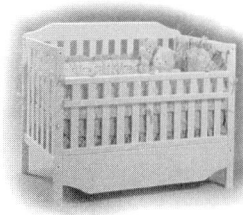

◆ **Cribs with fold-down railings or attached dressers.** Some cribs have a side rail that drops to give you access to an infant. However, a few models have fold-down railings. To gain access to the crib, the upper one-third of the railing is hinged and folds down. These are also called swing gate cribs (see picture above).

What's the problem? Actually, there are two problems. First, the folding rail can be a pinch point (a 1998 recall of Baby's Dream cribs focused on this problem). While Baby's Dream has fixed their fold-down rail, we're still leery of other brands that have this type of rail release.

The second problem: toddlers can get a foothold on the hinged rail to climb out of the crib, injuring themselves as they fall to the floor. It's much harder for a child to climb out of a crib with a traditional drop side. (Another disadvantage to the fold-down rail: most requires TWO hands to release, which is a hassle if you have a baby in your arms!)

Attached dressers pose a similar problem. Children can climb onto the dresser and then out of the crib. One mother we interviewed was horrified to find her ten month-old infant sitting on top of a four-foot-high dresser one night. Unfortunately, there are no federal safety standards that apply to attached dressers. Yet it's clear to us there is a risk here.

So what's the appeal of these cribs? We're not sure what the appeal of the fold-down rail is . . . there really is no advantage. As far as the attached dressers, we can see how space-crunched nurseries would cry out for this solution. But we say resist the call.

◆ **Stripped screws.** Cheap cribs often have screws that attach directly to the wood of the headboard. The problem? The screws can strip over time (especially if the crib is set up several times) and that can weaken the crib's support . . . which is very dangerous. If you ever discover you are not able to tighten the screws or bolts used to hold your crib together, immediately stop using it. When you are crib shopping, look at how the mattress support is attached to the headboards—look for metal screwed into metal.

◆ **Watch out for sharp edges.** It amazes us that any company today would market a baby furniture item with sharp edges. Yet, there are still some on the market. We've seen changing tables with sharp edges and dressers with dangerous corners. A word to the wise: be sure to check out any nursery item carefully before buying—look in less-than-obvious places, like the bottom edges of a dresser or the under-crib drawer.

◆ **Be aware of the hazards of putting a baby in an adult bed.** Co-sleeping is where a baby shares a bed with adults. While common in other parents of the world, co-sleeping is controversial here in the US—on one side are attachment parenting advocates, who insist it is safe, a big convenience for nursing moms and an important part of parent/child emotional bonds.

On the other side are some safety advocates, including the Consumer Product Safety Commission and the American Academy of Pediatrics. A CPSC report released in 2002 blamed 122 deaths of babies in a previous three year period on co-sleeping. Of those deaths, many were caused when a child's head became entrapped between the adult bed and another object (a headboard, footboard, wall, etc). Other deaths were caused by falls or suffocation in bedding. The American Academy of Pediatrics weighed into this debate in 2005, issuing a recommendation against co-sleeping.

We have an expanded discussion of this debate in our other book, *Baby 411*. Since this book focuses on gear, here is our quick take: whatever sleep routine you choose (co-sleeping in a family bed or solitary sleep in a crib), make sure you set up a SAFE sleeping environment. One compromise to this debate is to keep a newborn in a product like the Arm's Reach Co-Sleeper (we'll discuss this more in-depth later in the chapter). In a nutshell, the Arm's Reach is a bassinet that attaches to the adult bed, providing easy access for nursing, but a separate sleep space.

◆ **Some stylish cribs can make bumper tying a challenge.** Those thick corner posts on expensive cribs sure look pretty, but they can create problems—using a bumper pad (a bedding item discussed in the next chapter) on these cribs can be darn near impossible. Why? Many bumper pads have short ties that simply don't fit around thick corner posts. And other cribs have solid headboards or footboards—this prevents the tying of a bumper. We'll discuss bumpers in the next chapter (our position: they're optional)

. . . but if you decide you want to use them, be sure to get a crib that is bumper-compatible.

◆ **When assembling a crib, make sure ALL the bolts and screws are tightened**. A recent report on *Good Morning America* pointed out how dangerous it can be to put your baby in a miss-assembled crib—a child died in a Child Craft crib when he became trapped in a side rail that wasn't properly attached to the crib. How did that happen? The parent didn't tighten the screws that held the side rail to the crib. All cribs (including the Child Craft one here in question) are safe when assembled correctly; just be sure to tighten those screws! A smart safety tip: check your crib once a month to make sure all screws and bolts are firmly attached.

◆ **What about the finish?** Some crib makers are now touting "non-toxic water-based finishes" for their cribs. Example: on an eco-baby web site, we saw a $720 crib that is "hand rubbed with pure beeswax and tung oil." The implication: traditional oil-based finishes for baby furniture are somehow dangerous. Really? We've seen no evidence that a baby that sleeps in a crib finished/painted with an oil-based product is somehow at risk for health problems. In 1978, the federal government required ALL cribs to be finished with *non-toxic* materials. Of course, there is no requirement that the finish be water-based or oil-based—each is equally safe in our opin-ion. While we realize some eco-sensitive parents might shell out extra for the water-based finish, we don't see a problem or a rea-son to spend more.

◆ **Recalls: where to find information.** The U.S. Consumer Product Safety Commission has a toll-free hotline at (800) 638-2772 and web site (cpsc.gov) for the latest recall information on cribs and other juvenile items. Both are easy to use—the hotline is a series of recorded voice mail messages that you access by following the prompts. You can also report any potential hazard you've discov-ered or an injury to your child caused by a product. Write to the U.S. Consumer Products Safety Commission, Washington, D.C. 20207 or file a complaint online at cpsc.gov. FYI: The CPSC takes care of all juvenile product recalls, except for car seats—that's the purview of the National Highway Traffic Safety Administration (nhtsa.gov).

A great "all-in-one" site for recalls is Recalls.gov. Also: check our blog (you can subscribe to its RSS feed). We list recalls and post reader email about safety issues. Go to BabyBargains.com and click on "News/Updates" to get to the blog.

◆ **Safety is more than a crib.** Be sure to have a smoke and carbon monoxide detector for your baby's nursery. And if you haven't had your home tested for radon yet, this would be a good time. (We discuss radon and other environmental hazards in our book, *Toddler 411*. See the back of this book for details).

Smart Shopper Tips

Smart Shopper Tip #1
Beware of "Baby Buying Frenzy."

"I went shopping with my friend at a baby store last week, and she just about lost it. She started buying all kinds of fancy accessories and items that didn't seem that necessary. First there was a $50 womb sound generator and finally the $200 Star Trek Diaper Changing Docking Station. There was no stopping her. The salespeople were egging her on—it was quite a sight. Should we have just taken her out back and hosed her down?"

Yes, you probably should have. Your friend has come down with a severe case of what we call Baby Buying Frenzy—that overwhelming emotional tug to buy all kinds of stuff for Junior—especially when Junior is your first child. Baby stores know all about this disease and do their darnedest to capitalize on it. Check out this quote from trade journal *Juvenile Merchandising* advising salespeople on how to sell to expectant parents: "It's surprising how someone who is making a purchase (for baby) sometimes can be led into a buying frenzy." No kidding. Some stores encourage their staff by giving them bonuses for every additional item sold to a customer. Be wary of stores that try to do this, referred to in the trade as "building the ticket." Remember what you came to buy and don't get caught up in the hype.

Smart Shopper Tip #2
The Art and Science of Selecting the Right Crib.

"How do you evaluate a crib? They all look the same to me. What really makes one different from another?"

Selecting a good crib is more than just picking out the style and finish. You should look under the hood, so to speak. Here are our 11 key points to look for when shopping for a crib:

◆ **Brand reputation.** Later in this chapter, we will rate and review the biggest crib brands. Our advice: stick with a brand that gets a B or better rating. We formulate these ratings from parent feedback (some of which is posted on our web site, where readers rate and review various crib brands) as well as our analysis of a brand's track record. We look at recall history, customer service, delivery reliability and overall quality to assign a rating.

◆ **Mattress support.** Look underneath that mattress and see what is holding it up. You might be surprised. Some lower-end cribs use cheap vinyl straps. Others use metal bars. One crib maker uses a piece of MDF (a wood composite) to hold up the crib mattress. What's best? In our opinion, either a set of metal springs or a wood slat platform.

◆ **Ease of release.** Cribs come in two basic flavors: those with drop-sides and those with static (or stationary) rails. Up until a few years ago, most cribs had at least one side that lowered. While drop-side cribs are still on the market, the new rage are "static" rail cribs—yep, cribs with rails that do not lower. Here are the pluses and minuses of each type of crib rail release:

1 **STATIC/STATIONARY.** As the name implies, these cribs have rails that do NOT lower. Why would crib designers do this? Well, these crib styles are easier to convert to full-size beds (the side rails become the head and footboards). The advantage to this design: there are no moving parts to break and these cribs seem much more stable/solid than other models. The downside: for shorter parents, it can be a long reach to put a sleeping infant down on the mattress when set in its lowest position. Our advice: try these cribs out in the store before buying. Note: these cribs meet the same safety standards as drop-side cribs.

2 **KNEE-PUSH.** By lifting the side rail and pushing against it with your knee, the drop side releases. First seen on cribs imported from Italy, in recent years nearly all crib makers have turned to this type of release. This is probably the quietest release, although that can vary from maker to maker. Another plus: the hardware is often hidden inside the crib posts, so there are no rods and springs like the foot-bar release. We should note that one version of the knee-push rail has exposed plastic brackets on the crib posts.

3 **FOOT-BAR.** You release the crib drop side by lifting up the side rail while depressing a foot bar. This used to be the most common rail release type. But many crib makers have abandoned the foot-bar in recent years for alternatives like the knee-push. The negatives to the foot-bar seemed to spell its doom—some parents found the foot-bar release awkward, requiring them to balance on one foot while lowering the rail with one hand. Another negative: the foot-bar release required exposed hardware (rods, springs, etc.) that was noisy and unattractive. While we think there is no safety concerns with the foot-bar release or exposed hardware, Canada has banned the use of the foot bar release. Corsican's wrought iron cribs (see review later) is one of the few holdouts still using the foot-bar release.

4 **DOUBLE TRIGGER.** This release is used on low-price cribs from makers like Stork Craft and Delta. The drop side is released by simultaneously pulling on two plastic triggers on either side of the rail. Crib makers that use this type of release tout its safety (only an adult can release the rail) and the lack of exposed hardware like that used on foot-bar releases. However, we see two major drawbacks: first, you need *two* hands to operate the release, not really possible if you have a baby in your arms (unless you can grow extras!). Also, the double trigger release uses plastic hardware that can be a problem if you live in a dry climate. Why? The wood posts can shrink, causing the plastic hardware to crack.

5 **FOLD DOWN/SWING-GATE.** Rarely used in the market today, the fold-down rail release does what it sounds like—instead of lowering, the rail has a hinge that allows the top portion to fold down. The biggest user of the fold-down release is Baby's Dream. As we discussed earlier, we're not big fans of fold-down rails—we believe the rail gives an opportunity for larger toddlers to gain a foothold to climb out of the crib.

◆ *Hardware: hidden or exposed?* Crib rail releases have hardware that enables the side to drop. Less expensive cribs have exposed hardware, typically plastic brackets mounted on the crib ends. More expensive cribs have "hidden" hardware, which is tucked inside the headboard and footboard. Is there a difference in safety or durability? No, it often boils down to aesthetics—some parents like hidden hardware because it gives the crib a cleaner, sleeker look. Hidden hardware does have another benefit over exposed hardware: it tends to be quieter. The trend over the last few years has been a move toward hidden hardware. Now you can find hidden hardware on cribs for as little $200 at discounters. And don't forget about the trend toward stationary drop sides—these cribs have no rail release hardware at all!

One safety note: some crib headboards have an exposed plastic track where the rail slides up and down—even if they have hidden hardware. This is a safety hazard in our opinion, as little fingers can get caught in the track. The safest option is a hidden track.

◆ *Mattress height adjustment.* Most cribs have several height levels for the mattress—you use the highest setting when the baby is a newborn. Once she starts pulling up, you adjust the mattress to the lowest level so she won't be able to punt herself over the railing. You have two choices when it comes to this topic: bolt/screws or a hooked bracket. The first system requires you to loosen a bolt or screw that connects a strap to each of the four posts. Then you lower the mattress and screw the bolt back to the post. The only problem with the bolt/screw method: cheap cribs use uncoated bolts that over time can strip the holes on the post, weakening the support system. The bolt/screw is used on cribs with knee-push or double trigger rail releases. The alternative is the hooked brackets—the mattress lies on top of springs, anchored to the crib frame by hooked brackets. Some makers use this system on their cribs with foot-bar releases. Yet, as we mentioned, those makers are phasing out the foot-bar release and, with it, the hooked bracket hardware.

◆ *How stable is the crib?* Go ahead and abuse that crib set up in the baby store. Knock it around. The best cribs are very stable. Unfortunately, cheap models are often the lightest in weight (and hence, tend to wobble). Cribs with a drawer under the mattress are probably the most stable, as are those with stationary side rails. Unfortunately, all this extra stability comes at a price—models with these features start at $400 and can go up to $500 or $600. Keep in mind that some cribs may be wobbly because the store set them up incorrectly. Check out the same model at a couple of different stores if you have stability concerns.

◆ *Are there casters?* In years past, most cribs came on wheels (casters). This made it easier to vacuum or clean behind a crib. Yet in recent years, however, most static convertible cribs have jettisoned the wheels. Today, we see wheels/casters only on a few crib models, typically low-end brands sold at discount stores. Bottom line: wheels are purely optional.

◆ *How easy is it to assemble?* Ask to see those instructions— most stores should have a copy lying around. Make sure they are not indecipherable. Yes, some stores offer set-up and delivery, but with chain superstores, you are typically on your own. Sadly, some crib makers don't put a high priority on easy-to-understand assembly instructions—check first before you buy! The good news: some crib makers now have instructions you can download from their web sites.

◆ **Compare the overall safety features of the crib.** In a section earlier in this book, we discuss crib safety in more detail.

◆ **Which wood is best?** Traditionally, cribs were made of hardwoods like maple, oak, ash and cherry. Crib makers considered these woods superior since they were more durable and easier for them to stain/paint. In the last couple of years, however, the latest craze is pine furniture. The problem? Pine is a softwood that tends to nick, scratch and damage. Of course, not all pine is the same. North American pine is the softest, but pine grown in cold climates (Northern Europe, for example) is harder. Hence, the pine you're most likely to see used in baby furniture is hardwood pine.

So, which wood is best? To be honest, it doesn't really matter much. Cribs imported from Asia (which are most common today) typically use birch or beech hardwoods. Occasionally, you'll see oak, maple and mahogany.

The only wood we would caution parents against: ramin, a wood from Asia that's often called the poorman's mahogany. Ramin doesn't have the durability of other hard woods, but is so cheap you'll see it on promotional cribs sold at rock-bottom prices.

We'd also caution against pine furniture—even "hardwood pine" can be more susceptible to nicks, scratches and damage than other woods like birch or beech. If you decide to buy pine baby furniture, just prepare yourself for the inevitable ding here or there.

Of course, dressers are another subject that we'll cover later in this chapter. Wood choices (including man-made substitutes like MDF) are more of a factor in that decision than with cribs. And if you want your furniture to match, you may want to read the section on dressers before making a crib decision.

Another note: some stores and web sites tout "cherry" cribs when they are actually referring to the finish, not the actual wood. It may be a "cherry" stain, but the wood is probably not.

◆ **Consider other special needs.** As we noted above, noisy crib railing release mechanisms can be a hassle—and this seems especially so for short people (or, in politically correct terms, the vertically challenged). Why? Taller folks (above 5′ 8″) may be able to place the baby into a crib *without* lowering the side rail (when the mattress is in the highest position). Shorter parents can't reach over the side rail as easily, forcing them to use the release mechanism more often than not. Hence, a quieter release on a more expensive brand might be worth the extra investment.

Disabled parents also may find the foot bar difficult or impossible to operate. In that case, we recommend a crib that has a knee-push rail release, described earlier.

Smart Shopper Tip #3
Cyber-Nursery: Ordering furniture online

"We don't have any good baby stores nearby, so I want to order furniture online. How do you buy items sight unseen and make sure they arrive in one piece?"

As we discussed earlier, the growth in online nursery furniture sites continues, despite the hurdles of high shipping costs and freight damage. Folks clearly like shopping online for furniture and smart sites are responding to this demand by figuring out how to package orders to minimize damage.

So how can you be a savvy shopper when buying furniture online?

First, deal with an established seller that has a good customer service track record. We mentioned the top online sellers of nursery furniture earlier in this chapter; take a second to surf our message boards (BabyBargains.com; navigate to the Nursery Necessities board) to find recent parent experiences.

Confirm shipping policies: how will furniture be delivered? What if you live on the third floor of an apartment building—confirm door to door delivery. What happens if there is damage? Is assembly required? The best web sites have detailed FAQ's on these subjects.

While we realize it is tempting to do all your furniture shopping online, here are some caveats. First, leave PLENTY of time to order. Shipment delays are common. If a site quotes 4-8 weeks delivery,

E-MAIL FROM THE REAL WORLD
Spending $385 for a $50 dresser

A reader in Ohio shared this bad experience with shopping for a dresser online:

"I ordered a three drawer combo dresser from BabyUniverse.com. It had all of the things suggested in your book and was $385 (the Rumble Tuff line around here was $700 for the same thing). The manufacturer is Angel Line. The item arrived with split wood on the corner, a knob missing, a missing wall strap and one of the drawers didn't shut completely and was crooked. I called Baby Universe and they said I had to contact the manufacturer directly to get the problem resolved. It took four calls and the best I could get was another knob and drawer sent to me with corners that did not fit together. So, I essentially paid $400 for something that looks like it was $50 at a garage sale."

double that time to be safe. Next, quickly and thoroughly inspect any delivered items and report damage immediately. Be familiar with the web site's return and shipment policies, in case you have to file a claim.

Before you order online, check with local stores first to see if their prices are competitive–it might be worth paying an extra $50 or $100 to order a piece from a local retailer, especially if that store will take care of delivery, set-up and damage claims. Remember that some chains (Wal-Mart, for example) are experimenting with online orders shipped to a local store for pick-up . . . that might be a smarter move than trusting UPS won't mangle your crib.

Wastes of Money

1 LOW QUALITY "BABY" FURNITURE THAT WON'T LAST. Baby furniture stores (both chains and independents) are sometimes guilty of selling very poor quality furniture. Take a dresser, for example. Many dressers made by juvenile furniture companies have stapled drawers, veneer construction (instead of solid wood), cheap drawer glides and worse. Now, that wouldn't be so bad if such dressers were low in price. But often you see these dressers going for $500 and up in baby stores–it's as if you are paying a premium to merely match the color of your crib. While we don't see a problem buying low-end "disposable" furniture at a good price (IKEA is a prime example), paying a fortune for a poorly-made dresser seems ridiculous. In this chapter, we will point out brand names that provide more quality for the dollar. Look for solid wood construction, dove-tail drawers, and smooth drawer glides if you want that dresser to last.

2 UNDER-CRIB DRAWERS. It sounds like a great way to squeeze out a bit more storage in a nursery–the drawer that slides out from under a crib. Getting a crib with such a feature usually costs an extra $100 or $150. The problem? These drawers do NOT have tops . . . therefore anything kept in there will get dusty in a hurry. So that nixes storing extra blankets or clothes. We say skip the extra expense of an under-crib drawer.

3 THE TODDLER BED. Some crib makers tout cribs that convert to toddler beds. Smaller than a twin bed, a toddler bed uses the crib mattress and is pitched as a transition between the crib and a big boy/girl bed. But, guess what? Most kids can go straight from a crib to a regular twin bed with no problem whatsoever. So, the toddler bed business is really a joke.

4 **CRADLE.** Most pediatricians recommend "rooming in" with your newborn to help with breastfeeding. But where will the baby sleep? Cradles and bassinets are one option, but can be pricey. Cradles (basically a mini crib that rocks) run up to $400, while separate bassinets (a basket on a stand) can cost $200. A more affordable solution: just set up the crib in your room. After you establish that breastfeeding rhythm, the baby and crib can move to the nursery. If you don't have room in your master bedroom to set up the crib, consider a playpen with bassinet feature like the Graco Pack N Play. A co-sleeper like the Arm's Reach (discussed later in this chapter) is another option. We'll discuss the best buys on bassinets later in this chapter; playpens like the Pack N Play are reviewed in Chapter 7, Around the House.

5 **CRIBS WITH "SPECIAL FEATURES."** Some stores carry unique styles of cribs and that might be tempting for parents looking to make a statement for their nursery. An example: round cribs. The only problem: special cribs like this may require additional expenses, such as custom-designed mattresses or bedding. And since few companies make bedding for round cribs, your choices are limited. The best advice: make sure you price out the total investment (crib, mattress, bedding) before falling in love with an unusual brand.

6 **CHANGING TABLES.** Separate changing tables are a big waste of money. Don't spend $70 to $200 on a piece of furniture you won't use again after your baby gives up diapers. A better bet: buy a dresser that can do double duty as a changing table. Many dressers you'll see in baby stores are designed with this extra feature—just make sure the height is comfortable for both you and your spouse. Other parents we interviewed did away with the changing area altogether—they used a crib, couch or countertop to do diaper changes.

Top 9 Things Baby Stores Won't Tell You About Buying Nursery Furniture

◆ *Our store may disappear before your nursery furniture arrives.* It's a sad fact: baby stores come and go. Most retailers that close do so reputably—they don't take special orders for merchandise they can't fill. A handful are not so honest . . . they take deposits up until the day the landlord padlocks their doors. Our advice: always charge your purchase to a credit card. If the store disappears, you can dispute the charge with your credit card and (most likely) get your money back. Another red flag: stores that ask for payment up front on a special order. The typical deal is half down with the balance due upon delivery. Stores that are desperate for cash might demand the entire purchase price upfront. Be suspicious. Another piece of advice: keep a close eye on what's going on with your furniture maker. How? Read our blog or surf our message boards at BabyBargains.com. Over the years, we've seen it all–strikes, floods, fires, port shutdowns and more. You name it, it can happen to the factory that makes your furniture. When we get a whiff of a problem, we send out the news to our readers via our e-newsletter, blog or on our message boards. That way you can switch to another brand if you've haven't placed an order yet . . . or for-mulate a plan B if your furniture is caught by a delivery delay.

◆ **Never assume something in a sealed box is undamaged.** Always OPEN boxes and inspect furniture before taking it out of a store. Yes, that is a hassle, but we've had numerous complains about boxed furniture that someone has driven 50 miles home, only to discover a major gash or other damage. Or the wrong color is in the right box. Or a major piece is missing. A word to the wise: inspect it BEFORE going home.

◆ **If it is in stock, BUY IT.** Let's say you see a crib that is in stock, but the matching dresser is on back order. Do you get the crib now and wait on the dresser? Or special order both? Our advice: if an item is sitting there in a store (even if it is a floor sample), it is ALWAYS better to take the in-stock item now. Will the stain match since the furniture will be from two different batches? Mismatched finishes are rare and usually not an issue. Most furniture makers make their cribs in one factory and their case pieces in another; hence the dye lot thing is not relevant. Even if there is a slight dif-ference in coloration, you probably won't put the dresser right next to the crib anyway. And you'll use the crib for two to four years, but the dresser for much longer—so if there is a slight color differ-ence, you won't notice it when you've long put away the crib!

◆ **Your special order merchandise will be backordered until 2011, despite our promise to get it to you before your baby is born.** Almost all furniture today is imported . . . we are not talking from close-by countries like Canada or Mexico. Nope, odds are your furniture will be made in China, Eastern Europe or South America. And a myriad of problems (labor strikes, port shutdowns, Latvian Independence Day) can delay the shipment of your nursery furniture. Our advice: ORDER EARLY. If the furniture store says it will take six weeks, plan on 12. Or 15.

◆ *Just because the crib maker has an Italian name doesn't mean your furniture is made in, say, Italy.* Not long ago, you had domestic makers of cribs (Child Craft, Simmons) and the imports, most of which were from Italy. As we mentioned above, nearly all cribs are imported today, most from China and Eastern Europe, but some from South America and Canada. And yes, the Italians are still players in the crib business.

Here's where it gets confusing: sometimes the very same brand will import furniture from different countries. Sorelle, for example, started out as an Italian importer. Today, Sorelle still sells some cribs from Italy, but now also imports cribs and dressers from China, Brazil and Latvia (Eastern Europe). Ditto for Bonavita, which now supplements its Italian imports with collections from Vietnam and China. Munire imports some cribs from Italy, makes a few dressers in New Jersey and imports other entire collections from Indonesia.

An important point: don't assume you are getting a crib made in Italy because the brand has an Italian name.

Bottom line: key on the brand's reputation for quality and customer service, not so much the country the crib is made in. Yes, Italian-made cribs are still considered the gold standard in the biz. But we've seen great quality cribs from Brazil, Eastern Europe and yes, even China and Indonesia. Because of currency exchange rates, these other cribs will be a better value than Italian cribs. In the reviews in this section, we will give you our opinion about a brand's quality and customer service. We consider the furniture's construction and safety in assigning our ratings as well.

◆ *That special mattress we insist you buy isn't necessary.* Some baby stores are trying a new tactic to sell their pricey in-house brand of crib mattress: scaring the pants off new parents. We've heard all the stories—only OUR mattress fits OUR crib, a simpler foam mattress is DANGEROUS for your baby and so on. Please! Government standards require both cribs and mattresses to be within standard measurements. Yes, fancy boutiques might make their mattress a bit larger to give a tighter fit . . . but that doesn't mean a regular mattress won't work just as well (and safely). It's no wonder stores push the in-house mattress—it can cost $250 or more. Our advice: save your money and get a plain crib mattress for half the price at another store.

◆ *Just because we say this item is discontinued does NOT mean you can't find it anywhere else.* This is especially true for chain stores—just because Babies R Us says the crib you've fallen in love with is now discontinued, that does NOT mean you can't find it from another store. That's because chains discontinue items all the time . . . and not just because the manufacturer is discontinuing it. Chains replace slow moving merchandise or just make way for something new. Meanwhile, the very same furniture (or for that matter, any baby gear) is sold down the street at another store.

◆ *This beautiful sleigh style crib will make it impossible to tie a crib bumper.* Cribs with solid panel ends (like sleigh styles) are hip these days . . . but if you want to use a bumper, you may be disappointed. That's because many crib makers forget to design these cribs with any place to tie a bumper; and a poorly attached bumper is a safety hazard. (More on bumpers and whether you really need one in the next chapter). Cribs with very thick corner posts also make it hard to tie a bumper (some cribs from Natart, Dutailier, and Bonavita are often guilty of this design flaw). Our advice: if in doubt, take a bumper from another crib and try to tie it on the style you want.

◆ *The stain on your expensive nursery furniture may match . . . or not.* Here's something baby stores don't advertise: the finishes on that expensive nursery furniture you special ordered may not match. Why? Many furniture companies use different wood for different pieces—say birch for a crib, but pine for a dresser. The problem: each takes stain differently. As a result, a birch crib in cherry may not match a pine dresser in the same cherry stain. While the difference may be small, it bugs some folks more than others. The take home message: if matching stain is important to you, confirm all the pieces of your furniture are made of the same wood—and try to see a sample of the stain on a real piece of furniture to confirm colors (don't rely on online photos).

Money Saving Secrets

1 CHECK OUT REGULAR FURNITURE STORES FOR ROCKERS, DRESSERS, ETC. Think about it—most juvenile furniture looks very similar to regular adult furniture. Rockers, dressers, and bookcases are, well, just rockers, dressers, and bookcases. And don't you wonder if companies slap the word "baby" on an item just to raise the price 20%? To test this theory, we visited a local discount furniture store. The prices were incredibly low. A basic three-drawer dresser was $60. Even pine or oak three-drawer dressers were just $129 to $189. The same quality dresser at a baby store by a "juvenile furniture" manufacturer would set you back at least $400, if not twice that. We even saw cribs by such mainstream names as Bassett at decent prices in regular furniture stores. What's the disadvantage to shopping there? Well, if you have to buy the crib and dresser at different places, the colors might not match exactly. But, considering the savings, it might be worth it.

2 **THINK TWICE ABOUT MOD.** Modern furniture is the rage in high-end boutiques, but what do you get for that ultra-mod look? Many "modern" cribs and furniture are made of MDF, particle board and laminates . . . and for this you're supposed to shell out $800 for a crib and $1600 for a dresser? Can someone explain to us why modern furniture costs TWICE as much as "regular" cribs and dressers that are made of all wood? Sure that mod furniture has a few extra coats of lacquer and looks all shiny. But we still don't get it—especially since nearly all nursery furniture (yes, even the mod stuff) is imported from Asia. Our advice: If you decide to go mod, stick with the more affordable options like IKEA (even Wal-Mart now sports a modern furniture collection at reasonable prices).

3 **COMPARE ONLINE PRICES.** Do you wonder if that local baby store has jacked up the price of nursery furniture? We know some of you live in towns or communities with little or no local competition for nursery items. One obvious solution: hit the web. Now, we realize we listed all sorts of caveats for online orders earlier in the book (high shipping fees, problems with damage, etc)—but let's face it. In some parts of the country, this is really your best option. As always, don't ASSUME local stores will be higher price than the web. Do your homework first. And always ask local retailers if they will price match what you see online. Many quietly do! One good source to compare crib prices: BabyCribCentral.com doesn't sell cribs, but provides a handy price comparison engine.

A caveat to online shopping: if you live in Alaska or Hawaii (or are overseas military with an APO address), you may be out of luck. While Wal-Mart and Target will ship some items to Alaska and Hawaii, others sites refuse.

4 **ONE WORD: IKEA.** Sure, it's basic and no frills . . . but it's hard to beat the price! IKEA's ultra affordable cribs and dressers make even Wal-Mart look expensive. Example: the DIKTAD crib for $159 and matching dresser for $169. Yes, you will have assemble it yourself. And no, it won't last through three kids. But hey—its hard to beat the price. (See the brand reviews later for more in IKEA, including some key things to know before you buy).

5 **GO NAKED.** Naked furniture, that is. An increasing number of stores sell unfinished (or naked) furniture at great prices. Such

E-MAIL FROM THE REAL WORLD
**Get all the details on delivery
before you mail-order furniture**

*A mom-to-be in Chicago discovered Sears was a much better
deal than JCPenney for her nursery furniture. Here's her story:*

"While I was searching for baby furniture, I thought JCPenney's
would be a good choice. The catalog gave me a large selection to
choose from and it would be less time consuming than hitting all
the little shops. So, I put in an order for a crib and mattress and a
four-drawer dresser. The prices on the furniture were pretty good
(about $150 less than in other stores). However, the furniture has to
be shipped directly from the warehouse to your home. Shipping
and handling would have been $110 and the shipping company
would only drop off the material at the front door—not into the
home (or, in our case, a second floor apartment!) I could hardly
believe it! If I had to spend over a hundred dollars extra on shipping, I would rather spend it on a higher quality crib and dresser
than on shipping and handling. Hence, the search continued.

"Next I went to Sears where they had a 'Sculptured' series
Child Craft crib and matching flip-top dresser. The prices were
reasonable, you could pick the delivery day (including Saturdays)
and they would deliver for just $25! They had these items in stock,
so we got it in two days. Even if it did have to be shipped from
the main warehouse, however, we would still only be charged the
$25 fee and would have to wait at most four weeks. Needless to
say, we bought the crib and dresser at Sears!"

places even sell the finishing supplies and give you directions (make
sure to use a non-toxic finish). The prices are hard to beat. At a local
unfinished furniture store, we found a three-drawer pine dresser (23"
wide) for $100, while a four-drawer dresser (38" wide) was $175.
Compare that to baby store prices, which can top $400 to $700 for
a similar size dresser. A reader in California e-mailed us with a great
example of this trend in the Bay Area: "Hoot Judkins" has three locations (Redwood City, Fremont, Millbrae; hootjudkins.com) that sell
unfinished furniture. She found a five-drawer dresser in solid birch for
just $229 and other good deals on nursery accessories. Another idea:
Million Dollar Baby (see review later in this chapter) is one of the few
crib makers to offer unfinished crib models (Jenny Lind, M0301).
While unfinished cribs are somewhat rare, naked furniture stores at
least offer affordable alternatives for dressers, bookcases, and more.

6 **SKIP THE SLEIGH CRIB.** Lots of folks fall in love with the look of
a sleigh-style crib, which looks like, well, a sleigh. The only

problem? Most sleigh cribs have solid foot and headboards. All that extra wood means higher prices, as much as $100 to $300 more than non-sleigh crib styles. If you have your heart set on a sleigh style, look for one with slats on the headboard instead of solid wood.

7 **CONSIDER AN AFFORDABLE CONVERTIBLE CRIB.** Now, the key word here is "affordable." In past editions of our book, we derided most "convertible" cribs for their high prices and expensive conversion kits. And then there is the whole issue of whether you really want a crib to morph into a double bed. But we realize that many parents like the convertible concept, so let's talk about how to get a deal. Good news: several companies (among them Munire, Child Craft/Legacy and Sorelle) have rolled out affordable convertible cribs. Walk into Babies R Us and you'll find convertible cribs around $500 . . . that buys you a decent crib that converts to a toddler bed and then to a real-size double bed with the addition of simple bed rails. One tip: make sure the design has a true headboard and shorter footboard (many low-end convertible cribs cheat on this point by having the same size head and foot boards). This looks much better when converted to a double bed.

8 **TRY CRAIGSLIST.ORG.** As you probably know, Craigslist's popular online classified site has versions for three dozen cities, with a special "for sale" section for baby/kids stuff. Use Craigslist to find a local family that is unloading unneeded nursery furniture, gear and other items (but do NOT buy a used cribs, as we've discussed earlier).

Baby Superstore Reviews: The Good, Bad & Ugly

There's good news and bad news when it comes to shopping for baby. Good news: there are an amazing number of stores to shop for baby gear. Bad news: there are an amazing number of stores to shop for baby gear.

And as a first-time parent, you probably have never been in these stores (except for that time you bought a gift for a pregnant co-worker). Walking into a baby superstore for the first time can give even the most levelheaded mom or dad-to-be a case of the willies. It is a blizzard of pacifiers, strollers, cribs and more in a mind-numbing assortment of colors, features and options. So, as a public service, here's our overview of the major players in the baby store biz.

Babies R Us *(888-BABYRUS; web: babiesrus.com).* The 800-pound gorilla of baby stores, Babies R Us has 230+ stores nationwide and is the country's leading baby gear retailer. Love 'em or hate 'em, you'll probably find yourself in a BRU at some point—in some communities, BRU is the only game in town.

For the uninitiated, Babies R Us is your typical chain store—big on selection, decent prices . . . but service? That's not the point. Sure, our readers occasionally report they found a knowledgeable sales clerk. But other times, you are lucky to find a person to check you out, much less give advice on a car seat.

As for brands, BRU is middle of the road—yes, there are entry level brands like Graco and Delta, but also more premium options from Perego and Maclaren. As for nursery furniture, BRU has expanded into private-label, exclusive merchandise in recent years, most recently with their deal with designer Wendy Bellissimo (see brand review later). BRU also teamed with Dorel/Cosco to do a line of furniture under the Jardine and Bella D'Este name plates. The results so far have been a mixed bag—we haven't been that impressed with these in-house brands, quality-wise.

It's a much brighter picture for Babies R Us' web site. After dissolving a disastrous partnership with Amazon in the past year, BRU has built its own independent site and the results are a stark improvement. BRU's dot-com entry is easy to navigate and features user reviews of products plus decent pricing.

Best of all, BRU's web site is now better integrated with the chain's popular gift registry. When you sign up at the store, you get a slick spiral-bound packet stuffed with info on how to register, FAQ's and so on. There are several "quick start" registries, with suggestions for basics (layette, bedding, feeding, etc.) and then beyond the basics (strollers, playpens, etc.). Sure, some of the suggested items are a little nutty (no, you don't need the Diaper Genie or Floating Bath Pal Thermometer). But it is a good starting point and well organized.

Like all gift registries, there are always hiccups and BRU isn't immune—given our reader email, we could probably start an entire new blog with just BRU registry snafus. But the complaints have been on the decline in recent months, as the Amazon divorce has helped BRU put the registry on a better footing.

So, how to grade Babies R Us? For selection, make it an A-, service gets a C, pricing a B+ and the new registry, an A. Overall, let's call it a B. **Rating: B**

Baby Depot (800-444-COAT; web: burlingtoncoatfactory.com). Baby Depot is a store-within-a-store concept. Tucked inside the cavernous Burlington Coat Factory, Baby Depot is a nook stuffed with nursery furniture, strollers and a smattering of other gear.

Even though there are more Baby Depots than Babies R Us stores (300+ at last count), Baby Depot has always played second-fiddle to BRU. Part of the problem has been marketing strategy: Baby Depot could use one. Burlington/Baby Depot operates in a wide range of locations, some in shiny new suburban power centers and others in dingy warehouses. The company has experimented with free-standing baby superstores and now runs a couple of "Super Baby Depots" in New Jersey and California.

The selection of brands at Baby Depot is decent: you'll see Perego strollers and name-brand furniture like Child Craft and Sorelle (C&T) cribs. Merchandising isn't Baby Depot's strong suit—the aisles of Baby Depot are often disorganized and cluttered. Ditto for Baby Depot's web site—don't come here looking for user reviews (there aren't any) or easy navigation (you can't search by brand).

The service at Baby Depot makes Babies R Us look like Nordstrom's. We get frequent letters from Baby Depot furniture customers, complaining about late orders, botched orders and worse.

And don't get us started on Baby Depot's draconian return policy, which for years generated voluminous (negative) reader mail. At least there is good news to report on that front: in September 2006, Baby Depot adopted a new return policy—you can now return an item within 30 days and get your cash back (as long as you have a receipt and the tags are still attached).

So, here's our advice: if you see something here that is in stock and the price is right, go for it. But forget about special ordering anything such as furniture. ***Rating: C-***

Buy Buy Baby Web: BuyBuyBaby.com. Run by the sons of the family that founded the Bed, Bath & Beyond chain, Buy Buy Baby is the East Coast baby store chain that is our top pick in this category. Yes, you have to be lucky to live near one of their eight locations in New York, New Jersey, Maryland or Virginia . . . but it is worth the trip if you are nearby.

Service is the strong point here—folks at Buy Buy Baby know their stuff. Now, we realize that this might not be a fair fight—can Babies R Us (with 230+ stores) ever compete on service with a much smaller rival? It will be interesting to see if Buy Buy Baby can maintain that advantage as it slowly expands from its East Coast base.

Given the urban slant to its locations, the brands and selection skew toward the expensive. Yes, there are Graco travel systems here . . . but also Bugaboo's $800 models. Ditto for the furniture, with Million Dollar Baby sharing floor space with more pricey options from Young America (by Stanley), Berg and Westwood.

The stores are merchandised a bit like Bed Bath and Beyond—that is crowded, with stacks of merchandise rising to the ceiling. While Babies R Us is a bit easier to navigate, Buy Buy Baby has more selection in several categories.

If we had to pick one point on which Buy Buy could improve, it would have to be their lackluster web site. No user reviews, poor organization and little in the way of buying advice—Buy Buy Baby's web site might have done the trick five years ago, but now it is among the weakest online entries. When you click on a category like strollers, you get a long list of links . . . for both stroller types (umbrella, double) and brands. A better brand search engine would be most helpful.

Despite their web site, we still give Buy Buy Baby our top rating among chain stores—if you happen to be near one, this store is a keeper. **Rating: A**

The Discounters: Target, Wal-Mart, K-Mart

What's Cool: Any discussion of national stores that sell baby items wouldn't be complete without a mention of the discounters: Target, Wal-Mart, K-Mart and their ilk. In recent years, the discounters have realized one sure-fire way to drive store traffic—discount baby gear! As a result, you'll often see formula, diapers and other baby essentials at rock-bottom prices. And there are even better deals on "in-house" brands. The goal is to have you drop by to pick up some diapers . . . and then walk out with a big-screen TV.

Of all the discounters, we think Target is best (with one big caveat—their draconian return policy, see below for a discussion). Target's baby department is a notch above Wal-Mart and K-Mart when it comes to brand names and selection. Yes, sometimes Wal-Mart has lower prices—but usually that's on lower-quality brands. Target, by contrast, carries Perego high chairs and a wider selection of products like baby monitors. The best bet: Super Targets, which have expanded baby products sections.

One important trend: discounters have bulked up their web sites with brands, products and models that are NOT carried in their stores. Sometimes you'll even find an upscale brand online at discount prices. We'll discuss the discounter web sites specifically below.

Needs work: If you're looking for premium brand names, forget it. Most discounters only stock the so-called mass-market brands: Graco strollers, Cosco car seats, Gerber sheets, etc. And the baby departments always seem to be in chaos when we visit, with items strewn about hither and yon. K-Mart is probably the worst when it comes to organization, Wal-Mart the best. We like Target's selection (especially of feeding items and baby monitors), but their prices are somewhat higher than Wal-Mart. What about service? Forget it—no matter which store you're in, you're on your own.

While we do recommend Target, we should warn readers about

their return policy. Once among the most generous, Target now requires a receipt for just about any return. A raft of new rules and restrictions greet customers (sample: exchanges now must be made for items within the same department). This has understandably ticked off a fair number of our readers, especially those who have unfortunately chosen to register at Target for their baby gifts. Among the biggest roadblocks: Target won't let you exchange duplicate baby gifts if you don't have a gift receipt (and there are numerous other rules/restrictions as well). Of course, your friends may forget to ask for a gift receipt or throw it away. And watch out: gift receipts have expiration dates; be sure to return any item before that date. Target also limits the number of returns you can do in one year.

After receiving a fair amount of consumer complaints about this, Target now allows returns of registry gifts without a gift receipt IF the item is listed on your registry. The rub: you will get the lowest sales price in the last 90 days, not necessarily what your guest paid for it. That's a special gotcha for new parents—many baby products and clothes go on sale frequently, rendering your gift almost worthless on an exchange. This and other beefs with Target have spawned many complaints about their registry and even blogs dedicated to dissing the chain.

Our advice: think twice about registering at Target. While we get complaints about all baby registries (even industry leader Babies R Us), be sure to read the fine print for ANY baby registry before signing up. Ask about returns and exchange policies, including specifically what happens if you have to return/exchange a duplicate item without a gift receipt. And check for limits on the number of returns you can do within a certain time period. Finally, ask about HOW the store integrates your registry with the web site—if someone buys an item online instead of at a store, will this be reflected on your registry? Check our blog and message boards for the latest buzz on baby registries.

Web: Each of the major discounters sells baby products online. Here's an overview of each site:

◆ *WalMart.com:* Hit the baby tab and you'll find yourself in Wal-Mart's extensive online baby gear department. We like how the chain has expanded online offerings in recent years—there's much more on the web site than in the stores (particularly for strollers). Wal-Mart has steadily improved the site over the last year or so—now you can search by brand, read product reviews and get a product delivered to nearby store at no charge. And, of course, the prices are excellent.

◆ **Kmart.com**: K-Mart's online outpost is a winner—we liked the graphics and easy navigation. You can search by brand, price and more. We also liked the "This Just In" section for new arrivals. The only bummer: unlike Target, K-Mart's online selection brand-wise is much the same as the store—heavy on low-end brands like Kolcraft. The depth of merchandise on Kmart.com is also quite thin: go to convertible car seats and you'll see only a half dozen choices. Compare that to Target, which posts 30+ options online.

◆ **Target.com** is our pick as the best discounter web site—their online offerings go way beyond what's in the stores. We also like the user reviews, as well as the ability to sort any category by brand, price or best-sellers. Perhaps the biggest drawback with Target.com (as with other sites) is the rather skimpy product descriptions. You can often find more about a product by reading the user reviews than Target's own descriptions. Example: for a $200 crib,

Baby Gift Registries: Disappointing

We have a plea for tomorrow's computer science college graduates: fix the gift registries at chain stores—please!

Sure, computers can pilot a spaceship to Pluto or solve the most complex microbiology problem . . . but for some reason, such computer smarts elude the baby gift registry programmers at chains stores.

No matter how sweet the promises are about computerized registries ("Look Ma! I'm changing an item on the registry at 2am!") the reality falls WAY short of utopia. Judging from our reader mail and message boards, folks are steamed when they must deal with registry snafus . . . and who can blame them.

While the process of registering at any chain is relatively straightforward (you can scan items in the store or pick them off a web site), USING the registry is where things start to fall apart. You name it, we've heard it: duplicate gifts, out of stock items (with no notice to the parent), endless backorders and other goofs.

Here's a typical story from one of our readers:

"I decided to register at Target since that is where most of my family shops and I figured it would be an easy thing to do. Boy, was I wrong. The first time I registered, they 'lost' my list and then found it only to connect it to the wrong name! I ended up spending over an hour on hold with their help desk while they corrected the problem. Much to my dismay, I real-

Target neglects to mention the crib's antiquated double-trigger rail release . . . something a buyer complained about in a review posted online.

Specialty Chains: More Baby Stores To Shop!

Inspired by the success of Pottery Barn Kids, several chains have ventured into the nursery business. An example: Room & Board (web: RoomandBoard.com), a nine-store chain with locations in California, Colorado, Illinois, Minnesota and the New York City Area. Their well-designed web site has a nursery section with a couple of cribs ($600 to $700), dressers and accessories. Quality is good and prices are reasonable, say our readers who've ordered from them.

And that's just the beginning: Land of Nod, a subsidiary of Crate & Barrel, has an extensive website with nursery offerings

ized that I needed to add a few things to the list about a week later, so I went back in and repeated the process. Once again, I've had to call the help desk because my new items are not showing up on the list. And again, my list is 'lost' and this time they said it could be up to 48 hours before it can be fixed! And each person I talked to seemed to blame me for the initial problem."

Some of the problems with a gift registry only become apparent AFTER you've received a gift. Example: Pottery Barn's policy on gift certificates. If you want to use a gift certificate for an online or telephone purchase at Pottery Barn Kids, you must MAIL the certificate in and cool your heels for a two to three week processing period. How convenient.

Babies R Us runs the country's biggest gift registry—and comes in for a regular barbequing from our readers. To its credit, BRU has fixed many of the glitches that were apparent in recent years . . . the gift registry is now in sync with BRU's web site and yes, now you can use a gift card to pay for an online purchase.

Bottom line: take a second and read the gift registry feedback from recent parents on our web site (hang out in the "Lounge" forum or do a search on the site). Always READ the return policies of any gift registry BEFORE you sign up—is there a time limit for returns? Must you have a gift receipt? Are you limited to X number of returns or exchanges? Know ALL the fine print before you plunge in!

(ten cribs as of press time) as well as four stores plus an outlet. Bombay Kids, the offshoot of Bombay Company of Ft. Worth, Texas, now has three dozen stores that sell baby and kids furniture (as well as online).

What's driving this is a boom in babies, especially to older moms and dads. Tired of the cutesy baby stuff in chain stores, many parents are looking for something more sophisticated and hip. Of course, it remains to be seen what this means for bargain shoppers. On one hand, more competition is always good—having a wide diversity of places to buy nursery furniture and accessories is always a plus. On the downside, most of these chains are chasing that "upscale" customer with outrageously priced cribs and bedding. "As much as parents love the furniture at Pottery Barn Kids, some wince at the prices," said the *Wall Street Journal* in a recent article on this trend. And we agree—while we love the PBK look, our goal in life is to try to find that same look . . . at half the price!

Outlets

There are dozens of outlets that sell kids' clothing, but when it comes to furniture the pickings are slim. In fact, we found just a handful of nursery furniture outlets out there. Here's a round up:

Pottery Barn Kids has eight outlets for their kids catalog, scattered around the country (go to outletbound.com and search for Pottery Barn to see if there is one near you). Readers report some good deals there, including a changing table for $99 (regularly $199) and a rocker for $199 (down from $700). The outlet also carries the PBK bedding line at good discounts. A reader in Georgia said the PBK outlet there features 75% off deals on furniture and you can get a coupon book at the food court for an additional 10% discount. "The best time to shop is during the week—they run more specials then," she said. "And bring a truck—they don't deliver." One final tip: call AHEAD before you go. The selection of nursery furniture can vary widely from outlet to outlet . . . some may have no stock during certain months.

If you are looking for Child Craft cribs and live near Indianapolis, check out the **Décor 4 Kids** store in Noblesville, IN (317-770-7700; decor4kidsonline.com). This store is the official outlet for Child Craft and Legacy's discontinued furniture—you'll 2500 square feet of cribs, dressers and other items at about 30% to 40% off retail. (Note: Décor 4 Kids has a second store in Carmel, IN, but only the Noblesville location carries the Child Craft outlet deals).

Live in the Northeast? Check out **Baby Boudoir Outlet,** an off-shoot of a baby store in New Bedford, MA (800-272-2293, 508-998-2166) that is also authorized by Child Craft to sell their discontinued furniture at wholesale prices or below. The Baby Boudoir Outlet has 1000 cribs in stock at any one time at prices that start under $100 (most are $150 to $300). The store also carries glider rockers, bedding and other baby products at 30% to 70% off retail. FYI: There is both a Baby Boudoir store and a warehouse outlet—you want to visit the outlet for the best deals. The outlet is around the corner from the main store. Of course, Baby Boudoir sells more than just Child Craft—they also sell discontinued Sorelle cribs (30% to 70% off) and certain discontinued Munire styles, as well as factory seconds from such bedding lines as Kids Line, Lambs & Ivy and more. A caveat to this outlet: a reader who recently visited the outlet described it as a "rusty warehouse in a bad neighborhood. I would put a HUGE disclaimer on this outlet to warn folks it is very bare bones."

Along the same lines, **Baby Furniture Warehouse**, with stores in Reading and Braintree, MA (781-942-7978 or 781-843-5353; web: BabyFurnitureWarehouse.com, see below), specializes in selling overstock and discontinued cribs from Pali, Bonavita, Sorelle and Baby's Dream. You can save up to 30% off regular retail prices here—cribs run $260 to $500 and case pieces are also available. The store sells many furniture sets, including a three-piece package (crib please two dressers) from Baby's Dream for $1150 or Pali for $1300. A reader who bought her furniture at this outlet thought the store

Hotel cribs: hazardous at $200 a night?

Sure, your nursery at home is a monument to safety, but what happens when you take that act on the road? Sadly, many hotels are still in the dark ages when it comes to crib safety. A recent survey by the CPSC found unsafe cribs in a whopping 80% of hotels and motels checked by inspectors. Even worse: when the CPSC invited hotel chains to join a new safety effort to fix the problem, only the Bass Hotel chain (Inter-Continental, Holiday Inn, Crowne Plaza) agreed to join. That chain pledged to have their staff inspect all cribs, making sure they meet current safety standards. We urge other hotels to join this effort, as research shows children under age two spend more than seven MILLION nights per year in hotels and motels. And if you find yourself in a hotel with your baby, don't assume the crib you request is safe—check carefully for loose hardware, inadequate size sheets and other problems. Another tip: consider bringing your own sheets to ensure safety.

was fine, but delivery and customer service after the sale left much to be desired. Her order took much longer to arrive than estimated; then a dresser door arrived damaged. It took three months to get a replacement door and, meanwhile, Baby Furniture failed to promptly return the customer's calls, missed delivery appointments and so on.

Bassett sells its cribs and nursery furniture from its namesake outlet in Bassett, Virginia (276) 629-6446. A reader recently visited the outlet for a good selection of cribs. She snagged a $500 retail crib at the Bassett outlet for $157 (new and in the box)!

Don't forget that **JCPenney** has 15 outlet stores nationwide. The stores carry a wide variety of items, including children's and baby products (always call before you go to confirm selection). Check out the web site Outlet Bound (outletbound.com) for a current listing of locations.

Finally, for our Canadian readers in Ontario (or Buffalo, NY), check out the **Mother Hubbard** factory outlet in Toronto (416) 572-0486. This outlet sells the company's namesake cribs and dressers—discontinued styles, samples and more at 20% to 60% off retail. The outlet also offers bedding from Bebe Chic.

The Name Game:
Reviews of Selected Manufacturers

Here's a look at crib brands sold in the U.S. and Canada. Our focus is on the most common nursery furniture brands you see in chains stores, independents and other furniture outlets. If you've discovered a brand that we didn't review, feel free to share your discovery by calling or emailing us (see our contact info at the end of the book).

How did we evaluate the brands? First, we inspected samples of cribs at stores and industry trade shows. With the help of veteran juvenile furniture retailers, we checked construction, release mechanisms, mattress supports, and overall fit and finish. Yes, we did compare styling among the brands but this was only a minor factor in our ratings (we figure you can decide what looks best for your nursery).

Readers of previous editions have asked us how we assign ratings to these manufacturers—what makes one an "A" vs. "B"? The bottom line is quality *and* value. Sure, anyone can make a high-quality crib for $500 or $800. The trick is getting that price down to $300 or less while maintaining high-quality standards. Hence, we give more bonus points to brands that give more value for the dollar.

What about the crib makers who got the lowest ratings? Are their cribs unsafe? No, of course not. ALL new cribs sold in the U.S. and Canada must meet minimum federal safety standards. As we mentioned earlier in this chapter, a $100 crib sold at Wal-Mart is just as safe as a $700 designer brand sold at a posh boutique. The only difference is styling, features and durability—more expensive cribs have thick wood posts, fancy finishes, features like "hidden hardware" on the rail release, under-crib storage drawers and durability to last through two or more kids.

Brands that got our lowest rating typically have had a problem with recalls in previous years. Some were fined by the CPSC for failing to report injuries or problems with their products. That doesn't mean that their current production cribs are unsafe; but we were troubled enough by their past track record to assign that lower rating.

Please note: we've included phone numbers and web sites in this section so you can find a local dealer. These manufacturers do NOT sell directly to the public, unless otherwise noted. Most web sites will feature a selection of cribs, if not the entire line.

The Ratings

A **EXCELLENT**—*our top pick!*

B **GOOD**— *above average quality, prices, and creativity.*

C **FAIR**—*could stand some improvement.*

D **POOR**—*yuck! could stand some major improvement.*

AFG Furniture. *This crib brand is reviewed on our free web site, BabyBargains.com (click on Bonus Material).*

Alta Baby *This crib brand is reviewed on our free web site, BabyBargains.com (click on Bonus Material).*

Amby Baby Motion Bed *Call 1-866-519-2229 for a dealer near you. Web: AmbyBaby. com* Invented by an Australian dad for his colicky daughter, the Amby baby hammock is just that—a hammock that is designed as a safe sleep environment to replace a bassinet, cradle or even crib. It looks like a swing, with a wide base (18") and comes with a mattress, pair of sheets, frame, spring and cross bar. The basic version  runs $228, while a couple of deluxe versions (which include accessories like a mosquito net and more sheets) can cost up to $295.

So, should you get one? Well, we agree with the science behind this idea—a cocooned environment like a hammock mimics the womb, which soothes colicky babies. So, is it safe? Yes, we think it is—the exception would be preemies. We don't recommend a baby hammock for preemies (despite the fact the company sells an accessory to better accommodate smaller infants). If you have a preemie, discuss your baby's sleeping arrangement with your pediatrician. And, while Amby says you can use the hammock up to 59 lbs. with a second spring (the first spring that comes with the unit is good up to 29 lbs), we suggest you transition your baby out of the hammock around three months. Why? First, that's when colic usually ends (it starts around three weeks and can continue until three months. For more about colic, which affects 15% of babies, see our other book *Baby 411*).

Second, around three to four months of age, babies become more aware of their surroundings and that's why most pediatricians suggest this is the right time to transition a baby out of a cradle or bassinet (or in this case, a hammock). After four months, babies start to establish a permanent sleep routine. A crib would be best then. Why? Babies need to roll over and learn how to pull themselves up—something that can't be done in a hammock. Yea, Amby dismisses this concern by saying baby can learn these developmental milestones during the daytime on the floor, but considering how much time a baby spends in a "sleep environment," that seems a bit misguided.

The take home message: if you have a history of colic in your family or your baby develops colic, consider the Amby Baby Motion Bed hammock (after consulting with your pediatrician first). Use it until around three months. No, Amby does NOT cure colic, but it could help lessen it. ***Rating: A***

Angel Line *Call (800) 889-8158 or (856) 863-8009 for a dealer near you. Web: angelline.com.* Angel Line is a low-priced import furniture brand that makes a decent crib for the dollar. No, there's nothing fancy or high-style about this furniture—we spied a simple Jenny Lind crib on sale for $150 (regular price $230) on BabyUniverse.com. This crib features exposed rod/cane hardware and a foot-bar rail release, which you rarely see on the market these days. Other styles

Who Is Jenny Lind?

You can't shop for cribs and not hear the name "Jenny Lind." Here's an important point to remember: Jenny Lind isn't a brand name; it refers to a particular *style* of crib. But how did it get this name? Jenny Lind was a popular Swedish soprano living in the 19th century. During her triumphal U.S. tour, it was said that Lind slept in a "spool bed." Hence, cribs that featured turned spindles (which look like stacked spools of thread) became known as Jenny Lind cribs. All this begs the question—what if today we still named juvenile furniture after famous singers? Could we have Britney Spears cribs and Jessica Simpson dressers? Nah, bad idea.

run $200 to $400 and feature knee-push rail releases and other more contemporary touches. Most cribs come in a variety of finishes, including natural, white, maple, white wash, oak and cherry. While we thought Angel Line's crib represented a good value (especially for Grandma's house), their case goods and rockers were less of a deal. The quality on these items is poor (dressers featured stapled drawers and low-end drawer glides); a reader gave her Angel Line rocker-glider a C+ on our site after it started squeaking after six months, no matter how much oil was applied to the bolts. On the plus side, we do like Angel Line's detailed web site (primitive yes, but still lots of info there) . . . and Angel Line is one of the few furniture brands you can buy online. We've lowered Angel Line's rating a bit this year . . . while the brand is much the same as previous years, their competition has upped the ante on quality and pricing, making this line seem a bit behind the times. **Rating: C+**

A.P. Industries *Call (800) 463-0145 or (418) 728-2145. Web site: apindustries.com.* Quebec-based crib maker A.P. Industries (also known as Generations) offers stylish cribs and case pieces, which are available in a dozen different collections. A.P. has survived the recent shake-out of Canadian crib makers, thanks in part to its emphasis on high-quality finishes and construction. A.P. offers 19 finishes, available on any of its cribs and dressers (that's impressive). Yet even A.P. isn't immune to the pressure to import from Asia—in the past year, A.P. has added Chinese-made cribs to its line, as well as two dressers from Vietnam. Considering how expensive A.P. is (a crib typically runs $600, a dresser $800), we found this development to be a bit disappointing. Yes, A.P.'s quality has always been quite good (and most of the dressers are still made in Canada) . . . but we don't have much feedback yet on their new Asian imports. Customer service for this brand has been up and down through the years. Delivery takes about four weeks. New for 2008, A.P. is rolling out a contemporary, modern collection ($500 for a crib, $900 for a dresser), as well as 12 new two-tone finishes. **Rating: B+**

Babee Tenda *See box on page 54-55.*

Baby Appleseed *Web: babyappleseed.com. See Nursery Smart.*

Baby Cache *This Babies R Us exclusive is made by Munire (see review later in this chapter).*

Baby Trilogy Corner Cribs *This crib brand is reviewed on our free web site, BabyBargains.com (click on Bonus Material).*

Baby Mod. *This contemporary-style furniture is sold at Wal-Mart. It is made by Million Dollar Baby—see review later in this chapter.*

Baby's Dream *Call (800) TEL-CRIB or (229) 649-4404 for a dealer near you. Web: babysdream.com.* It's been a rough last year at Baby's Dream—in January 2007, the company's main manufacturing plant in Chile burned to the ground. As a result, the company struggled in the past year to fill orders and customers faced some

---

Babee Tenda's "safety" seminar: Anatomy of a Hard Sell

We got an interesting invitation in the mail during our second pregnancy—a company called "Babee Tenda" invited us to a free "Getting Ready For Baby" safety seminar at a local hotel. The seminar was described as "brief, light and enjoyable while handing out information on preventing baby injuries." Our curiosity piqued, we joined a couple dozen other expectant parents on a Saturday afternoon to learn their expert safety tips.

What followed was a good lesson for all parents—beware of companies that want to exploit parents' fears of their children being injured in order to sell their expensive safety "solutions." Sure enough, there was safety information dispensed at the seminar. The speaker started his talk with horrific tales of how many children are injured and killed each year. The culprit? Cheap juvenile equipment products like high chairs and cribs, he claimed. It was quite a performance—the speaker entranced the crowd with endless statistics on kids getting hurt and then demonstrated hazards with sample products from major manufacturers.

The seminar then segued into a thinly veiled pitch for their products: the Babee Tenda high chair/feeding table and crib. The speaker (really a salesperson) spent what seemed like an eternity trying to establish the company's credibility, claiming Babee Tenda has been in business for 60 years and only sells its products to hospitals and other institutions. We can see why—these products are far too ugly and expensive to sell in retail stores.

How expensive? The crib sells for $600+ and the feeding table for about $400.

We found Babee Tenda's sales pitch to be disgusting. They used misleading statistics and outright lies to scare parents into thinking they were putting their children in imminent danger if they used store-bought high chairs or cribs. Many of the statistics and "props" used to demonstrate hazards were as much as 20 years old and long since removed from the market! Even more reprehensible

---

delays in getting their furniture (the company switched some of their production to a Georgia plant to pick up the slack).

The latest saga at Baby's Dream reflects a company that has seen its share of ups and downs in recent years. Readers of past editions of this book may remember our criticism of Baby's Dream and their failing to report safety problems with their folding rail release (also called a drop gate). Not only were 13,000 defective cribs recalled, but the company was also cited for hiding the problem from safe-

---

were claims that certain popular juvenile products were about to be recalled. Specifically, Babee Tenda's salesperson claimed the Evenflo Exersaucer was "unsafe and will be off the market in six months," an accusation that clearly wasn't true.

The fact that Babee Tenda had to use such bogus assertions raised our suspicions about whether they were telling the truth about their own products. Sadly, the high-pressure sales tactics did win over some parents at the seminar we attended—they forked over nearly $800 for Babee Tenda's items. Since then, we've heard from other parents who've attended Babee Tenda's "safety seminars," purchased the products and then suffered a case of "buyer's remorse." Did they spend too much, they ask?

Yes, in our opinion. While we see nothing wrong per se with Babee Tenda's "feeding table" (besides the fact it's god-awful ugly), you should note it costs nearly four times as much as our top recommended high chair, the very well made Fisher Price Healthy Care. (At some seminars, the price for the feeding table is $400, but you get a free car seat with your purchase. Whoopee). There's nothing wrong with the crib either—and yes, Babee Tenda, throws in a mattress and two sheets. But you can find all this for much less than the $500 or so Babee Tenda asks.

A new twist to the Babee Tenda pitch: invitations sent by a Babee Tenda distributor in Virginia in 2004 carried a line that their seminar is sponsored "in conjunction with the Consumer Product Safety Commission and the National Highway Traffic Safety Administration." Whoa, sounds official! Except it isn't true—neither the CPSC nor NHTSA have anything to do with Babee Tenda's seminars . . . in fact, the federal government successfully sued Babee Tenda to stop the practice. In 2007, a federal judge ruled Babee Tenda committed mail fraud, calling their sales tactics "deceitful and reprehensible."

So, we say watch out for Babee Tenda (and other similar companies like Babyhood, who pitches their "Baby Sitter" in hotel safety seminars). We found their "safety seminar" to be bogus, their high-pressure sales tactics reprehensible and their products grossly overpriced.

ty regulators. As you might guess, we took a dim view of this and rated Baby's Dream accordingly.

On the upside, the company replaced its management a few years ago and cleaned up its act. While you still see the folding rail on many of their model, the company re-designed the hinge and it's now safe. The company's new managers have also beefed up quality and lowered prices, which have contributed to the strong growth of the brand in recent years.

Baby's Dream's line consists of stationary side models, folding rails (drop gates) and traditional knee push rail releases. All models are JPMA certified and most feature spring mattress platforms . . . some have under crib drawers and most convert to adult beds. The majority of crib styles are in the $300 to $550 range.

In the past year, Baby's Dream launched Cocoon, four collections of cribs and dressers that start at $470 (for cribs) and $600 (dressers). Cocoon started out as a copy of Bambino (a former division of Ragazzi) but has evolved over the last year to offer a touch more style and flourish than Baby's Dream regular line. FYI: Cocoon is imported from China while Baby's Dream is made in Chile.

All in all, Baby's Dream's quality is excellent and retailers tell us the deliveries and customer service of this brand is better than most in the industry (despite last year's hiccups). No, we still aren't wild about the folding rail releases, but there are plenty of other styles here to choose from. So we will give Baby's Dream a much better rating this time out, reflecting their improvements. FYI: Be sure to check out Baby's Dream's web site—the company occasionally offers coupons online and has a free pregnancy calendar and nursery guide, as of this writing. ***Rating: A***

Babi Italia *This is a special brand made by Bonavita for chain stores. See the Bonavita review later in this section for more info.*

Babies Love by Delta *See the review of Delta later in this section.*

Bambino *See Ragazzi.*

BassettBaby *Call (276) 629-6000 for a dealer near you. Web: bassettbaby.com.* Pop into chains stores like Target or Babies R Us (BRU) and you'll find Bassett. While Bassett sells furniture under its own name (BassettBaby) in stores like Sears and JCPenney, the brand has teamed with BRU in-house stylist Wendy Bellissimo to create "exclusive furniture" for the chain: a crib for $500 and matching armoire for $600. While the Wendy B furniture does have a bit more pizzazz than what you'd see at Target under the Bassett brand, we couldn't quite justify the price difference (Bassett cribs at

Target are $200 to $370; dressers are $220-$370). Generally, it's been Bassett's strategy to add a bit of bling to its line (dressers with glass knobs, for example) to help distinguish it from low-price imports such as Jardine. How's quality? Like most brands, Bassett has shifted its production to China, but a few pieces are also imported from Vietnam. Overall, we found Bassett to be a good

Certifications: Do they really matter?

As you shop for cribs and other products for your baby, you'll no doubt run into "JPMA-Certified" products sporting a special seal. But who is the JPMA and what does its certification mean?

The Juvenile Products Manufacturers Association (JPMA) is a group of over 300 companies that make juvenile products, both in the United States and Canada. Twenty five years ago, the group started a volunteer testing program to head off government regulation of baby products. The JPMA enlisted the support of the Consumer Products Safety Commission and the American Society of Testing and Materials to develop standards for products in several categories, including cribs, high chairs and more.

Manufacturers must have their product tested in an independent testing lab and, if it passes, they can use the JPMA seal.

So is a product like a crib more safe if it has the JPMA seal? No, not in our opinion. In fact, the biggest crib recall in history (one million Simplicity cribs in 2007) involved cribs that were JPMA certified. How did that happen?

Well, the JPMA certification is a MINIMUM set of standards that mostly address adequate warning labels. While detailed warning labels for products are helpful, it doesn't stop defective design or faulty instructions (the problem in the Simplicity recall).

The Simplicity recall tarnished the JPMA's certification program—and the JPMA's actions in the past year (accusations of misleading the public on the safety of crib bumpers and lobbying against baby bottle regulations) have undermined the association's safety message. See our blog at BabyBargains.com (click on news/updates) for details about these stories on bedding and bottles.

So is the JPMA seal worthless? No—it does indicate that a company has the financial backing to get the certification (it costs $10,000 or more). As a result, you'll see that most JPMA-certified products are from the big juvenile product companies.

But the JPMA seal hardly makes a crib or any other baby product more safe than those without the seal.

value (more so for the $200 to $300 cribs; less for the Babies R Us furniture), although we'd stay away from their collections made of pine (too soft and susceptible to damage). While we like the cribs, the case pieces are another story. A hi-lo dresser we recently saw had drawer glides that were sticky—and the drawers themselves are stapled, not dove tailed. You're supposed to spend $560 for this?

New this year, Bassett will attempt to launch a specialty-store version of BassettBaby, with $600 to $850 cribs and $700 to $800 dressers. We say "attempt to launch" because given what we saw of this new furniture, Bassett will have a tough time convincing either retailers or consumers that it can compete in the high-end market. Sure, the furniture is an upgrade style-wise from what you'd see in Target, but Bassett's high-end line is no match for quality, features or styling when compared to Munire, Baby's Dream or Natart in this price range. Back to the drawing board, guys.

Bottom line: Bassett's cribs in chain stores (not counting Babies R Us) are a good value, but skip the dressers. **Rating: B+**

Bedford Baby *This brand is made by Westwood (see review later in this chapter).*

Bella D' Este *See Jardine.*

Bellini *Call (805) 520-0974, (800) 332-BABY or (516) 234-7716 for a store location near you. Web: bellini.com.* Bellini is an odd duck in the world of baby retailers: it is a franchised chain with some three dozen locations, mostly on the East and West Coasts that rack up $70 million in sales annually. While most baby retailers are either big-box chains (Babies R Us) or small mom-and-pop stores, Bellini occupy the middle ground (stores average 5000 square feet).

Bellini had its heyday in the 80's and 90's—then its business model of importing Italian furniture was unique. Selling $600 private-label cribs and other Bellini-exclusive furniture and linens, the chain's offerings were nicer than anything you could find in big-box stores.

However, the competition soon caught up with Bellini. Italian crib importers flooded the market in the 90's and then came the wave of low-cost Asian imports in recent years . . . at prices that were 20% to 40% less than Bellini. Competitors such as Pottery Barn and online luxe baby gear sellers further eroded Bellini's position. As a result, the chain has shrunk, losing both stores (down to 36 locations from 48 in years past) and sales (off 14% in 2006).

Bellini's sagging fortunes have hit the chain's reputation—as stores have closed (some of whom disappeared with customer's deposits), parents have posted numerous negative reviews on our site. The chain has been its own worst enemy here—by not helping out stranded customers, Bellini's corporate owners have ensured more negative publicity. That reflects poorly on the remaining franchisees, many of whom still provide good customer service.

How's the quality? Inconsistent, say our readers. Given the premium prices, we shouldn't hear reports of peeling paint on $800 dressers (but we do). While most of their furniture is still imported from Italy and Canada, it's clear the quality isn't what it used to be. Given the disappearing act of some of the franchisees, we have lowered Bellini's rating this time out. **Rating: C+**

Berg (908) 354-5252. Web: bergfurniture.com. In business since 1984, Berg branched out into juvenile furniture in the late 90's. Sold in stores like Buy Buy Baby, Berg offers several different crib models. Solid pine cribs (made in Russia and China) run $400 to $500, while convertible cribs (that convert to twin beds) are $650. That is pricey, but the convertible models do include the conversion kit. We liked the hidden hardware on the knee-push rail releases, but the attached dressers on their "Crib N Beds" were a turn-off (for safety reasons, as we discussed earlier). As for dressers, Berg has dramatically improved its offerings here: their newer styles feature smooth glides and quality detailing. Feedback from parents on Berg has been quite positive. One caveat: Berg's pine groupings. Berg uses a soft pine, which is susceptible to nicks and scratches. As a result, Berg's pine furniture in baby stores often looks beaten up. . . obviously, this is less of an issue in a nursery, as long as you're careful. Or just skip the pine groups and get a different Berg style. **Rating: A-**

Bethany James Collection *This is a Wal-Mart exclusive brand made by Cosco/Dorel. See Cosco later in this section.*

Bonavita *Call (888) 266-2848 or (732) 346-5150 for a dealer near you. Web site: LaJobi.com.* Bonavita's theme song must be that disco chestnut, "I Will Survive." What else could explain this company's history, which has had more ups and downs than a Six Flags thrill ride?

A brief history: La Jobi (Bonavita's parent) started as an importer of Italian furniture, sold to both chain stores like Babies R Us and indie retailers. To avoid raising the ire of specialty stores, Bonavita has marketed its wares under a plethora of aliases—it currently uses "Babi Italia" and "Issi" in Babies R Us, "Europa Baby" in Baby Depot and its own moniker (Bonavita) in specialty channels. (Each brand has its own web site—go to LaJobi.com to access these sites).

When the Euro rose sharply against the dollar (making Italian furniture costly to import), Bonavita switched to Asian imports (mostly Vietnam and Thailand). This transition was bumpy—quality glitches and delivery problems dogged this line for several years earlier in this decade. Yet the company survived (again) and now has put most of that behind it.

Bonavita's main market niche is value—and unlike their competitors at Pali or Munire, they've always been aggressive about marketing their goods in chain stores. While Bonavita typically is the most expensive price point for chains, the company gives you more style and features for the buck. Look at their $400 Europa Baby convertible crib in Baby Depot or the $500 Issi crib in Babies R Us and compare these to low-end models by Delta or Stork Craft in the same stores. You'll see how Bonavita furniture not only out-does these other brands style-wise, but also with quality touches like fit and finish. A particularly good buy: the Baby Italia Mon Cheri crib at Babies R Us for $300.

New this year, Bonavita has licensed the Graco name and is selling cribs, gliders, cradles and dressers under that moniker in Target and Wal-Mart. A Bonavita-made Graco convertible crib sells in Target and Wal-Mart for $160-$170—a good deal. Of course, these are bare-bones models with exposed rail-release hardware (but still a great deal for the dollar). For a regular Bonavita crib, expect to shell out $450 for a drop-side model or $500-$600 for a convertible style. Dressers from this line can be pricey, with prices ranging

Rug Burn: How to save on nursery rug prices

Yes, it's always exciting to get that new Pottery Barn Kids catalog in the mail here at the home office in Boulder, CO. Among our favorites are those oh-so-cute rugs Pottery Barn finds to match their collections. But the prices? Whoa! $300 for a puny 5′ by 8′ rug! $600 for an 8′ by 10′ design! Time to take out a second mortgage on the house. We figured there had to be a much less expensive alternative out there to the PBK options. To the rescue, we found *Fun Rugs* by General Industries (www.funrugs.com; 800-4FUN-RUGS). This giant kids' rug maker has literally hundreds of options to choose from in a variety of sizes. Fun Rugs makes matching rugs for such well-known bedding lines as California Kids and Olive Kids. Now, their web site lets you see their entire collection, but you can't order direct from Fun Rugs. Instead, go to one of their dealers *like American Blind & Wallpaper*, *RugsUSA* (RugsUSA.com) and *NetKidsWear* (netkidswear.com search for rugs). All of those web sites sell Fun Rugs at prices that are significantly below similar rugs at PBK. Example: a 5′ by 8′ log cabin quilt design rug is only $155; PBK's price is $300 for a similar size rug. We found most of those web sites sell rugs for 40% less than PBK or posh specialty stores.

from $500 for a simple chest to $900 for an armoire.

Also new this year at Bonavita: eco-nursery furniture. The company is debuting its first "eco-friendly" collection (Madre) which has water-based finishes and is made from wood from certified "sustainable" forests.

How's the quality? Again, it's been an up and down story. We always thought Bonavita's Italian cribs (a few are still sold in chain stores) were well-made and a good value. We weren't as impressed with Bonavita's first attempts at Asian imports, but subsequent models are much better. Inconsistency has haunted Bonavita over the years, but to be fair, other importers (Sorelle) have also faced similar problems. FYI: While Bonavita's competitors sell many of their cribs via online sites, even drop-shipping for e-tailers. . . . Bonavita is a no-show when it comes to e-commerce.

Customer service has also been uneven. Readers of past editions of our book may recall Bonavita customer service meltdowns and recalls; but in the past year, we haven't heard many complaints about Bonavita and the parent reviews of the line on our web site have been quite positive.

So, we will tick Bonavita's rating up this year to reflect their improved efforts. Kudos to their affordable cribs and generally good quality. One caveat: if you decide to order Bonavita furniture, be sure to deal with a store that has a good customer service reputation in case there are any snafus. And be sure to check the box BEFORE leaving the store to make sure nothing is damaged. ***Rating: A-***

Bratt Décor *Call (888)-24-BRATT or (410) 327-4600 for a dealer near you. Web: brattdecor.com.* Well, at least you have to give this company bonus points for creativity—Bratt Decor made their name with offerings like the "Casablanca Plume" crib that was topped with (and we're not making this up) ostrich feathers. That (and the $1050 price tag) enabled Bratt Décor to earn a distinguished place on our list of the most ridiculous baby products in a previous edition of this book. In the past year, Bratt has expanded their line to include a series of wood cribs in various "vintage" and whimsical looks. Their Heritage Four Poster Crib with Stars is a take-off of a 1940's design with four finials that can be changed from stars to bunnies, flowers, planes or balls. Price: $725. All in all, we've noticed Bratt Décor's prices have drifted downward in recent years—gone are most of the $1000+ options, replaced by cribs that now sell for $600 to $900. What parents seem to like here is the style and colors of the cribs (Bratt Décor is one of the few crib makers out there today that does a navy blue or bright red finish). Bratt Décor also has matching accessories such as nightstands, mirrors, bookcases and other decorative options. FYI: Bratt Décor is one of the few crib brands that sells direct via their web site (one collection is available only online). Bratt also has a company store in Baltimore, in addition to regular retail dealers. All in all, we'll give Bratt Décor thumbs up for style—but you're going to pay for it. **Rating: B**

Bright Future See JCPenney.

C&T International This company is the same as Sorelle; see their review later in this section.

Canalli This private label furniture is made by Munire (see review later) and sold in a small number of stores in New Jersey and New York, most notably the Crib & Teen City chain (cribteencity.com).

Capretti Home Web: CaprettiHome.com. Launched in 2007, Capretti Home is the brainchild of Mitchell Schwartz, one of the key players who worked at the old Ragazzi label. After Ragazzi was

E-Mail from The Real World
Leg got stuck in crib slats

"Yesterday, my nine month old somehow wedged his leg between two slats of the crib. I heard him scream shortly after I put him to bed for his afternoon nap and found his leg entrapped up to the thigh. I couldn't pull the slats apart and get his leg out myself, so I called 911. A police officer was able to pull the slats apart just enough so I could gently guide by son's leg back through. I took him to the doctor and he's fine, other than a bruise on his leg. Any tips on how we can avoid this in the future?"

Crib slats are required by federal law to be a certain maximum distance apart (2 3/8"). This is done to prevent babies from getting their heads trapped by the crib spindles or slats, a common problem with cribs made before 1973 when the rule was enacted. Of course, just because baby can't get a head stuck in there doesn't mean an arm or leg can't be wedged between the slats. A solution: Trend Lab makes a "Crib Shield System" ($30) and "Breathable Crib Bumper" ($25 to $30) that uses Velcro to attach to a crib (it is compatible with most, but not all cribs). It is made of breathable mesh and is sold online at BabiesRUs.com and OneStepAhead.com. Does everyone need this? No—it is rather uncommon for baby to get their arms or legs wedged in the slats. But if you do discover this is a problem, there's your solution!

cribs

sold to Stork Craft, Schwartz launched Capretti Home as his own label. It's perhaps no big surprise that the furniture takes design cues from the old Ragazzi—but Capretti tries to up the quality quotient with solid poplar construction, cribs that include a toddler guard rail and conversion kit to a full-size bed and more. Among the most popular features: self-closing drawer glides that prevent pinching. We've had a chance to demo Capretti's furniture and were impressed with the quality touches (including those drawers, which are unique to the nursery biz). It's clear that Capretti's owners have used their extensive experience at Ragazzi to craft an excellent furniture line.

The prices, however, are hard to swallow—$800 for a convertible crib, $600 for a drop-side model. A double dresser can run $1000. While Capretti did drop prices a smidge after its debut (cribs at one point were $900), we still find the line to be a bit out of sync with the rest of the market (compare a Capretti to Munire and you'll notice the price premium). Another criticism: Capretti only offers a handful of finishes and the accessories selection (mirrors, other accents) is also thin compared to say, Stanley.

Yet Capretti does provide value—we liked the included conversion kits for their cribs (that can run $100 to $200 with other lines). And even though this furniture is made in China, this isn't cheap furniture masquerading as the real thing—it is the real thing.

All in all, we've been impressed with Capretti's track record—so far, this young company has done an excellent job at deliveries, customer service and fixing glitches that are inevitable with any start up. Watch for new "contemporary" style furniture from Capretti in 2008—that may help the company distinguish itself from the pack. Bottom line: if you can afford it, Capretti is an excellent choice for quality. **Rating: A**

Cara Mia Call (877) 728-0342 or (705) 328-0342 for a dealer near you. Web: CaraMiaFurniture.com. These cribs (most are $300 to $550) are sold in specialty stores and touted as "European crafted." This apparently has a better ring than "Made in Slovenia in the former Yugoslavia." Actually, Cara Mia makes/imports furniture from a variety of countries, including pine groupings from Brazil and birch furniture from China. A typical offering is the Sedona group, a $500 convertible crib and matching dresser with hutch for $600. Delivery is six to eight weeks on average, which is rather zippy in this industry. How about the quality? We consider Cara Mia to be in the middle of the pack—not the best, but not the worst. Most folks are happy with Cara Mia's cribs, although we did get a complaint from one mom whose crib rail slats separated one day when she was pulling up the side rail. Fortunately, the baby wasn't in the crib at the time, but this incident raises questions about Cara Mia's quality control. Cara Mia's dressers aren't that impressive either . . . most are made with MDF and feature very plain styling at too-high prices. **Rating: B-**

Chanderic *Call 800-363-2635 or 819-566-1515 for a dealer near you. Web: shermag.com.* It's been a rough couple of years for Canadian furniture makers—a falling U.S. dollar has made their products more expensive, just as competition from Asian imports has intensified. The result: some companies have gone out of business (Status) while others have retrenched or been sold (EG). Canadian furniture behemoth Shermag has been buffeted by the same forces and has tried to diversify—their "Chanderic" line is an attempt to crack the upper end of the nursery market. When Chanderic debuted in 2003, we weren't that impressed . . . they had just a handful of styles and prices seemed high. Well, the line has expanded and now includes five collections (a total of 12 cribs). The cribs are imported from Croatia, while the case goods are made in Canada. We liked the birch wood and expanded color choices; all the cribs feature hidden hardware and good stability. Yet, the prices are still on the high side: cribs run $550 to $700. The dressers ($700 to $900) feature all-wood drawers with dovetail joints and wall straps to prevent tipping.

Chanderic's parent, Shermag, is in a free fall—the company's sales are down by 30% and Shermag hasn't made a profit since 2005. To deal with a strong Canadian dollar, Shermag/Chanderic has raised its prices . . . and that, of course, has further eroded sales. You can see the declining fortunes in Chanderic's nursery furniture line—there are few new or innovative designs. Chanerdic's conservative styling now looks dated. Bottom line: competition in the upper-end of the business is fierce and Chanderic appears to be falling behind. While the Canadians still make good quality dressers, we noticed that about half of this line is now imported from China (the Chinese collections were new as of press time).

Given how much turmoil is happening here, we have dropped our rating of this brand. Quality is still good, but the company's uncertain future tempers any enthusiasm for this brand. **Rating: C+**

Child Craft *Call (812) 206-2200 for a dealer near you. Web: child-craftind.com.* Here's a sad parable for the crib business. Child Craft, the Indiana-based crib maker that traces its roots back to 1910, was once among the top brands of nursery furniture. In recent years, however, the company has had a slow, painful slide into obscurity. Some of this has been bad luck (a 2004 flood knocked the company offline for several months) . . . while most of the blame can be laid at the company's leadership, which never fully adapted to the flood of Asian-produced nursery furniture, both on the high and low ends of the market.

As a result, you rarely see Child Craft (or its sister brand, Legacy) in stores these days. Sure, Coscto.com has collections of their furniture ($1400 for a three-piece set). And yes, you can see Child Craft cribs online at Target or Wal-Mart for $180 to $250. But you rarely see CC in person at chain stores like Babies R Us . . . and Child Craft's "upper-end" line Legacy has slowly disappeared from specialty stores.

All this is too bad: Child Craft pioneered several innovations in the biz, including the first crib that morphed into a full-size bed. We like Child Craft's emphasis on safety: CC tests all their case goods with 50-pound weights hanging from a top drawer. That would prevent a climbing toddler from tipping a dresser over. Child Craft even adds weight to the bottom of their case goods to make sure they pass this 50 pounds test.

Despite the company's lower profile in recent years, we still think Child Craft's entry-level cribs sold at Target for about $200 and other discounters represent a solid value. Dressers run $200 to $400.

Child Craft imports most of their furniture from a plant it owns in Honduras—some final finishing is done in Indiana. Other furniture is imported from China. One Child Craft collection (the Winston) is still made in the US, although you'll pay for it: a crib is $900 and five-drawer chest is $1200.

Legacy is Child Craft's "upper-end" brand that features fancier finishes and detailing. A Legacy crib runs $400 to $500, with similar prices for dressers. Reviews for Legacy from parents are mostly positive, although one dissenter emailed us her disappointed with a Legacy armoire—uneven doors didn't close properly and other

E-MAIL FROM THE REAL WORLD
Tricks from the sale floor

Reader Jennifer Gottlieb shared an interesting story about a trick some baby stores use to convince parents to buy more expensive cribs:

"Here's an interesting tidbit we heard recently and wanted to pass along: A guy in our childbirth education class works at a baby furniture store, and let us in on a marketing ploy. Evidently, some stores purposely loosen the screws on the floor models of less expensive cribs so that when you're checking them out they seem more rickety than their pricey counterparts. This makes most nervous parents naturally turn to the cribs that appear to be more solid—not to mention expensive!"

quality issues marred the product. Let's be honest here: Legacy's case pieces are stylish, but at prices that approach $500, you'd be better off investing in a brand with higher overall quality (such as Westwood or Munire), even if it means spending another $100 or $200 for a dresser.

Bottom line: while we aren't as hot on the Legacy line for quality and value, Child Craft's affordable cribs and dressers are a good buy for the dollar. **Rating: B+**

Childesigns *This company went out of business in 2005.*

Chris Madden *See Bassett.*

Concord *This crib brand is reviewed on our free web site, BabyBargains.com (click on Bonus Material).*

Corsican Kids *Call (800) 421-6247 or (323) 587-3101 for a dealer near you. Web: Corsican.com.* Looking for a wrought iron crib? California-based Corsican Kids specializes in iron cribs that have a vintage feel, with detailed headboard and footboard decoration. Before you fall in love with the look, however, be sure to turn over the price tag. Most Corsican Kids iron cribs sell for a whopping $1300 to $3000! Yes, you can choose from a variety of cool finishes like pewter and antique bronze but these prices are hard to swallow. And there are some downsides to wrought iron cribs: first, they are darn noisy when raising or lowering the side rail. And Corsican's drop-sides are those exposed (rod/cane) hardware foot bar releases that most of the market abandoned long ago (most parents find knee push easier to use). And those side rails (made out of solid metal) are heavy. So, it's a mixed review for these guys. Yes, they are cool to look at but the practical drawbacks of wrought iron cribs (as well as the stratospheric prices) score only an average rating in our book. **Rating: C+**

Cosco *Call (800) 544-1108 or (812) 372-0141 for a dealer near you. Web: coscoinc.com.* The Cosco name has just about disappeared from the crib market, as parent Dorel has concentrated on their Jardine line for the Babies R Us chain. It's no wonder—Cosco must translate as "recall" in Canadian. The company suffered through several high-profile recalls (and sadly, injuries and deaths) due to their poorly made cribs in the 1990's. Yes, you can still see a handful of Cosco cribs on the market today—an $80 portable crib and $130 metal cribs, most of which are sold online. We say skip it.

FYI: we have rated Cosco separately from Jardine; Cosco is owned by Dorel Juvenile Group, based in Canada. Jardine is made by Dorel Asia, a separate subsidiary. While both Cosco and Jardine

Co-sleepers

If you can't borrow a bassinet or cradle from a friend, there is an alternative: the **Arm's Reach Bedside Co-Sleeper** (call 800-954-9353 for a dealer near you; web: armsreach. com). This innovative product is essentially a bassinet that attaches to your bed under the mattress and is secured in place. The three-sided co-sleeper is open on the bedside. The result: you can easily reach the baby for feedings without ever leaving your bed, a boon for all mothers but especially those recuperating from Caesarean births. Best of all, the unit converts to a regular playpen when baby gets older (and goes into a regular crib). You can also use the co-sleeper as a diaper changing station. The cost for the basic model? $160 to $230, which is a bit pricey, considering a plain playpen with bassinet feature is about $100. But the unique design and safety aspect of the Arm's Reach product may make it worth the extra cash layout.

In recent years, Arm's Reach has rolled out several variations on its co-sleeper. The "Universal" model ($200 to $230) is re-designed to fit futons, platform and European beds. The removable sidebar and new liner can also be positioned at the top level of the play yard to create a four-sided freestanding bassinet.

One of Arm's Reach most popular modes is the "Mini-Bassinet Co-Sleeper," which does not convert to a playpen ($140). Also new this year, a sleigh-style wooden co-sleeper for $300.

If you like the functionality of a co-sleeper but not the look, there is good news. Arm's Reach web site (see above; click on accessories) now sells 13 floor-length liners in various colors to camouflage the co-sleeper.

Of course, Arm's Reach isn't the only co-sleeper on the market. **The Baby Bunk** (BabyBunk.com) is a wood co-sleeper that is either purchased for $300 or rented by the month. That's right, you can rent one for just $30 a month (with a $50 refundable deposit) in case you want to see if this is for you. That might be the best bargain of all when it comes to co-sleepers. Baby Bunk also sells a series of accessories for their co-sleepers, including sheets, mattresses, bumpers and more.

While we like the co-sleeper, let us point out that we are not endorsing the concept of co-sleeping in general. Co-sleeping (where baby sleeps with you *in your bed*) is a controversial topic that's beyond the scope of this book. We discuss co-sleeping (along with other hot parenting issues) in our other book, *Baby 411* (see back of this book for details).

are owned by parent Dorel, they are marketed and manufactured as separate brands.

New this year, Dorel is selling furniture under the Vintage Estate label at Sears. This furniture ($200 for a crib, $240 for a hi-lo dresser) was new as of press time, so we don't have any parent feedback on its quality. Another exclusive brand: Bethany James Collection is made by Cosco for Wal-Mart. This furniture (crib $150, dresser/changer for $130) has received positive marks from parents. While this sub-brand has fared well, overall we do not recommend Cosco given their history of recalls in this category. **Rating: F**

Creations *Web: CreationsBaby.com. 602-269-5811.* Well, this looked good on paper.

When industry veteran Michael Schaffer (Child Craft, Baby's Dream) teamed with adult furniture maker SLF, Inc. to launch Creations in 2007, we thought they had the formula right: following in the footsteps of Munire and Westwood, Creations told us they want to take quality to the next level. That meant multi-step finishes on cribs and dressers, armoires with double hinges, hutches with three-light settings and more. The goal was nursery furniture that was more like adult furniture—Creation's dressers will be 21″ deep (as are most adult dressers) versus the 18″ seen in most juvenile furniture.

Yet, Creations first shipments were a disaster—readers reported furniture with "major cracks and imperfections," poor finish and other glitches. Retailers told us about similar problems, noting that long waits for special orders (five months plus) was adding to the pain.

To say this was disappointing is an understatement—Creations is trying to launch a high-end brand (although cribs start at $400, most cribs and dressers are $500 to $700), yet clearly stumbled out of the gate.

Now, that said, the company is trying to turn things around. After switching production facilities to China from Vietnam, quality has improved, say retailers. As we were going to press, stores tell us that Creations current shipments are defect-free and running on time (Creations goal is delivery of special orders in eight to 10 weeks). Creations' management has been honest about its screw-ups and is trying to right the ship.

But the jury is still out—while we like the concept here (adult furniture quality and design at prices a notch below other brands), Creations is going to have to actually ship quality product for a sustained period before they will earn our recommendation. The next few months will be crucial—watch our blog for updates.

As for a rating, we'd give Creations an F for their botched launch . . . but the most recent shipments give us hope. As a result, we'll be generous and give them a passing grade for now. **Rating: C**

Cub. *See NettoCollection.*

DaVinci *See Million Dollar Baby later in this chapter for contact info.*
Million Dollar Baby was one of the first crib importers to grasp the
importance of ecommerce—the company launched the "DaVinci"

Two guys, a container and a prayer

Back in ancient times (say, the 1970's), if you wanted to make
and sell cribs, you needed a factory. This required a significant
amount of capital, as well as the know-how to engineer cribs to
comply with safety standards, finish cribs to match dressers and
market the resulting furniture nationwide.

Fast forward to today: most start-up nursery furniture companies
today are two guys, a shipping container from China . . . and a
prayer.

We realize the days of domestic manufacturing are long gone
for many basic items like furniture . . . yet the stark new reality of
imported goods creates challenges for new parents—which brands
can a parent trust to make safe furniture for their baby's nursery?
Will their special ordered furniture arrive sometime before the child
goes to college? Will the company be around in a few years to fill
a parts or service request?

The biggest challenge for today's nursery furniture suppliers and
buyers: will the furniture ever ship? Since nearly all furniture is
imported from China or other Asian countries, it can take 12 weeks
or more to land a container of nursery furniture at a West Coast
port. Then it must be trucked to a distribution center and finally,
out to stores (and consumers). And that doesn't count any disruptions (Chinese New Year, port strikes, bad weather, etc). It's no surprise that delayed shipments is a common complaint in our reader email and message boards.

Customer service is another issue for today's furniture imports.
Let's be honest: customer service in the baby business ranges from
grossly inadequate to the merely abysmal. And that's being charitable. Whether you are talking the big baby gear companies or
the smallest furniture importer, customer service often means one
lone person sitting at a phone or answering emails. You are lucky
to get a reply to an email (beyond a canned response) or a
returned phone call.

The take home message for new parents: go into this process
with your eyes open. Don't wait until the last minute to place an
order—leave PLENTY of lead time. Stick to the better brands
reviewed in this chapter. And once your furniture arrives, carefully
inspect items for damage or incorrect installation.

label as an online alias way back in the late 90's. Sold on sites like BabyCenter and BabyUniverse, prices range from $200 for a simple Jenny Lind style to $300 to $400 for convertible cribs. And despite the Italian sounding name, most of these cribs are NOT made in Italy (rather imported from Asia). Our parent feedback on DaVinci/Million Dollar Baby runs both hot and cold—for every parent who posts a positive review of their furniture, another will complain about late deliveries, quality issues or customer service problems. So ordering this furniture is a roll of the dice . . . something you probably don't want to hear when you are spending hundreds of dollars! **Rating: C**

Delta *Call (212) 736-7000 for a dealer near you. Web: deltaen-terprise.com.* Imported from Indonesia, Delta (also known as Delta Luv and Babies Love by Delta) is sold in chain stores like Wal-Mart, Sears and Target, as well as online. Delta scored a coup recently when one of their basic Jenny Lind cribs (style 4750-1) scored a top ranking from *Consumer Reports*. And we agree—it's a good value for $110. In fact, most Delta cribs are low in price, about $130 to $240 on average. So, what is Delta's quality like? Well, this is low-end furniture . . . and you get low-end quality. For example, most of Delta's cribs don't have a spring mattress platform—instead you get a flat piece of MDF. Delta's dressers are nothing to write home about, with stapled drawers and other production shortcuts (read-ers report uneven paint jobs, etc). That said, Delta does have sev-eral advantages (in addition to price): first, all its cribs are easy to assemble, requiring no tools. That might be just the trick for Grandma's house, where you'll need to quickly set up a crib for short trips. Second, Delta is one of the few crib brands that is big into cartoon licenses. So if you just have to have a SpongeBob-themed nursery, Delta is your brand. On a serious note, however, Delta has had several high profile recalls in recent years, including a 2004 recall of a crib with high levels of lead paint. Then in 2005, Delta recalled 10,000 portable cribs for slats that separated form the headboard. Shame on Delta for these serious safety lapses. As a result, we have lowered our rating for Delta. FYI: Delta also owns the Simmons brand, reviewed later in this chapter. **Rating: C+**

Disney *The Disney Pooh crib sold at Wal-Mart is made by Delta; see review above.*

Domusindo *Web: domusindo.com. See JcPenney.*

Dorel Dorel is the parent of Cosco, which also sells their cribs under the names Bridgeport and Jardine. See the Cosco review for Dorel, Bridgeport and Cosco cribs; Jardine is reviewed separately later.

Bait and Switch with Floor Samples

Readers of our first book, *Bridal Bargains,* may remember all the amazing scams and rip-offs when it came to buying a wedding gown. As you read this book, you'll notice many of the shenanigans that happen in the wedding biz are thankfully absent in the world of baby products.

Of course, that doesn't mean there aren't ANY scams or rip-offs to be concerned about. One problem that does crop up from time to time is the old "bait and switch scheme," this time as it applies to floor samples of baby furniture. A reader in New York sent us this story about a bait and switch they encountered at a local store:

"We ordered our baby furniture in August for November delivery. When it all arrived, the crib was damaged and both the side rails were missing paint. We were suspicious they were trying to pass off floor samples on us—when we opened the drawer on a dresser, we found a price tag from the store. The armoire's top was damaged and loose and the entire piece was dirty. There was even a sticky substance on the door front where a price tag once was placed. Another sign: both the changing table and ottoman were not in their original boxes when they were delivered."

The store's manager was adamant that the items were new, not floor samples. Then the consumer noticed the specific pieces they ordered were no longer on the sales floor. After some more haggling, the store agreed to re-order the furniture from the factory.

Why would a store do this? In a tough economy, a store's inventory may balloon as sales stall. The temptation among some baby storeowners may be to try to pass off used floor samples as new goods, in order to clear out a backlog at the warehouse. Of course, you'd expect them to be smarter about this than the above story—the least they could have done was clean/repair items and make sure the price tags were removed! But some merchants' dishonesty is only matched by their stupidity.

Obviously, when you buy brand new, special-order furniture that is exactly what you deserve to get. While this is not an everyday occurrence in the baby biz, you should take steps to protect yourself. First, pay for any deposits on furniture with a credit card—if the merchant fails to deliver what they promise, you can dispute the charge. Second, carefully inspect any order when it arrives. Items should arrive in their original boxes and be free of dirt/damage or other telltale signs of wear. If you suspect a special-order item is really a used sample, don't accept delivery and immediately contact the store.

Dream on Me *Web: DreamOnMe.com.* The portable/folding crib market has been rife with problems in recent years, with major players like Evenflo and Delta recalling their models for safety reasons. Yet small player Dream on Me has a winner with their "3 in 1 Folding and Adjustable crib." Sold online at Wal-Mart and other sites for about $200, this crib is a good bet for Grandma's house. This might be the best choice in a category with limited options. (We should note Dream On Me also makes full-size cribs; we have not reviewed those models yet. Our rating applies only to the portable crib model). **Rating: B**

ducduc *For a dealer near you, call 212-226-1868. Web: ducducnyc.com.* Looking for high-style nursery furniture? Got $1500 to spend on a crib? Like orange? If you answered yes to those questions, then take a look at ducduc, a New York-based design company that aims to

give the nursery biz a shot of glam. The result is a group of five nursery collections (and matching linens) that are rather retro in design . . . and oddly, heavy on orange as a design accent. "A new aesthetic, a new generation" is the theme and we will give ducduc points on creativity—the pieces emphasize lacquered veneers and contrasting colors, a fusion between the Brady Bunch and a European cable access show. We suppose this is going to appeal to hipsters in San Francisco or Soho, but it's hard imagine the rest of the country going wild over ducduc. How's the quality? What little feedback we've heard from parents (this line is still relatively new) has been positive. **Rating: B**

Dutailier *For a dealer near you, call 800-363-9817 or 450-772-2403. Web: dutailier.com or egfurniture.com.* Canadian rocker-glider maker Dutailier launched its furniture line in 2004 after acquiring fellow Canuck crib maker EG. The new line (at one point marketed under the name Petite Cheris) features a dozen collections of conservatively designed furniture. Cribs are made in Romania and China; the dressers in Canada. Typical prices are $500 to $700 for a crib, while a dressers runs $800 to $1100. You can choose from 32 finish choices—Dutailier's "Design Center" web site lets you morph the color of any collection, which is a neat touch.

We only gave this line a C+ last time out, as we were nervous about quality with the production switch overseas. Yet Dutailier has done a good job of making sure quality is high, based on recent parent reviews on our web site. One caveat: waits can be long for some items—up to 18 weeks for her crib, emailed one frustrated reader.

Given Dutailier's overall track record for quality, however, we'll go with a higher rating this time out. Perhaps the biggest negative here is the price—a three-piece nursery can easily top $2500. ***Rating: B+***

EA Kids. *See Ethan Allen below.*

Eden *Web: EdenBaby.com.* This LA-based crib importer sells a small collection of traditional and convertible cribs to a handful of independent stores nationwide (including USA Baby stores). Along with cribs, Eden also has five collections of furniture with matching dressers, armoires, hutches and combo dressers. The styling is very plain vanilla, with prices running $250 to $300 for a regular crib, $400 or more for convertible models. A three-drawer dresser is about $400. Imported from China, we found the quality to be unimpressive (some dressers featured stapled drawers, which lacked a smooth glide). Given the competition on the market, Eden needs to step up the styling, features and quality in order to better compete. ***Rating: C+***

EG Furniture *See Petite Cheris.*

El Greco *Web: ElGrecoFurinture.com; Paintboxdesigns.com. An archived review of El Greco and Paintbox is on our web site BabyBargains.com (click on bonus material).*

Ethan Allen *(888) EAHELP1; web: ethanallen.com.* We love the look of the EA Kids furniture, which is available in any of Ethan

An Amish Paradise

They may shun electricity, but the Amish do make some darn good furniture—and the quality puts most other juvenile makers to shame. But how to do you buy Amish furniture if you don't live in, say, Amish country? The web, of course. Reader Andrea L. bought all her nursery furniture from the Amish and gave us the lowdown. First, consider go to SimplyAmish.com for an overview of the buying process. Most Amish do not sell direct to the public; they sell through mom and pop dealers who have small showrooms (and web sites).

Among the best Amish furniture web sites are AmishOak.com, AmishEtc.com, StoneBarnFunishings.com, AmishOakInTexas.com and PureOak.com. Our reader's advice: compare prices and beware of some dealers who take huge mark-ups. "Be leery of any dealer who can't give you a quick price quote," she said. "Research prices online to get an idea of usual pricing so you can spot any price gouging."

Allen's 300 stores nationwide . . . but the prices! Whoa! A basic crib, $650. double dresser $1400, armoire $2500. Even when EA puts this stuff on "sale," the prices are hard to swallow if you haven't won the lotto. That said, readers who've bought Ethan Allen furniture for their nursery sing their praises for quality and durability. "We found their furniture isn't much more expensive than Morigeau or Ragazzi, but is much better quality. I'm confident the EA furniture we purchased will last for a very long time." Point well taken. The downside? We've heard several complaints from readers about late deliveries . . . but that seems to plague many furniture brands from time to time, not just EA. Nonetheless, if you plan to order EA furniture, leave plenty of time (double their estimated delivery time frame). All in all, we'll give this line a "B" rating—great quality, style and features—if you can afford it. ***Rating: B***

Europa Baby See Bonavita.

Evenflo For a dealer near you, call (800) 233-5921. Web: evenflo.com. Evenflo is just a bit player in the crib market, but occasionally you'll see one of their simple Jenny Lind styles at chain stores or online. We've never been impressed with Evenflo's crib offerings—while the price is low, so is the the quality and lack of features. And the safety record of this brand has been marked by recalls—the most recent in 2003 for 364,000 fold-away mini-cribs. We recommended these fold-away cribs in a previous edition of our book, so if you have one sitting in your home or grandma's house, you need to call (800) 233-5921 for an upgrade kit that will fix the problem. ***Rating: C***

Fisher Price See Stork Craft.

Generation 2 This company is out of business.

Golden Baby See Sorelle.

Graco See Bonavita.

Hart See Westwood.

IKEA. Web: ikea.com. European furniture mega-store Ikea combines the best of both worlds: simple baby furniture . . . at very affordable prices. How affordable? IKEA's most popular model, the Hermelin runs $119. Too much? IKEA also offers an even simpler crib (Sniglar) for $80. All together, Ikea sells five crib models from $80 to $139. So what's the catch? Well, as with most of IKEA's offerings, all furniture comes flat-packed and the assembly is do-it-yourself. One upside:

despite IKEA's European pedigree, standard crib mattresses and sheets fit IKEA's cribs. IKEA also sells matching dressers for $140. So you can basically outfit an entire nursery for $300 to $500 (depending on how many pieces you buy). That's rather amazing, considering $500 won't even buy you a crib from certain brands.

The downsides to IKEA: there are only 35+ stores in the US and Canada, so unless you live in a major city, you will only be able to see (and order) online. But IKEA has been expanding beyond its original locations on the coasts, so odds are good one may be near you. Other drawbacks: you'll either love or loathe the minimalist IKEA look. The cribs are safe and sturdy . . . but Spartan is the word. The cribs lack drop sides and it's hard to use crib skirts (due to the design of some of IKEA's cribs). While the crib slats are solid beech, side panels tend to be made of fiberboard/MDF. And we weren't thrilled with IKEA's thin and insubstantial crib mattress (get a standard mattress from another source). But, given our reader feedback, IKEA cribs and furniture are quite durable and will last through more than one child. A plus: the furniture's somewhat smaller outside dimensions might be just the ticket for those who need to turn a tight space into a nursery. And if your budget is tight, IKEA is among the best options on the market. ***Rating: A***

Issi *See Bonavita earlier in this chapter.*

Jardine *(See Cosco's review for contact information and web site).* Jardine is owned by Dorel Asia, part of the Canada-based Dorel Industries conglomerate that also owns Dorel Juvenile Group USA (Cosco, Safety 1st). This brand is an exclusive for Babies R Us and judging from the line's ever-expanding group of cribs and dressers, it is a hit. Imported from China, Jardine (and its sister brand Bella D'Este) is sold both in Babies R Us stores and online. Sample offerings range from a simple "Natural Spindle Crib" for $100 up to a top of the line "Bella" model with molding accents for $400. Most Jardine cribs are in the $200 to $300 range; matching dressers from $400 to $500. So, how's the quality? Well that is a story with two endings. Most parents we interviewed like Jardine's *cribs*—you get a lot of crib for the dollar (the exposed bolts are the only clue that these are low-end models from China). But the dressers and changing tables? The quality here is much lower—one reader who bought a Jardine changing table posted to our web sit that "there must have been 50 parts with four of them broken . . . the stain on the furniture was not consistent and most of the table is made of cheap particle board." Other readers criticized Jardine for missing parts and other woes. Reviews of Jardine's gliders have been mixed: some readers are happy with Jardine (affordable for both a rocker and ottoman for

$350), but others say Dutailier is a better bet quality-wise. So, it's a mixed bag for Jardine/Bella D'Este: the cribs aren't bad, but the case goods stink. ***Rating (cribs): B+ Rating (dressers, changing tables): F***

Jenny Lind *This is a generic crib style, not a brand name. We explain what a Jenny Lind crib is in the box on page 52.*

Jesse. *See Natart.*

JCPenney (800) 222-6161, web: jcpenney.com. Penney's is a big player in the online/mail-order crib business—their site has nearly three dozen crib styles to choose from, along with a raft of other nursery furniture accessories. In the past, Penney's used to carry well-known names like Bassett or Simmons . . . today, it is all private-label goods imported from Asia. Occasionally, Penney's will note a supplier's name (such as Domusindo), but most items are Penney's private label. The site sells everything from a $150 mini crib to a $500 convertible style. Watch out for shipping charges, which are $100 or more for most furniture items.

While we were pleased with most styles design-wise, we did note that Penney's sells a crib with attached dresser (Rockland). As we explained earlier in this chapter, we aren't wild about this style of nursery furniture for safety concerns.

So, how's the quality? Penney's nursery furniture has a good reputation for quality, durability and safety. The company dispatches its own representatives to suppliers to make sure quality is up to snuff. Customer service, however, is another subject. We have received an increasing number of complaints about order snafus at Penneys: late deliveries, backorder nightmares, the wrong style/color shipped—you name it. Sure, we also get a few positive reviews of Penney's . . . these folks must have won the backorder lottery. Yet the overwhelming number of complaints makes us issue a huge caution flag for this retailer. Bottom line: we only can recommend Penney's if you live in a place few other retail baby store alternatives. ***Rating: C-***

LA Baby Web: LABabyCo.com. Importer LA Baby's main business is commercial-grade, less-than-full-size cribs sold to hotels and day care centers. In addition, LA Baby also has a line of full-size convertible cribs made in China for $350, with matching dressers (also $350). We saw LA Baby's furniture at a recent trade show and weren't impressed. Drawers on the dressers are stapled, not dovetailed. The $350 cribs are simple, but we expect more than exposed bolts and basic finishes at this price level. ***Rating: C***

La Jobi *This is the parent company for Babi Italia and Bonavita. See their review earlier in this section.*

Land of Nod *Web: landofnod.com.* An off-shoot of the Crate and Barrel chain, the Land of Nod catalog and web site offers nine cribs and a selection of matching accessories (including bedding, bassinets, and other gear.) Nope, this stuff ain't cheap: cribs range from $330 to $740. And shhh! Here's something Land of Nod doesn't mention online—that Jenny Lind Crib sold for $330 is actually made by Million Dollar Baby . . . and sold on other sites like Amazon for just $160 under the DaVinci label. (And you think we call this book *Baby Bargains* for nothing, eh?). Parents who have discovered this after the fact have been quite miffed . . . understandably so. However, fans of Land of Nod point out that the catalog frequently offers a custom finish for their MDB cribs that isn't available elsewhere. So you have to decide if that "buttercream" hue is worth the price premium.

As for Land of Nod's customer service and quality, readers give the brand a high marks. But one reader was upset that her furniture order arrived damaged—twice. Land of Nod was accommodating in shipping out replacement pieces, but getting it right in the first place would be nice for a brand that sells such pricey items. Another black mark for Land of Nod: in 2006, the company had to recall 2,000 cribs and dressers in their Cottage collection because they were finished with paint that contained lead. ***Rating B***

Legacy *See Child Craft.*

Li'l Angels. *This crib brand is reviewed on our free web site, BabyBargains.com (click on Bonus Material).*

Little Miss Liberty *This crib brand is reviewed on our free web site, BabyBargains.com (click on Bonus Material).*

Litto *310-798-1788; Web: LIttoKids.com.* Asian-influenced design marks Litto's first efforts, including an $850 crib covered in a zebra laminate veneer. The California company joins a wave of new modern baby furniture companies that debuted in the past year. Since this furniture is still so new as of this writing, we don't have a read on their quality or parent feedback. While the zebra wood laminate (which appears on both Litto's crib and dressers) is a unique touch, we're a bit skeptical how this would hold up in the real world, with humidity extremes and other factors. We'll take a wait and see on this brand. ***Rating: Not Yet.***

Luna *This crib brand is reviewed on our free web site, BabyBargains.com (click on Bonus Material).*

Million Dollar Baby *Call (323) 728-9988 for a dealer near you. Web: milliondollarbaby.com.* Hong Kong entrepreneur Daniel Fong started Million Dollar Baby (MDB) in 1989 and was one of the first successful importers of cribs from Asia. MDB got its start selling low-end $99 cribs to discounters, but over time has broadened its line to include convertible cribs and more upscale resellers (you'll find their Jenny Lind crib at Land of Nod, for example). With prices today ranging $150 to $500, MDB was one of the first crib importers to sell its goods online, although it uses an alias (DaVinci) so as to not offend retail customers. An example: the DaVinci Emily pine crib sold online at Target, Amazon and BabyCenter.com for $200 to $300, depending on the site. The Emily crib has been a popular seller, thanks in part to several new darker finishes.

So, how's the quality? The cribs are good, the case goods are average. Our biggest beef with MDB: their Asian pine is softer (and more prone to damage) than other pine cribs on the market. We wish MDB had more hardwood groupings in their line and less pine. How is MDB's customer service? We've heard mixed reports. Retailers seem happy with MDB's customer service and deliveries. Consumers are less enthusiastic, telling us about unreturned emails, poor assembly instructions and overall lackluster customer service.

New in the past year, Million Dollar Baby has been selling a contemporary line of furniture under the "Baby Mod" moniker at Wal-Mart (there's no mention of MDB in the description). These two-tone cribs ($300) and dressers ($250) aim for that contempo/sleek look (glossy "espresso" finish matched with antique white) at a fraction of the price of other modern nursery furniture. And the quality? It's much the same as MDB's other furniture—no one will mistake Baby Mod as heirloom-quality furniture, but you are getting decent value for the dollar. The caveats: most of the pieces are made of composites (not solid wood) . . . and what solid wood there is is soft pine. And like all MDB furniture, the instructions are poor and confusing.

So it's a mixed review for Million Dollar Baby—this brand is defi-

---

Craigslist & eBay deals

Tempted by the nursery furniture bargains on eBay or Craigslist? While these sites can offer some great deals, there are caveats: unsafe cribs, outrageous shipping fees, damaged items and worse. We've prepared a free special report on buying nursery furniture on eBay or Craigslist—check it out on BabyBargains.com (Bonus Material).

---

nitely better than other low-end competitors like Delta or Simplicity. But be aware of the caveats to MDB (soft pine wood, poor instructions, etc) before purchasing. ***Rating: B-***

Mondi *This crib brand is reviewed on our free web site, BabyBargains.com (click on Bonus Material).*

Morigeau/Lepine *Call (800) 326-2121 or (724) 941-7475 or (970) 845-7795 for a dealer near you Web: morigeau.com.* Here's an oddity: a crib maker that still makes furniture in Canada. Sure, Morigeau/Lepine has a 50 year history as a family-run business in Quebec—but, considering that nearly every other furniture company in North America now imports all its goods from Asia, you have to wonder whether is Morigeau is insane . . . or insanely smart.

Morigeau's niche is nursery furniture that looks smart and sophisticated—more adult than baby, with an emphasis on quality construction and numerous finish options. But it's going to cost you . . . a crib from Morigeau runs $600 to $800. Ditto for the dressers, while an armoire can set you back a cool $1000 or more. Hence a three-piece nursery from Morigeau can easily top out at $2500 to $3000.

What do you get for those bucks? Solid wood construction for most groupings (a few items are MDF), drawers with dovetailed joints and cribs with completely hidden hardware and self-lubricating nylon tracks. Safety-wise, Morigeau's dressers have side-mounted glides with safety stops. We also liked the fact that most of Morigeau's dressers are oversized with 21" deep drawers to give you extra storage.

New in the past year, Morigeau debuted modern baby furniture groupings that looks much like ducduc. Why Morigeau decided it needed to knock-off another line is a bit of a head-scratcher. Expect to pay $1200 for a modern Morigeau crib, while a dresser is $1000.

Also new: Morigeau joins the "green" furniture trend this year with the cleverly named Green Collection, featuring eco-harvested wood, water-based finishes and soy-based glue—$1000 for crib or dresser.

So, assuming you have the bankroll, is Morigeau worth it? Reading the parent reviews on our web site, you'll note Morigeau gets mixed reviews. Retailers give them high marks for quality, service and delivery. Consumers, on the other hand, have been divided. Some love the brand; others are disappointed that certain Morigeau pieces are made of MDF. Still others knock the noisy crib rail release, which latches with a loud click. That bugs some, but not others—try it out in the store first. Finally, in the past year, we blogged about several cases of Morigeau cribs whose paint peeled after only a year or so of normal use. The company blamed this on a batch of bad paint—sure, something you might expect on a $150 Wal-Mart crib . . . but not when you are spending serious coin. These hiccups keep this brand from earning our top rating this time out. **_Rating: B+_**

Mother Hubbard's Cupboard _Call (416) 661-8201 for a dealer near you. Web: mhcfurniture.com._ Canadian-based furniture maker Mother Hubbard's Cupboard (MHC) scored a coup a few years ago when they landed their dressers in the Buy Buy Baby chain. Since then, they've expanded by adding cribs to their line. MHC has six collections of conservatively designed furniture with different dresser configurations (four or five drawer chests and double dressers, as well as armoires). Cribs run $500 to $600; dressers are $500 to $900. That puts MHC somewhat in the middle of the crib market—more expensive than the stuff you see at Babies R Us, but less than Morigeau or Pali. While the style isn't cutting edge or overly adult, the emphasis here is on construction (all the case pieces are made in Canada) and finish choices (30 at last count).

So how's the quality and delivery? Our readers are split on this. Fans of MHC like the fact it is made in Canada instead of China (to be precise, a couple of MHC crib styles are imported from Bulgaria, but finished and painted in Canada). Quality and finish are generally good, but one frustrated dad emailed us a story of a changing table with miss-drilled holes for the handles. After many calls, they got a replacement drawer fronts—but they weren't pre-drilled. Other parents complain of long waits for delivery (up to 15 weeks), even though others say it took just eight weeks (which is MHC's goal). And, yes, MHC's painted pieces are made of MDF (not solid wood), but the overall construction (dove-tailed drawers, etc) is good. FYI: If you live near Toronto, check out the MHC outlet for close-outs at 20% to 60% off retail. **_Rating: B+_**

Munire _For a dealer near you, call 732-339-6070. Web: MunireFurniture.com._ Munire is a rising star in the baby furniture biz. Although the brand is not as well known as others, Munire has actually been making juvenile furniture since 1987 for other companies. About five years ago, the company began to expand and market its wares under the Munire brand.

Munire's niche is adult-looking nursery furniture (with an emphasis on style and quality) at prices that are few notches below the other players on the market. A typical offering is Munire's best-selling Majestic collection, a mahogany grouping featuring a crib ($500), double dresser ($630) and armoire ($850). So, a three-piece Munire nursery will set you back around $2000. Sure, the finish choices are limited (four for Majestic) but you get quality touches like dove-tail drawers and architectural details such as bun feet on the dressers. In fact, it is the quality that most impressed us about Munire: drawers feature a double-track, ball-bearing system for smooth glides, center supports, corner blocks and more. Most of Munire's collections are made of solid wood, although a few have painted MDF veneers.

New this year is Munire's first collection for chain stores: Baby Cache. Sold online at JCPenney.com and in Babies R Us stores, Baby Cache features a trio of cribs with Munire's trademark adult touches (hand-carved columns on one crib; bun feet on another). A Baby Cache convertible crib is $500 from Penney's (dressers are $600). Pricing on the Babies R Us version of Baby Cache wasn't available as of press time, but we'd bet it will be similar to Penney's. Since these are completely new styles, we don't have any parent feedback yet on Munire's new venture.

Munire's rapid growth in the US has not been without a few hiccups. When the company switched production from Mexico to Indonesia in 2006, snafus left customers waiting for orders for weeks beyond delivery dates. Worse still, Munire admitted the "finish and color which Indonesia shipped on its first production run was not to our specifications." Translation: colors didn't match and other quality complaints piled up. To the company's credit, Munire owned up to its mistakes and replaced the defective items.

Readers have generally been positive in their reviews of Munire, with many citing their sturdy and solid cribs plus overall level of craftsmanship as Munire's strengths. A few dissenters say Munire doesn't quite live up to the hype, citing delivery delays for some items and the aforementioned production snafus. As of this writing, all is back to normal with Munire for quality and delivery, albeit the wait times for certain collections sometimes stretch to ten to 12 weeks.

When it comes to Munire versus other brands, here's the best analogy: Munire is like the Toyota Camry of baby furniture—good quality and solid construction, albeit somewhat conservative in styling. Yes, you could get a Lexus (brands like Natart and Pali are a step up in both styling and craftsmanship)—but you'd have to pay 20% to 40% more for the sizzle.

Given Munire's popularity, the brand's biggest challenge for the coming years will be maintaining its quality, service and value as it grows into one of the industry's key players. All in all, we recommend Munire. ***Rating: A***

Natart Call (819) 364-3189 for a dealer near you. Web: natartfurniture.com. Natart—a company in desperate need of a catchier name—is one of a number of Quebec-based nursery furniture makers to come to the U.S. market in recent years (Natart debuted in 2001). At least Natart deserves bonus points for creativity—it's recent collections feature unique touches like a changing table that morphs into a computer desk. Clever design squeezes extra storage out of other items, while whimsical touches like the floral wood appliqués on the Victorian-inspired Paris crib are sassy without being overly cutesy. Best of all, the quality is very high—so if you are going to spend the big bucks on Natart (a crib is typically $700; dressers can top $1000), at least you know you are getting your money's worth. Take a look at Natart's dressers. Made in Canada, the dressers have dovetail drawers and stabilizer bars for a smooth glide. All the cribs have hidden hardware for the knee-push rail releases. Delivery is eight to ten weeks. New this year: Natart introduces an entry-level crib (Emily) for $600 and the first convertible crib (Alex) that morphs from crib to twin to double for $800. If you have the bankroll to invest in top-quality furniture and want something that's a cut above the furniture sold in chain stores, Natart is for you. ***Rating: A***

NettoCollection *Web: NettoCollection.com.* New York designer David Netto helped launch the modern/minimalist design wave rolling over the nursery market with his NettoCollection in 2002. An interior designer by trade, Netto's furniture comes in two collections: Netto (which is more expensive) and the new mid-price line, Cub. On the upper end, the "Modern Crib" ($1440) is typical of the Netto aesthetic with solid white lacquer panels and natural ash side rails. A shelf under the crib can hold optional $115 linen boxes (or buy your own boxes). A matching dresser is $1420. The new Cub line features a crib for $500 in white ($525 for mixed white/pine), a changing table for $550 and bookshelf for $300. A few caveats to this line: all the furniture comes "IKEA"-style—that is flat-packed for do-it-yourself assembly. Also: Netto's cribs have fixed side rails, so this might be a no-go for shorter parents. Netto is sold in just a handful of boutiques nationwide, including the Giggle chain. All the furniture is made in Vietnam or Poland. As for a rating on this line, we'll have to give it mixed reviews—while we realize this is supposed to appeal to minimalist parents with cash to burn, we still can't get over the four-figure price tags for this stuff. Yes, the new Cub line is closer to the mark, but we can't help but think you can get a similar look at IKEA for a fraction of this price. And if you want to spend big bucks on contemporary nursery furniture, you'd be better off with Morigeau's modern groupings. Overall, we found the quality of Netto to be only average.

And we were disappointed to learn about a safety recall of Netto's Moderne and Loft cribs in 2007 for crib slats that separated from the side rails—we expect a bit more quality control on $1400 cribs. FYI for New York City parents: Netto's Soho store runs occasional sample sales with prices up to 60% off. ***Rating: C+***

Newport Cottage *Web: NewportCottages.com.* When it comes to over-the-top furniture, Newport Cottage turns the knob to 11.

With their trademark look of two-toned case pieces with distressed finishes, Newport Cottage is a mix of both vintage and contemporary aesthetics. But this will cost you: a simple, colorful crib is $1200 to $1400. A dresser will set you back $1500. Yep, that is pricey . . . but at least the furniture is manufactured in the U.S. (which makes Newport Cottage one of the last domestic makers of nursery furniture). We got a look at Newport Cottage's furniture at a trade show and thought the quality was good—but it's hard to justify these prices (unless you just have to have that lavender finish). Given this line's limited distribution and high prices, we've heard from few parents who's actually bought the furniture. As a result, we'll have to wait on assigning a rating for a future edition. **Rating: Not Yet.**

Nursery Smart Web: nurserysmart.com; babyappleseed.com. 626-333-1919. Newcomer Nursery Smart injects a bit of eco-activism into their Baby Appleseed furniture collection: when you buy one of their cribs, the company will plant ten trees in your baby's name, thanks to a partnership with the non-profit American Forests.

Pricing is reasonable: most Nursery Smart cribs run $300 to $350; the Baby Appleseed Millbury crib is the most pricey at $550. A limited selection of dressers are in the $500 range. While Baby Appleseed consists of just two collections (Millbury and Davenport),

True Colors: Swatches and samples

What's the difference between oak and pecan? When you order baby furniture, those terms don't refer to a species of wood, but the color of the stain. And many parents have been stymied when their expensive nursery furniture arrives and it looks nothing like the "cherry" furniture they expected. Here's our advice: when ordering furniture, be sure to see ACTUAL wood samples stained with the hue you want. Don't rely on a web site picture or even a printed catalog. And remember that different types of wood take stain, well, differently. If you order your furniture in a pecan finish, but the crib is made of beech wood and the dresser is pine, they may NOT match. That's because beech and pine would look slightly different even when stained with the exact same finish.

Ordering online makes this more of a challenge, of course. Most sites don't offer wood samples—you have to rely on a web site picture (and how that is displayed on your monitor). Bottom line: you'll have to be flexible when it comes to what the final stain looks like. But if you have your heart set on a particular hue for your nursery furniture, it might be best to order off-line . . . and see a stained wood sample first.

Nursery Smart has three groupings.

In the last printing of this book, we gave Nursery Smart/ Baby Appleseed an A, complementing the furniture's quality and construction based on their successful initial run in stores like Buy Buy Baby. But like many young companies, Nursery Smart had teething problems in 2007—after quality slipped, the company switched production from Vietnam to China. This prompted further complaints of delayed shipping, miss-matched finishes and other quality woes.

On the plus side, the company's newest shipments from China show a marked improvement in quality (the drawer construction on Baby Appleseed's dresser is excellent, for example). And Nursery Smart/Baby Appleseed has switched from pine to hardwoods, which is an improvement. To catch its breath, the company isn't introducing any new furniture collections in 2008.

So it is a mixed review for this newcomer—we liked the company's eco-consciousness and the furniture's architectural style. But the company's production problems in the last year lead us to lower their rating this time out—we will be watching to see if they can regain their footing in the coming months. **Rating: B**

Nurseryworks *Web: Nurseryworks.net* Describing its furniture as "mid-century inspired baby furniture and bedding designed to fit a modern home," Nurseryworks is a LA-based company that adds a bit of a twist to the modernist trend: color. Their Aerial crib enables to you to customize the colors for the end panels, rails and slats—you can pick from cotton candy, citrus, lime, navy and something called slumber (a pale yellow). All yours for $990, plus $300 for an optional drawer. Nurseryworks' Studio crib features zebra laminate (apparently a popular trend today in modernist circles) and a built-in changing table for $1780. If all this is too much, Nurseryworks budget option (the Loom crib) runs $590-$650 but only has a fixed side rail. Nurseryworks cleverly markets a line of complimentary bedding for its cribs—a six-piece set runs $330-$355. Of all the modern crib designers, Nurseryworks has the biggest distribution, both in stores and online. We also liked the wide range of accessories. So, if your heart's desire is a modernist nursery (and you have the bank account

Replacement parts

What if you are missing a part to assemble your crib? Most crib makers are happy to supply a missing bolt or other hardware . . . but what if your crib maker goes out of business? The solution: ProductAmerica.com. This web site is one of the few sources for crib hardware replacement parts.

to drop $3000+ on a nursery), Nurseryworks is probably the best bet. But we still find it hard to justify these prices ($1350 for a dresser? $1000 for a crib?), given that most of the furniture (imported from Asia) is MDF, veneers and laminate. ***Rating: B+***

Oeuf Web: Oeufnyc.com. Oeuf (literally, egg in French and pronounced like the "uff" in stuff) traces its roots to 2002, when French-American designers Sophie Demenge and Michael Ryan launched the company (and a family) in Brooklyn, New York. Their goal: pair eco-consciousness with modernist design elements. The result: the Oeuf crib, which takes its cues from minimalist Euro styling. The Oeuf crib's fixed side rails, headboard and footboard remove, converting the whole unit to a toddler bed. Like many modern cribs, the Oeuf crib has a wood base (in this case, birch) and MDF panels covered in a white lacquer finish. Price: $824 to $848. A matching three drawer dresser is $870. Oeuf also makes a "baby lounger" (bouncer) for $100 and has a knit clothing line ($38 mittens, anyone?). New this year, Oeuf has debuted a slightly-less expensive line of furniture (Sparrow), with cribs at $650 and dressers for $680. Sparrow features more natural wood accents, paired with a grayish/brown MDF. All in all, we liked Oeuf—their prices are a bit lower than their modernist peers and the quality (considering all the items are made of MDF with just a dash of solid wood) is good. ***Rating: B***

Pacific Rim Woodworking *This crib brand is reviewed on our free web site, BabyBargains.com (click on Bonus Material).*

Paintbox *See El Greco.*

Pali For a dealer near you, call (877) 725-4772. Web: paliitaly.com. Italian furniture maker Pali has had its ups and downs over the years, but still retains the crown as one of the industry's top brands. Why? Pali makes among the best quality and beautifully detailed cribs and dressers on the market. Tracing its roots to 1919 as a chair maker, family-owned Pali focused its efforts on juvenile furniture in 1962 and then rode a wave of popularity in the 1990's.

Solid beech wood construction and Italy's reputation for meticulous craftsmanship give Pali's cribs a leg up on competitors, despite the high price tags. A Pali crib runs $600 to $800; a three-piece Pali nursery typically runs $2500 at retail, making it one of the most expensive brands. (One slight negative to Pali's cribs: the side rail latches with a loud click, which annoys some parents).

But even Pali isn't immune to market forces—buffeted by a soaring Euro and low-cost Asian imports, Pali has seen its market share shrink in recent years. As a response, Pali now imports four if its collections from Thailand and Vietnam. These still maintain the brand's quality touches (birch wood construction, dovetail drawers, for example). A three-piece nursery set of Thailand-made Pali furniture sells for a touch under $2000 (a crib is $600), in line with competitors like Munire. About 40% of Pali's furniture is now made in Asia, with the balance being made up of Canadian-made dressers and Italian-produced cribs.

How's the quality of these new imports? Good, report both retailers and consumers. That's comforting, as other companies have stumbled when they tried to move production to Asia.

In other news, Pali has opened a big distribution center in Montreal (Pali makes dressers in Canada) which has helped reduce previously long waits for delivery. And true enough, we hear fewer complaints about Pali delivery delays or customer service than in the past. Overall, we recommend Pali—both their Italian and Asian collections are excellent. FYI: you won't find Pali sold online or in chain stores; it's only at specialty stores. The only exception: the Buy Buy Baby chain. **Rating: A-**

Pamela Scurry *See Bassett.*

Petite Cheris. *See Dutailier.*

PJ Kids *This company went out of business in 2005. An archived review of PJ Kids is on our web site (click on Bonus Material) in case you discover some of their furniture for sale second-hand.*

Pottery Barn Kids *(800) 430-7373 or potterybarnkids.com.* It's rare that one retailer/catalog can change an entire industry. Pottery Barn Kids (PBK) scored that coup earlier this decade when their contemporary nursery décor (accented by vintage motifs and a bright color palette) literally changed the rules. Out went cutesy baby-ish décor; PBK ushered in a more modern yet still whimsical look.

Despite its success, we are still put off by PBK's sky-high prices—cribs run $600 to $700, with one round-crib style running a whopping $1000. Imported from Asia as their own private label, PBK's cribs are convertible and made of beech wood . . . but you can find the same looks/quality elsewhere for $200 to $300 less. And watch out for the shipping charges Pottery Barn slaps on their cribs—10% of the order, on top of the already high prices. A double dresser is $700; a five-drawer dresser is $800.

While most parents are happy with PBK (they sell a wide variety of accessories, including glider rockers, changing tables and dressers), we've had more than one parent tell us about quality woes with PBK furniture: peeling paint on a crib, splintering wood on a dresser, etc. To PBK's credit, the web site or store usually takes care of the problem and replaces the defective item. But at these prices, it would be great if PBK could get it right the first time.

Bottom line: use this catalog for décor items like bedding or lamps and order the furniture elsewhere. **Rating (furniture): C**

Ragazzi *Web: ragazzi.com.* We once compared Ragazzi to the Lexus of the baby furniture market—expensive, stylish, and exclusive. Well, Ragazzi ended its 34-year run as a nursery furniture leader in May 2006, when it suddenly shuttered its Quebec plant. In a terse fax to retailers, Ragazzi blamed the company's collapse on "today's economic realities." That news pretty much stunned Ragazzi's dealers and customers, who had little warning of the company's demise.

Enter Stork Craft, the Vancouver, Canada-based furniture importer best known for its low-end cribs sold in Wal-Mart. For an undisclosed figure, Stork Craft bought the rights to the Ragazzi name and planned to re-launch the brand as an upper-end line in 2007.

This was a real head-scratcher—Stork Craft buying Ragazzi is a bit like Hyundai buying Lexus. Sure, Hyundai could make a luxury car and declare it to be a Lexus . . . but that doesn't make it a Lexus. Ditto for Stork Craft—we're skeptical that the new Ragazzi (made in China) will be able to live up to the reputation of its former owners.

Ragazzi plans to debut with nine collections in five finishes—a drop-side crib will run $600, while a sleigh-style convertible crib will be $700 to $800. Ragazzi's dressers will feature felt-lined, self-closing drawers and premium hardwoods (a five-drawer chest will run $750). Ragazzi will also debut a slightly-less expensive line (Bambino) made of New Zealand pine—same styling, but about 10% lower in price. Bambino will also have fewer finishes (four), limited accessories and less fancy features (no felt lined drawers, for example).

What really sticks in our craw about the Stork Craft/Ragazzi buyout was the way Stork Craft decided to treat former Ragazzi customers. Readers told us when they contacted Stork Craft with warranty problems or parts requests for Ragazzi models, they were told Stork Craft just bought the name rights to Ragazzi—there would be no support for past products. Guess if you bought a $700 Ragazzi crib and needed a small part, that's your tough luck.

This seems incredibly short-sighted. Failing to honor past warranties or fulfill parts requests is a sure way to evaporate whatever goodwill Ragazzi had left among consumers or retailers.

So, how's the quality on the new Ragazzi? As of this writing, the company just started shipping after a lengthy delay (Stork Craft said it needed to iron out production wrinkles). The initial reports: the quality is quite good. But it is too early to get an accurate reading—we like to see six to 12 months of a track record before assigning a rating.

In our last printing, we gave the new Ragazzi an F, reflecting our disappointment over Stork Craft's initial ham-handed transition of the brand. But now that the new company is finally shipping furniture, we will wait on a rating until the dust settles. ***Rating: Not Yet.***

Relics Furniture *This crib brand is reviewed on our free web site, BabyBargains.com (click on Bonus Material).*

Restore & Restyle *Web: target.com. Target's in-house brand of baby furniture is reviewed on our free web site, BabyBargains.com (click on Bonus Material).*

Romina *Web: RominaKidsFurniture.com.* Who knew that Ragazzi (the Canadian luxury nursery furniture maker that closed in 2006 and was sold to Stork Craft) didn't make their own cribs? And that Ragazzi imported these unfinished items from a factory in Romania? That was news to us. And the even bigger news is that Ragazzi's Romanian supplier (Romina) is now coming to the US to sell its cribs direct. Yes, these are the same (or very similar models) that Ragazzi sold. Romina sells both regular cribs ($600) and convertible models ($700-$1000), as well as dressers (five-drawer for $700; armoire for $1100).

Romina started out modestly, with two collections—but within each collection there is a good number of accessories (nightstands, mirrors, etc). For 2008, Romina will add a couple of new styles, including its first collection of contemporary furniture and a line of organic finishes based on beeswax.

So, how's the quality? We are impressed with Romina's solid wood (beech) construction and details like dovetail drawers, corner blocks on drawers and so on. But we have heard a few initial reports of finish problems—misapplied finish, a clear coat overspray that was rough in areas, etc. This makes sense to a degree: while Romina made Ragazzi's cribs, they shipped them unfinished (the finishing was done in Ragazzi's Canada facility). To the company's credit, they have worked to resolve problems quickly. So the craftsmanship is there, but Romina probably needs to work out a few kinks in its finishing department. Overall, however, we will recommend Romina—while the prices make this no bargain, the quality is high. ***Rating: B+***

Room & Board *Web: roomandboard.com. This nine-store chain with locations in Chicago, San Francisco and New York is reviewed on our free web site, BabyBargains.com (click on Bonus Material).*

Rumble Tuff. *See RT Furniture.*

RT Furniture (aka Rumble Tuff). Web: rtfurnitureusa.com. RT Furniture is a Utah-based maker and importer of nursery furniture that got its start by popularizing the "hi-lo" combo dresser in the 90's. (A quick word on RT and Rumble Tuff–RT is the furniture maker; Rumble Tuff makes changing pads and other soft goods. Both companies used to have the same owners, but Rumble Tuff spun off on its own in 2006. Confusingly, some stores still refer to the furniture by the brand name Rumble Tuff, although it really is now RT). Like most furniture makers, RT has turned to imports in the past year (previously, all of RT's furniture was made in Utah).

We were fans of RT's dressers and have recommended them in past years, but we'll have to take a wait-and-see approach when it comes to the new imports. Just to confuse the situation further, RT still makes some furniture domestically, while other items are imported from Thailand and Vietnam. RT's convertible cribs ($500 to $600), which are relatively new to the line, are imported from Slovenia and Italy. RT's dressers run $500 for a five-drawer chest. So far, we think the quality of the samples we've seen is good, but we've heard complaints of long delays on orders from readers (one of whom waited seven weeks beyond the original delivery date to get her furniture). So we will temper our rating a bit as RT transitions its line from domestic to imports, to see how things shake out. **Rating: B**

Sauder *This brand is reviewed on our free web site, BabyBargains.com (click on Bonus Material).*

Shermag *See Chanderic.*

Simmons Web: simmonskids.com. Here's a sad story about the fall of an American company. Simmons Juvenile was once one of the country's biggest nursery furniture makers, selling cribs and dressers to many generations of parents. Started in 1917 by Thomas Alva Edison to provide wooden cabinets for one of his recent inventions (the phonograph), Simmons morphed into a furniture company that also made mattresses. The company spun off its juvenile division in the 1980's (just to confuse you, there is still a Simmons company that makes mattresses). Then the company began its slow decline. Simmons made a couple major mistakes, chief among them a decision in the 1990's to concentrate on selling its furniture in chain stores (forsaking the independent stores that built its business over the decades). Yet the company never adapted to the changing nursery furniture market, which soon became flooded with low-cost imports from Asia. Simmons stuck to making its cribs and dressers in plants in Wisconsin and Canada.

By 2004, the company's deteriorating fortunes prompted the

management to sell their crib mattress biz back to Simmons and then shutter the Wisconsin plant. Simmons sold the rights to their name to Delta, which then relaunched Simmons as a separate, upscale division aimed at specialty stores. Ironic, no? Delta's first Simmons collection (imported from China) was a bust—$800 cribs, $700 dressers that were met with little enthusiasm among consumers.

Yes, you can find Simmons in chain stores like Babies R Us—last we looked, a Simmons crib was $400 to $500, with matching five-drawer chest for $470. This is a much more realistic price point for Simmons. How's the quality of the new imported line? About average—not the best, but not the worst. Given Delta's lackluster overall reputation for quality and customer service, we can only give the new Simmons a lukewarm rating. One warning about Simmons: readers report that since Delta moved all the production to China, deliveries are taking "forever." ***Rating: C***

Simplicity *(800) 448-4308. Web: simplicityforchildren.com.* This brand showed so much promise when it emerged as a major importer of affordable cribs and furniture from China. Sold in chain stores like Wal-Mart and Target, Simplicity got its start selling licensed furniture under the Graco label. That license deal has since expired (Bonavita now makes Graco furniture), but Simplicity pressed on, emphasizing its own brand.

Simplicity's main biz is ready-to-assembly (RTA) dressers, although the brand launched a few already-assembled items in 2007. Simplicity's cribs run $140 for a simple drop-side model to $250 to $300 for a convertible crib. Dressers like a high-low combo unit are $250. The new high-end (already assembled) items will run $600 for a crib and $600 for a dresser.

Several high profile stumbles have hurt Simplicity. The biggest was a 2007 recall of nearly one MILLION Simplicity cribs, which killed two children after the side rails separated from the crib (there were 55 incidents in all). The problem was blamed on confusing assembly instructions and faulty design, said the CPSC. Simplicity earned the notoriety of being responsible for the largest crib recall in history. Among the most troubling aspects of the recall: a mom who contacted Simplicity about her crib rail detaching told the *Chicago Tribune* that the company never returned her calls.

As a result of this and other previous recalls (Simplicity had two previous safety recalls on its cribs), we can not recommend this brand. ***Rating: F***

Sorelle *Call 201) 531-1919 for a dealer near you. Web: sorellefurniture.com.* Sorelle is the main brand for C&T, an importer that has been in the market since 1977 (FYI: Sorelle cribs are sold under the name Golden Baby or C&T at Babies R Us and Baby Depot).

Sorelle started out as an Italian importer, but in recent years, the company has begun importing cribs from Brazil and Latvia (in addition to Italy). Case pieces are made in all those locales, as well as Canada. Sorelle also imports three furniture collections from China. A good example of the line: the popular Lana crib sold at Baby Depot (and elsewhere) for $220—that's a great value for a birch crib with hidden hardware, knee push rail release and under crib drawer. Other Sorelle models run $250 to $400, which is affordable in today's market. Sorelle's dressers run $600 for a combo to $700 for an armoire.

So, how's the quality? If you take a look at the two dozen reviews of Sorelle posted to our web site, you'll note the opinions are all over the board. For every parent who tells us they are pleased with the quality and finish of their Sorelle furniture, another will write to blast a series of problems—defective side rails, "nonexistent and rude" customer service, poor assembly instructions, missing parts and more. At one point in 2005, Sorelle switched the mattress support system in their cribs from metal springs to wooden slats . . . but neglected to change the crib's assembly instructions.

Bottom line: ordering furniture from this brand is a bit of a crapshoot. Be sure to deal with a reputable store or web site in case you have problems. Sorelle must concentrate on better quality control and customer service—given the consumer feedback we hear, they are missing the mark at this point. ***Rating: B-***

Stanley *See Young America.*

Stokke/Sleepi *Call (877) 978-6553 for a dealer near you. Web: stokkeusa.com.* Color us skeptical when we first heard about this Norwegian company's ultra-expensive crib "system:" The Sleepi morphs from a bassinet to a crib, then a toddler bed and finally two chairs . . . for a cool $1000. A separate changing table (the Care) converts to a play table and desk for $450. As with all these funky European products, you'll have to buy specially made bedding with limited choices ($30 for a sheet; $165 to $225 for a set).

Yet the parent feedback on the Sleepi has been very positive—fans love its clever oval shape (fits through narrow doorways) and overall ease of use. The Sleepi is perhaps best suited to urban apartment dwellers with little space for a standard-size crib. Given positive reader reviews, we will up the rating of the Stokke Sleepi—yes, it is outrageously expensive and a niche product, but for those who are space-deprived, this is a good solution. ***Rating: A-***

Stork Craft *For a dealer near you, call (604) 274-5121. Web: storkcraft.com.* Stork Craft is probably the best known as an entry-level brand that's sold in discount chain stores. You'll find their wares in stores and online at places like Wal-Mart and Target, as well as in Babies R Us, Costco, JCPenney, and Burlington's Baby Depot.

Stork Craft's entry level cribs run about $100 online at Wal-Mart, although most offerings are in the $150 to $300 range. At the top end, the $300 crib model features sleigh-styling and the ability to convert to a full-size bed. Stork Craft also makes a wide array of matching accessories, including dressers, rocker gliders and other items—the dressers are an affordable $200 to $300. Stork Craft both manufacturers furniture in Canada and imports some items from Asia.

So, let's talk quality. Parents generally give Stork Craft low marks,

8 tips to lower the risk of SIDS

Sudden Infant Death Syndrome (SIDS) is the sudden death of an infant under one of year of age due to unexplained causes. Sadly, SIDS is still the number one killer of infants under age one—over 2000 babies die each year.

So, what causes SIDS? Scientists don't know, despite studying the problem for two decades. We do know that SIDS is a threat during the first year of life, with a peak occurrence between one and six months. SIDS also affects more boys than girls; and the SIDS rate in African American babies is twice that of Caucasians. Despite the mystery surrounding SIDS, researchers have discovered several factors that dramatically lower the risk of SIDS. Here is what you can do:

Put your baby to sleep on her back. Infants should be placed on their back (not side or tummy) each time they go to sleep. Since the campaign to get parents to put baby to sleep on their backs began in 1992, the SIDS rate has fallen by 50%. That's the good news. The bad news: while parents are heeding this message, other care givers (that is, grandma or day care centers) are less vigilant. Be sure to tell all your baby's caregivers that baby is to sleep on his back, never his tummy.

Encourage tummy time. When awake, baby should spend some time on their tummy. This helps prevent flat heads caused by lying on their backs (positional plagiocephaly). Vary your child's head position while sleeping (such as, turning his head to the right during one nap and then the left during the next nap). Minimize time spent in car seats (unless baby is in a car, of course!), swings, bouncer seats or carriers—any place baby is kept in a semi-upright position. A good goal: no more than an hour or two a day. To learn more about plagiocephaly, go online to plagiocephaly.org.

Forget gadgets. Special mattresses, sleep positioners, breathing monitors—none have been able to reduce the risk of SIDS, says the American Academy of Pediatrics. Just put baby to sleep on her back.

Use a pacifier. Consider giving baby a pacifier, which has been based on reviews posted to our web site. Fans like the affordable pricing and the fact you can order most of this furniture online. But detractors say items often arrive damaged, with missing parts and worse. One parent who paid $450 for a Stork Craft crib said she was extremely disappointed in the poor finish which looked very cheap—and the under-crib drawer's bottom constantly fell off its track when moved. Another parent who bought a $300 Stork Craft dresser said it arrived severely damaged and "looks as if it were purchased at a garage sale." Stork Craft's customer service also came in for criticism, with delays in fixing defective merchandise and parts among the top gripes. And we've been less than

shown in studies to reduce the rate of SIDS. Why? Scientists don't know exactly, but some speculate pacifiers help keep the airway open. Okay, we should acknowledge that pacifiers are controversial— key concerns include breastfeeding interference, tooth development and ear infections. But if you introduce the pacifier after breast-feeding is well-established (around one month), there are few problems. Stop using the pacifier after one year (when the SIDS risk declines) and there are no ill dental effects. While pacifiers do increase the risk of ear infections, ear infections are rare in babies when the risk of SIDS is highest (under six months old). Bottom line: Use pacifiers at the time of sleep starting at one month of life for breastfed babies. If the pacifier falls out once the baby is asleep, don't re-insert it. Stop using pacifiers once the risk of SIDS is over (about a year of life).

Don't smoke or overheat the baby's room. Smoking during pregnancy or after the baby is born has shown to increase the risk of SIDS. Keep baby's room at a comfortable temperature, but don't overheat (do not exceed 70 degrees in the winter; 78 in the summer). Use a sleep sack or swaddle baby with a blanket.

Bed sharing: bad. Room sharing: good. Why does bed sharing increase the risk of SIDS? Scientists say the risk of suffocation in adult linens (pillows, etc) or entrapment between bed frame and mattress, or by family members is a major contributor to SIDS. That said, *room sharing* (having baby in the same room as the parents, either in a bassinet or a product like the Arm's Reach Bedside co-sleeper) is shown to reduce the rate of SIDS. Again, researchers don't know exactly why, but it's possible parents are more attuned to their baby's breathing when baby is nearby.

No soft bedding. Baby's crib or bassinet should have a firm mattress and no soft bedding (quilts, pillows, stuffed animals, etc). Bumpers are optional—we will discuss this topic in the next chapter.

Make sure all other caregivers follow these instructions. Again, you might be vigilant about back-sleeping . . . but if another caregiver doesn't follow the rules, your baby could be at risk. Make sure your day care provider, grandma or other caregiver is on board.

impressed with the way Stork Craft has handled the Ragazzi acquisition (see earlier review).

Finally, Stork Craft has downgraded the quality of its cribs in the past year, in our opinion. Example: gone are the spring mattress supports. Now Stork Craft uses a MDF board to support the mattress, which is not our preferred choice.

Bottom line: if you want to order this brand online, stick with the low-price items (the $150 cribs at Wal-Mart are a good bet). Skip the dressers, glider rocks and anything expensive (those $250+ cribs). And be sure to set your expectations accordingly. As a result of the increased complaints about this brand, we've dropped their rating. **Rating: C**

Today's Baby *This crib brand is reviewed on our free web site, BabyBargains.com (click on Bonus Material).*

Vermont Precision *This company exited the nursery furniture biz in 2006; an archive of our previous review of this brand appears on our free web site, BabyBargains.com (click on Bonus Material).*

Vintage Estate *This crib brand is sold at Sears and made by Dorel/Cosco—see Cosco's review earlier in this chapter.*

Wendy Bellissimo. *These cribs sold at Babies R Us are made by Bassett (see review earlier).*

Westwood Design *For a dealer near you, call 908-719-4707. Web: westwoodbaby.com.* New kid on the block Westwood Design was launched in 2005 by several veteran nursery furniture executives who partnered with an adult furniture company for distribution expertise. The result is Westwood, a company that imports all its designs from China, Vietnam and Thailand. All the cribs are static (no moveable drop sides) and retail for $420 to $600. The dressers are made of pine, Italian beech and Asian hardwoods and veneers—a pine six drawer retails for about $450 to $500. As you can see from the prices, Westwood is positioning itself to compete with the likes of Munire and Pali. Design-wise, Westwood is going for a more traditional look—not as ornate as Munire or over the top as ducduc. We did like the samples we saw at a recent trade show, which featured thoughtful design points like dressers that had adjustable heights.

New this year at Westwood, the company has launched two sister brands to be sold at chains: Hart at Baby Depot and Bedford Baby at JCPenney. The latter collection features a convertible crib ($400), five-drawer dresser ($500) and dresser and hutch for $800. Also new: Westwood will launch its first contemporary collection

(Pacific) with both a crib and dresser running $600 each. Westwood also plans to launch a entry-level price crib in 2008 (the Jonesport) for $400.

As for quality, the first reviews from parents are in and the word is quite positive (including Westwood's chain store brands, Hart and Bedford Baby). "Sturdy and high quality" is how one mom described her Westwood crib and dresser. While a few complained about delivery delays and backordered items, the overall view is Westwood is worth the money (and possible wait). One telling review: when one reader's Westwood hutch arrived cracked, the president of Westwood himself personally contacted the customer to apologize and pledged to make it right. In an era of customer service in the nursery biz that ranges from abysmal to abhorrent, *that* is refreshing. **Rating: A**

Young America by Stanley *Call 888-839-6822 for a dealer. Web: stanleyfurniture.com.* Adult furniture maker Stanley entered the juvenile market in 2003 with "Young America," a collection of a dozen styles with sculpted headboards and other high-end details. In our first report on Young America, we complained about Stanley's prices (initially, cribs were priced at $700 or so). There is good news to report on that front: Stanley has dropped their prices this year, with cribs ranging from $500 to $650. Yeah, that's still pricey but now at least Stanley is in the ballpark. And the quality of this line makes it worth a look-see—we liked the thoughtful design touches like a full bed that can be adjusted in height to allow for under-bed storage drawers. You'll find dovetail construction with the dressers ($700 to $800), anti-tipping restraints on most pieces and more. The cribs have hidden hardware, solid construction with two dowels for stability and spring mattress platforms.

FYI: Stanley's cribs (and bunk beds) are made in China and Slovenia (only the natural finish models are imported from Slovenia). The dressers are still made in the USA.

Stanley has both standard cribs (seven styles in 12 finishes) and convertible options (four styles in 17 finishes). All together, you can choose from 30 items in any one of 40 colors—that's an impressive amount of accessories and customization. Stanley is available in both juvenile stores and regular furniture shops. Check out Stanley detailed web site, which includes their entire catalog with extensive additional info and even pricing. Bottom line: it is pricey but the quality may make it worth the investment. **Rating: B+**

See the chart on the following pages for a summary of the major crib brands. For our picks for best cribs, see page 98.

CRIB RATINGS

NAME	RATING	COST	WHERE MADE?
Angel Line	C+	$ to $$	Taiwan
A.P. Industries	B+	$$$	Canada/Asia
Baby's Dream	A	$$ to $$$	Chile/USA
BassettBaby	B+	$$ to $$$	Asia/USA
Bellini	C+	$$$	Italy
Berg	A-	$$$	Russia/China
Bonavita/Babi Italia	A-	$ to $$$	Italy/Asia
Bratt Decor	B	$$$	Asia
Capretti Home	A	$$$	China
Cara Mia	B-	$$ to $$$	Slovenia/China
Chanderic	C+	$$$	Croatia
Child Craft	B+	$ to $$$	E. Europe/Asia
Corsican Kids	C+	$$$	USA
Creations	C	$$$	Vietnam
Da Vinci	C	$$	Asia
Delta	C+	$	Asia
Ducduc	B	$$$	USA
Dutailier	B+	$$$	Romania
Eden Baby	C+	$$	China
Ethan Allen	B	$$$	Asia
IKEA	A	$	Asia
Jardine	B+ (cribs)	$ to $$	Asia
JcPenney	C-	$ to $$$	Asia
Land of Nod	B	$$ to $$$	Asia
Million $ Baby	B-	$ to $$$	Asia
Morigeau/Lepine	B+	$$$	Canada
Mother Hubbard	B+	$$$	Bulgaria/Canada
Munire	A	$$$	Indonesia
Natart	A	$$$	Canada
NettoCollection	C+	$$$	Vietnam
Nursery Smart	B	$$ to $$$	Vietnam
Nurseryworks	B+	$$$	Asia
Oeuf	B	$$$	Asia
Pali	A-	$$$	Italy/Thailand
Pottery Barn Kids	C	$$$	Asia
Romina	B+	$$$	Romania
RT Furniture	B	$$$	Asia/USA/Europe
Simmons	C	$$$	Asia
Simplicity	F	$ to $$$	Asia
Sorelle	B-	$$	Italy/Brazil/Asia
Stokke/Sleepi	A-	$$$	Norway
Storkcraft	C	$ to $$	Asia/Canada
Westwood	A	$$$	China/Vietnam
Young America	B+	$$$	Asia

Key:	**RATING:** Our opinion of the manufacturer's quality and value. **COST:** $=under $200, $$=$200-400, $$$=over $400. **JPMA:** Are these cribs JPMA-certified? See page 57 for details.

JPMA   COMMENTS

	Makes decent Jenny Lind crib; sold online.
	Good quality; lots of color choices.
◆	Still have some folding rails; very good quality.
◆	Cribs good; case pieces bad. Big at Babies R Us.
◆	Sold only in namesake pricey boutiques.
	Big on pine groupings, but watch out for scratches.
	New Graco line starts at just $180 at chain stores.
	Vintage looks, bright colors. Sells direct via own site.
	New high-end line set to debut this year.
	Average quality, but watch out for MDF dressers.
	Good quality and emphasis on safety; pricey.
◆	Affordable, but quality/service has slipped slightly.
	Very pricey wrought-iron cribs; vintage feel.
	New line focusing on adult looks; good quality.
◆	Only available online; quality and service so-so.
◆	Low prices but low quality; easy to assemble.
	Retro, modernist furniture; high gloss finish.
	Quality improving; expensive but two dozen finishes.
	Unimpressive quality, especially for dressers.
	Very expensive; excellent quality. Sold only in own stores.
	Do-it-yourself assembly; low prices; very simple styling.
◆	Cribs good; dressers bad. Exclusive at Babies R Us.
◆	Good quality but very poor service and delivery.
	Stylish but pricey; good customer service.
◆	Make Jenny Lind style crib for Land of Nod.
	Very good quality; one of the last made in Canada.
	30 finishes; good quality but some MDF in dressers.
	Excellent quality; adult looks. Delivery can be slow.
	Innovative storage; whimsical touches; high quality.
◆	Modern/minimalist; do-it-yourself assembly.
	Excellent quality; new to market. Use New Zealand pine.
◆	Can customize colors; mix and max. Modernist looks.
	Eco-style meets modernism; lowest price of modern group.
	High quality but high prices; Thai line less expensive.
	Design leader but overpriced; high shipping charges.
	Pricey, but very well-made furniture.
	Quality good, but long delays on orders.
◆	Owned by Delta; average quality, high prices.
◆	Do-it-yourself assembly for most; recall problems.
	Decent prices; mixed customer service reputation
	Pricey crib "system" best for those with little space.
◆	Quality has slipped; New high-end line to debut soon.
◆	Traditional looks; high quality. Pricey but worth it.
◆	20 color finishes; Great quality. Thoughtful design.

Brand Recommendations: Our Picks

Good. On a tight budget? IKEA is the answer: their simple cribs sell for $80 to $139. IKEA's Hermelin crib (pictured) is no frills (the side rail is fixed and assembly is do-it-yourself), but safe and sturdy. If you don't have IKEA near you,

IKEA sells all their cribs online. Other top picks in the bare-bones crib category include Jardine's Natural Spindle Crib ($100; Babies R Us) and the Child Craft's Prairie crib for $200 at Target. All are good, basic choices.

Better. Babi Italia (Bonavita) and Sorelle (C&T) are our top brand picks in the "better" niche. Both are sold in specialty chains like Babies R Us and are a step-up in features and quality, most in the $200 to $400 range. Examples: $315 will buy

a Babi Italia "Mon Cheri" single crib from Babies R Us—for the extra bucks, you get a under-crib storage drawer and a headboard with decorative carving. A similar crib is the Sorelle (C&T) Lana Crib (pictured) for $220 at Baby Depot.

Best. The choices here are mind-boggling . . . you have your pick of over a dozen brands. Who's got the very best quality? Munire, Natart and Westwood are our top picks of you've got the bankroll for a $500 to $700 crib and similarly priced dressers. A close runner-up would be Pali and Morigeau—great quality, but the prices are higher.

A convertible crib is more expensive to start, but you actually get two products—a crib that later converts to a full-size bed. Baby's Dream probably has among the best selection in this category, but most of the top brands we mentioned above now carry convertible models. These models will set you back $400 to $600 or more, depending on the finish.

If space is tight (yes, we are talking to you, New Yorkers), we'd suggest the Stokke Sleepi system. Ok, it isn't cheap ($1000), but when your urban lifestyle requires a compact crib/bassinet, the Sleepi is the answer.

Grandma's house. If you need a secondary crib for Grandma's house, consider a foldaway crib from Dream on Me for $250 (pictured). Or Delta's simple Jenny Lind style for $100 can be quickly assembled without any tools. Both of these products can be found at Wal-Mart or other chain stores as well as online.

Bassinets/Cradles

A newborn infant can immediately sleep in a full size crib, but some parents like the convenience of bassinets or cradles to use for the first few weeks or months. Why? These smaller baby beds can be kept in the parents' bedroom, making for convenient midnight feedings.

What's the difference between a bassinet and a cradle? Although most stores use the terms interchangeably, we think of bassinets as small baskets that are typically put onto a stationery stand (pictured at top right). Cradles, on the other hand, are usually made of wood and rock back and forth.

A third option in this category is "Moses baskets," basically woven baskets (bottom right) with handles that you can use to carry a newborn from room to room. (Moses-Baskets.com has a good selection; but you can even find Moses baskets on sites like Target.com). Moses baskets can only be used for a few weeks, while you can typically use a bassinet or cradle for a couple of months.

As for bassinets, we noticed a Badger Basket bassinet (a rather common brand, badgerbasket.com) runs about $50 at chain stores, but that price doesn't include the "soft goods" (sheets, liners, skirts and hoods). Models that include soft goods typically run closer to $100 and up to $180. Cradles, on the other hand, run about $100 to $400 but don't need that many soft goods (just a mattress, which is usually included, and a sheet, which is not. Bumper pads are optional). Moses baskets run $50 to $200 and include all the soft goods.

So, which should you buy? We say none of the above. As we mentioned at the beginning of this section, a newborn will do just fine in a full-size crib. If you need the convenience of a bassinet, we'd suggest skipping the ones you see in chain stores. Why? Most are very poorly made (stapled together cardboard, etc) and won't last for more than one child. The bedding is also low-quality. One reader said the sheets with her chain store-bought bassinet "were falling apart at the seams even before it went into the wash" for the first time. And the function of these products is somewhat questionable. For example, the functionality of a Moses basket, while pretty to look at, can be easily duplicated by an infant car seat carrier, which most folks buy anyway.

Instead, we suggest you borrow a bassinet or cradle from a friend. . . or buy a portable playpen with a bassinet feature. We'll review specific models of playpens in Chapter 7, but basic choices like the Graco Pack 'N Play run $80 to $200 in most stores. The bassinet feature in most playpens (basically, an insert that creates a small bed area at the top of the playpen) can be used up to 15 pounds, which is about all most folks would need. Then, you simply remove the bassinet attachment and voila! You have a standard size playpen. Since many parents get a playpen anyway, going for a model that has a bassinet attachment doesn't add much to the cost and eliminates the separate $100 to $200 expense of a bassinet. (See the next chapter for a discussion of bassinet sheets).

Another way to save: check out second-hand stores and garage sales. Just make sure the bassinet or cradle is in good repair and not missing any pieces. Most parents use these items for such a short period of time that there is little wear and tear. You'll need a new mattress for your second-hand cradle or bassinet—sites like BabyUniverse.com or BabyCatalog.com are two sources.

Of course, you can also go for the Arm's Reach Co-Sleeper (reviewed earlier) as an alternative to the bassinet as well.

Mattresses

Now that you've just spent several hundred dollars on a crib, you're done, right? Wrong. Despite their hefty price tags, most cribs don't come with mattresses. So, here's our guide to buying the best quality mattress for the lowest price.

Safe & Sound

The key issue in mattress safety is Sudden Infant Death Syndrome (SIDS), the leading cause of death among infants under one year of age, claiming about 2500 lives per year. We have a detailed discussion of SIDS in our book, *Baby 411* (see back of this book for info), but here is the take-home message when it comes to SIDS and mattresses: buy a FIRM mattress that correctly fits your crib, bassinet or cradle.

Babies don't have the muscle strength to lift their heads up when put face down into soft or fluffy bedding—some have suffocated as a result. The best defense: NEVER place your baby face down in soft, thick quilts, wool blankets, pillows, or toys. (Futon mattresses are also a no-no). Babies should ALWAYS be put down to sleep on their backs.

More advice: never put the baby down on a vinyl mattress without a cover or sheet since vinyl can also contribute to suffocation. In addition, several studies into the causes of Sudden Infant Death

Syndrome (SIDS) have found that a too-soft sleep surface (such as the items listed above) and environmental factors (a too-hot room, cigarette smoke) are related to crib death, though exactly how has yet to be determined. Experts therefore advise against letting infants sleep on a too-soft surface.

See the box on page 92 for more tips on preventing SIDS.

Another point to remember: while mattresses come in a standard size for a full-size crib, the depth can vary from maker to maker. Some mattresses are just four inches deep; others are six. Some crib sheets won't fit the six-inch thick mattresses; *it's unsafe to use a sheet that doesn't snugly fit OVER the corner of a mattress and tuck beneath it.*

Mattresses should fit your crib snugly with no more than two finger's width between the mattress and all sides of the crib when *centered* on the mattress platform. Since most cribs and mattresses are made to a standard size, this is usually not a major problem. Occasionally, we hear from a parent who has purchased a crib in Europe only to find that they can't find a mattress here that fits (Europe has a different standard for crib sizes).

Smart Shopper Tips

Smart Shopper Tip #1
Foam or Coil?

"It seems the choice for a crib mattress comes down to foam or coil? Which is better? Does it matter?"

Yes, it does matter. After researching this issue, we've come down on the foam side of the debate. Why? Foam mattresses are lighter than those with coils, making it easier to change the sheets in the middle of the night when Junior reenacts the Great Flood in his crib. Foam mattresses typically weigh less than eight pounds, while coil mattresses can top 20 or 30 pounds! Another plus: foam mattresses are less expensive, usually $100 to $150. Coil mattresses can be pricey, with some models running $200+.

Sounds easy, right? Just buy a foam mattress? Well, as always, life can be complicated—many baby stores (and even chains like Babies R Us) only sell coil mattresses, claiming that coil is superior to foam. One salesperson even told a parent that foam mattresses aren't safe for babies older than six months! Another salesperson actually told a parent they should expect to replace a foam mattress two to three times during the two years a baby uses a crib. Oh sure.

We've consulted with pediatricians and industry experts on this issue and have come to the conclusion that the best course is to choose a *firm* mattress for baby—it doesn't matter whether it's a firm coil mattress or a firm foam one. What about the claim that foam mattresses need to be replaced constantly? In the 12 years we've been researching this topic, we've never heard from even one parent whose foam mattress had to be replaced!

What's going on here? Many baby stores try to make up for the thin profit margins they make on furniture by pitching parents to buy an ultra-expensive mattress. The latest rage are so-called "2 in 1" mattresses that combine foam *and* coil (foam on one side; coil on the other). These can run $200 or more! While these mattresses are nice, they are totally unnecessary. A $100 foam mattress will do just as well.

So why all the pressure to get the fancy-shmancy double dip mattress? Such mattresses cost stores just $40 at wholesale, yet they sell for $200 or more!

Bottom line: foam mattresses are the best deal, but can be hard to find (hint: web sites like BabyCatalog.com sell foam mattresses). As a result, we'll recommend mattresses in both the coil and foam categories just in case the baby stores near you only stock coil.

Smart Shopper Tip #2
Coil Overkill and Cheap Foam Mattresses
"How do you tell a cheap-quality coil mattress from a better one? How about foam mattresses—what makes one better than the next?"

Evaluating different crib mattresses isn't easy. Even the cheap ones claim they are "firm" and comparing apples to apples is difficult. When it comes to coil mattresses, the number of coils seems like a good way to compare them, but even that can be deceiving. For example, is a 150-coil mattress better than an 80-coil mattress?

Well, yes and no. While an 80-coil mattress probably won't be as firm as one with 150 coils, it's important to remember that a large number of coils do not necessarily mean the mattress is superior. Factors such as the wire gauge, number of turns per coil and the temper of the wire contribute to the firmness, durability and strength of the mattress. Unfortunately, most mattresses only note the coil count (and no other details). Hence, the best bet would be to buy a good brand that has a solid quality reputation (we'll recommend specific choices after this section).

What about foam mattresses? The cheapest foam mattresses are made of low-density foam (about .9 pounds per cubic foot). The better foam mattresses are high-density with 1.5 pounds per cubic foot. Easy for us to say, right? Once again, foam mattresses don't list density on their packaging, leaving consumers to wonder whether they're getting high or low density. As with coil mattresses, you have to rely on a reputable brand name to get a good foam mattress (see the next section for more details).

One good, basic test for crib mattress firmness: take the mattress between your two hands and push your hands together. Okay, that sounds silly but you'll notice some differences in firmness right away!

Smart Shopper Tip #3
Flatulent foam mattresses?

"I read on the 'net that some foam mattresses have an out-gassing problem. Is this true?"

We've noticed that several eco-catalogs and web sites have raised concerns that standard crib mattresses are a possible health hazard. One even went so far as to say that such mattresses are "unhealthy combinations of artificial foams, fluorocarbons, synthetic

E-MAIL FROM THE REAL WORLD
Colic remedy turns mattress into magic fingers.

Colic, that incessant crying by young infants at night, can drive parents to distraction. A mom in Tennessee writes about one solution she found:

"After several relatively sleepless nights with our two-week old infant, I found a product called the Sleep Tight Infant Soother. This product basically makes sleeping in the crib similar to riding in the car. A vibration device attaches underneath the mattress and you can either get a sound box for the crib, which plays white noise, or get a 90-minute cassette tape. If you opt for the sound box, the price is $140; it is $100 if you go for the cassette tape. The product has a 15-day trial period and can be ordered online at www.colic.com or by calling 1-800-NO COLIC. The FDA has approved it as a medical device so insurance may reimburse the cost."

One caution: a recent study by researchers at the University of California, San Francisco warned against exposing babies to continuous white noise, which may damage the auditory region of the brain. The study, which appeared in an April 2003 issue of the journal Science (www.hhmi.org/news/chang.html), convinced us to recommend AGAINST white noise generators for infants. Hence, we recommend you use the above product just for the vibration and not the sound component. For more information about colic, please check out our other book Baby 411 (see the back of this book for details)..

fibers and formaldehyde, all materials that give off toxic fumes." The solution? Buy *their* organic cotton crib mattress for a whopping $650 and your baby won't have to breathe that nasty stuff.

Hold it. We checked with pediatricians and industry experts and found no evidence that such a problem exists. While it is possible that a foam or coil mattress might give off a few vapors when you first take it out of the packaging, there's no ongoing fume problem in our opinion. There are also no medical studies linking, say, lower SAT scores to kids who slept on foam mattresses as babies. While it is possible that a few children who have extreme chemical sensitivities might do better on "organic" mattresses, it's doubtful such products will make any difference to the vast majority of infants. We think it's irresponsible of such eco-crusaders to raise bogus issues intended to scare parents without providing corresponding proof of their claims.

What about mattresses that are hypoallergenic with special antimicrobial covers? These all-natural, organic mattresses are again pitched to parents as the ultimate safe place for baby to sleep. Even regular "conventional" crib mattress makers are jumping on the bacteria hysteria wagon by coating their mattress covers with Microban and other additives. Yet there are no studies showing these mattresses give babies a better night sleep, stop sickness or prevent allergies. If your baby develops severe allergies (which is rare for infants), then we can see a reason for attempting to outfit a nursery with such pricey special products. But for the vast majority of parents, these mattresses are a waste of money.

We will discuss organic mattress brands later in this section.

Here are a few more shopping tips/myths about crib mattresses:

◆ **What's the best way to test the firmness of a crib mattress?** Test the center of the mattress (not the sides or corners)—place the palm of one hand flat on one side of the mattress and then put your other hand on the opposite side. The greater the pressure needed to press your hands together, the more firm the mattress.

◆ **Are all crib mattresses the same size?** No, they can vary a small amount—both in length/width and thickness. Most coil mattresses are 5" to 6" in depth. What's the best thickness? It doesn't matter, but 5" should be fine. Remember the safest crib mattress is the one that snugly fits your crib—you shouldn't be able to fit more than two fingers between the headboard/side rails and the mattress. A tip: the mattress should be CENTERED on the crib mattress platform, not jammed up to one side or the other!

FYI: For the curious, full-size cribs sold in the US and Canada must be between 27 5/8" and 28 5/8" wide (and 51 3/4" to 53" in length). Hence most crib mattresses are about 27 1/4" to 28 5/8" in width.

◆ *All foam mattresses look alike—what separates the better ones from the cheaper options?* Test for firmness (see above). The more firm, the better. Another clue: weight. A slightly heavier foam mattress usually means they used a better-quality foam to make the product. Finally, look at the cover: three layers of laminated/reinforced vinyl are better than a single or double layer. What about quilted covers? They are a waste of money, in our opinion.

Top Picks: Brand Recommendations

◆ **Foam Mattresses.** *Top pick:* the **Colgate** "Classica I" mattress ($100, colgatekids.com) is our top pick in this category—this five-inch thick mattress has top-quality foam and a reasonable price.

We should note that Colgate makes about a dozen foam crib mattresses and they are quite similar—some have fancier covers, others have "dual firmness" (a firmer side for infants; less firm for toddlers). In 2007, Colgate is launching a new "preferred line" of upgraded mattresses with more foam and five-ply anti-microbial covers (price: $150). While all these are fine, we still think the basic Classica I is fine. FYI: Colgate is sold in specialty stores only (no chains). Check their web site for a current list of dealers.

Runner up: **Moonlight Slumber's** "Starlight Support" foam mattress ($190; moonlightslumber.com) is more expensive than Colgate, but gets very good marks form our readers. Folks love the dual-zone firmness, with a less-firm side for toddlers. FYI: Moonlight Slumber makes a standard and supreme version of its mattress—the latter ($220) has a layer of memory foam.

◆ **Coil Mattresses.** *Top Picks:* the **Simmons** Super Maxipedic 160 coil mattress for $100 at Babies R Us is a best buy for the dollar. Good quality and price. Also good: the **Sealy** Baby Soft Premium coil mattress (204 coils, $90), again at Babies R Us.

Also worth a recommendation: **Sealy's** Nature Rest Mattress ($70 at Target) features 220 coils and a double laminated cover.

If you can find the Colgate brand, they too make a decent coil mattress—a 150-coil model is about $150.

Yes, most major crib makers also have mattress lines, most notably Child Craft and Pali. Prices typically run $150 to $250. Are they any better than the Sealy or Simmons coil mattresses found in chain stores? No. Save your money and get a basic mattress.

What about those fancy vibrating mattresses? Kolcraft makes a "Tender Vibes" mattress for $100 to $160 which features 150 coils, a vibrating feature and an automatic timer that turns off the vibration after 15 minutes. Is this necessary? Unless you have a history of colic (that never-ending crying that afflicts some babies) in your family, it's overkill. Nothing wrong with it, but save your money and get a regular non-vibrating mattress.

Bottom line: there isn't much difference between coil mattress brands—each does a good job. Stick with the ones at 150 coils (80 is too little; 250 is overkill).

Still can't decide between foam or coil? Well, Colgate has a solution—a "2 in 1" mattress that is half foam and half coil. The company suggests the extra-firm foam side for infants. When your baby reaches toddler hood, you flip the mattress over to the coil side. The price: $140. As we pointed out earlier, the "2 in 1" mattress isn't something we'd recommend (it really isn't necessary), but we realize some parents will consider it.

◆ **Organic Mattresses.** Let's be honest: there is no evidence that organic crib mattresses are safer for babies than conventional mattresses. Yes, there is concern about environmental exposure of babies to toxic chemicals—and yes, most conventional mattresses are made of vinyl (PVC), polyurethane foam and chemical fire retardants. But the scientific research and evidence does NOT support the conclusion that babies are at any risk for sleeping on conventional mattresses.

Despite that, there is growing interest in organic mattresses—so here are our top picks if you plan to go this route.

Top pick: NaturePedic's "No-Compromise" coil mattress (web: naturepedic.com) comes in both natural ($220) and organic cotton versions ($260). These mattresses feature 252 coils and a food-grade polyethylene cover. If you want to go entirely organic, NaturePedic's Organic Cotton Ultra coil mattress ($340) has a quilted organic cotton cover. Between the two, we think the No Compromise mattress balances the best of both worlds: organic cotton filling, a firm coil innerspring AND a waterproof cover. All of NaturePedic's mattresses have no PVC's, polyurethane foam or chemical fire retardants.

Runner-up: Natura's Naturlatex crib mattress ($400, web: NaturaWorld.com) is made from a natural form of latex and has an unbleached cotton cover. No, the cover isn't water-proof—the company sells a wool "puddle pad" that repels moisture.

Watch for even more organic crib mattresses to debut this year. Devon, England-based **NaturalMat** (naturalmat.com) plans to debut three organic mattress made of coir (the husk of a coconut), latex or mohair. Prices range from $375 to $625. Even traditional mattress maker Colgate is jumping into the organic market with the Natural 1 ($329), made of coconut fiber and an all-natural cotton cover.

Dressers & Changing Tables

Now that you've got a place for the baby to sleep (and a mattress for her to sleep on), where are you going to put all those cute outfits that you'll get as gifts from Aunt Bertha? The juvenile trade refers to dressers, armoires, and the like as "case pieces" since they are essentially furniture made out of a large case (pretty inventive, huh?).

Of course, a dresser is more than just a place to store clothes and supplies. Let's not forget that all-too-important activity that will occupy so many of your hours after the baby is born: changing diapers. The other day we calculated that by our baby's first birthday, we had changed over 2400 diapers! Wow! To first-time parents, that may seem like an unreal number, but we're not exaggerating. On average, that is about SEVEN diaper changes a day during the first year . . . but for a newborn, expect up to 15 diaper changes a day. So, where are you going to change all those diapers? Most parents use the dresser top, but we'll also discuss changing tables in this section.

What are You Buying

DRESSERS. As you shop for baby furniture, you'll note a wide variety of dressers—three drawer, four drawer, armoires, combination dresser/changing tables, and more. No matter which type you choose, we do have three general tips for getting the most for your money.

First, choose a model whose drawers glide easily. Test this in the store—drawers with an easy glide typically have tracks on BOTH sides of the drawer. Cheaper dressers have drawers that simply sit on a track at the bottom center of the drawer. As a result, they don't roll out as smoothly and are prone to coming off the track.

Our second piece of advice: look at the drawer sides—the best furniture makers use "dove-tailed" drawer joints. There are two types of dove-tail drawers: English and French (see pictures at right). Either is OK; the cheapest dressers do not have dove-tailed drawers. Instead, the drawer and drawer front are merely stapled together.

English Dove-tail

A third quality indicator: drawers with corner blocks (see picture on next page). Pull the drawer out and turn it over to look at the corners—if there is

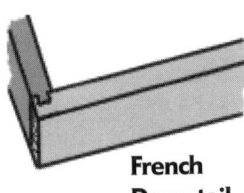

French Dove-tail

a small bock that braces the corner, that's good. Cheaper dressers omit this feature, which adds to the stability of the drawer.

Corner Block

Take a second to look at the dresser . . . do the drawers or doors fit? Or are they askew? It's amazing to see cheap dressers in chain stores whose sloppy construction is obvious.

What about wood substitutes like medium density fiberboard (MDF)? MDF, a composite wood product similar to particleboard, is made by compressing/gluing together wood waste fibers. MDF is used in furniture because it is a) cheap and b) is smooth (and easier to finish) and won't warp, compared to wood.

MDF by itself isn't necessarily good or bad. It really depends on the overall construction (drawer glides, joints, etc.), not so much the wood content. Yes, some high-priced furniture makers tout their "all wood" construction (where even the sides and backs of the dressers are wood), but that might be overkill. How often will you be looking at the back of your child's dresser anyway? Our concern with MDF is when it is covered in laminate, which can chip or warp in humid environs.

Many modern/minimalist furniture designers are using MDF (usually coated with a high-gloss lacquer) as a design statement. While we don't see anything wrong with that, we do object to the sky-high prices for this—paying $1500 for a dresser made of MDF is like spending four-figures for a fake-leather jacket.

Another major change: more adult furniture looks and features. Credit newcomers like Munire, Westwood and Creations for upping the quality of dressers in the nursery—parents will now see more features common on adult furniture (example: hutches with built-in lights) as well as more detailed finishes.

2 **CHANGING AREA.** Basically, you have two options here. You can buy a separate changing table or a combination dresser/changing table. As mentioned earlier, we think a separate changing table is a waste of money (as well as a waste of space).

So most folks look for dressers to do double duty: not only a place to store clothes, but also change diapers. Basically, you need a changing area of the right height to do this—evaluate your and your spouse's heights to see what you'd need.

In the past, one popular solution to this issue was the hi-low dresser or combo dresser (see picture at right). The two-tier design of these dressers provides a convenient space to change diapers while not looking like a diaper-

changing table. Most parents keep diaper-changing supplies in the upper drawer, while the lower dresser functions as clothing storage, etc. Combo dressers start at $500 and range up to $700. As an option, some manufactures offer a hutch that attaches to a dresser to provide additional shelf space.

Hi-lo dressers aren't as popular as they used to be, but you'll see some out there on the market. Instead, we see more double dressers doing double duty as changing areas. Also new: the chiffarobe (pictured), which is a combination dresser and armoire (that is, a place to hang clothes). In the past year, we noticed more furniture companies rolling out chiffarobes, which are smaller versions of armoires.

Where do you keep the diaper changing supplies? Well, you can use a drawer in the combo or chiffarobe. Or, a rolling storage cart is another solution (cost: about $25 in many catalogs and stores such as Container Store 800-733-3532; web: containerstore.com; Sam's Club has a plastic "six drawer mini chest" for $24). One disadvantage to changing baby in the crib: if you have a boy, he could spray the crib sheets, bumper pads, and just about anything else in the crib with his little "water pistol." Hence, you might find yourself doing more laundry. If you have back problems, leaning over into the crib to change a diaper may also be uncomfortable.

One mom sent us an e-mail with a solution to the changing table dilemma—she bought a "Rail Rider," changing table that fits across a crib and can be removed when the baby is sleeping. For about $30, it did the trick. Made by Burlington Basket Company (for a dealer near you, call 800-553-2300 or 319-754-6508) and sold online at BabyCenter.com, the Rail Rider does have a few drawbacks: it doesn't fit all cribs and shorter folks find it difficult to use.

E-Mail from The Real World
Antique bargains

A reader reminds us that antique stores can be great sources for dressers and storage units for baby's room.

"You might remind readers not to overlook the local antique store when shopping for nursery furniture. We found a great English dresser from the 1930s with ample drawer and cupboard space for $325 that has a lot of character than anything we've seen in baby stores, plus it can be easily moved to another room/use when our baby outgrows it."

Safe & Sound

Safety doesn't stop at the crib—consider these items:

◆ **Anchor those dressers and shelves.** A nice bookcase or dresser become a tip-over hazard as the baby begins pulling up on objects. The best advice is to attach any furniture that can be climbed to a wall to provide stability. Some of the best furniture brands include anchor straps with their dressers—use them!

◆ **Baby proof the diaper station.** If your diaper changing area has open shelves, you may have to baby proof the bottom shelves. As the baby begins to climb, you must remove any dangerous medicines or supplies from easily accessible shelves.

◆ **Choose a dresser that doesn't have drawer pulls.** Those little knobs can make it easy for baby to open the drawers—and it's those open drawers that can be used as a step stool to scale the dresser. A good tip is to buy a dresser without drawer pulls; a few styles have drawers with grooves that let you open them from below. (While this isn't totally baby proof, it reduces the attraction for baby.

◆ **Air out all that new nursery paint, furniture and decor.** A University of Maryland School of Medicine study suggests new parents should air out freshly painted or wallpapered rooms before baby arrives. New furniture and mattresses also "out-gas" fumes for a brief time, so consider ventilating the nursery when they arrive as well. How much ventilation? The study suggested four to eight weeks of open window ventilation, which seems a bit excessive to us. But it makes sense to do some air-out of the nursery before baby arrives. Another idea: look for environmentally friendly paints that have lower out-gas emissions. If you install new carpet in the house, leave during the installation and open the windows (and turn on fans) for two days.

◆ **Stay away from wicker.** Sure, those wicker storage baskets and other accessories look nice . . .but watch out. Most wicker is treated with gasoline before it's painted. When the weather warms up, the fumes from wicker furniture can be noticeable. Wicker is great for other parts of the house or an outside deck—but we say skip it for the nursery.

Our Picks: Brand Recommendations

Our picks for dressers mirror what we picked for cribs. For contact information on these brands, refer to the reviews earlier in this chapter. Here's a round up:

Good. Just as in cribs, *IKEA's* affordable dressers (about $100) are our top pick if money (or space) is tight. Let's be honest: IKEA's dressers aren't for the long haul and are nothing to fancy to look at. Plus you have to assemble everything yourself. But if you need something on a temporary basis (and plan to swap out all the nursery furniture as your child grows older), IKEA is the answer.

Better. The dressers from brands like *Babi Italia* and *Sorelle* are better quality than what you'd see in discount stores like Wal-Mart. A simple four-drawer dresser from these brands would run around $400 to $600. The look is basic, but the quality is there.

Best. Our top picks for nursery dressers and other case pieces are *Munire*, *Westwood* and *Natart*. The first two brands are imported from Asia and emphasize adult-furniture looks (and features). Canadian Natart is more of an innovator, adding clever storage options and other touches.

At this price level, you'll find quality touches like drawers with dove-tail joints and fancy glide systems. You'll also have the choice of a wide range of finishes. But it will cost you: a dresser from these brands runs $500 to $800, with armoires topping $1000. Westwood is probably the most affordable; Natart the most pricey. Either way, you are getting your money's worth.

Yet Even More Nursery Stuff

Just because to this point you have spent an amount equivalent to the gross national product of Peru on baby furniture doesn't mean you're done, of course. Nope, we've got six more items to consider for your baby's room:

ROCKER-GLIDER. We're not talking about the rocking chair you've seen at grandma's house. No, we're referring to the high-tech modern-day rockers that are so fancy they aren't mere rockers—they're "glider-rockers." Thanks to a fancy ball-bearing system, these rockers "glide" with little or no effort.

Is a glider-rocker a waste of money? Some parents have written to us with that question, assuming you'd just use the item for the baby's first couple of years. Actually, a glider-rocker can have a much longer life. You can swap the cushions after a couple of years (most makers let you order these items separately) and move the glider-rocker to a family room. Making this transition even easier is the trend toward all upholstered gliders (earlier models had exposed wood; the newer ones are all fabric). Yep, they are more expensive, but they can go from the nursery to the family room in a single bound.

Here are some shopping tips when looking at rocker gliders:

a) Go for padded armrests. You'll be cradling a newborn and spending many hours here—go for the padded armrests . . . and while you're at it, get the best padded chair overall.

b) Consider a chair with a locking mechanism. Some brands (notably Shermag) have an auto-locking feature; when you stand up, the chair can no longer rock. Very helpful when you have a curious toddlers who might end up with pinched fingers.

c) Extra width is always smart. Some of the cheapest glider rockers are quite narrow, which might not seem bad if you are a small person. But remember you will most likely be using a nursing pillow with your newborn . . . and having the extra width to accommodate this pillow is most helpful!

Here is an overview of the biggest players:

◆ **Best Chair** *Call 812-367-1761 web: bestchair.com* This Indiana-based rocking chair maker just entered the baby biz in 2002, although they trace their roots to the 1960's. We were very impressed with their quality and offerings. Basically, Best specializes in upholstered chairs with over 100+ fabric choices. Delivery is four weeks and prices are reasonable for an all-upholstered look: most are $400 to $500. A matching ottoman is $200. Best is only sold in specialty stores. **Rating: A**

◆ **Brooks** *Call 800-427-6657 or 423-626-1111* Tennessee-based Brooks sells glider-rockers that lack the style or pizzazz of Dutailier— these traditional chairs feature basic fabrics and exposed wood. Prices run $230 to $550 for the glider rockers, while the ottomans are $100-$150. One plus: all Brooks fabrics are available on any style chair. Brooks chairs feature solid base panels (Dutailier has an open base), which the company touts as more safe. While we liked Brooks' quality, one baby storeowner told us he found the company very disorganized with poor customer service. **Rating: B**

◆ **Crypton** *Call 248-432-5718; web: cryptonfabric.com* Crypton is one of the more exciting new entrants to the glider category. A textile company that specializes in stain-resistant, hi-tech fabrics, Crypton has two offerings: the Aanabelle rocker and the Ultimate Glider, which rocks and swivels. Both are $800 to $900, feature dozens of fabrics and take six weeks for delivery. We were amazed at the comfort of the chairs—and the stain, water and bacterial-resistant fabric is impressive. **Rating: Not Yet.**

◆ **Dutailier** *Call 800-363-9817 or 450-772-2403; web: dutailier .com.* Quebec-based **Dutailier** is to glider-rockers what eBay is to online auctions—basically, they own the market. Thanks to superior quality and quick delivery, Dutailier probably sells one out of every two glider rockers purchased in the U.S. and Canada each year.

Dutailier has an incredible selection of 45 models, seven finishes, and 80 different fabrics. The result: over 37,000 possible combinations. All wood is solid maple or oak and features non-toxic finishes. You have to try real hard to avoid seeing Dutailier—the company has 3500 retail dealers, from small specialty stores to major retail chains.

Prices for Dutailier start at about $200 for their "Ultramotion" line sold at discount stores like Target.com. The Ultramotion gliders are entry-level: you get basic fabric cushions and exposed wood accents.

Dutailier's mid-price line (about $400) sold at chains like Babies R Us and feature upgraded fabric and more fabric choices. Of course, the price can soar quickly from there—Dutailier's specialty store line lets you customize a glider-rocker to your heart's content . . . add a swivel base, plush cushions or leather fabric and you can spend $600. Or $1000. The latest rage: all upholstered glider rockers.

New this year at Dutailier: the Matrix line of ergonomic gliders

Upholstered chairs at a discount

The all upholstered rocking chair is the rage for nurseries—but the prices for these models can be exorbitant. $1000 for a chair, anyone? Yet, we've found some ways to save.

First, consider Wal-Mart—the chain's "Classic Upholstered Glider Rocker and Ottoman" runs less than $100; readers were surprised with the quality of Wal-Mart's entry. Another option: adult furniture stores, many of which sell upholstered rockers in the $300 range. Finally, try the catalog Plow & Hearth (web: plowhearth.com). Their cottage rocker is $500 (plus $60 shipping) and is available in nine colors. Readers loved the look and quality of the Plow & Hearth rocker—while not the cheapest option, it is half the cost of those $1000 rockers you see in specialty stores!

echoes the look of those high-end office chairs with mesh backs ($700 to $900). The Matrix gliders have memory-foam seats and are aimed at the modern nursery market.

If we had to criticize Dutailier on something, it would have to be their cushions. Most are not machine washable (the covers can't be zipped off and put into the washing machine). As a result, you'll have to take them to a dry cleaner and pay big bucks to get them looking like new. A few of our readers have solved this problem by sewing slipcovers for their glider-rockers (most fabric stores carry pattern books for such items). Of course, if the cushions are shot, you can always order different ones when you move the glider-rocker into a family room.

It can take 10-12 weeks to order a custom Dutailier rocker (more for leather options), but the company does offer a "Quick Ship" program—a selection of 17 chair styles in two or three different fabric choices that are in stock for shipment in two weeks. We have received occasional complaints about how long it takes to order a Dutailier—one reader special-ordered a Dutailier from Babies R Us, only to find out some weeks later that the fabric was discontinued (Dutailier "forgot" to tell Babies R Us, who, to their credit, tried to fix the problem immediately). Other readers complain about fabric backorders, which cause more delays in delivery. Our advice: make sure the store double checks the order with Dutailier.

While Dutailier's web site lacks a product catalog, this is one of those products that is easy to research (and buy) online. Several sites carry the brand at a discount, including BabyCatalog.com—much of the Dutailier line (both wood and metal) is on that site.. An additional site that has a great selection of Dutailier is Rocking Chairs 100% (web: rocking-chairs.com; 800-4-ROCKER), a web site off-shoot of the San Rafael, CA store of the same name. The site is easy to navigate, with thumbnails of different models and little color chips for available colors. Unfortunately, Dutailier prohibits this site from listing prices online, so you have to email for a quote.

So, who's got the best deals on Dutailier? At the moment, we'd have to give the crown to Target. At both their Super Target locations and online (target.com), you can get a Dutailier for just $200 to $230. Yes, Target only carries one or two styles, so your choices are limited. If you want a discount on a Dutailier you saw online or at another store, check out the above mentioned sources like BabyCatalog.com.

An optional accessory for glider rockers is the ottoman that glides too. These start at $80 at discounters like Target, but most cost about $170 to $250. We suggest forgetting the ottoman and ordering an inexpensive "nursing" footstool (about $30 to $40 from sites like Motherwear.com, 800-950-2500). Why? Some moms claim the ottoman's height puts additional strain on their backs while breastfeeding. While the nursing footstool doesn't rock, it's lower height puts less strain on your back. (That said, we should note that some ottoman fans point out that once their mom/baby get the hang of nursing, that gliding ottoman is a nice luxury).

One safety note: don't leave an older child sitting in a glider-rocker. Many can be tipped over by a toddler when they climb out of it. (Hint: some glider rockers have a lever that locks it in position when not in use). ***Rating: A***

◆ ***Jardine*** Made by Dorel Asia, Jardine's rocker gliders are sold at Babies R Us; prices range from $150 for a basic model to $300 for all upholstered styles. One model with a deep recline even runs $400. The quality is disappointing—these chairs don't rock as easily as a Dutailier or Shermag. We say pass on this one. ***Rating: D***

◆ ***Little Castle*** Web: LittleCastleInc.com. Expensive, but high quality is how we'd describe Little Castle's glider rockers. Little Castle specializes in all-upholstered, swivel gliders made in California. An example is their Cottage Chase, a soft, over-stuffed chair for $800. Other styles start at $600. As you'd expect for that price level, you get a wide choice of fabrics (all of which are online at Little Castle's web site) and other perks like a hidden release button to recline the chair. While Little Castle has two chair styles in five colors available for quick shipping, most custom chair orders take six to eight weeks (and sometimes, up to 12 weeks). So plan in advance. ***Rating: A***

◆ ***Shermag/Chanderic*** In the U.S., call 800-363-2635 for dealer near you or 800-556-1515 Canada. Web: shermag.com. Shermag plays second fiddle to Dutailier, despite Shermag's size as a major furniture maker in Canada. Shermag's strategy seems to be to under-price Dutailier. Their $150 to $200 gliders (which include an ottoman) are sold at stores like Target.com. Shermag's focus is the entry glider market, similar to Dutailier's Ultramotion rockers.

So what's the catch with Shermag's affordable line sold at Target? First, these styles are a bit smaller in size than other glider-rockers—they fit most moms fine, but those six-foot dads may be uncomfortable. The color choices are also limited (just one or two, in most cases). And you should try to sit in these first to make sure you like the cushions (no, they aren't as super comfy as more expensive options but most parents think they're just fine).

Shermag's pricier options are found at stores like Babies R Us, where one $500 model includes a multi-position recline feature. Other mid-price Shermag gliders can be found under their Chanderic label for $300 to $450 online.

How's the quality of Shermag gliders? While the low-end glider rockers get good marks from our readers, we did hear more complaints about Shermag's mid and upper price models. Perhaps the expectations are much higher here, but we were disappointed to note that readers thought the quality and durability of these $300 to $500 was not as good as Dutailier. As a result, we've dropped Shermag's rating in this edition. ***Rating: B***

◆ ***Stork Craft*** Like their cribs and dressers, Stork Craft's glider rockers are priced for the entry-level part of the market: about $175 to $240. The quality here is only average; for the same price, we'd suggest a better brand like Dutailier, whose Ultramotion line is about the same price. And we have not been happy with the way Stork Craft has handled its acquisition of the Ragazzi brand (see earlier review). Bottom line: there are better options than Stork Craft when it comes to gliders. ***Rating: C***

◆ ***And more ideas.*** What about plain rocking chairs (without cushions)? Almost all the glider-rockers we recommend above can be ordered without cushions. Of course, just about any furniture store also sells plain rocking chairs. We don't have any preference on these items—to be honest, if you think you want a rocker, we'd go for the glider-rocker with cushions. Considering the time you'll spend in it, that would be much more comfortable than a plain rocking chair with no padding.

2 **CLOSET ORGANIZERS.** Most closets are a terrible waste of space. While a simple rod and shelf might be fine for adults, the basic closet doesn't work well for babies. Wouldn't it be better to have small shelves to store accessories, equipment and shoes? Or wire baskets for blankets and t-shirts? What about three more additional rods at varying heights to allow for more storage? The solution is closet organizers and you can go one of two routes. For the do-it-yourself crowd, consider a storage kit from such brands as Closet Maid (call 800-874-0008 for a store near you; web: closetmaid.com) or Mill's Pride (800-441-0337; web: millspride.com). Closet Maid's web site (closetmaid.com) is particularly helpful, with a useful "Design Selector" and how-to guide. Another favorite catalogs that sell storage items is Container Store (800) 733-3532 web: containerstore.com.

What if you'd rather leave it to the professionals? For those parents who don't have the time or inclination to install a closet organizer themselves, consider calling Closet Factory (call 310-715-1000 for a dealer near you; web: closetfactory.com) or California Closets (call 888-36-9709 for a dealer near you; web: californiaclosets. com). You can also check Craigslist.org for local companies that install closet organizers. Professionals charge about $500 to $1000 for a typical closet.

While a closet organizer works well for most folks, it may be especially helpful in cases where baby's room is small. Instead of buying a separate dresser or bookshelves, you can build-in drawer stacks and shelves in a closet to squeeze out every possible inch of storage. Another idea: a deep shelf added to a closet can double as a changing area.

3 STEREO. During those sleep deprivation experiments, it's sure nice to have some soothing music to make those hours just whiz by. Sure, you could put a cheap clock radio in the baby's room, but that assumes you have decent radio stations. And even the best radio station will be somewhat tiring to listen to for the many nights ahead. Our advice: buy (or register for) one of those CD boom box radios that run $100 to $300 in most electronics stores. Or go for a mini-stereo that holds an iPod.

4 DIAPER PAIL. Well, those diapers have to go somewhere. We'll review our top picks for diaper pails in Chapter 7, Around the House.

5 A CUTE LAMP. What nursery would be complete without a cute lamp for Junior's dresser? A good web site for this is Baby-Center.com, which has a decent selection of lamps and nightlights.

6 MORE FUN STUFF. Need a small light to see baby during 2am diaper changes? We like the BabeeBrite, a hands-free mobile light source with an automatic on/off timer. $20; web: MommyBeeHappy.com.

If you have a preemie and your doctor wants you to track feedings and diaper changes, the Itzbeen Baby Care Timer is a good solution. The handheld timer tracks when baby last napped, ate or had a diaper change. Optional alarms will remind you if a time limit has been reached. Cost: $50; Web: Itzbeen.com.

The Bottom Line:
A Wrap-Up of Our Best Buy Picks

For cribs, you've got two basic choices: a simple model that is, well, just a crib or a "convertible" model that eventually morphs into a twin or full size bed. For a basic crib, IKEA's affordable DIKTAD ($159) is nothing fancy, but will do the job. We also liked Child Craft's Shaker Ridge Stationary Crib (model 10001) for $200 at Target.

Look for a crib that has hidden hardware and a quiet rail release—and check under the hood to look at the mattress support. We like metal springs or wood slats; avoid the cheap "posture" boards made of MDF. Safety wise, see if the crib is JPMA-certified and watch out for cribs with fancy detailing that can snag clothing. Choose a crib made of hard wood that will resist scratches and nicks (stay away from soft pine for that very reason).

If a convertible crib makes sense to you, look at Baby's Dream, Munire or Westwood. Their models run $400 to $600. Yep, it costs more money up-front but you get a crib that converts to an attractive looking full-size bed.

The best mattress? We like the foam mattresses from Colgate ($100 for the Classica I). Or, for coil, go for a Simmons Super Maxipedic 160 coil mattress at Babies R Us for $100. For organic mattresses, we liked the NaturePedic "No Compromise" coil mattress in natural cotton ($220).

Where to buy a crib and other nursery furniture? Our readers say chains like Babies R Us and Target have the lowest prices, but the web can be a great source for discounts on less-bulky items like rocker gliders. For design inspiration, consider the Pottery Barn Kids catalog for ideas (but few deals).

The best dressers for your baby's nursery should have dove-tail drawers and smooth glides; solid wood construction is best. Avoid pine and other soft woods, since these show scratches and other damage. As for brands, Munire, Westwood and Natart are our top picks.

For glider rockers, Dutailier and Little Castle earn our top marks. A simple glider rocker runs $200, but fancy all-upholstered styles can push $1000.

So, let's sum up some of our recommendations:

Child Craft Shaker Ridge (10001)	$200
Simmons 160 coil mattress	$100
Munire dresser	$600
Dutailier Ultramotion glider-rocker	$200
Miscellaneous	$200
TOTAL	**$1300**

By contrast, if you bought a Bellini crib ($600), a 200-coil mattress ($200), a Morigeau dresser ($750), a fancy glider-rocker ($500), separate changing table ($200) and miscellaneous items ($200) at full retail, you'd be out $2450 by this point. Of course, you don't have any sheets for your baby's crib yet. Nor any clothes for Junior to wear. So, next we'll explore those topics and save more of your money.

CHAPTER 3

Baby Bedding & Decor

H ow can you find brand new, designer-label bedding for as much as 50% off the retail price? We've got the answer in this chapter, plus you'll find nine smart shopper tips to help get the most for your money. We'll share the best web sites and mail-order catalogs for baby linens. Then, we'll reveal nine important tips that will keep your baby safe and sound. Finally, we've got reviews of the best bedding designers and a must-read list of seven top money-wasters.

Getting Started: When Do You Need This Stuff?

Begin shopping for your baby's linen pattern in the sixth month of your pregnancy, if not earlier. Why? If you're purchasing these items from a baby specialty store, they usually must be special-ordered—allow at least four to eight weeks for delivery. If you leave a few weeks for shopping, you can order the bedding in your seventh month to be assured it arrives before the baby does.

If you're buying bedding from a store or catalog that has the desired pattern in stock, you can wait until your eighth month. It still takes time to comparison shop, and some stores may only have certain pieces you need in stock, while other accessories (like wall hangings, etc.) may need to be special ordered.

Sources

There are six basic sources for baby bedding:

1 **BABY SPECIALTY STORES.** These stores tend to have a limited selection of bedding in stock. Typically, you're expected to choose the bedding by seeing what you like on sample cribs or by looking through manufacturers' catalogs. Then you have to special-order your choices and wait four to eight weeks for arrival. And that's the main disadvantage to buying linens at a specialty store: THE WAIT. On the upside, most specialty stores do carry high-quality brand names you can't find at discounters or baby superstores. But you'll pay for it—most specialty stores mark such items at full retail.

2 **DISCOUNTERS.** The sheer variety of discount stores that carry baby bedding is amazing—you can find it everywhere from Wal-Mart to Target, Marshall's to TJ Maxx. Even Toys R Us sells baby bedding and accessories. As you'd expect, everything is cash and carry at these stores—most carry a decent selection of items in stock. You pick out what you like and that's it; there are no special orders. The downside? Prices are cheap, but so is the quality. Most discounters only carry low-end brands whose synthetic fabrics and cheap construction may not withstand repeated washings. There are exceptions to this rule, which we'll review later in this chapter.

3 **DEPARTMENT STORES.** The selection of baby bedding at department stores is all over the board. Some chains have great baby departments and others need help. For example, JCPenney carries linen sets by such companies as Cocalo and Cotton Tale (see the reviews of these brands later in this chapter), while Macy's seems to only have a few blankets and sheets. Prices at department stores vary as widely as selection; however, you can guarantee that department stores will hold occasional sales, making them a better deal.

4 **BABY SUPERSTORES.** The superstores reviewed in the last chapter (Babies R Us, Baby Depot, etc.) combine the best of both worlds: decent prices AND quality brands. Best of all, most items are in stock. Unlike Wal-Mart or K-Mart, you're more likely to see 100% cotton bedding and better construction. Yet, the superstores aren't perfect: they are often beaten on price by online sources (reviewed later in this chapter). And superstores are more likely to sell bedding in sets (rather than a la carte), forcing you to buy frivolous items.

5 **THE WEB.** If there were a perfect baby product to be sold on-line, it would have to be crib bedding and linens. The web's full-color graphics let you see exactly what you'll get. And bedding is lightweight, which minimizes shipping costs. The only bummer: you can't feel the fabric or inspect the stitching. As a result, we recommend sticking to well-known brand names when ordering online.

6 **MAIL-ORDER CATALOGS.** In the last few years, there's been a marked increase in the number of catalog sellers who offer baby linens, and that's great news for parents. Catalogs like Pottery Barn Kids, Land's End and Company Kids offer high quality bedding (100% cotton, high thread counts) at reasonable prices. Best of all, you can buy the pieces a la carte (eliminating unnecessary items found in sets) while at the same time, mixing and matching to your heart's content. If you want "traditional" bedding sets, JCPenney's catalog won't disappoint. We'll review these and more catalogs later in this chapter.

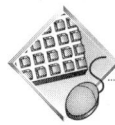

Parents in Cyberspace: What's on the Web?

Baby Catalog of America

Web: babycatalog.com

What it is: One of the best all around baby product retailers online.

What's cool: Whatever bedding item or brand you want, this site has it. Want sheets and bumpers for a cradle? Need a custom-sized bassinet mattress? How about comfortable, good quality portable crib sheets? BabyCatalog.com has got it. As for bedding, you'll find lines like Kids Line, Hoohobbers, and Lams & Ivy to name a few. All these items are priced 20% to 50% off retail. And you can get another 10% off with the purchase of an annual membership ($25 per year or $45 for three years).

Needs work: The site is not fancy, but functional. User reviews of products would be a nice addition.

Baby Supermarket

Web: babysupermarket.com

What it is: The online outlet for an independent baby store in Jackson, MS.

What's cool: Over 20 bedding lines, including some of our top picks (Cotton Tale, Pine Creek and Sweet Kyla). Prices are good. Example: a four-piece set from Glenna Jean for $292 (regular price $334). Some designs are available a la carte, while others are only sold in sets. And they do have a decent selection of separates including the Ultimate Crib Sheet. Free shipping on orders over $250.

Needs work: We found the navigation of the site a bit confusing. It takes a couple of clicks to get to a brand listing for bedding. But some of the brand links are empty.

Baby Universe

Web: babyuniverse.com

What it is: The web's largest selection of bedding.

What's cool: Over 75 bedding brands are here— best of all, you can buy many designs a la carte (including extra fabric). The site is easy to navigate and includes helpful hints, which note when matching twin bedding sets are available for a certain pattern. We liked the ability to search by gender, nursery theme or brand name. The shop-by-theme section included 70 choices under animal, 97 for floral & lace, etc. Brand names include Picci, Glenna Jean, California Kids, Lambs & Ivy and more. On a recent visit, we noted many free shipping offers and other discounts.

Needs work: Some bedding items are special order—leave six weeks or more.

Overstock

Web: overstock.com

What it is: A huge resource for overstocked and discontinued items.

What's cool: It's hit or miss, but some bargains are amazing. For example, we saw a round crib set of 21 pieces (yes, 21) for $469. You can sort crib sets by price, and top sellers among other options. And we definitely like the candid reader reviews of the sets. Savings is about 50% off retail.

Needs work: This site wins the award for the most clicks to get to a bedding section. First, you have to choose Home & Garden, then Bedding & Bath followed by Bedding, and finally Crib Sets. Insane, no? Tip: use the search function to go straight to crib sets. A big frustration Overstock.com often omits brand names from their product listings, making it hard to tell if you are scoring a real deal.

◆ *Other web sites to check out:* Most bedding companies have their entire catalogs online. The best include California Kids (calkids.com), Kids Line (kidslineinc.com) and Glenna Jean (glennajean.com).

For parents looking for accessories and bedding with a Beatrix Potter theme, check out *Country Lane* (countrylane.com). This site sells 750 different accessories and bedding pieces available in the Beatrix Potter line. Country Lane also has Pooh themed merchandise and Precious Moments. Discounts are up to 40% off.

Finally, don't forget *PotteryBarnKids.com*—a style leader with great design inspiration for decorating the nursery. We'll review their products later in this chapter

What Are You Buying?

Walk into any baby store, announce you're having a baby, and stand back: the eager salespeople will probably pitch you on all types of bedding items that you MUST buy. We call this the "Diaper Stacker Syndrome," named in honor of that useless (but expensive) linen item that allegedly provides a convenient place to store diapers. Most parents aren't about to spend the equivalent of the Federal Deficit on diaper stackers. So, here's our list of the absolute necessities for your baby's linen layette:

◆ **Fitted sheets**—at least three to four. This is the workhorse of your baby's linens. When it comes to crib sheets, you have three choices: woven, knit and flannel. Woven (also called percale) sheets are available in all cotton or cotton blend fabrics, while knit and flannel sheets are almost always all cotton. As to which is best, it's up to you. Some folks like flannel sheets, especially in colder climates. Others find woven or knit sheets work fine. One tip: look for sheets that have elastic all-around the edges (cheaper ones just have elastic on the corners). See the "Safe & Sound" section for more info on crib sheet safety issues.

If you plan to use a bassinet/cradle, you'll need a few of these special-size sheets as well . . . but your choices here are pretty limited. You'll usually find solid color pastels or white. Some specialty linen manufacturers do sell bassinet sheets, but they can get rather pricey. And you may find complete bassinet sets that come with all the linens for your baby. Just be sure to check the fabric content (all cotton is best) and washing instructions. By the way, one mom improvised bassinet sheets by putting the bassinet mattress inside a king size pillowcase. You may want to secure the excess fabric under the mattress so it doesn't un-tuck.

◆ **Mattress Pads/Sheet Protector.** While most baby mattresses have waterproof vinyl covers, many parents use either a mattress pad or sheet protector to protect the mattress or sheet from leaky diapers. A mattress pad is the traditional way of dealing with this problem and is placed between the mattress and the crib sheet. A more recent invention, the sheet protector, goes on top of the crib sheet.

A sheet protector has a waterproof vinyl backing to protect against leaking. And here's the cool part: it Velcro's to the crib's posts, making for easy removal. If the baby's diaper leaks, simply pop off the sheet protector and throw it in the wash (instead of the fitted crib sheets). You can buy sheet protectors in most baby stores or catalogs. See an "Email from the Real World" on the next page for information on sheet savers.

◆ *A Good Blanket.* Baby stores love to pitch expensive quilts to parents and many bedding sets include them as part of the package. Yet, all babies need is a simple, thin cotton blanket. Not only are thick quilts overkill for most climates, they can also be dangerous. The latest report from the Consumer Product Safety Commission on Sudden Infant Death Syndrome (SIDS) concluded that putting babies face down on such soft bedding may contribute to as many as 30% of SIDS deaths each year in the U.S. (As a side note, there is no explanation for the other 70% of SIDS cases, although environmental factors like smoking near the baby and a too-hot room are suspected). Some baby bedding companies have responded to these concerns by rolling out decorative flannel-backed blankets (instead of quilts) in their collections.

But what if you live in a cold climate and think a cotton blanket won't cut it? Consider crib blankets made from fleece (a lightweight 100% polyester fabric brushed to a soft finish) available in most stores and catalogs. For example, *Lands End* sells a polar fleece crib blanket (called the Bunny Belly blanket) for $20. Of course, polar fleece blankets are also available from mainstream bedding companies like *California Kids* (reviewed later in this chapter). Or how about a "coverlet," which is lighter than a quilt but more substantial than a blanket? Lightweight quilts (instead of the traditional thick and fluffy version) are another option for as little as $30 in catalogs.

We found a great product to keep baby warm and avoid a blanket altogether. *Halo Innovations* (halosleep.com), the manufacturer of a crib mattress reviewed in the last chapter, also makes a product called the SleepSack. This "wearable blanket" helps baby avoid creeping under a blanket and suffocating. Available in three sizes and fabrics, the SleepSack is $20 to $30. A portion of the sale price goes to the SIDS Alliance. *Kiddopotamus* also has a couple options: the BeddieBye Zip-Around Safety Blanket for $14 to $16 and the Swaddle Me infant wrap for $13.

Swaddling blankets are now the rage (although most folks can figure out how to swaddle a baby without much effort). Examples include the *Miracle Blanket* ($30), which is nice for those sleep-deprived nights.

◆ *Bumper Pads.* Bumpers are fabric pads designed to go around a crib to prevent an infant from knocking their head against the crib sides. Once considered a "must have" for new parents, crib bumper pads have become ensnared in controversy in recent years. Why? Numerous warnings about SIDS and soft bedding (see previous sec-

E-Mail from The Real World
Sheet savers make for easy changes

Baby bedding sure looks cute, but the real work is changing all those sheets. Karen Naide found a solution:

"One of our best buys was 'The Ultimate Crib Sheet.' I bought one regular crib sheet that matched the bedding set, and two Ultimate Crib Sheets. This product is waterproof (vinyl on the bottom, and soft white poly/cotton on the top) and lies on top of your regular crib sheet. It has six elastic straps that snap around the bars of your crib. When it gets dirty or the baby soils it, all you have to do is unsnap the straps, lift it off, put a clean one on, and that's it! No taking the entire crib sheet off (which usually entails wrestling with the mattress and bumper pads)... it's really quick and easy! While the white sheet may not exactly match your pattern, it can only be seen from inside the crib, and as you have so often stated, it's not like the baby cares about what it looks like. From the outside of the crib, you can still see the crib sheet that matches your bedding. Anyway, I think it's a wonderful product, and really a must."

Basic Comfort makes the **Ultimate Crib Sheet** *(call 800-456-8687 for a store near you; web: www.basiccomfort.com). It sells for $18 and is available at Babies R Us or we've seen it for as little as $15 on other baby web sites. FYI: older versions of the Ultimate Crib Sheet generated a few complaints. Some of our readers report that their children were able to get under the Ultimate Crib Sheet as they got a bit older. This scary scenario can be avoided by using their new, improved version with snaps on the ends, not just the sides.*

Of course, there are several other companies that sell similar sheets; we've seen them in general catalogs like One Step Ahead and Baby Catalog of America.

One of the coolest new products we found was the **Quick Zip** *crib sheet from Clouds and Stars (www.cloudsandstars.com). Here's how it works: the sheet base covers the bottom of the mattress and stays in place. The top of the sheet is secured via a plastic zipper. Baby's diaper leaks at two in the morning, you zip off the top of the sheet and zip on a spare. No lifting of the mattress (except when you first set it up) and no untying bumpers. The white or ecru sheet sets are $35 and additional top sheets are $17.50. They even make a version for portable cribs. Hand painted and custom sheets are available for a bit more.*

tion) have led some safety advocates to advise against bumpers.

For example, the CPSC "recommends that infants under 12 months be put to sleep in a crib with no soft bedding of any kind under or on top of the baby." Note the CPSC doesn't specifically say anything about banning bumpers, but some safety experts have extrapolated their warning to include crib bumpers.

As you would guess, that warning didn't sit well with crib bedding makers, who felt bumpers were getting a bad wrap. The industry's trade association (the JPMA) asked the CPSC to examine the data on infant injuries and deaths due to bedding in order to better determine if bumpers were the culprits. The CPSC released a report in 2004 which found that 94 infant deaths between 1995 and 2003 were caused by bedding . . . but here's the rub: in most cases, authorities didn't specify exactly WHICH bedding item caused the death. In a third of the cases, the "sleep environment was cluttered with adult sized blankets, quilts and pillows." The bottom line: the CPSC concluded "although bumper pads and stuffed toys were mentioned as being in the crib in some of the other deaths, there was insufficient detail to conclude these were the causative agents in the infants' deaths."

Now that clears it up, doesn't it?

One important point for this study: the CPSC excluded any SIDS deaths from their examination of crib bumpers, for reasons unknown. Yet it stands to reason that if you want to decide whether bumpers are safe or dangerous, you should include ALL the data (both SIDS and other deaths due to bedding).

Adding more fuel to this debate: a study in the *Journal of Pediatrics* (September 2007) found 27 cases of infant death involving bumper pads in a 20 year period. The study concluded that bumpers were dangerous and any benefit (preventing minor injuries when baby rolls in the side of the crib) was outweighed by the risk of suffocation.

Here's the take-home message: *you do **NOT** need crib bumpers*, which we believe can be dangerous. However, if you decide to use bumpers (say, your baby starts banging into the side of the crib or gets her arms/legs stuck), consider a bumper alternative like the **CribShield**, which we will discuss in detail later this chapter. The CribShield is a breathable, thin mesh that attaches with Velcro to the crib rail—this avoids the entrapment or suffociation risk of traditional bumpers.

If you still insist on using traditional bumpers, don't buy the ultra-thick or pillow-like bumpers. Instead choose firm bumpers that are made to properly and securely fit the crib (that means no overlapping sections or wide gaps between the ends at the corner sections). We recommend machine-washable bumpers with ties on the top and bottom, which let you attach the bumper more securely to a crib. Avoid any bumpers that are dry-clean only.

We'll have more comments on the safety aspects of bumpers in the Safe & Sounds section later in this chapter.

More Money Buys You . . .

Baby bedding sets vary from as little as $40 in discount stores up to nearly $1000 in specialty stores. The basic difference: fabric quality and construction. The cheapest bedding is typically made of 50/50 cotton-poly blends with low thread counts (120 threads per inch). To mask the low quality, many bedding companies splash cutesy licensed cartoon characters on such low-end bedding. So what does more money buy you? First, better fabric. Usually, you'll find 100% cotton with 200 thread counts or more. Better quality bedding sets include more substantial bumpers with more ties. Some may even have slipcovers removable for easy cleaning. Cheap quality crib sheets often lack elastic all the way around and some shrink dangerously when washed (see Safe and Sound next for details).

Beyond the $300 price point, you're most likely paying for a designer name and frilly accessories (coordinating lamp shade, anyone?). At the upper end of the crib bedding market, you find luxury fabrics—silks, brocades, matte lasse, etc.

Safe & Sound

While you might think to cover your outlets and hide that can of Raid, you might not automatically consider safety when selecting crib sheets, comforters, and bumpers. Yet, your baby will be spending more time with these products than any others. Here are several safety points to remember:

◆ **Make sure the crib sheets snugly fit the mattress.**
Let's talk about crib sheets. As you might guess, it is the elastic on a sheet that helps it fit snugly to a mattress. But not all sheets have the same amount of elastic.

One quality sign: check to make sure the sheet's elastic extends around the ENTIRE sheet (cheaper quality crib sheets only have elastic on the ends, making a good fit more difficult to achieve).

Another issue to consider with crib shrinks: shrinkage. Never use a sheet that has shrunk so much it no longer can be completely pulled over the bottom corners of the mattress. Unfortunately, some sheets shrink more than others. Generally, the cheapest sheets sold in discount stores shrink the most. We will review and rate bedding brands later in this chapter—those brands we recommend have sheets that are pre-shrunk.

Our advice: for any crib sheet you buy, be sure to wash it several times according to the directions and see if it correctly fits your crib. If not, return it to the store.

In response to concerns about ill-fitting cribs sheets, a few new crib sheet alternatives have come on the market. Example: The **Stay Put** safety sheet (babysheets.com; $19 each) works like a pillowcase on your mattress. Another option to consider: "pocket" sheets wrap around the crib mattress and close easily with Velcro manufactured by **Halo** (halosleep.com), the makers of the SleepSack.

J. Lamb (jlambandfriends.com) makes a 100% cotton, 200-thread count Safety Sheet with "Stay-Put" elastic safety bands (see picture). Four colors are available; there's even a "chemical free" version. Price: about $15.

You can also consider the Ultimate Crib Sheet and the QuickZip sheet discussed earlier in this book as another safe sheet option.

Finally, if you want a safety sheet that is customized to your nursery décor, take a look at **Sweet Pea's Heirlooms** (sweetpeasheirlooms.com). These sheets completely encase the mattress (like a pillowcase) then snap on the end. And, best of all, you can get the sheet made-to-order (with a print on one side and a solid on the other, or any combination of fabric). Regular sheets can be converted to safety sheets for a small fee. A 200-thread count cotton sheet from Sweet Pea starts at $25, with flannel and fleece options as well.

◆ **No soft bedding in the crib.** Studies on Sudden Infant Death Syndrome (SIDS, also known as crib death) have linked SIDS to infants sleeping on fluffy bedding, lambskins, or pillows. A pocket can

---

Sheets with All Around Elastic

Here is a partial list of manufacturers who make their crib sheets with elastic all around the sheet:

Amy Coe	Cotton Tale	Hoohobbers
Circo	Fleece Baby	Lands End
Baby Basics	Baby Gap	Patch Kraft
Baby Gap	Gerber	Sweet Kyla

form around the baby's face if she is placed face down in fluffy bedding, and she can slowly suffocate while breathing in her own carbon dioxide. The best advice: put your infant on her back when he or she sleeps. And don't put pillows, comforters or other soft bedding or toys inside a crib.

In the late 90's, the Consumer Product Safety Commission issued new guidelines regarding SIDS and soft bed linens. The CPSC now recommends that parents not use ANY soft bedding around, on top of, or under baby. If you want to use a blanket, tuck a very thin blanket under the mattress at one end of the crib to keep it from moving around. The blanket should then only come up to baby's chest. Safest of all: avoid using any blankets in a crib and put baby in a blanket sleeper (basically, a thick set of pajamas) and t-shirt for warmth. (More on blanket sleepers in the next chapter). See the picture above for an example of the correct way to use a blanket.

One mom wrote to tell us about a scary incident in her nursery. She had left a blanket hanging over the side of the crib when she

E-MAIL FROM THE REAL WORLD
Lack of Bumper Ties Cause a Scare for Parents

Nicole Morely of Chicago wrote to tell us of a frightening incident with borrowed bedding that did not have ties on the bottom of the bumper. (Keep in mind, there is no requirement for bumpers to have ties top and bottom. We recommend it highly, however.)

"We were spending the holidays with grandparents who bought a crib and borrowed bedding so that our five-month-old would sleep comfortably. We failed to check the crib bumpers for ties at the top and bottom and woke up in the middle of the night to shrieking—we found our baby's head and arms trapped under the crib bumper! Scary and unbelievable! Fortunately, we got there in time. I can't believe that so many manufacturers still make them that way. We've called nearby stores and all the bumpers they sell only tie at the top. The one our daughter was trapped under is Classic Pooh made by Red Calliope. I can't imagine that it doesn't happen more often!"

put her son down for a nap. He managed to pull the blanket down and get wrapped up in it, nearly suffocating. Stories like that convince us that putting any soft bedding in or near a crib is risky.

How much bedding is too much? A new father emailed us this question: "With all the waterproof liners, fitted sheets and ultimate crib sheets we're worried that our firm mattress is now becoming soft and squishy. How many layers are safe?"

Good point. We know that some parents figure it is easier to change crib sheets at 2 am if they simply pile on several layers of sheets on the crib mattress. (This way, you simply remove the top wet layer when changing the sheets). While we admire the creative thinking, we suggest NOT doing this. One sheet over a waterproof liner is enough. Or use a Ultimate Crib Sheet over your sheet—you won't need a additional liner since the Ultimate Crib Sheet is waterproof. The take-home message: any more than TWO layers on top of a mattress is dangerous.

♦ **_Beware of ribbons and long fringe._** These are possible choking hazards if they are not attached properly. Remove any questionable decoration.

♦ **_We do not recommend crib bumpers,_** for safety reasons discussed earlier. If you wish to ignore this advice, purchase bumpers with well-sewn ties at the top *and* bottom (at least 12 to 16 total). Ties should be between seven and nine inches in length. That's the industry's voluntary standard for safety—ties that are too short can't be tied correctly around a crib post. If ties exceed nine inches, they can be a strangulation hazard.

We should note that while there is a voluntary standard on bumper ties, our investigation of baby bedding found many manufacturers exceed the limit—one even had ties that were 14" in length! In their defense, expensive bedding makers claim their customers put their bedding on high-price Italian cribs, whose thick corner posts require longer ties. We think that's a weak excuse—14" is too long, even for cribs with the thickest posts. If you buy bumpers with ties that exceed 9", we recommend cutting off any excess length after you install them on the crib. (See the previous chapter's Safe & Sound section for a discussion of Italian cribs and bumper pads).

A related issue to the length of the ties is their location: some companies have ties ONLY on the top of bumpers. In this case, we've had many reports of babies scooting under the bumper and getting trapped (see our Email from the Real World on the previous page). If you fall in love with bedding that has ties only on the top, consider adding additional ties yourself. Just be sure to sew them on securely. A chart later in this chapter will compare the tie length and location among different brands.

As we noted earlier, make sure the bumpers fit well with no overlapping and no gaps at the ends. And avoid bumpers that are too thick and fluffy. They pose the same kind of risk as pillows. Look for firm, flat bumpers. Before you decide to use bumpers, read the section earlier in this chapter for the latest research on bumper safety.

As a side note, Canada heavily discourages the use of bumpers. A Canadian reader emailed: "We are not supposed to use bumper pads due to the increased risk of SIDS. No one I know uses them. When the health nurse comes to visit you in the home, she checks to make sure you don't have bumper pads." You can find out more on Canada's crib bedding recommendations on the Health Canada web site: www.hc-sc.gv.ca.

◆ *If you use bumpers, remove them immediately when your child starts to pull up or stand.* Why? Bumpers make a great step stool that lets baby launch herself out of the crib! This usually happens around six months of age.

◆ *Never use an electric blanket/heating pad.* Babies can dangerously overheat, plus any moisture, such as urine, can cause electric shock.

◆ *Avoid blankets that use nylon thread.* Nylon thread melts in the dryer and then breaks. These loose threads can wrap around your baby's neck, fingers or toes or break off and become a choking hazard. Cotton thread is best.

◆ *Look out for chenille.* It's the hip new thing and sort of like the shag carpeting of fabric—chenille is all over the market (sweaters, blankets, etc.) and now it has come to baby products. At a recent trade show, we saw many bedding manufacturers who had chenille groupings. Some use it as an accent on bumpers, while others have chenille blankets. Yet, some safety advocates wonder if this trim is safe for baby's bedding—with some chenille, you can actually pull out fibers from the fabric backing with little effort. And that might be a choking hazard for baby.

◆ *Travel.* Now that you've created a safe nursery at home, what about when you travel? Parents who frequently travel are often frustrated by hotels, which not only have unsafe cribs (see previous chapter) but also questionable sheets. At one hotel, we were given queen size bed sheets to use in a crib! A solution: one reader recommended bringing a crib sheet from home. That way you know your baby will be safe and sound. (When you reserve a crib at a hotel, find out if it is a portable crib or a standard crib so you know what size sheet to bring.) Check with some of our recommended safety sheet manufacturers listed earlier in this chapter and consider buying their port-a-crib versions for travel.

◆ **All linens should have a tag** indicating the manufacturer's name and address. That's the only way you would know if the linens were recalled. You can also contact the manufacturer if you have a problem or question. While this is the law, some stores may sell discounted or imported linens that do not have tags. Our advice: DON'T buy them.

Smart Shopper Tips

Smart Shopper Tip
Pillow Talk: Looking for Mr. Good Bedding

"Cartoons or more cartoons—that seems to be the basic choice in crib bedding at our local baby store. Since it all looks alike, is the pattern the only difference?"

There's more to it than that. And buying baby bedding isn't the same as purchasing linens for your own bed—you'll be washing these pieces much more frequently, so they must be made to withstand the extra abuse. Since baby bedding is more than just another set of sheets, here are nine quality points to look for:

1 RUFFLES SHOULD BE FOLDED OVER FOR DOUBLE THICKNESS— INSTEAD OF A SINGLE THICKNESS RUFFLE WITH HEMMED EDGE. Double ruffles hold up better in the wash.

2 COLORED DESIGNS ON THE BEDDING SHOULD BE PRINTED OR WOVEN INTO THE FABRIC, NOT STAMPED (like you'd see on a screen-printed t-shirt). Stamped designs on sheets can fade with only a few washings. The problem: the pieces you wash less frequently (like dust ruffles and bumpers) will fade at different rates, spoiling the coordinated look you paid big money for. In case you're wondering how to determine whether the design is printed rather than stamped, printed fabrics have color that goes through the fabric to the other side. Stamped patterns are merely applied onto the top of the fabric.

3 MAKE SURE THE PIECES ARE SEWN WITH COTTON/POLY THREAD, NOT NYLON. Nylon threads will melt and break in the dryer, becoming a choking hazard. Once the thread is gone, the filling in bumpers and quilts can bunch up.

4 **CHECK FOR TIGHT, SMOOTH STITCHING ON APPLIQUÉS.** If you can see the edge of the fabric through the appliqué thread, the work is too skimpy. Poor quality appliqué will probably unravel after only a few washings. We've seen some appliqués that were actually fraying in the store—check before you buy.

5 **HIGH THREAD-COUNT SHEETS.** Unlike adult linens, many packages of baby bedding do not list the thread count. But, if you can count the individual threads when you hold a sheet up to the light, you know the thread count is too low. High thread-count sheets (200 threads per inch or more) are preferred since they are softer and smoother against baby's skin, last longer and wear better. Unfortunately, most affordable baby bedding has low thread counts (80 to 120 thread counts are common)—traditionally, it's the design (not the quality) that sells bedding in the baby biz. But there is good news on this front: several upstart brands (reviewed later) actually tout high thread counts for their sheets.

Another telltale sign of a quality sheet is the elastic. The best sheets will have elastic that encircles the entire sheet.

6 **FEEL THE FILLING IN THE BUMPER PADS.** If the filling feels gritty, it's not the best quality. Look for bumpers that are firm when you squeeze them (Dacron-brand filling is a good bet).

7 **THE TIES THAT ATTACH THE BUMPER TO THE CRIB SHOULD BE BETWEEN SEVEN AND NINE INCHES IN LENGTH.** Another tip: make sure the bumper has ties on both the top and bottom and are securely sewn. For more discussion on this issue, see "Safe & Sound" earlier in this chapter.

8 **THE DUST RUFFLE PLATFORM SHOULD BE OF GOOD QUALITY FABRIC**—or else it will tear. Longer, full ruffles are more preferable to shorter ones. As a side note, the dust ruffle is sometimes referred to as a crib skirt.

9 **REMEMBER THAT CRIB SHEETS COME IN DIFFERENT SIZES—** bassinet/cradle, portable crib, and full-size crib. Always use the correct size sheet.

 *Wastes of Money/Worthless Items*

"I have a very limited budget for bedding, and I want to avoid spending money on stuff that I won't need. What are some items I

should stay away from?"

It may be tempting to buy every new fad and matching accessory. And you'll get a lot of sales pressure at some stores to go for the entire "coordinated" look. Yet many baby-bedding items are a complete waste of money—here's our list of the worst offenders:

1 **DIAPER STACKER.** This is basically a bag (in coordinating fabric, of course) used to store diapers—you hang it on the side of a changing table. Apparently, bedding makers must think stacking diapers on the shelf of your changing table or storing them in a drawer is a major etiquette breach. Take my word for it: babies are not worried if their diapers are out in plain sight. Save the $30 to $50 that bedding makers charge for diaper stackers and stack your own.

2 **PILLOWS.** We are constantly amazed at the number of bedding sets that include pillows or pillowcases. Are the bedding designers nuts, or what? Haven't they heard that it's dangerous to put your baby to sleep on a pillow? What a terrible safety hazard, not to mention a waste of your money. We don't even think a decorative pillow is a good idea—what if another caretaker puts your baby to sleep in her crib and forgets to remove the decorative pillow? Forget the pillow and save $20 to $30.

3 **SETS OF LINENS.** Sets may include useless or under-used items like those listed above as well as dust ruffles and window valances. Another problem: sets are often a mixed bag when it comes to quality. Some items are good, while others are lacking. A better bet: many baby stores or even chains now sell bedding items a la carte. That way you can pick and choose just the items you need—at a substantial savings over the all-inclusive sets.

4 **CANOPIES.** Parents-to-be of girls are often pressured to buy frilly accessories like canopies. The emphasis is on giving baby a feminine look for her nursery. Don't buy into it. The whole set-up for a canopy is going to be more expensive (you'll need a special crib, etc.)—it'll set you back $75 to $175 for the linens alone. And enclosing your baby's crib in a canopy won't do much for her visual stimulation or health (canopies are dust collectors).

5 **ALL-WHITE LINENS.** If you think of babies as pristine and unspoiled, you've never had to change a poopy diaper or clean spit-up from the front of an outfit. We're amazed that anyone would consider all-white bedding, since keeping it clean will probably be a full-time job. Stick with colors, preferably bright ones. If you buy all-white linens and then have to go back to buy colored ones, you'll be out another $100 to $200. (Yes, some folks argue that white linens are easier to bleach clean, but extensive bleaching over time can yellow fabric.)

6 **HEADBOARD BUMPERS.** Whatever side you come down on in the bumper debate (some parents think they're a good safety item; we don't recommend them because of the suffocation risk), there is a certain bumper that definitely is a waste of money—the headboard bumper. This bumper is designed to cover the entire headboard of the crib. Regular bumpers are just a six to nine-inch tall strip of padding that goes around the crib . . . and that's all you need if you want bumpers. Headboard bumpers are more expensive than regular bumpers, running another $25 to $100, depending on the maker. Skip them and save the money.

7 **SLEEP POSITIONERS.** These $10 to $20 blocks of foam are supposed to hold baby in place on their back, but they are unnecessary. The current recommendation is to put baby to sleep on her back . . . and nearly all infants will stay right there through out the night until they reach six months of age (when they are strong enough to roll over on their own). Positioners are a waste of money.

 *Money Saving Secrets*

1 **IF YOU'RE ON A TIGHT BUDGET, GO FOR A GOOD BLANKET AND A NICE SET OF HIGH THREAD-COUNT SHEETS.** What does that cost? A good cotton or fleece blanket runs $10, while a fitted sheet runs $10 to $20. Forget all the fancy items like embroidered comforters, duvet covers, window valances, diaper stackers and dust ruffles. After all, your baby won't care if she doesn't have perfectly coordinated accessories.

2 **DON'T BUY A QUILT.** Sure, they look pretty, but do you really need one? Go for a nice cotton blanket, instead—and save the $50 to $200. Better yet, hint to your friends that you'd like receiving blankets as shower gifts.

3 **SKIP EXPENSIVE WALL HANGINGS—DO DECOR ON THE CHEAP.** One of the best new products we've discovered for this is Wall Nutz (wallnutz.com). These innovative iron-on transfers let you create paint-by-number masterpieces in your baby's room. Paint a six-by-eight foot mural or just add some decorative borders. Cost:

$35 (plus the cost of paints).

A new idea: wall decals. These creative graphic "stickers" can be positioned and repositioned, removed and replaced. Choose from animals, flowers, abstract designs and more. Two companies offer these cool décor options: *Blik Re-Stik* (whatisblik.com; six decals for $5) and *WallPops!* (wall-pops.com; $13 each exclusively at Lowe's). *Wallies* (wallies.com) are similar to decals except that they are pre-pasted shapes. You wet the backing and stick wherever you like. FYI: Wallies aren't reusable—you have to strip them off like wallpaper. A pack of 12 small flowers runs about $13.

Of course, crafts stores are another great source for do-it-yourself inspiration. Michaels Arts & Crafts (800-MICHAELS; web: michaels.com) sells stencils and supplies for nursery decor.

4 MAKE YOUR OWN SHEETS, DUST RUFFLES AND OTHER LINEN ITEMS. Think that's too complicated? A mom in Georgia called in this great tip on curtain valances—she bought an extra dust ruffle, sewed a curtain valance from the material and saved $70. All you need to do is remove the ruffle from the fabric platform and sew a pocket along one edge. I managed to do this simple procedure on my sewing machine without killing myself, so it's quite possible you could do it too. A good place for inspiration is your local fabric store—most carry pattern books like Butterick, Simplicity and McCalls, all of which have baby bedding patterns that are under $10. There are other pattern books you can purchase that specialize in baby quilts—some of these books also have patterns for other linen items like bumpers. Even if you buy good quality fabric at $10 per yard, your total savings will be 75% or more compared to "pre-made" items.

5 SHOP AT OUTLETS. Scattered across the country, we found a few outlets that discount linens. Among the better ones Garnet Hill and Carousel (also known as babybeddingonline.com)—see their reviews in this chapter. Another reader praised the Pottery Barn Outlet. They have six locations at the time of this writing. The discounts start at 50% on bedding and furniture from their catalog and retail stores. Other outlets: Carter's, Baby Gap, and Nautica. Check Outlet Bound (www.outletbound.com) for locations.

6 DON'T PICK AN OBSCURE BEDDING THEME. Sure, that "Exploding Kiwi Fruit" bedding is cute, but where will you find any matching accessories to decorate your baby's room? Chances are they'll only be available "exclusively" from the bedding's manufacturer—at exclusively high prices. A better bet is to choose a more common theme with lots of accessories (wall decor, lamps, rugs, etc.). The more plentiful the options, the lower the prices. Winnie the Pooh is a good example, although you'll find quite a few accessories for other common themes like Noah's Ark, teddy bears, rocking horses, etc.

7 **GO FOR SOLID COLOR SHEETS AND USE THEMED ACCESSORIES.**
Just because you want to have a Disney-themed nursery does-n't mean you have to buy Disney *bedding*. A great money-saving strategy: use low-cost solid color sheets, blankets and other linen items in the crib. Get these in colors that match/compliment theme accessories like a lamp, clock, poster, wallpaper, rugs, etc. (Hint: register for these items, which make nice shower gifts). You still have the Disney look, but without the hefty tag for Beatrix Potter bedding. Many of the mail-order catalogs we review later in this chapter are excellent sources for affordable, solid-color bedding. Another bonus: solid color sheets/linens from the catalogs we recommend are often much higher quality (yet at a lower price) than theme bedding.

8 **SURF THE WEB.** Earlier in this chapter, we discussed the best web sites for baby bedding deals. Later in this chapter you'll find additional mail-order sources for bedding on a budget. The savings can be as much as 50% off retail prices. Even simple items like crib sheets can be affordably mail ordered. Next up: the best outlets for saving on baby bedding.

The Name Game: Reviews of Selected Manufacturers

Here are reviews of some of the brand names you'll encounter on your shopping adventures for baby bedding. Note: we include the phone numbers, web sites and addresses of each manufacturer—this is so you can find a local dealer near you (most do not sell directly to the public, nor send catalogs to consumers). We rated the compa-nies on overall quality, price, and creativity, based on an evaluation of sample items we viewed at retail stores. We'd love to hear from you—tell us what you think about different brands and how they held up in the real world by emailing authors@BabyBargains.com.

The Ratings

A EXCELLENT—*our top pick!*
B GOOD— *above average quality, prices, and creativity.*
C FAIR—*could stand some improvement.*
D POOR—*yuck! could stand some major improvement.*

Amy Coe *For a dealer near you, call (203) 221-3050. Web: amy-coe.com.* Designer Amy Coe turned her hobby of collecting vintage fabrics into a business when she launched her eponymous baby bedding line in 1993. The result is a linen collection with a flair for nostalgia: Coe takes fabrics that replicate patterns from the 1930's to the 1950's and crafts a full line of bedding items.

Coe has two lines: one for specialty stores (Amy Coe) and another for Target (amy coe). While both play off the same design inspiration, as you might expect, there are some major differences. The Amy Coe in specialty stores features more sumptuous fabrics and (no surprise) bigger price tags. The more expensive line runs $400 to $500 for a set and accessories are pricey too (chenille throws for $115, velour blankets for $80 and so on). Quality is high and most fabrics are all cotton.

At Target, you get a more muted version of Amy's designs, although the fabric is still all-cotton and the sheets boast 200-thread counts and all-around elastic. Four-piece sets run just $80 to $100, extra sheets are $10 and chenille blankets $10. How's the quality? In a past edition of this book, we noted many readers complained about the sheet shrinkage and other quality snafus. Recently, however, reviews are much more positive. Most parents noted that the sheets washed well and one mom thought the quality was as good as Pottery Barn Kids. ***Rating (Target version): B+ (Specialty stores version): A-***

Baby Bedding Online*. See Carousel.*

Baby Basics*. See Carter's.*

Baby Gap *Web: babygap.com.* In the past we reported that Baby Gap had five bedding collections sold a la carte. However, at the time of this writing, Baby Gap is no longer selling bedding sets. They do have a few crib sheet options sale priced at $10 to $17. It's unclear whether Baby Gap plans to bring back bedding sets in the near future. ***Rating: A-***

Baby Martex *CoCaLo distributes this brand. See their review later in this section.*

BananaFish *For a dealer near you, call (800) 899-8689 or (818) 727-1645. Web: bananafishinc.com.* "Sophisticated" and "tailored" is how we'd describe this California-based bedding maker. BananaFish's emphasis is on all-cotton fabric with adult-like finishes (such as pique) and muted color palettes. It's not cheap—prices range from $240 to $400 at retail for a four-piece set. Quality is high. FYI: You can see most of the collection at BabyUniverse.com. Final note: in the past year, we learned that BananaFish was acquired by mass-market bedding maker Betesh Group. ***Rating: B***

Beatrix Potter *This brand was a license by Crown Craft (see review later in this section), but the company no longer makes it. We still see a few closeout sets online for this brand, however.*

Beautiful Baby *For a dealer near you, call (903) 295-2229. Web: bbaby.com.* Next to Nava's (reviewed later), this is probably the most over-the-top bedding in the market today. There's nothing subtle about Beautiful Baby's linens, which feature satin, lace and tulle. The bumpers are so huge they're like king-size pillows sewn together (okay, that's an exaggeration, but trust us, they are BIG) but they do have the most bumper ties of any manufacturer (26). Good news, though, you can customize the bumper thickness. As we noted earlier, thinner bumpers are safer, in our opinion. In fact, you can custom change just about anything in this line. Another plus: their sheets all have safety straps, an added feature we applaud. With over 1300 fabrics to choose from, Beautiful Baby says it takes four to six weeks to ship most orders. Prices are high: expect to shell out $400 to $800 for a three-piece set,. Most but not all fabrics are 100% cotton. Bottom line: this line isn't cheap, but if you're looking for bedding you can customize with an over-the-top style, this is the brand for you. ***Rating: B***

Bedtime Originals *Lambs & Ivy make this brand. See their review later in this section.*

Blue Moon Baby *For a dealer near you, call (626) 455-0014.*

Affordable Artwork

Framed artwork for baby's room has to be very expensive, right? Nope, not if you buy a framed print from **Creative Images** (call 800-784-5415 or 904-825-6700 for a store near you; web: www.crimages.com). This Florida-based company sells prints, growth charts, wall hangings and more at very affordable prices—just $30 to $100. Each print is mounted on wood and laminated (no glass frame) so baby can enjoy it at eye-level (just sponge it off if it gets dirty). Best of all, there are hundreds of images in any theme to choose from: Pooh, bunnies, Noah's Ark, plus other collections of animals, sports and pastels. Check out their web site for samples.

Web: bluemoonbaby.com. In business for seven years, California-based Blue Moon Baby specializes in chenille bedding (although they've expanded the line recently and included designs without chenille accents). Their 16 collections feature chenille in a variety of patterns and designs for both boys and girls. One of the best bets: The Cody Collection with its red bandanna trim and denim accents, along with a chenille cowboy. For girls, the Christina collection featured an antique rose print accented with windowpanes of chenille that is sure to draws ooh's and aah's from grandparents. Blue Moon Baby also sells coordinating furniture, stuffed animals and other decorative accents. Prices are about $330 to $420 for a four-piece set, which includes slip-covered bumpers, skirt, jersey sheet and quilt. The fabric is all cotton. We thought the quality was very good and we really like the unique designs—no one else is doing sculptured chenille. However, the use of chenille in baby bedding is quite controversial. See the Safe and Sound section earlier in this chapter. Another downside: the price is rather high. In the past, because of the controversy over chenille, we gave this line only an average rating. This year thanks to some non-chenille options, we'll up the rating a bit. ***Rating: B-***

Brandee Danielle *For a dealer near you, call (800) 720-5656, (714) 957-1240. Web: brandeedanielle.com.* In the past, we highly recommended Brandee Danielle bedding—but recent complaints have caused us to rethink our rating.

Brandee Danielle offers three bedding lines: Posh Baby, BD Baby and Brandee B.

Designs are typically simple looks with some embroidery and appliqué. Posh Baby has the most sophisticated look while BD Baby and Brandee B are more traditional in design. Prices range from $150 to $350 for a four-piece set and most of the fabrics are 100% cotton.

Overall, parents are pleased with the quality of embroidery and appliqué. One reader described the embroidery as "prettier in real-life than in the photos on the web site." And the machine washable pieces seem to stand up well to repeated washings.

So what's the problem? Some readers have complained that sets have elastic only on the corners of sheets. Some items (namely, quilts) are spot-clean only while other items are hand-wash only.

Customer service has been another sore spot. When one reader had a problem with a stain on her brand new, out-of-the-bag bumper, the company offered her no help in solving the problem. Other readers have complained about excessive shipping delays.

In light of these problems, we've decided to lower Brandee Danielle's rating this time around. ***Rating: C***

LICENSE TRANSLATOR

Who makes what brand of bedding

One of the hottest trends in crib bedding is licensed characters–just about every cartoon character imaginable has been licensed to one of the big bedding makers for use in juvenile bedding. But how can tell you tell who makes what? Here is a list of popular licensed characters and their bedding makers:

LICENSE	SEE BEDDING MAKER
BABY LOONEY TUNES	GERBER
BABY MARTEX	COCALO
BEATRIX POTTER	CROWN CRAFTS
BENETTON	BABY BOOM
DISNEY BABY	CROWN CRAFTS
EDDIE BAUER	CROWN CRAFTS
HELLO KITTY	LAMBS & IVY
HOLLY HOBBIE BABY	CROWN CRAFTS
J. GARCIA	QUILTEX
KELLY B RIGHTSELL DESIGNS	CROWN CRAFTS
LAURA ASHLEY	SUMERSAULT
LITTLE TIKES	SPRINGS
NAUTICAKIDS	CROWN CRAFTS
NOJO	CROWN CRAFTS
OPBABY!	CROWN CRAFTS
OSH KOSH B'GOSH	COCALO
PRECIOUS MOMENTS	CROWN CRAFTS
SESAME STREET	CROWN CRAFTS
SNOOPY	LAMBS & IVY
SUZY'S ZOO	GERBER
TODD PARR	QUILTEX
WAMSUTTA	SPRINGS
WAVERLY BABY	CROWN CRAFTS
WINNIE THE POOH	CROWN CRAFTS

California Kids For a dealer near you, call (800) 548-5214, (650) 637-9054. Web: calkids.com. One of our favorite bedding lines, California Kids specializes in bright and upbeat looks. In the past few years, they've added more girl-oriented themes as well as a line of coordinating lamps. The quality is excellent; everything is 100% cotton and made in California. Prices run $250 to $550 for a four-piece set (the average is about $300). With an amazing array of options (60+ patterns at last count), California Kids is sold in specialty stores and upper-end department stores. Available accessories include wall hangings, lampshades and fabric by the yard. Finally they've added a website, after all these years. The only problem? Their web site hasn't been updated in two years. **Rating: A**

The Marketing of Baby Linens: Dangerous Impressions?

Flip through any bedding catalog or web site and you'll see decked-out cribs, stuffed with sumptuous linens. Some linen companies like Baby Martex even use long ago recalled cribs (with dangerous corner posts) to market "antique" looking patterns. Yet, in their haste to market their products, baby linen makers may be sending a wrong (and dangerous) message to parents—that it's OK to put soft bedding items like pillows, comforters and the like in cribs. Safety advocates clearly warn against this, but it still amazes us to see bedding brochures with many offending items loaded into cribs, some of which are missing a drop-side (in order to show the merchandise more clearly, of course). The reason why this happens is obvious: linen manufacturers make fat profits off of such "decorative" accessories. And what better way to sell such items for baby than to deck out cribs? But we wonder if this sends the wrong message to parents—some folks may think that's how their crib should look. Yeah, many bedding makers include warning labels (in six-point type) that say you shouldn't put such items in a crib—but that's usually in the fine print if it exists at all. All bedding makers should eliminate this practice at once.

Back in 2000, retailers including JCPenney, Sears, Babies R Us, Target, Ikea and Lands End promised the CPSC they would discontinue displaying soft bedding in cribs including quilts, pillows and stuffed animals. But . . . checking the web sites for all these retailers, we continue to see most of them market cribs with quilts draped over the railings. In one case, we even saw a stuffed animal inside the crib. As for store marketing, Babies R Us continues to market its cribs with thick bumpers and quilts hung over the sides. We're disappointed that these companies continue to send out mixed messages to parents, preferring to emphasize marketing over safety.

Carousel/Baby Bedding Online Web: *babybedding.com.*
Carousel/Baby Bedding Online use to sell its line of bedding exclusively through retail stores at about $250 to $450 per set. Several
years ago, however, they decided to change to an Internet-only
sales model and started up their site BabyBeddingOnline.com.
Selling directly to consumers resulted in lower prices—today their
sets run $99 to $300. Can't beat those prices for an all cotton, 200+
thread count bedding line. And best of all, Carousel doesn't do this
half way. The web site offers free fabric swatches and other goodies. Looking for quality portable crib sheets or matching cradle
sheets? How about rocking chair pads and high chair pads? They've
got them. Lastly, Baby Bedding has an outlet store near Atlanta;
check the web site for their latest schedule (it was open to the public only on the third Saturday of the month last we checked).

What do parents think about Carousel? Universally parents
praise Carousel's great prices and quality. One mom noted that not
only were the prices great, but after repeated washing of the crib
set "it still looks new!" And best of all, it can all be ordered online,
with UPS tracking and more. So, overall, we recommend
Carousel—good designs, great quality and affordable prices.
Rating: A

Carter's *See Kidsline.*

Celebrations *Call (310) 532-2499 for a dealer near you. Web:
baby-celebrations.com.* Celebrations specializes in feminine, sophisticated looks—patchwork motifs, eyelet laces, chenille trim and lay-
ered dust ruffles. The all-cotton linens range from $300 to $590.
Quality is excellent; we noticed the bumpers sported ties on the
top and bottom (16 total). Most fabrics are all cotton. In recent
years, Celebrations has branched out into matching accessories and
now sells hand-painted lamps, cradle sets, wall hangings and more.
This line is only sold in specialty stores. **Rating: B+**

Circo *See Target*

Classic Pooh *See Crown Craft*

CoCaLo *Call (714) 434-7200 for a dealer near you. Web: coca-
lo.com.* You could say baby bedding runs in the family at CoCaLo.
Owner Renee Pepys Lowe's mother (Shirley) founded Nojo in 1970
and Renee worked at the family business before it was sold to
Crown Crafts. Since then, Renee has branched out on her own,
launching the CoCaLo line in 1999 (the name comes from the first
two letters of Renee's daughters, Courtenay and Catherine Lowe).

CoCaLo is made up of four lines: Osh Kosh, Baby Martex, an eponymous collection and Kimberly Grant, which CoCaLo acquired in 2002 and is reviewed separately later in this section. The lowest priced (and largest) group is Osh Kosh, ranging from $170 to $250 for a four-piece set. Unfortunately, not all of this collection is all-cotton (some sets are blends). CoCaLo has their own line of bedding that features extra long ruffles for $150 to $300 per set. Design-wise, the Osh Kosh line features their trademark denim look in most groupings, while CoCaLo is more whimsical, in brighter hues. Baby Martex (priced around $190 at Babies R Us and up to $250 at specialty stores) is simpler with checks, plaids and seersucker looks, although one grouping also showcased vintage floral prints. Quality-wise, we were impressed with Baby Martex and Kimberly Grant (which are all cotton) compared with the Osh Kosh sets. We'd stick with the 100% cotton selections. ***Rating: B+***

Company Kids *Call (800) 323-8000 for a catalog or to place an order. Web: companykids.com.* A subsidiary of the Company Store, Company Kids offers a complete catalog catering to the bedding whims of parents and little ones alike. Basically, Company Kids offers a selection of quilts for infants, which can then be paired with sheets in solids or checks. There are also some bedding sets (sold a la carte with matching bumpers, sheets and dust ruffles) as well. Duvets are also available. Sheets run $14 each while quilts are about $80 each. Not a bad deal at all for 100% cotton percale fabrics.

While the prices are decent, we've received complaints about Company Kids' poor customer service and quality. Backordered items are a common gripe. Another reader was frustrated when her sheets ripped after several washings. Overall, quality reviews were mixed—some fans say the brand is good, comparable to Pottery Barn Kids. Others are less generous.

Given the mixed reviews, we'll tick down the Company Kids rating this time out. While the web site is easy to navigate and the prices are decent, quality and customer woes drag down this brand. ***Rating: B***

Cotton Tale *Call (800) 628-2621 or (714) 435-9558 for a dealer near you. Web: cottontaledesigns.com.* In our last edition we noted that Cotton Tale had been bought by Baby's Dream, the crib manufacturer. Recently, however, designer Nina Selby bought back the company she founded and has released a new high fashion line under her own name: N. Selby Designs.

Cotton Tale has been one of our favorite bedding lines for a long time and for one reason: originality. There are no licensed cartoon characters or trendy fabrics like chenille here. Instead, you'll see beautiful soft pastels, whimsical animal prints and adorable appliqués. Best of all, Cotton Tale's prices are affordable—most range from $200 to $300 with an average of $270 for a four piece set. Most of the fabrics are 100% cotton, although some trim may be a blend.

The new N. Selby line kicks up the sophistication a notch with more luxurious looks. You'll find more bold colors as well as fun accents like tiers of ruffles and lots of polka dots. A four-piece set of N. Selby Designs sells for $250 to $500.

All in all, we'll give Cotton Tale a big thumbs up for the innovative designs and beautiful patterns. ***Rating: A***

CribShield & Breathable Bumper *Made by Trend-Lab. Call 866-873-6352 for a dealer near you. Web: cribshield.com.* Here's a mom-invented product that is a simple solution to babies who get their arms or legs caught in the crib spindles: a "breathable" bumper made of mesh that Velcros on to the crib. Unlike other thicker bumpers, this one allows for airflow and baby can't get trapped between it and the mattress. And it's affordable: $25 to $40 and available in stores or online (Wal-Mart.com carries it). The company makes two versions of the product: one is the Breathable Bumper (11" tall) and the other is the CribShield. The latter covers the entire crib from bottom rail to top rail, while the bumper is just a bumper. Detractors of these products say it doesn't fit all cribs (given the wide variety of models out there, that isn't a big surprise) and older babies can rip it off the crib. (It can only be used up to nine months of age, as recommended by the manufacturer). Yes, we see the last point . . . but this is a good solution for most folks. FYI: Don't rush out and get this product before baby is born. Only AFTER your baby develops a habit of getting arms or legs stuck in the crib spindles (only a small percentage will do that), do we recommend getting this product! ***Rating: A***

Crown Crafts *Call (800) 421-0526 or (714) 895-9200 for a dealer near you. Web: www.ccipinc.com.* Baby bedding behemoth Crown Crafts seems to have snapped up every possible character license you can imagine. Their current line up includes Eddie Bauer Baby, Disney Baby, Classic Pooh, Kelly B. Rightsell, Precious Moments, Holly Hobby, Nojo, Waverly, Nautica Kids, Sesame Street and Kimberly Grant (reviewed separately). Depending on the brand, sets run $40 to $200 and are sold at chain stores like Target (which has the company's Classic Pooh as an exclusive), Babies R Us, Baby Depot and other chains. In the past, we knocked Crown Craft's emphasis on cartoon characters instead of quality. And there is still room for improvement here (we noted the company's high end sets have bumpers with both top and bottom ties; the cheaper sets just have top ties). But the company has made a renewed effort to improve quality, particularly with the Nojo line ($100 to $270). Most of Crown Crafts' sheets are 100% cotton, which is better than in years past when the sheets could be blends. New this year at Crown Crafts are sets made of organic cotton ($190 per set). Bottom line, you get what you pay for with this manufacturer. Stick with the better quality sets (Nojo, Eddie Bauer) and avoid the cheap-o character-theme sets (Disney Baby). ***Rating: C+***

Disney Baby *See Crown Craft*

Dwell *Web: dwellshop.com.* If you've bought an expensive, modern-style crib, the bedding picks are slim. We'd guess that frilly bedding you see in chain stores won't work.

To the rescue comes Dwell, which matches that modern aesthetic with pricey bedding sets. Made of 210 to 320-thread count and 100% cotton, Dwell isn't cheap, but they offer a simple, yet sophisticated look. Example: Motif is a '60's flashback with aqua, green and yellow hues. The price: $295 for a set that includes a fitted sheet, padded bumper, crib skirt and blanket (items are also available a la carte). We should note that prices on Dwell's web site are significantly higher than from online retailers (Dwell lists their prices from $385 to $456 while online we saw them for $295 to $350). Parent reviews have been positive on this brand complimenting them for their softness and fit. One reader commented that the bedding is "expensive, but worth it." ***Rating: B+***

Eddie Bauer. *See Crown Craft*

Fleece Baby *Web: fleecebaby.com.* So, you live in a part of the country where winter is colder than (fill in your own punch line here)? Given all the warnings about soft bedding and heavy quilts, how do you keep baby warm during those cold winter months? One solution is fleece baby sheets. Fleece Baby makes a wide variety of crib sheets, blankets, play yard sheets and more . . . all of 100% polar fleece. Crib sheets run $25 and are sold online at BabyCenter.com and various other sites. We had a reader road test the play yard version of the Fleece Baby sheet ($15) and she gave it two thumbs up. The only concern: after washing, the sheet lost a bit of its softness, but still overall it was a winner—one user recommended using unscented dryer sheets to retain the softness. ***Rating: A***

Garnet Hill *Call (800) 622-6212 for a catalog or to place an order. Web: garnethill.com.* If you want to spend the big bucks on bedding, check out Garnet Hill. This catalog makes a big deal out of its "natural fabric" offerings, and they do sell products we haven't seen elsewhere.

Garnet Hill sells woven and knit crib bedding. Unfortunately, they've scaled back their crib bedding options since our last edition. Last time we complained that it was difficult to figure out which Garnet Hill bedding was available in crib sizes. Well, thankfully they've fixed that flaw and you can now go straight to the crib size items. Regardless, we still recommend checking out the quilts first rather than the sheet sets. For example, you'll find that the Solar System Quilt ($78) comes in crib size. Next you can find coordinating Rockets percale sheets to coordinate ($20). There are also basics available like the Dot-To-Dot sheets in flannel ($15) and percale $18) if you don't want a themed nursery. Quality is high: all sheets are 200-thread count. **Rating: B**

George *See Wal-Mart.*

Gerber *For a dealer near you, call (800) 4GERBER Web: gerber.com.* While Gerber offers some cute patterns in their bedding line and they're available almost everywhere, the bedding's quality leaves much to be desired. One reader emailed us this typical story: "I bought several of the Gerber Everyday Basics knit sheets. They fit my 5" thick Sealy mattress well when I bought them, they were super soft, and had elastic all the way around for safety. BUT THEN . . . I washed them on the delicate cycle in cold water and dried them on low/delicate as instructed in the package, and they shrunk so much I couldn't even get them on the mattress anymore!" Other parents complained about colors that faded after just a couple washes and bumpers that lost their form as well. Gerber's biggest licenses are Suzy's Zoo and Baby Looney Tunes. And yes, the prices are cheap—a three-piece set of Baby Looney Tunes from Babies R Us is a mere $60. But the designs are screen printed on low quality cotton/poly fabrics. We can't recommend this brand. **Rating: D**

Glenna Jean *For a dealer near you, call (800) 446-6018 or (804) 561-0687. Web: glennajean.com.* Glenna Jean has notched 28 years in the bedding biz by adapting to the times—their current line features dressed-up designs with velvets, brocades, and bright color palettes. Example: the Dynasty collection—a rosy, floral design showcasing velvet edging on the quilt and bed skirt, with cool tassel trim on the edge of the skirt. Coordinating stripes and solids complete the look for $270 for a four-piece set.

Overall, Glenna Jean sets start at $225 and go up to $450. Most of the designs are 100% cotton with the exception of some of the trim. Our only caution: Glenna Jean's bumpers have top and bottom ties at the corners—the center of the bumper only has top ties. As you know, we aren't big fans of bumpers—but if you use one, make sure entire bumper has ties on the top and bottom. Glenna Jean's bumpers fail that test.

New this year from Glenna Jean: Sweet Potato, a lower-priced line (starting at $200) with a more mod look. Yes, this departs a bit from Glenna Jean's traditional look, but we liked the geometric designs—and the prices are certainly more reasonable than other mod bedding brands. ***Rating: B+***

Graham Kracker *Call (800) 489-2820 for a catalog or to place an order. Web: grahamkracker.com.* This mail order company specializes in custom bedding. You can mix and match your own selections from 108 different fabrics or you can provide your own fabric. The price? A whopping $495 for a five-piece set, which includes a headboard bumper and baby pillow (don't use this in the crib, please!). But, everything is 100% cotton and there are all sorts of matching accessories. Most of the choices are bright, cheerful colors, but not too cutesy. Shipping time is two to three weeks. ***Rating: B***

Holly Hobby *See Crown Craft*

Hoohobbers *For a dealer near you, call (773) 890-1466. Web: hoohobbers.com.* The quality of this brand was impressive—all of the bumpers are made duvet-style with zippers. The result: it's easy to remove the covers for washing. Hoohobbers' 19 designs tend to have interesting color combinations in both bright jewel tones and pastels. Prices for all their four-piece collections are $380; that's expensive, but everything is 100% cotton and well constructed (the sheets feature all-around elastic, and the bumpers have top and bottom ties, for example). The good news is you can see and buy any of their patterns on their web site. All bedding is made at Hoohobbers' Chicago factory. Finally, we should mention Hoohobbers' bassinets and Moses baskets come in coordinating fabrics as well. In fact, the company makes a wide range of accessories including furniture, bouncer seat covers and more. ***Rating: B+***

Jessica McClintock *For a dealer near you, call (719) 947- 1170. Web: PacificCoastHomeFurnishings.com* Remember those lacy Jessica McClintock homecoming and prom dresses? Or her old-fashioned wedding gowns? We do (maybe we're showing our age), so it's not surprising that Jessica McClintock is bringing that lacy, Victorian look to crib bedding. Made by Pacific Coast Home

Furnishings (which is a JM licensee), the designs are 100% cotton with satin, silk, and plush accents. Good news: even with the fancy fabrics and lace, the whole line is machine-washable. Prices range from $250 to $400 for a five-piece set and yes, there is even one organic offering (made of organic cotton) for $160. And here's a unique offering: one set features an illustration of Our Lady of Guadalupe. Jessica McClintock crib bedding had not hit the stores yet as of this writing, so we don't have any parent feedback yet. ***Rating: Not Yet.***

JoJo Designs *Web: Amazon.com and other web sites.* JoJo Designs offers a rather amazing bedding deal: a nine-piece bedding set for only $120 to $179. What does that include? You get a comforter, bumper (ties on top only), sheet, skirt, two valances, diaper stacker, toy bag and throw pillow (never use this in your crib!). The 100% cotton sets come in all the popular themes (24 of them, in fact): firefighting, car racing, bugs (bees or dragonflies), Hawaiian, patchworks, and toile.

But how's the quality? Unfortunately, this line is so new that we haven't yet received any parent feedback. So we'll have to take a wait and see on this one. ***Rating: Not Yet.***

Kelly B. Rightsell *See Crown Craft*

Kids Line *151 W. 135th St., Los Angeles, CA 90061. Call (310) 660-0110 for a dealer near you. Web: Kidslineinc.com.* Kids Line has been on a roll in recent years, designing sets with luxury touches while keeping prices affordable (most Kids Line sets are $100 to $200 for a six-piece set). New in the past year are several sets that include fleece, velvet burnout, corduroy and chenille. They've expanded their accessories line to include bath coordinates as well as blankets, wall hangings, lamps and more. And that seems to have resonated with our readers: parents tell us they love all the accessory options with Kids Line's patterns. How's the quality? Well, reviews are mixed. Some items are cotton-poly blends and parents have reported that shrinkage is sometimes a problem. On the plus side, colors hold up well in the wash, Kids Line added ties to both the tops and bottoms of bumpers and their sheets have elastic all around.

FYI: Kids Line also makes the Tiddliwinks line of bedding available mostly at Target. This lower end line runs $66 for a three-piece set. While it has 100% cotton sheets with all around elastic, we found the overall quality of Tiddliwinks to be disappointing. And we suspect these sheets will shrink, since the washing instructions are cold-water only. Our advice: avoid Tiddliwinks.

Finally, Kids Line is now producing the Carter's line of bedding (with a separate web site at carters.kidsline.com). Kids Line has given the Carter's bedding a much needed style-upgrade—there are three complete collections as well as a baby basics mix and match line. A four-piece set is priced at $160. Sheets ($10 each) are 200 thread-count, 100% cotton and quite a step up from the old Carter's sheets we reviewed in the past. Kids Line has definitely improved both the quality and design.

Overall it is a mixed review for Kids Line—nice designs and great accessories . . . but a bit iffy on the quality (especially Tiddliwinks, the Target-exclusive). The Carter's separates are a better bet, quality wise. **Rating: B**

Kimberly Grant *Call (714) 546-4411 for a dealer near you. Web: kimberlygrant.com.* If you're looking for bedding designs that are a bit lower key and not too cutesy, Kimberly Grant is a great option. Now produced by Crown Crafts (see review above), Grant continues to create sophisticated looks (floral prints, plaids) using luxe fabrics (velvets, satins, cotton), all in a warm palette. Prices run $175 to $400 for a four-piece set. Pricey but good quality. **Rating: A-**

Koala Baby *Available exclusively at Babies R Us.* Koala Baby is Babies R Us' attempt at establishing an in-house brand of bedding. In an earlier edition, we noted that a six-piece Koala Baby bedding set sold for $150 to $170 and included the quilt, bumper, sheet, dust ruffle, diaper stacker and valance. Apparently, Koala Baby has now decided to market the line only a la carte. Bumpers cost $25 and bed skirts are $18, a two pack of sheets is $15 and a blanket will run $17. Pretty darned affordable. So what's the downside? Quality, for one. As one reader put it, "This brand is TERRIBLE!!!! I washed the fitted sheet before putting it on my crib mattress and it shrunk about 6" in length! I wouldn't recommend these sheets to anyone." Another reader knocked the Koala Baby dust ruffle she bought, which was very poor quality and didn't wash well. While the concept is admirable (private-label bedding at affordable prices), it seems that Babies R Us has missed with their Koala Baby line. **Rating: D+**

Lambs & Ivy *For a dealer near you, call (800) 345-2627 or (310) 839-5155. Web: lambsivy.com.* Barbara Lainken and Cathy Ravdin founded this LA-based bedding company in 1979. Their specialty: cutesy baby bedding that is sold in discount and mass market stores (you'll also see them sold in JCPenney's catalog and on many web sites). This year they've added some whimsical looks along with vintage prints and licensed characters. In fact, they've expanded their Snoopy license to include three options now. Quality of the Snoopy line is actually good. Instead of using stamp printing, Lambs & Ivy uses photo-quality heat transfer technology. This is a clever way of achieving a nicer look without big cost (you have to see the bedding in person to note the difference). Prices are still reasonable at $150 to $285 for a six-piece set. Bedtime Originals, a sub-line of Lambs & Ivy, is lower in price (around $60 to $85 for a three piece set) and quality. We'd rank the overall quality of Lambs & Ivy a bit ahead of other mass-market bedding brands. Yes, some of the fabrics are blends (50-50 cotton/poly), but the stitching and construction is a cut above. **Rating: B+**

Land of Nod *Call (800) 933-9904 for a catalog or to place an order. Web: landofnod.com.* This stunning catalog (now owned by Crate & Barrel) features attractive layouts of baby's and kid's rooms, replete with cute linens and accessories. Even if you don't buy anything, the Land of Nod is a great place to get decorating ideas.

Crib bedding is sold a la carte and some designs only have the quilt, bed skirt and bumpers available. The fabric is 100% cotton, 200-thread count. And they have ties on the top and bottom of their bumpers. A four-piece set runs $200 to $236, while a single sheet can cost $19. The prices are good, maybe even a bit less than last time. We loved the color palettes, which ranged from patchwork denim to bright pastels. Check out the whimsical lamps and other accessories. **Rating: A-**

Lands End *Call (800) 345-3696 for a catalog or to place an order. Web: landsend.com.* Lands' End changes their options so frequently, it's tough to nail them down for you. While they've always made great quality sheets with all-around elastic, availability of specific colors and fabrics can vary. For example, a recent visit to Lands End site revealed only one sheet option in 100% cotton knit fabric. Sold in sets of two sheets for $39.50, you can choose from five sold colors (pink, blue, gold, green and white). Blankets, on the other hand come in a variety of options: fleece, cotton, lace and cashmere. Parent comments are universally positive: "incredibly soft, yet durable," "soft fabric, washes great" and "minimal shrinkage."

While the offerings change each season, Land's End designs have tended toward the simple, with no cartoons or appliqués to clutter up the basic look. Another bonus: Lands' End web site has fantastic overstock deals, posted twice weekly. **Rating: A**

Laura Ashley *This is a licensed line of Sumersault. See their review later in this section.*

Little Bedding *See Crown Crafts.*

Luv Stuff *Call (903) 450-1300 for a dealer near you. Web: luvstuff-baby.com.* Texas-based Luv Stuff's claim to fame is their unique, hand-trimmed wall hangings, which match their custom bedding. You can mix and match to your heart's content (all items are sold a la carte). The quality is high: the company's exclusive fabrics are mostly 100% cotton with high-thread count, plus all their collections are made in-house in Texas. As you might expect, however, all this quality isn't free—a four-piece ensemble (sheet, comforter, bumper, dust ruffle) runs $550 to $750. And Luv Stuff's bumpers aren't very consumer friendly—they are surface clean (with a mild detergent) or dry-clean only. Despite this, we liked the brand's unique and bold styles. This bedding is a tour de force of color and contrast. ***Rating: B***

Maddie Boo *Web: maddieboobedding.com.* You can just imagine seeing Maddie Boo baby bedding in an *Architectural Digest* spread. And we will give this line bonus points for sophistication—some of their designs would look great on adult beds! Of course, you'll be paying *Architectural Digest* prices. Four-piece sets run $600 to $800.

Made in Houston, Texas, the sets are 100% cotton with high thread counts, and the accent fabrics include silk and linen. Ties are both top and bottom and sheets have all around elastic.

Surprisingly, Maddie Boo bedding can be found on sites as diverse as Amazon.com, BabyUniverse.com, and tiny specialty sites and stores. That doesn't mean you'll be able to find it at a discount, however, but the wide distribution is a nice surprise. Quality of the samples we viewed was high; but the prices drag down their over-all rating. ***Rating: B***

Mr. Bobbles Blankets *Web: MrBobblesBlankets.com.* We love the Graco Pak N Play and other playpens for their convenience . . . with one exception: those darn cheap sheets! Active babies easily pull off the sheets that come with most playpens and the thin, low-thread count cotton makes them a cold place for baby during winter months. To the rescue comes Mr. Bobbles Blankets, which besides its namesake blankets, also makes a No-Slip Play Yard Sheet for $19. We had a reader give this product a test-run and the verdict was positive. Made of 100% cotton flannel, the "very soft" sheets come in "cute fabrics" and "held up well after several washings," said our reviewer. And true to its claims, the sheet does not slip off the mattress—it is designed like a pillow sham so it doesn't easily pull off the corners. FYI: Another no-slip playpen sheet our readers like is by Kushies, the brand better known for their cloth diapers. Kushies' fitted flannel playpen sheet is $8. ***Rating: A***

My Baby Sam *Web: MyBabySam.com.* This bedding line is an off-shoot of a baby gift dot-com (NewArrivalsInc.com) and is widely available, both in specialty stores and online at sites like Target.com, BabiesRUs.com and even WalMart.com. The latter site sells a three-piece set for $140, a good value for an all-cotton set (bumpers have ties on the top and bottom). But . . . we noticed the set is cold-water wash only, which is not a good sign when it comes to shrinkage.

My Baby Sam's specialty store offerings are more elaborate than the denim and floral looks you see in discount stores and start at around $170 for a four-piece set. At this point, we haven't received any parent feedback on My Baby Sam. So, we'll take a wait and see approach on their rating. **Rating: Not Yet.**

NauticaKids *See Crown Craft*

Nava's Designs *For a dealer near you, call (818) 988-9050. Web: navasdesigns.com.* Okay, Warren Buffet is your uncle . . . and he wants to give you a gift of baby bedding. Who you gonna call? Try Nava's, the most over-the-top bedding on the market today. The fabrics in this line are simply amazing—damask, silk dupioni, matte lasse and so on. Owner Nava Shoham has been designing nurseries since 1986 and her credits include numerous celebrities such as (and we are not making this up) Slash's nursery. Yes, Slash from Guns N Roses. Fill in your own joke here. So, how much does this cost? Are you sitting down? Nava's bedding runs $800 to $1100 for a set. And, yes, some of the fabrics have to be dry-cleaned. But seriously, we dare you to find more sumptuous bedding on the market. We're impressed with Nava. . . making it over 20 years in this biz by selling these linens at these prices, well, that's an achievement in its own right. **Rating: B**

NoJo *See Crown Craft.*

N. Selby Designs *See Cotton Tale.*

Nurseryworks *For a dealer near you, call (626)676-6287; web: NurseryWorks.net.* Modern crib maker Nurseryworks has a matching bedding line that features nine sets of 100% cotton bedding. Price are $300 to $400 for a six-piece set—pricey, yes, but not as high as some modernist bedding makers. Nurseryworks' design inspiration is the "use of uncommon visual vocabularies derived from common objects, nature and everyday things." Translation: interesting graphics of flowers, macaroni and, oddly, sugar cubes. Bumpers have top and bottom ties and sheets have elastic all around. Quality of this bedding is above average. **Rating: B+**

OshKosh B'Gosh *See CoCaLo.*

Patchkraft *This crib brand is reviewed on our free web site, www.BabyBargains.com (click on Bonus Material).*

Picci *Imported by Inglesina. Web: picci.com.* And now for something completely different. Stroller maker Inglesina's U.S. distributor decided to bring Italian bedding maker Picci to the U.S. after sensing there was a niche for high-end bedding made in Europe. And that points up an oddity of the baby market here: many European-made products are a big hit here (Baby Bjorn, Perego strollers), but bedding is not among them. Why? Part of the blame is that what sells well in Europe for nurseries (garish colors, frilly treatments like canopies) just doesn't translate well across the Atlantic. To solve that dilemma, Picci researched American design sensibilities and went with a more toned down look. The result is impressive. In a market stuffed with cheaply made imports from Asia, Picci actually pulls off a tasteful line with a high-end feel. The only caveat is the prices: $280 to $400 for a set. Some of the silk, velvet and embroidered groups can top $900. But we give Picci bonus points for creativity and quality. ***Rating: B+***

Pine Creek *Call (503) 266-6275 for a dealer near you. Web: pinecreekbedding.com.* Oregon-based Pine Creek Bedding has come back to their signature look with more flannel options, while offering sets with a new vintage feel. Look for old-fashioned graphics and soft colors. All the fabrics are 100% cotton. Considering the quality, we thought Pine Creek's prices were pricey at $280 to $450 for a four-piece set. Pine Creek also sells accessories like lampshades and curtain valances, plus fabric is available by the yard. ***Rating: A-***

Pitter Patter *For a dealer near you, call 505-751-9067 Web: pitterpattercollections.com.* Taos, New Mexico-based Pitter Patter has a unique take on baby bedding. Independent artists design their Hawaiian themed nursery linens, so many of the patterns and designs are one-of-a-kind. We loved the embroidered accents and playful prints. And yes, you can get a fabric-covered surfboard as an accessory. Quality is high, but the price is as well–this might be a suggestion for grandma to buy. A four-piece set runs $520 to $600 and features all cotton and some linen-cotton blends. And Pitter Patter offers one of the few (only?) crib bedding collections made from hemp, which some eco-parents laud for its environmentally friendly and hypoallergenic qualities. The hemp sets are $700, so you may need to whip out the Sierra Club American Express Platinum to pay for that. All in all, we liked Pitter Patter. It's refreshing to see a newcomer like Pitter Patter offer a different twist on baby bedding. ***Rating: B+***

Pooh *Classic Pooh/Disney Pooh bedding are made by Crown Craft.*

Pottery Barn Kids *Call (800) 430-7373 for a catalog or to place an order. Web: potterybarnkids.com.* No catalog has shaken up the baby bedding and décor business in recent years like the Pottery Barn Kids (PBK) catalog. Their cheerful baby bedding, whimsical accessories and furniture blew past competitors. PBK isn't cutesy-babyish or overly adult. It's playful, fun and bright. And hot. We get more questions about this catalog than any other.

So let's answer a few of those questions. PBK's bedding is 100% cotton, 200-thread count. The sheets have 10" corner pockets . . . and they *used* to have elastic that went all the way around the edge. We're disappointed to say that they now only make their crib sheets with elastic on the ends. And that elastic is the source of frustration among some parents we talked to—one PBK customer said she had to exchange several sheets after the elastic popped off or simply wore out after only one washing.

Several readers have also complained about the bumpers, which are knocked as "thin and insubstantial." One reader wrote saying "they are very thin and my child can get his arms and legs out of the slats of the crib because the bumpers smush down so easily!" Another reader complained that the ties kept pulling off her bumper. On the plus side, recent parent feedback has consistently praised the softness of PBK sheets. Their "chamois" sheets ($29; polyester fleece) have also come in for great praise. Moms say PBK's fleece sheets stay softer than Fleece Baby's sheets.

Prices for quilts range from $70 to $90, bumper sets are $70 to $80, sheets are $14 to $16 and dust ruffles are about $60. While the prices are affordable, the nagging quality issues give us pause in recommending PBK's crib bedding. On the plus side, frequent sales make more expensive items like lamps and rugs even more affordable. The best deal: PBK's outlet stores. One reader saw sheets on sale for $8, duvet covers for $15 and even a crib for $175 at the outlet (see earlier in the chapter for locations). What really seems to be PBK's strong suit is accessories. The catalog is stuffed with so many rugs, lamps, storage options and toys, you can shop one place for a complete look.

So, it is a mixed bag for PBK: kudos to this retailer for shaking up the staid baby bedding biz. But poor quality gives us pause in recommending this brand, unless you get an unbelievable deal at their outlet store. ***Rating: C+***

Precious Moments *See Crown Craft*

Quiltex *For a dealer near you, call (800) 237-3636 or (212) 594-2205. Web: quiltex.com.* Quiltex is famous for their licensed bedding items, including Hello Kitty, Precious Moments and Thomas the Tank Engine. Style-wise, we'd put Quiltex into the "cutesy, baby-ish" category—the groupings are heavy on the pastel colors and frilly ruffles. Unfortunately, most of the line is blends (50/50 cotton-poly fabric). The quality of the Quiltex designs is middle-of-the-road: some appliqué work leaves a bit to be desired, while other designs are merely stamped on the fabric. Their prices ($60 to $150 for a three-piece set) are a bit more reasonable. **Rating: C-**

Red Calliope *See Crown Craft.*

Sesame Street *See Crown Craft*

Sleeping Partners *Call (212) 254-1515 for a dealer near you. Web: sleepingpartners.com.* Sleeping Partners' mojo is embroidered bedding sets—their simple animal-theme designs echo that of Wendy Bellissimo . . . nice but pricey. How pricey? We noticed a simple five-piece set was $225 to $500 online (Sleeping Partners is sold on sites like BabyUniverse.com and in some stores like Buy Buy Baby). Good news though: their Tadpole Basics line sells at Target for as little as $120 to $150 for five pieces. Both lines are all cotton, 200 thread count with top and bottom ties and wash well, but beware: some of the higher priced bumpers are DRY CLEAN ONLY. Whoops! That just shot down their rating by an entire letter grade considering the price range here. **Rating: C+**

Springs *Web: springs.com.* Springs Industries sells five different bedding lines, including Wamsutta and Little Tikes. At the high end, the Wamsutta line has two options (one for boys, one for girls). With 230-thread count, 100% cotton sheets and elastic all around, Wamsutta offers decent quality for the dollar (around $200). Springs other bedding options are less impressive, however: the Little Tikes line features cheap-o poly/cotton blends (but prices are only $60 for set).

Springs is sold in discounters like Wal-Mart. With the exception of the Wamsutta line, we found the overall quality disappointing. **Rating C-**

Sumersault *Call (800) 232-3006 or (201) 768-7890 for a dealer near you. Web: sumersault.com.* Owner Patti Sumergrade has an eye for beautiful fabrics which she turns into pleasing designs in her

Sumersault bedding collection. We loved the plaids and whimsical fabrics, all done with a sophisticated spin. Compared to other lines, Sumersault leaves most of the cutesy touches to optional wall hangings. A four-piece set retails for $150 to $330. FYI: Sumersault also makes the Laura Ashley Mother and Child bedding collection, which sells for $220 to $400 for four pieces. We like the touches of embroidery and a few mixed-texture sets, which were winners design-wise. This year they've added ties top and bottom to their bumpers. Overall, the quality of Sumersault is excellent. ***Rating: A***

Sweet Kyla *Call 800-265-2229 for a dealer near you. Web: sweetkyla.com.* Canadian bedding maker Sweet Kyla has popped up stateside in USA Baby Stores among other outlets. We liked their take on crib bedding, which often uses mixed textures (a touch of faux suede, for example) and patchwork motifs. Most fabrics are all-cotton and customer service and delivery is excellent. Readers who have purchased this line have been impressed with the quality (bumper ties top and bottom, elastic all around sheets, pre-shrunk 100% cotton). Sets are around $220 to $330 or you can order pieces a la carte. You can also buy their fabric by the yard. One parent who bought this brand for her son's nursery raved about their excellent fabric, saying the sheets in particular were "very soft and cozy." ***Rating: A-***

Sweet Pea *Call (626) 578-0866 for a dealer near you.* You gotta like Sweet Pea . . . their fun and funky fabrics are imported from places like the Vatican (which we didn't realize exported anything other than Popes). Sweet Pea's 100% cotton knit bedding features a variety of very-adult finishes including jacquards, satins and even crushed velvets (accent fabrics may be blends). New this year are different heights of bumper pads. Prices range from $279 to $495 for a four-piece set although Sweet Pea sells everything a la carte. For example a single sheet will cost you $30. We found it difficult to find this brand online so you'll have to search for it in specialty baby stores. ***Rating: B***

Tadpole *See Sleeping Partners.*

Target *Web: target.com.* Target not only sells bedding lines like Amy Coe, Tadpole (by Sleeping Partners) and Tiddliwinks (by Kids Line), they even have their own in-house line of basics called Circo. But Circo gets mixed reviews from our readers. They tell us they love the prices—$63 for a three-piece set—and the cute prints, but the quality is a mixed bag. Yes, it is all-cotton and the sheets feature elastic all around, but some complain of shrinkage and thin thread counts. Our advice: buy a sheet or two to test before investing much in this brand. ***Rating: B***

Tiddliwinks *See Kids Line.*

Trend Lab Baby *Web: trend-lab.com.* Trend Lab may sound more like a chemical beaker maker than a bedding designer, but this brand is a hit in the under-$150 crib bedding market. Sold on Target.com, Wal-Mart and other discounters, Trend Lab offers (mostly) 100% cotton bedding in the $50 to $150 range for a four-piece set. You'll see design elements like textured fabric (waffle weave and knit jersey, for example) as well as attractive embroidery and appliqué. The look is reminiscent of Wendy Bellissimo. And parents love their sheets. As one parent noted on our web site: "the crib sheets from Trend Lab are big enough to fit the mattress perfectly . . . and the quality is high." The downside: some items may shrink (note the cold-water washing instructions), bumper ties are only on the top and a few items are poly-cotton blends. But for the price, parents tell us Trend Lab is a decent value. ***Rating: B***

Wal-Mart *Web: Walmart.com.* Wal-Mart has been busy expanding it online baby bedding offerings, including several brands like Trend Lab and My Baby Sam (which are reviewed separately above).

George is Wal-Mart's in-house brand. Quality is rather impressive—100% cotton and 200-thread count sheets on a four-piece set we inspected. And the cost? A mere $80. The bumpers do have top and bottom ties. Since George is relatively new, we haven't received much parent feedback yet. But given our hands-on inspection, we'd give the line a thumbs-up. ***Rating: A-***

Wamsutta *See Springs.*

Waverly *See Crown Crafts.*

Wendy Bellissimo Baby N Kids *Call (818) 348-3682 for a dealer near you. Web: wendybellissimo.com.* Hotshot young designer Wendy Bellissimo hawked her pricey bedding at specialty boutiques until 2004, when she abruptly shifted gears to partner with Babies R Us. Now a BRU exclusive, Bellissimo has expanded her horizons beyond bedding to include all sorts of décor accessories, diaper bags, mobiles and more. As for the bedding, the designs look much the same as before: the typical Bellissimo look is a simple block pattern with a touch of embroidery or chenille. But the prices! $250 to $300 for a five-piece set that's sewn in China? While we thought the look was a notch above what is normally sold at BRU, we were unimpressed with the quality of the crib sheet, which seemed thin and low in thread count. And the reviews for this bedding have been similarly mixed to downright hostile (several folks knocked the bedding for low quality). Take your $300 and buy a better quality bedding set from any of the above-mentioned designers. **Rating: C-**

The Bottom Line: A Wrap-Up of Our Best Buy Picks

For bedding, we think Cotton Tale and Amy Coe (at Target) combine good quality at a low price. If you can afford to spend more, check out the offerings from Picci, Sumersault, and California Kids. And if money is no object, try Nava's.

Of course, there's no law that says you have to buy an entire bedding set for your nursery—we found that all baby really needs is a set of sheets and a good cotton blanket. Catalogs/web sites like Lands End and Baby Gap sell affordable (yet high-quality) basics like sheets ($35 for two) and blankets ($15). Instead of spending $300 to $500 on bedding sets with ridiculous items like pillows and diaper stackers, use creative solutions (like wall decals) to decorate the nursery affordably and leave the crib simple.

And if you fall in love with a licensed cartoon character like Pooh, don't shell out $300 on a fancy bedding set. Instead, we recommend buying solid color sheets and accessorizing with affordable Pooh items like lamps, posters, rugs, etc.

Who's got the best deals on bedding? Web sites like BabyCatalog.com, BabyUniverse.com, and Overstock.com have the best bargains. If you're lucky to be near a manufacturer's outlet, search these stores for discontinued patterns.

Let's take a look at the savings:

Lands End or Baby Gap cotton fitted sheets (two)	$34
Fleece coverlet blanket (Company Kids) or sleep sack	$20
Miscellaneous (lamp, other decor)	$100
TOTAL	**$154**

In contrast, if you go for a designer brand and buy all those silly extras like diaper stackers, you could be out as much as $800 on bedding alone—add in wall paper, accessories like wall hangings,

Continued on page 162

BEDDING RATINGS

Name	Rating	Cost
Amy Coe	A-/B+	$ to $$$
Baby Gap	A-	$$
Banana Fish	B	$$
Beautiful Baby	B	$$$
Blue Moon Baby	B-	$$$
Brandee Danielle	C	$ to $$
California Kids	A	$$
Carousel	A	$ to $$
Celebrations	B+	$$ to $$$
CoCaLo	B+	$ to $$
Company Kids	B	$
Cotton Tale	A	$$ to $$$
Crown Crafts	C+	$ to $$
Dwell	B+	$$$
Gerber	D	$
Glenna Jean	B+	$ to $$
Hoohobbers	B+	$$
Jessica McClintock	Not yet	$$
Kids Line	B	$ to $$
Kimberly Grant	A-	$$
Koala Baby	D+	$
Lambs & Ivy	B+	$ to $$
Land of Nod	A-	$$
Lands End	A	$
Luv Stuff	B	$$$
Maddie Boo	B	$$$
Nava's Designs	B	$$$
Nurseryworks	B+	$$
Picci	B+	$$ to $$$
Pine Creek	A-	$$ to $$$
Pitter Patter	B+	$$$
Pottery Barn	C+	$$
Quiltex	C-	$
Sleeping partners	C+	$ to $$$
Sumersault	A	$ to $$
Sweet Kyla	A-	$$
Sweet Pea	B	$$ to $$$
Target (Circo)	B	$
Trend Lab	B	$
Wendy Bellissimo	C-	$$

Key *See next page*

A quick look at some top crib bedding brands:

Fiber Content	Bumper Ties	Tie Length
100% COTTON	TOP/BOTTOM	10"
100% COTTON	TOP/BOTTOM	*
100% COTTON	TOP	6"
100% COTTON	TOP/BOTTOM	8"
100% COTTON	TOP/BOTTOM	*
MIX	TOP/BOTTOM	7"
100% COTTON	TOP/BOTTOM	10"
100% COTTON	TOP/BOTTOM	*
100% COTTON	TOP/BOTTOM	9"
MIX	TOP/BOTTOM	6.5"
100% COTTON	TOP/BOTTOM	*
100% COTTON	TOP/BOTTOM	7.5"
MIX	VARIES	8"
100% COTTON	TOP/BOTTOM	*
POLY/COTTON	*	*
MIX	** (SEE KEY)	10"
100% COTTON	TOP/BOTTOM	6"
100% COTTON	TOP/BOTTOM	*
MIX	TOP/BOTTOM	7" TO 9"
100% COTTON	TOP/BOTTOM	6.5"
100% COTTON	TOP	*
POLY/COTTON	TOP	10"
100% COTTON	TOP/BOTTOM	
100% COTTON	TOP/BOTTOM	*
100% COTTON	TOP	11"
100% COTTON	TOP/BOTTOM	*
100% COTTON	TOP/BOTTOM	14"
100% COTTON	TOP/BOTTOM	*
100% COTTON	TOP/BOTTOM	*
100% COTTON	TOP/BOTTOM	8"
100% COTTON	TOP/BOTTOM	*
100% COTTON	TOP/BOTTOM	*
POLY/COTTON	TOP	7"
100% COTTON	TOP/BOTTOM	10"
100% COTTON	TOP	7"-9"
100% COTTON	TOP/BOTTOM	9.5"
100% COTTON	TOP/BOTTOM	10"
100% COTTON	TOP	*
MIX	TOP	*
100% COTTON	TOP/BOTTOM	*

KEY

* N/A. In some cases, we didn't have this information by press time.
** Glenna Jean has bumpers with top and bottom ties only on the corners; the center section has top ties only.
Cost: Cost of a four-piece set (comforter, sheet, dust ruffle/bed skirt, bumpers) $=under $200; $$=$200 to $400; $$$=over $400
Fiber Content: Some lines have both all-cotton and poly/cotton blends—these are noted with the word "Mix."
Bumper Ties: refers to the location of bumper ties, top and bottom or top only.
Tie Lengths: the length of the bumper ties; these are approximate esti-

matching lamps and you'll be out $1100 or more. So, the total savings from following the tips in this chapter could be as much as $900 to $1000.

Now that your baby's room is outfitted, what about the baby? Flip to the next chapter to get the lowdown on those little clothes.

CHAPTER 4

The Reality Layette:
Little Clothes for Little Prices

Inside this chapter

W hat the heck is a "Onesie"? How many clothes does your baby need? How come such little clothes have such big price tags? These and other mysteries are unraveled in this chapter as we take you on a guided tour of baby clothes land. We'll reveal our secret sources for finding name brand clothes at one-half to one-third off department store prices. Which brands are best? Check out our picks for the best baby clothing brands and our nine tips from smart shoppers on getting the best deals. Next, read about the many outlets for children's apparel that have been popping up all over the country. At the end of this chapter, we'll even show you how to save big bucks on diapers.

When Do You Need This Stuff?

◆ **Baby Clothing.** You'll need basic baby clothing like t-shirts and sleepers as soon as you're ready to leave the hospital. Depending on the weather, you may need a bunting (a snug-fitting, hooded sleeping bag of heavy material) at that time as well.

You'll probably want to start stocking up on baby clothing around the seventh month of your pregnancy—if you deliver early, you will need some basics. However, you may want to wait to do major shopping until after any baby showers to see what clothing your friends and family give as gifts.

Be sure to keep a running list of your acquisitions so you won't buy too much of one item. Thanks to gifts and our own buying, we had about two thousand teeny, side-snap shirts by the time our baby was born. In the end, our son didn't wear the shirts much (he grew out of the newborn sizes quickly and wasn't really wild about them anyway), and we ended up wasting the money we spent.

◆ **Diapers.** How many diapers do you need for starters? Are you sitting down? If you're going with disposables, we recommend 600 diapers for the first six weeks (about 14 diapers a day). Yes, that's six packages of 100 diapers each (purchase them in your eighth month of pregnancy, just in case Junior arrives early). You may think this is a lot, but believe us, we bought that much and we still had to do another diaper run by the time our son was a month old. Newborns go through many more diapers than older infants because they feed more frequently. Also, remember that as a new parent, you'll find yourself taking off diapers that turn out to be dry. Or worse, you may change a diaper three times in a row because Junior wasn't really finished.

Now that you know how many diapers you need for the first six weeks, what sizes should you buy? We recommend 100 newborn-size diapers and 500 "size one" (or Step 1) diapers. This assumes an average-size baby (about seven pounds at birth). But remember to keep the receipts—if your baby is larger, you might have to exchange the newborns for size one's (and some of the one's for two's). Note for parents-to-be of multiples: your babies tend to be smaller at birth, so buy all newborn diapers to start. And double or triple our recommended quantity!

If you plan to use a diaper service to supply cloth diapers, sign up in your eighth month. Some diaper services will give you an initial batch of diapers (so you're ready when baby arrives) and then await your call to start up regular service. If you plan to wash your own cloth diapers, buy two to five dozen diapers about two months before your due date. You'll also probably want to buy diaper covers (6 to 10) at that time. We'll discuss cloth diapers in depth later in this chapter.

Even if you plan to use disposable diapers, you should pick up one package of high-quality cloth diapers. Why? You'll need them as spit-up rags, spot cleaners and other assorted uses you'd never imagined before becoming a parent.

Sources

There are ten basic sources for baby clothing and diapers:

I **BABY SPECIALTY STORES.** Specialty stores typically carry 100% cotton, high-quality clothes, but you won't usually find them affordably priced. While you may find attractive dressy clothes, play clothes are typically a better deal elsewhere. Because the stores themselves are frequently small, selection is limited. On the upside, you can still find old-fashioned service at specialty stores—and that's helpful when buying items like shoes. In that case, the extra help with sizing may be worth the higher price.

As for diapers, you can forget about it—most specialty baby stores long ago ceded the diaper market to discounters and grocery stores (who sell disposables), as well as mail-order/online companies (who dominate the cloth diaper and supply business). Occasionally, we see specialty stores carry an offbeat product like Tushies, an eco-friendly disposable diaper. And some may have diaper covers, but the selection is typically limited.

2 **DEPARTMENT STORES.** Clothing is a department store's bread and butter, so it's not surprising to see many of these stores excel at merchandising baby clothes. Everyone from Sears to Nordstrom sells baby clothes and frequent sales often make the selection more affordable.

3 **SPECIALTY CHAINS.** Our readers love Old Navy (see money-saving tips section) and Gap Kids. Both sell 100% cotton, high-quality clothes that are stylish and durable. Not to mention their price adjustment policies— if you buy an item at Gap/Old Navy and it goes on sale within seven days, you get the new price. Old Navy's selection of baby clothes is somewhat limited compared to Gap Kids. Other chains to check out include Gymboree, and Talbots for Kids. All are reviewed later in this chapter.

4 **DISCOUNTERS.** Wal-Mart, Target and K-Mart have moved aggressively into baby clothes in the last decade. Instead of cheap, polyester outfits that were once common at these stores, most discounters now emphasize 100% cotton clothing in fashionable styles. Even places like Toys R Us now stock basic layette items like t-shirts, sleepers and booties.

Target has vastly expanded their baby clothes with their in-store brand, Cherokee. Not only have they expanded, but also the quality is terrific in most cases. We shop Target for all cotton play clothes and day care clothes. They seem to last pretty well with the active play our kids indulge in.

Diapers are another discounter strong suit—you'll find both name brand and generic disposables at most stores; some even carry a selection of cloth diaper supplies like diaper covers (although they are the cheaper brands; see the diaper section later in this book for more details). Discounters seem to be locked into an endless price battle with warehouse clubs on baby items, so you can usually find deals.

5 **BABY SUPERSTORES.** Both Babies R Us and Baby Depot carry a decent selection of name-brand clothing at low prices. Most of the selection focuses on basics, however. You'll see more Carter's and Little Me than the fancy brands common at department stores. Over the years, Babies R Us has tried to upgrade their clothing options with a bit of embroidery here or an embellishment there. They've added sporty lines too like Nike track suits and more.

Diapers are a mixed bag at superstores. Babies R Us carries them, but Baby Depot doesn't. When you find them, though, the prices are comparable to discounters. We've seen diapers priced 20% to 30% lower at Babies R Us than grocery stores.

6 **WAREHOUSE CLUBS.** Members-only warehouse clubs like Sam's, Costco and BJ's sell diapers at rock-bottom prices. The selection is often hit-or-miss—sometimes you'll see brand names like Huggies and Pampers; other times it is an in-house brand. While you won't find the range of sizes that you'd see in grocery stores, the prices will be hard to beat. The downside? You have to buy them in "bulk," huge cases of multiple diaper packs that might require a forklift to get home.

Checkout their infant and toddler clothing as well. We'll talk later about some of the bargains we've found.

7 **WEB/MAIL-ORDER.** There are a zillion catalogs and web sites that offer clothing for infants. The choices can be quite overwhelming, and the prices can range from reasonable to ridiculous (don't worry, we'll give you the best bets). It's undeniably a great way to shop when you have a newborn and just don't want to drag your baby out to the mall. Another web strength: cloth diapers and related supplies. Chains and specialty stores have abandoned these items, so mail order suppliers have picked up the slack. Check out "Do it By Mail" later in this chapter for the complete lowdown on catalogs that sell clothing. Cloth diaper web sites are later in the diaper section of the chapter.

8 **CONSIGNMENT OR THRIFT STORES.** You might think of these stores as dingy shops with musty smells—purveyors of old, used clothes that aren't in great shape. Think again—many consignment stores today are bright and attractive, with name brand clothes at a fraction of the retail price. Yes, the clothes have been worn before, but most stores only stock high-quality brands that are in excellent condition. And stores that specialize in children's apparel are popping up everywhere, from coast to coast. Later in this chapter, we'll tell you how to find a consignment store near you.

9 **GARAGE/YARD SALES.** Check out the box on the next page for tips on how to shop garage sales like the pros.

Baby Clothing

So you thought all the big-ticket items were taken care of when you bought the crib and other furniture? Ha! It's time to prepare for your baby's "layette," a French word that translated literally means "spending large sums of cash on baby clothes and other such items, as required by Federal Baby Law." But, of course, there are some creative (dare we say, sneaky?) ways of keeping your layette bills down.

At this point, you may be wondering just what does your baby need? Sure you've seen those cute ruffled dresses and sailor suits in department stores—but what does your baby *really* wear everyday?

Meet the layette, a collection of clothes and accessories that your baby will use daily. While your baby's birthday suit was free, out-fitting him in something more "traditional" will cost some bucks. In fact, a recent study estimated that parents spend $12,000 on clothes for a child by the time he or she hits 18 years of age—and that sounds like a conservative estimate to us. That translates into a $20 *billion* (yes, that's billion with a B) business for children's clothing retailers. Follow our tips, and we estimate that you'll save 20% or more on your baby's wardrobe.

CPSC Issues Thrift Shop Warning

Do second-hand stores sell dangerous goods? To answer that question, the Consumer Product Safety Commission randomly surveyed 301 thrift stores a few years ago, looking for recalled or banned products like clothing with drawstrings (an entanglement and strangulation hazard). The results: 51% of stores were selling clothing (mostly outerwear) with drawstrings at the waist or neck. This is particularly disturbing since 22 deaths and 48 non-fatal accidents since 1985 have been attributed to drawstrings. If you buy clothing at a consignment or thrift store or from a garage sale, be sure to avoid clothes with drawstrings. Another disturbing finding: about two-thirds of the stores surveyed had at least one recalled or banned product on the shelves.

Parents in Cyberspace: What's on the Web?

Ella Bella Kids

Web: ellabellakids.com

What it is: Domestic and European baby clothing.

What's cool: Organized by brand, size and other helpful categories, this site is easy to navigate. They carry brands from Kitestrings, Sweet Potatoes, Mulberribush and more. Although prices can be quite high, the clothes are excellent quality and they offer up to 50% off sale items. Free shipping on orders over $99 is another plus.

Garage & Yard Sales
Eight Tips to Get The Best Bargains

It's an American institution—the garage sale.

Sure you can save money on baby clothes and products at an outlet store or get a deal at a department store sale. But there's no comparing to the steals you can get at your neighbor's garage sale.

We love getting email from readers who've found great deals at garage sales. How about 25¢¢ stretchies, a snowsuit for $1, barely used high chairs for $5? But getting the most out of garage sales requires some pre-planning. We interviewed a dozen parents who are garage sale experts for their tips:

1 **CHECK THE NEWSPAPER FIRST.** Many folks advertise their garage sales a few days before the event—zero in on the ads that mention kids/baby items to keep from wasting time on sales that won't be fruitful.

2 **GET A GOOD MAP OF THE AREA.** You've got to find obscure cul-de-sacs and hidden side streets.

3 **START EARLY.** The professional bargain hunters get going at the crack of dawn. If you wait until mid-day, all the good stuff will be gone. An even better bet: if you know the family, ask if you can drop by the day before the sale. That way you have a first shot before the competition arrives. One trick: if it's a neighbor, offer to help set-up for the sale. That's a great way to get those "early bird" deals.

4 **DO THE "BOX DIVE."** Many garage sale hosts will just dump kids clothes into a big box, all jumbled together in different sizes, styles, etc. Figuring out how to get the best picks while three

Needs work: Well, they're darned expensive. But if you're looking for items you saw in magazines like Baby Talk, check them out.

Patsy Aiken

Web: patsyaiken.com or chezami.com
What it is: The only source now for this well-liked brand.
What's cool: We've always loved Patsy Aiken's clothes, but their distribution used to be limited to fancy baby boutiques. The good news: their site now sells the entire collection online. The US-made clothes are all 100% cotton with amazing embroidery and appliqué. You'll find beautiful bright colors with fun accents. They've cut out a lot of the super dressy designs and seem to be

---

other moms are digging through the same box is a challenge. The best advice: familiarize yourself with the better name brands in this chapter and then pluck out the best bets as fast as possible. Then evaluate the clothes away from the melee.

5 CONCENTRATE ON "FAMILY AREAS." A mom here in Colorado told us she found garage sales in Boulder (a college town) were mostly students getting rid of stereos, clothes and other junk. A better bet was nearby Louisville, a suburban bedroom community with lots of growing families.

6 HAGGLE. Prices on big-ticket items (that is, anything over $5) are usually negotiable. Another great tip we read in the newsletter *Cheapskate Monthly*—to test out products, carry a few "C" and "D" batteries with you to garage sales. Most swings and bouncer seats use those type batteries, so you want to make sure they're working before you buy.

7 DON'T BUY A USED CRIB OR CAR SEAT. Old cribs may not meet current safety standards. It's also difficult to get replacement parts for obscure brands. Car seats are also a second-hand no-no—you can't be sure it wasn't in an accident, weakening its safety and effectiveness. And watch out for clothing with drawstrings, loose buttons or other safety hazards.

8 BE CREATIVE. See a great stroller but the fabric is dirty? And non-removable so you can't throw it in the washing machine? Take a cue from one dad we interviewed. He takes dirty second-hand strollers or high chairs to a car wash and blasts them with a high-pressure hose! Voila! Clean and useable items are the result. For a small investment, you can rehabilitate a dingy stroller into a showpiece.

concentrating on casual clothes. Prices average around $30 to $40 for the typical dress or overall. Not cheap but the quality is terrific. This is a great site for grandmas looking for a cute shower gift.

Since they've decided to discontinue selling their line in stores, they've added a new method of buying their designs. Called Chez Ami, it's a take off on the old Tupperware parties. You get a group of your friends together and have a Patsy Aiken clothing party. Check out the web site for more details.

Needs work: Patsy Aiken has upgraded their site so it's easier to use, but it seems like there are fewer infant sized clothes now.

One of a Kind Kid

Web: oneofakindkid.com, see Figure 1 on the next page.

What it is: Web site with extensive selection of high-quality kids clothes.

What's cool: This site specializes in the upper-end clothes you see in Nordstrom and Neiman Marcus. We saw brands like Hartstrings, Skivvydoodles and Funtasia among others. One of a Kind Kids has a great "sales rack" with clothes up to 70% off. New items appear weekly so check back frequently.

Needs work: Unfortunately, the site notes that many of the items on their site are "one of a kind." This means if you see something you like, you may have to order it on the spot. While the thumbnails of the clothes are expandable, their tiny size makes it hard to get a quick read on what's available.

◆ **Other great sites. Preemie.com** (preemie.com) is a wonderful oasis for parents of preemies. You'll find items like hospital shirts, basics, sleepwear, caps and booties and diapers. Not to mention, they have a selection of diaries and books as well as calendars. If you've got a preemie, this is the site for you.

Kid Surplus (kidsurplus.com) is another discounter/closeout store. They've expanded their layette to include Baby Zap, Lil' Jellybean and Kushies. We also saw sleep sacks and Goldbug socks and slippers. The site is a bit of a jumble and you'll have to scroll through lots of different stuff, but the prices are great.

A reader recommended **BargainChildrensClothing.com**, noting that it offers name brand kids clothes at 20 to 70% off. We checked it out and found clothes options from preemie sizes up to 16. Brands included Mulberribush, Tuti Fruiti and Bambolino.

We'd be remiss if we didn't also mention **eBay** (web: ebay.com) in this section. Their baby area is often stuffed with great deals on baby clothes. One tip: look for listings that say NWT—that's eBay-speak for "New With Tags." Obviously, these items are worth the most, yet often still sell for 50% off retail. Other eBay jargon to look

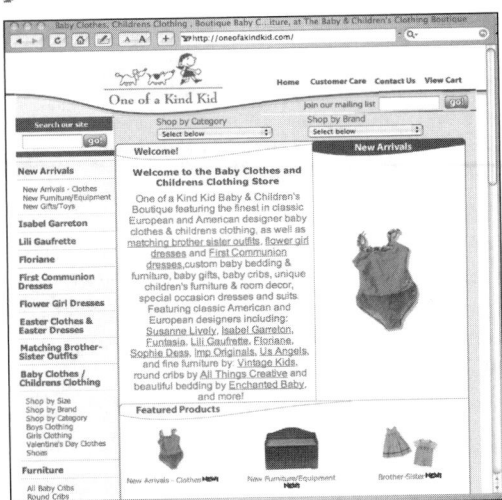

Figure 1: Great prices, high-quality brands and flat fee shipping make OneOfAKindKid.com a winner.

for: NWOT (new without tags), NIB (new in box) and EUC (excellent used condition). EBay has just about everything it comes to baby clothes, from basic items to luxury goods.

A bit of eBay strategy: one of our readers recommended shopping at an expensive baby boutique in town, noting the high-end brands and looking for them when you shop eBay. In fact, when looking on eBay for samples to show off on NBC's Today Show, we did just that. We located a snazzy, high end Geisswein jacket on eBay for only $122. The regular retail on the jackets is $225 in boutiques. (Of course, we'd never spend $100+ on a winter jacket for our child, but if you have to have that Geisswein look, eBay is da bomb).

 ## What Are You Buying?

Figuring out what your baby should wear is hardly intuitive to first-time parents. We had no earthly idea what types of (and how many) clothes a newborn needed, so we did what we normally do— we went to the bookstore to do research. We found three-dozen books on "childcare and parenting"—with three-dozen different lists of items that you *must* have for your baby and without which you're a very bad parent. Speaking of guilt, we also heard from relatives, who had their own opinions as to what was best for baby.

All of this begs the question: what do you *really* need? And how much? We learned that the answer to that last, age-old question was the age-old answer, "It depends." That's right, nobody really knows. In fact, we surveyed several department stores, interviewed dozens of parents, and consulted several "experts," only to find no consensus whatsoever. So, in order to better serve humanity, we have developed THE OFFICIAL FIELDS' LIST OF ALMOST EVERY ITEM YOU NEED FOR YOUR BABY IF YOU LIVE ON PLANET EARTH. We hope this clears up the confusion. (For those living on another planet, please consult our *Baby Bargains* edition for Mars and beyond).

Feel free to now ignore those lists of "suggested layette items" provided by retail stores. Many of the "suggestions" are self-serving, to say the least.

Of course, even when you decide what and how much to buy for your baby, you still need to know what *sizes* to buy. Fortunately, we have this covered, too. First, recognize that most baby clothes come in a range of sizes rather than one specific size ("newborn to 3 months" or "3-6 months"). *We recommend you buy "3-6 month" sizes (instead of newborn) so your child won't grow out of his clothes too quickly.* Stay away from newborn to three-month sizes unless you are having multiples.

If you have a premature baby or an infant who is on the small side (parents of multiples, take note), we have identified a couple of catalogs that specialize in preemie wear. And, if on the other hand, you deliver a 10-pounder, make sure you keep all receipts and labels so you can exchange the clothes for larger sizes—you may find you're into six-month sizes by the time your baby hits one month old! (Along the same lines, don't wash *all* those new baby clothes immediately. Wash just a few items for the initial few weeks. Keep all the other items in their original packaging to make returns easier).

Ever wonder how fast your baby will grow? Babies double their birth weight by five months . . . and triple it by one year! On average, babies grow ten inches in their first year of life. (Just an FYI: your child will average four inches in her second year, then three inches a year from ages 3 to 5 and two inches a year until puberty.) Given those stats, you can understand why we don't recommend stocking up on "newborn" size clothes.

Also: remember, you can always buy more later if you need them. In fact, this is a good way to make use of those close friends and relatives who stop by and offer to "help" right after you've suffered through 36 hours of hard labor—send them to the store!

We should point out that this layette list is just to get you started. This supply should last for the first month or two of your baby's life. Also along these lines, we received a question from a mom-to-be who wondered, given these quantities, how often do we assume you'll do laundry. The answer is in the next box.

The "Baby Bargains" Layette

One question we get frequently from expectant parents is "what makes a good quality outfit?" So before we tell you what makes up the baby's layette, let's talk quality.

First, you want clothing that doesn't shrink. Look at the washing instructions. "Cold water wash/low dryer setting" is your clue that this item has NOT been pre-shrunk. Also, do the instructions tell you to wash with "like colors?" This may be a clue that the color will run. Next check the detailing. Are the seams sewn straight? Are they reinforced, particularly on the diaper area?

Go online and check message boards for posts on different brands. On our boards (Babybargains.com), parents comment frequently on whether a brand shrinks, has plenty of diaper room, falls apart after a few washings, etc. Spend a little time online to get some intel on the best brands—and which ones to avoid.

Now, let's get to the list:

◆ **T-Shirts.** Oh sure, a t-shirt is a t-shirt, right? Not when it comes to baby t-shirts. These t-shirts could have side snaps, snaps at the crotch (also known as Onesies or creepers) or over-the-head openings. If you have a child who is allergic to metal snaps (they leave a red ring on their skin), you might want to consider

---

E-MAIL FROM THE REAL WORLD
How Much Laundry Will I Do?

Anna Balayn of Brooklyn, NY had a good question about baby's layette and laundry:

"You have a list of clothes a new baby needs, but you don't say how often I would need to do laundry if I go with the list. I work full time and would like to have enough for a week. Is the list too short for me?"

Our answer: there is no answer. Factors such as whether you use cloth or disposable diapers (cloth can leak more; hence more laundry) and how much your baby spits up will greatly determine the laundry load. Another factor: breast versus bottle-feeding. Bottle-fed babies have fewer poops (and hence, less laundry from possible leaks). An "average" laundry cycle with our layette list would be every two to three days, assuming breast feeding, disposable diapers and an average amount of spit-up.

over-the-head t-shirts.

(FYI: While some folks refer to Onesies as a generic item, the term Onesie is a trademarked clothing item from Gerber.)

By the way, is a Onesie t-shirt an outfit or an undergarment? Answer: it's both. In the summer, you'll find Onesies with printed patterns that are intended as outfits. In the winter, most stores just sell white Onesies, intended as undergarments.

HOW MANY? T-shirts usually come in packs of three. Our recommendation is to buy two packages of three (or a total of six shirts) of the side-snap variety. We also suggest buying two packs of over-the-head t-shirts. This way, if your baby does have an allergy to the snaps, you have a backup. Later you'll find the snap-at-the-crouch t-shirts to be most convenient since they don't ride up under clothes.

◆ **Gowns**. These are one-piece gowns with elastic at the bottom. They are used as sleeping garments in most cases. (We'll discuss more pros/cons of gowns later in this chapter.)

HOW MANY? This is a toss-up. If you want to experiment, go for one or two of these items. If they work well, you can always go back and get more later.

◆ **Sleepers**. This is the real workhorse of your infant's wardrobe, since babies usually sleep most of the day in the first months. Also known as stretchies, sleepers are most commonly used as pajamas for infants. They have feet, are often made of flame-retardant polyester, and snap up the front. As a side note, we've seen an increase in the numbers of cotton sleepers in recent years. Another related item: cotton long johns for baby. These are similar to sleepers, but don't have feet (and hence, may necessitate the use of socks in winter months).

One parent emailed us asking if she was supposed to dress her baby in pants, shirts, etc. or if it was OK to keep her daughter in sleepers all day long. She noted the baby was quite comfortable and happy. Of course, you can use sleepers exclusively for the first few months. We certainly did. As we've said all along, a comfortable baby is a happy parent!

HOW MANY? Because of their heavy use, we recommend parents buy at least four to eight sleepers.

◆ **Blanket Sleepers.** These are heavyweight, footed one-piece garments made of polyester. Used often in winter, blanket sleepers usually have a zipper down the front. In recent years, we've also seen quite a few fleece blanket sleepers, their key advantage being a softer fabric and a resistance to pilling.

HOW MANY? If you live in a cold climate or your baby is born in the winter, you may want to purchase two to four of these items. As an alternative to buying blanket sleepers, you could put a t-shirt on underneath a sleeper or stretchie for extra warmth.

Another option is a new product: the sleep sack. A couple manufacturers, Halo (halosleep.com) and Kiddopotamus (kiddopotamus.com) market these, which take the place of a blanket (in a sense, these are wearable blankets). Typically made of light-weight fleece, they are worn over t-shirts or light sleepers (see picture of the Halo at right).

Finally, swaddling has seen a resurgence in popularity. Most folks use a receiving blanket, but f you have trouble doing the "burrito wrap" with a blanket, you can try the Swaddleaze Startlefree Sleeper (www.2virtues.com). This $25 fleece sack has a swaddling wing that wraps around your baby and Velcros in the back. And we just had to mention the Cozy Cocoon baby bunting (cozyco-coon.com). What a simple and adorable concept. Basically a body sock made of organic cotton knit, this bunting simply rolls up over your baby. These would be especially cool for a preemie and are well priced at $24 each. These are also sold in the Acacia catalog (acaciacatalog.com).

 ◆ **Coveralls**. One-piece play outfits, coveralls (also known as rompers) are usually cotton or cotton/poly blends. Small sizes (under 6 months) may have feet, while larger sizes don't.

HOW MANY? Since these are really play clothes and small infants don't do a lot of playing, we recommend you only buy two to four coveralls for babies less than four months of age. However, if your child will be going into daycare at an early age, you may need to start with four to six coveralls.

 ◆ **Booties/socks**. These are necessary for outfits that don't have feet (like gowns and coveralls). As your child gets older (at about six months), look for the kind of socks that have rubber skids on the bottom (they keep baby from slipping when learning to walk).

HOW MANY? Three to four pairs are all you'll need at first, since baby will probably be dressed in footed sleepers most of the time.

◆ **Sweaters**. HOW MANY? Most parents will find one sweater is plenty (they're nice for holiday picture sessions). Avoid all-white sweaters for obvious reasons!

♦ **Hats**. Believe it or not, you'll still want a light cap for your baby in the early months of life, even if you live in a hot climate. Babies lose a large amount of heat from their heads, so protecting them with a cap or bonnet is a good idea. And don't expect to go out for a walk in the park without the baby's sun hat either.

HOW MANY? A couple of hats would be a good idea—sun hats in summer, warmer caps for winter. We like the safari-style hats best (they have flaps to protect the ears and neck).

♦ **Snowsuit/bunting.** Similar to the type of fabric used for blanket sleepers, buntings also have hoods and covers for the hands. Most buntings are like a sack and don't have leg openings, while snowsuits do. Both versions usually have zippered fronts.

FYI: Snowsuits and buntings should NOT be worn by infants when they ride in a car seat. Why? Thick fabric on these items can compress in an accident, compromising the infant's safety in the seat. So how can you keep your baby warm in an infant car seat? Check out Chapter 7 (Car Seats)—we'll discuss several car seat cover-ups/warmers that keep baby toasty without compromising the safety of the seat.

HOW MANY? Only buy one of these if you live in a climate where you need it. Even with a Colorado winter, we got away with layering clothes on our baby, then wrapping him in a blanket for the walk out to a warmed-up car. If you live in a city without a car, you might need two or three snowsuits for those stroller rides to the market.

♦ **Kimonos**. Just like the adult version. Some are zippered sacks with a hood and terry-cloth lining. You use them after a bath.

HOW MANY? Are you kidding? What a joke! These items are one of our "wastes of money." We recommend you pass on the kimonos and instead invest in good quality towels.

♦ **Saque Sets**. Two-piece outfits with a shirt and diaper cover.

HOW MANY? Forget buying these as well. We'll discuss later why saque sets are a waste of money.

♦ **Bibs**. These come in two versions, believe it or not. The little, tiny bibs are for the baby that occasionally drools. The larger versions are used when you begin feeding her solid foods (at about six months). Don't expect to be able to use the drool bibs later for feedings, unless you plan to change her carrot-stained outfit frequently.

HOW MANY? Skip the drool bibs (we'll discuss why later in this chapter under Wastes of Money). When baby starts eating solid foods, you'll need at least three or four large bibs. One option: plastic bibs for feeding so you can just sponge them off after a meal.

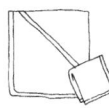

◆ **Washcloths and Hooded Towels**. OK, so these aren't actually clothes, but baby washcloths and hooded towels are a necessity. Why? Because they are small and easier to use . . . plus they're softer than adult towels and washcloths.

HOW MANY? At first, you'll probably need only three sets of towels and washcloths (you get one of each per set). But as baby gets older and dirtier, invest in a few more washcloths to spot clean during the day.

◆ **Receiving Blankets**. You'll need these small, cotton blankets for all kinds of uses: to swaddle the baby, as a play quilt, or even

---

Clothing: What you need, when

If you're new to this baby thing, you may be wondering how to pair the right clothing with your baby's developmental stage (if you're back for another round, think of this as a refresher). Here's a little primer for you on ages and stages.

◆ **0-3 months:** Newborns aren't even lifting their heads and they aren't able to do much besides eat, sleep and poop. Stick with sleepers, sleep sacks, and nightgowns for these guys. They don't need overalls or shirts and pants. Look for items sized by weight if possible since 0-3 month sizes can be all over the board.

◆ **3-6 months:** By the end of this stage your little one will be rolling over, sitting up and sleeping somewhat less. Still need those sleepers, but you're probably going to expand the wardrobe to include a few more play clothes. Two new items you will need now: bibs and socks. Depending on your baby's growth, you may find that you're buying nine and 12-month sizes.

◆ **6-12 months:** Finally, your baby is crawling, standing, maybe even cruising. At the end of a year she's likely tried her first tentative steps without you. Play clothes are a layette mainstay during these months. You'll also need good, no-skid socks that stay on (or very flexible shoes). Again, you may find you're buying into the 18-month sizes.

 for an extra layer of warmth on a cold day.

How MANY? We believe you can never have too many of these blankets, but since you'll probably get a few as gifts, you'll only need to buy two or three yourself. A total of seven to eight is probably optimal.

What about the future? While our layette list only addresses clothes to buy for a newborn, you will want to plan for your child's future wardrobe as well. For the modern baby, it seems clothes come in two categories: play clothes (to be used in daycare situations) and dress-up clothes. Later in this chapter, we'll discuss more money-saving tips and list several recommended brands of play and dress-up clothes.

More Money Buys You . . .

Even the biggest discounters now offer good quality clothing. But with more money you tend to get heavier weight cottons, nicer fasteners, better quality embellishments and more generous sizing. At some point, however, considering how fast your little one is growing, you'll be wasting money on the most expensive clothes out there.

Safe & Sound

Should your baby's sleepwear (that is, the items he'll wear almost non-stop for the first several months of life) be flame retardant? What the heck does "flame retardant" mean anyway?

According to the Consumer Product Safety Commission (CPSC), items made of flame retardant fabric will not burn under a direct flame. Huh? Doesn't "flame retardant" mean it won't burn at all? No—that's a common myth among parents who think such clothes are a Superman-style second skin that will protect baby against any and all fire hazards.

Prior to 1996, the CPSC mandated that an item labeled as sleepwear be made of "flame retardant fabric." More often than not, that meant polyester because the alternative (untreated cotton fabric) DOES burn under direct flame. While there are a few companies that make cotton sleepwear that is chemically treated to be fire retardant, the prices of such items were so high that the de facto standard for children's sleepwear for many years was polyester.

Then the government changed its mind. The CPSC noticed that

many parents were rebelling against the rules and putting their babies in all-cotton items at bedtime. After an investigation, the CPSC revised the rules to more closely fit reality.

First, pajamas for babies nine months and under were totally exempt from the flame-retardancy rules. Why? Since these babies aren't mobile, the odds they'll come in contact with a fire hazard that would catch their clothes on fire is slim. What if the whole house catches fire? Well, the smoke is much more dangerous than the flames—hence, a good smoke detector in the nursery and every other major room of your house is a much better investment than fire retardant clothes.

What about sleepwear for older babies? Well, the government admits that "close-fitting" all-cotton items don't pose a risk either. Only flowing nightgowns or pajamas that are loose fitting must meet the flame retardancy rules today.

If you still want to go with "flame retardant" baby items, there are a couple of options beyond plain polyester. Look for fleece PJ's—the Lands' End catalog now sells "Polar Fleece" pajamas for babies and young children ($25). The fabric, while polyester, is specially woven to breathe and be more comfortable. Another option: some catalogs listed later in this chapter sell cotton PJ's treated to be flame retardant.

Finally, one last myth to dispel on this topic: does washing flame-retardant clothing reduce its ability to retard flames? Nope—fabrics like polyester are *naturally* flame retardant (that is, there is no magic chemical they've been doused with that can wash out in the laundry). What about those expensive treated all-cotton clothes? We don't think that's a problem either. While we haven't seen any evidence to the contrary, we think those companies that sell these pricey items would be drummed out of business in a heartbeat if the flame-retardancy of their clothes suddenly disappeared after a few spins in the rinse cycle.

There is one exception to the laundry rule: if you do choose to buy flame-retardant clothing, be sure to avoid washing such clothing in soap flakes. Soap flakes actually add a flammable chemical residue to clothes. And so do dryer sheets and liquid softeners. For more advice on washing baby clothes, see the discussion on page 181.

What about other safety hazards with children's clothing? Here are a few more to consider:

◆ **Check for loose threads.** These could become a choking hazard, or the threads could wrap around fingers or toes, cutting off circulation. Be careful about appliques as well. "Heat-welded" plastic appliques on clothes can come off and cause choking. Poorly sewn appliques can also be a hazard.

One Size Does Not Fit All

A six month-size t-shirt is a six-month-size t-shirt, right? Wrong. For some reason, baby clothing companies have yet to synchronize their watches when it comes to sizes. Hence, a clothing item that says "six-month size" from one manufacturer can be just the same dimensions as a "twelve-month size" from another. All this begs the question: how can you avoid widespread confusion? First, open packages to check out actual dimensions. Take your baby along and hold items up to her to gauge whether they'd fit. Second, note whether items are pre-shrunk—you'll probably have to ask (if not, allow for shrinkage). Third, don't key on length from head to foot. Instead, focus on the length from neck to crotch—a common problem is items that seem roomy but are too tight in the crotch. Finally, forget age ranges and pay more attention to labels that specify an infant's size in weight and height, which are much more accurate. To show how widely sizing can vary, check out the following chart. We compared "six-month" t-shirts from six major clothing makers plus three popular catalogs, Hanna Andersson, Lands' End and Talbot's Kids. Here's what these six-month t-shirts really translated to in terms of a baby's weight and height:

What a six month t-shirt really means

MAKER	WEIGHT	HEIGHT
BABY GAP	17-22 lbs.	27-29"
CARTER'S LAYETTE	12-18 lbs.	25"
GYMBOREE	17-21 lbs.	25-27"
HANNA ANDERSSON	14-21 lbs.	26-30"
HEALTH-TEX	13-17 lbs.	25-28"
LANDS' END	19-22 lbs.	27.5-29"
LITTLE ME	12-16 lbs.	24-27"
OSHKOSH	16.5-18 lbs.	27-28.5"
TALBOT'S KIDS	13-17 lbs.	24-27"

Here's another secret from the baby clothing trade: the more expensive the brand, the more roomy the clothes. Conversely, cheap items usually have the skimpiest sizing. What about the old wives' tale that you should just double your baby's age to find the right size (that is, buying twelve-month clothes for a six-month old?). That's bogus—as you can see, sizing is so all over the board that this rule just doesn't work.

◆ *Avoid outfits with easy-to-detach, decorative buttons or bows—these may also be a choking hazard.* If you have any doubts, cut the decorations off.

◆ *Watch out for drawstrings.* In recent years, most manufacturers have voluntarily eliminated such drawstrings. But if you get hand-me-downs or buy second-hand clothes, be sure to remove any strings.

Laundry Conundrum: What's Best for Baby's Clothes?

Ever since Dr. Spock's best-selling tome on taking care of baby, most parenting authors have advised washing baby's clothes and linens in mild soap or detergents. The implication is that baby's skin is delicate and could be irritated by harsh chemicals.

Yet, it helps to take a second to talk about just WHAT we are washing our clothes, hands and hair with these days. Until World War II, most soaps were made of animal or vegetable products. After the war, new synthetic "detergents" debuted, which were chemical compounds that cleaned better and cost less than soap. Detergent use skyrocketed, while soaps languished. Today nearly all products we think of as "soap" are really detergents.

Over the past 20 years, we've seen an explosion in personal care detergents, including soft soaps, bath gels, anti-bacterial liquids, hair products and more. In the nursery, just look at the huge use of baby wipes (which contain alcohol and crude detergents) instead of the washcloths of old. At the same time, however the number of children with severe eczema has climbed sharply, from the single digits in the 1950's to nearly 20% today. That's right, one out of five children today suffers from severe eczema.

Is it possible the high-tech detergents we use today to wash our skin, clothes and dishes are contributing to the eczema epidemic? While there is no scientific data to prove this link, researchers in England have been actively studying this for the past decade. Dr. Michael Cork, a dermatologist at Sheffield University, suggests detergents strip the fat between cells, making the skin more susceptible to conditions like eczema.

Unfortunately, there is no known cure for childhood eczema, which can be painful in its most severe form. It is often treated with steroid creams, which may have harmful long-term side effects.

So, what should new parents do? First, look at your family's history of eczema and other skin diseases. If you DO have a family history of eczema, we'd suggest going on a detergent-free diet for your household. Why the entire house? That's because baby will be touching your hair, clothes and sheets and those of your family as well. It's not enough to wash your baby's clothes in non-detergent soap. The entire family will have to sign on to this. See below for specific suggestions of detergent-free products.

Even if you have no such history in your family, consider using the mildest soaps or detergents for your baby: products like Cetaphil and Dove bar soap among the options. Stick with laundry products that are dye and fragrance free as well. No, you don't have to use Dreft—any perfume and dye-free mild detergent will do. And consider a second rinse cycle—this helps remove detergent residue. Finally, if you use bleach in the laundry, add some distilled vinegar to the rinse cycle to remove some of the odor and help clothes last longer.

In our family, we've had success removing detergents from our house, where our youngest son suffers from severe eczema. We noticed a sharp improvement in his skin after banishing detergents. Here are our tips for families with severe skin allergies:

◆ **Wash baby's clothes** in pure soap. We use **Cal-Ben's Seafoam Liquid** laundry soap, which is made from natural soap (web: CalBenPureSoap.com). Another source for traditional soap flakes is soap-flakes.com. You may also find other pure soaps in natural food stores. Read the labels carefully, however, since some items still contain detergents and others may have allergenic fruit or vegetable ingredients. Do not use fabric softeners, drier sheets or other laundry products. WARNING: if you plan to use soap or soap flakes, only buy untreated cotton sleepers for your child. Polyester sleepers as well as fire retardant-treated cotton sleeper will lose their fire retardancy when washed in soap. Not sure, check the label on your sleepers to make sure.

◆ **Baby's hair and skin** should be washed with Dove or Cetaphil bar soap. Never use bubble baths, oils or kid's shampoo. For hand soap in the kitchen and bath, we use Cal-Ben's Seafoam liquid soap or the bar soap mentioned above. Yes, that means everyone in the house. We chucked our old shampoo and use a pure soap shampoo (Cal Ben's Gold Star shampoo) as well. Stay away from anti-bacterial soaps. They can cause painful flair ups for eczema sufferers. Wash hands frequently to avoid germs and follow with a good emollient moisturizer.

◆ **Dishes.** Yes, babies can be exposed to detergent residue by handing cups or dishes. Again, we use a Cal-Ben product (Seafoam Dish Glow) to wash our dishes.

A few caveats to this: pure soap products are hard to find and expensive—we order ours from the web site mentioned above, although some natural food stores carry these brands as well.

And, true enough, soap does NOT clean as well as detergent, especially in the laundry. That said, we are willing to put up with this hassle in order to see improvement in our son.

We understand this is quite a commitment—having mom or dad give up a favorite shampoo or hair gel isn't fun. But remember, baby is running her hands through your hair and touching your skin. Even a small detergent residue can cause a reaction in some kids.

While we follow this detergent-free diet and it seems to be offering huge relief for our son's eczema, we realize it may just be part of the puzzle. Some kids have eczema that is triggered by a food allergy . . . and drier times of the year (winter, for example) can aggravate the skin, even in a detergent-free house. For our son, allergy shots (plus cutting back on detergents) helped get is eczema under control. If your baby or toddler develops eczema, consult with a pediatrician, allergist or dermatologist for the best treatment course.

Someday we hope science is able to positively link eczema with environmental factors, then we as parents can take positive steps so our children don't have to suffer.

 *Smart Shopper Tips*

Smart Shopper Tip
Tips and Tricks to Get the Best Quality
"I've received several outfits from friends for my daughter, but I'm not sure she'll like all the scratchy lace and the poly/cotton blends. What should she wear, and what can I buy that will last through dozens of washings?"

Generally, we recommend dressing your child for comfort. At the same time, you need clothes that can withstand frequent washings. With this in mind, here are our suggestions for baby clothing:

1 **SEE WHAT YOUR BABY LIKES BEFORE INVESTING IN MANY GARMENTS.** Don't spend $90 on fancy sweaters, only to find baby prefers cotton Onesies.

2 **WE GENERALLY RECOMMEND 100% COTTON CLOTHING.** Babies are most comfortable in clothing that breathes.

3 **IF YOU DISCOVER YOUR CHILD HAS AN ALLERGY TO METAL SNAPS** (you'll see red rings on his skin), consider alternatives such as shirts that have ties. Another option is a t-shirt that pulls on over the head. Unfortunately, many babies don't like having any-thing pulled over their heads. Another alternative for allergic babies: clothes with plastic snaps or zippers.

4 **IN GENERAL, BETTER-MADE CLOTHES WILL HAVE THEIR SNAPS ON A REINFORCED FABRIC BAND.** Snaps attached directly to the body of the fabric may tear the garment or rip off.

5 **IF YOU'RE BUYING 100% COTTON CLOTHES, MAKE SURE THEY'RE PRE-SHRUNK.** Some stores, like Gymboree (see review later in this chapter), pre-wash their clothes to prevent shrinkage. With other brands, it's hard to tell. Our advice: read the label. If it says, "wash in cold water" or " tumble dry low," assume the garment will shrink (and hence buy a larger size). On the other hand, care instructions that advise "washing in warm water and tumble dry" usually indicate that the garment is already preshrunk.

6 **GO FOR OUTFITS WITH SNAPS AND ZIPPERS ON BOTH LEGS, NOT JUST ONE.** Dual-leg snaps or zippers make it much easi-er to change a diaper. Always check a garment for diaper accessi-bility—some brands actually have no snaps or zippers, meaning you would have to completely undress your baby for a diaper change! Another pet peeve: garments that have snaps up the back also make diaper changes a big hassle.

7 **BE AWARE THAT EACH COMPANY HAS ITS OWN WARPED IDEA ABOUT HOW TO SIZE BABY CLOTHES.** See the box "One Size Does Not Fit All" earlier in this chapter for more details.

8 **BEWARE OF APPLIQUES.** Some appliqué work can be quite scratchy on the inside of the outfit (it rubs against baby's skin).

9 **KEEP THE TAGS AND RECEIPTS.** A reader emailed us her strat-egy for dealing with baby clothes that shrink: until she has a chance to wash the item, she keeps all packaging, tags and receipts. If it shrinks, she returns it immediately.

 **Wastes of Money**

Waste of Money #1
Clothing that Leads to Diaper Changing Gymnastics
"My aunt sent me an adorable outfit for my little girl. The only problem: it snaps up the back making diaper changes a real pain.

In fact, I don't dress her in it often because it's so inconvenient. Shouldn't clothing like this be outlawed?"

It's pretty obvious that some designers of baby clothing have never had children of their own. What else could explain outfits that snap up the back, have super tiny head, leg and arm openings, and snaps in inconvenient places (or worse, no snaps at all)? One mother we spoke with was furious about outfits that have snaps only down one leg, requiring her baby to be a contortionist to get into and out of the outfit.

Our advice: stay away from outfits that don't have easy access to the diaper. Look instead for snaps or zippers down the front of the outfit or on the crotch. If your baby doesn't like having things pulled over his head, look for shirts with wide, stretchie necklines.

Waste of Money #2
The Fuzz Factor

"My friend's daughter has several outfits that aren't very old but are already pilling and fuzzing. They look awful and my friend is thinking of throwing them out. What causes this?"

Your friend has managed to have a close encounter with that miracle fabric known as polyester. Synthetics such as polyester will often pill or fuzz after washing, making your baby look a little rag-tag. Of course, this is less of a concern with sleepwear—the flame retardancy of polyester fabric outweighs the garment's appearance.

However, when you're talking about a play outfit, we recommend sticking to all-cotton clothes. They wash better, usually last longer, and generally look nicer—not to mention they feel better to your baby. Cotton allergies are rare, unlike sensitivities to the chemicals used to make synthetic fabrics. You will pay more for all-cotton clothing, but in this case, the extra expense is worth it. Remember, just because you find the cheapest price on a polyester outfit doesn't mean you're getting a bargain. The best deal is not wasting money on outfits that you have to throw away after two washings.

If you get polyester outfits as gifts, here's a laundry tip: wash the items inside out. That helps lessen pilling/fuzzing. And some polyester items are better than others—polar fleece sweatshirts and pajamas are still made of polyester, but are softer and more durable.

Waste of Money #3
Do I Really Need These?

"My mother bought me a zillion gowns before my baby was born, and I haven't used a single one. What the heck are they for?"

"The list of layette items recommended by my local department

store includes something called a saque set. I've never seen one, and no one seems to know what it is. Do I really need one?"

"A kimono with matching towel and washcloth seems like a neat baby gift for my pregnant friend. But another friend told me it probably wouldn't get used. What do you think?"

Baby Needs a New Pair of Shoes

As your baby gets older, you may find she's kicking off her socks every five minutes. And at some point she's going to start standing, crawling and even walking. While we suggest waiting to buy shoes until walking is firmly established, there will come a day when you will need to buy that first set of shoes. Here are some suggestions:

First, look for shoes that have the most flexible soles. You'll also want fabrics that breath and stretch, like canvas and leather—stay away from vinyl shoes. The best brands we found were recommended by readers. Reader Teri Dunsworth wrote us about Canadian-made **Robeez** (800) 929-2649 or (604) 435-9011; web: robeez.com. (See picture at right). "They are the most AWESOME shoes—I highly recommend them," she  said in an email. And Teri wasn't the only one who loves them. Our email has been blitzed by fans. Robeez are made of leather, have soft, skid-resistant soles and are machine washable. They start at $26 for a basic pair. Another reader recommended New Zealand-made **Bobux** shoes ($26, at www.bobuxusa.com). These cute leather soft soles "do the trick by staying on extremely well," according to a reader. Another reader recommended **Scootees** (www.scootees.com). These slippers "really stay on babies' feet!" And they only cost $11. Finally, we saw some great shoes recently at a trade show called **PediPeds** (www.pedipeds.com). The soft soled shoes are hand stitched and made of leather. They are sized from 0 to 24 months and sell for around $30.

What about shoes for one or two year olds? We've found great deals at Target, where a wide selection of sizes and offerings was impressive. Another good source: Gap Kids/Baby Gap. Their affordable line of sneakers are very good quality. Parents have also told us they've had success with Babies R Us' in-house brand; others like Stride Rite shoes, which are often on sale at department stores. If none of these stores are convenient, consider the web or mail order—see the Do It By Mail section later in this chapter for possibilities. We discuss how to get more deals on shoes for toddlers in our *Toddler Bargains* book. See back of this book for details..

All of these items come under the heading "Do I Really Need These?" Heck, we didn't even know what some of these were when we were shopping for our baby's layette. For example, what in the world is a saque set? Well, it turns out it's just a two-piece outfit with a shirt and diaper cover. Although they sound rather benign, saque sets are a waste of money. Whenever you pick up a baby under the arms, it's a sure bet her clothes will ride up. In order to avoid having to constantly pull down the baby's shirt, most parents find they use one-piece garments much more often than two-piece ones.

As for gowns, the jury is still out on whether these items are useful. We thought they were a waste of money, but a parent we interviewed did mention that she used the gowns when her baby had colic (that persistent crying condition; see our other book *Baby 411* for a discussion). She believed that the extra room in the gown made her baby more comfortable. Other parents like how gowns make diaper changes easy, especially in the middle of the night. Finally, parents in hot climates say gowns keep their infants more comfortable. So, you can see there's a wide range of opinions on this item.

There is no question in our minds about the usefulness of a baby kimono, however. Don't buy it. For a baby who will only wear it for a few minutes after a bath, it seems like the quintessential waste of your money (we saw one Ralph Lauren baby kimono for $39. And that was on sale). Instead, invest in some good quality towels and washcloths and forget those cute (but useless) kimonos.

Waste of Money #4
Covering Up Those Little Piggies
"I was looking at baby shoes the other day and I saw a $43 pair of Merrell JungleMoc Juniors! This is highway robbery! I can't believe babies' shoes are so expensive. Are they worth it?"

Developmentally, babies don't need shoes until after they become quite proficient at walking. In fact, it's better for their muscle development to go barefoot or wear socks. While those expensive Merrells might look cute, they're really a waste of time and money. Of course, at some point, your baby will need some shoes. See the next box for our tips on how to buy babies' first shoes.

Waste of Money #5
To Drool or Not to Drool
"I received a few bibs from my mother-in-law as gifts. I know my baby won't need them until she's at least four to six months old when I start feeding her solids. Plus, they seem so small!"

What you actually received was a supply of *drool* bibs. Drool bibs are tiny bibs intended for small infants who drool all over everything. Or infants who spit-up frequently. Our opinion: they're pretty useless—they're too small to catch much drool or spit-up.

When you do buy bibs, stay away from the ones that tie. Bibs that snap or have Velcro are much easier to get on and off. Another good bet: bibs that go on over the head (and have no snaps or Velcro). Why? Older babies can't pull them off by themselves.

Stay away from the super-size vinyl bibs that cover the arms, since babies who wear them can get too hot. However, we do recommend you buy a few regular-style vinyl bibs for travel. You can wash them off much more easily than the standard terry-cloth bibs. As for sources of bibs, many of the catalogs we review in this book carry such items. Readers have also recommended the long sleeve bib from A Better Bib (abetterbib.com). Made of soft, breathable fabrics, these bibs run $16.

Another bib we like: the SnugEase ($8, snugease.com), a mom-designed terry cloth bib with a clever design—it doesn't require Velcro or snaps to stay on baby. Instead, "memory arms" keep it in place. And the Snugease has extra gathered fabric at the neck to prevent food from dribbling down onto baby's clothes (which seems to happen with regular bibs). Two thumbs up for Snugease.

Waste of Money #6
The Dreft Syndrome
"I see ads in parenting magazines that say infant clothes should be washed in special laundry detergent. Is this true?"

See our earlier discussion of this topic, "The Laundry Conundrum."

Money Saving Secrets

REMEMBER THESE TWO STORES: OLD NAVY AND THE CHILDREN'S PLACE. Old Navy (oldnavy.com) is the hip, discount offshoot of the Gap (gap.com) with 700+ stores nationwide. Readers rave about the buys they find at Old Navy (sample: "adorable" 100% cotton Onesies for just $12 per 3-pack; gripper socks, 8 to $10), although most admit the selection is limited. The options change rapidly and Old Navy's sales and clearance racks are "bargain heaven," say our spies. An insider tip to Old Navy and Gap Kids: the stores change out their merchandise every six weeks, moving the "old" stuff to the clearance racks rather quickly. Ask your local Old Navy or Gap Kids which day they do their markdowns (typically it is mid-week).

Here's another tip for folks who shop Old Navy or the Gap regularly: check to see if your recent purchases have been marked down. You may be able to get a refund if items you've bought are marked down even more. One reader emailed us her great deal: "Last month I found a hooded sweatshirt for baby on clearance. It was originally $15 marked down to $10.50. The next week, I went back and the same sweatshirt had been marked down from $10.50 to $1.99. So they refunded me $8.60!" Both Old Navy and the Gap allow you a price adjustment within 14 days of purchase. But you don't have to bring the clothes back, just your receipt.

The Children's Place (childrensplace.com) has over 851 stores in the US and Canada. They're about as ubiquitous as Old Navy, and the prices are just as good. They offer their clothing in sizes newborn to 4T. One reader wrote: "I found that this chain has really great looking and durable clothes for extremely reasonable prices." She did note that sizes run a bit small, so buy up a size. An example of their offerings: we saw a white, velour girl's cardigan for a mere $14.50. If you order online, the site offers a flat $5 shipping fee plus you can make returns at their stores.

2 WAIT UNTIL AFTER SHOWERS AND PARTIES TO PURCHASE CLOTHES.

Clothing is a popular gift item—you may not need to buy much yourself.

E-MAIL FROM THE REAL WORLD
Second-hand bargains easy to find

Shelley Bayer of Connecticut raved about Once Upon A Child, a nationwide chain of resale stores with 100+ locations (call 614-791-0000 for locations; web: www.OnceUponAChild.com).

"We have two locations of Once Upon A Child in Connecticut and I love them! The clothes and toys are of great quality and very affordable. The good thing about these stores is that when you take something in to be sold, they pay you cash. You do not have wait for something to be sold and keep checking your account like a traditional consignment shop."

One caution about second-hand stores—if you buy an item like a stroller or high chair at a resale shop, you may not be able to get replacement parts. One mom told us she got a great deal on a stroller that was missing a front bar . . . that is, it was a great deal until she discovered the model was discontinued and she couldn't get a replacement part from the manufacturer.

---

3 **STICK WITH BASICS—T-SHIRTS, SLEEPERS, CAPS, SOCKS AND BLANKETS.** For the first month or more, that's all you need since you won't be taking Junior to the opera.

4 **TAKE ADVANTAGE OF BABY REGISTRIES.** Many baby stores offer this service, which theoretically helps avoid duplicate shower gifts or too many of one item. This saves you time (and money) in exchanging gifts.

5 **SALES!** The baby area in most department stores is definitely SALE LAND. At one chain we researched, the baby section has at least some items that are on sale every week! Big baby sales occur throughout the year, but especially in January. You can often snag bargains at up to 50% off the retail price. Another tip: consider buying for the future during end-of-season sales. If you're pregnant during the fall, for example, shop the end-of-summer sales for next summer's baby clothes. Hint: our research shows the sale prices at department stores are often better deals than the "discounted" prices you see at outlets.

6 **CHOOSE QUALITY OVER LOW PRICE FOR PLAYCLOTHES AND BASICS.** Sure that polyester outfit is 20% cheaper than the cotton alternative. HOWEVER, beware of the revenge of the washing machine! You don't realize how many times you'll be doing laundry—that play outfit may get washed every couple of days. Cheap polyester clothes pill or fuzz up after just a few washings—making you more likely to chuck them. Quality clothes have longer lives, making them less expensive over time. The key to quality is thicker or more heavyweight 100% cotton fabric, well-sewn seams and appliques, and snaps on reinforced fabric bands.

7 **FOR SLEEPWEAR, TRY THE AFFORDABLE BRANDS.** Let's get real here: babies pee and poop in their sleepers. Hence, fancy designer brands are a money-waster. A friend of ours who lives in Texas uses affordable all-cotton Onesies as sleepwear in the hot summer months. For the winter here in Colorado, we use thermal underwear, which we've found for as little as $12 in Target.

8 **CAN'T RETURN IT?** Did you get gifts of clothing you don't want but can't return? Consign it at a local thrift store. We took a basketful of clothes that we couldn't use or didn't like and placed them on consignment. We made $40 in store credit or cash to buy what we really needed.

9 **SPEAKING OF CONSIGNMENT STORES, HERE IS A WONDERFUL WAY TO SAVE MONEY:** Buy barely used, consigned clothing for your baby. We found outfits ranging from $5 to $7 from high quality designers like Alexis. How can you find a consignment or thrift shop in your area specializing in high-quality children's clothes? Besides looking in the phone book, check out web sites like the National Association of Resale & Thrift Shops (narts.com, click on the shopping guide icon). Here are two tips for getting the best bargains at second-hand stores: First, shop the resale stores in the richest part of town. Why? They are most likely to stock the best brands with steep discounts off retail prices. Such stores also have clothes with the least wear (we guess rich kids have so many clothes they don't have time to wear them all out)! Second: ask the consignment store which day is best to shop. Some stores accept new consignments on certain days; others tell us that days like Tuesday and Wednesday offer the best selection of newly consigned items.

10 **CHECK OUT DISCOUNTERS.** In the past, discount stores like Target, Wal-Mart and Marshall's typically carried cheap baby clothes that were mostly polyester. Well, there's good news for bargain shoppers: in recent years, these chains have upgraded their offerings, adding more all-cotton clothes and even some brand names. We've been especially impressed with Target.

For basic items like t-shirts and play clothes that will be trashed at day care, these stores are good bets. Wal-Mart sure impressed one of our readers: "I spent $25 for a baby bathing suit in a specialty store, and for a little over twice that (about $60) I bought my daughter's entire summer wardrobe at Wal-Mart—shorts, t-shirts, leggings, Capri pants, overalls and matching socks. Some of the pieces were as low as $2.88." And don't forget other discounters like Marshalls, TJ Maxx and Ross. Bargain tip: ask the manager when they get in new shipments—that's when selection is best.

By the way, Carter's makes Child of Mine brand clothing sold at Wal-Mart and Just One Year brand at Target.

11 **WAREHOUSE CLUBS.** Warehouse clubs like Sam's, BJ's and Costco carry baby clothes at prices far below retail. On a recent visit to Costco we saw Carter's fleece sleepers for only $7.29. All-cotton play clothes were a mere $13 while all-cotton pajamas (2T-10) were $12. Even baby Halloween costumes and kids outerwear (raincoats, fleece jackets) are terrific seasonal deals.

12 **DON'T FORGET ABOUT CHARITY SALES.** Readers tell us they've found great deals on baby clothes and equipment at church-sponsored charity sales. Essentially, these sales are like large garage/yard sales where multiple families donate kids' items as a fund-raiser for a church or other charity.

Outlets

Here's a round up of our favorite outlet stores for baby and kids clothes. Remember: outlet locations open and close frequently—always call before you go.

CARTER'S

Locations: Over 140 outlets.
Call (888) 782-9548 or (770) 961-8722 for the location nearest you.

It shows you how widespread the outlet craze is when you realize that Carter's has over 146 outlets in the U.S. That's right, 146. If you don't have one near you, you probably live in Bolivia.

We visited a Carter's outlet and found a huge selection of infant clothes, bedding, and accessories. Prices were generally marked 50% off retail although sharp-eyed readers noted that department store sale prices are often just as good.

The best deals, however, are at the outlet's yearly clearance sale in January when they knock an additional 25% to 30% off their already discounted prices. A store manager at the Carter's outlet we visited said that they also have two other sales: back-to-school and a "pajama sale." In the past, we noted that all the goods in their outlet stores were first quality. However, they have added a couple "seconds" racks (called "Oops" racks) in most of their stores with flawed merchandise. Our readers report that most seconds have only minor problems and the savings are worth it.

HANNA ANDERSSON

Outlets Stores: Lake Oswego, OR (503) 697-1953; Michigan City, IN (219) 872-3183; Albertville, MN (763) 497-7885; Kittery, ME (207) 439-1992; Woodinville, WA (425) 485-7998.

If you like Hanna Anderson's catalog, you'll love their outlet stores, which feature overstocks, returned items and factory seconds. For more information on Hanna Anderson, see "Do It By Mail" later in this chapter.

HARTSTRINGS

Locations: 29 outlets, mostly in the eastern U.S. Call (610) 687-6900.

Hartstrings' 30 outlet stores specialize in first-quality apparel for infants, boys, and girls and even have some mother/child outfits. Infant sizes start at three months and go up to 24 months. The savings range from 30% to 50%.

HEALTH-TEX

Locations: 80 outlets. Call (800) 772-8336 for the location near you.

Health-Tex children's clothing is owned by Vanity Fair Corporation, which also produces such famous brands as Lee jeans, Wrangler, and Jantzen. The company operates over four-dozen outlets under the name VF Factory Outlet. They sell first-quality merchandise; most are discontinued items. Most of the VF outlets carry the Health-Tex brand at discounts up to 70% off retail.

JCPENNEY

Locations: 7 outlets; call (800) 222-6161, Web: JCPenney.com

A reader in Columbus, Ohio emailed her high praise for the Penney's outlet there. She snagged one-piece rompers for $5 (regularly $25) and hand-loomed coveralls for $2.99 (compared to $28 in stores). She also found satin christening outfits for both boys and girls for just $5 that regularly sell for as much as $70! The outlet carries everything from layette to play clothes, at discounts of 50% or more. (Hint: the outlet stores also have maternity clothes).

OSHKOSH

Locations: 154 outlets. Call (920) 231-8800 for the nearest location.

OshKosh, the maker of all those cute little overalls worn by just about every kid, sells their clothes direct at over 154 outlet stores. With prices that are 30% to 70% off retail, buying these play clothes staples is even easier on the pocketbook. For example, footed sleepers were $7.70 (regularly $11), and receiving blankets were $18.20 (regularly $24).

We visited our local OshKosh store and found outfits from infant sizes up to size 16. They split the store up by gender, as well as by size. Infant and toddler clothes are usually in the back of the store.

The outlet also carries OshKosh shoes, socks, hats, and even stuffed bears dressed in overalls and engineer hats. Seasonal ensembles are available, including shorts outfits in the summer and snowsuits ($42) in the winter. Some clothes are irregulars, so inspect the garments carefully before you buy.

One complaint: a parent wrote telling us she was disappointed that OshKosh had cheap elastic around the legs and didn't wash well. In her opinion, the quality of Carter's was much better in comparison.

By the way, OshKosh was purchased by Carter's in 2005.

Talbot's Kids

Location: 3 stores, most of which are in the Eastern U.S. and Texas. Call (800) 543-7123 or (781) 740-8888. Web: talbots.com

A reader who calls herself a "devoted Talbot's shopper" emailed in her compliments for Talbot's outlet stores, which carry a nice selection of baby and children's clothes that didn't sell in their stores or catalog. "The deals can be fantastic, especially given the quality," she said, adding that you can get on the outlet's mailing list to get notices about additional markdowns. She estimated she saved 40% to 60% on items for her baby. Hint: Talbot's regular stores hold major sales twice a year (after Christmas and the end of June). What doesn't get sold then is shipped to the outlets.

◆ *Other outlets.* A great source for outlet info is **Outlet Bound** magazine, which is published by Outlet Marketing Group ($13 plus $5 shipping, 1-888-688-5382; web: outletbound.com). The magazine contains detailed maps noting outlet centers for all areas of the U.S. and Canada, as well as store listings for each outlet center. We liked the index that lists all the manufacturers, and they even have a few coupons in the back.

Outlet Bound also has an excellent web site with the most up-to-date info on outlets in the U.S. and Canada. We did a search on children's clothing outlets (you can search by location, store, brand or product category) and found several additional interesting outlets. These included outlets for Little Me (33 outlets), the Disney catalog outlet (18 locations) and the Oilily catalog (two outlets).

If you can't get enough of the **Gap**, check out their outlet stores (they have 159) (650) 952-4400 (web: gap.com). With several locations nationwide, most Gap outlets have a baby/kid's clothing section and great deals (50% off and more).

Yet another outlet: **Pingorama** offers periodic factory sales. Check their web site, (pingorama.com, click on the where to buy link) for dates and directions.

Did you discover an outlet that you'd like to share with our readers? Call us at our office at 303-442-8792 or e-mail authors@ BabyBargains.com.

The Name Game: Our Picks for the Best Brands

Walk into any department store and you'll see a blizzard of brand names for baby clothes. Which ones stand up to frequent washings? Which ones have snaps that stay snapped? Which are a good value for the dollar? We asked our readers to divide their favorite clothing brands/stores into three categories: best bets, good but not great and skip it.

The Best Bets tend to be clothes that were not only stylish but also held up in the wash. The fabric was usually softer and pilled less. Customer service also comes into play with the best brands. Hanna Andersson is a great example of a company that bends over backwards for their customers. Gymboree, on the other hand, seems to be less than satisfactory for many parents, souring them on the brand.

Good but not Great clothes were pretty good, just not as soft or as stylish as Best Bets. The Skip-It brands were most likely the poorest quality: they shrunk in the wash, pilled up or fell apart. Inconsistent sizing was also a problem with brands like Babies R Us' Koala Kids.

Check these brands web sites to find local stores; some brands sell direct, of course.

Best Bets

Baby Gap	(800) GAP-STYLE	BABYGAP.COM
Baby Lulu		BABYLULU.COM
Carter's	(770) 961-8722	CARTERS.COM
Cozy Toes		COZYTOES.COM
Flap Happy	(800) 234-3527	FLAPHAPPY.COM
Flapdoodles	(302) 731-9793	FLAPDOODLES.COM
Funtasia! Too	(214) 634-7770	FUNTASIATOO.COM
H & M		HM.COM
Hanna Andersson		HANNAANDERSSON.COM
Hartstrings/Kitestrings	(212) 868-0950	HARTSTRINGS.COM
Hedgehog		HEDGEHOGUSA.COM
Jake and Me	(970) 352-8802	JAKEANDME.COM
Janie and Jack		JANIEANDJACK.COM
Little Lubbaloo		LITTLELUBBALOO.COM
Little Me	(800) 533-5497	LITTLEME.COM
LL Bean		LLBEAN.COM
MiniBoden		MINIBODEN.COM
MulberriBush (Tumbleweed Too)		MULBERRIBUSH.COM
Naartjie		NAARTJIE.COM
Old Navy		OLDNAVY.COM
OshKosh B'Gosh	(800) 692-4674	OSHKOSHBGOSH.COM
Patsy Aiken	(919) 872-8789	PATSYAIKEN.COM
Pingarama		PINGORAMA.COM
Sarah's Prints	(888) 477-4687	SARASPRINTS.COM
Sweet Potatoes/Spudz	(800) 634-2584	SWEETPOTATOESINC.COM
Wes & Willy		WESANDWILLY.COM
Zutano		ZUTANO.COM

REALITY LAYETTE

Good But Not Great

CHILDREN'S PLACE		CHILDRENSPLACE.COM
GOOD LAD OF PHILA.	(215) 739-0200	GOODLAD.COM
GYMBOREE	(877) 449-6932	GYMBOREE.COM
LANDS END		LANDSEND.COM
LE TOP	(800) 333-2257	LETOP-USA.COM
SPROCKETS (MERVYN'S)		MERVYNS.COM
TARGET (LITTLE ME, CLASSIC POOH, HALO, TYKES, CIRCO)		TARGET.COM
WAL-MART (FADED GLORY)		WALMART.COM

Skip It: GERBER, HANES, KOALA KIDS (BABIES R US), DISNEY, HEALTH-TEX, CARTER'S JUST ONE YEAR AT TARGET

Do it by Mail

CHILDREN'S WEAR DIGEST (CWD)

To Order Call: (800) 242-5437; Fax (800) 863-3395.
Web: cwdkids.com.
Outlet: "CWD Outlet," Gayton Crossing Shopping Center, Richmond, VA.
Also two company stores in Virginia. Call or visit the web site for more info.

If you're looking for name brands, check out Children's Wear Digest (CWD), a catalog that features clothes in sizes newborn to 14 years for both boys and girls. In a recent catalog, we saw clothes by Sweet Potatoes, Mulberribush, Wes and Willie, Baby Lulu, and Sarah's Prints. Unlike other catalogs that de-emphasize brand names, CWD prominently displays manufacturer info.

Children's Wear Digest doesn't offer much of a discount off regular retail, but it does have a selection of sale clothes from time to time with savings of 15% to 25%. A best buy: CWD's web site (cwdkids.com) has online bargains, with savings of up to 50% on quite a few items and the latest news on their outlet store.

HANNA ANDERSSON

To Order Call: (800) 222-0544; Fax (503) 321-5289.
Web: hannaandersson.com
Discount Outlets: Yes. Check outlet section earlier in the chapter

Hanna Andersson says it offers "Swedish quality" 100% cotton clothes. Unfortunately, Swedish quality is going to set you back some big American bucks. For example, a simple coverall with zippered front (called a zipper) was a whopping $36. Good news: the price hasn't gone up on these coveralls since the last edition. Even so, while Andersson's clothing features cute patterns and attractive colors, it's hard to imagine buying a complete wardrobe at those prices.

These aren't clothes you'd have your baby trash at daycare–Hanna Andersson's outfits are more suitable for weekend wear or going to Grandma's house. One note of caution: while the quality is very high, some items have difficult diaper access (or none at all). Another negative: Hanna Andersson uses "European sizing," which can be confusing. (Yes, there is an explanation of this in the catalog and on the website, but we still found it difficult to follow). Furthermore, some items (like dresses) are cut in a boxy, unstructured way.

On the plus side, we liked their web site (hannaandersson.com), which features an online store, sizing info and more. The site has a sale page that offers 20% to 40% off on overstock items; you can quickly glance at the specials by category.

Lands' End

To Order Call: (800) 963-4816; Fax (800) 332-0103.
Web: landsend.com
Discount Outlets: They also have a dozen or so outlet stores in Iowa, Illinois and Wisconsin–call the number above for the nearest location.

Lands' End children's catalog features a complete layette line–and it's darn cute. The clothes are typically 100% cotton although you'll see some fleece as well as velour. Choose from playsuits, Onesies, hat/bib sets, even cashmere sweaters and pants–all in sizes birth to 24 months. Most items were $14.50 to $24.50 (cashmere sweater $65). Don't look for fancy dress clothes from this catalog; instead Lands' End specializes in casual playwear basics like sweat pants, overalls and cute caps (for toddlers no doubt).

Lands' End web site is a continuation of the catalog's easy-to-use layout–you can buy items online, find an outlet store and more. Best bet for deals: check the great overstock deals, posted twice weekly.

LL Bean

To Order Call: (800) 441-5713; Fax (207) 552-3080
Web: llbean.com
Retail store: Freeport, ME

LL Bean used to have a separate site for kids clothes called LL Kids. They have since combined everything into one catalog and reduced the items they carry. They still emphasize outdoor gear: coats, snowsuits, hats, gloves, etc. But they also sell pants, sleepwear, jumpers and more. You may be confused a bit by their sizing as they group infant sizes under their Toddler section. Infant sizes start at 3 months. Prices are not cheap although sales items can be as much as 60% off.

PATAGONIA KIDS

To Order Call: (800) 638-6464; Fax (800) 543-5522.
Web: patagonia.com

Outdoor enthusiasts all over the country swear by Patagonia's scientifically engineered clothes and outerwear. They make clothing for skiing, mountain climbing, and kayaking—and for kids. That's right, Patagonia has a just-for-kids catalog of outdoor wear. In their recent kids' section on line, we found a few pages of clothes for babies and toddlers. They offer synchilla (Patagonia's version of polar fleece) clothes like cardigans ($48), overalls ($68), and baby buntings ($64-88). We bought our baby a bunting from Patagonia and found that it had some cool features. For example, with a flick of its zipper, it converts from a sack to an outfit with two leg openings, making it more convenient to use. It also has a neck to knee zipper (speeding up diaper changes), flipper hands, and a hood. When your baby's bundled up in this, you can bet she won't get cold.

Other gear for tots includes sets of capilene long underwear ($42), romper ($48) and interesting accessories like "Baby Pita Pocket" mittens ($18) and assorted hats and booties. The on line store also has a section called "Environmental Action," a series of essays and info on Patagonia's environmental efforts.

The bottom line: this is great stuff. It ain't cheap, but their cold weather gear is unlike that from any other manufacturer in terms of quality and durability.

TALBOT'S KIDS

To Order Call: (800) 825-2687.
Web: talbots.com
Retail stores: 600 stores in the U.S., Canada and the United Kingdom.
Outlets: Yes, Check outlet section earlier in the chapter.

Talbot's splashes its bright colors on both layette items for infants (three months to 12 months) and toddlers (up to 4T sizes). For baby, the catalog features a good selection of t-shirts, sleepwear, and overalls. Prices, as you might expect, are moderate to expensive. We saw cotton cardigans for $34, cotton turtlenecks with crotch snaps for $15. Nearly all of Talbot's Kids offerings are 100% cotton. The web site is easy to use.

clothing

WOODEN SOLDIER

To Order Call: (800) 375-6002; Fax (603) 356-3530.
Shopping Hours: Monday-Friday 8:30 am to midnight, Saturday and Sunday 8:30 am to 9 pm Eastern Time.

If you really need a formal outfit for your child, Wooden Soldier has the most expansive selection of children's formalwear we've ever seen. Unfortunately, the prices are quite expensive—a girls' plaid dress with velvet collar is $52; a boy's vest and knickers set with shirt is $94. And those are for infant sized clothes (6 to 24 months)!

On the plus side, the quality of the clothes is certainly impressive. And you won't find a bigger selection of dressy clothes around. They even offer some matching adult outfits. Wooden Soldier also continues to expand their casual offerings, which now include overalls, jumpsuits and cotton sweaters.

Finally, Wood Soldier entered the Internet Age with a web site (WoodenSoldier.com). We've been complaining for years that they didn't offer online shopping, so we're really happy to see they finally got their act together. Weirdly, though, they still won't let you order online. You have to call or download their order blank and mail it in. Come on guys! What are you waiting for?

◆ *Other catalogs.* Looking for Disney cartoon clothing and accessories? ***Disney's*** Catalog (800) 237-5751 (web: disneyshopping. com) has a few infant options. We liked the too-cute Halloween costumes as well as the winter gear. We found the quality from the Disney catalog to be quite good; most items wash and wear well.

Fitigues (fitigues.com) sells casual baby clothes at outrageous prices. Yes, the items are made of thermal knit or French terry with velvet trim, but we couldn't see ourselves spending $78 for a mesh romper. One plus: the kid's outfits do coordinate with the pricey adult clothes Fitigues offers.

If you need outdoor gear, check out ***Campmor*** (800) 226-7667 (web: campmor.com) or ***Sierra Trading Post*** (800) 713-4534 (web: sierratradingpost.com). Both heavily discount infant and children's outerwear, including snowsuits. Campmor even had some Sarah's Prints PJs for 50% off last we looked. They both also have backpacks. Since these items are closeouts, the selection varies from issue to issue.

Our Picks: Brand Recommendations

What clothing brands/catalogs are best? Well, there is no one correct answer. An outfit that's perfect for day care (that is, to be trashed in Junior's first painting experiment) is different from an outfit for a weekend outing with friends. And dress-up occasions may require an entirely different set of clothing criteria. Hence, we've divided our clothing brand recommendations into three areas: good (day care), better (weekend wear) and best (special occasions). While some brands make items in two or even three categories, here's how we see it:

Good. For everyday comfort (and day-care situations), basic brands like Carter's, Little Me, and OshKosh are your best bets. We also like the basics (when on sale) at Baby Gap (Gap Kids) for day-care wardrobes. For great price to value, take a look at Old Navy and Target. As for catalogs, most tend to specialize in fancier clothes.

Better. What if you have a miniature golf outing planned with friends? Or a visit to Grandma's house? The brands of better-made casual wear we like best include Baby Gap, Flapdoodles, and Gymboree. Also recommended: Jake and Me, MulberriBush, and Sweet Potatoes. For catalogs, we like the clothes in Hanna Andersson and Talbot's Kids as good brands.

Best. Holidays and other special occasions call for special outfits. We like Patsy Aiken, and the dressier items at Baby Gap. Of course, department stores are great sources for these outfits, as are consignment shops. As for catalogs, check out Wooden Soldier.

Note: For more on finding these brands, check out the Name Game earlier in this chapter. See "Do it By Mail" for more information on the catalogs mentioned above.

Diapers

The great diaper debate still rages on: should you use cloth or disposable? On one side are environmentalists, who argue cloth is better for the planet. On the other hand, those disposable diapers are darn convenient.

Considering the average baby will go through 2300 diaper changes in the first year of life, this isn't a moot issue—you'll be dealing with diapers until your baby is three or four years old (the average girl potty trains at 35 months; a boy at 39 months). Yes, you read that last sentence right . . . you will be diapering for the next 35 to 39 MONTHS.

Now, in this section, we've decided NOT to rehash all the environmental arguments pro or con for cloth versus disposable. Fire up your web browser and you'll find plenty of diaper debate on parenting sites like BabyCenter.com or ParentsPlace.com. Instead, we'll focus here on the FINANCIAL and PRACTICAL impacts of your decision.

Let's look at each option:

Cloth. Prior to the 1960's, this was the only diaper option available to parents. Fans of cloth diapering point to babies that had less diaper rash and toilet trained faster. From a practical point of view, cloth diapers have improved in the design over the years, offering more absorbency and fewer leaks. They aren't perfect, but the advent of diaper covers (no more plastic pants) has helped as well.

Another practical point: laundry. You've got to decide if you will use a cloth diaper service or launder at home. Obviously, the latter requires more effort on your part. We'll have laundry tips for cloth diapers later in this chapter. Meanwhile, we'll discuss the financial costs of cloth in general at the end of this section.

Final practical point about cloth: most day care centers don't allow them. This may be a sanitation requirement governed by state day care regulators and not a negotiating point. Check with local day care centers or your state board.

Disposables. Disposable diapers were first introduced in 1961 and now hold an overwhelming lead over cloth—about 95% of all households that have kids in diapers use disposables. Today's diapers have super-absorbent gels that lower the number of needed diaper changes, especially at night (which helps baby sleep through the night sooner). Even many parents who swear cloth diapers are best often use disposables at night. The downside? All that super-absorbency means babies are in no rush to potty train—they simply don't feel as wet or uncomfortable as babies in cloth diapers.

The jury on diaper rash is still out—disposable diaper users tell us they don't experience any more diaper rash than cloth diaper users.

Besides the eco-arguments about disposables, there is one other disadvantage—higher trash costs. In some communities, the more trash you put out, the higher the bill. Hence, using disposable diapers may result in higher garbage expenses.

The financial bottom line: Surprisingly, there is no clear winner when you factor financial costs into the diaper equation.

Cloth diapers may seem cheap at first, but consider the hidden costs. Besides the diapers themselves ($100 for the basic varieties; $200 to $300 for the fancy ones), you also have to buy diaper covers. Like everything you buy with baby, there is a wide cost variation with diaper covers. The cheap stuff (like Dappi covers) will set you back $3 to $6 each. And you've got to buy several in different sizes as your child grows, so the total investment could be nearly $100. If you're lucky, you can find diaper covers second-hand for $1 to $3. Of course, some parents find low-cost covers leak and quick-ly wear out. As a result, they turn to the more expensive covers—a single Mother-Ease (see later for more info on this brand) is $9.75. Invest in a half dozen of those covers (in various sizes, of course) and you've spent another $200 to $400 (if you buy them new).

What about laundry? Well, washing your own cloth diapers at home may be the most economical way to go, but often folks don't have the time or energy. Instead, some parents use a cloth diaper ser-vice. In a recent cost survey of such services across the U.S., we found that most run $600 to $1400 a year. While each service does supply you with diapers (relieving you of that expense), you're still on the hook for the diaper covers. Some services also don't provide enough diapers each month. You'll make an average of eight changes a day (more when a baby is newborn, less as they grow older), so be sure you're getting about 60 diapers a week from your service.

Proponents of cloth diapers argue that if you plan to have more than one child, you can reuse those covers, spreading out the cost. You may also not need as many sizes depending on the brands you use and the way your child grows.

So, what's the bottom line cost for cloth diapers? We estimate the total financial damage for cloth diapers (using a cloth diaper service and buying diaper covers) for just the first year is $600 to $800.

By contrast, let's take a look at disposables. If you buy disposable diapers from the most expensive source in town (typically, a grocery store), you'd spend about $600 to $650 for the first year. Yet, we've found discount sources (mentioned later in this chapter) that sell dis-posables in bulk at a discount. By shopping at these sources, we figure you'd spend $345 to $400 per year (the lowest figure is for private label diapers, the highest is for brand names).

The bottom line: the cheapest way to go is cloth diapers laun-dered at home. The next best bet is disposables. Finally, cloth dia-pers from a diaper service are the most expensive.

Parents in Cyberspace: What's on the Web?

All Together Diaper Company

Web: clothdiaper.com

What it is: Home of the all-in-one cloth diaper made in house by the All Together Diaper Company.

What's cool: We loved the simplicity of this site. In business since 1990, the All Together Diaper Company sells its own cloth diaper system in various packages. The accompanying FAQ, washing instructions and analysis of diaper costs are really helpful. While some of their price comparisons between cloth and disposable are a bit inaccurate (slanted toward cloth, of course), the information on the cost of home washing was helpful.

What about the diapers? We were impressed with the cool design—the all-in-one system has cotton inside against baby's skin, a waterproof outer shell, adjustable snaps and elastic leg openings. These diapers (the Deluxe) are $8 to $12 each or $84 to $132 per dozen. Less expensive are the prefold diapers, which do not have the waterproof shell. Price: $11 to $30 per dozen (quantity discounts available). Packages are another plus on the All Together Diaper Company site. You can even buy a package called All the Cloth Diapers Your Baby Will Ever Need! This includes 30 small, 24 medium, 24 large and 24 toddler diapers. Cost: $700 to $730 (priced separately this would cost $990).

Needs work: The web site seems to load a bit slowly.

The Baby Lane

Web: thebabylane.com
What it is: A comprehensive baby product and information site with a selection of cloth diapers and accessories.
What's cool: This is really the Mother of All Cloth Diaper sites. You'll find offerings from Under the Nile, Bumkins, Kushies, Plushies, Imse Vimse, Bummis and Kissaluv. Kushies Ultras were $9.50 for infant sizes (discounts available for five packs).
Needs work: If you choose the cloth diapers link, you'll have to wander through three really long pages of diapers to find what you want. We recommend clicking on links to specific manufactures to make this go faster.

Diapers 4 Less

Web: diapers4less.com
What it is: The web site for Diaper Factory Plus, a manufacturer of generic disposable diapers.
What's cool: Even with shipping costs, this site's diapers are about 20% less than any other discount diaper sites. And their diapers have Velcro closures, a foam waistband and a cloth-like cover like national brands.

Small (7-14 lbs) size diapers range in price from 20¢¢ to 22¢¢ per diaper. You have to buy 4 packs of 64 each (256 diapers) for a total of $47. Not bad, especially because shipping is free. In the chart following this section, you'll see this price (18¢¢ per diaper) compares well with grocery stores (which of course don't usually deliver to your home). In fact, prices have fallen slightly since our last edition. Sample packs are available if you want to check out the quality. Note: they will accept unopened packages as returns for refund or exchange.

Needs work: Plan ahead since UPS ground shipping can take seven to ten days to get to you.

Baby Works

Web: babyworks.com

What it is: Cloth diapers and a range of other eco friendly baby gear.

What's cool: You'll find diaper covers like Nikkys and Bummis, all-in-one diaper systems, cotton diapers, laundry products, and accessories. We saw the Bumkins all-in-one system for $15-16 per diaper. We liked all the washing instructions included on each page for the different items. Other nice features: Baby Works has a recommended layette for cloth diapers, you can order samples and they can troubleshoot leaking problems for you.

Needs work: Prices aren't anything to shout about, but the selection is good.

◆ *Other sites to consider:*

Disposables: We found several more sites that sell disposable diapers on line. Among the best: **CVS Pharmacy** (cvspharmacy.com) and **Diaper Site** (diapersite.com).

Cloth: Noel Howell, one of our readers, emailed us with great suggestions for sites to help newbee moms interested in using cloth diapers. **Diaperpin.com** is good for parents still trying to decide whether cloth is for them. **Mothering.com** is another site with advice on specific brands of cloth diapers. There are also plenty of articles on cloth diapering but be ready to preached at a bit!

Several readers have recommended **Baby J** (babyj.com) as a cloth diaper source. You'll find all-in-ones, folded diapers, wraps, liners and more with such brands as Kushies, Fuzzy Bunz, and Bummis. **Barefoot Baby** (barefootbaby.com) is another site recommended by readers. Besides their own brand of diapers, they carry Bumkins, Bummis, Cot'n Wrap and Fuzzi Bunz.

Check out any of the following web sites as well: *kellyscloset. com, cottonbabies.com, aunaturalbaby.com* and *babybunz. com*. Reader Sherri Wormstead noted that all three of these sites are competitively priced and have a nice wide variety of supplies. Finally, check out **Baby Because** (babybecause.com). They carry a huge assortment of folded diapers, all-in-one systems and diaper covers. Samples are available as well as diaper bags and accessories.

Our Picks: Brand Recommendations

Disposables. The evolution of disposable diapers is rather amazing. They started out in the 1960's as bulky and ineffective at stopping leaks. In 40 years, disposables morphed into ultra-thin, super-absorbent miracle workers that command 95% of the market.

And writing about disposable diaper brands is like trying to nail Jell-O to a wall—every five minutes, the diaper makers come out with new features and new gimmicks as they jostle for a piece of the $3.6 billion diaper market. In the 11 years since the first edition of this book came out, the constant innovation in this category is amazing. We used to talk about three types of diapers: basic (thick, tape tabs), ultrathin (with the gel and tape tabs) and supreme (fabric-like outer layer, Velcro tabs). But in recent years, almost all diapers have added Velcro tabs, nicer outer layers and the ubiquitous super absorbent gels. So what separates the good from the bad diapers? Parents are still looking for good fit, no leaks and comfort for baby.

Who's got the cheapest diapers?

What's the best place to buy disposable diapers? We did a price comparison among several major sources, listed here from least to most expensive:

Store or Web Site	Diaper Type	Count	Price	Per Diaper
Costco	Huggies #2	258	$37.99	15¢
Sam's Club	Huggies #2	228	$34.88	15¢
Wal-mart	Huggies #1	112	$17.47	16¢
Babies R Us	Huggies #1-2	192	$30.00	16¢
Diapers4Less.com**	House Brand	256	$47.00	18¢
Target	Huggies #1	48	$9.54	20¢
Grocery Store*	Huggies #1	56	$11.00	20¢
DiaperSite.com†	Huggies #1-2	228	$70.00	31¢

Price: Includes shipping.
Per Diaper: The cost per diaper.

* Checked at Kroger (King Soopers).
** Free shipping.
† Flat shipping fee regardless how many you order.

Note: Prices checked as of 2007.

No matter what brand you try, remember that sizing of diapers is all over the board. The "size two" diaper in one brand may be cut totally different than the "medium" of another, even though the weight guidelines on the package are similar. Finding a diaper that fits is critical to you and your baby's happiness.

Now, let's answer some common questions about disposables:

Q. What makes one brand different from another?

A. Surprisingly, the absorbency of diapers varies little from brand to brand. A *Consumer Reports* test of 8000 diaper changes on 80 babies at a day care center found that of 13 diaper types tested, eight were judged excellent. And three more were "very good." Translation: no matter what brand you choose, you'll probably have a diaper that fits well and doesn't leak. Yes, the premium/supreme diapers scored highest in CR's tests, but the difference between them and the cheaper options was minimal (except for the price, of course).

Besides absorbency, gimmicks and marketing ploys are the only differences between brands. This market goes through fads faster than Madison Avenue. We remember gender-specific diapers, which were on the market for about five minutes. That was more hype than real benefit and now they're gone (we're back to unisex versions). Another fad that came and went: "Pampers Rash Care," a premium diaper which "contains the same active ingredients as many diaper rash creams" to prevent diaper rash. Now Pampers offers "Caterpillar-Flex" while Huggies touts their Hugflex feature. Next week we expect Luvs to come out with a brand that promises higher college entrance scores. Call it Luvs "Ultra SAT Boosters."

Q. What about store brands like Babies R Us and others? Is there much difference?

A. Although store diapers used to be less impressive than name brands, in the last few years they've caught up in terms of cloth like covers, Velcro fasteners and ultra absorbency. And they cost as much as 30% less too.

Q. Do certain brands work better for boys or girls?

A. We used to hear anecdotal evidence from our readers that Huggies were better with boys and Pampers better with girls. In recent years, however, parents tell us there doesn't seem to be a gender difference at all.

Q. How many diapers of each size is a good starting point?

A. Most babies go through 12 to 14 diapers *per day* for the first few months. That translates into about 500 to 600 diapers for the first six weeks. As you read at the beginning of the chapter we recommend buying 100 "newborn" size diapers and 400 to 500 "size one" diapers before baby is born. Caveat: some families have large babies, so keep the receipts just in case you have to exchange some of those newborns for size 1.

So how many do you need of the larger sizes? Starting with a case of each size as you transition to larger diapers is a good idea. There are typically 100 diapers or more in a case. As you near a transition to a larger size, scale back the amount of smaller size diapers you buy so you don't have any half opened packs lying around.

Finally, remember that as your baby grows, she will require fewer diaper changes. Once you add solid foods to her feeding schedule you may only be doing eight to ten changes a day (we know—eight to ten a day still seems like a ton of changes; but it will feel much less than baby's first few weeks). Plus you'll be much more experienced about when a diaper really is wet.

So which diaper brand is best? While Consumer Reports may not note much difference between brands, our readers have different ideas. We'll include comments from our Reader Poll in the reviews below.

◆ **Huggies.** Huggies has been a strong brand for years. They now offer four diaper options: Huggies Supreme Gentle Care, Huggies Supreme Natural Fit, just plain Huggies, and Huggies Overnights. Most of our readers panned regular Huggies saying they leaked, but many really like the Supreme line.

The Gentle Care version is for newborns, with a u-shaped waistband for umbilical cords. They come in newborn up to size 2.

The Natural Fit diapers are intended for older babies. They claim their hourglass shape fits babies better. These are available in sizes 3 to 6.

Overnights are made to be even more absorbent so babies can actually sleep through the night (and parents too!). And they still have their "Little Swimmers" swim diapers—great for the pool or beach.

As for wipes, Huggies offers six varieties from Extra Sensitive to Shea Butter to Nourishing. Feedback from parents was a thumbs up on the wipes, no matter the type/

Huggies web site (huggies.com) is easy to use with buttons for deals and explanations of each diaper. The website also offers parenting advice on both pregnancy and child development with expert interviews and articles.

◆ **Pampers.** Pampers continues to offer a huge line of diapers to cover baby's stages of development and growth. Swaddlers are intended for newborns to size two. Claiming to "swaddle your baby in comfort" these diapers are for very young, inactive babies.

Eco Friendly Disposables

Is there a diaper that combines the convenience of disposables with the ecological benefits of cloth diapers? Yes—here's an overview of so-called eco-friendly disposables:

Tushies, first invented by a Denver pediatrician in the late 1980's, bills its diapers as a gel-free, latex-free, perfume-free alternative to name brand disposables. Made with non-chlorine bleached wood pulp surrounding an absorbent cotton core, they also offer a "cloth-like" cover. Tushies mentions that without the gel, their diapers won't "explode" in the swimming pool. The disadvantages to Tushies? They are considerably thicker than regular diapers. And like most "all-natural" versions of consumer goods, Tushies ain't cheap. They sell a case of 160 size small diapers for $58.81. That's 37¢¢ per diaper. Compare that to grocery store prices of 20¢¢ per diaper and warehouse clubs of 15¢¢ per diaper. Prices are slightly lower if you join their online club at www.tushies.com. They are also sold in health food stores like Whole Foods and Wild Oats.

Seventh Generation (seventhgeneration.com) is another website offering an "organic" (mostly chlorine-free) disposable diaper. When we recently visited the site, Seventh Generation was touting a new thinner design but the same absorbency as their previous line. The diapers have a cloth like outer layer, reusable tabs, and are latex and fragrance free. Made of wood pulp, a poly backing and a poly outer cover, Seventh Generation also includes an absorbent polymer get. They are careful to explain that the gel they use is non-toxic, non-carcinogenic and non-irritating.

Unfortunately, Seventh Generation's site does not sell diapers online, but there are a dozen online shopping options including Amazon.com. Or you can use their store search. We noticed that Wild Oats, Whole Foods and Vitamin Cottage carry the brand. On Amazon.com, a pack of 56 stage 1 Seventh Generation diapers was $16.47 (29¢¢ per diaper). We also priced these same diapers at a grocery store for 21¢¢ a diaper. Coupons are available on Seventh Generation's web site.

Ultimately, while these products are promising options for parents looking for a natural alternative to mainstream disposables, the price is certainly going to be a factor in getting parents to use them. And there is still an issue of where these diapers will go. Until recycling centers with composting options become more widely available, there's a question as to whether these diapers won't still end up buried under tons of earth and trash waiting to decompose.

Pampers claims they have "grow-with-me" fit—basically extra stretchy sides that can be easily adjusted.

For the next stage when babies begin to kick, roll over, crawl and stand, Pampers has introduced their Cruisers. These are supposed to have more elasticity and give for active babies as well as less bulk. Cruisers are sized from three to six. Baby Dry diapers are yet another line of diapers in sizes from newborn to toddler. They've added "caterpillar-flex" (only sizes 3-6) to allow the waistband to expand and contract giving the diaper a better fit.

Readers who responded to our disposable diaper poll gave both Swaddlers and Cuddlers high ratings over all. The Baby Dry line came in for lots of criticism, however—parents complained that these diaper leak. As for Pampers wipes, again parents seemed to like them although some complained that the wipes were too wet. Like Huggies, Pampers offer five versions of their wipes including sensitive, unscented and lavender scented.

Pampers' easy to use web site (pampers.com) explains the new offerings pretty well, and there is an easy-to use chart that helps you figure out what's available for your baby at any particular stage. Pampers also has a coupon program and will send out free samples if sign up as a member.

◆ **Luvs.** Made by Procter & Gamble, the company that also makes Pampers, Luvs are marketed as a lower-price brand. All in all, based on reader feedback, we didn't see much difference between Luvs and Pampers . . . or Huggies.

New this year, Luvs adds a blue Leakguard Core that is supposed to improve leak protection. Like the more expensive diapers, Luvs have an hourglass shape, fabric-like outer layer and reusable fasteners. Luvs is also offering a money-back guarantee—if you're not satisfied with their diapers, they offer your money back on a pack of Luvs. But there is some fine print (you'll have to send in your original receipt, it's limited to one refund per household, they deduct a dollar for postage and it take six to eight weeks to get the refund). Still, no one else is offering a guarantee.

Readers were mixed in their appraisal of Luvs. Some said they leaked, but others praised the low price and thought they worked fine.

Luvs' web site (luvs.com) has a simple layout. Besides products info, you can find message boards and other advice online.

◆ **White Cloud by Wal-Mart.** We mentioned White Cloud (Wal-Mart's private label brand) in our last edition, but we think it deserves a full-blown recommendation this time around. Parents seem universally pleased with the quality and impressed with the price of White Cloud. Parents told us these diapers don't leak, nor any strange chemical or perfume smell. But price was the biggest reason parents gave for trying White Cloud—they're affordable everyday, not just when they're on sale.

◆ **Store brands**. We've received numerous emails from parents who love store-brand diapers at Target, K-Mart, Walgreens and CVS Pharmacy. Even grocery stores are getting into the game with private label diapers at prices to rival the discounters. Generally, these diapers are 20% to 30% cheaper than name brands. In the past, generic diapers were inferior in terms of features and quality but no more—most have the same ultrathin design, cloth-like covers and reusable tabs.

Who's got the best store-brand diapers? Target and CVS brands got mixed reviews, while Walgreens had a few thumbs up from our readers. Bottom line: give store brand diapers a try. If you find one that works, you can find significant savings over the name brands.

Cloth Diapers. If you ask 100 parents for their recommendations on cloth diapers (as we recently did on our web site), you're likely to get 100 different opinions—it seems everyone has their special system or favorite brand! Unlike with disposable diapers, there aren't three or four market leaders that everyone uses or recognizes. Instead, there are at least 20 different options from simple prefold diapers with pins to fancy all-in-one diapers. And prices are all over the board too. So what's an aspiring CD'er to do? First let's take you through the basics with Karen F., our CD guru from our message boards:

A cloth diaper has three basic functions. Working from the inside out:

1. Wick it away. This layer is intended to keep baby from sitting in her pee. This layer lets moisture through in one direction but not back towards the skin. In cloth diapers, this layer is fleece or suede-cloth, but only certain kinds of fleece will do this. Some people just cut rectangles of fleece and lay them in inside the diaper. Some diapers are lined with fleece, sewn in place while others are pocket diapers with the fleece next to the skin. And there are some people who skip this layer and change the diaper as soon as baby pees.

2. Soak it up. Typically, the absorbent layer in cloth diapers is made of cotton or hemp and is sewn in layers. There are also some diapers with a micro fiber towel for the absorbent layer. Some people add an extra layer called a "doubler" which is just layers of cloth sewn together. This allows parents to increase absorption when needed (overnight, for example). See below for a discussion of the different options for this layer.

3. Keep the rest of the world dry. Remember those awful plastic/rubber pants of yesteryear? Uncomfortable for baby and noisy too! Today's options are much more comfortable to wear and touch. Cloth diaper covers can be polyurethane laminate (PUL) over cotton or polyester, nylon, wool or fleece. Wool is naturally water repellent when it has natural lanolin in it. (Otherwise sheep would bulk up like a sponge in a rainstorm!). The type of fleece that is used as diaper covers is water repellent."

Okay, now that you know the mechanics of cloth diapering, what should you use for your little guy or gal? First, here's the lingo you'll need to master:

1 **PREFOLDS** (CPF for Chinese prefolds or DSQ for diaper-service quality). These are what most parents think of when they envision cloth diapers. They are heavyweight 100% cotton cloths that have been prefolded so that there is extra padding in the middle then sewn down. This process leads to a diaper with six to eight layers in the middle and two to four layers on the sides. They can then be pinned onto your baby (not our favorite idea) or folded into a diaper cover. Avoid flat fold diapers—these are really just burp pads and great dust cloths!

2 **FITTED DIAPER:** Sometimes called prefitteds, these are prefold diapers that have elastic sewn in for the leg openings. They don't have snaps or Velcro so they have to be secured with pins or in a cover. You'll get a more snug fit around the leg openings with these.

3 **DOUBLER (ALSO CALLED LINERS).** Available in paper, cotton or even silk, doublers are used when you need extra absorbency. They are inserted between the diaper and baby's bottom. These would be a great option at night or on a long car trip.

4 **DIAPER COVER/WRAP.** This item is placed over the diaper to stop leaks. One style of diaper cover is called a wrap—think of it as baby origami. You'll wrap your baby up and secure the Velcro tabs to the front strip. Some covers snap in place and there are other pants that can be pulled on (elastic waist).

5 **ALL-IN-ONE.** Just what you'd think, an all-in-one (AIO) is a diaper and cover sewn together. There are plusses and minuses to this design. Yes, the convenience of grabbing one item and snapping or velcroing it on your baby is great but if your baby makes a mess, you have to wash the whole thing. With a traditional diaper/cover combination, you won't have to wash the cover every time unless baby gets poop on it. So you'll end up buying more all-in-ones to keep yourself from doing laundry constantly.

6 POCKET DIAPER. Made famous by Fuzzi Bunz, the pocket diaper is an all-in-one with a pocket sewn into the lining. You can then customize the diaper for more absorbency by adding an insert or a prefolded diaper.

7 SNAPPI FASTENERS. Made in South Africa, these cutting-edge diaper fasteners replace the traditional (and potentially painful) diaper pin. Check out their website at www.snappi.co.za for a look at how they work.

Whew! That's a lot to remember. So anyway, what's the bottom line? What should you buy? Great question. Here's what our cloth diaper guru recommends if you're just starting out and have a new-

---

E-Mail from The Real World
Cloth diaper laundry tips

Once you make the decision to use cloth diapers, you'll want to research the "art" of cleaning them. Too many harsh chemicals can damage and fade cloth diapers and covers, not enough will leave diapers looking less than pristine. So what's a parent to do? Here's some advice from readers who've experienced lots of diaper cleaning.

Rowan Cerrelli writes:

"I do not like to use chlorine bleach to wash out diapers since they are expensive and the chlorine ruins them. There are some products out there that use natural enzymes to predigest 'stuff' out of the diapers, therefore eliminating the need for bleach. Companies that have these products include Seventh Generation and Ecover. They are also available in natural food grocery stores."

Catherine Advocate-Ross recommends:

"I use Bio-Kleen laundry powder on the diapers. Works great and you need very little."

Bio-Kleen's web site bi-o-kleen.com explains their products and directs consumers to stores or web sites that carry them. They have an extensive line including liquid as well as powder detergent and stain and odor eliminator. The main ingredient in the line is grapefruit seed and pulp extract.

Kelly Small, from Wallingford, CT emailed us to say:

"I highly recommend OxyClean— it is great on the poop stains!!!"

---

born: Buy two to three dozen prefold diapers and four to six diaper covers. You may also want to get a few pocket diapers or all-in-ones and a couple Snappis.

Now you probably want to know which brands to buy. So we polled our readers to find out their favorites. Right off the bat, they told us "it depends." Depends on your baby's body type, whether you're looking for nighttime leak protection and many other factors. A couple of the brands readers *could* agree on were Fuzzi Bunz and Snap-EZ Fleece Pocket diapers. Here is a list of the many other brands parents mentioned:

◆ *Fitted Diapers:*
   Sugar Plum Babies (monkeytoediapers.com/sugarplumbaby)
   Bizzy B Hive (hyenacart.com/bizzybhive)
   Bijou Baby Gear (bijoubabygear.com)
   Benjamuffins (benjamuffins.com)

Finally, Rebecca Parish has some practical advice on cloth diapers:
"We (my friends and I) have run across a shortcut that I had not heard about before we attempted cloth diapering. Mainly, we have found it entirely unnecessary to rinse diapers out at all before laundering them. We own a four-day supply of pre-fold diapers and wraps. When our baby poops, we take an extra diaper wipe with us to the toilet, and use it to scrape what easily comes off into the toilet. Then we throw the dirty diaper into our diaper pail, right along with all the other dirty diapers. There's no liquid in the pail for soaking—they just sit in there dry. About every three or four days we throw the entire contents of the diaper pail into the laundry machine, add regular detergent (we use Cheer) and two capfuls of bleach (about 4 teaspoons), and run the machine. The diapers and wraps all come out clean. Just two extra loads of laundry a week (which is nothing compared to the extra loads of clothes we now wash), and no dipping our hands into toilet water. I generally use about five diaper wipes every time I change a messy diaper as it is, so using one extra one for scraping poop into the toilet seems like no big deal.

I think washer technology has improved significantly enough in recent years to allow for this much easier diaper cleaning. We own a fairly new front-loader washer. I don't think the brand name is important; we have a friend who owns a different brand of front-loader, and gets equally good results. However, one of our friends with an older top-loader uses our same system but ends up with stains; she doesn't care but I would. "

Bottom line: new technologies (detergents, additives and washers) have led to great improvements in the cleaning of cloth diapers.

◆ *Diaper Covers:*
  AngelDry (wool) (angeldrydiapers.com)
  Aristocrat (wool)
  Bummis (bummis.com)
  Windro (wool)
  Imse Vimse Bumpy
  Luxe (wool) (luxebabydiapers.com)
  Bizzy B Hive (wool) (hyenacart.com/bizzybhive)
  Proraps (prodiaper.net)

◆ *All-In–Ones:*
  Girl Woman Goddess (girlwomangoddess.com)
  Lullaby Diapers (lullabydiapers.com)
  Bum Genius
  Daisy Doodles (daisy-doodles.com)
  Cuddlebuns (cuddlebunsdiapers.com)
  DryBees (drybees.com)

◆ *Pockets:*
  Happy Heiny's (happyheinys.com)
  Olive Branch Baby Marathon (olivebranchbaby.com)

◆ *A source for all of the above:*
  Swaddlebees (swaddlebees.com)

Notes: Keep in mind that many of these companies are small, run by a couple friends or by a family. We've noticed that they often don't have fancy web sites and occasionally run out of stock for a while. Some websites sell directly to customers, others do not. And still others don't have websites but do sell online through retailers.

Need more information? A good book on using cloth diapers is *Diaper Changes* by Theresa Rodriquez (M. Evans and Co., publisher; $15). Also, check out our online message boards on our web site at babybargains.com. They have extensive commentary from cloth diaper parents with tips and recommendations.

Wipes. Like diapers, you have a basic choice with wipes: name brand or generic. Our advice: stick to the name brands. We polled our readers and their top picks were: **Huggies Natural Care** and **Target Sensitive Skin** brands. The reviews were more mixed with Pampers wipes: some parents thought they were too wet and too expensive.

We found most cheap generic wipes to be inferior. With less water and thinner construction, store brand wipes we sampled were losers. There is one exception to this rule, however: Costco's Kirkland brand wipes, which many readers have said are fantastic. One mom emailed: "They are not as rigid as Huggies or Pampers, have a lighter scent and are stronger than any other wipe we tried." And it's hard to beat the price: $16 for 704 (that's 2¢¢ per wipe).

Money Saving Secrets

Here are some tips for saving on disposable diapers (cloth diaper bargain advice is at the end of this section):

1 BUY IN BULK. Don't buy those little packs of 20 diapers—look for the 80 or 100 count packs instead. You'll find the price per diaper goes down when you buy larger packs.

2 GO FOR WAREHOUSE CLUBS. Both Sam's (samsclub.com) and Costco (costco.com) wholesale clubs sell diapers at incredibly low prices. For example, Costco sells a 258-count package of Huggies stage 2 for just $37.99 or about 15¢ per diaper. We also found great deals on wipes at the wholesale clubs. Another warehouse club is BJ's (bjs.com), which has over 100 locations in 16 states, most in the Eastern U.S. By the way, one reader noted that the size 1-2 diapers she's seeing in warehouse clubs are really size 1. She's been frustrated with this sizing issue since the size 3 diapers are too big but there isn't anything in between the 1-2 and the 3 sizes.

3 BUY STORE BRANDS. As mentioned earlier, many parents find store brand diapers to be equal to the name brands. And the prices can't be beat—many are 20% to 30% cheaper. Chains like Target, Wal-Mart and Toys R Us/Babies R Us carry in-house diaper brands, as do many grocery stores. In fact, Wal-Mart's White Cloud brand is a favorite among our readers.

4 CONSIDER TOYS R US. You may not have a wholesale club nearby, but you're bound to be close to a Toys R Us (or their sister division, Babies R Us). And we found them to be a great source for affordable name-brand diapers. The best bet: buy in bulk. You can often buy diapers (both name brand and generic) by the case at Toys R Us, saving you about 20% or more over grocery store prices. As you might have noted in the earlier diaper cost comparison, Babies R Us was one of the lowest-priced sources for diapers we found. Don't forget to check the front of the store for copies of Toys R Us' latest catalog. Occasionally, they offer in-store coupons for additional diaper savings—you can even combine these with manufacturer's coupons for double savings.

5 **WHEN BABY IS NEARING A TRANSITION POINT, DON'T STOCK UP.** Quick growing babies may move into another size faster than you think, leaving you with an excess supply of too-small diapers.

6 **DON'T BUY DIAPERS IN GROCERY STORES.** We compared prices at grocery stores and usually found them to be sky-high. Most were selling diapers in packages that worked out to 20¢ per diaper. We should note there are exceptions to this rule, however: some grocery chains (especially in the South) use diapers as a "loss-leader." They'll sell diapers at attractive prices in order to entice shoppers into the store. Also, store brands can be more attractively priced, even at grocery stores. Use coupons (see below) to save even more at grocery stores.

7 **USE COUPONS.** You'll be amazed at how many coupons you receive in the mail, usually for 75¢ off diapers and 50¢ off wipes. One tip: to keep those "introductory" packages of coupons coming, continue signing up to be on the mailing lists of the maternity chain stores (apparently, these chains sell your name to diaper manufacturers, formula companies, etc.) or online at diaper manufacturers' web sites.

8 **ASK FOR GIFT CERTIFICATES.** When friends ask you what you'd like as a shower gift, you can drop hints for gift certificates/cards from stores that sell a wide variety of baby items—including diapers and wipes. That way you can get what you really need, instead of cute accessories of marginal value. You'd be surprised at how many stores offer gift certificate programs.

9 **FOR CLOTH DIAPER USERS, GO FOR "INTRODUCTORY PACKAGES."** Many suppliers have special introductory deals (Mother-Ease offers their One-Size diaper, a liner and a covers for $17US; $20 Canadian, which includes shipping). Before you invest hundreds of dollars in one brand, give it a test drive first.

10 **BUY USED CLOTH DIAPERS.** Many of the best brands of cloth diapers last and last and last. So you may see them on eBay or cloth-diaper message boards. Buy them—you can get some brands for as little a buck or two. As long as you know the quality and age of the diapers you're buying, this tip can really be a money saver.

11 REUSE THEM. Okay, we know this may be obvious, but hang onto your cloth diapers and use them for your next child. Every child is different, so even if you buy a brand and it doesn't fit your baby well, it may work on your next child. And of course, you can always sell them on eBay when you're all finished.

The Bottom Line: A Wrap-Up of Our Best Buy Picks

In summary, we recommend you buy the following layette items for your baby (see chart on next page).

QUANTITY	ITEM	COST
6	T-shirts/onesies (over the head)	$22
6	T-shirts (side snap)	$25
4-6	Sleepers	$64-$96
1	Blanket Sleeper	$10
2-4	Coveralls	$40-$80
3-4	Booties/socks	$12-$16
1	Sweater	$16
2	Hats (safari and caps)	$30
1	Snowsuit/bunting	$20
4	Large bibs (for feeding)	$24
3 sets	Wash cloths and towels	$30
7-8	Receiving blankets	$42-$48
TOTAL		**$335 to $417**

These prices are from discounters, outlet stores, or sale prices at department stores. What would all these clothes cost at full retail? $500 to $600, at least. The bottom line: follow our tips and you'll save $100 to $300 on your baby's layette alone. (Of course, you may receive some of these items as gifts, so your actual outlay may be less.)

Which brands are best? See "Our Picks: Brand Recommendations" earlier in this chapter. In general, we found that 100% cotton clothes are best. Yes, you'll pay a little more for cotton, but it lasts longer and looks better than clothes made of polyester blends (the exception: fleece outerwear and sleepwear). Other wastes of money for infants include kimonos, saque sets, and shoes.

What about diapers? We found little financial difference between cloth and disposable, especially when you use a cloth diaper service. Cloth does have several hidden costs, however—diaper covers can add hundreds of dollars to the expense of this option although the cost can be spread out among additional children.

For disposables, we found that brand choice was more of a personal preference—all the majors did a good job at stopping leaks. The best way to save money on disposable diapers is to skip the grocery store and buy in bulk (100-diaper packages) from a warehouse club. Diapers from discount sources run about $300 to $375. The same diapers from grocery stores could be $600 or more. Another great money-saver: generic, store-brand diapers from Wal-Mart, Target, K-Mart and the like. These diapers performed just as well as the name brands at a 20% to 30% discount.

CHAPTER 5

Maternity & Nursing

Inside this chapter

Love 'em or hate 'em, every mother-to-be needs maternity clothes at some point in her pregnancy. Still, you don't have to break the bank to get comfortable, and, yes, fashionable maternity items. In this chapter, we tell you which sources sell all-cotton, casual clothes at unbelievably low prices. Then, we'll review the top maternity chains and reveal our list of top wastes of money. Finally, you'll learn which nursing clothes moms prefer most.

Maternity & Nursing Clothes

Getting Started: When Do You Need This Stuff?

It may seem obvious that you'll need to buy maternity clothes when you get pregnant, but the truth is you don't actually need all of them immediately. The first thing you'll notice is the need for a new bra. At least, that was my first clue that my body was changing. Breast changes occur as early as the first month and you may find yourself going through several different bra sizes along the way.

Next, its' time for the bump. Yes, the baby is making its presence known by making you feel a bit bigger around the middle. Not only may you find that you need to buy larger panties, but you may also find that skirts and pants feel tight as early as your third month. Maternity clothes at this point may seem like overkill, but some women do begin to "show" enough that they find it necessary to head out to the maternity shop.

If you have decided to breastfeed, you'll need to consider what type of nursing bras you'll want. Buy two or three in your eighth month so you'll be prepared. You may find it necessary to buy more nursing bras after the baby is born, but this will get you started. As for other nursing clothes, you may or may not find these worth the money. Don't go out and buy a whole new wardrobe right off the bat. Some women find nursing shirts and tops to be helpful while others manage quite well with regular clothes. More on this topic later in the book.

Sources

1 **MATERNITY WEAR CHAINS.** Not surprisingly, there are quite a few nationwide maternity clothing chains. Visit any mall and you'll likely see the names Pea in the Pod, Motherswork, Mimi Maternity, and Motherhood, to mention a few. Soon you may see a new maternity superstore, Destination Maternity, which will combine all the above chains plus skincare, fitness, nutritional products and classes for pregnant moms in one huge store. More on these chains later in the chapter.

2 **MOM AND POP MATERNITY SHOPS.** These small, independent stores sell a wide variety of maternity clothes, from affordable weekend wear to high-priced career wear. Some baby specialty stores carry maternity clothes as well. The chief advantage to the smaller stores is personalized service—we usually found salespeople who were knowledgeable about the different brands. In addition, these stores may offer other services. For example, some rent formal wear for special occasions, saving you big bucks. Of course, you may pay for the extra service with higher prices. While you're shopping at the independents look for lines from manufacturers like Meet Me in Miami, Juicy Maternity and Olian. Readers have been pleased with the quality and style of these brands.

3 **CONSIGNMENT STORES.** Many consignment or thrift stores that specialize in children's clothing may also have a rack of maternity clothes. In visits to several such stores, we found some incredible bargains (at least 50% off retail) on maternity clothes that were in good to excellent condition. Of course, the selection varies widely, but we strongly advise you to check out any second-hand stores for deals.

4 **DISCOUNTERS.** When we talk about discounters, we're referring to chains like Target, Wal-Mart and K-Mart. Now, let's be

honest here—these discounters probably aren't the first place you'd think of to outfit your maternity wardrobe. Yet, each has a surprisingly nice selection of maternity clothes, especially casual wear. Later, we'll tell you about the incredible prices on these all-cotton clothes.

5 DEPARTMENT STORES. As you might guess, most department stores carry some maternity fashions. The big disadvantage: the selection is usually rather small. This means you'll often find unattractive jumpers in abundance and very little in the way of fashionable clothing. Selection is much greater, however, on store websites. And department stores like Penney's and Sears often have end-of-the-season sales with decent maternity bargains.

6 WEB/MAIL-ORDER. Even if you don't have any big-time maternity chains nearby, you can still buy the clothes they sell. Many chains offer a mail-order service, either from printed catalogs or online stores. In the "Do It By Mail" section of this chapter, we'll give you the run-down on these options.

7 NON-MATERNITY STORES. Maternity stores don't have a monopoly on large-size clothes—and you can save big bucks by shopping at stores that don't have the word "maternity" in their name. One of our favorites: Old Navy & the Gap. Their maternity clothes are both stylish and affordable.

8 YOUR HUSBAND'S CLOSET. What's a good source for comfy weekend wear? Look no further than the other side of your closet, where your husband's clothes can often double as maternity wear.

9 OUTLETS. Yes, there are several outlets that sell maternity clothes and the prices can be a steal. We'll discuss some alternatives later in this chapter.

10 YOUR FRIENDS. It's a time-honored tradition—handing down "old" maternity clothes to the newly pregnant. Of course, maternity styles don't change that much from year to year and since outfits aren't worn for a long time, they are usually in great shape. Just be sure to pass on the favor when you are through with your pregnancy. And if your friend or neighbor is clearly not going to fit in your old maternity clothes (you're six feet tall, she's under 5'5"), don't dump your old gear on her just to get rid of it. You're trying to do someone a favor, not avoid a trip to Good Will.

Parents in Cyberspace:
What's on the Web?

Expressiva

Web: expressiva.com

What it is: Terrific source for *stylish* nursing clothes.

What's cool: Wow! That's all we could say when we took a look at Expressiva's designs. You really never would know they were nursing clothes. And they don't make you look like a sack of potatoes. Tops, dresses, casual clothes, workout gear, bras and even maternity clothes are available here. Sizes range from extra small to 3X and the site includes hints about sizing for specific outfits. We love the special collection for plus sizes. Three styles of nursing openings are available: vertical, crop top and concealed with zippers or snaps underneath a top layer. And the site shows you exactly how each type works. Prices are reasonable for the quality. If you want to look good and still offer the best first food for your baby, this is a site to check out.

Motherwear

Web: motherwear.com

What it is: More nursing clothes plus maternity clothing as well.

What's cool: "This catalog makes the best clothes for nursing!" gushed one mom in an email to us and we have to agree—this is a great catalog and web site. The quality is excellent with prices in the reasonable range (a baby blanket hoodie for $49). They have a clearance section as well and don't forget to check their weekly specials. A cool feature: want to see what the nursing openings look like on each garment? Just click on the little icon on each page and a window pops open with clear photos of each opening. Maternity options are pretty basic: t-shirts, a few dresses and some pants. Motherwear has a satisfaction guarantee and easy return policy.

eStyle

Web: estyle.com

What it is: A "lifestyle" retailer targeting pregnant women and new moms with fashions, tips and information.

What's cool: A fast-loading, color-saturated site with easy navigation, it's easy to see why eStyle is a favorite among new and expecting parents. Not only can you shop for maternity fashions, you'll also find tips, calendars, sizing and style suggestions and more. When we last reviewed this site, they carried a plethora of brands including Belly Basics, Diane Von Furstenburg, Belly Beautiful,

Figure 1: Gap Maternity's web site lets you return items bought online to Gap stores.

Michael Stars and more. Now, however, they are focusing on their in-house brand, BabyStyle, All the items we saw were quite stylish. **Needs work:** But don't expect cut-rate prices for all that fashion. How 'bout a pair corduroy pants for $88? Remember, you'll only be wearing these for a few months. If you really want to buy something here, check for their specials and deals.

eBay

Web: ebay.com

What it is: A surprising source of maternity bargains.

What's cool: Here are the deals just one of our readers, Alison Lewis of Winston-Salem, NC found: "I got five long sleeve cotton maternity shirts and two pairs of corduroy pant (mostly Motherhood brand) for a total of $21.50 and the shipping was $4." She notes too that the selection on eBay is "pretty much endless."

Needs work: Expect to find some real duds in the fashion department here. There's bound to be a lot of junk you'll have to sift through to find the jewels.

◆ *Other sites:* Years ago, maternity clothes were meant to cover up a pregnancy. Women were encouraged to wear the fashion equivalent of a burlap sack. But no more. Check out the sassy maternity t-shirts on **2 Chix** (www.2chix.com). Potato sacks these are not. Form fitting tank tops as well as short and long sleeved t's are the rule here, many with cutesy sayings like "what's kickin'" and "knocked up." Prices ranged from $30 to $52. We also chuckled at the dad shirts with sayings like "he shoots, he scores." Not that you'd want him to wear this around your dad, but his friends would be amused.

While most folks know **Gap** as a great place for kids clothes, few realize that Gap also does maternity. While most moms will only be able to find Gap Maternity online (gap.com), some BabyGap bricks and mortar stores offer maternity in store as well. You'll find classics like cardigans and jeans as well as stretch shirts, capri pants and more. Nice feature: photos showcase their four different types of waistbands for pants. And sizes range from 0 to 20. Check frequently for sale items—they seem to offer more sales than most maternity retailers. Readers have been impressed with the quality of Gap maternity, according to our email. **Old Navy**, Gap's low price sister chain is also selling maternity on line (oldnavy.com). As with other Old Navy clothes, the quality is a bit less but the so are the prices.

Chatter on our message boards has mentioned the website Due Maternity (duematernity.com) as a great place for maternity clothing. You'll see many fashion-forward brands on this site, including Chiarakruza, Momzee and Duet Designs. The prices are in the upper range, but they have an extensive sale section.

Maternity 4 Less (maternity4less.com) received a parent recommendation for speedy delivery. Our reader reported that they exchanged a pair of maternity pants for her in only a matter of days, not the usual weeks other mail-order sources take. They carry the gamut of maternity and nursing clothes and accessories. Maternity 4 Less also has a section of the site for plus sizes. The site isn't much to look at but the prices are darned reasonable.

One of our readers raved about the jeans on **Fashion Bug's** web site (fashionbug.com). "They were awesome!" she wrote. Prices ranged from $20 to $45 and plus sizes are available.

For a wide range of styles and sizes (up to 3X plus talls and petites), check out **Mom Shop** (momshop.com). With great full size photos and an easy to use site, we think MomShop.com is a top site.

Nursing clothes are where **One Hot Mama** (onehotmama.com) got their start, but they have expanded into maternity clothes as well. Either way, they attempt to showcase hip styles from manufacturers like Japanese Weekend. Just don't read the long-winded sermons on nursing from the site's owners.

Isabella Oliver (isabellaoliver.com) is a great site we stumbled upon when researching this book. What we liked best about the site was its categories: petite, tall, curvy and more. Instead of sifting through tons of styles, the site brings up only those clothes that meet your criteria. And the designs are very hip although expensive. Sale items however, are a great deal.

For our Canadian readers, check out **Thyme Maternity** (thymematernity.com), recommended by a reader in Ontario. She thought the styles were more "real world," the sizing was great and prices were reasonable. They no longer offer mail order, but their web site has a directory of stores in Canada. As a side note, another Canadian mom wrote to recommend that her countrywomen consider going to Buffalo or other US cities to shop for maternity clothes.

We could go on and on with all these maternity/nursing web sites, but let's condense it a bit for you. The following are yet more options to check out for maternity and nursing clothing:

Birth and Baby	birthandbaby.com
Mommy Gear	mommygear.com
Fit Maternity	fitmaternity.com
Liz Lange Maternity	lizlange.com
Naissance Maternity	naissancematernity.com
Pumpkin Maternity	pumpkinmaternity.com
Twinkle Little Star	twinklelittlestar.com

What Are You Buying?

What will you need when you get pregnant? There is no shortage of advice on this topic, especially from the folks trying to sell you stuff. But here's what real moms advise you to buy (divided into two topic areas, maternity clothes and then nursing clothes):

Maternity Clothes

◆ **Maternity Bras.** What is a maternity bra? Maternity bras are designed to grow with you as your pregnancy progresses; these bras also offer extra support (you'll need it). Maternity bras are available just about everywhere, from specialty maternity shops to department stores, mail order catalogs and discount chains. More on this topic later in this chapter; look for our recommendations for maternity underwear.

HOW MANY? Two in each size as your bust line expands. I found that I went through three different sizes during my pregnancy, and buying two in each size allowed me to wear one while the other was washed.

◆ **Sleep Bras.** Why a sleep bra, you ask? Well, some women find it more comfortable to have a little extra support at night as

Plus-size Maternity Clothing

What's the number one frustration with maternity wear? Finding decent plus-size maternity clothes, say our readers. Some maternity clothing manufacturers think only women with super-model bodies get pregnant. But what to do if you want to look attractive and your dress size starts at 16 or above? Our readers have recommended the following sites:

Baby Becoming	babybecoming.com
JCPenney	jcpenney.com
MomShop	momshop.com
Motherhood	maternitymall.com
Expressiva	expressiva.com
Plus Maternity	plusmaternity.com

their breasts change. Toward the end of pregnancy, some women also start to leak breast milk (to be technical, this is actually colostrum). And once the baby arrives, a sleeping bra (cost, about $10) will keep those breast pads in place at night (to keep you from leaking when you inadvertently roll onto your stomach—yes, there will come a day when you can do that again). Some women just need light support, while others find a full-featured bra a necessity. HOW MANY? Two sleep bras—one to wear while one is in the wash.

◆ **Underpants.** In the past, our recommendation for maternity underpants extolled the virtues of traditional maternity underwear. But time rolls on—and fashion has changed. Most women today are wearing bikini-style underpants as standard gear. And, readers note, you can continue to wear those same styles when you're pregnant. They're right—so save yourself some money and forget the maternity underpants. If you're already wearing bikini styles, stick with them. But, now is a good time to consider upgrading your underpants wardrobe in case you've let your skivvies wear out a bit. After all, you'll be going to lots of check ups and eventually the hospital—your mom would be embarrassed if your unmention-ables were full of holes!

HOW MANY? If you need new underpants or plan to ignore our advice and buy maternity underpants, we recommend at least eight pairs.

◆ **Maternity belts and support items.** Pregnancy support belts can be critical for some moms. For example, Pam A., one of our readers sent the following email when she was 7 1/2 months along:

maternity

"Last week I got the worst pain/cramp that I have ever had in my life. It kept coming and going while I was walking, but it was so bad that I doubled over in pain when it hit. I went to my doctor and she said that the baby was pushing on a ligament that goes between the abdomen and the leg. She recommended that I get a "Prenatal Cradle" (prenatalcradle.com). I'll tell you what—it is the most wonderful purchase I have ever made in my life. It was about $50, but it works wonders. It does not totally eliminate the pain, but it gives enough support that it drastically reduces the pain and even gives me time to change positions so that it does not get worse. I have even found that wearing it at night helps to alleviate the pain at night rolling over in bed."

Your best bet, if you find you need some support, is to check with your doctor as Pam did. Many of these belts are available on general web sites like OneStepAhead.com, BuyBuyBaby.com and some drugstore sites.

By the way, Candy from San Diego wrote to us about a product called the Bella Band (bellaband.com). Here's what she had to say: "I bought the Bella Band early on in my pregnancy and love it so much that I recently bought another one. It was perfect for keeping my "normal" clothes on when I couldn't button them anymore. Then it helped me keep maternity pants on when they were still a little too big but I couldn't fit in my regular clothes anymore." While the Bella Band isn't a support item like the Prenatal Cradle, it is a great product to help keep your clothes on!

How many? Kind of obvious, but one should be enough. And most likely you'll need this late in your pregnancy unless you are carrying multiples.

◆ **Career Clothing.** Our best advice about career clothing for the pregnant mom is to stick with basics. Buy yourself a coordinating outfit with a skirt, jacket, and pair of pants and then accessorize. Now, we know what you're saying. You'd love to follow this advice, but you don't want to wear the same old thing several times a week—even if it is beautifully accessorized. I don't blame you. So, go for a couple dresses and sweaters too. The good news is you don't have to pay full price. We've got several money-saving tips and even an outlet or two coming up later in this chapter. At some point, you'll notice that regular clothes just don't fit well, and the maternity buying will begin. When this occurs is different for every woman. Some moms-to-be begin to show as early as three months, while others can wait it out until as late as six months. But don't wait until you begin to look like a sausage to shop around. It's always best to scope out the bargains early, so you won't be tempted to buy outfits (out of desperation) at the convenient—and high-priced—specialty maternity chain.

By the way, thanks to casual office wear trends, pregnant woman can spend hundreds of dollars LESS than they might have had to ten or twenty years ago. Today, you can pair a knit skirt with a sweater set for most office situations.

◆ **Casual Clothes.** Your best bet here is to stick with simple basics, like jeans and cords. You don't necessarily have to buy these from maternity stores. In fact, later in this chapter, we'll talk about less-expensive alternatives. If you're pregnant in the summer, dresses can be a cooler alternative to pants and shorts.

◆ **Dress or Formal Clothes.** Forget them unless you have a full social calendar or have many social engagements associated with your job. Sometimes, you can find a local store that rents maternity formalwear for the one or two occasions when you might need it.

News from Down Under: Maternity Bras for the Real World

What makes a great maternity bra? Consider the following points while shopping:

◆ *Support—part I*. How much support do you need? Some women we interviewed liked the heavy-duty construction of some maternity bras. For others, that was overkill.

◆ *Support—part II* Once you decide how much support you need, consider the *type* of support you like. The basic choices: under wire bras versus those that use fabric bands and panels. Some moms-to-be liked stretchy knit fabric while others preferred stiffer, woven fabric.

◆ *Appearance*. Let's be honest: some maternity bras can be darn ugly. And what about the bras that claim they'll grow with you during your pregnancy? Yes, they may stretch some—but one bra won't work for the entire nine months of pregnancy.

◆ *Price*. Yes, the best maternity bras can be pricey. But I've found it doesn't pay to scrimp on underwear like bras and panties. Save money on other items in your maternity wardrobe and invest in comfortable undergarments.

Nursing Clothes

◆ ***Nursing Bras.*** The one piece of advice every nursing mom gives is: buy a well-made, high quality nursing bra *that fits you.* Easier said than done you say? Maybe. But here are some tips we gleaned from a reader poll we took.

First, what's the difference between a nursing bra and a maternity bra? Nursing bras have special flaps that fold down to give baby easy access to the breast. Access is usually with a hook or snaps either in the middle or on top of the bra near the straps. Readers insist new moms should look for the easiest access they can find. You'll need to be able to open your nursing bra quickly with only one hand in most cases.

Next, avoid under wire bras at all cost. They can cause plugged ducts, a very painful condition. If you sport a large cup size, you'll need a bra that is ultra supportive. Check out Motherhood Maternity bras. Some of our readers told us they have a good selection of large cup sizes. And in most cases, nursing moms require a sleep bra too—some for support, some just to hold nursing pads.

Mothers living near a locally owned maternity shop or specialized lingerie store recommended going in and having a nursing bra fitted to you. One reader reported that "I was wearing a bra at least three cup sizes too small. The consultant fitted me properly and I couldn't believe how comfortable I was!" If you don't have the luxury of a shop full of specialists, Motherwear (motherwear.com) has terrific online consultants and Bravado (www.bravadodesigns.com) offers extensive sizing tips for different models.

If you plan to nurse, you should probably buy at least two bras during your eighth month (they cost about $30 to $45 each). Why then? Theoretically, your breast size won't change much once your baby is born and your milk comes in. I'd suggest buying one with a little larger cup size (than your eighth month size) so you can compensate for the engorgement phase. You can always buy more later and, if your size changes once the baby is born, you won't have invested too much in the wrong size. If you want more advice on nursing bras, you can check out Playtex's cool web site at playtex.com. Click on the apparel section, then "Find the Perfect Fit." "Expectant Moments" is their maternity brand.

HOW MANY? Buy one to two bras in your eighth month. After the baby is born, you may want to buy a couple more.

◆ ***Nursing Pads.*** There are two options with nursing pads: disposable and reusable. Common sense tells you that reusable breast pads make the most economical sense, particularly if you plan to have more children. Still, if you aren't a big leaker, don't plan to breast feed for long or just need something quick and easy when you're on the go, disposables are handy.

When we polled our readers, we were surprised to learn that the majority preferred disposables. Those by Lansinoh (lansinoh.com; $9.60 for 60 at drugstore.com) were by far the favorite followed by Johnson and Johnson ($6 per 50), Gerber (60 for $5.60) and Curity (12 for $2.20). What's the secret to these disposables? The same type of super absorbent polymer that makes your baby's diapers so absorbent. That makes them super thin too so you aren't embarrassed by telltale "bulls-eyes" in your bra. Moms also love the indi-

Reader Poll: Nursing clothes brands

When we polled our readers about nursing clothes we were immediately chastised by at least half the respondents for even considering recommending them. "A waste of money," "ugly!" and "useless" were a few of the more charitable comments from these readers. As many as one third had never even used a single nursing top. They preferred to wear button up shirts or t-shirts and loose tops that they just pulled up. One mom told us "I got pretty good at being discreet in public with my regular clothes and no one was the wiser."

But other moms loved nursing clothes. And their favorites were those from **Motherwear**, the catalog and web site we reviewed earlier in this chapter. In our poll over 100 respondents mentioned Motherwear as the best source for well-made, comfortable nursing clothes. The biggest complaint about Motherwear was that their clothes are expensive. Readers suggested buying them used from ebay.com. The next closest company was **One Hot Mama** (onehotmama.com) with 17 votes.

Other sites recommended by parents included **Expressiva** (expressiva.com), **Birth and Baby** (birthandbaby.com) and **Breast Feeding Styles** (breastfeedingstyles.com). Breast Feeding Styles received special mention for their easy to use zippered openings.

Regardless of where nursing clothes were purchased, moms were universal in thinking that the best tops have two vertical openings over the breasts. Forget the single center opening! And no buttons either. Too hard, our moms said, to open with one hand while baby is screaming in your ear. Twin sets and cardigan sweaters were the preferred styles. Readers thought they looked least like nursing clothes. And lots of moms thought just having a few nursing camisoles and t-shirts to wear under a regular shirt was the way to go. Finally, several parents recommended the Super Secret Nursing Shirt from One Hot Mama.

Want to make your own nursing clothes? Creative sewers will find great patterns on **Elizabeth Lee's** web site (elizabethlee.com).

vidually wrapped pads because they can just grab a couple and throw them in the diaper bag on the way out of the house. Interestingly, moms were divided on whether they like contoured or flat pads or those with adhesive strips or without.

While there wasn't one discount source mentioned for disposable breast pads, moms tell us when they see their favorite brands on sale at Wal-Mart, Target or Babies R Us, they snapped up multiple boxes.

For the minority who preferred reusable, washable pads, Medela ($6 per pair), Avent ($6 for three pair) and Gerber ($4 for three pair) made the top of the list. Some moms recommend Bravado's (bravadodesigns.com) Cool Max pads ($16 for five pair) for superior absorption. A few parents have raved about Danish Wool pads (danishwool.com). These soft, felted pads contain natural lanolin, a godsend for moms with sore, cracked nipples. They aren't cheap ($15 to $25 per pair) but we thought them worth the mention. Another pad recommended by a reader is LilyPadz by Lilypadz.com. She told us they are streamlined and reusable, can be worn with or without a bra and cost about $20 per pair.

If you have nipple soreness (you have our sympathies!), Jeri from Stoneham, MA recommended a product called Soothies (soothies.com). These reusable gel pads can be slipped into your bra to cool and soothe painful nipples. You can find them online or in drugstores for $12.

◆ **Nursing Clothes.** You may not think so (especially at 8 1/2 months), but there will come a day when you won't need to wear those maternity clothes. But what if you want to nurse in public after baby is born? Some women swear by nursing clothes as the best way to be discreet, but others do just fine with loose knit tops and button front shirts. Bottom line: one obvious way to save money with nursing clothes is not to buy any. If you want to experiment, buy one or two nursing tops and see how they work for you. By the way, parents of twins found it difficult if not impossible to use a nursing top when nursing both babies at the same time. See the previous box for more reader feedback on nursing clothes.

Reader Tracy G. suggested that working moms who are nursing or expressing milk might want to check into getting a nursing camisole or tank top. "I wear them under a regular shirt and don't feel so exposed when I pump at work or nurse in public." Her favorite: a Wal-Mart brand camisole. She thought it was softer than Mimi Maternity or Motherhood Maternity options.

◆ **Nursing Pajamas.** Looking for something comfortable to sleep in that allows you to nurse easily? Nursing PJ's are one answer, although only a few moms we interviewed use them. Most hated nursing gowns and found it much simpler to sleep in pajamas with tops they could pull up or unbutton quickly

If you are interested in a specific nursing pajama, check out **Majamas** (majamas.com). One of our product testers tried out their cotton/lycra t-shirt with her newborn and thought it was great, worthy of a recommendation. It allowed her to sleep without wearing a nursing bra since it had pockets for holding breast pads and had easy nursing access. They have several pajama designs as well as t-shirts and have expanded the line to include maternity clothes.

 ## More Money Buys You . . .

Like any clothing, the more you spend, the better quality fabric and construction you get. Of course, do you really need a cashmere maternity sweater you'll wear for only a few months? Besides fabric, you'll note more designer names as prices go up. For example, Lilly Pulitzer, Nicole Miller, Juicy Couture and Vivian Tam are making maternity clothes now.

 ## Smart Shopper Tips

Smart Shopper Tip #1
Battling your wacky thermostat
"It's early in my pregnancy, and I'm finding that the lycra-blend blouses that I wear to work have become very uncomfortable. I'm starting to shop for maternity clothes—what should I look for that will be more comfortable?"

It's a fact of life for us pregnant folks—your body's thermostat has gone berserk. Thanks to those pregnancy hormones, it may be hard to regulate your body's temperature. And those lycra-blend clothes may not be so comfortable anymore.

Our advice: stick with natural fabrics as much as possible, especially cotton. Unfortunately, a lot of lower-priced maternity clothing is made of polyester/cotton blend fabrics.

Smart Shopper Tip #2
Seasons change
"Help! My baby is due in October, but I still need maternity clothes for the hot summer months! How can I buy my maternity wardrobe without investing a fortune?"

Unless you live in a place with endless summer, most women have to buy maternity clothes that will span both warm and cold seasons. The best bets are items that work in BOTH winter or summer—for example, lightweight long-sleeve shirts can be rolled up in the summer. Cropped pants can work in both spring and fall. Another tip: layer clothes to ward off cold. Of course, there's another obvious way to save: borrow items from friends. If you just need a few items to bridge the seasons (a coat, heavy sweater, etc), try to borrow before buying.

Smart Shopper Tip #3
Petites aren't always petite

"I'm only 5 feet 2 inches tall and obviously wear petite sizes. I ordered a pair of pants in a petite size from an online discounter, but they weren't really shorter in the leg. In fact, I'd have to have the pants reconstructed to get the right fit. What gives?"

Many maternity web sites advertise that they carry a wide range of sizes but in truth you may find the choices very limited. And in some cases, "petite" is really just sizes 2 to 4. Translation: these pants aren't really shorter in the leg. How can you tell without ordering and then having to return items? Your best bet is to try on items before you buy. That's not always easy, of course, especially when ordering online. In that case, check the size charts on each site to be sure they offer *real* petites. And if a manufacturer (like the Gap, for example) makes petites that fit you in their regular clothing, chances are they also will in their maternity line.

Here are our readers recommendations for petite maternity: Kohl's, JCPenney, Old Navy, Gap, Japanese Weekend, Mimi Maternity, Juicy Couture, Rebel jeans and Lands End.

Smart Shopper Tip #4
Tall is easy either

"At nearly six feet, I can't find any maternity pants that don't look dorky. Help!"

Just as with petites, we see lots of sites promising a wide range of sizes . . . only to find they have one style that comes in a 31" inseam. And you need a 34." I feel your pain. At 5'9" myself, I recall finding almost nothing in the right length for me. There are more choices today for tall women, but you may find yourself forced to wear more skirts and dresses than pants during your pregnancy. Here's a partial list of sites that carry tall maternity: JC Penney, Jake and Me Clothing Company (jakeandme.com), Eva Lillian (evalillian.com), Mom Shop (momshop.com), Isabella Oliver (isabellaoliver.com), Gap, and Old Navy. If you discover any new sites or stores with tall sizing, email the us and we'll add them.

Fetal Monitors: Good idea?

If you're like us, you waited with baited breath to hear your baby's heartbeat at about ten to 12 weeks. Finally, a real indication that you're about to become parents (as if the morning sickness wasn't clue enough)!

Your doctor used a fetal heart monitor to listen to your baby's heartbeat. And now you've discovered you can buy your own fetal heart monitor online. So should you?

The *Wall St. Journal* recently asked this question of both doctors and the Food and Drug Administration (they regulate these monitors). In response, the FDA noted that fetal heart monitors are a medical device and, as such, require a prescription from a doctor. While some sites will not rent or sell a monitor to a parent without the prescription, others assume you have your doctor's okay.

Why do you need a prescription? After all, isn't a heart monitor just a Doppler ultrasound that checks the heartbeat? What's the big deal?

Doppler ultrasound devices use acoustical energy that is emitted continuously from the unit. It's the "continuous" part that has doctors and the FDA concerned. In your doctor's office, he or she will use a fetal heart monitor for a few minutes. But unsupervised parents at home may decide to use it every day for longer periods of time. The risk: the unit could heat up causing damage to the fetus.

Our advice: don't bother with a fetal heart monitor. If you want to use a fetal heart monitor to make sure your child doesn't have a defect or problem, don't bother. It's unlikely that an untrained person would be able to detect a defect. Doctors are trained to listen for and identify defects or disruptions in a baby's heartbeat; parents are not. And most likely you'll be seeing your doctor enough in the next several months to allow her to find any problems.

As for the "entertainment value" of hearing your baby's heartbeat and sharing it with others we'd recommend a simple option—consider buying a good stethoscope. Then have your doctor teach you how to use it to hear your baby's heartbeat. By about 18 weeks you can usually hear a heartbeat with a stethoscope. And you can buy one for as little as $100.

Our Picks: Brand Recommendations for Maternity Undergarments

Thank goodness for e-mail. Here at the home office in Boulder, CO our e-mail (authors@BabyBargains.com) has overflowed with great suggestions from readers on maternity undergarments.

God bless Canada—those Maple Leaf-heads make one of the best maternity bras in the world. Toronto-based **Bravado Designs** (for a brochure, call 800-590-7802 or 416-466-8652; web: bravadodesigns.com) makes a maternity/nursing bra of the same name that's just incredible. "A godsend!" raved one reader. "It's built like a sports bra with no under wire and supports better than any other bra I've tried . . . and this is my third pregnancy!" raved another. The Original Bravado bra comes in three support levels, sizes up to 42-46 with an F-G cup and six of wonderful colors/patterns (you can also call them for custom sizing information). Available via mail order, the bra costs $35. New models now available from Bravado include the Supreme design for fuller-breasted women and the Lifestyle bra is a microfibre design with a "cotton-flex" lining for extra comfort.

Another plus: the Bravado salespeople are knowledgeable and quite helpful with sizing questions. In the past, some of our readers criticized the Bravado for not providing enough support, but the new Supreme should answer those concerns. Our readers have noticed great prices on Bravado Bras at WeartheBaby.com ($32 including shipping).

Some readers have complained that Bravado bras don't have enough support or that the chest elastic curls up. One reader recommended the **YES! Bra** from YES! Breastfeeding (yesbreastfeeding.com) instead. She noted that "the chest elastic doesn't curl and it's much more supportive than Bravado." At $20, it's also very affordable.

Playtex Expectant Moments brand was mentioned by our readers as a good choice as well. They offer two nursing bra choices, an underwire and an underwire alternative. Sizes range from B to DDD cups and 34" to 44". A nice touch, they offer sizing advice specifically for maternity and nursing customers on their web site at playtex.com. You'll find these bras at stores like JCPenney. **Medela**, as you'd imagine, also has a good following for their bras. Four options are available: Comfort, Classic, Seamless and a new Sleep bra. Some are also available in extended sizes from 36F to 46H. Prices average around $32.

Finally, one reader recommended a nursing bra she found on line at **iMaternity.com** for those with larger bra sizes:

"As a 36 H, the Original Bravado Bra just didn't do much to stop inertia from taking over! I have to recommend instead a bra found at imaternity.com. On the site it is called the Cotton Under wire Nursing Bra, but the label reads Leading Lady Style #488. It comes in sizes up to or past H and does wonders for me! Just wanted to try to spare someone else the hassle of ordering so many bras at 30$ each in order to find one that gets the job done." (Update: when last we checked the site still had the underwire option but only up to an F. Their Soft Cup bra does go up to an H.) Leading Lady bras are available in many department stores at maternity outlets. Their web site is leadinglady.com and they manufacturer quite a wide assortment of bras is a huge range of sizes.

Looking for maternity shorts/tights for working out? One of the best is *Fit Maternity* (fitmaternity.com; 800-961-9100). They offer an unbelievable assortment of workout clothes including unitards, tights, swimsuits, tennis clothes and more. Also check out their books and work out tapes. On the same subject, *Due Maternity* (duematernity.com; 800-342-4448) offers several yoga and workout pants as well as swimsuits.

Our Picks: Brand Recommendations for Nursing Bras, Pads and Clothes

Nursing pads are a passionate topic for many of our readers with disposables beating out reusables as moms' favorites. They loved both *Lansinoh* and *Johnson & Johnson* disposable by an overwhelming number. *Medela*, *Advent* and *Bravado* make great reusable nursing pads.

Bravado is also quite popular as a nursing bra for all but the largest of cup sizes as are *Playtex* and *Medela*. If you need a size larger than DD, consider *Motherhood Maternity's* brand as well as *Leading Lady*. The web is the best place to find bras on deal including *Decent Exposures* (decentexposures.com) and *Birth and Baby* (birthandbaby.com).

Most moms found that specialized nursing clothes weren't a necessity, but for those who want to try them, nearly everyone recommended *Motherwear* (motherwear.com). *One Hot Mama* (onehotmama.com) and *Expressiva* (expressiva.com) were other stylish sites to consider. Look for discounts on clearance pages or eBay.com.

 *Wastes of Money*

Waste of Money #1
Maternity Bra Blues
"My old bras are getting very tight. I recently went to my local

department store to check out larger sizes. The salesperson suggested I purchase a maternity bra because it would offer more comfort and support. Should I buy a regular bra in a larger size or plunk down the extra money for a maternity bra?

We've heard from quite a few readers who've complained that expensive maternity bras they've bought were very uncomfortable and/or fell apart after just a few washings. Our best advice: try on the bra before purchase and stick to the better brands. Compared to regular bras, the best maternity bras typically have thicker straps, more give on the sides and more hook and eye closures in back (so the bra can grow with you). Most of all, the bra should be comfortable and have no scratchy lace or detailing. Readers tell us that a good sports bra can also be a fine (and affordable) alternative.

Waste of Money #2
Over the Shoulder Tummy Holder

"I keep seeing those 'belly bras' advertised as the best option for a pregnant mom. What are they for and are they worth buying?"

Belly bras provide additional support for your back during your pregnancy. One style envelopes your whole torso and looks like a tight-fitting tank top. No one can argue that, in many cases, the strain of carrying a baby is tough even on women in great physical shape. So, if you find your back, hips, and/or legs are giving you trouble, consider buying a belly bra.

However, in our research, we noticed most moms don't seem to need or want a belly bra. The price for one of these puppies can range from $35 to an incredible $55. The bottom line: hold off buying a belly bra or support panty until you see how your body reacts to your pregnancy. Also, check with your doctor to see if she has any suggestions for back, hip, and leg problems.

Waste of Money #3
Overexposed Nursing Gowns/Tops

"I refuse to buy those awful nursing tops! Not only are they ugly, but those weird looking panels are like wearing a neon sign that says BREASTFEEDING MOM AHEAD!"

"I plan to nurse my baby and all my friends say I should buy nursing gowns for night feedings. Problem is, I've tried on a few and even though the slits are hidden, I still feel exposed. Not to mention they're the ugliest things I've ever seen. Can't I just wear a regular gown that buttons down the front?"

Of course you can. And considering how expensive some nursing gowns can be ($35 to $50 each), buying a regular button-up nightshirt or gown will certainly save you a few bucks. Every mother we interviewed about nursing gowns had the same complaint. There isn't a delicate way to put this: it's not easy to get a breast out of one of those teenie-weenie slits. Did the person who designed these ever breastfeed a baby? I always felt uncovered whenever I wore a nursing gown, like one gust of wind would have turned me into a centerfold for a nudist magazine.

And can we talk about nursing shirts with those "convenient button flaps for discreet breastfeeding"? Convenient, my fanny. There's so much work involved in lifting the flap up, unbuttoning it, and getting your baby positioned that you might as well forget it. My advice: stick with shirts you can pull up or unbutton down the front. These are just as discreet, easier to work with, and (best of all) you don't have to add some expensive nursing shirts (at $30 to $50 each) to your wardrobe. See box earlier for more feedback from real moms.

Another tip: if possible, try on any nursing clothing BEFORE you buy. See how easy they are to use. You might be surprised how easy (or difficult) an item can be. Imagine as you are doing this that you have an infant that is screaming his head off wanting to eat NOW, not five seconds from now. You can see why buying any nursing clothes sight unseen is a risk.

Waste of Money #4
New shoes

> *"Help! My feet have swollen and none of my shoes fit!"*

Here's a little fact of pregnancy that no one tells you: your feet are going to swell and grow. And, sadly, after the baby is born, those tootsies won't be shrinking back to your pre-pregnancy size. A word to the wise: don't buy lots of new shoes at the start of your pregnancy. But no need to despair. After your baby is born, you'll likely have a built-in excuse to go shoe shopping!

Another suggestion from reader Gretchen C. of Rochester, WA: "It is never too early to buy shoes that don't tie! I go to the gym every morning, and it was getting to be a huge ordeal just to get my shoes tied. I bought some slip on shoes at 20 weeks and I still think it's one of the smartest things I've done."

 *Money-Saving Secrets*

CONSIDER BUYING "PLUS" SIZES FROM A REGULAR STORE.
Thankfully, fashion lately has been heavy on casual looks . . .

even for the office. This makes pregnancy a lot easier since you can buy the same styles in larger ladies' sizes to cover your belly without compromising your fashion sense or investing in expensive and often shoddily-made maternity clothes. We found the same fashions in plus-size stores for 20% to 35% less than maternity shops (and even more during sales).

One drawback to this strategy: by the end of your pregnancy, your hemlines may start to look a little "high-low"—your expanding belly will raise the hemline in front. This may be especially pronounced with dresses. Of course, that's the advantage of buying maternity clothes: the designers compensate with more fabric in front to balance the hemline. Nonetheless, we found that many moms we interviewed were able to get away with plus-size fashions for much (if not all) of their pregnancy. How much can you save? In many cases, from 25% to 50% off those high prices in maternity chains like Pea in the Pod.

2 **DON'T OVER-BUY BRAS.** As your pregnancy progresses, your bra size is going to change at least a couple times. Running out to buy five new bras when you hit a new cup size is probably foolish—in another month, all those bras may not fit. The best advice: buy the bare minimum (two or three).

3 **TRY BRA EXTENDERS.** You may be able to avoid buying lots of maternity bras by purchasing a few bra extenders. Available from fabric stores, OneHanesPlace.com and even Amazon.com among other sites, these little miracles cost as little as $1.50. You simply hook the extender onto the back of your bra and you can add up to two inches around the bust. You may still need to purchase new bras at some point, but with extenders, you can continue to use your pre-pregnancy bra for quite a while.

4 **BUT DON'T SKIMP ON QUALITY WHEN IT COMES TO MATERNITY BRAS AND UNDERWEAR.** Take some of the money you save from other parts of this book and invest in good maternity underwear. Yes, you can find cheap bras for $19 at discount stores, but don't be penny-wise and pound-foolish. We found the cheap stuff is very uncomfortable and falls apart, forcing you to go back and buy more. Investing in better-quality bras and underwear also makes sense if you plan to have more than one child—you can actually wear it again for subsequent pregnancies.

5 **CONSIDER DISCOUNTERS FOR CASUAL CLOTHES.** Okay, I admit that I don't normally shop at K-Mart or Target for my clothes. But I was surprised to discover these chains (and even department stores like Sears) carry casual maternity clothes in 100% cotton at very affordable prices. Let's repeat that—they have 100% cotton t-shirts, shorts, pants, and more at prices you won't believe. Most of these clothes are in basic solid colors—sorry, no fancy prints. At Target, for example, I found a 100% cotton white maternity t-shirt (long sleeves) for $10. Velour lounge pants were only $25; jeans were $27. Even a knit skirt was a mere $17. If you buy from one of these discounters, just be sure that you check the fabric and try everything on before you buy. You don't want to have to lug the stuff back to the store. And Target now has maternity apparel from designers like Liz Lange. Our readers say the quality is a bit less than the regular, specialty store version, but the style is good and the prices can't be beat. Don't forget to check Target's sale rack too. One reader found items for as little as $4 on sale.

While the discounters don't carry much in the way of career wear, you'll save so much on casual/weekend clothes that you'll be ecstatic anyway. Witness this example. At A Pea in the Pod, we found a white, cotton-knit top and stretch twill pants. The price for the two pieces: a heart-stopping $290. A similar all-cotton tank top/shorts outfit from Target was $50. Whip out a calculator, and you'll note the savings is an amazing 80%. Need we say more? Not to mention that nice casual clothes are acceptable for office wear these days anyway.

By the way, don't forget to check out stores like Kohls, Marshall's, Ross and TJ MAXX. One reader told us she found maternity clothes at 60% off at TJ MAXX. Old Navy and the Gap have added maternity to their web sites and many readers have found great, comfortable clothes at good prices. Corrie, a reader from Chicago, did all her maternity shopping on line at Old Navy. She spent a total of $365 for eight pairs of pants, one pair of jeans, eleven sweaters, eight long sleeve tops, three button-down shirts, five sleeveless tops and two cardigans. This works out to less than $10 per piece!

6 **RENT EVENING WEAR—DON'T BUY.** We found that some indie maternity stores rent eveningwear. For example, a local shop we visited had an entire rack of rental formalwear. An off-white lace dress (perfect for attending a wedding) rented for just $50. Compare that with the purchase price of $200+. Sadly, places that rent maternity wear are few and far between, but it might be worth a look-see in your local community.

7 **CHECK OUT CONSIGNMENT STORES.** You can find "gently worn" career and casual maternity clothes for 40% to 70% off the original retail! Many consignment or second-hand stores carry only designer-label clothing in good to excellent condition. If you don't want to buy used garments, consider recouping some of your investment in maternity clothes by consigning them after the baby is born. You can usually find listings for these stores in the phone book or online. (Don't forget to look under children's clothes as well. Some consignment stores that carry baby furniture and clothes also have a significant stock of maternity wear.) One web source to find consignment shops is narts.org.

8 **FIND AN OUTLET.** Check out the next section of this chapter for the low-down on maternity clothes outlets.

9 **BE CREATIVE.** Raid your husband's closet for over-sized shirts and pants.

10 **SEW IT YOURSELF.** A reader in California emailed in this recommendation: she loved the patterns for nursing clothes by Elizabeth Lee Designs (435-454-3350; web: elizabeth-lee.com). "I would think anyone with a bit of sewing experience could handle any of the patterns, which don't LOOK like nursing dresses or tops." In addition to patterns, Elizabeth Lee also sells ready-made dresses and tops. Another bonus: the company has one of the largest selections of nursing bras we've seen, including Bravado Bras.

Pattern companies like Simplicity (simplicity.com) and McCall (mccall.com; includes Butterick and Vogue as well) have their patterns online and in fabric stores. You'll find a limited selection of designs, but if you're a sewing maven, here's a way to avoid the high prices and frustrating return policies of retail maternity stores.

11 **BEG AND BORROW.** Unless you're the first of your friends to get pregnant you know someone who's already been through this. Check around to see if you can borrow old maternity clothes from other moms. In fact, we loaned out a big box after our second baby was born and it has made the rounds of the whole neighborhood. And don't forget to be generous after your baby making days are over too.

12 **CHECK OUT CLEARANCE AREAS IN CATALOGS AND ONLINE.** Many of our most devoted discount shopping readers have scored big deals on their favorite web sites' clearance pages. For example, on Motherwear.com we noticed a "Safari Wrap Nursing Dress," regularly marked at $65 but on sale for only $19. Old Navy had some herringbone trousers marked down to $18 and the Gap had a v-neck cable sweater, regularly $48 for only $25.

13

WHEN ORDERING MATERNITY CLOTHES FROM WEB SITES, POOL YOUR ORDERS! Most web sites offer a free shipping option on orders of $75 to $100 or more (especially after holidays and during end of season sales). Check to see what deals they're offering when you visit. Also, chain stores like the Gap will let you return items to your local store, saving you the return-shipping fee.

Outlets

MOTHERHOOD MATERNITY OUTLETS

Locations: 85 Motherhood outlets and 10 Maternity Works outlets. For location info, call (800) 466-6223.

The offspring of the catalog and retail stores of maternity giant Motherhood Maternity (see review later in this chapter), these outlets have started springing up in outlet malls across the country. On a recent visit, the outlet featured markdowns from 20% to 75% on the same designs you see in their catalog or retail stores.

GAP CLEARANCE CENTER

Location: Prime Outlets, Birch Run, MI; Rockvale Square Outlets, Lancaster, PA; 2050 Global Way, Hebron, KY .(859) 586-3320

Reader Michelle R. of Cincinnati, OH recently emailed us about the Gap Clearance Center in Hebron, KY (15 minutes outside Cincinnati). "Not only do they sell regular Gap and Old Navy clothing for kids and adults, they also have a rather large maternity department. On my last trip there, they had racks and racks of maternity jeans for $5 a piece! All pants, skirts, shorts, long sleeve and short sleeve shirts were also $5 a piece. Sweaters were a bit pricier at $10, but when you're saving all that money you don't feel bad about the splurge. My girlfriend was able to pick up a couple of maternity blazers at great prices as well. The store is usually jam packed but the staff runs a very orderly process in the dressing rooms and at the check out lines."

The Name Game:
Reviews of Selected Maternity Stores

Usually this section is intended to acquaint you with the clothing name brands you'll see in local stores. But now there is only one giant chain of maternity wear in North America—Mothers Work Inc., which operates stores under three brand names and the Internet. This company is the 800 pound gorilla of maternity clothes with over 1500 locations (739 leased departments in Macy's and other stores) in the US, Canada and Puerto Rico. Mothers Work has over a 40% share of the $1.2 billion maternity clothing market in the US. So let's take a look at these three divisions, a new concept they've added, and their Internet site.

◆ **Motherhood.** With 690 stores, Motherhood is the biggest sister in the chain. While most stores are located in malls and power centers, 232 are also leased departments within department stores like Sears. Motherhood carries maternity clothes in the lowest price points. As an example, dresses at Motherhood range from $17 to $50. They also have 95 outlets. By the way, you may see Motherhood's line, Oh! Baby in Kohl's Department stores, while they make Two Hearts brand for Sears.

Watch out for return policies!

Have you bought a maternity dress you don't like or that doesn't fit? Too bad—most maternity stores have draconian return policies that essentially say "tough!" Most don't accept returns and others will only offer store credit. A word to the wise: make sure you REALLY like that item (and it fits) before you give any maternity store your money. A reader in Brisbane, California emailed us with the most horrific story we've ever heard about maternity stores' return policies.

"I recently visited a Dan Howard (now owned by Mothers Work) maternity store in San Francisco and was shocked to find their return policy stands even when you haven't left their store yet! They overcharged me for a sale item that was miss marked and then said all they could give me was store credit for the difference! I hadn't stepped one foot outside the store! They refused to credit my charge card, so now I'm stuck with a $65 store credit for a place I despise!"

Remember: ALL Motherswork stores (including Mimi and Pea in the Pod) share their appalling return/refund policies.

◆ ***Mimi Maternity.*** Mimi is intended to be the middle price point of the three divisions. Mimi supposed to be a more hip, youthful take on maternity. Here you'll find a more fashion-forward look with dresses in the $78 to $200 price range. They have 125 stores. Their target is the JCrew customer or Banana Republic shopper.

◆ ***A Pea in the Pod.*** Finally, A Pea in the Pod (APIP) is Mothers Works' most expensive division. With dress prices ranging from $145 to $300, you can see what we mean. APIP has only 37 stores and is positioned to be more of a designer boutique. Hence you'll find them in locations like Beverly Hills and Madison Ave. On their web site, they describe their target shopper to be someone with "closets filled with Prada, Gucci and Armani."

◆ ***Destination Maternity Superstore.*** These superstores (check their web site at destinationmaternity.com for locations) combine A Pea in the Pod, Mimi Maternity and Motherhood Maternity under one roof. They also include a spa called Edamame Spa offering a wide range of classes with topics like yoga, scrap booking 101 and financial planning. Only the New York City location is open at this time.

All these stores carry mostly merchandise designed in house, exclusively for the different divisions.

Now that you know the basics, what do real moms think of Mothers Works' stores? First and foremost, moms dislike, no, hate their return policy. The policy is pretty basic, once you've bought an item, you have ten days to return it for store credit or exchange only (you must have the tags and receipt too). No refunds. What if it falls apart in the wash on day 11? Too bad for you. By the way, if you order an item online from Mother Works web site, you'll find a more generous return policy: *Items can be returned for refund or exchange and you have 30 days to return the clothing.* You cannot return items bought online to the store or vice versa, but at least you get extra time and even the money back with an online return. Our advice, if you see it in the store, try it on. If you like it, go home and order it online.

And don't forget that some of these chain stores lease space in larger department stores like Macy's and Sears. In those cases, the leased stores have to comply with the same generous return policy of the department store where they lease space. Good news for you.

As for individual chains, most moms agreed that the quality at Motherhood is poor. Although some readers have praised their maternity and nursing bras, in general, most agree with the following: "I have found the quality to be inconsistent. I've bought shirts that have unraveled within a few months. . . trashy!" The consensus seems to be that if you buy at Motherhood, you should stick to the sale rack and don't expect high quality except for their bras.

Mimi Maternity received better marks from our readers for their clothes. Prices are higher than at Motherhood, but so is the quality. We've received fewer complaints about this division. And many moms liked the more stylish clothing. They sell the Olga line of bras, which many readers liked as well.

A Pea in the Pod is just way too expensive. That's the general feeling among our readers about this store. Most moms don't feel the style of clothing at this chain is anything special. Certainly not to spend $85 for a cotton t-shirt. Considering how short a time a pregnancy is it's a huge waste of money to spend over $180 on a Pea in the Pod shorts outfit. And what about their "legendary" service, as Pea in the Pod likes to tout? It's a joke, say our readers. One mom summed it up best by saying: "For the price that one is paying, one expects a certain degree of customer service and satisfaction, both of which are lacking in this over-priced store. What a complete and utter disappointment!"

Consumer alert: one new mom warned us about giving personal info to a maternity chain when you make a purchase (clerks may ask you if you want to receive sales notices). The problem: you often end up on junk mailing lists. In the case of our reader, even though she specifically requested the chain not sell her information to third parties, they did so. Once on those lists, it's tough to stop the junk from arriving in your mailbox.

Do it By Mail

JCPENNEY

To Order Call: (800) 222-6161. Ask for "Maternity Collection" catalog.
Web: JCPenney.com/shopping

Perhaps the best aspect of Penney's maternity offerings is their wide range of sizes—you can find petites, talls, ultra-talls and women's petites and women's regular sizes. It's darn near impossible to find women's sizes in maternity wear today, but Penney's carries sizes up to 32W and some styles are available in petites and talls.

What most impressed us about Penney's maternity catalog was their career clothes. For example, we saw a nice wrap dress for just $40. This polyester outfit was available in women's and misses sizes. Most of JCPenney's career wear this time around is separates, giving the option of mixing and matching with pieces you may already have. We saw a wide array of affordably priced cotton maternity shirts and jeans. A selection of nightgowns, swimsuits, nursing shirts and lingerie round out the offerings.

One bargain hint: Penney's has quite a few unadvertised sales and discounts on maternity wear. When placing your order, inquire about any current deals.

E-MAIL FROM THE REAL WORLD
Stay fit with pregnancy workout videos

Sure, there are plenty of workout videos targeted at the preggo crowd. But which are the best? Readers give this their top picks, starting with Margaret Griffin:

"As a former certified aerobics instructor, I have been trying out the video workouts for pregnancy. I have only found three videos available in my local stores, but I wanted to rate them for your readers.

"**Buns of Steel: Pregnancy & Post-Pregnancy Workouts** with Madeleine Lewis ($13) gets my top rating. Madeleine Lewis has excellent cueing, so the workout is easy to follow. Your heart rate and perceived exertion are both used to monitor your exertion. There is an informative introduction. And I really like the fact that the toning segment utilizes a chair to help you keep your balance, which can be off a little during pregnancy. Most of the toning segment is done standing. This is a safe, effective workout led by a very capable instructor and I highly recommend it."

"A middle rating goes to **Denise Austin's: Fit & Firm Pregnancy** ($15). Denise has a good information segment during which she actually interviews a physician. She also provides heart rate checks during the workout. However, there are a couple of things about this workout that I don't particularly like. First, during the workout, there are times when safety information is provided regarding a particular move. This is fine and good, but instead of telling you to continue the movement and/or providing a picture-in-a-picture format, they actually change the screen to show the safety information and then cut back into the workout in progress. Surprise! You were supposed to keep doing the movement. Second, Denise Austin is a popular instructor, but I personally find that her cueing is not as sharp as I prefer and sometimes she seems to be a little offbeat with the music. My suggestion is get this video to use in addition to other videos if you are the type who gets easily bored with one workout."

Reader Laura McDowell recommended a few different workout DVDs. **Leisa Hart's FitMama** ($15) workout DVD was a favorite. "I loved it! Leisa has great energy and her peppy attitude made me smile through the whole workout. It has about 20 minutes of salsa dancing and then modified yoga." Laura also enjoyed *Kathy Smith's Pregnancy Workout* ($10). It was "a total 80s throwback; fun and energizing. She moves through the steps fast at times, but is always clear about offering ways to slow down if you need to. The hair, outfits and music are highly entertaining so the workout goes fast and feels great."

Another reader recommended **The Perfect Pregnancy Workout** DVD ($25). "It's by a former Cirque du Soleil acrobat, who leads the exercises with a French accent. It also offers beginner, intermediate and advanced options for each exercise."

Yoga is a terrific low impact exercise that does a wonderful job of stretching muscles you'll use while carrying and delivering your child. It's a terrific option for pregnant moms. And it's definitely become one of the most popular exercise options in North America. So it was only a matter of time before our readers began reviewing yoga DVDs. Here are some of their comments:

Another reader, Sheri Gomez, recommended Yoga Zone's video **Postures for Pregnancy** ($15), calling it "wonderful for stretching and preventing back problems. It's beginner friendly and not too out there with the yoga thing." Her only complaint: there is no accompanying music, so she played her own CDs along with the tape.

Eufemia Campagna recommended Yoga Journal's **Prenatal Yoga** with Shiva Rea ($20). She noted that each segment of the tape is done using three women different stages of pregnancy. "The segments are all accompanied by lovely, relaxing music and the instructor's directions are so clear that you don't even have to look at the TV to know what you need to do!" Another reader, Carolyn Oliner, also complimented this tape: "It's not so much of a traditional yoga workout but a

great series of poses and stretches that work for pregnant women and leave you feeling warm and stretched and (more gently) exercised." Finally, another reader noted that this workout is "really gentle (pretty easy for experienced yogini)." Available on DVD.

Finally, we should note that pilates has also been adapted for pregnancy exercise. You'll find several options on DVD including **Pilates During Pregnancy, Jennifer Gianni's Fusion Pilates for Pregnancy**, and **Prenatal Pilates** as well as many others.

Note: Amazon.com is a great source to find these videos. If you have any favorite DVDs, email us your review of them and we'll add them to our collection. One of our readers noted that NetFlix (netflix.com) has a huge assortment of pregnancy DVDs for rent if you don't want to buy.

The Bottom Line:
A Wrap-Up of Our Best Buy Picks

For career and casual maternity clothes, we thought the best deals were from the Old Navy, the Gap and Motherhood stores. Compared to retail maternity chains (where one suit can run $300), you can buy your entire wardrobe from these two places for a song.

If your place of work allows more casual dress, check out the prices at plus-size stores or alternatives like Old Navy. A simple pair of jeans that could cost $135 at a maternity shop are only $35 or less at Old Navy. And if you prefer the style at maternity shops, only hit them during sales, where you can find decent bargains. Another good idea: borrow from your husband's closet—shirts, sweat pants and sweatshirts are all items that can do double-duty as maternity clothes.

For weekend wear, we couldn't find a better deal than the 100% cotton shirts and shorts at discounters like Target, Wal-Mart and K-Mart. Prices are as little as $9 per shirt—compare that to the $80 price tag at maternity chain stores for a simple cotton shirt.

Invited to a wedding? Rent that dress from a maternity store and save $100 or more. Don't forget to borrow all you can from friends who've already had babies. In fact, if you follow all our tips on maternity wear, bras, and underwear, you'll save $700 or more. Here's the breakdown:

1. Career Wear: $240. Old Navy featured cuffed stretch pants, a blazer and t-shirt for a mere $75. Buy two versions of these in different colors, add a couple nice dresses (another $60) and skirts ($60) and you're set.

2. Casual Clothes: $100. Five outfits of 100% cotton t-shirts and shorts/pants from Target run $100. Don't forget sale items on Gap Maternity as well as Old Navy's maternity line.

3. Underwear: $200 to $300. We strongly suggest investing in top-quality underwear for comfort and sanity purposes. For example, a Bravado bra is $35. Some readers have found good deals on affordable underwear at Target or online. Either way, you need eight pairs of underwear, plus six bras, including regular/nursing and sleep bras. One tip: see if you can wear your pre-pregnancy panties . . . this works for some moms, saving the $100 expense in "maternity" underwear.

Total damage: $540 to $640. If you think that's too much money for clothes you'll only wear for a few months, consider the cost if you outfit yourself at full-price maternity shops. The same selection of outfits would run $1200 to $1400.

CHAPTER 6

Feeding

Inside this chapter

How much money can you save by breastfeeding? What are the best options for pumps? Which bottles are best? We'll discuss these topics as well as ways to get discount formula, including details on which places have the best deals. And of course, we'll have tips and reviews on the next step in feeding: solid food. Finally, let's talk about high chairs—who's got the best value? Durability? Looks?

Breastfeeding

As readers of past editions of this book know, we are big proponents of breastfeeding. The medical benefits of breast milk are well documented, but obviously the decision to breast or bottle-feed is a personal call for each new mom. In the past, we spent time in this chapter encouraging breast-feeding . . . but we realize now we are preaching to the choir on this one. Our time is better spent discussing how to save on feeding your baby, no matter which way you go. So, we'll leave the discussion of breast versus bottle to other our other book *Baby 411* (as well your doctor and family). Let's talk about the monetary impact of the decision, however.

Breastfeed Your Baby and Save $500

Since this is a book on bargains, we'd be remiss in not mentioning the tremendous amount of money you can save if you breast-feed. Just think about it: no bottles, no expensive formula to prepare, no special insulated carriers to keep bottles warm/cold, etc.

So, how much money would you save? Obviously, NOT buying formula would be the biggest money-saver. Even if you were to use the less-expensive formula powder, you would still have to spend nearly $25 per 25.7-ounce can of powdered formula. Since each can makes 188 ounces of formula, the cost per ounce of formula is about 13¢.

That doesn't sound too bad, does it? Unless you factor in that a baby will down 32 ounces of formula per day by 12 weeks of age. Your cost per day would be $4.16. Assuming you breastfeed for at least the first six months, you would save a grand total of $759 *just on formula alone*. The American Academy of Pediatrics recommends breastfeeding for 12 months (with solid foods added to the mix at six months), so in that case your savings could be as much as $1500! That doesn't include the expense of bottles, nipples and accessories! By the way, statistically speaking, nearly 70% of American moms breastfeed their babies at birth. By six months, however, the number of breastfeeding moms drops to nearly 33%.

To be fair, there are some optional expenses that might go along with breastfeeding. The biggest dollar item: you might decide to buy a breast pump. Costs for this item range from $60 for a manual pump to $300 for a professional-grade breast pump. Or you can rent a pump for $45 a month (plus a kit—one time cost of about $50 to $60). And of course, you'll also need some bottles—but arguably fewer than if you formula-fed.

If $759 doesn't sound like a lot of money, consider the savings if you had to buy formula in the concentrated liquid form instead of the cheaper powder. A 32-ounce can of Enfamil ready-to-eat liquid costs about $5.60 at a grocery store and makes up only eight 4-ounce bottles. The bottom line: you could spend over $1000 on formula for your baby in the first six months alone!

Of course, we realize that some moms will decide to use formula because of a personal, medical or work situation—to help out, we have a section later in this chapter on how to save on formula, bottle systems and other necessary accessories.

Sources: Where to Find Breast Feeding Help

The basis of breastfeeding is attachment. Getting your new little one to latch onto your breast properly is not a matter of instinct. Some babies have no trouble figuring it out, while many others need your help and guidance. In fact, problems with attachment can lead to sore nipples and painful engorgement. Of course, you should be able to turn to your pediatrician or the nurses at the hospital for breastfeeding advice. However, if you find that they do not offer you the support you need, consider the following sources for breastfeeding help:

1 **La Leche League** (800) LA LECHE or web: lalecheleague. org. Started over 35 years ago by a group of moms in Chicago, La Leche League has traditionally been the most vocal supporter of breastfeeding in this country. You've got to imagine the amount of chutzpah these women had to have to buck the bottle trend and promote breastfeeding at a time when it wasn't fashionable (to say the least).

In recent years, La Leche has established branches in many communities, providing support groups for new moms interested in trying to nurse their children. They also offer a catalog full of books and videotapes on nursing, as well as other child care topics. Their famous book *The Womanly Art of Breastfeeding* is the bible for huge numbers of breastfeeding advocates. All in all, La Leche provides an important service and, coupled with their support groups and catalog of publications, is a valuable resource.

2 **Nursing Mothers' Council** (408) 272-1448, (web: nursingmothers.org). Similar in mission to La Leche League, the Nursing Mothers' Council differs on one point: the group emphasizes working moms and their unique needs and problems.

3 **Lactation Consultants.** Lactation consultants are usually nurses who specialize in breastfeeding education and problem solving. You can find them through your pediatrician, hospital, or the International Lactation Consultants Association (703) 560-7330 web: iblce.org. Members of this group must pass a written exam, complete 2500 hours of clinical practice and 30 hours of continuing education before they can be certified. At our local hospital, resident lactation consultants are available to answer questions by phone at no charge. If a problem persists, you can set up an in-person consultation for a minimal fee (about $40 to $90 per hour, although your health insurance provider may pick up the tab).

Unfortunately, the availability and cost of lactation consultants seems to vary from region to region. Our research shows that, in general, hospitals in the Western U.S. are more likely to offer support services, such as on-staff lactation consultants. Back East, however, the effort to support breastfeeding seems more spotty. Our advice: call area hospitals before you give birth to determine the availability of breastfeeding support. Another good source for a referral to a lactation consultant is your pediatrician.

4 **Hospitals.** Look for a hospital in your area that has breastfeeding-friendly policies. These include 24-hour rooming in (where your baby can stay with you instead of in a nursery) and breastfeeding on demand. Pro-nursing hospitals do not supplement babies with a bottle and don't push free formula samples.

5 **Books.** Although they aren't a substitute for support from your doctor, hospital, and family, many books provide plenty of info and encouragement. Check the La Leche League catalog for titles.

6 **The web.** We found several great sites with breastfeeding information and tips. Our favorite was **Medela** (medela.com), which is a leading manufacturer of breast pumps. Medela's site features extensive information resources and articles on breastfeeding, as well as advice on how to choose the right breast pump.

The catalog **Bosom Buddies** (bosombuddies.com or call 888-860-0041) has a web site with a good selection of breastfeeding articles, product information and links to other breastfeeding sites on the web.

Of course, our message boards are also a good place to find help—we have a special board on feeding where you can ask other moms for advice, tips and support. Hint: use our boards to find a discount web site that has the lowest price on a breast pump you want; there's always lots of discussion on who's the cheapest, who's offering free shipping and more. Go to BabyBargains.com and click on message boards.

7 **Your Health Insurance Provider.** Contact your health insurance provider as soon as you become pregnant. They often have a variety of services available to policyholders, but you have to ask.

8 **DVDs.** Yes there is a DVD available to teach you how to do just about anything. So why not a DVD on breastfeeding? Or two. The "Real Deal on Breastfeeding" ($23; RealDealVideos.com) covers issues like latching on, how to position your baby, different holds, trouble shooting and increasing your supply of milk. They've also included a selection of experiences from real breastfeeding moms to help remind you that you aren't alone in this.

Stephanie Neurohr is the mother of seven children (hence her company name: Mother of 7, Inc.), so you can't say she doesn't have experience. And with a film degree as well, it seems natural that she would produce a series of baby care videos. As part of her video series, Stephanie offers four breastfeeding DVDs (most of which are $37 to $47). These DVDs include interviews with 28 experts, as well as moms from around the world plus 3-D animation to help moms understand the mechanics of breastfeeding. You can see trailer for one of the videos on her web site at MotherOf7.com.

Parents in Cyberspace: What's on the Web?

Medela

Web: medela.com

What it is: A treasure trove of info on breastfeeding.

What's cool. Medela's web site is a great example of what makes the 'net so helpful—instead of just a thinly veiled pitch for their products, Medela stuffs their site with reams of useful info, tips and advice. Yeah, you can read about their different breast pumps, but the site is full of general breastfeeding tips, links to other sites and more. "Problems and Solutions" is an excellent FAQ for nursing moms. You'll also find instructions for all their products on line in case you misplace them!

Needs work: Although they've improved the site, you'll find it takes a lot of clicks to get where you want to go. And we'd still like to see approximate retail prices for Medela's products on the site.

Nursing Mother Supplies

Web: nursingmothersupplies.com

What it is: An extensive nursing supply resource.

What's cool: Not only does this site carry breast pumps and supplies from Medela and Ameda Egnell (among others), they offer support to customers after they buy. They have extensive FAQs on the site and even a breast pump comparison chart. They claim they discount all their pumps off regular retail, although we found the same prices elsewhere. Nursing pillows, storage options (the Mothers Milk Mate is $25), slings, Avent bottles and pads are also available.

Needs work: Not much to complain about here. The site is a bit primitive in design, but it does the job—loads fast, has a shopping cart feature, clear photos, etc. We also like the gentle approach to encouraging breast-feeding. These guys aren't too preachy.

Breast Pumps Direct

Web: breastpumpsdirect.com

What it is: A discount nursing supply resource.

What's cool: The prices. You can buy a Medela Pump in Style Advanced Backpack for $100 off retail. And that's not all. Breast Pumps Direct have Avent's new iQ, Ameda's Purely Yours and the Whisper Wear pumps as well—all on sale. Manual pumps and accessories are also sold on the site. And you can find reviews of pumps, comparison charts, tips on breastfeeding and more.

◆ *Other web sites:* Here are a couple sites with names that speak for themselves: *Affordable-medela-pumps.com* and *SelfExpressions.com*. Readers have mentioned both as great sites for pumps from Medela, Ameda, Nurture III and Whittlestone to name a few.. *Mommy's Own* (mommysown.com) carries nearly every brand of recommended pump, bottle, breast pad and more. You'll find Boppy pillows, Majamas nursing clothes and LilyPadz breast pads at decent prices plus advice and forums you can join. Finally, a reader, Cherie Kannarr, thought that *BreastFeeding.com* "is a wonderful site, filled with facts, stories, humor, and support for nursing mothers."

What Are You Buying?

Even if you are dedicated full-time to breastfeeding, you probably will find yourself needing to pump a bottle from time to time. After all, you might want to go out to dinner without the baby. Maybe you'll have an overnight trip for your job or just need to get back to work full or part time. Your spouse might even be interested in relieving you of a night feeding (in your dreams; anything's possible). The solution? Pumping milk. Whether you want to pump occasionally or every day, you have a wide range of options. Here's our take on them:

◆ *Manual Expression:* OK, technically, this isn't a breast pump in the sense we're talking about. But it is an option. There are several good breastfeeding books that describe how to express milk manually. Most women find that the amount of milk expressed, compared to the time and trouble involved, hardly makes it worth using this method. A few women (we think they are modern miracle workers) can manage to express enough for an occasional bottle; for the majority of women, however, using a breast pump is a more practical alternative. Manual expression is typically used only to relieve engorgement.

◆ *Manual Pumps:* Non-electric, hand-held pumps are operated by squeezing on a handle. While the most affordable option, manual pumps are generally also the least efficient—you simply can't duplicate your baby's sucking action by hand. Therefore, these pumps are best for moms who only need an occasional bottle or who need to relieve engorgement.

	Manual	Mini-Elec.	Piston Elec.	Rental*

BREAST PUMPS

Which pump works best in which situation?

Do you need a pump for:	Manual	Mini-Elec.	Piston Elec.	Rental*
A missed feeding?	■	◆		
Evening out from baby?	■	◆		
Working part-time.	■	◆		
Occasional use, a few times a week.	■	◆		
Working full-time.			●	●
Premature or hospitalized baby?			●	●
Low milk supply?			●	●
Sore nipples/engorgement?	■		●	●
Latch-on problems or breast infection?			■	●
Drawing out flat or inverted nipples?	■	◆	●	●

Key: ■ = Good ◆ = Better ● = Best
*Rental refers to renting a hospital-grade pump. These can usually be rented on a monthly basis.
Source: Medela.

pumps

◆ **Mini-Electrics:** These battery-operated breast pumps are designed to express an occasional bottle. Unfortunately, the sucking action is so weak that it often takes twenty minutes *per side* to express a significant amount of milk. And doing so is not very comfortable. Why is it so slow? Most models only cycle nine to fifteen times per minute—compare that to a baby who sucks the equivalent of 50 cycles per minute!

◆ **High-End Double Pumps:** The Mercedes of breast pumps—we can't sing the praises of these work horses enough. In just ten to twenty minutes, you can pump *both* breasts. And high-end double pumps are much more comfortable than mini-electrics. In fact, at first I didn't think a high-end pump I rented was working well because it was *so* comfortable. The bottom line: there is no better option for a working woman who wants to provide her baby with breast milk.

Today, you have two options when it comes to these pumps: rent a hospital-grade pump (which often is called a piston-electric) or buy a high-end consumer grade double-pump.

Rental Pumps. These are what the industry refers to as "hospital-grade pumps" or piston electric pumps." They are built to withstand continuous use of up to eight to ten times a day for many years. Often they are much heavier than personal use pumps like the Medela Pump-In-Style. And all the interior parts are sealed to prevent contamination from one renter to the next. *In fact, rental pumps are certified by the Food and Drug Administration (FDA) for multiple*

The best milk storage options

Once you've decided to express breast milk for your child, you'll need to consider how to store it. Freezer bags are the most common method and most major pump manufactures and bottle makers sell bags. So, who's got the best storage bags? **Lansinoh** (sold in Target) is the hands-down winner. "They are sturdy, stand on their own and have an excellent double lock seal closure," said one mom. Others echoed that recommendation.

In the past, we criticized **Medela**, the king of breastpumps, of having a dismal storage bag. Good news: apparently Medela took this criticism to heart and redesigned their collection/storage bags, which are now greatly improved. You can attach the bags directly to all Medela's pumps with a self-stick strap. They also added a zipper top-and Medela's new bags are made it out of special plastic that retains more of the milk's benefits.

A completely different alternative is **Mothers Milk Mate** (www. mothersmilkmate.com). For $30, you get a ten-bottle storage system with rack. Some parents have complained, however, that there are no nipples that will attach directly to the storage bottles. So they have to thaw the milk then pour it into another bottle/nipple. But if you can handle the extra steps, these bottles may be one of the best options for milk storage. Why? All those great antibodies in mom's milk stick to some types of bags and don't get to baby's mouth. That's why most lactation professionals prefer the hard polypropylene bottles (frosted plastic) for breast milk storage.

And finally, a brand new option for freezer storage: **Milk Trays** by Sensible Lines (SensibleLines.com). It's hard to believe no one has thought of this before-Milk Trays are like old-fashioned ice cube trays but with a twist. The tray's 16 one-ounce capacity cubes are shaped like skinny cylinders, small enough to fit into any baby bottle. It comes with a sealed lid to block freezer burn and is made from BPA-free plastic. The trays sell for $16 for two trays with lids.

use. The only item each renter must buy is a new collection kit.

Where to find: Pediatricians, lactation consultants, doulas, mid-wives, hospitals, maternity stores and home medical care companies are sources to find rental pumps. You can also call La Leche League (800-LALECHE; web: lalecheleague.org) or other lactation support groups for a referral to a company that rents piston electric pumps.

How much: Prices generally average about $45 per month to rent a breast pump. Most common brands of hospital grade rental pumps are Medela's Lactina Select (medela.com), White River Concepts Models WRC 9050 or 9600 (lactationconnection.com), Ameda Elite and Egnell Lact-E. Collection kits cost about $45 to $60 for the bottles, shields and tubes.

Professional-Grade Electric Pumps. These electric pumps are available for sale to consumers and are intended to be used no more than three or four times a day. Unlike rental pumps, they are lighter weight and easier to carry around (to work or elsewhere). These pumps have an open system without sealed parts and are therefore only recommended as a single use item. *The FDA, lactation consultants, pediatricians and manufacturers DO NOT recommend using a second-hand personal pump.* Even if you change the tubes and shields, there is a possibility of cross contamination. Examples of these pumps include the Medela Pump-In-Style and the Ameda Purely Yours.

Where to find: Online is a primary source. Also: most independent baby stores and Babies R Us stores carry a selection of electric breast pumps. See earlier in the chapter for some of our favorite sources.

How much: Prices range from about $150 to $350 depending on the brand and accessories included. Typically the collection kit is included in the price. We will review pumps next and include prices.

Breast Pumps (model by model reviews)

Manual Pumps

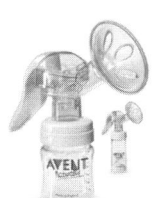

Avent Isis
Web: AventAmerica.com
Price: $50.
Type: Manual.
Comments: The best manual pump on the market. Our readers love this pump, which Avent claims is as efficient as a mini-electric (it takes about eight to ten minutes to empty a breast). You can buy the Isis by itself, or as part of a kit that includes extra bottles, cooler packs and

Breastfeeding in public: Exposing yourself for onlookers' fun and your baby's health

Here's a controversial topic to discuss around the office water cooler: breastfeeding in public. Since our society tends to see a woman's breasts as sexual objects rather than as utilitarian milk delivery systems, you will occasionally hear stories of moms who run into problems when they nurse their babies in public. Ironically, one of the chief advantages of breastfeeding is its portability. No hauling and cleaning bottles, mixing formula, and your child gets nourishment exactly when he needs it.

Amazingly, some parts of this country still manage to equate breastfeeding in public with indecent exposure. Florida recently repealed a law forbidding public breastfeeding after several women were cited by the "breast" police for whipping it out at a local mall. It's hard to believe that until just recently laws in this country branded one of life's most basic needs—eating—as illegal. You can call your local La Leche League or other breastfeeding sources to find out if your city or state still has laws like these. If they do, consider getting involved in trying to get them repealed.

The irony is that breastfeeding in public involves very little flashing. As an admitted public breast feeder, I can attest to the fact that it can be done discreetly. Here are some suggestions:

1 **USE EXPRESSED MILK.** If the thought of breastfeeding in public is not your cup of tea, consider bringing a bottle of expressed milk with you.

2 **USE THE SHAWL METHOD**. Many women breastfeed in public with a shawl or blanket covering the baby and breasts.

more ($60 to $75). Yes, there are other manual pumps on the market, but we think the Isis is tops. (One caveat to the Isis, however: a reader recommends going for the model with the reusable bottle, instead of the disposable one. Why? The reader says Avent's bottle liners for the disposable bottles are terrible—you have to double bag to freeze them or they leak). FYI: Avent now sells a version of the Isis that works with their VIA reusable bottles. Overall, the Isis is a winner.

Rating: A

While this works well, you must start practicing this early and often with your baby. Otherwise, you'll find that as she gets more alert and interested in her surroundings, she won't stay under the shawl.

3 FIND ALL THE CONVENIENT REST ROOM LOUNGES IN YOUR TOWN. Whenever we visited the local mall, I nursed in one of the big department store's lounge areas. This is a great way to meet other breastfeeding moms as well. Of course, not every public rest room features a lounge with couches or comfy chairs, but it's worth seeking out the ones that do. We applaud stores like Babies R Us for having "breastfeeding rooms" with glider-rockers and changing tables for easy nursing.

Wonder where to find the best spots to nurse? Nursing Room Locator (http://nursingrooms.wordpress.com) is a fantastic blog that posts reviews of nursing rooms all over the country. In the postings for our home state, we noticed there were two for our local mall with information on how clean they were, what amenities were offered and even details on the lighting! Great for moms who don't feel comfortable nursing in public or who want a quite, comfy place to relax.

Another creative alternative: stores will usually let you use a dressing room to breastfeed. Of course, some stores are not as "breastfeeding friendly" as others. New York City, for example, has 10 million people and about seven public rest rooms. In such places, I've even breastfed in a chair strategically placed facing a wall or corner in the back of a store. Not the best view, but it gets the job done.

4 TRY YOUR CAR. Yep, the backseat of a parked car is a good place to nurse. I found it easier and more comfortable to feed my child there, especially when he started to become distracted in restaurants and stores. The car held no fascination for him, so he tended to concentrate on eating instead of checking out the scenery. I suggest you keep some magazines in the car since you may get bored.

MEDELA HARMONY
Web: Medela.com
Price: $35 to $40.
Type: Manual.
Comments: It has fewer parts to wash than the Avent and is easier to assemble, but the reviews on it are not as universally positive as on the Isis. One mom with larger breasts found this pump worked better for her than the Isis. All in all, a good second bet to the Isis.
Rating: A-

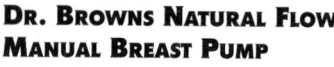

DR. BROWNS NATURAL FLOW MANUAL BREAST PUMP

Web: Handi-Craft.com

Price: $50.

Type: Manual.

Comments: This is a new entry to the manual pump category—so new that we don't have any feedback on it yet. It is made for Dr. Brown's by Whittlestone and utilizes the same express cups as the Whittlestone Breast Expresser electric pump. The company claims this pump allows for "faster let downs, more breast milk for baby and unmatched comfort for mom." The company also claims the pumps "air-barrier" protects moms and babies from bacteria that may cause breast infections. The jury is still out on this one, however.

Rating: Not Yet

Mini Electric Pumps

EVENFLO COMFORT SELECT SINGLE ELECTRIC BREAST PUMP

Web: Evenflo.com

Price: $40.

Type: Mini-electric.

Comments: It's not nick-named the Evil-Flo for nothing—this one hurts. Yep, it's cheap and that's about the only thing going for it.

Rating: D+

MEDELA DOUBLE SELECT BREAST PUMP

Web: Medela.com

Price: $100 to $130.

Type: Mini electric.

Comments: In our last edition, this mini electric pump had just debuted and we didn't have much feedback on it. This time around, though, we have a verdict: thumbs down. This dual pump alternates between breasts to more quickly express milk and has five pressure settings. But. . .many moms complained about the motor losing suction and even dying after a short time. There are instructions for cleaning the motor if it does lose suction, but what a drag. While this pump has promise, we can't recommend it until Medela fixes those motor problems.

Rating: D

MEDELA SWING BREAST PUMP

Web: Medela.com
Price: $130-$150.
Type: Mini electric.
Comments: This single electric pump offers Medela's 2-Phase Expression (the same system as the Symphony), which is supposed to copy baby's natural sucking rhythm. The pump has two different modes: first to stimulate let-down and then to simulate baby's normal sucking pattern. Moms applaud this pumps ease of use and comfort. The only negative: it's a single pump. In fact, some moms wished it came as a double version. Despite that, we will give it our highest rating. **Rating: A**

Professional-Grade Pumps

AMEDA PURELY YOURS

Web: Ameda.com
Price: $150 for the pump only; $200 for the CarryAll version; $230 for the Backpack
Type: Professional.
Comments: It's smaller! It's lighter! And its less expensive—the Ameda Purely Yours has won a large legion of fans for its Purely Yours Pump, which comes in two versions: CarryAll and Backpack. Both weigh about five pounds and have the same number of suction settings (eight) and speeds (nine), but the backpack includes a car adapter (that is optional with the CarryAll). The Ameda has a built-in AA battery pack, versus the Medela, which has a separate battery pack. Best of all, the Ameda is easy to maintain (milk can't get into the tubes, which means less cleaning than the Medela). The downside? Medela is sold in many more retail outlets than Ameda meaning you can get spare parts and supplies easier (although to its credit, Ameda has great customer service). The Lansinoh is a branded version of the same pump for $150. *FYI: As we were going to press, Ameda was acquired by Evenflo. No word yet on how this will change the line.*. **Rating: A**

AVENT ISIS iQ

Web: AventAmerica.com
Price: $135 for the Uno and up to $350 for the Duo (pictured).
Type: Professional.
Comments: Perhaps the coolest thing about Avent's ISIS iQ is the customization feature. Moms can adjust the suction strength, the length of suction time and the rest

period—that's fantastic.

So how does it work? You start by pumping manually, then the pump "copies" your preferences (that's explains the iQ moniker). You can continue to tweak the settings with "infinite variable controls" and it remembers your latest settings.

So what's the downside to the ISIS iQ? Not much. There are a lot of parts to assemble, but most moms noted that with practice it's pretty easy. We did hear from one mom who complained that when set up on a desk, the Isis iQ can be rather tippy to use. She also noted that milk gets stuck in the diaphragm and has to be emptied at the end. And finally, the price is a big stumbling block. For $350 you get the pump, two Avent feeding bottles, two breast milk storage containers, two storage bags, eight gel packs, an electric adapter and power cord in an insulated tote bag. That's a lot of bucks compared to the Ameda Purely Yours, but comparable to the top-of-the-line Pump In Style Advanced.

Aside from the price, moms thought it was quiet, comfortable and easy to clean. And it does the job.

Rating: A

Lansinoh Lightweight Double Electric Breast Pump

Comments: This pump is a repackaged version of the Ameda Purely Yours reviewed above. Priced at $150 at Target.

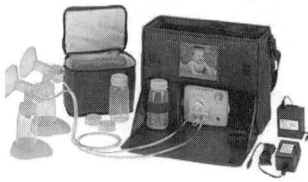

Medela Pump In Style

Web: Medela.com
Price: $290 to $370.
Type: Professional
Comments: It's the 800 pound gorilla of the breast pump category: the Medela Pump In Style.

So what's all the fuss about? If you are serious about pumping every day, the Pump In Style allows you to carry a high quality pump with you to work and home. You can empty both breasts in a short amount of time with great comfort. As a nursing mom, I remember using the Original version and found it pretty comparable to a hospital-grade pump.

There are two basic versions of the Pump In Style: Original and Advanced. The Original (which is being discontinued) comes with a cooler carrier to refrigerate breast milk, a built-in bottle holder and a battery pack in case you can't plug in. All this in a black carry pack for $250.

The Advanced model features Medela's new "2-Phase Expression" technology that mimics the way infants nurse at the breast. At first, infants apparently nurse quickly to simulate let down.

Then they settle into a deeper, slower sucking action—the Pump In Style Advance simulates this pattern. Cost: $279 to $329.

The Advanced is available in several versions, which are basically different carrying cases. There is a "Metro" bag (messenger style), a backpack and "limited edition" colors. The pump is the same; only the case is different.

So what's the disadvantage of the Pump In Styles? Cost is a biggie: these pumps run about $80 to $100 more than the leading competitor, the Ameda Purely Yours, which is smaller, lighter and has several other attractive features. And Medela has been aggressive in cutting off online discounters that sell its pumps for less than full retail—while we realize this practice is legal, we think it stinks. Ironically, Medela's heavy handedness has only fueled competitors' success, whose lower-priced pumps are attracting more attention.

Despite the price and Medela's online business policies, we will still give this pump our top rating. The Pump In Style is a winner.
Rating: A

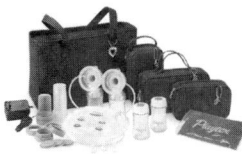

PLAYTEX EMBRACE DELUXE
Web: playtex.com
Price: $180 to $200
Type: Professional.
Comments: Playtex entered the breast pump market with both a professional grade and manual pump in the past year. The Embrace Deluxe features soft silicone breast shields, a closed system design and the included accessories (car adapter, etc) that are often extra with other brands. The downsides? Since Playtex is a new player, it's harder to find accessories (like extra breast shields) at retail—you'll have to order them online and wait for shipment. And the Playtex breast shields have multiple parts to assemble, which is frustrating. But the biggest downside: the pump is NOISY and very slow (about 50% slower than Medela or Ameda). The weak suction is a deal-killer—we don't recommend this pump. **Rating: D**

WHISPER WEAR
DOUBLE BREAST PUMP
Web: whisperwear.com
Price: $110 to $200
Type: Professional.
Comments: This is the "world's first hands-free pump." Yep, this one has generated much buzz on our message boards, with reviews decidedly mixed. Whisper Wear has cups that mold to each breast and tuck inside a bra. Moms who really like this pump are often commuters, those who need to

Nursing Extras

Many nursing moms find a nursing pillow makes breastfeeding easier and more comfortable. Our readers have emailed us positive comments for **My Brest Friend** by Zenoff Products (800-555-5522; web: www. zenoffproducts.com). Okay, it probably qualifies as the Most Stupid Name for a Baby Product Ever award, but it really works—it wraps around your waist and is secured with Velcro. It retails for about $50. A similar product is the **Nurse Mate** nursing pillow, which sell for $56. It looks like half a donut with a Velcro strap to secure it. Don't forget the **Boppy** pillow. Sold for $25 online this perennial favorite doesn't have a waist strap, but many moms swear by it as a simple, affordable nursing pillow.

Got twins? Check out **EZ-2-NURSE's** pillow (800-584-TWIN; we saw it on www.everythingmom.com). A mom told us this was the "absolute best" for her twins, adding, "I could not successfully nurse my girls together without this pillow. It was wonderful." Cost: $64.

If you're not sold in the idea of a big, bulky nursing pillow, we did find an alternative. **Utterly Yours** (www.utterlyyours.com) makes a small, hand-sized pillow that you position directly under the breast. It's a really different idea and one that may be especially useful if you need a breast lift to help baby latch on. Cost: $22 to 32 (including pillow cover), depending on the size.

pump on a long trek to or from the office. But beware: the suction is weaker than Medela's Pump In Style or the Ameda Purely Yours, meaning you have to pump longer to get the same amount of milk. Others complain it is difficult to assemble; it takes some practice to get right. So, it is a mixed bag—some love Whisper Wear and others curse it. "If it works for you," one mom told us, "it's amazing! The ability to use both your hands and wander around is great. I don't think I will use another pump unless I absolutely have to."
Rating: B

◆ *More pumps.* One reader recommended the **Nurture III** breast pump available on line at baileymed.com. Manufactured by Bailey Medical Engineering, it looks a lot like the Purely Yours. But the price is amazing at $130 to $160. Quite a deal for a professional pump. **Whittlestone** also makes a breast pump, the Breast Expresser, which uses a gentle massaging action to pump the breasts. The cost is $280, but we've had little to no feedback about this brand at this point.

Sure, you'll see lots of pumps in the discount stores. While these are all made by reputable companies (First Years, Gerber, Evenflo), we say stick to the quality pumps by Medela, Avent or Ameda.

Our Picks: Brand Recommendations

◆ **Manual Pump:** The best manual pump is the Avent "Isis" ($45). Second runner-up is the Medela Harmony.

◆ **Mini Electric Pump:** Medela's new Swing mini-electric is pricey ($130) but very good quality. Yes, you can find other brands of mini-electric pumps in discount stores for $40 and $50, but we have one word of advice: don't.

◆ **Professional Grade Pump:** You can't go wrong with either, so we'll make it a tie: the Medela Pump In Style ($270 to $350) and Ameda Purely Yours ($137 to $200) are the co-champs. The Avent ISIS iQ ($350) is gaining popularity too and challenging the Medela and Ameda pumps. One side issue: we prefer the Medela collection bottles, which do not contain bisphenol-A (BPA). See more on this topic on page 278.

Before you buy a pump, we suggest RENTING a hospital-grade pump first for a week or two (or a month). After you decide you're serious about pumping and you're comfortable with the double-pumping action, then consider buying one of your own. Given the hefty retail prices, it makes sense to buy only if you plan to pump for several months or have a second child.

Bottom line: a hospital rental pump is probably best for most moms. But if you need portability and plan to have additional children, investing in a good quality pump from Medela or Ameda is worth it.

 *Safe and Sound*

As we mentioned earlier in the What Are You Buying section, we don't recommend buying a used breast pump. Models like Medela's Pump In Style can actually collect milk in the pump mechanism. So, let's state it clearly: DO NOT PURCHASE A USED BREAST PUMP. The risk of exposing your baby to any pathogens in the previous user's breast milk is not worth it.

Of course, it is fine to re-use your own breast pump for another child down the road. Just replace the tubing and collection bottles to make sure there are no bacteria left over from previous uses.

One more safety tip: if it hurts stop. No kidding! Pumping to express milk for your baby should not be a painful experience. The last thing you want to do is damage breast tissue.

Smart Shopper Tip

Smart Shopper Tip #1
When to buy that pump.

"I don't know how long I want to breastfeed. And I'll be going back to work soon after my baby is born. When should I get a pump?"

We'd suggest waiting a bit before you invest in a breast pump or even nursing clothes. Many moms start with breast-feeding, but can't or don't want to continue it after a few weeks. For them investing in a pump would be a waste of money. If you aren't sure how long you want to breast feed, but you'd like to pump some extra bottles of milk anyway, consider renting a hospital grade pump first and trying it out before you invest a couple hundred dollars. You can often rent for as little as one month, which will be much cheaper than buying a pump that can run $200 to $350.

Waste of Money

Even Cows Opt for the Electric Kind

"I'm going back to work a couple of months after my baby is born. My co-worker who breastfeeds her baby thinks manual and mini-electrics pumps are a waste of money. Your thoughts?

While they may be useful to relieve engorgement, manual pumps aren't very practical for long-term pumping when you're at work. They are very slow, which makes it hard to get much milk. Mini-electric breast pumps are better but are really best only for occasional use—for example, expressing a small amount of milk to mix with cereal for a baby who's learning to eat solids. The problem with mini-electrics: some are painful and most are too slow.

Your best bet if you plan to do some serious pumping is to rent a hospital-grade pump. These monsters maintain a high rate of extraction with amazing comfort. A lactation consultant we interviewed said these pumps can empty both breasts in about ten to 15 minutes—contrast that with 20 to 30 minutes for mini-electrics and 45 minutes to an hour for manual pumps.

As mentioned earlier, the manual pump that received top rating from our readers is the Avent Isis—and even though it is a vast improvement over previous options, it still is a MANUAL pump. It may not work well for moms who plan to work part or full-time and still nurse their baby. That said, one solution is to use two pumps— a mom we interviewed uses a Pump In Style when she's tired (during the evening or night-time) and an Avent Isis at work (it's much quieter; doesn't need electricity, etc).

Money Saving Tips

1 **GET A FREE PUMP—COURTESY YOUR HEALTH INSURANCE.** One reader noted that her insurance provider will pay $50 toward the purchase of a breast pump; yet another reader found her medical insurance covered the *entire* cost of a $280 pump! You'll have to ask about this benefit; insurance companies don't always volunteer this info. And other insurance providers will only pay for a pump if there is a medical reason (premature birth, etc). You may have to get a "note from your doctor" to qualify. FYI: Medela has downloadable forms on their web site that are templates to request insurance reimbursement.

2 **CONSIDER EBAY.** Many readers have noted that breast pumps, including Medela's Pump In Style (PIS), are available for sale on eBay.com at huge discounts. We saw one, new in the box, for only $182. Some of them are older models or even used, so you'll need to educate yourself on what you're buying. Again, our advice: don't buy a used pump—only a new one.

3 **DON'T FEEL LIKE YOU HAVE TO BUY THE "TOP BRAND."** There are several manufacturers of breast pumps besides Medela. And our readers say their products work just as great for a lot less money (we discuss these alternative brands earlier in this chapter). For example, the Ameda Purely Yours pump retails for only $200, while the Medela Pump in Style Advanced is a whopping $370 retail and the Avent ISIS iQ is $350. The Nurture III pump is only $115! We recommend sticking with manufacturers who specialize in breastfeeding. The First Years, for example, makes a ton of other products from spoons to bath tubs as well as breast pumps. We aren't as impressed with the quality of their pumps compared to other brands, however.

Formula

Is there any nutritional difference between brands of formula? According to our research, the answer is no. The federal government closely regulates the ingredients in baby formula. Formula is extensively tested and required by the Infant Formula Act (1986) to include minimum levels of 29 nutrients. That's right—the "generic" formula sold at Wal-Mart and Target is nutritionally no different than pricey Similac. But you may notice that the ingredients on the labels aren't always exactly the same. Why? Some manufacturers add additional vitamins, fatty acids and other ingredients to differentiate their products from the competition. You'll see an explanation of some of these additive below.

What does formula cost these days? First realize that formula comes in three different versions: powder, liquid concentrate and ready-to-drink. Powder is least expensive, followed by liquid concentrate. Ready-to-drink is the most pricey. A recent check of grocery stores revealed a 25.7-ounce can of powdered Enfamil Lipil with Iron was running about $24.50. This can makes 188 fluid ounces of formula, so the cost per ounce is 13¢.

What Are You Buying?

In the past, formula was just formula. You basically had the regular version (with or without iron) and soy (also iron fortified or plain). Now the choices are mind numbing: organic formula, toddler versions, formula with or without additives and more. Here is our overview of some of the newer options:

◆ **DHA/ARA additives.** Scientists have been researching breast milk for years to find out what makes it the perfect food for our babies. The media has widely reported that the presence of two fatty acids in breast milk (DHA and ARA—also called lipids) may be responsible for the purported difference in IQ levels in breast-fed babies versus those that are formula-fed. As a result, formula companies have added DHA and ARA to their formulas as some kind of a "brain-boost." But the jury is still out on whether these additives really provide any benefit to formula. A 2002 report from the American Council on Science and Health stated: "experts disagree about whether it is necessary to include DHA and ARA in infant formulas to promote optimal brain and visual development." It's getting harder and harder to find plain formula (without DHA/ARA). Enfamil still sells a version, but Similac seems to have phased it out.

◆ *Organic formula.* With the boom in all things organic, the formula biz has seen its share of new entrants. In 2003, Horizon Organic (horizonorganic.com) debuted Horizon Organic Infant Formula with Iron, a powdered formula made from organic lactose with 27 other vitamins and minerals. Horizon feeds its cows only organic grain and hay grown without fertilizers or insecticides, and they use no growth hormones or antibiotics. Recently, Horizon sold its infant formula business to Hain-Celestial, the makers of Earth's Best baby food. Although they continue to use Horizon's organic milk protein in the manufacture of infant formula, it is now sold as *Earth's Best Infant Formula.*

We found this brand in Whole Foods Markets, although it may not yet be in every store. A 13.2 oz can runs $19 (that's 19¢ per ounce; 30% more than the cheapest store brand formula bought at a discount store). This formula is USDA certified organic. By the way, Earth's Best does not make a soy version of its organic formula.

Baby's Only Organic baby formula (babyorganic.com) is manufactured by Nature's One, (naturesone.com). The product is made with no genetically engineered organisms, no bovine growth hormones, no antibiotics or steroids, and no insecticides or chemical fertilizers. Available only in a powder, Baby's own comes in regular, soy and a DHA/ARA option. FYI: Baby's Only is marketed as a "toddler" formula for babies 12 months and up. Why? The FDA has a strict certification program for infant formula, which the Baby's Only formula has not gone through. The concern: we fear some parents may give this to younger infants, missing the small disclaimer and "toddler" typeface. We would not feed an infant any formula that was not certified by the FDA.

Similac has released its own version of organic formula produced without growth hormones, antibiotics or chemicals and certified by the USDA. The cost: $28 for a 25.7 oz. can or 15¢ per fluid ounce. We also noticed Private Selection Organic Formula for sale at our local Kroger grocery store. This private label option was $20 for 25.7 oz (11¢ per fluid ounce). Finally, Parent's Choice (see later in the chapter) also sells an organic infant formula sold at Wal-Mart.

◆ *Gourmet formula.* Formula makers have been busy rolling out additional formula to accommodate a range of baby needs. For example, there is a lactose-intolerant formula (Bright Beginnings Lactose-Free, Enfamil LactoFree and others), Isomil DF for babies

The most popular formula brands
Market share by brand, 2007

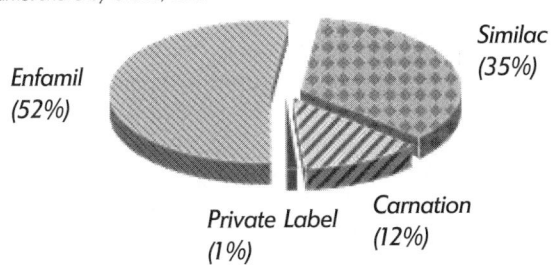

Enfamil (52%)

Similac (35%)

Private Label (1%)

Carnation (12%)

experiencing a stomach virus and Enfamil AR for babies with gastro esophageal reflux. We discuss these formulas in greater detail in our other book, *Baby 411* (see our web site for more information).

◆ **Toddler formula.** First created by Carnation ("Follow Up" formula, now marketed under the Nestle name), then copied by other formula manufacturers, "toddler" formulas are intended to be used for older children (typically nine months old and up) instead of regular cows milk or soymilk. Most parents move to whole milk or soymilk when their child reaches one year of age, leaving formula behind forever. In order to hang on to consumers longer, formula manufacturers have developed these toddler formulas. So what's the big difference between baby formula and toddler formula? Nestle/Carnation adds extra calcium to their formula while Enfamil (Next Step) and Similac (Similac 2) have upped the amount of vitamins C and E as well as iron. We'll comment on the usefulness of these formulas later in this chapter.

For more comments and information on formula, check out our *Baby 411* book. Co-written with a pediatrician, Dr. Ari Brown, the book extensively discusses breastfeeding, formula and feeding challenges for all infants. It's all in a fun-filled chapter called "Liquids." Check our web site (Baby411.com) for Dr. Brown's blog, which covers breaking news items on infant feeding.

Safe and Sound

Formula is one of the most closely regulated food items in the US. The Food and Drug Administration has strict guidelines about what can and cannot go into baby formula. The FDA requires expiration dates, warning labels and so on. So what are the safety hazards you might run up against? Here are a couple:

1 CONFUSING CANS CONFRONT SOY FORMULA USERS. Soy formula now accounts for 17% of the infant formula market. Yet, a case of mistaken identity has led some parents to nearly starve their infants. Apparently, some parents mistakenly thought they were feeding their babies soy formula, when in fact they were using *soymilk*. The problem: soymilk is missing important nutrients and vitamins found in soy formula. As a result, babies fed soymilk were malnourished and some required hospitalization. Adding to the confusion, soymilk is often sold in cans that look very similar to soy formula. The government has asked soymilk makers to put warning labels on their products, so most should be labeled. If you use soy formula, be careful to choose the right can at the grocery store.

Another concern: low-iron formula. A myth among some parents is that the iron in standard formula causes constipation—it does not, says Dr. Ari Brown, a pediatrician who co-authored our other baby book, *Baby 411*. Yes, constipation can be a problem with ALL formulas. But, babies should NEVER be on low-iron formula unless instructed by a pediatrician.

2 EXPIRED FORMULA. We realize those cans of formula look like they could survive a nuclear attack (they remind us of the "bomb-proof" cans of Hawaiian Punch our moms used to buy in the '70's), but they do have expiration dates on them. And many of our readers have written to tell us that stores don't always remove expired formula from the shelves in a timely manner. That includes grocery stores, discounters and even warehouse clubs. So read the label carefully and check your own stores of formula before you open a can. Also, some formula sold on auction sites has been expired as well. Be sure to ask.

Money Saving Tips

1 STAY AWAY FROM PRE-MIXED FORMULA. Liquid concentrate formula and ready-to-drink formula are 50% to 200% more expensive than powdered formula. Yes, it is more convenient but you pay big time for that. We priced name brand, ready to drink formula at a whopping 20¢ per ounce.

Guess what type of formula is given out as freebies in doctors' offices and hospitals? Yes, it's often the ready-to-drink liquid formula. These companies know babies get hooked on the particular texture of the expensive stuff, making it hard (if not impossible) to switch to the powdered formula later. Sneaky, eh?

What's the most popular type of formula in the US? Powder. Over 60% of the formula sold in the US is powdered while liquid concentrate accounts for only 27% of formula sales.

2 CONSIDER GENERIC FORMULA. Most grocery stores and discounters sell "private" label formula at considerable savings, at least 30% to 40%. At one grocery store chain, their generic powdered formula worked out to just 9¢ per fluid ounce of formula, a 40% savings.

The largest maker of generic formula is PBM Products (PBMProducts.com). This company makes generic formula under several different brand names including Bright Beginnings (BrightBeginnings.com), Member's Mark (sold at Sam's Club) and Parent's Choice (sold at Wal-Mart). Generic formula has come a

Baby Formula Manufacturers: Out of Control?

In the past few editions of this book, we issued a long rant about the marketing tactics of the formula manufacturers. And we still feel that way today. When you check into the hospital to give birth, you start the long promotional parade of formula freebies—most new parents emerge after birth with formula samples, diaper bags emblazoned with formula logos and more. Is this good for parents? For the country?

Considering the fact that breast-feeding rates still trail national goals, we say no. We realize formula makers have the right to market their wares as they see fit . . . but we argue that hospitals and doctors' offices should be no-pitch zones. The subtle and not-so-subtle effect of all the endless formula freebies is to undermine moms who choose to breastfeed. While we realize most moms and dads are intelligent enough to recognize the formula hype as just that, we are concerned that less-educated parents are led to believe that hospitals and doctors are endorsing formula over breast-feeding. And statistics bear that out—moms who are from lower socioeconomic groups are most likely to turn to formula instead of trying breastfeeding.

Nestle, maker of Carnation Good Start formula, deserves special scrutiny. In 2004, Nestle started targeting Hispanic mothers in California with its Nan formula, a leading formula brand in Latin America. Unlike other brands that shun direct consumer marketing, Nestle has run ads in Spanish language magazines and radio, plastering the Nan brand on billboards in Hispanic sections of Los Angeles and handing out free samples at baby fairs.

The key question: is Nestle exploiting a vulnerable population that gets very little or no info on the health benefits of breastfeeding, in order to fatten market share?

Ironically, Nestle does not advertise this brand in countries like Mexico. Why? In 1981, the World Health Organization devised a voluntary code to curb the marketing of formula after allegations that—guess who? Nestle exploited the world's poor to pitch formula, which was often misused. While the U.S. signed the code, it never passed laws to enforce it. Hence, that's why we have a formula marketing free-fire zone in hospitals, doctors' offices and billboards in the barrio.

As a country, we have to ask ourselves—shouldn't hospitals and doctor's offices be a pitch-free area for formula? And should formula companies be allowed to target vulnerable populations with formula pitches?

long way in recent years—now you can buy generic organic formula as well as several other special varieties.

We should note that some pediatricians are concerned about recommending generic formula—doctors fret that such low-cost formula might discourage breastfeeding. Ironic, when so many pediatricians hand out all those free samples of formula. We'd love to see them stop accepting samples from Similac, Enfamil and Carnation and start discouraging hospitals from doling them out to moms in the maternity wards.

3 **BUY IT ONLINE.** Yep, you can buy formula online from eBay. You can save big but watch out—some unscrupulous sellers try to pawn off expired formula on unsuspecting buyers. Be sure to confirm the expiration date before buying formula online. And watch out for shipping charges—formula is heavy and shipping can outweigh any deal, depending on the price you pay. We saw six cans of formula (12.9 oz. each) go for $21.50 on eBay. Considering a case could cost as much as $81, the savings is astonishing. But beware the shipping costs—in the above case they were $15.

4 **BUY IN BULK.** We found wholesale clubs had the best prices on name brand formula. For example, Costco (Costco.com) sells a 36 oz. can of Enfamil for $24 (3.6¢ per fluid oz.). That is 67% less than grocery stores. And generic formula at wholesale clubs is an even bigger bargain. Costco's Kirkland brand formula was $19.97 for two 25.7-ounce cans.

5 **ASK YOUR PEDIATRICIAN FOR FREE SAMPLES.** Just make sure you get the powdered formula (not the liquid concentrate or ready to pour). One reader in Arizona said she got several free cases from her doctor, who simply requested more from the formula makers. OK, we know this sounds hypocritical since we just said we think doctors should take a stand against all the formula giveaways in their offices and hospitals. However, as long as doctors' offices are stuffed with such freebies, you might as well ask for them.

6 **SHOP AROUND.** Yes, powdered formula at a grocery store can run $20 to $25 for a 28-ounce can (approximately)—but there's no federal law that says you must buy it at full retail. Readers of our book have noticed that formula prices vary widely, sometimes even at different locations of the same chain. In Chicago, a reader said they found one Toys R Us charged $1.20 less per can for the same Similac with Iron ready-to-feed formula than another TRU across town. "They actually have a price check book at the registers with the codes for each store in the Chicagoland area," the reader said. "At our last visit, we saved $13.20 for two cases (about 30% of the cost), just by mentioning we wanted to pay the lower price."

Another reader noticed a similar price discrepancy at Wal-Mart stores in Florida. When she priced Carnation Good Start powdered formula, she found one Wal-Mart that marked it at $6.61 per can. Another Wal-Mart (about 20 miles from the first location) sells the same can for $3.68! When the reader inquired about the price discrepancy, a customer service clerk admitted that each store independently sets the price for such items, based on nearby competition. That's a good lesson—many chains in more rural or poorer locations (with no nearby competition) often mark prices higher than suburban stores.

7 FORGET TODDLER FORMULA. When your child is ready for whole milk (usually at one year of age, according to most pediatricians), you can switch from formula (about 10¢ per ounce) to milk (about 2¢ per ounce). Yep, that is a savings of 80%! No, you don't need toddler formula.

What about the claim that toddler formulas have extra calcium, iron and vitamins? Nutritionists point out that toddlers should be getting most of their nutrition from solid foods, not formula. Toddlers should only be drinking about two cups a day of whole milk. Additional calcium can be found in foods as diverse as yogurt and broccoli; iron in red meat and spinach; vitamins in a wide variety of foods.

But what if you don't think your child isn't getting enough of those nutrients? Adding a vitamin and mineral supplement to your child's diet would *still* be less expensive than blowing your money on toddler formulas.

You may be wondering, in the day of increasing concern about obesity, why whole milk is recommended. Pediatricians tell us toddlers between 12 and 24 months of age need the fat in whole milk to foster brain development. At age two, you can switch to skim milk or 1%. For more on toddler development and nutrition, check out our *Toddler 411* book. See the back of this book for more information.

8 CHECK OUT AMAZON. Yep, Amazon sells formula (and even diapers) in their health and personal care store. Prices for formula were about 10% to 15% cheaper than full retail and if you order more than $25 (which is pretty easy, considering most options on Amazon are by the case or six pack), you get free shipping. Compare Amazon's prices with the lowest discount source in your area to see if it makes sense.

9 JOIN A FORMULA CLUB. Several formula makers have frequent buyer clubs. Example: Enfamil's Family Beginnings offers checks for purchasing formula, a free diaper bag, and more. It's free (sign up at Enfamil.com) but be prepared to fill out lots of stupid forms asking for information on where you live, when your baby is due and your attitudes toward breast and formula feeding. Bonus savings idea: Sam's Club accepts Enfamil's checks, which lets you stretch those freebies even farther! And you can find lots of checks for sale on eBay.com at great prices.

Bottles/Nipples

What's the best bottle for baby? Actually, it's more than just the bottle. The nipple—how the milk is delivered to baby is just as important as the container.

When it comes to nipples, there are a myriad of choices. At the low end, Playtex and Gerber are available in just about every grocery store in the U.S. and Canada. Mid-price options like Evenflo and Munchkin's Healthflow (formerly made by Johnson & Johnson) are also widely available. At the high end, brands such as Avent and Dr. Brown bottle systems are sold in baby specialty stores and chains like Target and Babies R Us.

So, which nipple (and bottle) system is best? This is like asking folks to name their favorite Thanksgiving dish—everyone will have a different opinion. For many parents, the bottle/nipple system they start with is the one they stick by. And the low-end options can work just as well as the premium brands.

That said, **Avent** and **Dr. Brown's** are the two brands with the most positive parent feedback, according to our research. Why? Avent gets a nod for its well-designed nipple, which is clinically proven to reduce colic (uncontrollable, extended crying that starts in some babies around one month of age). Ditto for Dr. Brown's Natural Flow bottle (handi-craft.com), which has a patented vent system that eliminates bubbles and nipple collapse. Avent and Dr. Brown's are pricey, however—they cost about $5 a bottle. That compares to $2 to $4 for other bottles from makers like Evenflo and Playtex.

Of course, the nipple is just half the equation: the bottle (and what is made of) is the other important factor. Baby bottles come in several flavors: polycarbonate, glass, polypropylene and polyethylene. By far, polycarbonate bottles are the most popular (with about 90% of the market)—this durable, rigid plastic stands up to repeated washings/dryings without losing its shape. FYI: Most bottle brands make several different types of bottles (Evenflo makes both glass and polycarbonate bottles, for example).

In the past, we recommended polycarbonate bottles from Avent and Dr. Brown's, but we changed our recommendation in

2007. That's when a federal panel cited health concerns with bisphenol-A (BPA), a chemical used to make polycarbonate bottles. For a Q&A about BPA, see the box on page 278. (FYI: Nipples are made of silcone which does NOT contain BPA.)

So if you want to avoid polycarbonate bottles, what is best? There are four alternatives: glass, polyethylene, polypropylene and BPA-free plastic.

Bottle Warmers & Sterilizers

When you are a first-time parent, how do you know you will really need an item? Which ones are wastes of money? Take bottle sterilizers and warmers, for example. Will your child die from some bacterial agent if you don't sterilize your baby bottles? Will Junior scream bloody murder if his bottle isn't a perfect 85 degrees Fahrenheit? The answer to both questions is: probably not. In most cases washing baby bottles in the dishwasher cleans them just fine—and a room temperature bottle will make a hungry baby just as happy as a warmed bottle of formula or milk. But what if you decide you want a bottle sterilizer or warmer? Here are our recommendations:

Like the competition in bottles, Avent also seems to win the sterilizer war with their "Sterilizer Express," a new model that is even zippier than their previous sterilizers. The Express comes in a microwave ($30) or electric version ($70) that can sterilize six bottles in just four to six minutes (the lower figure is for the microwave; the higher one for the electric version). Their newest option, the iQ 24 Electronic Steam Sterilizer offers two modes. Both modes sterilize in six minutes but mode 1 keeps bottles sterile up to six hours while mode 2 keeps items sterile for 24 hours. It can also sterilize up to two ISIS breast pumps or up to six 9 oz. bottles. Cost: a whopping $90

While Avent makes a good sterilizer, we would suggest getting the matching sterilizer for your bottle brand. For example, if you decide to use Born Free bottles, then the Born Free sterilizer ($45) is a good bet. Why? Sterilizers for one brand can sometimes damage other brand's bottles—for example, we did receive a report that Medela's Quick Clean Micro-Steam bags can melt Born Free bottles.

What about bottle warmers? Avent makes a pretty good one, the "Express Bottle and Baby Food Warmer" ($40). It can heat a bottle in four minutes. It also fits baby food jars and all types of baby bottles (not just Avent). However, in general, bottle warmers are unnecessary for most parents—you can skip this purchase.

- ◆ Glass. **Evenflo** makes glass bottles ($2 each).
- ◆ Polyethylene. The **Playtex Nurser** is a drop-in liner system that is made of polyethylene (you put the milk/formula in a plastic liner that then drops into the bottle).
- ◆ Polypropylene. All of **Medela's** bottles are made of polypropylene. Other examples are **Gerber Clear View** bottle and the **Avent Tempo**, which is a drop-in system.
- ◆ BPA-free plastic. **Born Free** bottles ($10; pictured) are made of a plastic that is hard and clear . . . and free of BPA. Another option: **Sassy's Mam Assure** bottles ($5; sassybaby.com), which get high marks from our readers.

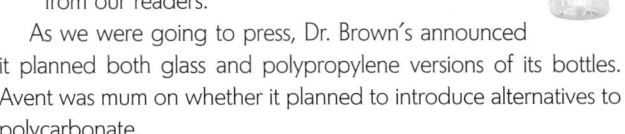

As we were going to press, Dr. Brown's announced it planned both glass and polypropylene versions of its bottles. Avent was mum on whether it planned to introduce alternatives to polycarbonate.

One quick note: in most cases, bottles and nipples aren't interchangeable. You can't use an Avent nipple on a Gerber bottle and so on. The exception: Dr. Brown's nipples DO fit on Evenflo's glass bottles, report our readers (a bit of trimming on the vent tube is required).

We realize this is confusing, so let's go over our recommendations: we do NOT recommend polycarbonate bottles, so that rules out the Avent Natural Feeding bottle and the Dr. Brown's Natural Flow polycarbonate bottle.

We DO recommend any of these alternatives: drop-in systems like the Playtex Nurser or Avent Tempo. OR BPA-free plastic bottles like the Born Free or Sassy Mam Assure (pictured). OR the new Dr. Brown's polypropylene bottle. Finally, glass bottles like those from Evenflo or Dr. Brown's are an option, but there is an obvious drawback: glass bottles can shatter if dropped.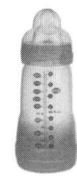

Finally, there is another facet to the BPA issue: breast pumps, many of which use polycarbonate collection bottles. Here we would suggest Medela's pumps—all of their collection bottles are made of polypropylene, which is BPA-free. We do realize in the last chapter we recommended pumps that use polycarbonate collection bottles (Ameda, for example). If you decide to go for one of these pumps, consider hand-washing the bottles. It is the repeated washing/drying in a dishwasher that causes the concern.

FYI: While Ameda pumps come with polycarbonate collection bottles, the company does sell polypropylene bottles as an accessory.

Where can you find bottles at a discount? Chains like Target and Wal-Mart carry even premium bottle brands like Avent and Dr. Brown's at good prices. We also like Kid Surplus (kidsurplus.com), which also has great deals on bottles.

Smart Shopper Tip

Smart Shopper Tip #1
Nipple confusion?

"When I check the catalogs and look in baby stores, I see bottles with all different shaped nipples. Which one is best for my baby? How do I avoid nipple confusion?"

Nipple confusion occurs when a baby learns to suck one way at the breast and another way from a bottle. This happens because the "human breast milk delivery system" (that is, the breast and nipple) forces babies to keep their sucking action forward in their

---

Are plastic baby bottles toxic? An FAQ

So just what the heck is bispenol-A? And what is it doing in my baby's bottle? Here's an FAQ for answers.

Q. What the heck is BPA? Why is it dangerous?

Most clear plastic baby bottles (as well as some breast pump collection bottles and water bottles) are made of polycarbonate, which contains a chemical called bisphenol A (BPA). It is the BPA that makes the hard, clear plastic bottles . . . well, hard and clear.

Here's the rub: BPA's chemical bond with polycarbonate breaks down over time—especially with repeated washings or heating of the bottle. As a result, BPA leaches out of the plastic bottle or sippy cup . . . and into the liquid (that is, breast milk or formula).

While most data on BPA comes from animal research, studies show even low-levels of BPA MAY be linked to everything from early puberty to breast cancer, to attention and developmental problems.

The debate on BPA heated up in 2007 when, in an article in a peer-reviewed medical journal (***Reproductive Toxicology***), 38 researchers said BPA caused a significant health risk. Then a federal panel convened by the National Institutes of Health said there is "some concern" the chemical could cause behavioral and neurological problems in young children.

Q. Do we really know that these bottles are dangerous to humans?

No, we don't. There have been no human studies on BPA—so far, researchers have only found problems in animal research.

There is a split opinion here among scientists. The same federal panel that said it had "some concern" about behavioral and developmental problems in babies also stated that links to other ailments like birth defects and adult ailments were "negligible." Of course,

---

mouth. The result: they have to work harder to get milk from a breast than from a conventional baby bottle.

So if you want to give an occasional bottle, what bottle is least likely to cause nipple confusion? Unfortunately, the answer is not clear—some parents swear that Avent's nipple is best. Fans of Dr. Brown's bottle say it is better. Others find less expensive options like the Playtex Nurser work just as well.

Are there really that many differences between nipples, besides shape? Not really. All major brands are dishwasher-safe, made of latex and have very similar flow rates. The bottom line: you may have to experiment with different nipples/bottles to find one your baby likes.

bottles

the plastics industry says BPA is completely safe.

But the fact the federal panel said there were "some concerns" for the health of babies tipped the balance for us.

As parents, we realize it can be hard to decide what to do when the debate is so heated. As always, our mantra is "show us the science." We believe enough science is now in to recommend a change in course.

Q. Isn't it a bit alarmist to say stop using these bottles? When will we know for certain BPA is harmful to humans?

The truth is we won't know for YEARS if there is a human health problem from BPA. And it could be YEARS more before the government decides to take some regulatory action.

We have consulted with pediatricians and other experts before making this decision. The consensus of these experts is: if concerns exist today (and that is backed up by reputable scientific research), then why not limit your baby's exposure to this chemical? Babies are especially at risk when it comes to exposure to harmful chemicals—that's one thing we all can agree on.

The bottom line: we suggest parents stop using polycarbonate baby bottles and sippy cups NOW. Since there are quite a few BPA-free bottles on the market (see page 277 for alternatives) we believe this is an easy call for parents.

Q. What about sippy cups?

A. Basically, the same advice applies: avoid those made of polycarbonate plastic. Sippy cups made of opaque plastic are fine. Check the bottom of the cup for its recycling number (#7 should be avoided). Metal sippy cups are a good alternative to polycarbonate.

For a primer on how to spot polycarbonate plastic, see our blog at BabyBargains.com (click on news/updates and then bottles). Look to our blog for updates on this issue.

Smart Shopper Tip #2
Bottle confusion?

"How many bottles will I need if I formula feed? What nipple sizes do I need? Do I need a bottle sterilizer?"

Yes, it the questions about bottles and feeding baby can be rather endless! To help, we've posted to our web site a great email from a mom who's been there, done that. This email actually appeared first as a thread on our message boards, but we thought it was the most comprehensive discussion of bottle-feeding we've ever seen. Since it is eight pages long, however, we didn't have room to reprint it here. Go to Babybargains.com and click on Bonus Material to read it online.

Baby Food

At the tender age of four to six months, you and your baby will depart on a magical journey to a new place filled with exciting adventures and never-before-seen wonders. Yes, you've entered the SOLID FOOD ZONE.

Fasten your seat belts and get ready for a fun ride. As your tour guide, we would like to give a few pointers to make your stay a bit more enjoyable. Let's take stock:

Pacifiers: Good or Bad?

Should your baby use a pacifier? Surprisingly, this is a controversial topic.

Some experts argue that early use of pacifiers may interfere with breastfeeding. But new studies show that pacifier use in children actually reduces the risk of Sudden Infant Death Syndrome (SIDS). It's unclear why pacifiers work, but studies clearly show a lowered risk of SIDS.

So, here are our recommendations for pacifier use: wait to give your child a pacifier until breastfeeding is well established (about a month of age). Discontinue pacifier use by six months of age. Why? Ninety percent of SIDS deaths occur between one month and six months of age. For more on the health benefits of pacifiers, see our other book, *Baby 411*.

So, now that you know what's good about a pacifier, which type of pacifier is best? There are two types—regular pacifiers have round nipples, while "orthodontic" pacifiers have flat nipples. Either is fine— but consult with your pediatrician if you have concerns on this topic.

Parents in Cyberspace: What's on the Web?

Looking for a schedule of what foods to introduce when? Earth's Best's web site has a comprehensive chart with suggestions (earthsbest.com, click on Health & Nutrition, then Doctor's Corner, then Infant Feeding Schedule). Gerber's slick web site (gerber.com, click on Start Healthy, then look for the online feeding plan download) also has baby development info (including when to start different stage foods). We also liked Beechnut's site (beechnut.com), which includes "suggested menus," "feeding FAQ's" and "making feeding fun." Although it is designed for Canadian parents, Heinz's baby food web site, heinzbaby.com contains extensive nutritional advice and other helpful info. Canadians can take advantage of rebate offers and other deals on this site (hopefully, they'll add the rest of North America to the coupon deals soon).

Safe & Sound

1 FEED FROM A BOWL, NOT FROM THE JAR. Why? If you feed from a jar, bacterium from the baby's mouth can find their way back to the jar, spoiling the food much more quickly. Also, saliva enzymes begin to break down the food's nutrients. The best strategy: pour the amount of baby food you need into a bowl and feed from there (unless it's the last serving from the jar). And be sure to refrigerate any unused portions.

2 DON'T STORE FOOD IN PLASTIC BAGS. If you leave plastic bags on the baby's high chair, they can be a suffocation hazard. A better solution: store leftover food in small, Tupperware-type containers.

3 DO A TASTE TEST. Make sure it isn't too hot, too cold, or spoiled. We know you aren't dying to taste the Creamed Ham Surprise from Gerber, but it is a necessary task.

4 CHECK FOR EXPIRATION DATES. Gerber's jarred food looks like it would last through the next Ice Age, but check that expiration date. Most unopened baby food is only good for a year or two. Use opened jars within one to two days. Formula cans also have expiration dates. The quality of the formula will deteriorate after the expiration date.

5 **AVOID UNPASTEURIZED MILK, MILK PRODUCTS AND JUICES.**
Babies don't have the ability to fight off serious bacterium like
e. coli. Avoid these hazards by feeding your child only pasteurized
dairy and juice products.

Also steer clear of feeding honey to children less than one year
of age. Botulism spores can be found in honey—while not harmful
to adults and older kids, these spores can be fatal to infants.

6 **A FINAL WORD OF ADVICE ON FEEDING BABY:** don't introduce
nuts (like peanuts or peanut butter) until your child is at least
three years old. This advice comes from a nationally known allergist
we interviewed who's a specialist in nut allergies. He points out that
nut allergies are potentially fatal and lifelong. . . and early exposure
(before age three) tends to heighten the risk. So the longer you wait
to introduce nuts, the better chance you have of avoiding these
deadly allergies. FYI: Watch out for foods that are processed on the
same production lines as those that process nuts—these can contain
trace amounts of nuts, even if they are not listed as an ingredient.
You'll see this warning noted on labels.

For a comprehensive discussion of food allergies and intoler-
ances, see our new book, Baby 411. Dr. Ari Brown, an award winning pediatrician and mother includes the most up-to-date information on this topic as well as other feeding issues.

Smart Shopper Tips

Smart Shopper Tip #1
Tracking Down UFFOs (Unidentifiable Flying Food Objects)

*"We fed our baby rice cereal for the first time. It was really cute,
except for the part when the baby picked knocked the bowl to the
floor . . . multiple times! Should we have bought some special stuff
for this occasion?"*

Well, unless you want your kitchen to be redecorated in Early Baby
Food, we do have a few suggestions. First, a bowl with a bottom that
suctions to the table is a great way to avoid flying saucers. Plastic
spoons that have a round handle are nice, so baby can't stick the
spoon handle in her eye (yes, that does happen—babies do try to
feed themselves even at a young age). Spoons with rubber coatings
are also nice; they don't transfer the heat or cold of the food to the
baby's mouth and are easier on the gums. One clever spoon is
Munchkin's "White Hot Infant Spoon" (web: munchkininc.com, four
for $6). This spoon uses a special coating that changes color when
baby's food is too hot (over 110°°).

"Toddler" foods: a waste of money?

When the number of births leveled off in recent years, the baby food companies began looking around for ways to grow their sales. One idea: make foods for older babies and toddlers who have abandoned the jarred mushy stuff! To boost sales in the $1 billion baby food market, Gerber rolled out "Gerber Graduates" while Heinz debuted "Toddler Cuisine," microwaveable meals for kids as old as 36 months. Heck, even Enfamil has rolled out the "EnfaGrow" line of foods and snacks. So, what do nutritionists and doctors think of these foods? Most say they are completely unnecessary. Yes, they are a convenience for parents but, besides that, so-called "toddler foods" offer no additional nutritional benefit. In their defense, the baby food companies argue that their toddler meals are meant to replace the junk food and unhealthy snacks parents give their babies. We guess we can see that point, but overall we think that toddler foods are a complete waste of money. Once your baby finishes with baby food, they can go straight to "adult food" without any problem—of course, that should be HEALTHY adult food. What's best: a mix of dairy products, fruits, vegetables, meat and eggs. And, no, McDonald's French fries don't count as a vegetable.

Smart Shopper Tip #2
Avoiding Mealtime Baths
"Our baby loves to drink from a cup, except for one small problem. Most of the liquid ends up on her, instead of in her. Any tips?"

Congratulations! You have a child who is ready to join the rest of the world and give up the bottle or breast. You may have mixed feelings about this, especially when you have to wash all those additional bibs, the floor and yourself more frequently. But this is a cool milestone. Babies are developmentally able to use a cup between ten and 16 months.

So what's the solution to the inevitable mess your baby will make when learning to drink from a cup? Most parents turn to sippy cups. But we don't recommend them. Why? Sippy cups aren't exactly beloved by doctors and dentists. Turns out babies use the same sucking action to get milk from a sippy cup as they do when sucking from a baby bottle. Hence they are not learning how to drink from a cup. Plus, sippy cups direct the flow of liquid straight for the back of baby's top front teeth—this promotes tooth decay. That's why dentists are no fans of these products

Is there an answer to this dilemma? When being clean and pristine aren't that important (say when eating at home in the kitchen with lots of clean up gear handy) let your baby practice with a regular plastic cup. But also try to teach her to use a straw. That way, when you're out at a restaurant, she won't be taking a bath in public.

Money-Saving Tips

1 **MAKE YOUR OWN.** Let's be honest: baby foods like mashed bananas are really just . . . mashed bananas. You can easily whip up this stuff with that common kitchen helper, the food processor. Many parents skip baby food altogether and make their own. One tip: make up a big batch at one time and freeze the leftovers in

ice cube trays. Check the library for cookbooks that provide tips on making baby food at home. A reader suggestion: the "Super Baby Food" book ($19.95, published by F. J. Roberts Publishing, web: superbabyfood.com). This 590-page book is about as comprehensive as you can find on the subject.

2 **BELIEVE IT OR NOT, TOYS R US AND BABIES R US SELL BABY FOOD.** If you think your grocery store is gouging you on the price of baby food, you might want to check out the prices at Babies R Us. We found Gerber 1st Foods in a four-pack of 2.5-

---

E-MAIL FROM THE REAL WORLD
Making your own baby food isn't time consuming

A mom in New Mexico told us she found making her own baby food isn't as difficult as it sounds:

"My husband and I watch what we eat, so we definitely watch what our baby eats. One of the things I do is buy organic carrots, quick boil them, throw them in a blender and then freeze them in an ice cube tray. Once they are frozen, I separate the cubes into freezer baggies (they would get freezer burn if left in the ice tray). When mealtime arrives, I just throw them in the microwave. Organic carrots taste great! This whole process might sound complicated, but it only takes me about 20 minutes to do, and then another five to ten minutes to put the cubes in baggies."

ounce jars for $2.09—that works out to about 50¢ per jar or about 15% less than grocery store prices. Toys R Us also sells four-packs of assorted dinners from Gerber's 2nd and 3rd Food collections.

3 **COUPONS! COUPONS! COUPONS!** Yes, we've seen quite a few cents-off and buy-one-get-one-free coupons on baby food and formula—not just in the Sunday paper but also through the mail. Our advice: don't toss that junk mail until you've made sure you're not trashing valuable baby food coupons. Another coupon trick: look for "bounce-back" coupons. Those are the coupons put in the packages of baby food to encourage you to bounce back to the store and buy more.

4 **GO FOR A LESSER-KNOWN BRAND.** Example: Bay Valley Foods Nature's Goodness (formerly owned by Del Monte) makes good quality baby food, but is not as well known as Gerber or Earth's Best, but it is priced about 20% less than the competition. The only drawback: it isn't available everywhere.

5 **SUBSTITUTE COMPARABLE ADULT FOODS.** What's the difference between adult applesauce and baby applesauce? Not much, except for the fact that applesauce in a jar with a cute baby on it costs several times more than the adult version. (One caveat: make sure the regular applesauce is loaded with extra sugar). Another rip-off: "next step" foods for older babies. Gerber loves to tout its special toddler meals in its "Graduates" line. What's the point? When baby is ready to eat pasta, just serve him small bites of the adult stuff. Bottom line: babies should learn to eat the same (hopefully healthy) foods you are eating, with the same spices and flavors. Toddler or graduate foods are a waste of time and money.

6 **GO FOR THE BETTER QUALITY.** That's a strange money-saving tip, isn't it? Doesn't better quality baby food cost more? Yes, but look at it this way—the average baby eats 600 jars of baby food until they "graduate" to adult foods. Sounds like a lot of money, eh? Well, that only works out to $300 or so in total expenditures (using an average price of 48¢ to 75¢ per jar). Hence, if you go for the better-quality food and spend, say, 15% to 20% more, you're only out another $90. Therefore it might be better to spend the small additional dollars to give baby better-quality food. And feeding baby food that tastes more like the real thing makes transitions to adult foods easier.

By the way, a recent article in *Consumer Reports*, recommends serving your baby organic baby food as often as possible. Because pesticide residues affect the tiny bodies of small infants and children more than our grown-up bodies, CR suggests avoiding such residues. Organic baby foods brands include Earth's Best and Gerber Organic.

The Name Game: Reviews of Selected Manufacturers

Here's a round up of some of the best-known names in baby food. We should note that while we actually tried out each of the foods on our baby, you may reach different conclusions than we did. Unlike our brand name ratings for clothing or other baby products, food is a much trickier rating proposition. We rated the following brand names based on how healthy they are and how much they approximate real food (aroma, appearance, and, yes, taste). Our subjective opinions reflect our experience—always consult with your pediatrician or family doctor if you have any questions about feeding your baby. (Special thanks to Ben and Jack for their help in researching this topic.)

The Ratings

A EXCELLENT—*our top pick!*

B GOOD— *above average quality, prices, and creativity.*

C FAIR—*could stand some improvement.*

D POOR—*yuck! could stand some major improvement.*

Beech-Nut (800) BEECHNUT; Web: beechnut.com. Beech-Nut was one of the first baby food companies to eliminate fillers (starches, sugar, salt) or artificial colors/flavors in its 120 flavors. While Beech-Nut is not organic, the company claims to have "stringent pesticide standards." Our readers generally give Beech-Nut good marks (some like it better than Gerber). New this year, Beech-Nut is now adding DHA and ARA (see the formula discussion above for more about these important lipids) to its First Advantage baby food. Available for sale on their website, the First Advantage foods cost about 72¢ per 4 oz. jar.

The only bummer about Beech-Nut baby food: it can be hard to find (not every state has stores that carry it). You can use their where to buy function or order directly from the website. Look for online deals and coupons on the site as well. **Rating: B+**

Del Monte See below for review of Natures Goodness.

Earth's Best *(800) 442-4221. Web: earthsbest.com.* Organic is everywhere in every grocery. It's even trickled down to baby food. The first organic baby food manufacturers and one of our favorite brands is Earth's Best. Started in Vermont, Earth's Best was sold in 1996 to Heinz, one of the baby food giants. Heinz couldn't figure out what to do with the company and decided to sell it to natural foods conglomerate Hain Celestial (parent of Celestial Tea). Despite all the changes in ownership, Earth's Best still has the largest line of "natural" baby foods on the market—all vegetables and grains are certified organically grown (no pesticides are used), and meats are raised without antibiotics or steroids. Another advantage: Earth's Best never adds any salt, sugar or modified starches to its food. And the foods are only made from whole grains, fruits and vegetables (instead of concentrates). Yes, Earth's Best is more expensive (about 15% to 20% more) but as we pointed out earlier, that's works out to only about $90 more per year. We tried Earth's Best and were generally pleased. All in all, Earth's Best is a much-needed natural alternative to the standard fare that babies have been fed for far too many years. ***Rating: A***

Gerber *Web: gerber.com.* Dominating the baby food business with a whopping 70% market share (that's right, three out of every four baby food jars sold sport that familiar label), Gerber sure has come a long way from its humble beginnings. Back in 1907, Joseph Gerber (whose trade was canning) mashed up peas for his daughter, following the suggestion of a family doctor. We imagine those peas looked quite different from Gerber's peas today. Now, thanks to scientific progress, Gerber's peas are put through such a rigorous canning process that they don't even look like peas . . . instead more like green slime. And it's not just the look, have you actually smelled or tasted any of Gerber's offerings? Yuck. Sure it's cheap (about 45¢ for a 2 1/2 ounce jar of Gerber 1st Foods), but we just can't feed our baby this stuff with a clear conscience.

On the upside, Gerber offers parents one key advantage: choice. The line boasts an amazing 200 different flavors. Gerber is sold in just about every grocery store on Earth. And we have to give Gerber credit: a few years ago, the company announced it would respond to parents' concerns and reformulate its baby food to eliminate starches, sugars and other fillers. Gerber also rolled out "Tender Harvest," a line of organic baby food to compete with Earth's Best. The new line is made with "whole grains and certified organic fruits and vegetables" (note that Gerber's regular line still uses fruit and vegetable concentrates). Finally, we noticed that Gerber is now packing its first foods in plastic rather than glass. No shattered jars when feeding your squirming baby. While we like the changes Gerber has made, we still have problems with the brand: we think their "Graduates" line of "toddler" foods is a waste of money. And their juice line is overpriced compared to others on the market. ***Rating: C***

Healthy Times *Web: healthytimes.com.* Healthy Times got its start selling one of the first health-food baby products back in 1980: a teething biscuit. Since then, the company has expanded their baby food offerings to include 22 jarred baby foods, baby cereal, snacks and toiletry items. The baby food line is certified organic and contains no soy, flour or other fillers. You'll find single fruits and vegetables (stage 1), fruit and veggie blends (stage 2) and dinners (combos of several veggies, and meat and veggies). You can buy Healthy Times online on the company's web site for 89¢ per 4 oz. jar for stage one foods—that's slightly less than Earth's Best stageone foods. We also saw Healthy Times foods on Amazon.com and at Whole Foods, Trader Jo's and Vitamin Cottage. ***Rating: A-***

Naturally Preferred *Web: kroger.com.* Launched in 2003, Kroger's own in-house brand of baby food is dubbed Naturally Preferred. You'll find it in grocery stores like Ralph's, Fry's, City Market and King Soopers to name a few. For a complete listing of stores in the Kroger chain, check their website. Like all private label brands, the big draw here is the price. Sample: a four-ounce jar of Naturally Preferred is 50¢, compared to Gerber Tender Harvest at 73¢ for the same size item. However, Naturally Preferred did suffer a recall of some of their products in July 2004 for glass contamination. The manufacturer, J.R. Wood, noted that there were no injuries associated with the recall. ***Rating: B***

Natures Goodness *Web: naturesgoodness.com.* Formerly owned by Heinz and Del Monte, Nature's Goodness was sold to Baby Valley Foods in 2006. Oddly enough, the company's web site and labels still sport the Del Monte name just to confuse you. We like the fact that the website posts its nutritional labels online—and we noted the lack of added sugars or starches in most of the line. As for price, Del Monte/Nature's Goodness is priced about 15% to 20% less than Gerber, making it a good deal. A 2.5-ounce jar of bananas goes for 38¢ versus a similar Gerber natural fruit for 45¢ per 2.5 ounces. The feedback from parents on this line is positive; the only drawback is availability—Del Monte's Nature's Goodness isn't in as many stores as Gerber. ***Rating: A***

◆ ***Frozen organic baby food.*** This is a new category of baby food we're seeing in health food stores like Whole Foods. But the prices are astronomic: anywhere from $1.44 to $3.12 per 4 oz container. That's six times the cost of Gerber jarred food. There are even companies that will deliver fresh baby food or customize a menu of baby food for you (if you live in New York, Los Angeles, Boston and Seattle). Again, it's ridiculously expensive: up to $3.50 per jar plus delivery.

If you're still interested, here are some sources for frozen baby food: Evie's Organic Edibles (eviesorganicedibles.com), Plum Organics (plumorganics.com) Homemade Baby (homemadebaby.com), Little Potatoes Baby Food (littlepotatoesbabyfood.com), Bohemian Baby (bohemian-baby.com), Sprouts (sproutsbabyfood.com), Happy Baby (happybabyfood.com).

High Chairs

As soon as Junior starts to eat solid food, you'll need this quintessential piece of baby furniture—the high chair. Surprisingly, this seemingly innocuous product generates over 7000 injuries each year. So, what are the safest high chairs? And how do you use them properly? We'll share these insights, as well as some money-saving tips and brand reviews in this section.

 *Safe and Sound*

STRAP ME IN. *Most injuries occur when babies are not strapped into their chairs.* Sadly, four to five deaths occur each year when babies "submarine" under the tray. To address these types of accidents new high chairs now feature a "passive restraint" (a plastic post) under the tray to prevent this. Note: some high chair makers attach this submarine protection to the tray; others have it on the seat. We prefer the seat. Why? If it is on the tray and the tray is removed, there is a risk a child might be able to squirm out of the safety belts (which is all that would hold them in the chair). As a side note, wooden high chairs (except for the Eddie Bauer model) only seem to have a crotch strap—no plastic post. This may mean it is easier for a baby to squirm out when the tray is removed.

FYI: Even if the high chair has a passive restraint, you STILL must strap in baby with the safety harness with EACH use. This prevents them from climbing out or otherwise hurting themselves. Finally, never put the high chair near a wall—babies have been injured in the past when they push off a wall or object, tipping over the chair. This problem is rare with the newest high chairs (as they have wide, stable bases), but you still can tip over older, hand-me-down models.

2 **THE SAFETY STANDARDS FOR HIGH CHAIRS ARE VOLUNTARY.**
This means not all high chairs on the market today meet all these voluntary standards. Perhaps the safest bet: look for JPMA-certified high chairs. The JPMA requires a battery of safety tests, including checks for stability, a locking device to prevent folding, a secure restraining system, no sharp edges, and so on.

3 **INSPECT THE SEAT—IS IT WELL UPHOLSTERED?** Make sure it won't tear or puncture easily.

4 **LOOK FOR STABILITY.** It's basic physics: the wider the base, the more stable the chair.

5 **CAREFULLY INSPECT THE RESTRAINING SYSTEM.** Straps around the hips and between the legs do the trick. The cheapest high chairs have only a single strap around the waist. Expensive models have "safety harnesses" with multiple straps.

6 **SOME HIGH CHAIRS OFFER DIFFERENT HEIGHT POSITIONS, INCLUDING A RECLINING POSITION THAT SUPPOSEDLY MAKES IT EASIER TO FEED A YOUNG INFANT.** The problem? Feeding a baby solid foods in a reclining position is a choking hazard. If you want to use the reclining feature, it should be exclusively for bottle-feeding. We do think the recline feature is a plus for another reason, however: it is easier to move baby in and out of the high chair when it is reclined. And when babies start out with solid foods, they may go back and forth between the bottle and solid food during meals. Hence, the recline feature is helpful when they need to take a bottle break.

 *More Money Buys You*

Whether you spend $30 or $200, most high chairs do one simple thing—provide you with a place to safely ensconce your baby while he eats. The more money you spend, however, the more comforts there are for both you and baby. As you go up in price, you find chairs with various height positions, reclining seats, larger trays, more padding, casters for mobility and more. From a safety point of view, some of the more expensive high chairs feature five-point restraint harnesses (instead of just a waist belt). As for usability, some high chairs are easier to clean than others, but that doesn't necessarily correspond to price. Look for removable vinyl covers that are machine-washable (cloth covers are harder to clean). Nearly all high chairs sold today are made of plastic and metal, replacing the wooden high chairs that previous generations of babies used. But there are a few wood high chairs still out there—we'll review these in the Name Game section.

Smart Shopper Tips for High Chairs

Smart Shopper Tip #1
High Chair Basics 101

"What's the difference between a $50 high chair and one that's $200? And does it matter what color you get? I like white best."

The high chair market is basically divided into two camps: the low-end chairs from companies like Graco and Cosco and high-end models from Peg Perego and Chicco. New in the past year are both ultra-modern high chairs (the Calla, the Flair) and retro wood versions (Eddie Bauer). The key differences: styling (cutesy versus sleek/modern) and quality/durability.

Peg Perego's Prima Pappa, for example, became a runaway success, thanks to its stylish looks and compact fold for storage. At $170 to $190, however, the Pappa is TWICE the price of Graco's top-of-the-line high chair. And, as you'll read later, some readers gripe that the Pappa is a nightmare to clean.

There finally is good news to report on the high chair front, however. In the past year, several new competitors have debuted in the market in the "mid" price range (that is, between the $50 Graco chairs and the $170 Peregos) with decent looks AND good features. Examples include Baby Trend, Fisher-Price, Zooper and Combi. We'll discuss each later in this section. Here are some basic features and new trends to keep an eye out for:

◆ *Tray release.* Nearly all high chairs now have a "one hand" tray release that enables you to easily remove the tray with a quick motion. The problem: not all releases are the same. The more expensive chairs generally have a release that's easier to operate. Warning: some models have a one-handed "pull" release that is under the tray. Some kids learn they can kick the release and send the tray flying across the kitchen. Check under the tray to make sure the release can't be kicked off! Note: to address this problem, some manufacturers are adding a "kick-guard" to the release. Other trays have a "push" release button that eliminates the kick issue.

◆ *Tray wars.* High chair makers like to battle their competitors by touting the newest gimmick on their trays. Hence, you'll now see trays with cup holders, compartmentalized snack areas and so on. Do you really need a cup holder? Don't worry—your baby will spill their juice, cup holder or not. The latest trend is dishwasher-safe tray liners or double trays (where one can go in the dishwasher). This is a cool feature that helps with clean up.

◆ *Tray height.* Some parents complain the tray height of certain high chairs is too high—making it hard for smaller babies to use. A smart tip: take your baby with you when you go high chair shopping and actually sit them in the different options. You can evaluate the tray heights in person to make sure the chair will work for both you and baby. We'll note which chairs have the best/worst tray heights later in our reviews. Generally, a chair with a tray height of less than 8″ should work for most babies. A few models have tray heights over 8″—those can be a major problem since a child can't reach the food on the tray. Why is this important? Some day (we know it seems light years away), your baby will feed himself . . . and being able to see and reach the food is important!

◆ *Seat depth.* Most chairs have multiple tray positions and reclining seats. But what is the distance between the seat back when it is upright and the tray in its closest position? A distance of 5″ to 7″ is acceptable. Over 7″ and you run the risk that there will be a large gap between your baby and the tray—and all their food will end up in their lap. Again, take your baby with you when shopping for a chair, as smaller babies may be harder to fit.

◆ *Less convertibility.* Here's an ironic twist: while the rest of the baby products market is awash in "convertible" products, high chairs are moving the other way. Gone are the myriad high chairs that converted into a table and chair set, or some other future use with the exception of Combi's Transition high chair. Parents seem to like high chairs that are just, well, high chairs.

◆ *Washability.* Here's an obvious tip some first-time parents seem to miss: make sure the high chair you buy has a removable washable seat cover OR a seat that easily sponges clean. In the latter category, chairs with VINYL covers trump those made of cloth—vinyl can be wiped clean, while cloth typically has to be washed. This might be one of those first-time parent traps—seats with cloth covers sure look nicer than those made of vinyl. But cloth can't be wiped clean and requires washing—some cloth covers can't be thrown in the dryer either! That means waiting a day or more for a cover to line dry. Nojo does make a high chair cover ($24) that may be a handy option for parents who choose a high chair with a fabric seat pad. You could use the Nojo cover while you're washing and drying the original pad.

Of course, the cloth/vinyl issue becomes somewhat confusing when you consider some vinyl seats have cloth edging/piping. Our advice: be careful of any seat with cloth accents, as it might be very hard to clean. (Make sure the seat is washable *and* machine dryable).

What color cover should you get? Answer: anything but white. Sure, that fancy white "leatherette" high chair looks all shiny and new at the baby store, but it will forever be a cleaning nightmare once you start using it. Darker colors and patterns are better. Another tip: avoid high chairs that have lots of cracks and crevices near the tray and seat, which makes cleaning difficult.

Smart Shopper Tip #2
Tray Chic and Other Restaurant Tips

"We have a great high chair at home, but we're always appalled at the lack of safe high chairs at restaurants. Our favorite cafe has a high chair that must date back to 1952—no straps, a metal tray with sharp edges, and a hard seat with no cushion. Have restaurateurs lost their minds?

We think so. People who run restaurants must search obscure foreign countries to find the world's most hazardous high chairs. The biggest problem? No straps, enabling babies to slide out of the chair, submarine-style. The solution? When the baby is young, keep her in her infant car seat; the safe harness keeps baby secure. When your baby is older (and if you eat out a lot), you may want to invest in a portable booster seat. We'll discuss and recommend hook on chairs and booster seats later in this chapter.

The Name Game: Reviews of Selected Manufacturers

Here's a round up of the best high chairs on the market today:

The Ratings

    A **EXCELLENT**—*our top pick!*
    B **GOOD**— *above average quality, prices, and creativity.*
    C **FAIR**—*could stand some improvement.*
    D **POOR**—*yuck! could stand some major improvement.*

Baby Trend *(800) 328-7363, (909) 902-5568, Web: babytrend. com.* Baby Trend's high chair was one of our top picks in a previous edition of this book, but our rating of this chair continues to drift down as complaints from readers stack up. Yes, it is a credible knock-off of the Perego and Chicco chairs, yet sells for 40% less (about $70 to $100 in most stores). You get all the standard features you'd expect: five-point harness, four-position reclining seat, three-position tray with one hand release, six height positions, compact fold and casters. Some models have a separate dishwasher-safe tray. And, yes, the Baby Trend high chair is generally easier to use than competitors (it requires little assembly and the seat recline is easy to adjust, for example).

So, why all the complaints? The pad is this chair's Achilles' heel. We've received several reports that the cloth pad (which has a reversible vinyl side) fell apart or bunched up after machine washing. Even Baby Trend, in an email to us, admitted the pad "responds best to hand washing." Gee, that's nice—too bad the instructions for the chair say to machine wash the pad on the gentle cycle . . . with no mention of hand washing. Add that to the fact the pad has to be line dried and you have a deal-breaker here. Another major complaint centers on the tray height, which is way too high for average-size babies. Of course, not all the reviews are negative: some parents have had success with this high chair. And we give Baby Trend bonus points for improving the chair over the years. But Baby Trend's customer service stumbles and the pad washing issue have convinced us that this chair isn't worthy of a recommendation. ***Rating: C+***

Boon *(888) 376-4763, Web: booninc.com.* Boon's Flair high chair debuted in 2007, part of the modernist wave sweeping the baby products biz. At least this chair features something unique: a pneumatic lift, which gives the chair "effortless height adjustment." Basically, a button on the base will automatically lower the chair. We do like the seamless seat, which is easier to clean than other high chairs (where food finds its way into every last crack and crevice). The pad and harness remove for cleaning and a dishwasher-safe tray within a tray is easy to use. The Flair comes in two versions: standard (which has a translucent frosted glass seat, white pad and plastic base) and elite (high-gloss white seat, orange pad, stainless steel base; pictured). The standard Flair is $200, the Elite Flair $370 to $400. (We can't help but wonder if the folks at Boon were watching a DVD of *Office Space* when they named this chair).

The only negative for the Flair: the seat doesn't recline, making this chair inappropriate for smaller infants who are bottle feeding. A reclining seat is a standard feature on almost all high chairs, so we wonder why Boon left this out. As for parent feedback, this chair is so new that what we've heard so far is limited—folks love the sleek look and cleanability of the Flair. The only complaints are the lack of recline and a harness that lacks a chest buckle (hence the harness can slide off the shoulders of some kids). Those negatives hold the Boon Flair back from getting our highest rating. **Rating: A-**

Bloom *Web: BloomBaby.com* Bloom's Fresco high chair is the latest entrant in the space-age, Jetsons-style high chair category. It's egg-shaped, seamless seat and circular base echo the Boon Flair with one big exception: the Bloom Fresco can recline, making it suitable for infants. And we liked the micro-suede seat upholstery (in nine colors) and pneumatic-assist height adjustment. But the price? $400 is a bit high, in our opinion. Since the Fresco is so new, we don't have much parent feedback—but one parent who did buy it was disappointed with the twisty straps that are hard to adjust. For $400, you'd think Bloom would get that right.

Bloom has a second high chair model: the Nano, which is tagged as an "iconic minimalist" model with a flat fold and "micro leather" seat in six colors. Price: $180—that's about three times the price of other simple high chairs that don't recline, lack wheels and fold up flat. Again, the Nano is too new for much parent feedback at this writing. **Rating: Not Yet.**

Calla Chair *Web: callachair.com.* This high chair is reviewed on our web site BabyBargains.com (click on Bonus Material).

Carter's. This high chair is made by Kolcraft, see review later.

Chicco *(877) 4CHICCO or (732) 805-9200. Web: chiccousa.com.* Chicco's Polly high chair is the successor to the Mamma, a high chair we only gave a C in our last report. So is the Polly an improvement? Yes it is.

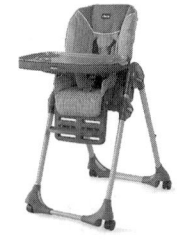

The Polly comes in three different versions: a basic model for $110 and a deluxe model with double pad for $130. The Polly features an adjustable footrest, compact fold, three-position seat recline, seven height positions and removable dishwasher-safe tray. So, how does the Polly differ from the Mamma? Well, the biggest difference is a lower tray, which addresses our biggest gripe with the previous model. The Polly folds more compactly than the Mamma—a nice plus. We also like the re-designed tray, which is easy to take off with one hand and can be hung off the back of the chair on pegs. Even the colors of the Polly are an improvement, ranging from stylish grey and taupe to more whimsical patterns with orange accents.

As for negatives, the Polly's pad is not machine washable, which is a bummer. We've also had several reports that Chicco's dish-washer-safe tray insert is too large to fit in a dishwasher (as Homer would say, Doh!). And yes, this chair can be a bear to clean: crevices in the tray and chair collect food, plus the harness straps can't be removed to be washed.

So it's a mixed review for the Chicco Polly: fans like the stylish design and easy fold. But the negatives are creeping up for this model, so we've lowered our rating a bit this time out. **Rating: B**

Combi *(800) 992-6624, (803) 802-8416; Web: combi-intl.com.* Best known for its strollers, Combi has been trying to crack the high chair category but its efforts have met with little success. Typical Combi high chairs had some gimmick (at one point, they sold a "gliding" high chair that rocked back and forth), but for their current offering (the Breeze), Combi has played it safe. The Breeze is a traditional high chair with a three-position recline, washable seat cushion and double tray with toy. Yet when folded, the tray doesn't lay flat but instead sticks out horizontally—that might make the Breeze a bit hard to stash in the pantry when company comes. We do think the price is right ($90), but overall the Breeze is a bit disappointing. It lacks the adjustable footrest you see on other models. And fashion-wise, the Combi Breeze doesn't stack up to Chicco's and Perego's offerings.

Combi plans to phase out the Breeze in 2008 and replace it with a new model: the Hero. This $150 high chair features a washable pad, five-point harness, three position recline and (here's the unique feature) the ability to attach to a kitchen chair as a booster chair for older kids. The price seems high to us—and we were turned off by the Hero's dinky dishwasher-tray insert. Sorry, the Hero looks like a zero.

Combi's other major high chair offering is the Transition ($120), which goes back to the gimmick playbook. The Transition morphs into a table and chair once a child outgrows the high chair. Evenflo tried this concept a few years ago and it bombed, mostly because of the huge amount of space this chair takes up (it doesn't fold up like most other models).

As for feedback on Combi's high chairs, that is hard to come by. The Combi Breeze, for example, is sold in very few stores (Target.com has it), so it's no surprise we haven't heard much from parents on this one.

Bottom line: Combi needs to try harder to innovate in this category; and having flaws like a tray that doesn't fold flat won't cut it.
Rating: C

Cosco *Web: djgusa.com.* Like most things Cosco
makes, their high chairs define the entry-level price
point in this market. The Cosco Convenience (also
known as the Beginnings Simple Start) high chair
(pictured) is a bare bones model ($30 at Wal-Mart).
This would do the trick for grandma's house—the
simple chair has a tray with one-hand release, four-position seat
recline and vinyl pad. Nothing too fancy to look at, but how many
bells and whistles does Grandma need? A similar model called Little
Blessings is sold at Kmart for $30.

While these high chairs are fine for occasional use at Grandma's
house, we aren't keen on these offerings as a primary high chair.
Why? A lack of safety features (example: three-point harnesses
instead of a five-point) make these chairs better for occasional use.
Rating: C-

Eddie Bauer *Web: djgusa.com.* Cosco has had
big success with their Eddie Bauer brand in car
seats and strollers, so it's no big surprise they
decided to bring the name to high chairs. We
were impressed with their creative offering here: a
hybrid wood chair with plastic tray. Yep, in the category of "everything old is new again," Cosco's
high chair combines the look of wood with the
convenience of plastic (the tray has a removable dinner tray, like
most competitors). All for $100 to $125, which is a great price. So,
what are the trade-offs? Well, you can forget about many of the
features you'll find in plastic chairs—Eddie Bauer's chair lacks wheels,
height adjustments, seat recline and more. Yet, did we mention
how sweet it looks? Parents who love this chair seem to accept the
trade off in features versus aesthetics.

We had a mom road test the EB high chair and the verdict was
a thumbs up—the one-hand adjustable tray and storage compartment (under the seat) is a nice design touch. The downsides? The
three-point restraint belts were hard to figure out and adjust. And
the slide slats of the seat (exposed wood not covered by any
padding) were a food magnet, making this chair harder to clean
than others. Another complaint: when the tray removes, there is a
permanent snack tray on the chair—that can make it hard to put a
wiggly baby in or out of the chair. That said, most parents like this

high chair and the feedback is positive overall (most folks think the wood design outweighs the flaws).

FYI: Babies R Us version of this chair (B is for Bear; pictured above) is probably best because it comes with a vinyl seat pad, which is much easier to clean than the cloth cover on other versions (such as the one sold at Target). Wal-Mart sells a version of this high chair under the Safety 1st (Sundance) moniker—it's basically the same chair with a simpler pad.

In the past year, Eddie Bauer rolled out new versions of this chair that feature darker wood (oak or cherry stain). Oddly, the cherry stain version does not have a full pad—but still carries the full price of the other models. We suppose Cosco is guessing that some parents wanted to see more wood on the chair . . . but it sounds to us like more to area to clean. We'd suggest the full pad versions.

So, it is mixed review for the Eddie Bauer—go for this high chair if the wood design is important to you . . . and you can live with the trade-offs (lack of seat recline, wheels, cleanability, no height adjustment). ***Rating: A-***

Evenflo *(800) 233-5921 or (937) 415-3300. Web: evenflo.com.* Evenflo has always been an also-ran in the high chair market, thanks to quality woes and designs that lack pizzazz. And that lackluster record continues with Evenflo's current high chair offerings: the Expressions and Majestic (pictured).

Evenflo prices its offerings in a niche between Cosco's bare-bones models sold at Wal-Mart and the more pricey stuff you see at specialty stores. Take the Expressions chair, for example. This $60 chair looks good on paper: one-hand tray release, compact fold, seven height positions, reclining seat, wheels and so on. The Expressions come in several versions: the Plus adds a dishwasher-safe tray, the Premier throws in an electronic toy, etc.

The Majestic is an upgraded model includes a dishwasher-safe tray, swing-out removable snack tray, foot rest, machine washable pad, four position recline and storage in the base. The Majestic comes in several versions, from a basic model for $60 to a "Discovery" version with toys for $100.

Parent feedback on Evenflo's high chairs is a mixed bag. The Expressions gets better marks as a good, simple high chair (and a decent value at $60). But parents are more caustic when it comes to the Majestic—a too-high tray, a seat that doesn't fully adjust upright and difficult assembly are key gripes.

Overall, we've been unimpressed with Evenflo's quality control—we've heard many stories of parts that break, screws that come out of a seat and so on. It seems that Evenflo cuts corners . . . and that comes back to bite you. So it is a tepid review for Evenflo: the Expressions is ok, but the Majestic is a loser. **Rating: C**

Fisher-Price *(800) 828-4000 or (716) 687-3000. Web: fisher-price.com.* Folks, we have a winner! After years of fumbling around in this category, Fisher-Price finally has hit a home run with the Healthy Care high chair. It features a three-position seat recline, five-point restraint, one-hand tray removal, dishwasher-safe tray liner, and various height adjustments. All in all, a good value—the Healthy Care starts at $80 for a basic version at Target and goes to $90 to $100 for an "Aquarium" or "Rainforest" (pictured) model. The basic model omits the one-hand tray release; the premium version has toys and an upgraded pad.

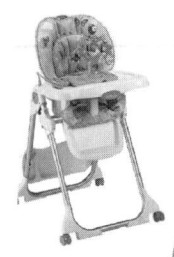

Parents universally praise the Healthy Care for its ease of use and cleanability (yep, those harness straps and toys can be thrown into the dishwasher). The only negative to this chair is the fashion—that cutesy color scheme on the chair turns parents off. Some complain the chair tends to collect food in crevices (the ruffles on the Aquarium model are food collectors; we suggest going for the ruffle-free Rainforest or plain model). And the Healthy Care requires quite a bit of assembly. Despite that, this is the best bet in the high chair market and we give the Healthy Care our highest rating.

Fisher Price makes two other high chairs: Space Saver and Easy Clean. The Space Saver ($50) is the first high chair that sits on a dining chair (sort of a suped-up booster). This model features a full-size tray, three-position recline and it converts to a toddler booster. If you are short of space (think New York City apartment), this might be a great option.

The Easy Clean ($70 to $85) features a curved tubular design that lets you pull the chair up closer to the dining table. The "easy clean" feature is a pad that easily pulls off for washing and even the straps are dishwasher-safe. A nice feature: the Easy Clean's tray height is adjustable.

New for 2008, Fisher Price will introduce its first wood hybrid high chair: the Zen. This $150 high chair will feature a plastic seat with three-position recline, a tray with dishwasher-safe insert and three-position height adjustment. The Zen is part of a collection that includes a cradle swing, bassinet, infant seat—all feature dark wood accents, green plastic and brown fabric.

The Zen is quite a departure for Fisher Price—we're not sure how folks will react to this from a company not exactly known for its design aesthetic. We like how the high chair has a wood base, but still features seat recline and height adjustment (features missing from other wood competitors like the Eddie Bauer).

All in all, Fisher Price does a good job with all their high chair offerings. Sure, no one's perfect: assembling these models can be a hassle, some readers say. Overall parent feedback is highest for the Healthy Care and Space Saver; the Healthy Start and Easy Clean get somewhat lower marks.

If you can live with the cutesy fashion, the Fisher Price Healthy Care makes a darn good high chair. **Rating: A**

Graco (800) 345-4109, (610) 286-5951. Web: gracobaby.com. Graco has had mixed results in the high chair category. For every innovation (the Graco Contempo high chair featured the most compact fold on the market), the company seems to also take a step backward. Graco had to recall 100,000 Contempo high chairs in 2006 after the chair collapsed when not fully opened and locked into place (Graco received 18 reports of the chair collapsing).

Graco divides its high chairs in two categories: standard and full-featured. The standard chairs include the Easy Chair, a bare-bones model that sells for as little as $39 at Wal-Mart (a good buy for Grandma's house) with a simple tray, three-position recline and vinyl pad.

As for full-featured chairs, Graco offers the Harmony, Meal Time and the aforementioned Contempo. The Harmony comes in several versions, ranging from a stripped-down version for $56 at Wal-Mart to a $130 "deluxe" model on Amazon (Babies R Us sells a $100 version). The Harmony's key selling point: a contoured design lets you pull baby up to the table easier than other models. The Harmony also features a one-hand height adjustment and seat recline, plus a "baby booster" insert that provides head and neck support for younger babies. The cushy padded vinyl seat and storage basket are nice features, as is the snap-off dinner tray.

What's the quality like? Parents give the Harmony mixed marks. Detractors point to the difficult assembly and a chair that doesn't adjust fully upright. Fans of the Harmony point out that the chair's many features make it a good value for the price. Overall, the Harmony isn't bad . . . but doesn't have the same positive feedback as Fisher Price's offerings.

The Graco Contempo ($100) lives on, despite the recall. Feedback on this model has been much more positive, with folks loving the ultra compact fold.

On the more affordable end, the Graco Meal Time high chair ($80 to $90) features a one-hand, three-position recline, dishwasher-safe tray, four height adjustments, casters and one-hand tray release. Feedback on this model has been sparse (it isn't as popular as the Contempo or Harmony), but what little we've heard has been positive—folks like the easy assembly and cleanability.

Out by the time you read this, Graco's wood high chairs. Available in three finishes, the "Classic Wood" high chairs ($130 to $150; pictured) feature a clear, dishwasher-safe cover for the wood tray and a wipe-clean, machine-washable seat pad. We saw a prototype of this chair and thought it was well-designed, but like most other wood high chairs, the Graco Classic Wood won't recline or adjust in height. And we thought it odd that Graco priced their version about $20 to $40 more than the competition. We don't see any reason for the price premium. **Rating: B**

high chairs

IKEA. *Web: ikea.com*. IKEA has two simple high chairs: the Antilop ($19; pictured) is a plastic chair with metal legs . . . but lacks a tray and doesn't fold up. The Gulliver ($50) is a simple wood high chair that includes a removable center support, but lacks a tray or safety harness. Obviously, this chair is more appropriate for an older toddler that needs a boost to a table (but doesn't need a safety harness or tray). We would not recommend these chairs for babies. **Rating: C**

Kolcraft *(773) 247-4494. Web: kolcraft.com.* Kolcraft's emphasis in this category is on being the low price leader and their current offerings are a case in point. The Recline N Dine is just $50. What do you get for that? Well, a rather basic high chair with one-hand tray release, vinyl pad and storage basket (but no wheels).

Kolcraft also sells a fancier high chair under their Sesame Street license (Sesame Beginnings, $70). This chair adds wheels, toys, three-position seat recline and one-hand tray release.

What about the quality? Let's be honest: these would be a great idea for grandma's house, where occasional use wouldn't tax them too much, but not as an everyday high chair. In the past, we heard many gripes about Kolcraft's previous high chairs . . . seat pads that ripped too easily, straps that were hard to adjust and more. **Rating: C+**

Inglesina *Web: inglesina.com.* Italian stroller company Inglesina jumps into the high chair market with the pricey Zuma, which attempts to be both high style and practical. The rounded seat echoes modern seats by Bloom and Boom, but

the more traditional base echoes a bit of Pali. The Zuma has eight height positions, three-position seat recline and a whopper of a price tag: $300. As a newcomer to the high chair market, Inglesina has made a few mistakes: the tray requires two hands to remove and the dishwasher-safe tray insert doesn't cover the entire main tray. Since the Zuma just debuted as of press time, we don't have any parent feedback yet.

FYI: Inglesina is also debuting a second, simpler high chair as well in 2008: the Club for $109. This chair doesn't really do anything but look pretty. ***Rating: Not yet.***

Peg Perego *(260) 482-8191. Web: perego.* *com.* Yes, the Prima Pappa has been a best seller but its day has come and gone. Sure, it looks stylish and features a four-position reclining seat, seven height adjustments, a dishwasher-safe dinner tray, five-point restraint and compact fold. And the fabrics! Very chic. But let's look at the chair's key flaw: the tray. It  sits a whopping 8.5" above the seat, making it too tall except perhaps for Shaq's kids. Another problem: the tray sits 7" from the back seat, creating a gap the size of the Grand Canyon between your baby and her food. Then let's talk about this chair's cleanability—it's notorious for collecting food in every little nook and cranny. All this for $200! Wow, what a deal.

Perego hasn't really changed this seat much in recent years, besides adding a rocking feature to the chair. And a parent needs a high chair that rocks . . . because? We don't see the point. Ditto for the Dondolino Prima Pappa, a version of the Pappa that runs on C batteries and has music for $230.

We should note that you can occasionally find Peg high chairs (especially last year models) for as little as $130 online.

New for 2008, Perego plans to introduce a premium version of the Pappa, dubbed the Prima Pappa Best. The only difference: the Best features an upgraded, tailored seat cushion. Price: $230.

So, we're not wild on this brand for high chairs. Instead of innovating in this category, Perego has been content to rest on its laurels . . . while competitors have knocked it off with better products at a lower price. Bottom line: if you like the looks of the Perego, save yourself $70 and get the Chicco Polly instead—same styling, just easier to use and clean. ***Rating: C+***

Rochelle *Web: rochellefurniture.com.* If plastic high chairs seem, well, too plastic-y, there is an alternative: a wooden high chair. Yes, kiddos, in the day before injection molded plastic, this was how babies sat at

the dinner table—in a high chair made of wood.

Rochelle has been making wooden high chairs in Michigan for 30 years. The company offers a half dozen models, most of which retail for $170 to $250. Example: the Charlotte ($190; pictured), which comes with a slide-on tray and safety harness. But let's be real: these chairs lack most of the modern features you see in plastic chairs—obviously, there is no seat recline, the wood tray can't be popped into the dishwasher and the chair lacks submarine protection (the simple harness isn't a match for modern five-point harnesses). Most parents add a foam pad, as the hard wood doesn't exactly make for comfortable seating.

While these high chairs are fine, the lack of safety features is the major negative. We understand why some folks like the look of wood . . . but the Eddie Bauer plastic/wood high chair hybrids are probably a more practical (and safe) alternative to the wood high chair. **Rating: C**

Safety 1st. While parent Cosco sells bare-bones high chairs to the discount chains, Safety 1st focuses on a slightly more upscale market. Example: Safety 1st has two hybrid wood models, much like their sister-brand Eddie Bauer chairs. The Safety 1st Sundance wood high chair ($90 at Wal-Mart) has a plastic tray with one-hand release and dishwasher-safe insert. This  chair comes with a three-point harness and a pad that only partially covers the chair (the Eddie Bauer version features a full pad and more deluxe tray). The Safety 1st Vineland wood high chair is similar to the Sundance, but comes in a darker wood color.

Safety 1st's other main high chair offering is the plastic All-in-On ($55). Positioned as a mid-price high chair, the All-in-One features a one-hand front tray release, three-position seat recline, dishwasher-safe tray, footrest and a "deluxe laminated pad." The downsides? That deluxe pad is hand-wash only, the chair only has a three-point harness and there are no wheels.

All in all, we don't quite see the point for Safety 1st's offerings. If you want a simple high chair for Grandma's house, Cosco's bare-bones offerings are half the price of the Safety 1st All-in-One. And if you want a wood chair, the Eddie Bauer wood high chairs have better pads, yet only cost $10 to $20 more than Safety 1st's version. **Rating: C+**

Sesame Beginnings. *Kolcraft makes this high chair, see review earlier in this chapter..*

Stokke *Web: stokkeUSA.com.* The Stokke Tripp
Trapp is the revised version of the Kinderzeat, which
we recommend in our Toddler Bargains book. This
$200 chair has a seat and footrest that adjust to mul-
tiple positions—the result is you can use it from six
months (once baby can sit up) to age eight or
beyond. The downsides? Well, the baby rail ($40)
and seat cushion ($40) are extras—making this a very

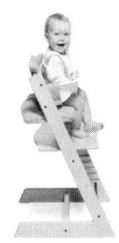

HIGH CHAIRS

High chairs, compared

NAME	RATING	PRICE	TRAY HEIGHT	TRAY DEPTH
BABY TREND	C+	$70-$100	8.5″	8
BOON FLAIR	A-	$200-$400	*	*
BLOOM FRESCO	N/A	$400	*	*
CHICCO POLLY	B	$110-$130	7.5	7
EDDIE BAUER	A-	$110-$125	8	5
EVENFLO EXPRESSIONS	C	$60	7	5
EVENFLO MAJESTIC	C	$60-$100	8	6
FISHER PRICE HEALTHY CARE	A	$80-$100	7.5	6
FISHER PRICE SPACE SAVER	A	$50	7.5	5
GRACO CONTEMPO	B	$100	7.5	6
GRACO HARMONY	B	$56-$130	7	7
GRACO CLASSIC WOOD	B	$130-$150	8	6.5
IKEA ANTILOP	C	$19	*	*
INGLESINA ZUMA	N/A	$300	*	*
KOLCRAFT RECLINE DINE	C+	$50	8.5	6
PEG PEREGO PRIMA PAPPA	C+	$200	8.5	7
SAFETY 1ST SUNDANCE	C+	$90	*	*
STOKKE TRIPP TRAPP	A-	$280	*	*
ZOOPER PEAS CARROTS	B-	$170	9	8.5

KEY

TRAY HEIGHT: Distance from the seat to the top of the tray. Any mea-
surement under 8″ is acceptable. Above 8″ is too tall.

DEPTH (tray to seat): Distance from the back of the seat to the tray. 5″
to 7″ is acceptable.

SUB?: Most high chairs have a special guard to prevent a child from
submarining under the tray. Some models attach this to the chair;
others to the tray. A better bet: those that attach to the seat. See discussion earlier in this chapter.

pricey investment. And the Tripp Trapp doesn't come with a tray . . . so baby will be making a mess on your table, not his high chair tray. Our view: the Tripp Trapp is probably best for older toddlers who have outgrown a regular high chair (as an alternative to a booster seat). The quality of the Stokke Tripp Trapp is excellent. ***Rating: A-***

Svan of Sweden (866) 782-6222; web: scandinavianchild.com. Svan is the latest multi-function high chair imported from Europe. The

Sub?	Pad	Comment
Seat	Cloth	Pad should be hand-washed, line dried.
Seat	Vinyl	Seamless seat; automatic height adjust.
Seat	Cloth	Seamless seat, auto height, seat reclines
Tray	Vinyl	$130 version w/ double pad; Italian fashion.
Tray	Both	Wood with plastic tray; two new finishes.
Seat	Vinyl	Complaints about seat recline.
Seat	Vinyl	Discovery version has toy for $100.
Seat	Vinyl	Better bet: version without seat ruffles.
Seat	Vinyl	Attaches to chair; great for little space.
Seat	Vinyl	Narrowest fold on market; recent recall.
Seat	Vinyl	Contoured design; infant head support.
Seat	Vinyl	New; one-hand tray release.
Seat	None	No tray; better for older toddlers.
Seat	Cloth	New; seamless seat, mod look.
Tray	Cloth	Lowest price; good option grandma.
Seat	Vinyl	Style leader; many colors.
None	Cloth	Wood hybrid; Pad isn't full coverage.
Seat	Cloth	No tray; better for older toddlers.
Tray	Vinyl	Stylish, but doesn't fold compact.

Pad: Is the seat made of cloth or vinyl? We prefer vinyl for easier clean up. Cloth seats must be laundered and some can't be thrown in the drier (requiring a long wait for it to line dry). Of course, this feature isn't black and white—some vinyl seats have cloth edging/piping.

* Not applicable or not available. Some of these models were new as of press time, so we didn't have these specs yet.

Svan Chair is unique for a couple of reasons: first, it is all wood, including the tray (a plastic dishwasher-safe tray cover is included). Second, the high chair converts to a toddler chair and finally a chair for older kids. The Svan is available in  three finishes (natural, cherry and whitewash) as well as five colors. We know some folks will go for this chair for the looks alone . . . but be prepared to spend twice the amount of other wood high chairs. The basic chair (18 months and up) goes for $200. But if you want to use it as a high chair for babies six months and up, you have to pay another $50 for an "infant kit." A matching cushion to make that wood seat more comfortable will run another $35. Total price: $285—yep, that's two to three times the cost of other wood high chairs (which, to be fair, do NOT convert to a chair for older kids).

Parent reviews of the Svan have been favorable—most folks like how sturdy the Svan is, yet it is light enough to move from room to room without much trouble. However, adjusting the chair's height requires an Allen wrench and there are lots of nooks/crannies to clean. And we've received some reports that it is hard to keep the infant tray level without constantly tightening the bolts (a pain to be sure). Parents who like the Svan most appreciate its aesthetic and small footprint, saying this outweighs the hefty price tag. **Rating: B+**

Zooper *(503) 248-9469; web: zooperstrollers. com.* Zooper's "Peas & Carrots" highchair's ultra-cool look (fashionable fabrics, brushed aluminum frame) makes it easy on the eyes. It features four height positions, mesh basket, five-point harness and locking wheels. Unfortunately, it is quite pricey  ($170 retail, although previous year models are on sale for less). Another bummer: the chair doesn't fold as flat as the Italian chairs and, when folded, the basket sticks out a good four inches from the chair. The result: the Peas & Carrots doesn't stand when folded because it isn't balanced. And we aren't wild about the tray height (too tall at 9″) nor the seat depth (8.5″ from the back of the seat to the tray). Readers picked up on this flaw as well and panned the Zooper overall. The passive restraint is on the tray instead of the seat, which is another negative.

The few fans of this high chair liked the big pad, which covers the entire chair and footrest (and hence, food didn't get stuck in hard to clean areas). But you can't remove the straps to wash them. FYI: This seat is hard to find in stores; it is sold online on Amazon and other sites.

Bottom line: this high chair has the looks . . . but doesn't deliver the goods. **Rating: B-**

◆ **Other Brands**. *Kettler* is a brand better known in this country for their tricycles, but their Tipp Topp high chair has won fans for its simple design. We found it for $200 on HighChairs.com, which also carry wooden high chairs by Geuther and Lipper. The best deal on a wood high chair: Angel Line's $90 Jenny Lind model, which includes a tray and safety harness.

If you like those wood high chairs at restaurants, you can buy a similar model online: the *Lipper* wood high chair for $55 at Amazon.

Our Picks: Brand Recommendations

Here is our round up of the best high chair bets.

Good. The *Fisher-Price Easy Clean* ($70 to $85) lives up to its name, with its easy to remove pad and straps that can go into the dishwasher. If space is tight, the *Graco Contempo* ($100) has the most compact fold of any high chair on the market and positive feedback (despite a 2006 recall).

Better. *Chicco's Polly* high chair is an improvement over their last effort and lands a spot as number two on our recommended list. Chicco has lowered the tray, added a compact fold and re-designed the tray for easy one-hand removal. Yep, the price is more than the Fisher Price pick we discuss next ($110 to $130, depending on the version) . . . but we'd bet many folks will view this chair's styling and fashion as worthy of the upgrade. The only bummer: the Chicco Polly's dishwasher-safe tray is so big it doesn't fit in a dishwasher.

Best. The *Fisher-Price Healthy Care* has got it all—great safety features, easy of use, cleanability and more. We like the snap-off dishwasher-safe tray, good design and easy-to-clean vinyl pad. The chair comes in two versions: $90 for the "Aquarium" version or $100 for "Rainforest." We like the latter, since it omits the seat ruffles (a food magnet). But the $90 version would do just as well for most folks. The only drawback to the Fisher Price high chair: you have to like the like the cutesy fashion.

Grandma's house. For grandma's house, a simple *Cosco Convenience* (aka Beginnings Simple Start) ($30) should do the trick. No, it doesn't have casters or other fancy features, but Grandma doesn't need all that. *The Kolcraft Recline N Dine* ($50) is another good choice.

Hook-on Chairs and Boosters

Your toddler has outgrown his high chair, but doesn't quite fit into the adult chairs at the kitchen table. What to do? Consider a booster. There are three types of kitchen booster seats on the market today:

1 **HOOK-ON CHAIRS.** As the name implies, these seats hook on to a table, instead of attaching to a chair. Pros: Lightweight; yet most can hold toddlers up to 35 to 40 lbs. Very portable—many parents use these chairs as a sanitary alternative when they dine out since many restaurants seemed to have last cleaned their high chairs during the Carter administration. Cons: May not work with certain tables, like those with pedestal bases. Fear of tipping an unstable table leads some restaurants to prohibit these chairs. Hook-on chairs do not recline, a feature you see on regular boosters.

2 **BOOSTER SEATS WITH TRAYS.** These boosters strap to a chair and usually have a tray. Pros: Most fold flat for travel. Some have multiple seat levels. Can use with or without a tray. Cons: Child may not be sitting up at table height. Some brands have too-small trays and difficult to adjust straps make for a loose fit.

3 **PLAIN BOOSTERS (NO TRAY).** These chairs are just boosters— nothing fancy, no trays. Pros: Better bet for older toddlers (age four or five) who want to eat at the table. Cons: No restraint system or belt, so this isn't a choice for younger toddlers.

Our Picks: Brand Recommendations

◆ *Hook-on chair. Top pick:* Graco *Travel Lite Table Chair* (gracobaby.com). This simple, safe and affordable ($35) hook-on chair is a great option when you need a chair for baby at a restaurant, grandma's house or when traveling. It is very portable, weighing only ten pounds,

and includes a tray. On the other hand, the padding isn't very cushy, the tray is small and you can only use it (or any hook-on) on a table with a flat underside. The weight limit is 37 pounds.

Runners Up: Chicco's two entrants in this category are also strong contenders. The *Caddy* ($40) has a compact fold, three point harness and "quick grip" table clamps. The seat pad is removable and machine washable. The *Hippo Travel Seat* ($50; pictured) has
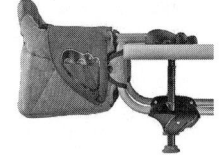

added a double locking attachment for extra safety.

♦ **Kitchen booster seat with tray.**
Top pick: *Fisher Price Healthy Care Booster Seat* (fisher-price.com). Fisher Price has a winner here: we liked the snap-off feeding tray that can go into a dishwasher, easy fold and shoulder strap for road trips

and three different height settings. When your child gets older, the tray removes so the seat becomes a basic booster. The only caveat: the back does not recline, so your baby must be able to sit up on his own to use it safely. (No biggie for most toddlers, but we know some folks consider these boosters as high-chair replacements—not a good idea unless your child can sit upright). Price: $25, making this a good value.

Runner Up: *Eddie Bauer 2 Level Wood Booster* (djgusa.com). Similar to Eddie Bauer's full size wooden high chair, this booster seat is mostly made of wood with a plastic tray. If you don't like the plastic look of most boosters, then this is a good alternative. No, it doesn't have all the bells and whistles of other chairs (it doesn't

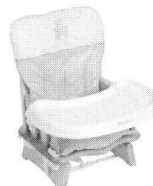

recline, you need two hands to remove the tray), but it functions well for most parents.

If you just want a cheap seat to use occasionally, check out the Babies R Us brand booster, Especially for Kids. At just $13 it's a steal.

♦ **Kitchen booster seat without tray.**
The BabySmart Cooshie Booster. This is our recommendation for older toddlers—the Cooshie Booster's super comfortable foam design is a winner. It's lightweight and non-

skid. No, there isn't a safety harness, but older kids don't really need it. How old? The manufacturer says this seat would work for babies as young as 12 months, but we think that is a stretch. The optimum time to use this booster would be for between ages three and five, in our opinion. Yes, we think some toddlers as young as two would be mature enough but any younger would be pushing it. We used this booster with our youngest son and it got raves. The seat costs $30 to $35 although we saw on ebay.com for less.

A brief warning: The *Bumbo Baby Sitter* ($40) is a popular seat designed for younger infants to sit upright. The problem? The Bumbo should ONLY be used on the floor (NOT on a raised surface like a chair or table). A recent

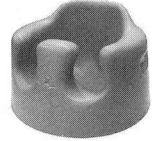

report by a San Francisco TV station chronicled several cases of

kitchen boosters

babies tipping out of their Bumbos . . . and toppling to the floor when the Bumbo was on a table. As we were going to press, the CPSC has opened an investigation into the matter.

The Bottom Line:
A Wrap-Up of Our Best Buy Picks

What's the more affordable way to feed baby? Breastfeeding, by a mile. We estimate you can save $500 in just the first six months alone by choosing to breast instead of bottle-feed.

Of course, that's easy for us to say—breastfeeding takes some practice, for both you and baby. One product that can help: a breast pump, to relieve engorgement or provide a long-term solution to baby's feeding if you go back to work. Which pumps are best? For manual pumps, we like the Avent Isis ($45) for that occasional bottle. If you plan to pump so you can go back to work, a professional-grade pump works best. Tip: rent one first before you buy. If you like it and decide you are serious about pumping, we liked the Medela Pump In Style Advanced ($350) or Ameda Purely Yours (about $150 to $230).

If you decide to bottle feed or need to wean your baby off breast milk, the most affordable formulas are the generic brands sold in discount stores under various private-label names. You'll save up to 40% by choosing generic over name brands, but your baby gets the exact same nutrition.

Who makes the best bottles? Our readers say Avent is tops, but others find cheaper options like Playtex and Munchkin Health Flow work just was well at half the price. A dark horse brand: Dr. Brown's bottles, which help eliminate colic.

Let's talk baby food—besides the ubiquitous Gerber, there are several other brands that are good alternatives. One of the best is Earth's Best, although it is more pricey than affordable brands like Del Monte/Nature's Goodness and Beechnut. How can you save? Make your own baby food for pennies or buy jarred baby food in bulk at discount stores. And skip the toddler meals, which are a waste of money.

Finally, consider that quintessential piece of baby gear—the high chair. We felt the best bets were those that were easiest to clean (go for a vinyl, not cloth pad) and had snap-off dishwasher-safe trays. Our top pick is the Fisher Price Healthy Care ($90 to $100), although the Chicco Polly ($110 to $130) is a stylish alternative.

Now that you've got the food and kitchen covered, what about the rest of your house? We'll explore all the other baby gear you might need for your home next.

CHAPTER 7

Around the House: Monitors, Diaper Pails, Safety & More

Inside this chapter

W hat's the best bathtub for baby? Which baby monitor can save you $40 a year in batteries? What's the best—and least stinky—diaper pail? In this chapter, we explore everything for baby that's around the house. From bouncer seats to the best baby monitors, we'll give you tricks and tips to saving money. You'll learn about playpens and swings. Finally, let's talk safety—we'll give you tips and advice on affordable baby proofing. So let's get cracking.

Getting Started: When Do You Need This Stuff?

The good news is you don't need all this stuff right away. While you'll probably purchase a monitor before the baby is born, other items like bouncer seats and even bath-time products aren't necessary immediately (you'll give the baby sponge baths for the first few weeks, until the belly button area heals). Of course, you still might want to register for these items before baby is born. In each section of this chapter, we'll be more specific about when you need certain items.

What Are You Buying?

Here is a selection of items that you can use when your baby is three to six months of age. Of course, these ideas are merely suggestions—none of these items are "mandatory." We've divided them into two categories: bath-time and the baby's room.

Bath

1 TOYS/BOOKS. What fun is taking a bath without toys? Many stores sell inexpensive plastic tub toys, but you can use other items like stacking cups in the tub as well. And don't forget about tub safety items, which can also double as toys. For example, Safety 1st (800) 739-7233 (safety1st.com) makes a *Bath Pal Thermometer*, a yellow duck or seal with attached thermometer (to make sure the water isn't too hot) for $6 at Kmart. *Tubbly Bubbly* by Kel-Gar (972) 250-3838 (web: kelgar.com) is a $10 elephant or hippo spout cover that protects against scalding, bumps and bruises. In fact, Kel-Gar makes an entire line of innovative bath toys and accessories.

If money is no object, consider the new digital spout cover with built-thermometer from *4 Moms*. It's $30, but it does tell you exactly how hot the water temperature is as it comes out the spout. And it changes color: blue for water that is too cold, red for too hot and green for "just right." Pretty cool, especially if you have a hard time setting your hot water heater to the right temperature.

2 TOILETRIES. Basic baby shampoo like the famous brand made by Johnson & Johnson works just fine, and you'll probably need some lotion as well. The best tip: first try lotion that is unscented in case your baby has any allergies. Also, never use talcum powder on your baby—it's a health hazard. If you need to use an absorbent powder, good old cornstarch will do the trick.

What about those natural baby products that are all the rage, like Mustela or Calidou? We got a gift basket of an expensive boutique's natural baby potions and didn't see what the big deal was. Worse yet, the $20-a-bottle shampoo dried out our baby's scalp so much he had scratching fits. We suppose the biggest advantage of these products is that they don't contain extraneous chemicals or petroleum by-products. Also, most don't have perfumes, but then, many low-price products now come in unscented versions as well. The bottom line: it's your comfort level. If you want to try them out without making a big investment, register for them as a shower gift.

If you have a history of allergies or skin problems in your family, consider washing baby's skin and hair with Dove or Cetaphil bar soap. These do not contain detergents that you find in even the most basic baby shampoo.

3 BABY BATHTUB. While not a necessity, a baby bathtub is a nice convenience (especially if you are bathing baby solo). See the section below for more info on bathtubs.

4 **POTTY SEAT.** Check our e-book *Toddler Bargains* (BabyBargains. com) for reviews and ratings of the best potty chairs.

Safe & Sound

◆ **BATH SEATS SHOULD NOT BE USED.** It looks innocuous—the baby bath seat—but it can be a disaster waiting to happen. These seats suction to the bottom of a tub, holding baby in place while she takes a bath. The problem? Parents get a false sense of security from such items and often leave the bathroom to answer the phone, etc. We've seen several tragic reports of babies who've drowned when they fell out of the seats (or the seats became un-suctioned from the tub). The best advice: AVOID these seats and NEVER leave baby alone in the tub, even for just a few seconds.

◆ **TURN DOWN YOUR WATER HEATER.** Ideally, your water heater should be set at no more than 120° F. at 140° F it poses a safety hazard. You can also consider installing anti-scalding devices on your showers and faucets. One such device is called *ScaldShield* and sells at hardware stores for about $40.

◆ **NO SKID RUGS IN THE BATHROOM.** Invest in rugs that have rub-berized no skid bottoms. You don't want to slip carrying your baby, and you don't want your new walking toddler to bang his head on the toilet or tub.

◆ **LOCK IT UP.** Install cabinet and toilet locks. This is just as impor-tant as safeguarding baby from dangers in the kitchen. And now is a great time to retrain your husband to put the lid down on the toilet seat. Locks don't work unless you actually use them.

Baby Bathtubs

Sometimes, it is the simplest products that are the best. Take baby bathtubs—if you look at the offerings in this category, you'll note some baby bathtubs convert to step stools and then, small compact cars. Okay, just kidding on the car, but these products are a good example of brand manager overkill—companies think the way to success with baby bath tubs is to make them work from birth to college.

So, it shouldn't be a surprise that our top pick for a baby bath-tub is, well, just a bathtub. The *EuroBath by Primo* ($30; web: primobaby.com; pictured right) is a sturdy tub for babies, age birth to two. It weighs less than two pounds and is easy to use—just add baby, water and poof! Clean baby. The EuroBath is well designed, although it is big—almost three feet from end to end. It may be a tight fit if you have a small bathroom. In that case, you might want to consider the **Comfy Duck Bath Center** by Safety 1st ($15; pictured). Nothing fancy, but it does have a foam liner and (as the name implies) a "ducky" sling to cradle a newborn. This might be a good choice for Grandma's house. FYI: Safety 1st also makes a Fun Time Froggy Bath Center with the same features, just a frog theme instead of duck.

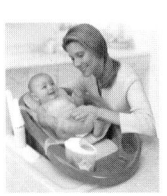

Got a big baby? Some parents tell us regular bathtubs (like the Safety 1st tub mentioned above) don't work as well when Junior is a linebacker in training. So, try out the **First Years Sure Comfort Deluxe** tub ($22; see at right). It's no frills but does have an anti-slip backrest. One reader writes with kudos for the **EZ Bather Deluxe** by Dex Products ($12, 800-546-1996; dexproducts.com), an L-shaped vinyl frame that keeps babies head above water in the bathtub or kitchen sink.

Finally, for something new, check out the **Cleanwater Infant Tub** with built in ther-mometer by 4 Moms (4momsonline.com; $40; pictured). This tub's clever design circulates clean water around baby, while dirty water leaves through a side drain. A built in color coded thermometer ensures the proper water temperature.

A baby bathtub is a great item to pick up second-hand or at a garage sale. Or borrow from a friend. Readers say they've snagged baby bath tubs for $2 or so at garage sales—with a little cleaning, they are just fine. What if you want to give baby a bath in a regu-lar tub or kitchen sink? A bath sling like Summer's Mother's Touch ($15) will do the trick!

Baby's Room

1 **A DIAPER PAIL.** Yes, there are dozens of diaper pails on the market. We'll review and rate the offerings in the next section.

2 **BABY MONITOR.** Later in this chapter, we have a special sec-tion devoted to monitors, including some creative money-saving tips. Of course, if you have a small house or apartment, you

may not even need a baby monitor.

3 **THE CHANGING AREA.** A well-stocked changing area features much more than just diapers. Nope, you need wipes and lots of them. We discussed our recommendations for wipe brands in Chapter 4, the Reality Layette. We should note that we've heard from some thrifty parents who've made their own diaper wipes—they use old washcloths or cut-up cloth diapers and warm water.

What about wipe warmers? In previous editions of this book, we've recommended these $20 devices, which keep wipes at 99 degrees (and lessen the cold shock on baby's bottom at three in the morning). However, we've been concerned with safety issues about wipe warmers that have arisen in recent years.

First, Dex recalled a half million of their wipe warmers in 1997 after one fire was allegedly caused by the unit (there were six additional instances "involving melting of the product," says the CPSC). While Dex fixed the problem, we were so miffed about how the company handled the recall, we don't recommend Dex warmers.

Then, we started getting complaints from readers about another brand of wipe warmers (Prince Lionheart) that damaged dresser tops. Prince Lionheart blamed the problem on the little feet under the warmer, which were apparently leaving marks on the dresser tops when the unit warmed up. The company claims it has now fixed the problem (and denies that wipe warmers "burn" wipes—they say the heat discolors the chemicals in the wipes), but we're still leery of these products in general.

If you still want a wipe warmer, we'd go for a newer model instead of a hand-me-down because of past safety recalls. Also: newer models from makers like Prince Lionheart work better to keep wipes moist and avoid discoloration. Better yet: just skip it.

Other products to consider for the diaper changing station include diaper rash ointment (A & D, Desitin, etc.), lotion or cream, cotton swabs, petroleum jelly (for rectal thermometers) and rubbing alcohol to care for the belly button area (immediately remove this item from the changing area once you finish belly button care—it's poisonous!). If you have a Container Store nearby (800) 733-3532 (containerstore.com), we noticed they sell simple plastic storage containers for $4 to $20 for all those diaper changing station items. Target has also expanded their storage departments.

4 **PORTABLE CRIBS/PLAYPENS.** While this item doesn't necessarily go in your baby's room, many folks have found portable cribs/playpens to be indispensable in other parts of the house (or when visiting grandma). Later in this chapter, we have a special section devoted to this topic.

5 **WHITE NOISE.** In the past, we noted that some parents swear they'd never survive without the ceiling fan in their baby's room—the "white noise" made by a whirling fan soothed their fussy baby (and quieted sounds from the rest of the house). We even recommended a white noise generator for babies who needed calming. However, in a study published in the journal *Science* (April 18, 2003), researchers say using white noise can be dangerous to your child's developing hearing. Our advice now is to avoid those white noise generators and find other ways to sooth your baby to sleep. (For the record, the slight hum of a ceiling fan or A/C unit is not a problem—the concern is noise generators put close to the crib).

6 **HUMIDIFIER.** See our web page (babybargains.com; click on bonus material) for advice on buying a humidifier for baby's room.

Diaper Pails

Pop quiz! Remember our discussion of how many diapers you will change in your baby's first year? What was the amount?

Pencils down—yes, it is 2300 diapers! A staggering figure . . . only made more staggering by figuring out what do with the dirty ones once you've changed baby. Yes, we can hear first-time parents raising their hands right now and saying "Duh! They go in the trash!"

Oh, not so fast, new parental one. Stick a dirty diaper in a regular trashcan and you may quickly perfume your home—not to mention draw a curious pet and we won't even go there.

So, most parents use a diaper pail, that specialized trashcan designed by trained scientists to limit stink and keep out babies, pets and stray relatives. But which diaper pail? Here's our Diaper Pail 411:

Diaper pails fall into two camps: those that use cartridges to wrap diapers in deodorized plastic and pails that use regular kitchen trash bags. As you'd guess, those plastic refill canisters are more expensive to use (they cost $4 to $8, depending on the size) and wrap about 140 or so diapers. The pail can hold 20-25 diapers at a time, which is about three days worth of diapers.

So, should you just get a diaper pail that uses regular kitchen trash bags? Yes, they are less expensive to use—but there is sometimes a major trade-off. Stink. These pails tend to stink more and hence, have to be emptied more frequently than the diaper pails that use special deodorized plastic—perhaps daily or every other day.

Obviously, the decision on which diaper pail is right for you and your baby's nursery depends on several factors. What is the distance to the trash? If you live in a house with easy access to an outside trashcan, it might be easier to go with the lower-cost alternatives and just take out the diapers more frequently. If you live in an apartment where the nearest dumpster is down three flights of stairs and a long walk across a parking lot, well, it might make sense to go with an option that requires less work.

Another factor: how sensitive are you to the smell? Some folks don't have a major problem with this, while moms who are pregnant again with a second child may need an industrial strength diaper pail to keep from losing it when walking into baby's nursery. A great tip from our readers: dump the poop. Before tossing the diaper, dump the poop into the toilet. No matter what you use to contain used diapers, this simple step will hugely mitigate the odor.

Whatever your decision, remember you'll live with this diaper pail for three or more YEARS (that's how long before most children potty train). And it's a fact of life: diapers get stinkier as your baby gets older . . . so the diaper removal strategy that works for a newborn may have to be chucked for a toddler. Yes, you may be able to use a plain trashcan with liner when your newborn is breastfeeding . . . but after you start solid foods, it will be time to buy a diaper pail.

Given those caveats, here is an overview of what's out there:

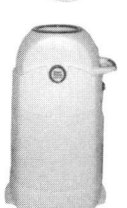

DIAPER CHAMP BY BABY TREND
Type: Kitchen trash bag.
Price: $30. Web: BabyTrend.com.
Pros: Did we mention no expensive refills? The Diaper Champ uses regular ol' kitchen bags, yet the contraption works to seal out odor by using a flip handle design. Very easy to use. Taller design means it holds more diapers than the Genie.
Cons: Not as stink-free as the Genie or Dekor, but close. Enterprising toddlers can learn how to put their toys into the diaper slot. Bigger footprint than other pails.
Comments: The Diaper Champ comes in two versions: the original (4000) and a revised version (4100). Unfortunately, most web sites and stores don't seem to distinguish between the two models, just referring to both as the Diaper Champ (see pictures at left—the older 4000 is top). That's a problem because Baby Trend's re-design has left some former fans disappointed. The new version has a wider opening, but parents tell us it doesn't work as well (diapers get stuck, the smell can be atrocious, etc). And the diaper removal process may require an EPA HazMat Rapid Response team, given the stink level. That said, fans love the Champ since it can use regular kitchen bags, saving hundreds of dollars in refill cartridges. But . . . most folks like the Champ

only until their child starts to eat solid foods. Then the smell can be overwhelming, forcing folks to buy Dekor or Genie. One tip: if you go with the Champ, put a fabric softener sheet in the pail with each load (this cuts down on the smell). And be prepared to scrub it every month or two with bleach, leaving it outside to air out. And the Champ probably isn't the best bet if you have an older toddler, who can put toys into the slot (trust us, not a pretty sight).

Bottom line: Not perfect, but good for the first few months. A bargain—but beware the stink trade-offs.

Rating: A-

DIAPER DEKOR

Type: Refill canister

Price: $30 to $40. Refill packs are $22 and wrap 590 newborn diapers. Web: regallager.com

Pros: Hands free operation—you hit the foot petal and drop in a diaper. Large size can hold 5+ days worth of diapers. Converts to a regular trashcan after baby is done with diapers. Parents say it is much easier to use than the Diaper Genie, reviewed below. And refills cost half as much as the Genie, on a per diaper basis. More attractive design than the Genie.

Cons: Still have to buy those expensive refill canisters. One complaint by some users: the plastic is cheap and breaks easily. Hinges on the "trap door" seem prone to breakage, as does the foot pedal. We've slightly lowered the rating this time to reflect this.

Comments: The Diaper Dekor debuted in 2002 and is giving the Diaper Genie a good run for its money. It comes in two versions: a regular model and a "plus" version that is a few inches bigger/taller and holds more diapers. As for the stink factor, the jury is still out on this one—some parents say it is just as good as the Genie at odor control, while others think it isn't quite as effective. Overall, however, the Dekor does seem to get better marks from parents for ease of use (love the hands free idea). Plus we like the fact it can convert to a regular trashcan later after the diaper days are over.

Bottom line: A worthy alternative to the Genie.

Rating: B+

DIAPER GENIE II BY PLAYTEX

Type: Refill canister

Price: $30. Refill cartridges ($6) hold 30 diapers.

Web: diapergenie.com

Pros: Wraps each diaper in deodorized plastic. One-hand operation. Easy to remove diapers. Some say better at stink control than Diaper Champ.

Cons: Expensive, since you have to keep buying those refills. Once pail starts to fill, stink can slip out when you put a new diaper in.

Comments: The revised Diaper Genie II addresses some of the key gripes with the original version: there's no more twisting when diapers go in, enabling one-hand operation. A clamp keeps the diapers (and the smell) inside the container. The Genie II also holds more diapers, since there are no more chains of sausages as with the original. The removal process has also been improved: Playtex actually designer a cutter that, well, cuts. When you talk to parents about the Diaper Genie, you get strong love/hate reactions. Fans think it is tops at odor prevention and the revised version is easier to use. Detractors point out that the high cost of refills make this a pricey purchase. And the smell issue comes up again with some parents, who complain they get hit with a wall of odor when they put a diaper in (this seems to be a problem when the pail is more full). FYI: Playtex still sells the original Genie, sold under the name "Twist Away" pail system. We don't recommend this old version.

Bottom line: Between the Genie II and the Dekor, we give the Dekor an edge when it comes to stink control and ease of use. But the Genie is a close second.

Rating: B-

CLEAN AIR ODOR FREE DIAPER DISPOSAL BY FIRST YEARS

Type: Kitchen trash bag.

Price: $40. Extra carbon filters $15 for two.

Pros: Uses a fan and carbon filter to trap odors. Holds 40 diapers. Uses standard kitchen trash bags.

Cons: LOUD! Requires 4 D batteries. Smell escapes.

Comments: Like the Graco diaper pail reviewed below, First Years must have figured it needed some catchy gizmo to break into the diaper pail market. Voila! The first diaper pail with a fan and carbon filter! Readers have one universal complaint: it is too LOUD! When you put a diaper in, the pail cranks up the decibels like a 747 (ok, an exaggeration, but you get the idea). Other readers report diapers that jam and a general lack of stink control.

Bottom line: A loser.

Rating: F

TOUCH FREE DIAPER PAIL BY GRACO

Type: Kitchen trash bag.

Price: $50. Extra carbon filters $4.

Pros: Motion sensor activates lid—just drop in diaper, without ever touching the diaper pail. Can switch pail to manual as well. Uses standard 10 or 13-gallon trash bags.

Cons: Requires 4 D batteries—lots of them! Must replace carbon filters. Pricey. Small size only holds a few diapers. Poor stink control.

Comments: We love gizmos and gadgets as much as anyone, so Graco's new "Touch Free" Diaper Pail has that novelty appeal . . . but then our cynical side kicks in. Is it really worth spending $20 more than the Baby Trend Diaper Champ to get a motion-sensor activated lid? Sure, you can switch the pail to "manual mode" if you have dogs or older kids, but that kind of defeats the whole whiz-bang nature of the Touch Free. And the verdict from consumers? Parents who've used the Touch Free tell us they aren't happy with it—it eats batteries (4 D's every week, which must be replaced each time by removing three small screws). And the Touch Free fails at stink control. Plus it is too small, say readers.

Bottom line: The Touch Free violates the cardinal rule of baby products: Keep It Simple. We say pass on this diaper pail.

Rating: C-

Bonus Material Online: Humidifiers, Toys, Pets

On our web site, BabyBargains.com, click on Bonus Material to read about humidifiers, toys (our top picks, including crib mobiles), and how to introduce your pet to a new baby. Plus a report on affordable baby announcements.

Bouncer Seat/Activity Gyms

◆ **ACTIVITY GYM.** Among our favorites is the *Gymini by Tiny Love* (for a dealer near you, call 800-843-6292; web: tinylove.com). The Gymini is a three-foot square blanket that has two criss-cross arches. You clip rattles, mirrors and other toys onto the arches, providing endless fun for baby as she lies on her back and reaches for the toys. The Gymini comes in four different versions: a basic version in black, white and red is $45 and the "super deluxe" model (Lights & Music) is about $60. The more expensive versions have more toys. Another plus for the Gymini: it folds up quickly and easily for trips to Grandma's.

◆ **ACTIVITY SEAT/BOUNCER WITH TOY BAR.** An activity seat (also called a bouncer) provides a comfy place for baby to hang out while you eat dinner, and the toy bar adds some mild amusement. The latest twist to these products is a "Magic Fingers" vibration feature—the bouncer basically

Coupon deals cut the cost of online shopping

How do baby product web sites generate traffic and sales? One tried and true method is the online coupon—a special discount, either in dollars or percentage off deals. Sites offer these as come-ons for new customers, returning customers . . . just about anyone. Coupons enable sites to give discounts without actually lowering the prices of merchandise. You enter the coupon code when you place the order and zap! You've saved big.

Yes, there are sites that list coupon deals across the internet (FatWallet.com, eDealFinder.com), but how do you find the best coupons for baby stuff? Check out our message boards (BabyBargains.com, click on Message Boards). On the Bargain Alert board, we keep a pinned thread with all the latest coupon deals, all submitted by our readers (spam isn't allowed). Updated regularly, this thread has all the best deals. (And there's even a separate pinned thread for freebies).

---

vibrates, simulating a car ride. Parents who have these bouncers tell us they'd rather have a kidney removed than give up their vibrating bouncer, as it appears the last line of defense in soothing a fussy baby, short of checking into a mental institution.

What features should you look for in a bouncer? Readers say a carrying handle is a big plus. Also: get a neutral fabric pattern, says another parent, since you'll probably be taking lots of photos of baby and a garish pattern may grate on your nerves.

What is the best brand for bouncers? Fisher Price (fisher-price.com) makes the most popular one in the category; most are about $20 to $60, depending on the version. A good choice: the *Fisher Price RainForest bouncer* ($50). Although some of sounds were a little loud, the toys and waterfall got high marks. Yes, other companies make similar products (Summer makes one for $50, Combi has some ranging in price from $40 to $80 version, etc.) but the feedback we get from parents is that Fisher-Price is the best.

The only caveat: most bouncer seats have a 25-pound weight limit. If you want something that will last longer, consider the *Baby Bjorn Babysitter 1-2-3*. Yes, it is more pricey than the Fisher-Price (anywhere from $85 to $150, depending on the store) and lacks a vibrating feature . . . but you can use it up to 29 lbs. Fisher-Price does have a bouncer that can even be used up to 40 lbs—the *Learning Patterns Infant-to-Toddler* rocker. It's a great deal at $35. Parent feedback on that model (as with most Fisher Price bouncers) is very positive.

New this year in the bouncer category: a "soothing center." The

Graco Sweet Peace ($170; pictured) provides four cradling motions, six speeds and the removable carrier doubles as a floor rocker (or you can use it with a Graco infant car seat). The Sweet Peace was too new as of press time for parent feedback.

◆ **Toy bars for your car seat.** Here's another money-saving tip: turn your infant car seat into an activity center with an attachable toy bar. Tiny Love (tinylove.com) makes a *Take Along Arch* with dangling toys for $16. Lamaze (learningcurve.com) also has a car seat toy that wraps around the seat handle. The *Happy Wrappy* includes crinkle and rattle toys, for $16. Another plus: your baby is safer in an infant car seat carrier than in other activity seats, thanks to that industrial-strength harness safety system. Safety warning: only use these toy bars when the car seat is NOT inside a vehicle (that is, at home, etc.). Toy bars are not safe in a vehicle as they can be a hazard/projectile in an accident.

One caveat: some parents and pediatricians believe that leaving an infant in a car seat for extended periods of time can contribute to breathing problems in very young infants. For older babies, excessive time in an infant seat could lead to flat head syndrome (plagiocephaly). Unfortunately, doctors don't agree on how much time in an infant seat is too much. Use your common sense and move your child out of the seat frequently.

Monitors

For her first nine months, your baby is tethered to you via the umbilical cord. After that, it's the baby monitor that becomes your surrogate umbilical cord—enabling you to work in the garden, wander about the house, and do many things that other, childless human beings do, while still keeping tabs on a sleeping baby. Hence, this is a pretty important piece of equipment you'll use every day—a good one will make your life easier . . . and a bad one will be a never-ending source of irritation.

Smart Shopper Tips for Monitors

Smart Shopper Tip #1
Bugging your house
    "My neighbor and I both have babies and baby monitors. No matter what we do, I can still pick up my neighbor's monitor on my receiver. Can they hear our conversations too?"

You better bet. Let's consider what a baby monitor really is: a radio transmitter. The base unit is the transmitter and the receiver is, well, a receiver. So anyone with another baby monitor can often pick up your monitor—not just the sound of your baby crying, but also *any* conversations you have with your mate in the nursery.

You'll notice that many monitors have two channels "to reduce interference," and some even have high and low range settings—do they help reduce eavesdropping? No, not in our opinion. In densely populated areas, you can still have problems.

We should note that you can also pick up baby monitors on many cordless phones—even police scanners can pick up signals as far as one or two miles away. The best advice: remember that your house (or at least, your baby's room) is bugged. If you want to protect your privacy, don't have any sensitive conversations within earshot of the baby monitor. You never know who might be listening.

Are there any monitors on the market that scramble their signal for privacy? Until just recently, the answer was no. But there is good news: several models feature "digital" technology—their signals can't be intercepted, unlike older analog monitors. See later in this chapter for details.

What about higher frequency monitors—are they harder to intercept? Well, yes and no. A 900 MHz or 2.4 GHz monitor may be a bit harder to snoop on with a police scanner, but if your neighbor has the exact same model, guess what? They can probably hear everything in your house (that is, unless you have one of the newer digital models, as discussed earlier).

The best advice: only turn on your monitor when baby is napping. Leaving it on all day means others can listen in to every noise and sound.

Smart Shopper Tip #2
Battery woes

"Boy, we should have bought stock in Duracell when our baby was born! We go through dozens of batteries each month to feed our very hungry baby monitor."

Most baby monitors have the option of running on batteries or regular current (by plugging it into a wall outlet). Our advice: use the wall outlet as often as possible. Batteries don't last long—as little as eight to ten hours with continual use. Another idea: you can buy another AC adapter from a source like Radio Shack for $10 or less—you can leave one AC adapter in your bedroom and have another one available in a different part of the house. (Warning: make sure you get the correct AC adapter for your monitor, in terms of voltage and polarity. Take your existing AC adapter to

monitors

Radio Shack and ask for help to make sure you are getting the correct unit. If not, you can fry your monitor).

Another solution: several new baby monitors (reviewed later in this chapter) feature rechargeable receivers! You'll never buy a set of batteries for these units—you just plug them into an outlet to recharge.

Smart Shopper Tip #3
Cordless compatibility

"We have a cordless phone and a baby monitor. Boy, it took us two weeks to figure out how to use both without having a nervous breakdown."

If we could take a rocket launcher and zap one person in this world, it would have to be the idiot who decided that baby monitors and cordless phones should share the same radio frequency. What were they thinking? Gee, let's take two people who are already dangerously short of sleep and make them real angry!

So, here are our tips to avoid frustration:

First, realize the higher the frequency, the longer the range of the monitor. Basic baby monitors work on the 49 MHz frequency—these will work for a few hundred feet. Step up to a 900 MHz monitor and you can double the distance the monitor will work (some makers claim up to 1000 feet). Finally, there are baby monitors that work on the 2.4 GHz frequency, where you can pick up your baby in Brazil. Ok, not that far, but you get the idea. Of course, "range" estimates are just that—your real-life range will probably be much less than what's touted on the box.

Now here's the rub: cordless phones can often interfere with your baby monitor. Old cordless phones worked on the 49 MHz frequency, but modern models are more likely to be found in the 900 MHz or the 2.4 GHz (or even 5.8 GHz) bands. If you've got a baby monitor at 900 MHz and a cordless phone on the same frequency, expect trouble. Ironically, as more and more devices use the higher frequency, the old 49 MHz for baby monitors now seems to be the most trouble free when it comes to interference.

So, to sum up, here is our advice: first, try to buy a baby monitor on a different frequency than your cordless phone. Second, always keep the receipt. Baby monitors have one of the biggest complaint rates of all products we review. We suspect all the electronic equipment in people's homes today (cell phones, Wi-Fi routers, fax machines, large-screen TVs the size of a Sony Jumbotrons), not to mention all the interference sources near your home (cell phone towers, etc.) must account for some of the problems folks have with baby monitors. Common complaints include static, lack of range, buzzing sounds and worse—and those problems can happen with a baby monitor in any price range.

So, read our monitor recommendations later with a grain of salt. ANY monitor (even those we rate the highest) can still run into static and interference problems, based on what electronics are in your home.

Again, the best advice: always keep the receipt for any baby monitor you buy—you may have to take it back and exchange it for another brand if problems develop.

Smart Shopper Tip #4
The one-way dilemma

"Our baby monitor is nice, but it would be great to be able to buzz my husband so he could bring me something to drink while I'm feeding the baby. Are there any monitors out there that let you communicate two ways?"

Yep, Evenflo and Safety 1st have models that do just that (see reviews later in this chapter). Of course, there is another alternative: you can always go to Radio Shack (radioshack.com) and buy a basic intercom for as little as $40. Most also have a "lock" feature that you can leave on to listen to the baby when he's sleeping. Another advantage to intercoms: you can always deploy the unit to another part of your house after you're done monitoring the baby. Of course, the only disadvantage to intercoms is that they aren't portable—most must be plugged into a wall outlet.

Here are other features to consider when shopping for monitors:

◆ *Out of range indicators.* If you plan to wander from the house and visit your garden, you may want to go for a monitor that warns you when you've strayed too far from its transmitter. Some models have a visual out of range indicator, while others beep at you. Of course, even if your monitor doesn't offer this feature, you'll probably realize when you're out of range—the background noise you hear in your home will disappear from the receiver.

◆ *Low battery indicator.* Considering how quickly monitors can eat batteries, you'd think this would be a standard feature for monitors. Nope—very few current models actually warn you when you're running out of juice. Most units will just die. At this writing, the new Philips Digital Baby Monitor, Evenflo's Whisper Connect line and Safety 1st's Digital 1 Monitoring System have low battery indicators.

◆ *What's the frequency?* As we discussed above, the right or wrong frequency can make a world of difference. Before selecting a monitor, think about the wireless gadgets you have in your home (particularly cordless phones). Then look carefully at packages . . . not all monitors put that info up front.

◆ *Extra receivers.* It is convenient to leave one receiver in your bedroom and then tote around another receiver when wandering in the house.

◆ *Digital technology.* New models use digital technology to prevent eavesdropping by your neighbors.

◆ *Great, but not necessary.* Some monitors have a temperature display, which might help you spot a nursery that's too warm. Others have an intercom feature . . . but we doubt the usefulness of this for most folks. And you'll see several new video monitors in the baby stores today—but the quality of the video is hardly HDTV, which limits its usefulness.

Smart Shopper Tip #5
The cordless phone trick

"A techie friend of mind mentioned that some of the new cordless phones can double as baby monitors. Which phone has that feature?"

Here's a clever way to avoid spending $50 on a baby monitor. Simply use your cordless phone to monitor the baby's room. Uniden (uniden.com), for example sells not one but 55 cordless phone models with a room monitor feature. One example is the DCT756-3 Compact Cordless Telephone (three handsets included for $70). Basically you put one handset in the baby's room, turn on the room monitor feature and you can listen in on a second handset. One caveat, with some models you can't both monitor a room and receive a phone call at the same time. Make sure your model can receive a call when in monitor mode.

The bottom line: if you need a new cordless phone for your house, consider buying one with a room-monitoring feature.

 *More Money Buys You*

Basic baby monitors are just that—an audio monitor and transmitter. No-frills monitors start at $20 or $25. More money buys you a sound/light display (helpful in noisy environments, since the lights indicate if your baby is crying) and rechargeable batteries (you can go through $50 a year in 9-volts with regular monitors). More expensive monitors even have transmitters that also work on batteries (so you could take it outside if you wish) or dual receivers (helpful if you want to leave the main unit inside the house and take the second one outside if you need to work in the garage, etc.). Finally, the top-end monitors either have digital technology or intercom features, where you can use the receiver to talk to your baby as you walk back to the room. The most expensive monitor on the market, Philips' $200 Digital Monitor, adds a room temperature thermometer, adjustable sound sensitivity, music and a night light.

And don't forget baby video monitors. Several models are available ranging in price from $100 to $150. They may not be very useful however, with poor picture clarity and excessive interference being the two most common complaints. Almost all have consistently bad parent reviews.

The Name Game: Reviews of Selected Manufacturers

Here's a look at the best baby monitors.

Major caveat to these reviews: ANY baby monitor, even those that earn our highest ratings, can have problems with static, poor reception or interference. Why? As we discussed earlier, houses today have a myriad of radio equipment (Wi-Fi, anyone?), cell phones and other interference-causing sources. The best advice: keep your receipt and buy a monitor from a store with a good return policy. You may have to try a few different models/brands before finding one that works.

The Ratings

A **EXCELLENT**—*our top pick!*
B **GOOD**— *above average quality, prices, and creativity.*
C **FAIR**—*could stand some improvement.*
D **POOR**—*yuck! Could stand some major improvement.*

Anglecare Web: bebesounds.com. BebeSounds Anglecare monitor ($75 single, $90 double receiver) preys on parents fear of Sudden Infant Death Syndrome—this "movement" monitor sounds an alarm if baby stops breathing (or moving) for 20 seconds. The problem? The American Academy of Pediatrics says monitors like Anglecare or Babysense don't work in preventing SIDS. And if you have a preemie whose breathing needs to be monitored, you need to get a *medical grade* monitor from your pediatrician. **Rating: F**

Babysense *Web:babysafeus.com.* Babysense V Movement Monitor ($130) is similar to the Anglecare—it detects baby's movements to prevent SIDS. We don't recommend monitors like the BabySense; see the Anglecare review above for more details. ***Rating: F***

BeBeSounds. *See Anglecare.*

Evenflo *(800) 233-5921 or (937) 415-3300. Web: evenflo.com.* Evenflo's Whisper Connect monitors are well designed and packed with features: all have rechargeable batteries, out-of-range indicators, low battery warnings and sound/light display. Evenflo makes three versions of these models: a basic monitor with one receiver ($20), a dual receiver model ($30) and a 900mhz "pro" version ($30 at Target). And there's even a "pet detection" version of this monitor (the Sensa) that "alerts consumers to unusual movement near baby." Price: $60. New in the past year is a model (the Tria) with dual receivers that can be used as walkie-talkies for $70. How's the quality? That's a mixed picture: *Consumer Reports* gave a previous version of the Evenflo monitor high marks, but our readers are less generous. Their complaints include static and an out-of-range beeper that goes off randomly among other gripes. And we're disappointed that Evenflo hasn't joined the rest of the market with new digital monitors—again, the company is behind the curve. So we'll drop Evenflo's rating this year and hope the company joins the digital crowd sometime before 2010. ***Rating: B***

First Years *(800) 225-0382 or (508) 588-1220. Web: thefirstyears.com.* First Years has pared their monitor offerings back to three models. A basic, dual-receiver 49 MHz model is $28 and features sounds/lights and a low battery indicator. The "Go Anywhere" monitor ($60) has two receivers—and a transmitter that attaches to wherever baby falls asleep (crib, playpen, etc). Finally, First Years offer a Digital Monitor ($50). One bummer: First Years has eliminated models that have rechargeable batteries, which is too bad. As for quality, First Years is a mixed bag. Design and feature-wise, these models are a good value. Feedback from parents for these monitors is generally lukewarm: not the best, but not the worst. Yet any time we consider recommending this brand, we are reminded of the Great Monitor Massacre of 2002—that year, we recommended one of First Years monitors, only to have the company run into production snafus that resulted in a flood of quality complaints. So, as always with any monitor, keep the receipt in case you need to return it. ***Rating: B+***

Fisher Price *(800) 828-4000 or (716) 687-3000. Web: fisher-price.com.* Fisher Price offers an impressive array of eight models, ranging from $20 to $50 (see the chart on next page for comparison of models/features). Our recommendation: stay with the simple units like the Sounds 'N Lights—this monitor comes in single ($20) and double ($33) receiver versions and features a sound/light display. Nothing fancy, but it does the trick.

Also good: the 900 MHz Long Distance monitor ($35), which the company claims has three times the range of its regular monitors (it also has a more compact design with no bulky antenna).

If your house is buzzing with electronics, the Fisher Price Private Connection monitor might do the trick ($35 single, $53 dual). This 900 MHz monitor has ten switchable channels and rechargeable batteries. This model gets good reviews form parents.

Fisher Price's Ready2Wear Digital Monitor ($60; once known as the anyWear) is the company's first digital offering. The monitor can be worn as a wristwatch, armband or on a belt. This model also has out-of-range and low-battery indicators. The Ready2Wear has a rechargeable battery. Parent feedback on this monitor has been negative, with complaints about static and other quality woes.

We wish Fisher Price would role out digital technology to more models, as Graco has done. But the quality on most of Fisher Price's models is high—we give the simple Sounds 'N Lights version and the Private Connection model (with rechargeable batteries) the top ratings. **Rating (Sound 'N Lights or Private Connection only): A-**

Graco (800) 345-4109, (610) 286-5951. Web: gracobaby.com. Graco has always played second fiddle in the monitor market to Fisher Price and others, but now the company is poised to take the

F-P's MONITORS	*An overview of Fisher Price's monitors*		
	Price	Dual Receiver	Range (in feet)
SOUND & LIGHTS	$20		400 FEET
DUAL SOUND/LIGHTS	$30	✔	400
900MHz LONG DISTANCE	$35		850
PRIVATE CONNECTION	$35		850
DUAL PRIVATE CONNECT.	$53	✔	850
AQUARIUM MONITOR	$40		400
2.4GHz ULTIMATE	$50		1500
READY2WEAR	$80		850

lead. Graco's aggressive push into digital monitors features three models that receive good marks from parents.

The imonitor ($55 single, $90 dual) is pricey, but features digital signal, a 2000-foot range and rechargeable battery. Feedback on this model has been positive—the only negative is the battery life (only about 90 minutes when not in the charging cradle). The digital feature on this model delivers as promised, with privacy and little to no interference. Feedback on this model has been generally positive, although complaints about too-short range and the aforementioned battery hold down the overall scores.

Memo to parents of twins: the imonitor also comes in a "multi-child" version ($130) that can monitor two rooms at once.

Out by the time your read this, Graco has debuted an imonitor Vibe ($60 single, $90 double), which (as the name implies) has a vibration feature similar to a cell phone.

Graco also makes a series of analog monitors: the Ultra Clear, Ultra Clear II, Respond and Décor. All these models work on the 49 MHz frequency, except the Respond, which is 900 MHz. The Respond ($50) records your voice for playback to sooth your child, while the $40 Décor model has a temperature read-out and front plates that swap out to match your nursery décor. The $30 Ultra Clear II has two parent units and rechargeable batteries. FYI: an older version of the Ultra Clear is still out that doesn't have rechargeable batteries.

If that weren't enough, Graco also jumped into the video baby monitor market in the past year with their imonitor Digital Color Video monitor. This $200 model features a rotating camera and color LCD screen. And the verdict from parents? Thumbs down, say our readers, who complained of poor resolution, a useless zoom feature, too short range and more.

Realizing the video monitor was a bust, Graco is trying a do-over: the Graco imonitor 2.0 version will be out by the time you read this and features better screen resolution, battery-saving mode and other software improvements. Will Graco get it right this time? Stay tuned.

Overall, we will raise Graco's rating this time out—quality has improved and the imonitor audio monitor is a winner. ***Rating: B+***

Mobicam Web: getmobi.com. Mobicam was among the first affordable video baby monitors ($120) with an LCD screen to score widespread distribution. While we recommended this monitor in a previous edition, we pulled that recommendation in the last printing of this book after a avalanche of consumer complaints. Numerous quality woes dogged Mobicam, including broken on/off switches, broken power cords, etc. Interference and static were another major issue for other users—some of this is caused by the 2.4 GHz frequency that Mobicam uses . . . the same as many WiFi internet routers.

Mobicam attempted to address these problems with an updated version dubbed Mobicam Ultra in 2006. The updated camera sports a larger display, voice activation and "new technology for clear sound and picture" (it now works on the 900 MHz frequency). And the verdict from consumers? While the complaints have dropped somewhat, there are still numerous gripes about constant static, poor night vision and poor customer service. Given these problems, we still don't recommend Mobicam. **Rating: C**

Philips Web: Consumer.Philips.com. Consumer products giant Philips is known for its innovative products. Yet, Philips is also known for its inept marketing and poor customer service. All of these qualities were in display earlier in the decade when Philips rolled out several award-winning baby monitors that were loaded with nice features (in-room temperature display, out of range indicator, rechargeable batteries). But the monitors bombed, mostly due to lack of distribution. And when consumers had problems, their complaints fell on deaf ears when they called Philips' anemic customer service.

So, it came as no big surprise when Philips withdrew from the market two years ago. But like a zombie movie, Philips is back—this time with an ultra-expensive monitor packed with more tech goodies. The SCD590 monitor guarantees zero interference, thanks to digital technology and a special radio frequency (1.9 GHz) that is reserved for digital devices. Other features include rechargeable batteries, an alarm, night-light and temperature alarm if the baby's nursery falls below a preset level.

And the price? Are you sitting down? $200. Yep, $200 for an audio baby monitor.

Now, we'd be hard pressed to find anyone who needs to spend $200 on a baby monitor. We guess someone who lives in dense urban area and whose apartment is bombarded with all sorts of radio interference, (wireless networks, cell phone towers, etc.) might consider this a good solution if other monitors fail. And the initial feedback on this monitor has been positive. But given Philips track record in the baby market and the monitor's sky-high price tag, we can't recommend it. **Rating: C-**

Safety 1st (800) 962-7233 or (781) 364-3100. Web: safety1st.com. Like Graco, Safety 1st offers both audio and video monitors.

In the audio category, the company starts with a bare bones model with no sound and light display (Crystal Clear, $17). The Safe Glow adds a sound and light display and comes in both single ($20) and dual receiver ($30) versions. The baby's unit has a glow light with a 15 minute auto-shut off.

Safety 1st is giving digital monitors another go this year with the

High-Def Digital Monitor ($70 at Babies R Us). The company's first effort (Digital 1 Monitor) bombed last year, probably thanks to a too-high price (a two-receiver model was $100). The new High-Def is iPod-esque with an all-white design, sound/light display, 1000 foot range, rechargeable batteries and out-of-range indicator.

New in 2008, Safety 1st will debut two lower-price analog monitors: the Glow & Go ($23 single, $33 double) and the simple Sound View ($21). The Glow & Go is similar to the Safe Glo, except it adds a temperature display in the baby's room. Both the Glow & Go and Sound View feature rechargeable batteries.

Safety 1st has several old-style video monitors with black and white screens (the In-Sight for $95 for example). This year, Safety 1st joins the world of color: the High-Def Video Monitor ($250) will feature a 1.8″ crisp LCD screen, digital zoom and pan, battery conservation options, night vision and out-of-range indicator. Since it is

BABY MONITORS

A quick look at various features and brands

Name	Model	Price
Evenflo	Whisper Connect	$20
	Whisper Connect Dual	$30
	Whisper Connect Pro	$30
First Years	Two-Receiver 49 MHz	$28
	Go Anywhere	$60
	Digital Monitor	$50
Graco	iMonitor	$55
	Respond	$50
	Decor	$40
	Ultra Clear II	$30
Philips	SCD 590 Digital	$200
Safety 1st	Crystal Clear	$17
	High-Def Digital	$70
	Glow & Go	$23
Sony	Baby Call NTM-910	$40
Summer	Baby's Quiet Sounds	$30
	Secure Sounds	$50

✔= Yes

Sound/Light: indicates whether the monitor has a sound and lights display.

digital, the High-Def should be free from interference or static.

How's the quality? Safety 1st audio monitors tend to earn middle-of-the-road marks . . . not the best, but not the worst. Their simple, least expensive audio monitors are probably the best bets. Parents are less enthusiastic about Safety 1st's video monitors, although this unhappiness extends to most video baby monitors (complaints about lack of range, interference, and static dog Safety 1st's In-Sight monitor). The digital Hi-Def monitors (both audio and video) weren't out as of this writing, so no parent feedback on these units yet. **Rating: C**

Sony *Web: sonystyle.com.* Sony has been a fringe player in the monitor market, thanks to prices that were always too high. But there is good news: Sony has woken up and lowered its prices. The Sony BabyCall NTM-910 is a 27-channel model with rechargeable batteries

monitors

RECHARGE. BATT.	SOUND/LIGHT	900MHz	DIGITAL
✔	✔		
✔	✔		
✔	✔	✔	
	✔		
	✔	✔	
	✔		✔
✔	✔		✔
✔	✔	✔	
✔			
✔	✔		
✔	✔		✔
✔	✔		✔
✔	✔		
✔	✔	✔	
✔	✔	✔	
✔	✔		✔

900MHZ: A higher frequency that eliminates interference with cordless phones and extended a monitor's range.

DIGITAL: Does the monitor have digital technology.

for $40. Yes, you read that right—the BabyCall has 27 channels (most monitors have at most one or two). The result is less chance for inter-ference and that's what parents seem to love about Sony's BabyCall—it works without static, buzzing, clicking and all the other complaints you read about monitors. No, Sony's monitor isn't packed with whiz-bang features (its analog, not digital), but it does have an out-of-range indicators and an optional sound-activated mode that silences the receiver until sufficient noise activates it. Given the positive reader feed-back for Sony, we'll give them our highest rating. ***Rating: A***

Summer Web: summerinfant.com. Summer has come from out of nowhere to be a big player in the monitor market. Its claim to fame is video monitors, including a $100 black and white CRT version and a $170 handheld color LCD model. Both have night vision tech-nology. While we give credit to Summer for bring down the price on video monitors (they used to run $300), we still found the video and audio quality on these units lacking. And parents seemed to agree—we received many complaints about static, poor quality reception and units that flat out broke after just a few months. New this year, Summer is debuting a multi-room video monitor ($250) and a flat-screen digital video monitor for $200.

Summer also makes audio-only monitors: in the past year, they've debuted three new models, including a $30 rechargeable 900 MHz model (Baby's Quiet Sounds) and a new digital 2.4 GHz model (Secure Sounds, $50). Summers audio monitors didn't impress us—yes, they are cool to look at, but the quality is poor. Given parent feedback, we can't give this brand more than an average rating. ***Rating: C-***

Our Picks: Brand Recommendations

Here are our picks for baby monitors, with one BIG caveat: how well a monitor will work in your house depends on interference sources (like cordless phones, wireless internet routers), the presence of other monitors in the neighborhood, etc. Since we get so many complaints about this category, it is imperative you buy a monitor from a place with a good return policy. Keep the receipts in case you have to make an exchange.

Good. The *Fisher Price Sounds 'N Lights* moni-tors are a good starting point. The basic version is $20; if you need two receivers, go for the $33 model. No, you don't get rechargeable batteries or fancy features like an intercom, but you do get a quality analog baby monitor that does its job well.

Better. Are the neighbors a bit too nosy? If so, you may want to consider a new digital monitor. *Graco's imonitor* ($55 single, $90 dual receivers) is a winner, with digital technology to 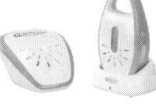 stop interference and eavesdropping. The imonitor has rechargeable batteries, out-of-range indicator and a 2000-foot range.

Best. If your house is buzzing with electronic equipment and you fear Baby Monitor Interference Hell, then it's time to check out our top-rated baby monitor, the *Sony BabyCall NTM-910*. For $40, you get a monitor with 27 selectable channels . . . odds are, 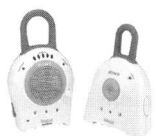 one will work. Add in rechargeable batteries, an out-of-range indicator and very positive parent reviews and we've got a winner.

Video. Sorry, but there are no video baby monitors on the market that we recommend. The two biggest players in this niche (Summer and Mobicam) have too many complaints. We hope that someday a company will make a great video baby cam . . . but that hasn't happened yet.

Twins. Need to monitor two different rooms in your house at once? The *Graco imonitor Multi Child monitor* ($130) is pricey, but you do get digital technology (for better reception and privacy), and rechargeable batteries. With two receivers and two transmitters, you can monitor two rooms at the same time.

Swings

You can't talk to new parents without hearing the heated debate on swings, those battery-operated or wind-up surrogate parents. Some think they're a godsend, soothing a fussy baby when nothing else seems to work. Cynics refer to them as "neglect-o-matics," sinister devices that can become far too addictive for a society that thinks parenting is like a microwave meal—the quicker, the better.

Whatever side you come down on, we do have a few shopping tips. First, ALWAYS try a swing before you buy. Give it a whirl in the store or borrow one from a friend. Why? Some babies love swings. Others hate 'em. Don't spend $120 on a fancy swing only to discover your little one is a swing-hater.

When we last wrote on the topic of swings, you still had a choice between wind-up swings and battery-operated models. While you may still find some wind-up models at garage sales or on eBay, most swings sold in stores are battery-operated. On Craigslist, we've seen wind-up swings for as little as $20. Of course, check with the CPSC (cpsc.gov) to make sure your used swing hasn't been recalled.

If you are in the market for a new swing, remember this rule: swings eat batteries faster than toddlers can scarf M&M's. Look for swings that use fewer batteries—some use as little as two or three (others up to four). See the email from the real world for more on this.

New swings range in price from $40 to $120. The more money you spend the more bells and whistles you get—see below for brand picks.

Remember to observe safety warnings about swings, which are close to the top ten most dangerous products as far as injuries go. You must always stay with your baby, use the safety belt, and stop using the swing once your baby reaches the weight limit (about 25 pounds in most cases). Always remember that a swing is not a baby-sitter.

Our picks: Brand recommendations

Swings today come in three flavors: full-size, compact or travel. As you might guess, the latter category folds up for easy transport. Each work fine—if you have the space, go for a full-size model. If

---

E-MAIL FROM THE REAL WORLD
Voracious swings eats batteries

Batteries are a necessity for modern life and no more so than when you own a baby swing. But as one of our readers discovered, you'd better be buying them in bulk at a warehouse store or you may go bankrupt!

Hilary W. from Chicago wrote to us about her Fisher Price cradle swing. She noted: *"There is no AC power outlet for this model, which really stinks as it eats batteries like you wouldn't believe. Four D batteries are required. If they're the regular ones (alkaline), they're all used up in a week. If they're rechargeable, it's one set a day. Yes, that's right, one set of four per day! It's cheaper for the rechargeable, so we have eight D batteries and four are charging in the charger at any time. Why there is no AC power is beyond me. Perhaps these guys are in cahoots with Energizer and Duracell? If we found a swing not this nice but with AC power that cost $10 more, we'd buy THAT one."*

Good news! Fisher Price now makes swings with A/C adapters. So you can avoid the batteries and just plug them in.

---

not, try a compact or travel version.

Who makes the best swings? We'd give the award to **Graco**. This brand has a mind-numbing 7 models with a total of 35 different versions. Quality-wise, these swings get the best marks from parents. The price difference usually has more to do with the amount of toys, music and other doo-dads that are added on to the mod-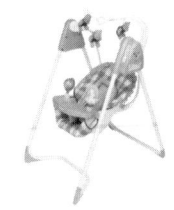els. We like the Silhouette models with three toys, three-position recline, six speeds and classical music or nature sounds. It also has a one-handed flip up tray and 5-point harness for $100.

A good second bet would be the **Rain Forest Open-Top cradle swing by Fisher Price** with its two different motions and inte-grated mobile for $120. (FYI: even though Fisher-Price calls this product a "cradle swing," that is really a misnomer. Baby sits in a seat, rather than lying flat in a cradle—we do not recommend swings that incorporate a bassinet or cradle, as we believe it is not safe to have infant in a prone position in a swing).

How about a swing for Grandma's house? We like the **Open Top Take-Along Swing**, again by Fisher-Price. This cool swing folds up for portability, making it a good bet for $40 to $65.

Safety

All parents want to create a safe environment for their baby. And safety begins at the place where baby spends the most time—your home.

First, let's discuss the biggest safety hazards . . . and what baby products cause the most injury. Next, we'll give you our picks for that ubiquitous safety item, the baby gate. Finally, we'll discuss our tips for making your baby's toys safe.

Getting Started: When Do You Need This Stuff?

Whatever you do, start early. It's never too soon to think about baby proofing your house. Many parents we interviewed admitted they waited until their baby "almost did something" (like playing with extension cords or dipping into the dog's dish) before they panicked and began childproofing.

Remember Murphy's Law of Baby Proofing: your baby will be

instantly attracted to any object that can cause permanent harm. The more harm it will cause, the more attractive it will be to him or her. A word to the wise: start baby proofing as soon as your child begins to roll over.

Safe &Sound: Smart Baby Proofing Tips

The statistics are alarming—each year, 100 children die and millions more are injured in avoidable household accidents. Obviously, no parent wants their child to be injured by a preventable accident, yet many folks are not aware of common dangers. Others think if they load up their house with safety gadgets, their baby will be safe. Yet, there is one basic truth about child safety: *safety devices are no substitute for adult supervision.* While this section is packed with safety must-haves like gates, you still have to watch your baby at all times.

Where do you start? Get down on your hands and knees and look at the house from your baby's point of view. Be sure to go room by room throughout the entire house. On our web site, BabyBargains.com (click on bonus material), we have room-by-room advice on how to baby proof on a shoestring.

Top 10 Baby Products That Should Be Banned

We asked Dr. Ari Brown, an award-winning pediatrician in Austin, TX and co-author of our new book *Baby411* for a list of baby products that should be banned. Some are dangerous, others simply foolish and unnecessary. Here is her take:

1 **BABY WALKERS: NEVER!** There are so many cases of serious injury associated with these death traps on wheels that Canada actually banned the sale, advertising and import of baby walkers. More on why walkers are dangerous later in this chapter.

2 **DON'T GET YOUR KIDS HOOKED ON BABY EINSTEIN.** TV and electronic media of any type, even "educational videos" designed for babies, are bad for developing brains. Babies need active, not passive learning, and getting them used to watching TV is a bad habit to encourage.

3 **THROW AWAY THE PACIFIER AT SIX MONTHS.** As we discussed in the feeding chapter, pacifiers are now recommended after breastfeeding is well established (about one month). But . . . remem-

ber to STOP the pacifier at six months! Your baby needs to learn to fall asleep and/or comfort herself without a crutch.

4 **AVOID EAR THERMOMETERS.** They are notoriously unreliable, and since fever in infants (over 100.3 degrees) could be serious, an inaccurate reading might give parents a false sense of security. Rectal thermometers are the most accurate.

What are the most dangerous baby products?

The Consumer Product Safety Commission releases yearly figures for injuries and deaths for children under five years old related to juvenile products. The latest figures from the CPSC are for 2005 and show a slight decline in the number of injuries. The following chart details the statistics:

PRODUCT CATEGORY	INJURIES	DEATHS
WALKERS/JUMPERS	3,000	2
STROLLERS/CARRIAGES	10,400	3
INFANT CARRIES/CAR SEATS*	14,000	16
CRIBS, BASSINETS, CRADLES**	10,700	81
HIGH CHAIRS	7,300	4
BABY GATES/BARRIERS	1,800	1
PLAYPENS	1,300	26
CHANGING TABLES	2,900	1
PORTABLE BABY SWINGS	1,800	4
BATH SEATS	***	26
OTHER	5,200	15
TOTAL	**59,800**	**182**

Key:
Deaths: This figure is an annual average from 2001 to 2003, the latest figures available.
*excludes motor vehicle incidents
** including crib mattresses and pads
***in the CPSC's latest report bath seat injuries were not tabulated due to a low sample size

Our Comments: The large number of deaths associated with cribs almost exclusively occurs in cribs that are so old they don't meet current safety standards. We encourage parents to avoid hand-me-down, antique and second hand cribs.

5 **DON'T FALL FOR THE BABY TOOTHPASTE HYPE.** The best way to clean your baby's teeth is to wipe them with a wet washcloth, twice daily. The sweet taste of baby toothpaste encourages your baby to suck on the toothbrush once in his mouth and you can't maneuver it around well.

6 **BEWARE OF NATURAL BABY SKIN-CARE PRODUCTS.** Over 25% of "natural" infant products contain common allergens including peanuts, which can sensitize infants to permanent food allergy.

7 **YOU DON'T NEED TEETHING TABLETS** from the health food store. Some of these contain *caffeine* as an ingredient! Save the espresso for kindergarten!

8 **FORGET SIPPY CUPS.** They promote tooth decay because the flow of liquid heads straight to the back of the top front teeth. If your baby hasn't quite mastered drinking from a cup yet, offer her a straw instead.

9 **HANGING MOBILES ARE ONLY FOR NEWBORNS.** Remove all toys and decorations hanging over your baby's crib by the

---

Kids in Danger

Nancy Cowles, executive director for Kids in Danger (kidsindanger.org) a non-profit advocacy group, offers some food for thought to parents about juvenile products and safety:

"Except for cribs, bunk beds, pacifiers, and small parts in toys meant for young children, there are NO requirements in the US that manufacturers meet standards or test their products for safety. While most parents believe that if it is on the store shelf and is a recognized brand name someone has made sure it is safe for their baby, that is not the case. Voluntary standards (like the JPMA) exist for many products, but companies are in no way required to test their products to these standards. Even the mandatory crib standard does not cover all known hazards.

"Don't forget to check the products your child uses outside your home, which you have carefully baby proofed. Don't let Grandma pull the old crib down from the attic, use a recalled portable crib at childcare, or any other hazards."

Kids In Danger has a brochure (Is My Child Safe?), which gives parents three easy steps to check their products for recalls and stay up to date on product safety. It is available on their website, KidsInDanger.org.

time he or she is five months old. They become hazardous when babies start to pull themselves up and grab for them.

10 ENJOY THOSE BEAUTIFUL QUILTS AS WALL HANGINGS, not in the crib.

Safety Gates: Our Picks

When you look at the options available in baby gates, you can get easily overwhelmed. KidCo, Safety 1st, Evenflo, SuperGate and First Years are just a few of the brands available. And you'll see metal, plastic, fabric padded, tall, short, wide, permanent mount, pressure mount and more. So, what to get? The temptation of many parents (including us) is to buy what's cheapest. But after buying and using at least six gates, here are our picks and tips:

Your best option from the start is to stick with the metal or wooden gates. Plastic never seems to hold up that well and looks dirty in short order from all those sticky fingerprints. Our favorite brand is **KidCo**. They make the Gateway, Safeway and Elongate models plus a variety of extensions and mounting kits. We used the per-

manent mount gate (the Safeway $65), which expands from 24.5 inches to 43.5 inches. We thought it was fairly easy to install and simple to use. The Gateway ($65; pictured) is the pressure-mounted version. The Elongate ($85) fits spaces from 48 inches to 60 inches wide. All three gates can be expanded further with inexpensive extensions.

Another interesting option for a pressure gate is the **First Years' Hands Free Gate** ($50). This metal gate has a foot pedal that adults can step on to open. If you have your hands full, this is a great way to get in and out. Soft gates have recently entered the market including the **Soft n´ Wide** from Evenflo ($35 to $45). It is a stationary gate (does not swing open) with nylon covered padding at the top and bottom to protect baby from the metal frame. This is useful if you don't want to move the gate often and don't need to open the gate for access. Otherwise swinging gates are a better bet.

Finally, check out the plastic **Supergate** from North States

Industries ($40), a gate our readers have recommended. This gate expands up to 62 inches and slides together and swings out of the way so you can easily clear a path. It is a permanent-mounted gate so it can be used at the top of stairs.

Pictured at right is the Supergate Superyard ($65). You may also notice a new gate, the ***Kiddy Guard***, which opens and retracts like a window blind. At $110, however, it's a bit on the expensive side.

Most of these gates can be found at Babies R Us.

Money-Saving Secrets

1 **OUTLET COVERS ARE EXPENSIVE.** Only use them where you will be plugging in items. For unused outlets, consider a cheaper option—moving heavy furniture in front to block access. What type of outlet cover should you buy? We like the Safe-Plate ($3 from babyguard.com), which requires you to slide a small plate over to access the receptacle. In contrast, those that require you to rotate a dial to access the outlet are more difficult to use.

E-MAIL FROM THE REAL WORLD
A solution for those coffee tables

Reader Jennifer K. came up with this affordable solution to expensive coffee table bumpers.

"When our son started to walk we were very worried about his head crashing into the glass top tables in our living room. We checked into the safety catalogs and found those fitted bumpers for about $80 just for the coffee table. Well, I guess being the selfish person that I am, and already removing everything else dangerous from my living room. I just didn't want to give up my tables! Where do we put the lamps, and where do I fold the laundry?

"My mother-in-law had the perfect solution. FOAM PIPE WRAPPING!!! We bought it at a home improvement store for $3. You can cut it to fit any table. It is already sliced down the middle and has adhesive, (the gummy kind that rolls right off the glass if you need to replace it). The only disadvantage that we've come across is that our son has learned to pull it off. But at $3 a bag we keep extras in the closet for 'touch-ups'.

"Now the novelty has worn off, so I have NOT had to replace it as often. And I'm happy to report that we've had plenty of collisions, but not one stitch!"

---

2 **MANY DISCOUNTERS LIKE TARGET, K-MART, AND WAL-MART SELL A LIMITED SELECTION OF BABY SAFETY ITEMS.** We found products like gates, outlet covers, and more at prices about 5% to 20% less than full-priced hardware stores. And don't forget to check home improvement stores like Home Depot. They also carry safety items.

3 **HOME IMPROVEMENT STORES SELL CHILD SAFETY PRODUCTS.** Yep, Home Depot, Lowe's and other hardware and home improvement stores carry cabinet locks, safety gates and more. Plus you'll find items like blank outlet plates for outlets you never use. We saw a KidKusion fireplace cushion at Lowe's for $39.

4 **SOME OF THE MOST EFFECTIVE BABY PROOFING IS FREE.** For example, moving items to top shelves, putting dangerous chemicals away, and other common sense ideas don't cost any money and are just as effective as high-tech gadgets.

5 **CRAIGSLIST.ORG.** Many parents have discovered this online classified site as a great source for used baby gear, including safety items. One reader scored a plethora of baby bargains there, including a Safety 1st Swing N Lock Gate (in the box, never installed) for just $10. Yep, used to sell for $30 in stores (it is now discontinued).

Bonus Material Online

For more safety tips and advice, go to our web site, BabyBargains.com (click on Bonus Material). There you'll find practical tips on baby proofing on a budget, as well as mail order sources for safety gadgets.

 ## Safe & Sound for Toys

Walk through any toy store and the sheer variety of toys will boggle your mind. Buying toys for an infant requires more careful planning than for older children. Here are nine tips to keep your baby safe and sound:

1 **CHECK FOR AGE APPROPRIATE LABELS.** Yes, that sounds like a no-brainer, but you'd be surprised how many times grandparents try to give a six-month old infant a toy that is clearly marked "ages 3 and up." One common misunderstanding about these labels: the age range has NOTHING to do with developmental ability of your baby; instead, the warning is intended to keep small parts out of the hands of infants because those parts can be a choking hazard. Be careful of toys bought at second-hand stores or hand-me-downs—a lack of packaging may mean you have to guess on the age-appropriate level. Another trouble area: "Kids Meal" toys from fast-food restaurants. Many are clearly labeled for kids three and up (although some fast food places do offer toys safe for the under-three crowd). One smart tip: use a toilet paper tube to see if small parts pose a choking hazard . . . anything that can fit through the tube can be swallowed by baby.

2 MAKE SURE STUFFED ANIMALS HAVE SEWN EYES. A popular gift from friends and relatives, stuffed animals can be a hazard if you don't take a few precautions. Buttons or other materials for eyes that could be easily removed present a choking hazard—make sure you give a stuffed animal the once over before you give it to baby. Keep all plush animals out of the crib except maybe one special toy (and that only after baby is able to roll over). While it is acceptable to have one or two stuffed animals in the crib with babies over one year of age, resist the urge to pile on. Once baby starts pulling himself up to a standing position, such stuffed animals can be used as steps to escape a crib.

3 BEWARE OF RIBBONS. Another common decoration on stuffed animals, remove these before giving the toy to your baby.

Oppenheim Toy Portfolio

While we do have a few basic baby toy recommendations on our web page (BabyBargains. com; click on bonus material), our specialty is really baby gear, not toys. As a result, we recommend this source for reviews on toys, books, video and software: The Oppenheim Toy Portfolio (web: www.toyportfolio.com). Readers concur; here's what one said about this great book:

"Once I bought this book, I understood better what to look for in a toy and what was skill/age appropriate—not what the manufacturers listed on the boxes! We have made many fewer return-the-toy trips and I am a much happier person. The book also includes games to play with your infants and no toy was required!"

4 **MAKE SURE TOYS HAVE NO STRINGS LONGER THAN 12 INCHES**–another easily avoided strangulation hazard.

5 **WOODEN TOYS SHOULD HAVE NON-TOXIC FINISHES.** If in doubt, don't give such toys to your baby. The toy's packaging should specify the type of finish.

6 **BATTERY COMPARTMENTS SHOULD HAVE A SCREW CLOSURE.** Tape players (and other battery-operated toys) should not give your baby easy access to batteries–a compartment that requires a screwdriver to open is a wise precaution.

7 **BE CAREFUL OF CRIB TOYS.** Some of these toys are designed to attach to the top or sides of the crib. The best advice: remove them after the baby is finished playing with them. Don't leave the baby to play with crib toys unsupervised, especially once she begins to pull or sit up.

8 **DO NOT USE WALKERS.** And if you get one as a gift, take it back to the store and exchange it for something that isn't a death trap. Exactly what are these invitations to disaster? A walker suspends your baby above the floor, enabling him or her to "walk" by rolling around on wheels.
The only problem: babies tend to "walk" right into walls, down staircases, and into other brain damage-causing obstacles. It's a scandal that walkers haven't been banned by the Consumer Products Safety Commission. How many injuries do these things cause? Are you sitting down? Over 3000 a year.

To be fair, we should note the baby gear industry has tried to make walkers safer–with a large amount of prodding from the CPSC. While the government decided not to ban walkers outright in 1993, the CPSC did work to strengthen the industry's voluntary standards over the past few years. The result: redesigned walkers with safety features that stop them from falling down stairs. Some have special wheels or "gripping strips" that prevent such falls.

The result of these new safety features: walker injuries have dropped dramatically since 1995. But we still think 3000 injured babies is 3000 too many. Our advice: don't put your baby into a walker, no matter how many new "safety" features are built-in.

By the way, in 2004, Canada announced an outright ban on baby walkers due to continuing concern over serious injuries from the products. The ban on these items includes second-hand walkers as well.

9 **STATIONARY PLAY CENTERS.** What about walker alternatives? So-called "stationary" play centers have made a big splash on the baby market in recent years, led by Evenflo's Exersaucer. Most stationary play centers run $40 to $150 and are basically the same— you stick the baby into a seat in the middle and there are a bunch of toys for them to play with. (The more money you spend, the better the toys, bells and whistles). While the unit rocks and swivels, it doesn't roll across the floor. And that's a boon to parents who need a few minutes to make dinner or take a shower.

So, should you get one? Well, our belief is these play centers are optional—and if overused, can be a problem. We're troubled by studies that have shown infants who use walkers and stationary play centers suffer from developmental delays when compared to babies who don't use them. According to a study in the October 1999 Journal of Developmental and Behavioral Pediatrics, researchers at Case Western Reserve University found "babies who were placed in walkers were slower to sit up, crawl and walk than those raised without walkers. The mental development of the children also appeared to be slowed," according to an Associated Press article on the study.

Researchers studied 109 infants, including 53 who did not use walkers. On average, babies who used the walkers were delayed at least a month in sitting up, crawling and walking. Non-walker using kids also scored 10% higher on mental development tests than walker users.

The researchers concluded that "restriction in a walker may exert its greatest influence on mental development during the six- to nine-month age period, a time regarded as transformational in a child's intellectual development," according to the AP article. Noticeably, walker babies were able to catch up to non-walker children after they started crawling—and hence used the walker less often.

Why do walkers and stationary play centers have such a dramatic effect on a child's development? Researchers speculate that "the opaque trays placed on the newer walkers as a safety device prevent the children from seeing their legs, blocking the feedback they get from moving a limb and seeing the leg actually move," the article stated.

While this study focused on walkers, we interpreted the results to also apply to stationary play centers. Why? Because both play centers and walkers use those "opaque trays" that keep baby from seeing their feet. Another study from 2002 conducted at the University of Dublin School of Physiotherapy in Ireland concurred with the results of the Case Western study. They concluded "this study provides additional evidence that baby walkers are associated with delay in achieving normal locomotor milestones . . .The use of baby walkers should be discouraged."

Bottom line: babies should spend a LIMITED time in a stationary play center. If you are going to use one of these items, your child should spend no more than 15 minutes a day in them (long enough for a quick shower). As for a brand of stationary play center, we recommend the **Evenflo ExerSaucer**, based on parent feedback.

And traditional walkers should never, ever be used in our opinion.

10 JUMPERS. These contraptions attach to a doorway and let baby bounce up and down, thanks to a large spring that acts like a bungee cord. Yet, we've been troubled by the large number of recalls and reported injuries attributed to jumpers. Unfortunately, the CPSC doesn't separately break out injuries for jumpers (it lumps them in the category with walkers—these products caused a total of 3000 injuries, according to a 2007 CPSC report). But given the large number of recalls, we would suggest parents avoid this item.

Wastes of Money

Waste of Money #1
Outlet plugs

"My friend thought she'd save a bundle by just using outlet plugs instead of fancy plate covers. Unfortunately, her toddler figured out how to remove the plugs and she had to buy the plates anyway."

It doesn't take an astrophysicist to figure out how to remove those cheap plastic outlet plugs. While the sliding outlet covers are pricier, they may be well worth the investment. Another problem: outlet plugs can be a choking hazard. If baby removes one (or an adult removes one and forgets to put it back), it can end up in baby's mouth. If you want to try plugs anyway, do a test—check your outlets to see how tight the plugs will fit. In newer homes, plugs may have a tighter fit than older homes. While we generally think the outlet cover plates are superior to plugs, we do recommend the plugs for road trips to Grandma's house or a hotel room (because they are easier to carry and install).

Waste of Money #2
Plastic corner guards

"The other day I was looking through a safety catalog and saw some corner guards. It occurred to me that they don't look a whole lot softer than the actual corner they cover. Are they worth buying?"

Tummy Time Toys: A Waste of Money?

"Friends keep telling me that Tummy Time for my baby is a must. I've heard that my daughter might suffer developmental delays if I don't include tummy time in her day. What is it and why is it so important?"

Do babies spend too much time on their backs? That's one concern parents and child development specialists have brought up in recent years. Before the advent of the Back to Sleep campaign, the SIDS awareness program that encourages parents to put their babies to bed on their backs, babies were more likely to be placed in a variety of positions. Nowadays, however, babies spend an inordinate amount of time on their backs. And some folks wonder if that is causing a delay in creeping, crawling and walking.

The solution is a simple one: just put your baby on her tummy for a few minutes a day when she is awake. Yes, there is research that shows that extra tummy time can help your child reach developmental milestones sooner. But keep in mind that normal babies who don't participate in increased periods of tummy time typically still meet developmental milestones within the normal time period. So there is no need to panic if your baby isn't getting "15 minutes of tummy time daily."

In fact, many parents have noted that their babies hate being on their stomachs. For those babies who object to being on their tummies, you simply don't have to force them. Of course, baby products manufacturers have jumped on this new craze to come up with more stuff you can buy to make Tummy Time more fun. For example, Camp Kazoo, the makers of Boppy pillows (www.boppy.com) make a Boppy Tummy Play pillow for $20. This smaller version of the famous Boppy has a few toys attached to entertain your baby.

Don't think you need to buy extra stuff to make tummy time successful in your house, however. Save your money and just get down on the floor with your baby face to face. After all, you're the thing in her life she finds most fun, so get down there and spend some quality tummy time with her.

You've hit (so to speak) on a problem we've noticed as well. Our advice: the plastic corner guards are a waste of money. They aren't very soft—and babies can easily pop them off a table. So what's the solution? If you're worried about Junior hitting the corner of your coffee table, you can either store it for a while or look into getting a soft bumper pad (up to $80 in catalogs—see our reader email earlier in the chapter for a more affordable alternative). Similar bumpers are available for your fireplace as well. On the other hand, you may decide that blocking off certain rooms is a more practical option.

Waste of Money #3
Appliance safety latches

"I can't imagine that my daughter is going to be able to open the refrigerator any time soon. So why do they sell those appliance latches in safety catalogs, anyway?"

There must be some super-strong kids out there who have enough torque to open a full-sized refrigerator. Most infants under a year of age don't seem to have the strength to open most appliances. However, toddlers will eventually acquire that skill. One point to remember: many appliances like stoves and dishwashers have locking mechanisms built in—so use them! And, keep all chairs and stools away from the laundry room to prevent your baby from opening the washing machine and dryer.

A Baby First Aid Kit

Wonder what should be in your baby first aid kit? As a childless couple, we were probably lucky to find a couple of bandages and an ancient bottle of Bactine in our medicine cabinet. Now that you're Dr. Mom (or Nurse Dad) it's time to take a crash course on baby medicine etiquette. By the way, do not administer any of the drugs mentioned here without first checking with your doctor. He/she will know the safest dosage for your infant. Here's a run-down of essentials.

◆ *Acetaminophen* (one brand name of this drug is Tylenol). For pain relief and fever reduction. If you suspect your child may have an allergy to flavorings, you can buy a version without all the additives. You may also want to keep acetaminophen infant suppositories in your medicine cabinet in case your infant persists in vomiting up his drops. Or refuses to take them at all. Do NOT keep baby aspirin in your house. Aspirin has been linked to Reyes Syndrome in children and is no longer recommended by pediatricians. Warn grandparents about this issue, as some may still think baby aspirin is OK.

◆ *Children's Ibuprofen* (one brand name of this drug is Motrin). This is another great option for pain relief and fever reduction. Typically, Ibuprofen will be a bit longer lasting than Acetaminophen.

safety

◆ *Children's Benadryl.* To relieve minor allergic reactions.

◆ *Antibiotic ointment* to help avoid bacterial infection from cuts.

◆ *Baking soda* is great for rashes.

◆ *Calamine lotion* to relieve itching. Some versions include Benedryl so check the label carefully.

◆ *A cough and cold remedy recommended by your pediatrician.* DO NOT use adult cough syrups. Incorrect doses can be dangerous—always ask a doc first.

◆ *A good lotion.* Unscented and non-medicated brands are best.

◆ *Measuring spoon or cup for liquid medicine.* For small infants, you may want a medicine dropper or syringe. Droppers often come in the box with some medications.

◆ *Petroleum jelly*, which is used to lubricate rectal thermometers.

◆ *Plastic bandages like Band-Aids.*

◆ *Saline nose drops* for stuffy noses.

◆ *Tweezers.* For all kinds of fun uses.

◆ *A card with the number for poison control.* You may want to call your local poison control center and ask them what poison remedies they recommend having on hand. Previously, Syrup of Ipecac was recommnded to induce vomiting. However, the American Academy of Pediatrics now recommends NOT keeping ipecac in your house. Why? The AAP says ipecac may cause more harm than good and is worried about misuse. Bottom line: call poison control if your child ingests a dangerous or unknown substance. DON'T try to remedy the situation by yourself. Here is the national number for poison control: 1-800-222-1222. You can also get your local poison control number from the web site of the American Association of Poison Control Centers (aapcc.org).

◆ *Thermometer.* Remember the old mercury thermometers of our childhood? They were so simple and straightforward. Today, you'll find digital thermometers, ear thermometers, strip thermometers, pacifier thermometers and more. Some use infrared technology and even solar-powered alternatives to mercury and simple batteries. But in the end, the most important job of a thermometer is to take an accurate temperature. And it would be nice if it could do it fast.

According to pediatricians we've interviewed, the most accurate thermometer is a digital rectal thermometer ($5 to $10). We know . . . your first reaction is "Ewww!" But accuracy is important, perhaps life saving, in infants under three months of age. If you're concerned about doing it correctly, ask your doctor to show you at one of your child's exams. It doesn't hurt, so you can practice once with the doctor just to make sure.

After one year of age, you don't necessarily need to use a rectal thermometer to take your child's temperature. At that point, you can use a digital oral thermometer ($5 to $10) under your baby's arm pit. No need for ear thermometers (too big for tiny ear canals), pacifier thermometers, temporal artery scanners or skin strips. In this case, simple really is best.

Top 11 Safety Must Haves

To sum up, here's our list of top safety items to have for your home (in no particular order).

◆ *Fire extinguishers*, rated "ABC," which means they are appropriate for any type of fire.

◆ *Outlet covers.*

◆ *Baby monitor*—unless your house or apartment is very small, and you don't think it will be useful.

◆ *Smoke alarms.* The best smoke alarms have two systems for detecting fires—a photoelectric sensor for early detection of smoldering fires and a dual chamber ionization sensor for early detection of flaming fires. An example of this is the First Alert "Dual Sensor" ($25 to $35). We'd recommend one smoke alarm for every bedroom, plus main hallways, basement and living rooms. And don't forget to replace the batteries twice a year. Both smoke alarms and carbon monoxide detectors can be found in warehouse clubs like Sam's and Costco at low prices.

◆ *Carbon monoxide detectors.* These special detectors sniff out dangerous carbon monoxide (CO) gas, which can result from a malfunctioning furnace. Put one CO detector in your baby's room and another in the main hallway of your home.

◆ *Cabinet and drawer locks.* For cabinets and drawers containing harmful cleaning supplies or utensils like knives, these are an essential investment. For fun, designate at least one unsecured cabinet or drawer as "safe" and stock it with pots and pans for baby.

◆ *Spout cover for tub.*

◆ *Bath thermometer or anti-scald device.*

◆ *Toilet locks*—so your baby doesn't visit the Tidy Bowl Man. One of the best we've seen in years is KidCo's toilet lock ($16), an award-winning gizmo that does the trick. Check their web site at kidco-inc.com for a store that carries it.

◆ *Baby gates.* See the section earlier for recommendations.

◆ *Furniture wall straps.* More than 100 deaths caused by tipping TVs and other furniture have been reported since 2000. We recommend you anchor all your large furniture to the wall, especially shelves and dressers in baby's room. Once your child becomes a climber, she'll climb anything so be prepared.

Playpens

The portable playpen has been so popular in recent years that many parents consider it a necessity. Compared to rickety playpens of old, today's playpens fold compactly for portability and offer such handy features as bassinets, canopies, wheels and more. Some shopping tips:

◆ *Don't buy a second-hand playpen or use a hand-me-down.* Many playpen models have been the subjects of recalls in recent years. Why? Those same features that make them convenient (the collapsibility to make the playpen "portable") worked too well in the past—some playpens collapsed with babies inside. Others had protruding rivets that caught some babies who wore pacifiers on a string (a BIG no-no, never have your baby wear a pacifier on a string). A slew of injuries and deaths have prompted the recall of ten million playpens over the years. Yes, you can search government recall lists (cpsc.gov) to see if that hand-me-down is recalled, but we'd skip the hassle and just buy new.

◆ *Go for the bassinet feature.* Some playpens feature bassinet inserts which can be used for babies under three months of age (always check the weight guidelines). This is a handy feature that we recommend. Other worthwhile features: wheels for mobility, side-rail storage compartments and a canopy (if you plan to take the playpen outside or to the beach). If you want a playpen with canopy, look for those models that have "aluminized fabric" canopies—they reflect the sun's heat and UV rays to keep baby cooler.

◆ *Check the weight limits.* Playpens have two weight limits: one for the bassinet and one for the entire playpen (without the bassinet). Graco and most other playpen versions have an overall weight limit of 30 lbs. and height limit of 35" The exception is the Arms Reach Co-Sleeper which tops out at 50 lbs. However, there is more variation in the weight limits for the bassinet attachments. Here are the weight limits for the *bassinet attachments* on various playpens:

Arms Reach Co-Sleeper	30 lbs.
Graco Pack N Play	15 lbs.
Chicco Lullaby	15 lbs.
Compass Aluminum	18 lbs.
Combi Play Yard	15 lbs.

Our Picks: Brand Recommendations

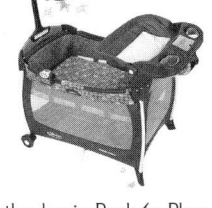

What are the best brands for playpens? Once again, we give it to **Graco**—their **Pack 'n Play** playpens are the best designed and least-recalled. Last we looked, they had seven models that ranged from $80 to $200. Most fall in the $100 range, however.

So, which model should you get? We like the basic Pack 'n Play with bassinet attachment, which runs $80 to $230 depending on the pattern. Pictured is a $140 deluxe version of the Pack 'n Play with bassinet, changer station, canopy, vibrating mattress, and more.

A brief word on the Graco playpen with bassinet feature: we recommend this as a good alternative to a stand-alone bassinet or cradle in Chapter 2. However, some readers note that Graco advises the product is "intended for naps and play" and question whether a newborn should sleep full time in the bassinet. We understand the confusion, but here's our advice: when it comes to newborns, there isn't much of a distinction between "naps" and nighttime sleep—day or night, most newborns are sleeping only four hours at a stretch (they need to feed at roughly that interval). Hence, Graco's advice to only use the Pack N Play for "naps or play" applies more to older babies—the product shouldn't take the place of a full-size crib (but is fine for occasional use at Grandma's house or a hotel room). The bottom line: we believe the bassinet feature is fine for full-time use for newborns who are under the weight limits (typically 15 pounds).

What about the other playpen brands? Yes, you can find playpens by Baby Trend, Evenflo, Kolcraft and Fisher Price, but we don't think their quality or features measure up to Graco's offerings.

So, what's new for playpens? In a word, extra padding. Graco has upgraded their Pack 'n Plays with quilted pads and bumpers. **Chicco** also jumped on this trend, debuting their first playpen with extra cushy padding (which will be machine-washable). The Chicco Lullaby is a winner—it sells for $150 and includes toy gym, electronic music and vibrations with remote and bassinet.

How about a playpen that's 20% lighter than others? Compass' new **Aluminum Play Yard** ($80-$100) weights only 17 lbs. so you can sherpa it more easily. Features are basic but it does have a bassinet. **Combi** has also added play yards to their product line, the Sport or the DX ($120 to $170). They offer a rocking, detachable bassinet, a diaper changing station, storage pockets and music, lights and vibration.

For something much lighter for Grandma's house, Graco's **Travel Lite Crib** ($80) is a good bet. It is 20% smaller than a standard Pack N Play, but still has a bassinet attachment and canopy, wheels and push button fold.

What if you need a no-frills playpen? Just the basics, no toys, bassinet, canopy and so on? A good basic choice is **J. Mason's Safe Surround Sport**, which is just $85 and has a non-folding rail that safety advocates cite as a great feature. The screw-in steel posts are easy to set up. Don't expect to easily move this from room to room, however, as it lacks wheels.

FYI: Be sure to check out some of our recommendations for playpen sheets in Chapter 3. While most parents love their playpen, the cheap-o sheets that come with most are a bane (they slip off the mattress too easily, etc). We discuss alternatives like Mr. Bobbles Blankets and Fleece Baby in Chapter 3 that solve this problem.

The Bottom Line:
A Wrap-Up of Our Best Buy Picks

In the nursery, we highly recommend the Diaper Champ as the best diaper pail . . . but Graco's new Touch-Free diaper pail is worth a look. Skip wipe warmers, which have safety concerns.

An activity/bouncer seat with a toy bar is a good idea, with prices ranging from $20 to $60—we like the Fisher Price bouncers best. An affordable alternative: adding a $10 toy bar to an infant seat.

As for bathtubs, we thought the EuroBath ($30) by Primo was the best bet, although it is big. A good option for Grandma's house might be the simple Comfy Duck Bath Center by Safety 1st ($15). We also recommend the Clearwater Infant Tub ($40).

For baby monitors, a simple Fisher Price Sound 'N Lights for $20 will work for most folks. If you want rechargeable batteries (highly recommended), consider the Graco imonitor for $50 or the Sony BabyCall NTM-910 for $40.

For swings and playpens, Graco is the brand of choice. Graco's swings set the standard for quality and features, although Fisher-Price's cradle swings are a good second bet. For playpens, the Graco Pack 'n Play with bassinet feature is our pick.

CHAPTER 8

Car Seats: Picking the right child safety seat

Inside this chapter

W hat's the best car seat for your baby? What is the difference between an infant and a convertible seat? We'll discuss these issues and more in this chapter. You'll find complete reviews and ratings of the major car seat brands as well as informative charts that compare the best choices.

Here's a sobering figure: last year, motor vehicle crashes killed 2,157 children under age 14 and injured another 246,000. And 572 infants under age one were killed in traffic accidents from 2001 to 2005.

While the majority of those injuries and deaths occurred to children who were not in safety seats, the toll from vehicle accidents in this country is still a statistic that can keep you awake all night. Just to make you feel a tiny bit better, the lives of 367 children under age five were saved last year because they were in a child restraint.

Every state in the U.S. (and every province in Canada) requires infants and children to ride in child safety seats, so this is one of the few products that every parent must buy. In fact you may find yourself buying multiple car seats as your baby grows older—and for secondary cars, grandma's car, a caregiver's vehicle and more.

So, which seat is the safest? Easiest to use? One thing you'll learn in this chapter is that there is not one "safest" or "best" seat. Yes, we will review and rate the various car seat brands and examine their recall/safety history. BUT, remember the best seat for your child is the one that correctly fits your child's weight and size—and can be correctly installed in your vehicle.

And that's the rub: roadside safety checks reveal 80% to 90% of child safety seats are NOT installed or used properly. Although the exact figure isn't known, a large number of child fatalities and injuries from crashes are caused by improper use or installation of seats. Realizing that many of today's child safety seats are a failure due to complex installation and other hurdles, the federal government has rolled out a safety standard (called LATCH) for child seats and vows to fix loopholes in current crash testing. We'll discuss these changes in-depth in this chapter.

Getting Started: When Do You Need This Stuff?

You can't leave the hospital without a car seat. By law, all states require children to be restrained in a child safety seat. You'll want to get this item early (in your sixth to eighth month of pregnancy) so you can install it in your car before baby arrives.

Sources to Find Car Seats

1 DISCOUNTERS. Car seats have become a loss leader for many discount stores. Chains like Target and Wal-Mart sell these items at small mark-ups in hopes you'll spend money elsewhere in the store. The only caveat: most discounters only carry a limited selection of seats, typically of the no-frills brands.

2 BABY SPECIALTY STORES. Independent juvenile retailers have all but abandoned car seats to the chains. With the exception of premium brands like Britax, you'll only see a few scattered offerings here.

3 THE SUPERSTORES. Chains like Babies R Us, Toys R Us and Burlington Coat Factory's Baby Depot (reviewed in depth in Chapter 2) tend to carry a wider selection of car seats than discounters. And, sometimes, that includes the better brands. Prices can be a few dollars higher than the discounters, but sales often bring better deals.

4 MAIL ORDER/THE WEB. Yes, you can buy a car seat through the mail or online. More on the 'net next. Prices are usually discounted, but watch out for shipping—the cost of shipping bulky items like car seats can outweigh the discount in some cases. Use an online coupon (see the previous chapter for coupon sites) to save and look for free shipping specials.

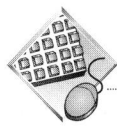

Parents in Cyberspace: What's on the Web?

The web is teeming with both information and bargains on car seats. Here's the best of what's out there.

◆ **NHTSA.** The National Highway Traffic Safety Administration site (nhtsa.dot.gov) is a treasure trove of car seat info—you can read about recalls, the latest news on changing standards and installation tips. The NHTSA's brochure "Buying a Safer Car For Child Passengers" is a good read (online or call 888-DASH2DOT). You can also contact the government's Auto Safety Hotline at 800-424-9393 to ask car seat related questions. Even better: NHTSA now ranks car seats on their *ease of use* (assembly, instructions, securing a child, etc). The most recent report covers 67 seats, from infant to booster. See the report here: nhtsa.gov/cps/cssrating or by calling 888-327-4236. Note: these ratings do NOT cover how well a seat does in crash tests or compatibility with different vehicles.

◆ *The American Academy of Pediatrics* (aap.org, go to "Parenting Corner") is an excellent resource for buying tips.

◆ *The National Safe Kids Campaign* (safekids.org) has a helpful interactive "safety seat guide" that helps you determine which seat is right for the age and weight of the child.

◆ *Safety Belt Safe USA* (carseat.org) has a good site with tips on picking the best seat for your child, as well as the latest recalls and info on child safety seats.

◆ *CarSeatData.org* has an "interactive compatibility database" that lets you search for which seats work in which vehicles. Very cool.

◆ *Our web site* has a message board dedicated to car seats. Plus: we have a brochure called "Buying a Better Car Seat Restraint" produced by a Canadian auto insurance company. This publication (downloadable as a PDF) has excellent advice on buying a seat. The institute's web site (icbc.com) has rating charts that compare major brands of car seats—go to "Road Safety," then "Child Seats" and then finally to "Buying a Child Seat." For a link to the brochure and the ratings web page, go to BabyBargains.com and click on the "Bonus Material" section for a link to this car seat guide.

◆ *Where to buy online.* Many of the large baby product web

sites (and catalogs) mentioned throughout this book sell car seats at competitive prices. When you find an online coupon for these sites (see Chapter 7, Around the House, for a list of such sites), the deals can be even better. Check out the Bargain Alert message board on our site BabyBargains.com for a regularly updated list of coupon deals and discounts.

More Money Buys You . . .

As you'll read later in this chapter, all child safety seats are regulated by the federal government to meet minimum safety standards. So whether you buy a $50 seat from Wal-Mart or a $250 brand from a specialty store, your baby is equally covered. When you pay extra money, however, there are some perks. First, on the safety front, the more expensive seats have shock-absorbing foam that protects a seat from side-impact collisions. The more expensive seats are also easier to use and adjust . . . and clearly that is a major safety benefit. For infant seats, when you spend more money, you get an adjustable base (which enables a better fit in vehicles), a canopy to block the sun and plush padding.

Speaking of padding . . . the more money you spend, the more cushy the seat—some makers throw in infant head pillows, body cushions and more to jack the price of a car seat. These are not marketed as a safety benefit, but more for the baby's "comfort." The problem? Newborns and infants don't really care. They are just fine in a seat with basic padding (versus the deluxe version). Of course, if you have a super long commute or an older child (say over two years), padding and comfort becomes more of a relevant issue. But for most babies, basic padding is just fine.

Smart Shopper Tips

Smart Shopper Tip #1
So many seats, so much confusion
"I'm so confused by all the car seat options out there. For example, are infant car seats a waste of money? Or should I go with a convertible seat? Or one of those models that is good from birth to college?

Children's car seats come in four flavors: "infant," "convertible," "boosters" and "hybrid." Let's break it down:

◆ **Infant** car seats are just that—these rear-facing seats are designed for infants up to 22 lbs. or so and 26″ in height (one model works up to 30 pounds and 32″ in height). On average, parents get about six months of use out of an infant seat (of course, that varies with the size/height of the child). Infant car seats have an internal harness (usually five-point) that holds the infant to the carrier, which is then snapped into a base. The base is secured to the car. Why the snap-in base? That way you can release the seat and use the carrier to tote your baby around.

◆ **Convertible** car seats (see right) can be used for both infants *and* older children (most seats go up to 40 lbs.)—infants ride rear facing; older kids over one year of age ride facing forward. Convertible seats have different harness options (more on this later); unlike infant seats, however, they do not have snap-in bases.

car seats

◆ **Booster** seats were once used exclusively to position the vehicle's safety belt to correctly fit a young child up to 80 pounds (hence, they are called belt-positioning boosters). In recent years, some boosters have added five-point harnesses (see picture) for use by younger children weighing less than 40 pounds (after that time, the five-point harness is removed and the seat is used with the vehicle's safety belt; see lower picture). These seats are called "transitional boosters" or "combo seats" (we'll use combo seat to refer to them later in the chapter). Later in this chapter we'll break booster seats down into several more categories.

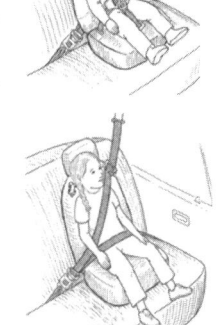

◆ **Hybrid** seats are forward-only facing seats, designed for older children—many can use a five-point harness up to 65 pounds, considerably more than the 40 lb. harness limit of combo boosters. After that, most of these seats convert to a belt-positioning booster. Some can be used as boosters up to 100 pounds.

Of course, real life doesn't always fit neatly into these categories—some seats pitch their use from birth to 100 pounds. The most well known is the Cosco Alpha Omega (also called the Eddie Bauer Three in One)—the pitch here is one seat that can be used for an infant, toddler and then older child. The Alpha Omegas is used rear facing from 5 to 30 pounds, then forward-facing to 40 lbs. From 40 lbs. to 100 lbs. the Alpha Omega converts to a booster seat that uses the auto safety belt to restrain an older child. We'll review this seat later in this chapter. (There will be a quiz on this later as well).

So does it make more sense to buy one car seat (that is a convertible car seat) and just skip the infant car seat? There is considerable debate on this subject. Some safety advocates point to recent crash tests (we'll discuss this shortly) where many infant seats failed. Others deride infant car seats for their overuse *outside* of a car (as a place for baby to nap), speculating that such babies are at risk for SIDS (Sudden Infant Death Syndrome, discussed in Chapter 2). Fuel was added to this fire in 2006, when a *British Medical Journal* study generated headlines, saying that babies in infant car seats are at risk for breathing problems.

But . . . we examined that study and found the researchers examined only nine babies in New Zealand to come up with that conclusion (see our *Baby 411* blog for a detailed discussion). And while babies born prematurely (less than 37 weeks in gestation) are at an increased risk for breathing problems while in a car seat, full term infants ARE NOT. Sure, you should always supervise a newborn in an infant seat (have someone ride in the back seat if possible). And limit your baby's time in an infant seat. But that doesn't mean infant seats are UNSAFE or dangerous for sleeping infants.

On the other side of the infant seat debate are advocates who say infant car seats fit infants better—most are designed to accommodate a smaller body and baby travels in a semi-reclined position, which supports an infant's head and neck. Yes, some convertible seats recline—but the degree of recline can be affected by the angle of your vehicle's seat back. And certain convertible seats (those with bar shields or t-shields instead of five-point restraints—more on this later) simply don't work well with infants. Furthermore, most babies don't reach the 22-pound mark until six months (and some as late as 12 months)—and that can be a very long period of time if you don't have an infant car seat.

Why? First, it's helpful to understand that an infant car seat is more than just a car seat—it's also an infant carrier when detached from its base. Big deal, you might say? Well, since infants spend much of their time sleeping (and often fall asleep in the car), this *is* a big deal. By detaching the carrier from the auto base, you don't have to wake the baby when you leave the car. Buy a convertible car seat, and you'll have to unbuckle the baby and move her into another type of carrier or stroller (and most likely wake her in the process). Take it from us: let sleeping babies lie and spend the additional $60 to $90 for an infant car seat, even if you use it for just six months.

Remember: babies should be REAR-FACING until they reach one year of age, regardless of weight. If your child outgrows his infant car seat before one year of age, be sure to use a convertible seat in rear-facing mode for as long as possible. Most convertible seats can be used rear-facing until baby is 30 or 33 lbs.

Smart Shopper Tip #2
Infant seats: Are they safe?

"I heard that in a recent crash test, many infant car seats failed. Are they safe?"

You are referring to now infamous *Consumer Reports* article from February 2007. Before we get into the details of how the *Consumer Reports* test went wrong, let's take a second to explain how car seat safety works. The federal government, through the National Highway Traffic Safety Administration (NHTSA), sets safety standards for car seats. You can't sell a car seat here in the U.S. that doesn't meet these safety requirements.

To be certified as meeting federal standards, car seat makers must crash test their seats. This is done either in an in-house facility or outside lab and reported to the government. Once a seat is on the market, the NHTSA performs spot checks, crash testing models from time to time.

While we won't delve into the technical details of federal standards, you should know that the basic crash test for a car seat is a frontal collision at 30 mph. Now, that number wasn't picked out of thin air—the vast majority of auto accidents occur at 30 mph or less. According to the Michigan Transportation Research Institute, the 30 mph test is "more severe than approximately 98% of frontal impact crashes nationwide."

Consumer Reports magazine independently crash test car seats—to confirm that seats actually meet standards These crash tests are proprietary—*Consumer Reports* hires an independent lab to run the test, but the results are not peer-reviewed (that is, independently verified).

So what happened with *Consumer Reports* in 2007? The magazine designed a new crash test that was flawed (the speeds were much higher than CR thought it was using). The results were dramatic—ten out of 12 infant car seats failed. Since CR doesn't used outside experts to check its test design or results, this flawed report made it into the magazine . . . and the media.

After a series of mea culpas and pressure from the NHTSA, *Consumer Reports* withdrew their report and vowed to re-test the seats using correct protocol (that is, the current government standards). CR's re-test, which was reported in late 2007, showed that *all infant car seats sold on the market today pass government safety standards.*

Smart Shopper Tip #3
New standards, new problems?

"I hear there are problems with LATCH. What is LATCH anyway?"

Stop any ten cars on the road with child safety seats and we'll bet eight or nine are not installed or used correctly. That's what road-side checks by local law enforcement in many states have uncovered: a recent study by the National Highway Traffic Safety Administration stopped 4000 drivers in four states and found a whopping 80% made mistakes in installing or securing a child safety seat.

What's causing all the problems?

In the past, many child safety seats have failed parents, in our opinion. Installation of a car seat was an exercise in frustration—even parents who spent hours with the instructions still made mistakes. The number one culprit: the auto seat belt—it is great at restraining adults, but not so good at child safety seats. And those seats simply won't work well if they aren't attached to a car correctly . . . that's the crux of the problem. Simply put, thanks to the quirkiness of auto safety belts (different auto makers have different systems), putting a child safety seat in a car is still like trying to fit a square peg into a round hole. Some seats wobble too much; others can't be secured tightly to the back seat.

The bottom line: some child safety seats simply DON'T FIT in some vehicles. Which cars? Which seats? It's hard to tell. There is one good web site with a car seat compatibility database (carseat-data.org), but it doesn't cover every seat and every vehicle. Often, parents find it's trial and error to see what works.

So, that's where LATCH comes in. The federal government recently rolled out a new, mandated "uniform" attachment (called LATCH or ISOFIX), required for all vehicles and safety seats made after September 2002. LATCH stands for "Lower Anchors and Tethers for Children." ISOFIX stands for International Standards Organization FIX, which is the international version of LATCH. (More on ISOFIX later in this section).

What is LATCH? Instead of using the auto's seat belt, car seats attach to two anchor bars in the lower seatback. The result: fewer confusing installations, no more locking clips or other apparatus needed to make sure the seat is correctly attached. (Another part of the new standard: tether straps, which are discussed later in this section.) See picture of a LATCH installed car seat at right.

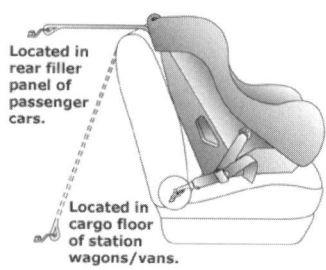

Located in rear filler panel of passenger cars.

Located in cargo floor of station wagons/vans.

Here is a sum up of frequent questions we get on LATCH seats:

◆ *Which manufacturers sell LATCH seats?* Answer: all. Every infant and convertible car seat sold now includes LATCH. Most belt-positioning booster seats do NOT have LATCH.

◆ *Will I have to junk my old car seat?* Yes, car seat safety advocates do NOT recommend using a seat that is over five years old. Why? Belts, clips and interior parts in car seats wear out over time . . . hence, seats five years old or older may no longer be safe to use. (The last time a non-LATCH seat would have been manufactured was 2002—and that is now beyond the five-year guideline).

◆ *My car does not have LATCH. What is the safest seat I can buy?* All LATCH seats are backward compatible—that is, they can be safely installed and used in older vehicles that do NOT have LATCH. Remember the safest seat is the one that best fits your car *and* your child. There is no one "safest" seat. Get the best seat you can afford (we'll have recommendations later in this chapter) and use it with a tether strap. And get your car seat safety checked to make sure you have the best installation and fit.

◆ *I need to move my LATCH seat to a second car that doesn't have the new attachments. Will it work?* Yes, see above.

◆ *I know the safest place for a baby is in the middle of the back seat. But my car doesn't have LATCH anchors there, just in the outboard positions! Where should I put the seat?* Our advice: use the LATCH positions, even if they are only on the side. Now, some car seat and vehicle makers say it is okay to use a LATCH seat in the middle of the back seat if you use the LATCH anchors in the outboard positions—check with your car seat and vehicle owner's manual to see if this is permissible. FYI: many General Motors vehicles have center LATCH connectors.

◆ *I got a LATCH seat that doesn't fit in my vehicle! I thought this was supposed to be universal.* LATCH has been sold to the public as some kind of magic pill that will instantly make all seats fit all vehicles. Hardly. Because of the wide variety of vehicles and seats (a SUV versus a compact, minivan versus pickup), it is unreasonable to expect any system would make this happen. While LATCH helps, it is not the cure-all.

◆ *I read that in crash tests, some seats attached with LATCH performed worse than those secured by a vehicle belt. Why did this happen?* You are referring to the now infamous 2007 *Consumer Reports* crash test. Yes, the magazine's crash tests showed SEVERAL seats (such as the Peg Perego Primo Viaggio) performed *much worse* with LATCH than with vehicle safety belts. (We'll note these issues in our ratings of seats later in this chapter). Why does that happen? We don't know—that's something the government is investigating.

But wasn't LATCH supposed to be BETTER than a vehicle belt? Yes, it was supposed to make attaching seats easier . . . but the crash test data should be the same (or better for LATCH). Again, we don't know why this has happened. Adding to the frustration with LATCH: LATCH connectors are hard to access in some vehicles.

As we were going to press, the NHTSA was holding a hearing to address LATCH problems—no wonder a recent survey showed that 40% of parents aren't using LATCH.

Smart Shopper Tip #4
Strap Me In

"What is a tether strap? Do I want one?"

Back in 1999, the federal government mandated that all convertible child safety seats be sold with a tether strap—these prevent a car seat from moving forward in the event of a crash. How? One end of the tether strap attaches to the top of the car seat; the other is hooked to an "anchor bolt" that is permanently installed on the back of the back seat or on the floor in your vehicle.

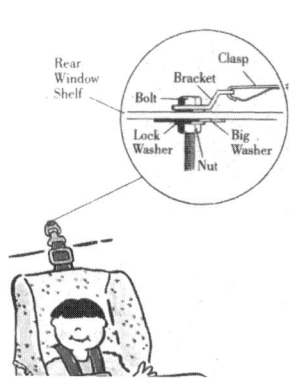

Most newer vehicles already have anchor bolts, making the use of a tether strap a snap. (Hint: check your vehicle's owner's manual to find instructions on using tether straps). Older vehicles may have pre-drilled anchorage points—just ask your car dealer for the "anchor bolt installation kit" (a part number that's listed in your owner's manual in the section on installing child safety seats). You can install the bolt or have the dealer do it.

Of course, really old cars are trickier since they lack anchor bolts or even pre-drilled holes—to install the anchor bolt, you may need to drill through your car's sub floor (a job for the car dealer, as you can guess). And just finding out the part number for the anchor bolt can be a challenge; some car dealers are clueless about this issue.

(One tip: call a CANADIAN dealer to find out the part number of the anchor bolt for child safety seats. Why? Tether straps have been required for years in Canada. Hence, car dealers there are more familiar with this request. You can find a Canadian dealer's phone number on most automobile maker's web sites.)

A side note: most seats can only use tether straps when FOR-WARD-FACING. Only four models (the Britax Roundabout, Marathon and Wizard and the Sunshine Kids Radian 65/80) have a tether which can be used in either rear or forward-facing positions. Note: tether straps are typically not used with infant seats or booster seats (but always consult your seat's directions for specific advice on this).

So, is the tether strap worth all the hassle? Yes—crash tests show car seats are SAFER when used with a tether strap. The strap keeps the car seat (and hence, your baby's head) from moving forward in a crash, lowering the chance of injury. Unfortunately, parents don't seem to be getting this message: a 2006 survey from the NHTSA revealed that only 55% of parents are using a top tether.

Are seats used *without* tethers unsafe? No, the federal government requires seats to be safe even when a tether is not in use. Of course, the tether adds that extra measure of safety and is always preferable to a tether-less installation.

Smart Shopper Tip #5
One Size Does Not Fit All

"My friend has a car seat that just doesn't fit very well into her car. Does anyone put out a rating system that says which seats are most compatible? Easiest to use? Safest?"

Yes, there is good news there. The National Highway Traffic Safety Administration rates car seats on their ease of use and posts the results on the web at nhtsa.gov/cps/cssrating or call 888-327-4236.

Note these are not crash test results. NHTSA rates seats on ease of use: how a seat assembles, installs and secures a child. In the latest report, 99 seats were rated from 14 manufacturers. The government updates the report every year.

Smart Shopper Tip #6
Recalls

"I saw online that a particular car seat is being recalled. Should I be skeptical of other seats by that manufacturer?"

Here's a sobering fact of car seat shopping: most major brands of car seats have had a recall over the past five years. We've seen recalls on cheap seats sold in Wal-Mart and $200 car seats sold in specialty stores, making recalls a reality no matter what brand you

CAR
SEATS

consider. So if all major brands have had recalls, how do you shop for the best seat?

First, realize that some recalls are more serious than others. Some car seats are recalled for minor problems, like incorrect warning labels. Other companies do voluntary recalls when their own testing reveals a problem. The key issue: look to see if there are any injuries associated with the defective product. Obviously, car seats that are so defective as to cause injury to babies are much more serious than minor labeling recalls.

Another issue: how does a company handle a recall? Do they fight the government, forcing regulators to order a recall? Or do they voluntarily recall the item and set up an efficient process (web site or toll-free phone number) to get replacements or retrofit kits to consumers? In the past, we have lowered our ratings for car seat manufacturers who bungled a recall effort.

When a company announces a recall, the product is typically removed from store shelves (if the recall is for the current production run). If the recall is for a product's previous production run, you may still see it on store shelves (since the defect may have been corrected months before). That's why it is key to see WHEN the recalled product was manufactured. Of course, different car seats in the same manufacturer's line may be totally unaffected by a recall.

Another tip: make sure to fill out the registration card that comes with any car seat you buy . . . and send it in! In theory, this will get you expedited recall information and repair kits. Also: sign up for a recall email list on Recalls.gov.

Unfortunately, with some car seat makers, even if you fill out a registration card you may not get a recall notice. For more on this problem, see the previous box on pages 368 and 369

Smart Shopper Tip #7
Watch the height limit
"My son isn't anywhere near the 22 lb. limit for his infant seat, but he's so tall I don't think it is safe anymore—he has to bend his legs when we put him in!"

Here's a little known fact about most infant seats: in addition to WEIGHT limits, all infant car seats also have HEIGHT limits. And like everything in the car seat world, each seat has different limits (check the sticker on the side of the carrier—by law, the manufacturer must list both height and weight limits). Once your baby exceeds EITHER the height or weight limit, you should move him to a convertible seat.

One note on this: while the weight limit is important, do one other test if your child is approaching the height limit—is there less than an inch of seat left above baby's head? If so, then move your baby to a convertible seat (facing the rear of the vehicle until they pass one year of age).

With the bigger babies everyone seems to be having these days, this isn't a moot point. A large infant might exceed the height limit BEFORE he or she passes the weight limit. Here's the scoop: height limits range from 26" for the Evenflo Discovery to 30" for the Britax Companion infant car seat. Most infant seats have weight limits of 22 lb. range, although one seat (the Graco SafeSeat) works to 30 lbs. Later in this section, we'll have a chart that lists the height and weight limits of all major infant car seats. See the box "How Big is Normal?" later in this chapter for more on this topic.

Smart Shopper Tip #8
Do I have to buy THREE seats?

"My baby has outgrown his infant seat. Can I buy a combo seat that converts to a booster?"

The short answer: yes. Do we recommend it? No. Why? We think the safest place for an infant who has outgrown an infant seat is in a CONVERTIBLE seat in rear-facing mode. Leave them there until they are AT LEAST a year of age—longer if they still are under the weight limit. Note: nearly all "combo" seats with five-point harnesses that convert to a belt-positioning booster are FORWARD-FACING only seats. Examples of combo seats include the Cosco Summit and Graco CarGo.

So, what is best? When your child outgrows her convertible seat, THEN we recommend a booster seat (combo or belt-positioning). Now, we realize what you are thinking: have we lost our minds? We are recommending you buy THREE seats for your child: infant, convertible, and then a booster. Wouldn't it be cheaper to get one of those all-in-one seats or at least one that combines the convertible/booster function? No, not in our opinion. The all-in-one-seats (like the Eddie Bauer Three-In-One or Cosco Alpha Omega) are a poor choice; see review later in this chapter. And while those combo boosters are a good choice for a three or four year old child who has outgrown his convertible seat but is not mature enough to sit in a belt-positioning booster, combo seats are NOT good for infants—they often don't recline and have less sleeping support than convertibles.

Smart Shopper Tip #9
European seats

"I saw a cool European car seat online—is that safe or legal to use in the U.S.?"

Short answer: no.

CAR
SEATS

Thanks to the web, you can order a car seat from Switzerland . . . or South Africa. Making this more tempting: the belief among some safety advocates that Europe has better car seats than the U.S. or Canada.

But let's do a reality check: European standards are DIFFERENT than the U.S. or Canada. Different does not necessarily mean better, however. European seats are designed to work in European cars, which have different safety features compared to vehicles sold in North America.

Bottom line: it is ILLEGAL (and foolish) to use a seat from over-

Registering a Complaint: Do Some Seat Makers Ignore Registered Users During Recalls?

As a new parent, you try to do everything you can to make sure your baby is safe. Besides researching which products are safe, many parents also diligently fill out warranty and registration cards with the expectation they will be contacted in case of a future safety recall.

Yet many parents are surprised to learn that baby product companies fail to mail out notices of defective products to registered users. Why? Companies complain that mailing costs are too high—instead they issue a press release to the media, hoping web sites, local newspapers, radio and TV will spread the word about a defective product.

Case in point: the March 2002 recall of the Graco SnugRide infant seat. Graco discovered that over 900,000 units of the popular infant car seat were defective. The problem: a number of the bases had missing components that were used to attach the carrier to the base (Graco has subsequently fixed the problem and we still recommend that seat).

Registered users of the SnugRide probably expected Graco to drop them a note about the problem. If so, they were sorely disappointed. Graco did send a press release to the media regarding the recall, but made no effort to contact registered users directly.

Hello? Is this insane or what? Parents take the time to fill out and mail those registration cards that manufacturers include in product boxes, but for what? Instead of receiving a courtesy call or postcard that the car seat you are using might be dangerous, you are supposed to be watching the local news at exactly the right moment to hear your car seat is recalled? Or see page 16A of the local paper?

Companies like Graco should be ashamed. Let's do the math—assuming only one-third of all SnugRide users actually registered their seats (and that is a conservative guess), Graco would have to send out notices to 300,000 parents. What does a postcard cost to mail these days? A whopping 24¢. So, Graco's total costs would be about $75,000 (assuming some printing costs). That seems a small price to pay for a company with $600 million in annual sales.

seas here in the U.S. (Ditto for you Canadians—seats must be certified to meet Canadian standards before they can be sold or used in Canada. So if you are a Canadian reading this book, you can't buy a seat in the U.S. and use it legally in Canada).

Smart Shopper Tip #10
Holding Your Baby Back: Safety Harness Advice
 "Which safety harness is best—the 5-point or bar-shield?

Car Seat Lesson 101: understanding the different harness systems

And what about email? Last we looked, most of the world used the 'net to communicate. Yet most big baby gear manufacturers still don't allow parents to register online. Emailed recall notices? Forget about it.

Last year, the Consumer Products Safety Commission (CPSC) issued 59 recalls of baby products, including toys. That's more than one per week! So, what can a parent do to keep up with what's safe and what's recalled? Here are our tips:

◆ *Track your purchases.* In order to know whether you have a recalled product, you first have to know what you've got to begin with. One parent told us she kept a spreadsheet with the following info for all her baby products: manufacturer, model, serial number, date manufactured, company phone number/web site, where purchased and price paid. Okay, perhaps that's a bit overboard for most parents. But at least put all your receipts and product manuals into a file or shoebox. The goal: create ONE place you go to when a recall is announced.

◆ *Stay informed.* Register for free email alerts about recalls. Our blog (BabyBargains.com, click on News) tracks the latest recalls. Of course, the Consumer Products Safety Commission also sends out recall notices—sign up at Recalls.gov or CPSC.gov.

◆ *Consider buying products from web sites that will inform you of recalls.* Case in point: Amazon.com does a good job of letting customers know of recalled products. One reader was amazed when Amazon sent her a recall notice (with detailed instructions on what to do) for a bassinet she bought over a year ago.

◆ *Be careful with eBay and other second-hand purchases.* Yes, Craigslist has great deals, but be sure you aren't buying a recalled product. Do a search of the CPSC's web site (cpsc.gov) to find whether that car seat deal is really a dud.

car seats

available on the market. For INFANT seats, you have two choices: three point or five-point belts (although nearly all infant seats now have five-point harnesses). For CONVERTIBLE seats, you have two choices: five-point or bar-shield. In the past there was a third type, a t-shield (a plastic shield that buckles in at baby's crotch). T-Shields are rarely seen today.

Three (or five) point belts refer to the number of points in which the belt attaches to the car seat. A bar shield lowers over the baby's head and snaps into a buckle—bar-shield car seats are often sold at discount stores.

Our recommendations: for INFANT seats, we recommend five-point harnesses, which have become the de facto standard. Yes, you will see an occasional three-point harness on a cheap infant car seat sold at Wal-Mart, but that is the exception to the rule. Our advice: go for the five-point harness.

For CONVERTIBLE seats, we also recommend the five-point version. Why? Safety experts say it's the best choice because you can tighten the belts to securely hold your baby in her seat. Bar shields have several problems. The biggest: most don't adjust well to growing children. Even those expensive models that feature *adjustable* shields only adjust so much—if your child grows quickly, they still might outgrow the car seat. The result? You'll have to move them into a booster seat (making an extra purchase) sooner than you want to.

Another major problem with bar shields: wiggling toddlers can get out of them way too easily. One mom told us she was horrified to look in her rear view mirror one day and find her 18 month-old child STANDING in his car seat while the vehicle was moving. We think five point harnesses are safer since it is very difficult for baby to wiggle out when the belts are tightened correctly.

Let's be honest, however: the five-point harness is the *least convenient* to use. You have to put each strap around baby's arms, find the lower buckle (which always seems to disappear under their rump) and then snap them in. Bar-shields and t-shields slip over the baby's head in one motion and are easier to buckle.

The fact that the five-point harness is inconvenient is just the way it goes (you'll get the hang of it, trust us). Simply put, it's the safest choice for your baby. And sometimes as a parent you have to do what's best for your child, even if that makes your life less convenient.

Here are ten more shopping tips for car seats:

◆ **How easily does it recline?** All convertible seats are supposed to have a recline feature to make sure baby is at a proper angle. Of course, how easily the seat reclines varies from model to model—and reaching that lever in a rear-facing seat may be a challenge. Check it out in the store before you buy.

◆ *No-twist straps.* Better car seats have thicker straps that don't twist. The result: it is easier to get a child in and out of a seat. Cheaper seats have cheaper webbing that can be a nightmare— "twisty straps" are a key reason why parents hate their car seats. Later in this chapter, we'll point out which seats have this problem.

◆ *Check the belt adjustments.* You don't merely adjust the car seat's belts just when your baby gets bigger—if you put Junior in a coat, you'll need to loosen the belts as well. As a result, it's important to check how easily they adjust. Of course, every car seat maker seems to have a different idea on how to do this. The best car seats let you adjust the belts from the *front*. Those models that require you to access the back of the seat to adjust the belts are more hassle. FYI: do not put your child in a bulky coat or snowsuit when sitting in a safety seat. In the case of an accident, the bulky coat might compress, compromising the safety of the seat. At most, only put a child in a thin coat (like a polar fleece) when they are riding in a child safety seat. (To keep an infant warm, consider a seat cover-up, which goes on the outside of the seat. We'll discuss examples of these products later in this chapter).

◆ *Change the harness height.* Some seats require you to re-thread the belts when you change harness heights. Try this in the store to see how easy/difficult it is. Note: the best seats have automatic harness height adjusters that require no re-threading.

◆ *Look at the chest clip.* The chest clip or harness tie holds the two belts in place. Lower-quality seats have a simple "slide-in" clip—you slip the belt under a tab. That's OK, but some older toddlers can slip out from this type of chest clip. A better bet: a chest clip that SNAPS the two belts together like a seat belt. This is more kid-proof.

◆ *Are the instructions in Greek?* Before you buy the car seat, take a minute to look at the set-up and use instructions. Make sure you can make sense of the seat's documentation. Another tip: if possible, ask the store for any installation tips and advice.

◆ *Is the pad cover machine-washable?* You'd think this would be a "no-brainer," but a surprising number of seats (both convertible and infant) have covers that aren't removable or machine washable. Considering how grimy these covers can get, it's smart to look for this feature. Also check to see if you can wash the harness.

◆ *Will the seat be a sauna in the summer?* Speaking of the seat pad, check the material. Plush, velvet-like covers might seem nice in the store, but think about next August. Will your baby be sitting in a mini-sauna? Cotton or cotton-blend fabric pads are better than heavier weight, non-breathable fabrics.

◆ **Does the seat need to be installed with each use?** The best car seats are "permanently" installed in your car. When you put baby in, all you do is buckle them into the seat's harness system. Yet a few models need to be installed with each use—that means you have to belt the thing into your car every time you use it. Suffice it to say, that's a major drawback.

◆ **Watch out for hot buckles.** Some inexpensive car seats have exposed metal buckles and hardware. In the hot sun, these buckles can get toasty and possibly burn a child. Yes, you can cover these buckles with a blanket when you leave the car, but that's a hassle. A better bet is to buy a seat with a buckle cover or no exposed metal.

◆ **Is it shopping cart compatible?** Some infant car seats are better at this than others. One simple test: while you are in a store like Babies R Us, Target or Wal-Mart, take the infant carrier and try snapping it into a shopping cart. You'll find some fit better than others. Now, we should point out that many safety advocates cringe when they see infant seats snapped into the upper part of a shopping cart—they say this makes the cart top-heavy, which could cause it to tip over. Advocates say the safest place for baby is in their infant seat

Are higher price seats better?

When you shell out $200 instead of $100 for a car seat, do you get a car seat that is twice as safe? Answer: no, price is not always an indicator of quality. Sometimes the most expensive seats merely feature fancier fabric or extra padding.

Now, that said, we should note that in some cases you DO get better safety features when you spend more. Example: Britax seats are pricey ($200 or so), but they have extra EPS foam for crash protection, no-twist straps and a slew of other safety and convenience features. Plus you can tether these seats either forward OR rear facing, unlike most of the competition, which is just forward-facing. The tether has been shown to greatly reduce seat movement in a crash. Now, THAT is a safety feature. And if a seat is loaded with features that make it easier to use, you could argue that parents would be less likely to miss-use the seat—and that makes it safer.

in the *main* part of the basket or carried by mom or dad. Some stores now realize this problem and have shopping carts with integrated infant seats, eliminating the need for you to bring your own. However, they can get rather grimy (or even broken) quickly.

◆ *How heavy is it?* This is a critical factor for infant car seats, but also important for convertibles. Why? First, remember you are lugging that infant seat WITH a baby that will weigh seven to ten lbs. *to start.* When your baby outgrows the infant seat, she will weigh 22 to 30 lbs. *in addition to the seat weight!* To help you shop, we list the weights for major infant car seat brands later in this chapter. What about convertible seats? If you buy one seat and plan to move it from car to car, realize weight may be a factor here as well.

◆ *Buying a new car?* Consider getting a built-in (also called integrated) child safety seat. The cost varies from car maker to maker, but is about $400. Remember that most built-in seats can only be used with children one year or older in a FORWARD-FACING position; you'll still need to buy an infant car seat for babies under one year of age. And if your child outgrows their infant seat before a year of age, you will need to use a convertible seat in rear-facing mode. That obviously eliminates some of the advantages of an integrated seat; that said, since the built-in seat is designed as part of the vehicle, you are getting a very safe seat. Note: the limits for integrated seats vary by vehicle maker, so check before purchasing.

Safe & Sound

NEVER BUY A USED CAR SEAT. If the seat has been in an accident, it may be damaged and no longer safe to use. Bottom line: used seats are a big risk unless you know their history. And the technology of car seats improves every year; a seat that is just five years old may lack important safety features compared to today's models. (And, as we discussed earlier, seats older than five years also have parts that may wear out and fail . . . a big reason not to use an old seat). Another tip: make sure the seat has not been recalled (see the contact info below for the National Highway Traffic Safety Administration). Safety seats made before 2000 may not meet current safety standards (unfortunately, most seats aren't stamped with their year of manufacture, so this may be difficult to determine). The bottom line: risky hand-me-downs aren't worth it. Brand new car seats (which start at $50) aren't that huge of an investment to ensure your child's safety.

2 **GET YOUR SEAT SAFETY CHECKED.** No matter how hard you try to buy and install the best seat for your child, mistakes with installation can still occur. There's nothing like the added peace of mind of having your car seat safety checked by an expert. Such checks are free and widely available. The National Highway Traffic Safety Administration's web site (nhtsa.dot.gov) has a national listing of fitting/inspection stations. Another cool program: Daimler Chrysler has a FREE car seat inspection—just take your car to a Chrysler dealer and they'll check your seat to see if it is safely installed. No, you don't need to have an appointment, nor do you have to own a Chrysler. Call 877-FIT-4-A-KID or web: SafetyCheck.org to find a local participating Chrysler, Jeep or Dodge dealer near you.

3 **DON'T TRUST THE LEVEL INDICATOR.** Yes, many infant car seats come with "level indicators" and instructions to make sure the seat is installed so the indicator is in the "green" area. When in the green, the seat is supposedly at the correct angle to protect your baby in case of a crash. Nice idea, but thanks to the myriad of back seat designs in dozens of cars, the seat may be incorrectly installed even if the indicator says it is fine. At car seat safety checks, many techs ignore the level indicator and instead use this test: They take a piece of paper and fold one corner to form a 45-degree angle. Then they place the side of the paper against the back of the infant car seat where the baby's back would lie. When the folded corner is level with the horizon, the seat is at the correct angle—even if the indicator says it ain't so. If you aren't sure your seat is installed to the correct angle, take it to a car seat safety check.

4 **FORGET CAR SEAT ADD-ONS.** We've seen all manner of travel "accessories" for kids in car seats, including bottle holders, activity trays and so on. The problem: all these objects are potential hazards in an accident, flying around the car and possibly striking you (the adult) or your child.

5 **HOW TALL IS TOO TALL?** You'll notice that most child safety seats utilize two types of limits: weight and height. It's the latter limit that creates some confusion among parents. Convertible seats have both a rear and forward facing height limit—this is required by federal law (for those inquiring minds, the standard is FMVSS 213). Most safety techs say the maximum height for a child is when their head is one inch below the top of the shell (the 1″ rule) or if your child's shoulders exceed the height of the top harness slot. The problem: some car seat makers have more strict height limits than the 1″ rule. Here's the frustrating part: kids often outgrow the seat's stated height limit *before* they reach that 1″ rule or their shoulders are taller than the top harness slot, leaving some parents to wonder if they should continue using the seat. The problem is one of interpretation: while the federal law requires every seat to have height limits, car seat makers are free to interpret this rule (and usage of the seat). Some seat makers just interpret the rules more strictly than others. Bottom line: while we understand seat makers might have their own take on federal safety standards, it is generally safe to use a seat until your child's head is 1″ below the top of the seat or their shoulders exceed the top harness slot—even if their height is slightly above the stated limit for the seat.

6 **READ THE DIRECTIONS VERY CAREFULLY.** Many car accidents end in tragedy because a car seat was installed improperly. If you have any questions about the directions, call the company or return the car seat for a model that is easier to use. Another tip: read your vehicle's owner's manual for any special installation instructions. Consult with your auto dealer if you have any additional questions.

What's the number-one problem with car seat installation? Getting a tight fit, say safety techs. Make sure the safety seat is held firmly against the back of the car seat and doesn't wobble from side to side (or front to back). One tip: put your knee on the seat and push down with your full weight while you tighten the seat belt. This eliminates belt slack and ensures a snug installation.

7 **USE YOUR CAR SEAT.** Don't make the mistake of being in a hurry and forgetting to (or just not wanting to) attach the restraints. Some parents merely put their child in the seat without hooking up the harness. It is more dangerous to leave your child in a car seat unrestrained by the safety harness than it is to put him or her in a regular seat belt. And always observe weight limits. As we mentioned earlier, children should ride REAR-FACING to one year of age, regardless of weight. Make sure your child's safety seat is able to accommodate her weight in that position.

8 **PUT THE CAR SEAT IN THE BACK SEAT.** Air bags and car seats don't mix—several reports of injuries and deaths have been attributed to passenger side air bags that deployed when a car seat was in the front seat. As a result, the safest place for kids is the back seat. In fact, whether the car has an air bag or not, the back is always safer—federal government statistics say putting a child in the back seat instead of the front reduces the risk of death by 27%.

And where is the safest part of the back seat? Safety experts say it's the middle—it is the furthest away from side-impact risks. The only problem with that advice is that some cars have a raised hump in the middle of the back seat that makes it difficult/impossible to safely install a car seat. Another problem: safety seats are best held against the car's back seat by a three-point belt—and many middle seats just have a two-point belt. Finally, consider the LATCH problem we noted above (where many vehicles have no LATCH anchors in the middle of the back seat, only the sides). Bottom line: while the middle of the back seat is the safest spot, sometimes you just can't install a seat there. The next best place is in an outboard position of the back seat with a lap/shoulder belt.

What about side curtain air bags you see in the back seats of some cars? Many new cars come equipped with side-impact air bags or curtains. These air bags are NOT as dangerous as front air bags, as they deploy with much less force in the event of a side impact crash. Therefore, putting a car seat next to a door that has a side curtain air bag is not a danger.

9 Register your seat. Don't forget to send the registration card back to the manufacturer. Yes, earlier we discussed how some manufacturers ignore sending notices to registered users when a car seat is recalled (instead, relying on a media announcement) . . . but register your seat anyway just in case.

10 Don't use a seat over five years old. Car seats don't last forever—parts wear out, extreme heat and cold in a vehicle takes a toll on a seat's internal mechanics and more. And safety standards change and improve over time. That's why experts say don't use a seat that is over five years old. What about seats sold on eBay that might have been sitting in a warehouse for several years? Again, don't take the risk.

Finally, let's talk about those seats that promise you can use them for kids up to 65 or 100 pounds. Britax makes one (the Marathon) which can be used up to 65 pounds with a five point harness (or about six to seven years of age), while Eddie Bauer/Cosco claims their Three-in-One (or Alpha Omega) seat will last up to 100 pounds as a belt-positioning booster. (FYI: On average, a child does not hit 100 pounds in weight until age 12 or 13!). Notice a problem here? If it is unsafe to use a seat for more than five years, does it make sense to go for that Eddie Bauer seat? No, not in our opinion.

While we do recommend the Britax seat (as 65 pounds or six/seven years would be the outer limit of any seat use), remember the PRACTICAL limits of any seat. Car seats can get pretty gross after a few years of use. Even if you are diligent about keeping the cover clean, you still might have to replace it after three to four years of use (and not all car seat makers sell replacement covers as an accessory).

11 Pickup Trucks are often NOT SAFE for car seats. "A pickup truck should not be considered a family vehi-

How big is normal?

A quick glance at the "average" growth charts for infants makes you realize why kids outgrow their infant seats so quickly. Most infant seats are only rated for babies up to 22 pounds and 29" height. The average male infant hits 22 pounds at about nine months (at the 50th percentile). But for boys at the top of the growth chart, that could happen at a mere six months! Girls are of course a bit behind that curve, hitting 22 pounds on average at 12 months of age (at the 50th percentile). Girls at the top of the chart might hit 22 pounds as soon as eight months.

When a child outgrows his infant seat, he must go into a convertible seat—and there is the rub. Safety advocates say babies should be rear facing to one year of age and AT LEAST 20 pounds. Our advice: make sure the convertible seat you buy is rear-facing to at least 30 pounds.

What about height? Boys hit 29" at around ten months (again the 50th percentile). But some really tall baby boys can hit 26" as soon as eight months. For girls, the average age when most infants hit 26" is 12 months, but it can happen as soon as eight months.

Bottom line: some kids may outgrow their seats by HEIGHT long before they hit the weight limit.

And here's the take home message: keep your child REAR-FACING as long as possible, given your seat's limits. It is the safest way for them to ride.

Source: National Center for Health Statistics, www.cdc.gov/ growthcharts.

car seats

cle," concluded an article by the Children's Hospital of Philadelphia on car seat safety—and we agree. Why? "Children in the rear seat of compact extended-cab pickups are nearly five times as likely to be injured as children seated in the back seat of other vehicles," according to a Partners for Child Passenger Safety study, sponsored by the same hospital.

Of course, not all pickup trucks are alike. Some larger pickup trucks with full-size rear seats do allow car seats (check your vehicle manual for advice). Depending on the vehicle maker, pickup trucks with these seats are called SuperCrew, Double cab, Crew Cab or Quad Cab. Yet pickup trucks with jump seats should NEVER be used with car seats—these are often referred to as Extended Cab or SuperCab trucks. If your pickup truck does not have a rear seat and you must use the front seat (again, not recommended), you must disable the passenger-side air bag.

Even if your pickup truck has a full-size rear seat that allows for car seat installations, think twice about using this vehicle with car seats. Studies show that all passenger cars are generally safer in an accident (for kids in a car seat) compared to pickup trucks.

Recalls

The National Highway Traffic Safety Administration (NHTSA) posts recalls online (nhtsa.dot.gov) and has a toll-free hot line to check for recalls or to report a safety problem. For info, call (800) 424-9393 or (202) 366-0123. You can have a list of recalled car seats automatically faxed to you at no charge (in case you don't have online access). Note that this is a different governmental agency than the Consumer Product Safety Commission, which regulates and recalls other juvenile products. (For Canadian recalls and safety seat rules, see the special section at the end of this book for more info).

Money-Saving Secrets

1 **GET A FREE SEAT!** A reader emailed in this great tip—her health insurance carrier provides free infant car seats to parents who complete a parenting class. No specific class is required . . . you just provide proof of completion. And health insurance providers aren't the only ones with car seat deals—check with your auto insurance provider as well. Of course, it is in insurance carriers' best interest to hand out free seats or rebates—each child safety seat used today saves auto insurers $100, private health insurers $45 and the government $45 in costs that would otherwise be incurred from unrestrained kids in auto crashes. Insurers pay out a whopping $175 million in claims annually resulting from crashes in which children age birth to four were traveling unrestrained in motor vehicles (source: "Child Safety Seats: How Large are the Benefits and Who Should Pay?" The Children's Safety Network). The take-home message: CALL your health and auto insurance providers to see what freebies, rebates and other deals they have for new parents. Another tip: check with your employer. Some companies sell discounted car seats as a family-friendly perk, so check that too.

2 **IF YOU HAVE TWO CARS, YOU DON'T NEED TO BUY TWO INFANT SEATS.** Instead, just buy one seat and then get an extra stay-in-the-car base. While it's not widely known, major infant seat makers sell their auto bases separately for $40 to $60. If you can't find them in stores likes Babies R Us, check out baby web sites that stock them.

3 **COUPONS!** Use Froogle (Froogle.google.com) to compare prices on seats—but then how to get a deal? Find out the latest coupons and discounts by popping over to our Bargain Alert message boards (BabyBargains.com, then Message Boards, then Bargain Alert). Right at the top, we keep a pinned thread with a list of the best online coupon codes, discounts and deals. The thread is updated regularly, so come back to visit when you need a code.

4 EXPENSIVE MODELS AREN'T NECESSARILY BETTER. If you spend $100 on a car seat, are you getting one that's twice as safe as a seat that's $50? Not necessarily. Often, all you get for that additional money is plush padding and extras like pillows. Do infants notice the extra padding? No, not in our opinion. Sure, you need SOME padding, but the minimum is fine for most infants. We do agree that this becomes more of an issue as a baby gets older—toddlers may be uncomfortable in less-padded seats for longer car trips. But since infants sleep most of the time, we think babies under a year of age don't notice the quilted fabric you paid extra bucks for. Bottom line: the $50 seat may be just as safe and probably as comfortable for baby.

The Name Game: Reviews of Selected Manufacturers

Here are our reviews of the major car seat makers sold in the U.S. and Canada. Many of the infant seats reviewed here are sold as part of stroller/car seat combo products; the strollers are reviewed separately in the next chapter. Of course, you don't have to buy a travel system—nearly all these seats are sold separately.

Special note: this section gives you an overview of each brand; we now review each model seat separately later in this chapter!

The Ratings

    A **EXCELLENT**—*our top pick!*
    B **GOOD**— *above average quality, prices, and creativity.*
    C **FAIR**—*could stand some improvement.*
    D **POOR**—*yuck! Could stand some major improvement.*

Baby Trend *For a dealer near you, call (800) 328-7363, (909) 902-5568, Web: babytrend.com.* Baby Trend scored a coup when their Flex-Loc infant car seat ($90) won top honors as a Best Buy in a *Consumer Reports* 2007 report. Yet Baby Trend, the company, has been dogged by poor customer service and other glitches. Example: the availability of Baby Trend's car seats has been inconsistent in recent years. In a past edition, we recommended their infant seat, only to have Baby Trend stop selling the seat as a stand-alone model (you could only buy it as part of a travel system—with one of Baby Trend's inferior strollers). As of this writing, you can buy their infant seats as a stand-alone item, but not all chain stores stock it. And Baby Trend's customer service is among the worst in the business, further dampening our enthusiasm for this brand.

Safety Track Record. There have been no recalls on these seats as of this writing.

Baby Trend's infant seats are reviewed on page 389.

Britax *(888) 4-BRITAX or (704) 409-1700. Web: britax.com.* European-based Britax came to the U.S. car seat market in 1996 and changed the rules of the game: the company introduced several premium car seats that were packed with extra safety features . . . and sold at premium prices. Britax was the first seat maker to cross the $200 price level (and some of its seats now approach $300).

Britax's success is due to both its innovation (side impact crash protection, a tether can that can be used in rear or forward facing position) and the seats' ease of use. On that latter score, Britax's seats are easy to install (they are a favorite of safety techs) and easy for parents to use (the harness adjustments, etc).

That said, Britax isn't perfect. The company has had a dozen safety recalls in the last ten years (most for minor issues) . . . and in the past couple of years, the company hasn't introduced many new models, instead content to sit on its big lead in the car seat biz. Britax has tried to launch a series of companion strollers to boost sales of its infant car seat—that effort has found little success. And a push to sell less-expensive (and scaled down) versions of its car seats under the Fisher Price label flopped in 2007.

That said, Britax still makes among the country's top-selling convertible seats (Roundabout, Marathon) and is among the best-respected brands in this category.

Safety track record: Despite its emphasis on safety, Britax hasn't been immune to recalls for production defects and other snafus—the company has had several major recalls in the past ten years. But the company has handled these responsibly, offering repair kits and fessing up to its mistakes in a timely manner. Yes, in the past, we complained about Britax's slow response to a 2004 recall, but the company has improved its customer service in recent years.

Britax's infant seat is reviewed on page 391. Britax's convertible seat reviews begin on page 404. Britax's booster seat reviews begin on page 434.

Century. *This brand, owned by Graco, was discontinued in 2002.*

Combi *(800) 992-6624, (803) 802-8416; Web: combi-intl.com.* While better known for its strollers, Combi has branched out with a line of car seats in recent years. The main emphasis here is on infant seats that pair with Combi strollers to form travel systems, although Combi does sell a couple of convertible and booster seats as well.

As of this writing, Combi's infant car seat line up includes the Connection and Centre (also known as the Shuttle). Even though the seats are similar, each works with a different Combi stroller (be sure to check their web site for compatibility).

New this year, Combi has debuted a convertible seat to replace the star-crossed Avatar, which was recalled in 2005 after failing a crash test. Combi's new convertible is the Zeus ($300), which rotates from rear to forward facing without having to reinstall it. The Zeus also has an anti-rebound bar and side impact protection.

Safety track record. In 2005, Combi recalled the Avatar convertible seat after the model failed a *Consumer Reports* crash test. Combi fixed the problem and a re-tested Avatar scored well in CR's tests. Combi has not had any recalls on its infant car seats.

Combi's infant seats are reviewed on page 393. Combi's convertible seats are reviewed on page 409.

Compass *(888) 899-2229. Web: compassbaby.com.* Ohio-based Compass is a new player in the car seat market. Founded by former Evenflo employees, Compass debuted in 2004 with a booster seat. In subsequent years, Compass has launched an infant car seat model, the 1410 and partnered with Inglesina to make an infant seat to match their strollers (although basically the same as the 1410, it's called the 1420). Compass added matching strollers to their line and, new as of this year, a convertible seat (True Fit). The company's niche seems to be car seats that are a step up in features, safety and design from the mass market brands like Dorel/Cosco . . . but are priced below the premium that Britax charges. Example: Compass seats have extra EPS foam for crash protection, plusher padding and so on.

In the past year, Compass was acquired by Learning Curve, which hopes to boost the brand's distribution. That's probably Compass biggest problem—while we like their innovative seats, Compass is sometimes hard to find at retail.

Safety track record. Compass recalled the 1420 infant car seat in 2006 because of a defective harness strap.

Compass' infant seat is reviewed on page 396. Compass' booster seat is reviewed on page 437.

Cosco *(812) 372-0141 or 514-323-5701 for a dealer in Canada). Web: djgusa.com.* Owned by Canadian conglomerate Dorel Industries, Cosco is a big player in the car seat market with over six million seats sold each year. As one blogger once put it, Dorel/Cosco puts the industrial in the Baby Industrial Complex.

Dorel/Cosco sells its seats under a variety of brand names: Eddie Bauer, Alpha Elite, Alpha Sport, Safety 1st and Maxi Cosi, which is Dorel's European subsidiary.

In previous years, Cosco would take the same basic seat, change the fabric pad and sell it under various brand names, depending on the outlet. Hence, you'd see the same seat sold in Wal-Mart under the Cosco brand, an upgraded version in Target sold under the Safety 1st nameplate and then a top-of-the-line model sold under the Eddie Bauer moniker at chains like Babies R Us.

Realizing parents aren't likely to be fooled by such small distinctions, Cosco told us they plan to make each brand more unique. So, you'll see basic seats under the Cosco name in discount stores . . . but Safety 1st car seats will now have brand-specific technology like "SecureTech" (to make sure a harness is latched correctly) and SofTech (foam cushions).

Perhaps Cosco's most unique brand is the Maxi Cosi line of car seats—since these are imported (and designed) by Cosco's European division, these seats aren't simply rehashes of Cosco's domestic seats. The Maxi Cosi car seats pair with a line of hot-selling strollers under the Quinny brand (another Dorel Euro import).

Safety track record: Cosco's safety track record has been marred by recalls—17 at last count since 1990. Now, you could point out that since Cosco is the largest seller of car seats in North America, it follows the company would have more recalls than a smaller competitor. True, but it's a consistent pattern of safety lapses that bothers us.

Example: Cosco allegedly sold hundreds of thousands of Touriva convertible seats AFTER the company knew a plastic notch in the seat caused skull fractures in low-speed crashes. That allegation came to light in an investigation by the *Chicago Tribune* (July 14, 2007, "When car-seat safety, commerce collide"). Despite Dorel's own engineers labeling the notch a "child safety concern," Dorel continued to make Tourivas with the notch for three years. Why? The Tribune alleges that Cosco didn't want to shut down its production lines (losing roughly $4 million in Touriva sales) to switch molds to a notch-less seat.

For the record, Dorel maintains it did investigate the notch allegation and its own testing confirmed "these recesses will not injure a child." When asked point blank if it delayed fixing the Touriva to rack up extra sales, the company replied: "The suggestion that Dorel would sacrafice the safety of children for a few extra dollars of profit is insulting and not worthy of further comment."

Yet, this isn't the first time Cosco allegedly put profits ahead of safety—in 1996, the American Academy of Pediatrics told parents

NOT to use shield boosters (a type of booster seat that uses a shield to hold a child in place) because of numerous injuries. Yet Dorel/Cosco continued to sell shield boosters until 2004, selling 10 million of the $20 boosters in a 20-year period. Cosco has settled dozens of shield-booster lawsuits (without admitting fault), according to the *Chicago Tribune*.

Reviews of Cosco's infant seats start on page 397, while Cosco's convertible seat reviews start on page 410. Cosco's booster seats are reviewed starting on page 438.

Eddie Bauer. *These seats are made by Cosco; see the previous review for details.*

Evenflo (800) 233-5921 or (937) 415-3300. In Canada, PO Box 1598, Brantford, Ontario, N3T 5V7. (905) 337-2229. Web: evenflo.com. Evenflo has struggled in this category, thanks to a string of disastrous recalls and other snafus. Yes, Evenflo has tried to add innovative features (mostly to their convertible seats), but the company has had a tough time overcoming its poor reputation in the marketplace. All in all, Evenflo often seems outflanked in the car seat market; Britax trumps them on safety features and Graco outguns

car seats

Seat cover-ups provide warmth

Okay, you aren't supposed to put baby in a car seat with a bulky coat. But what if you live in, say, Maine and its currently ten degrees outside as you read this? Try a cover-up that fits OVER the car seat and hence doesn't compromise the seat's safety. One of our favorites: **Kiddopotamus's**  "Poppit" ($28), a multi-purpose cover-up that can be used as a front carrier warmer. . . or on top of a car seat. The same company also offers several other innovative travel products, including the RayShade (a cover for strollers). For more details, call (800) 772-8339 or web: kiddopotamus.com.

What about other infant body pillows or warmers that fit between baby and the car seat? If it does not come in the box with your infant or convertible car seat, we wouldn't use it. Add-on or after-market products that are not manufacturer-tested may compromise the seat safety. The same thing goes for car seat toy bars or special mirrors so you can see baby from the front seat. We say don't use them. They could come loose in an accident, becoming a dangerous projectile.

them in infant seats and travel systems. Even downscale Cosco has a hotter license (Eddie Bauer).

Judging from parent reviews posted to our web site, Evenflo has a way to go to win the hearts of car seat buyers. Ease of use (or lack thereof) is a common gripe, with seats that have difficult-to-adjust belts and other frustrations.

Evenflo seems to be stuck in neutral—the company hasn't debuted a new infant or convertible seat for quite some time.

Safety track record: Most of Evenflo's recalls date to the 1990's, but the company did have a large recall of infant car seats (the Embrace) in 2006. The problem? The Embrace's handle unexpectedly released, causing some infants to tumble out of the seat. If that sounds familiar, you may remember the huge recalls of Evenflo infant car seats from the 1990's for a similar issue.

Reviews of Evenflo's infant seats start on page 397, while Evenflo's convertible seat reviews start on page 412. Evenflo's booster seats are reviewed on page 440.

Fisher-Price Fisher Price car seats were re-packaged Britax seats—scaled down with fewer features but with lower prices. This seats were discontinued in 2007.

Graco (800) 345-4109, (610) 286-5951. Web: gracobaby.com. Graco's success in the car seat market boils down to one model: its

What is the lightest infant car seat carrier?

Here at *Baby Bargains* we have Ivy League-trained scientists who help us determine important stuff like which infant car seat weighs the least (and hence, is easiest to lug around). Oh, we're just kidding. Actually, we the authors just went to our local baby store and stood there in the aisles lifting each infant seat and saying things like "Yep, this one is lighter!" For this edition, we actually employed a scale to get accurate readings (and you thought only the folks in lab coats at *Consumer Reports* got to play with such toys). Our official results: the lightest seat is the Evenflo Discovery (5.5 lbs.) followed by the Graco SnugRide (8 lbs.). The heaviest seats? That crown goes to the Britax Companion at a whopping 10 lbs. Weighing in at 9.9 lbs. is the Combi Centre DX while the Compass 1420, the Chicco KeyFit and Baby Trend Flex-Loc are 9 lbs. We list the weights for infant car seat carriers in a chart later in this chapter. Of course, the weight of an infant seat isn't the only factor we used to decide which was best, but it certainly is important.

best-selling infant seat, the SnugRide. That gave Graco a major leg-up in the travel system market (travel systems combine both an infant car seat and stroller). As a result, when you walk into chain stores, you'll see many Graco car seats.

In the past couple of years, Graco expanded its offerings to include the new Safe Seat line, which includes an infant and a tod-dler (forward-facing only) seat. This effort has had mixed results. The infant Safe Seat has been successful, while the forward-facing-only Safe Seat Step 2 hasn't lit the market on fire.

New this year, Graco will debut the Nautilus 3-in-1 Multi-stage car seat ($150), a new forward-facing seat that uses a five-point har-ness up to 65 pounds and then coverts to a high back booster up to 100 pounds. The same seat the becomes a backless booster for older kids (hence the 3 in 1 moniker).

Graco also makes a basic convertible seat (the ComfortSport) and a booster (the TurboBooster). Both receive good marks from par-ents and will be reviewed in depth later in this chapter.

Safety track record: In 2007, Graco recalled 277,000 ComfortSports for a misassembled anchor belt. Four years prior to that recall, Graco recalled 650,000 SnugRide infant seats for miss-ing hardware used to attach the carrier to the base. A recall for this same seat for a similar issue happened in 2002 as well.

Graco's infant seat is reviewed on page 399. Graco's convertible seat is reviewed on page 414. Graco's booster seats are reviewed starting on page 442.

car seats

Consumer Reports crash tests vs our ratings

Every time *Consumer Reports* comes out with a report on car seats, our phones and email light up—many readers want to know how we sometimes come to different conclusions as to which are the best car seats. It's quite simple: *Consumer Reports* actually crash tests car seats, something we don't have the budget to do here at *Baby Bargains*. When we rate a car seat, we look at the seat's overall features, ease of use and value based on parent feedback and our own hands-on inspections. We also look at the company's recall track record and (if available) any *Consumer Reports'* crash test reports. Even though we might use different rating methodologies, most of the time we agree with *Consumer Reports*. In the case of a major discrepancy, we'll often comment on this on our web page at BabyBargains.com (click on news).

IMMI. *See SafeGuard.*

Laura Ashley. *These seats are made by Graco; see review above.*

Orbit *(650)704-0985. Web: OrbitBaby.com* "High style" aren't two words you'd normally associate with a travel system, that combination of infant car seat and stroller often sold in discount stores. Orbit aims to change that—their high-end travel system is the brainchild of two Palo Alto-based designers who hope to inject a bit of style into the market.

Orbit's car seat is, well, different. Described on a parenting blog as looking like a crockpot (bummer that we didn't think of that first), the Orbit infant seat has two soft carrying straps and is only sold as part of a system (base and stroller) for a whopping $900. And yes, the toddler seat for the stroller frame is another $180.

Safety track record: No recalls as of this writing.
The Orbit infant seat is reviewed on page 401.

Peg Perego *(260) 482-8191. Web: perego.com.* After seeing their stroller sales eaten away by travel systems for years, Peg Perego finally decided to address this shortcoming with the debut of an infant seat (and travel system). Dubbed the Primo Viaggio, the infant seat has since gone on to be quite a success, despite two recalls (see below).

Safety track record: While Peg had two early recalls on their infant seat (in 2001 and 2002), the company has been subsequently recall-free (as of this writing). In recent years, Perego has only made a few small modifications to the seat, most notably adding "side impact protection."

Peg Perego's Primo Viaggio is reviewed on page 402.

Radian. *See Sunshine Kids below.*

Recaro *(800) 8-RECARO; 248-364-3818. Web: recaro.com.* Recaro is a 100-year old German-based company that is well known in Europe for their racing seats and other safety gear. After watching Britax's success on this site of the Atlantic, Recaro decided to give the market here a try. So far, Recaro has had limited success in cracking the market (their prices are too high), but we give them credit for persistence as well as rolling out innovative models. "These seats scream quality," said one of our readers—you can tell when you take a Recaro seat out of the box that the company does NOT skimp on construction details. So if you can afford it, we suggest giving these seats a look-see.

Recaro entered the U.S. market with three booster seat offerings (the Start, Young Style and Young Sport). In the past year, Recaro debuted its first convertible seat (the Como, $250), which has a five-point harness that works up to 70 pounds. The new Signo ($290) is similar to the Como, but adds an adjustable headrest. Finally, Recaro plans to debut its first infant car seat (the Picco) in 2008.

The NYC Taxi Dilemma

Here's a common email we get from parents in New York and other urban areas: are there any portable car seats that can be used in taxis? Something that is lightweight, easy to install and collapses to fit inside a small purse when not in use? Well, the answer is no—there's no perfect solution. But we have a few ideas. Let's break out our advice for New Yorkers by age:

◆ *Infant (birth to six months).* The safest way for an infant to ride in a taxi is in an infant car seat. Most (but not all) can be strapped in without the stay-in-the-car base. However, always check the manual BEFORE buying any seat to confirm this feature.

◆ *Older baby (six months to four years).*
This is where it gets trickier. Our advice here would be the Cosco Tote 'N Go ($30, formerly called the Travel Vest)—basically a small seat with a five-point harness for babies 25 to 40 pounds. It can only be used forward facing. Best of all, it weighs just 4 pounds—we can hear those parents on the way to Zabar's
cheering right now. Is it safe? Yes, for that occasional taxi ride. Would we use it every day in a vehicle? No—while the Cosco Tote 'N Go meets federal safety standards, parent testers we've interviewed say it is hard to get a good, tight fit, no matter whether they installed it with just a lap belt or with a lap and shoulder belt.

What about belt-positioning devices? The jury is still out on these products (lightweight devices that simply adjust a vehicle's belts to better fit a child). Some safety advocates say they don't provide any protection and the government has no data on them. The National Highway Traffic Safety Administration pledged to study belt-positioners back in 1999, but then backed off in 2004. Why? The NHTSA decided it didn't have enough crash test data on these products and couldn't rule on whether they are effective or not. Bottom line: we would avoid any after-market belt-positioning device and use a booster seat.

Also new for 2008: Recaro plans to release revised booster seats at new lower prices—the Vivo and Vivo Lite will sell for under $100 and work up to 100 pounds. Recaro's previous booster seats only worked up to 80 pounds and often sold for more than $200.

Will Recaro become the next Britax? Stay tuned.

Safety track record: No recalls as of this writing.

Recaro's infant seat is reviwed on page 403; convertible seats on page 416-17 and booster seats start on page 445.

SafeGuard *(317) 896-9531. Web: safeguardseat.com.* Safeguard is a new player in the car seat biz. Owned by IMMI, Safeguard's parent actually makes much of the hardware you see in other seats such as Britax. So why go into competition with your customers? IMMI has grown increasingly frustrated in recent years, as new innovations it pioneered went unused in car seats. So, it decided to roll out seats to demonstrate there is a market for advanced safety features.

SafeGuard's two offerings include the eponymous (and very

Leaving On a Jet Plane

Which car seats can be taken on an airplane? Most of the infant and convertible seats reviewed in this section are certified for use in an airplane. But will they fit? That's a tougher question—each airline has different size seats. Hence, wide car seats like the Evenflo Triumph may not fit (especially if you're required to keep the armrests down for take-off). Check with the airline before you get to the airport if you have questions about car seat compatibility. A better bet: simple seats like the Graco ComfortSport (which is narrow and light in weight) usually do the trick.

Here's a listing of convertible car seats with the narrowest bases: Graco ComfortSport (17.0″), Safety 1st Intera (16.5″) and Cosco Touriva (16.3″). By comparison, a seat like the Britax Marathon is 19.5″ wide.

FYI: There is a way to avoid lugging your own car seat on a plane: the FAA in 2006 approved the first child safety harness for airlines, the AmSafe Aviation Cares (KidsFlySafe.com). This $75 seat can be purchased online and provides additional belt and shoulder harnesses for a child weighing 22 to 44 pounds—perfect for infants that have outgrown their infant seat (and for parents who don't want to lug a heavy convertible seat in the airport).

expensive) SafeGuard, a forward-facing seat with five-point harness for toddlers weighing 22 to 65 pounds. SafeGuard's Go Booster works from 30 to 60 pounds with a five-point harness and up to 100 pounds as a booster.

While we're always happy to see more competition in the car seat market (there have been more players getting out than in recently), it's hard to really know whether IMMI wants to be a long term player as a manufacturer of car seats . . . or just convince other car seat makers to adopt its inventions. Time will tell, but meanwhile, at least parents have a new choice when it comes to upper-end seats.

Safety track record: No recalls as of this writing.

SafeGuard's toddler seat is reviewed on page 417. SafeGuard's booster seat is reviewed on page 446.

Safety 1st. *These seats are made by Cosco; see earlier review.*

Sunshine Kids *(888) 336-7909; sunshinekidsjp.com.* Sunshine Kids makes a variety of juvenile products, but it is their innovative Radian convertible car seats that have the market talking. The Radian's (which comes in two versions, one that works up to 65 pounds and another to 80) claim to fame is it is the only folding car seat. Sunshine accomplishes this by having omitting the typical base you see on a convertible seat—this clever design trick makes the Radian perfect for car pools. The Radian 80 is also the only convertible seat that works up to 80 pounds with a five-point harness—the highest capacity on the market.

New for 2008, Sunshine Kids will debut the Monterrey ($130), the company's first booster seat offering. The Monterrey will feature a deep seat with width adjustment.

The only bummer for Sunshine: its distribution is rather thin. You won't see these seats in chain stores—instead, you'll probably have to hunt down a seat in a specialty store or online.

Safety track record: No recalls as of this writing.

Sunshine Kids convertible seat is reviewed on page 420.

Infant Car Seats (model by model reviews)

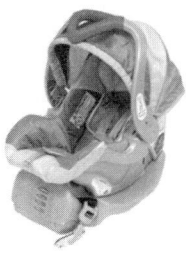

BABY TREND FLEX-LOC ADJUSTABLE BACK

Price: Latch-Lock Adjustable Back: $80-90. Extra bases $35-40.

Type: Infant seat, five-point harness.

Limits: 22 lbs. and 28.5″.

Pros: Top rated seat in recent crash test.

Cons: Carrier is quite heavy; Hard to find in some stores—mostly sold as part of a travel system with an inferior stroller.

Comments: Baby Trend scored a coup when the Flex-Loc infant seat landed a "Best Buy" rating in a *Consumer Reports* 2007 report.

The seat itself has nice features . . . you get two harness slots, an adjustable crotch strap, EPS foam for head protection and a machine washable pad. The base is adjustable and uses an all-steel connection for the seat—all that steel provides great safety, but

---

Mighty Big Controversy

In a past edition of this book, we recommended the Mighty-Tite car seat belt tightener, which removes slack and provides for a tighter car seat installation. It's $10 to $17 (web: skjp.com). Similar belt-tighteners are made by other companies. However, since our last edition, we noticed belt-tighteners like the Mighty-Tite are a bit controversial among safety advocates.

Their biggest concern about the Mighty-Tite: it might mislead parents into thinking the add-on belt tightener will make any car seat fit in any vehicle. As you've read in this chapter, there are simply some seats that don't work in some cars. Yes, you can check a web site like Car Seat Data (CarSeatData.org) to see what might work given your car's make and model, but sometimes you have to buy a seat on faith. The Mighty-Tite seems to promise that you can cheat car seat installation—enabling a tight fit even if you can't get the seat to work in a vehicle. Not true, say safety advocates— if a seat is incompatible with the back seat of a vehicle, no add-on product will fix it.

Safety advocates also blast the company's marketing tactics, which claim the Mighty-Tite passes federal crash standards. But those standard are written for seats, not add-on products, say advocates. And even Mighty-Tite's instructions say you should install your car seat according to the manufacturer's guidelines . . . which of course, should provide for a rock-solid fit, even without the Mighty-Tite. Car seat techs would rather parents learn how to correctly install a seat (or take it to a safety check) instead of using add-on products to shortcut the installation process.

So, what's the verdict on the Mighty-Tite? Well, we'd like to see some more testing on this product, preferably from a third-party to confirm add-on belt tighteners are truly safe. So, until that happens, we'll take a pass on recommending the Mighty-Tite.

FYI: The new LATCH system eliminates the need for any add-on belt tighteners like the Mighty-Tite—so if your vehicle is equipped with this system and you use a LATCH seat, this debate is moot for you!

---

makes the BASE quite heavy (in fact, the carrier is also heavy, weighing nine lbs.). You can buy a separate base for $40 for a second car or use the seat without the base in a car by strapping it in with the auto safety belt. All in all, this is a great seat—it scored well among our readers for ease of use. The downsides? The somewhat cheesy level indicator can get stuck, giving false readings. And the strange triangle handle takes a bit of getting used to.

While we will recommend this seat, let us warn you that Baby Trend is a flakey company to deal with: despite winning good reviews from several sources (including this book), Baby Trend often lets its seats run out of stock. Or it suddenly makes the seat only available as part of a travel system, paired with one of Baby Trend's inferior strollers. Part of this stems from Baby Trend's poor distribution—this seat is only sold in a handful chain stores (mainly, Babies R Us). While the recent good publicity for this seat will probably boost its visibility, we are still pessimistic Baby Trend will be able to keep it in stock.

We have also lowered this seat's rating a bit to reflect Baby Trend's customer service, or lack thereof. Unanswered emails, un-returned phone calls and a general "we don't care" attitude mar Baby Trend's brand.

Rating: B+

BABY TREND EZ-LOC ADJUSTABLE BACK

Comments: This seat is the same as the Flex-Loc above, but features a rigid or ISOFIX version of LATCH (the Flex-Loc has a flexible webbing-based LATCH like you see on most other seats). As of this writing, this seat was only sold as part of a travel system at Babies R Us.

Rating: B+

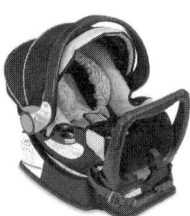

BRITAX COMPANION

Price: $200; extra base: $70.
Type: Infant seat, five-point harness.
Limits: 22 lbs., 30".
Pros: Anti-rebound bar, side-impact protection, EPS foam.
Cons: Price, low weight limit, not compatible with most strollers.

Comments: Britax's infant car seat is excellent: the Companion wins universal praise from other parents and safety techs. The anti-rebound bar, side-impact protection and ease of installation make this seat a solid, safe choice.

So why doesn't the Companion win our top recommendation? First, the price: at $200, it is nearly a $100 more than comparable seats. Next, consider the low weight limit: 22 lbs. makes the Companion less useful for bigger babies . . . and many competing seats now go to 30 pounds. Another bummer: the Britax Companion does not fit into most universal stroller frames. Hence, if you want to use this seat as a travel system, you'll have to pair it with one of Britax's strollers, which so far have been disappointing. Finally, this seat's carrier is HEAVY (a whopping ten pounds), which makes using it a hardy, upper-body workout.

Bottom line: get this seat if you have a smaller baby, don't care about pairing it with a stroller frame, have the strength to lift the carrier . . . and don't mind the $200 price tag.

Rating: A-

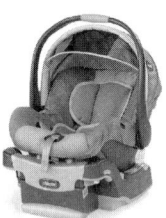

CHICCO KEYFIT 30

Price: $170, extra base $60.

Type: Infant seat, five-point harness.

Limits: 30 lbs., 30".

Pros: EPS foam, newborn insert, works with some Chicco strollers.

Cons: Doesn't work with most universal stroller frames. Skimpy sunshade.

Comments: The Chicco KeyFit scored at the top of *Consumer Reports* latest car seat report and that has helped propel the sales of this already popular seat into best-seller status. And it is well deserved.

The Chicco KeyFit boasts a nice list of features: a seat lined with EPS foam for improved side impact protection, thick seat padding,

---

Fabric vs. Model Names

When shopping for a car seat online, you'll note that some sites refer to seats by their fabric AND model name. For example, Amazon sells the Britax Granite Marathon. Britax is the manufacturer; Granite is the color or fabric pattern; Marathon is the model name.

Or sometimes Amazon and other sites omit the brand name altogether. As we went to press, Amazon was selling a Samba SafeSeat infant seat. This is made by Graco, but you won't see that in the title line. Again, Samba is the fabric name; SafeSeat is the model.

In this section, we refer to brands and models of car seats—since color or fabric patterns change frequently, we don't reference this. Just beware that a seat like the Graco Metropolitan SnugRide and Graco Family Tree SnugRide (as examples) are basically the same seat. Yes, the fabric might be fancier on one version, but you are talking the same basic seat! When we recommend a seat like the Graco SnugRide, we our recommendation applies to all the fabrics/versions of that seat.

---

multi-position canopy and comfort grip handle. Chicco hired a former Graco engineer who worked on the SnugRide to design the KeyFit and it shows in the details . . . the base has a "single-pull" LATCH adjustment, leveling foot to account for uneven back seats and even a smooth underside to keep from damaging your back seat upholstery. As you'd expect from Chicco, the fashion of this seat boasts Italian flair and there is even a newborn insert for a better fit.

FYI: Chicco makes two versions of the seat: the original KeyFit had a 22 pound limit. The KeyFit 30 has a (you guessed it) 30 pound limit. Between the two, we'd suggest the KeyFit 30 as it is only $10 more than the 22 pound version.

Our readers have been very positive about the KeyFit's ease of use, lauding the no-twist, easy-to-adjust straps, the ability to leave the handle in the up position when driving (most seats require it to be lowered), and overall ease of installation. Quibbles? The KeyFit carrier weighs nine pounds, a tad heavier than other seats. And the sunshade is too small.

New this year, the Chicco KeyFit 30 can fit into both Chicco's Cortina and (new) Trevi stroller. That's probably the KeyFit's key weakness: besides Chicco's own strollers, you can't fit the KeyFit into other strollers or stroller frames (which mostly work with Graco or Peg seats).

Between the Chicco KeyFit 30 and the Britax Companion, we give the edge to Chicco: their seat is $30 less expensive AND works up to 30 pounds (Britax is 22).

Rating: A

COMBI TYRO

Price: $100-$120; extra base $50.
Type: Infant seat, five-point harness
Limits: 22 lbs., 29".
Comments: Combi is phasing out this seat, but we still notice it is sold online as a clearance item. You can read an archived review of the Tyro on our web page (BabyBargains.com, click on Bonus Material).

COMBI CONNECTION & CENTRE / SHUTTLE

Price: $160-$180 (Connection), $110-$130 (Centre). Extra base: $50.
Type: Infant seat, five-point harness
Limits: 22 lbs., 29".
Pros: EPS foam, one-pull harness adjustment, nice padding.
Cons: Not easy to use.
Comments: The Combi Connection (top) and Centre (bottom) infant car seats have similar features: while the bases are slightly different, both have carriers with EPS foam for crash protection, comfort pads on the harness and one-pull harness adjustment.

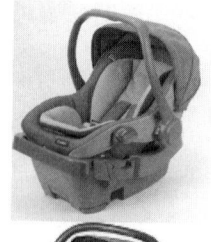

The Connection costs about $20 more than the Centre, but the Connection does add a bit more padding (Combi's "egg shock" foam in the head area) and an infant body pillow.

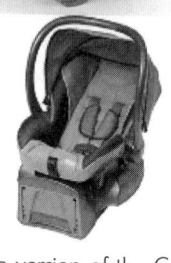

The Centre (also known as the Shuttle) comes in two trim levels, ST ($110) and DX ($130). The DX has a bit more padding and a deluxe canopy—but weighs a bit more as a result (9.9 pounds for the DX versus 8.6 for the ST). Given the choice, we'd skip the fancier padding, save $20 and go for the lighter weight carrier (ST).

Just to confuse you, Combi also sells a version of the Centre that is a Babies R Us exclusive: the Centre EX ($140) features even more padding and an anti-rebound bar. Combi appears to be phasing in the anti-rebound feature on this seat, as we also noticed some DX seats with the bar as well.

New this year, Combi is adding a anti-rebound bar to the Centre and re-christening it as the Shuttle. Other than this new bar, the Shuttle is very similar to the Centre (same weight limits, etc).

The big difference between the seats is which Combi stroller they work with—some Combi strollers work with the Connection as a travel system, while other models work only with the Centre. Yes,

SuddenStop

Driving around here in our home town of Boulder, CO, we have all manner of pedestrians and bicyclists who add new meaning to the word Kamikaze. Without warning, we'll have one of these daredevils throw themselves out in the street in the path of our car, forcing us to slam on our brakes. Of course, given the traffic in our town, this always puts us at risk at being rear-ended.

If this sounds familiar, one product we discovered may be a great solution: the SuddenStop license plate frame (web: SuddenStop.com). This $30 gizmo attaches to any license plate and rapidly flashes a bright red LED when you slam on your brakes. We saw a prototype of this product at a trade show and were impressed—the SuddenStop would make a great gift.

With over 2 million rear-end collisions a year in the U.S., we'd hope this technology would find its way into all vehicles.

Chocolate donuts with sprinkles?

Here's a confusing thing about car seat shopping: most car seat makers offer their models in a plethora of versions. At one point a couple of years ago, one infant seat maker had FIVE different versions of the same seat: the Classic, Plus, Elite, Supreme and the Extra Crispy. Okay, there wasn't an Extra Crispy, but you get the point. The key thing to remember: the seat was basically the very same seat in each configuration, just with minor cosmetic variations (an extra bit of padding here, a pillow there, etc). Yes, sometimes there are more significant variations like a five-point harness (versus three-point) or an adjustable base. But often there isn't much difference. Think of it this way: car seat makers produce a chocolate donut and top it with different color sprinkles–the rainbow sprinkle version goes to Wal-Mart, the green sprinkle donut goes to Target, etc. That way the companies can offer "exclusives" on certain "models" to large retailers, so the chains don't have the same exact offerings. But remember this: basically, it's the same donut. Bottom line: don't get caught up in all the version stuff. If the basic seat has the features you want, it doesn't really matter whether you buy the Plus or the Elite. Or the Extra Crispy.

leave it to Combi to sell a stroller frame (the Flash) that doesn't work with one its own car seats (the Centre). If you plan to pair a Combi car seat with a Combi stroller, it would be wise to surf Combi's web site to get the latest updates on compatibility.

In their most recent car seat report, Consumer Reports only tested the Centre, which scored at the bottom of their rankings. Why? Ease of use, or lack thereof. And our readers agree: the Centre has a hard-to-adjust handle, making the seat difficult to get in and out of car. Others knocked the flimsy canopy and hard to adjust belts. On the plus side, the Centre was easier to install . . . especially compared to the Connection.

As for the Connection, (with the exception of installation issues) parents were generally most positive in their ratings, although several noted the fabric started to pill and fuzz after just a few months of use. Unfortunately, the Connection tends to work only with Combi's more expensive strollers.

Combi's car seats are a prime example of what's wrong with this company: confusing, overlapping products that are overpriced and outmoded (note that Combi doesn't have an infant seat that goes to 30 pounds).

Rating: C

infant seats

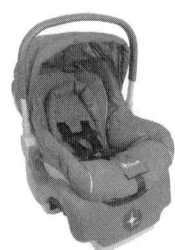

COMPASS I410 (VIA)

Price: $120

Type: Infant seat, five-point harness.

Limits: I410: 22 lbs., 30".

Pros: Carrier is completely lined with foam. Widest, deepest carrier. Light weight.

Cons: Must use carrier with base. Doesn't fit into shopping carts or stroller frames.

Comments: Compass is probably best known for their booster seats for older kids, but the company has been branching out lately: first with an infant seat and now a convertible (reviewed later in this chapter).

Now owned by Learning Curve, Compass' first effort this category-ry was the I400 (which later morphed into the I410). The 410, which is still sold online as of this writing, features a carrier entirely lined in EPS foam (yet still weighing only 8.4 lbs.), a padded handle, up front belt adjustment, washable pad, height adjustable base and more. We liked the built-in belt lock-off for non-LATCH installations and steel-on-steel construction for latching the carrier to the base (some cheaper seats use plastic hooks, which can break and have led to past recalls). While not the cheapest seat on the market, Compass is about $50 less than similar high-end seats by Britax and Peg Perego.

Compass plans to replace the I410 this year with an updated model: the Via. While similar to the I410, the Via will feature a shorter seat base, a more comfortable carrying handle and side-impact protection (courtesy of deep side wings).

While the Via wasn't out yet as we were going to press, we do have quite a bit of feedback on Compass I410 infant seat—and most of it is quite positive. Our readers give the I410 a thumbs up when it comes to ease of use—most liked the lightweight carrier, easy-to-adjust straps and built-in infant head support. The downsides? The skimpy canopy that always slides out of its plastic insert is a pain . . . and the Compass I410 can ONLY be used with its base (hence this isn't the best choice for urban dwellers who want to use it on the go in a taxi). Also: the Compass seat doesn't fit into shopping carts or universal stroller frames. As a result, you have to use the Compass infant seat with a one of Compass' strollers, which don't get very high marks.

As a side note, Compass makes an infant car seat for Inglesina as well. The I420 is nearly identical to the I410 seat so our rating would apply to both.

Bottom line: if you can still find the I410, it is a worthwhile choice. Our rating applies to the I410 (and I420); we'll wait for the new Via to debut before we assign a rating.

Rating (for the I410): A-

COSCO DESIGNER 22 *See the Eddie Bauer infant seat review later in this section. The Cosco Designer 22 is the same as this seat.*

EDDIE BAUER DELUXE (AKA DESIGNER 22, SAFETY 1ST STARTER)

Price: $100; extra base: $35.
Type: Infant seat, five-point harness
Limits: 22 lbs., 29".
Pros: Low price.
Cons: Recalled in 2006; problems with base.
Comments: Like most Cosco seats, the Eddie Bauer Deluxe infant seat is sold under a wide variety of aliases (the Designer 22, Safety 1st Starter, the Cosco Alpha Elite, etc.) . . . but the features are the same. Basically, this is a simple infant seat with the same features you see in most other seats on the market: an adjustable base, five-point harness, canopy, etc. The only difference: the Cosco version of this seat lacks a front adjustment to tighten the belts (that appears on all other models). What's missing? Side-impact protection, for one. EPS foam for additional crash protection (which is almost now a standard feature) isn't here either. Of course, this seat is sells for $90—that's about 30% to 50% less than seats with those features, so we guess you can call that a trade-off.

FYI: A scaled down version of this infant seat is sold as the Safety 1st Starter for $60 at Wal-Mart. A version of the Designer 22 with more padding is sold as the Safety 1st Designer for $70.

The Eddie Bauer Deluxe infant seat has seen its share of troubles in the past year. First, in 2006, Cosco recalled this seat for loose handle screws that were a choking hazard. Then Cosco launched a "customer satisfaction program" to handle complaints about the base not fitting in some vehicles. Notice we didn't say recall—Cosco changed the base and offered the fixed base to existing owners . . . but only if folks knew to call in and request it. Shame on Cosco— the company should have issued a formal recall and sent the new base to all registered owners.

Given Cosco's past safety record and troubles with this seat's base, we will take a pass on recommending this infant seat.
Rating: D+

EDDIE BAUER SUREFIT *See Safety 1st onBoard.*

EVENFLO DISCOVERY

Price: $45 to $60; extra base $25.
Type: Infant car seat, three-point harness.
Limits: 22 lbs., 26".
Pros: Lightweight carrier, low price. Z-shaped

infant seats

handle is easy to carry.

Cons: Not easy to use.

Comments: This bare-bones seat is sold in discount stores like Wal-Mart. The carrier (at 5.5 lbs.) is among the lightest on the market. And this year, Evenflo has added EPS foam to the seat (a few years after the competition). But . . . you don't get many features with this seat—the base doesn't adjust, there is just one crotch strap position and some versions of the Evenflo Discovery still have a three-point harness (although Evenflo is moving to a five-point harness for all models this year). Want to adjust the straps? You'll have to do that from the back of the seat, a major pain.

That probably explains how the Evenflo Discovery scored at the very bottom of *Consumer Reports* 2007 report on infant car seats—that report weighed ease of use heavily in their rankings. And our feedback from parents is similar: yes, this seat is cheap, but in this case, you get what you pay for.

Rating: D

EVENFLO EMBRACE

Price: $70-$90.

Type: Infant car seat, five-point harness.

Pros: Three-position adjustable base, easier to release base and handle.

Cons: Recalled in 2007 for faulty handle

Limits: 22 lbs., 29".

Comments: Here, in a nutshell, is why Evenflo is in last place in the car seat biz: the Embrace infant seat was supposed to a fresh start for Evenflo, after their last major car seat (the PortAbout) was recalled for failing a *Consumer Reports* crash test in 2005. The Embrace features a new, easier release mechanism for the carrier (this was a gripe for past models). The seat also has a three-position adjustable base and Z-handle with the "Press 'n' Go" system that releases the handle with one hand.

Yet, Evenflo had to recall 450,000 Embrace infant seats in 2007 after 679 reports of the handle of the carrier unexpectedly releasing, causing 160 injuries to children. (As a side note, 679 reports? 160 injuries? At what point did Evenflo think it was time to pull the plug?).

If that sounds familiar, then you may remember the massive recalls Evenflo suffered in the late 90's for their On My Way infant car seat with a very similar problem.

About the best we can say for this seat is a bit easier to install and use than the Evenflo Discovery . . . but that's not saying much. Given the past safety issues with this seat and Evenflo's track record, we say pass.

Rating: D+

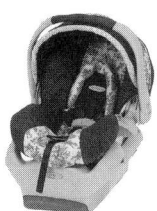

GRACO SAFESEAT

Price: $115 to $170 (average $130 to $150); extra base $45.

Limits: 30 lbs., 32".

Pros: One of the few seats to work up to 30 lbs. (great for bigger babies). EPS foam. Easy to use and install.

Cons: Heavy, bulky to carry.

Type: Infant car seat, five-point harness.

Comments: The Graco SafeSeat is part of Graco's new car seat line that includes a forward-facing toddler seat and booster. The key feature of the SafeSeat is its ability to work up to 30 pounds, joining the Chicco KeyFit 30 as one of the few seats on the market that works up to 30 pounds.

Why is that important? Well, babies are getting larger and heavier . . . and safety experts say it is best to keep a child rear-facing as long as possible. With some larger babies outgrowing a typical 22 lb. limit infant car seats as early as four months, the Graco SafeSeat will extend that time even for the largest of infants.

Our readers give the Graco SafeSeat high marks for ease of use: thanks to built-in safety belt lock offs, the SafeSeat is easy to install. And adjusting the harness is a snap. The negatives? The sunshade/canopy is wimpy. And the Graco SafeSeat is HEAVY (9.75 lbs. empty) and somewhat bulky (which is an unfortunate byproduct of the design to accommodate larger infants). Most parents found it to be manageable, but keep this in mind if you are petite.

Another small consideration: The Graco SafeSeat does not work with as many strollers brands as Graco's other infant seat (the SnugRide reviewed below). The SafeSeat DOES work with many Graco strollers and a few other brands—double check this before you buy the seat if you have your heart set on a specific stroller.

FYI: Graco makes several versions of the SafeSeat—one model goes for as little as $115, while others are near $170. The difference? Just the plushness of the fabric. And the most expensive SafeSeats add an all-weather boot and blanket. All SafeSeats feature EPS foam lining and a base with a dial adjustment for the proper angle.

Bottom line: this is a great seat. We highly recommend it.

Rating: A

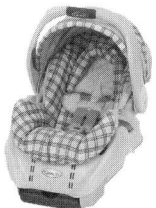

GRACO SNUGRIDE WITH EPS

Price: $72 to $150; extra base $33.

Type: Infant seat; comes in both three-point and five-point harness versions.

Limits: 22 lbs., 29".

Pros: Lightweight carrier (8 lbs.), level indicator,

canopy, easy to use. Front belt adjuster on some models. Works with many strollers.

Cons: Only one crotch position. Only works to 22 lbs.

Comments: Here is the country's top-selling infant car seat—and it deserves to be. The Graco SnugRide is an affordable (prices start at $72) infant seat with excellent features: EPS foam lining, adjustable base and good fit to most vehicles.

As for ease of use, our readers gave the SnugRide overall good marks. The few complaints centered on the "annoying" handle, which must be lowered when driving (it takes two hands). Parents with bigger babies rightfully complained their infants outgrew the SnugRide quickly with its 22 lbs. limit. And a few said that some fabrics (namely the Metropolitan) can get quite uncomfortable for baby in warm climates.

As always, Graco makes a zillion versions of the SnugRide, with the main difference being the fabric. A simple SnugRide in discount stores runs $72, while plusher versions with boot can top out at $150. One tip: newborns don't really care how much padding there is in the seat—that's really an issue for older kids in convertible seats. Hence, the less-expensive SnugRides are just fine.

What's missing? Well, the SnugRide does lack extra side-impact protection like you see on the Peg Perego and Britax seats (and even Graco's SafeSeat). And the seat lacks an anti-rebound bar, seen on the Britax seat.

On the other hand, one advantage to getting the ever-popular SnugRide: it is compatible with a wide range of strollers and stroller frames, much more than the Graco SafeSeat.

So, overall, this seat is a winner—good crash test ratings, excellent ease of use and features. Add in the affordable price and we have a winner.

Rating: A

INGLESINA FUCCO *This is the same seat as the Compass 1410 but called the 1420. See earlier review.*

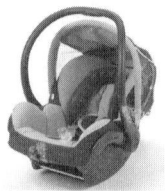

MAXI COSI MICO
Price: $170.

Limits: 22 lbs., 29".

Pros: Works with Quinny strollers, EPP foam, four harness heights, deep side wings.

Cons: Pricey, not sold in many stores, low weight limit.

Comments: Cosco imports this seat from their European subsidiary, adapted for the US market and designed to work with the hot-selling Quinny strollers.

The Mico is so new that we haven't heard much from readers who have used it, yet what little feedback we've had is positive. The seat is easy to use and install; fans like the high-tech fabric and padding, plus the EPP foam (which is softer than the EPS foam you see on most other seats).

But . . . this seat's high price and low weight limits (basically, you are paying the same as a Chicco KeyFit 30 but only getting a seat that works up to 22 lbs.) is a bit disappointing. That tempers our rating a bit. And forget about finding this seat in discount stores— as of this writing, it is only in a handful of boutiques and web sites. **Rating: B**

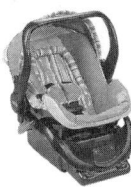

MIA MODA VIVA

Comments: New stroller maker Mia Moda launched this basic infant seat last year. The Viva sells for $100, works up to 22 lbs. and has EPS foam, three harness heights and a three-positioning reclining base. The carrier weighs only 7.5 lbs.

While we did see a sample of this seat at a trade show, there are few out there in the wild: we haven't heard any parent feedback on the Viva. Part of that may be the Viva's thin distribution: it is only sold online and at just few sites. New for 2008, Mia Moda plans to come out with the Viva Supra, which will add more padding. Given the lack of real world feed back, we don't have a rating for this seat yet.

ORBIT

Price: $900, as part of a travel system with stroller frame.

Limits: 22 lbs., 29″.

Pros: Well, it is stylish.

Cons: Did we mention it is sold as part of a travel system that's $900?

Comments: Orbit is a start-up company that aims to inject a bit of cache into the travel system market. Their first offering, the Orbit Baby Infant System, includes an infant car seat, in-car base and stroller frame that attempts a Bugaboo-like vibe. The infant car seat is a bit strange-looking (one parenting blog compared it to a crock pot), with an innovative soft-strap handle and rotating base. We liked Orbit's "SmartHub" base technology, that lets you "dock" the seat at any angle. The base also has a front knob that ensures a tight fit to the vehicle.

Given its high price, however, it's not surprising that we haven't heard much parent feedback on how the Orbit works in the real world. Yet those few reports have been positive: most love the technology, ease of use and ergonometric design. Detractors point out the Orbit's heavy weight (the carrier is just a shade under 10 lbs) and large size means it is a tight fit in smaller vehicles.

Once your baby outgrows the infant seat, Orbit sells a stroller seat for another $180 that pops into the stroller frame.

Overall, we give Orbit kudos for its innovative features and clever design. But $900 for an infant seat and stroller frame? Sure you could buy the Orbit . . . or buy the Graco SnugRide infant seat for $100 plus Graco SnugRider stroller frame for $60–then take the $740 savings and start a college fund for your infant.

Rating: B

PEG PEREGO PRIMO VIAGGIO SIP

Price: $220 extra base: $70.

Limits: 22 lbs., 30". (2008 version works up to 30 lbs., 30 inches).

Pros: Matches Perego's hot-selling strollers. Side impact protection, auto harness adjustment, improved canopy, luxe fabrics.

Cons: Uh, it's $220.

Comments: Peg Perego has had much success in this category, despite its high price tag and an earlier model that had some noticeable flaws. Peg revised the Viaggio back in 2006 (note the added SIP tag), aiming to fix the first seat's shortcomings. The SIP version of the Viaggio features side impact protection, an automatic adjustable harness and better canopy, which are all welcome improvements. Also new: the Viaggio can be used with or without the car base. Like the old seat, the Viaggio features plush padding, luxe fabrics and an adjustable base.

New for 2008, Peg plans to release a revised version of the Primo Viaggio that will work up to 30 lbs., and features a redesigned handle release and added side-impact protection. The new seat, dubbed the Viaggio 30/30 will be a whopping $250.

As for ease of use, most of our readers give the Viaggio good marks, although not quite as high as the Graco SafeSeat or SnugRide. Negatives include a bulky, heavy carrier for the SIP version (10.8 lbs.) and we can only imagine the 30/30 version will weigh even more.

Obviously, the price of the Viaggio is its biggest drawback–at $220 for the SIP version and $250 for the 30/30, it is more than *twice* the price of Graco's excellent SnugRide. If you're going to invest these bucks, we'd suggest the 30 pound version for its longer use. But beware when shopping for the new version: we'd guess there will be many Viaggio SIP (22 lbs.) out there at discount prices once the new seat arrives. It might be confusing as to which is which.

Rating: A-

QUINNY *See Maxi Cosi.*

RECARO PICCO

Comments: Recaro plans to debut an infant seat in 2008, although details were sketchy at press time. We did see a prototype of the Picco at a trade show: it will feature an anti-rebound bar (like the Britax Companion) and a $170 price tag. No word yet on the weight limits. Stay tuned to our blog for details.

SAFETY 1ST DESIGNER 22 *This is the same as the Eddie Bauer seat, reviewed earlier in this section.*

SAFETY 1ST ONBOARD

Comments: This new car seat from Safety 1st will debut in spring 2008. Features include a special insert for preemies (you can use the onBoard from four pounds and up), EPS foam and four harness heights. Price: $100 or part of the new Helix Travel system. FYI: The Eddie Bauer SureFit ($120) is the same as the Safety 1st onBoard.

SAFETY 1ST STARTER/DESIGNER

Price: $60-$70

Comments: This seat is the same as the Eddie Bauer Deluxe (Designer 22) reviewed earlier in this chapter.

◆ *Car beds.* How do you transport a preemie home from the hospital? The smallest infants may not be able to sit in a regular infant seat—in that case, a "car bed" enables an infant to travel lying down. Check with your hospital—some rent out car beds for preemies for free (one mom said she had to pay a $50 deposit, refundable when she returned the car bed). If you have to purchase a car bed, we'd recommend the **Cosco Dream Ride** ($70-$130, rating: A). Also: EliteCarSeats.com sells the **Angel Guard AngelRide** infant car bed for $100—it can be used for premature infants up to nine pounds. FYI: ALL premature infants should be given a car seat test at the hospital to check for breathing problems—ask your pediatrician for details.

Convertible and Forward Facing-Only Car Seats (model by model reviews)

ALPHA SPORT/ALPHA OMEGA THREE IN ONE

See Eddie Bauer Three In One convertible seat.

BRITAX BOULEVARD
Price: $300.
Type: Convertible, five-point harness.
Limits: 5 to 33 lbs. rear facing, 20 to 65 lbs. forward facing, 49″ tall.
Pros: Same as the Marathon (see page 409), but seat adds height-adjuster knob. Additional side impact protection with headrest.

Cons: Price. Big seat—may not fit into smaller vehicles. EPS foam only in headrest.

Comments: This seat is virtually the same as the Marathon (see later review), with two significant differences. First, you get a height adjuster knob that lets you make numerous adjustments to the harness heights (instead of being stuck with the four positions you see in the Marathon). Hence, you don't have to re-thread the belts every time your child grows. The second difference is what Britax calls "true impact protection." Basically, this is a reinforced headrest lined with EPS foam that protects your child in a side-impact collision. The first version of this seat (called the Wizard) had a headrest that many felt was too restrictive, so Britax revised the headrest to make it wider. Britax also added an infant pillow, like the Decathlon.

According to reader feedback posted to our web site, parents give the Boulevard high marks for ease of use. The only major drawback: you can only use a tether strap with this seat to 50 pounds. Britax issued a recall on the Boulevard in 2006 for this very reason—the Boulevard's tether broke when tested with a dummy that weighed over 50 lbs.

So, should you shell out $300 for the Boulevard? Given the tether issue, we'd say go for the Marathon if you'd like a seat that goes to 65 pounds with a five-point harness.
Rating: B

BRITAX DECATHLON
Price: $285
Type: Convertible, five-point harness.
Limits: 5 to 33 lbs. rear facing, 20 to 65 lbs. forward facing. 49″ tall.
Pros: Use up to 65 pounds, can be tethered rear- or forward-facing, adjustable crotch strap, plush padding.

Cons: Expensive. Very tall seat, which can block rear view in some cars. Some complain the harness is hard to adjust.

Comments: The Decathlon is a slight evolution of the more widely available Britax Marathon. Like the Marathon, the Decathlon works up to 65 pounds, can be tethered front or rear facing and has the HUGS strap system (read the Marathon review for the pros and cons of HUGS). So, what's different? And why is this seat about $30 more than the Marathon? Well, the Decathlon includes an infant body pillow, which the Marathon omits. So if you plan to use this seat from birth or you have a small infant that is graduating from their infant seat, the pillow may make for a better fit. The other key difference: the Decathlon has an automatic harness adjustment—basically a button you push to adjust the straps. While that sounds like a plus (the Marathon has a manual strap you pull on), parents give mixed reviews to the push-button harness adjustment. Some find it difficult to use (the button is stiff to press), while others say it is fine. Spend a few minutes with it in the store to see what you think before buying this seat.

Other than that, the Decathlon and Marathon are twins—and that means the Decathlon is just as tall as the Marathon. It may not fit well into the back seat of a small car . . . or your rear-view may be obstructed by the seat (depending on the vehicle). One plus for the Decathlon: you can use a tether to 65 pounds (if your vehicle allows this), unlike the Boulevard, which has a 50-pound limit.
Rating: B+

BRITAX DIPLOMAT
Price: $260
Type: Convertible, five-point harness.
Limits: 5 to 33 lbs. rear facing, 20 to 40 lbs. forward facing. 40″ tall.
Pros: Similar to the Roundabout, but adds side impact protection. Comfort foam, body pillow.
Cons: Can only use up to 40 lbs.
Comments: The Diplomat is basically the same as the Britax Roundabout—for an extra $40, you get side-impact protection wings and an infant body pillow. Realizing that its Marathon/ Boulevard seats are too big to fit rear-facing in the back of smaller cars, the Diplomat offers a compromise: you get the side impact protection of the Boulevard . . . but the smaller size of the Roundabout. The big trade-off: this seat only works up to 40 lbs.
Rating: A

BRITAX MARATHON
Price: $270.
Type: Convertible, five-point harness.
Limits: 5 to 33 lbs. rear facing, 20 to 65 lbs. forward facing, 49″ tall.
Pros: Up to 65 pounds with a five-point harness. Plush pad, EPS foam, same pros as Roundabout.

convertible seats

Cons: Did we mention it is $250? Taller, wider than the Roundabout—hence sometimes doesn't fit in smaller cars. Some parents don't like the HUGS harness system.

Comments: The Britax Marathon is one of the few convertible seats on the market that goes to 65 pounds—the pitch here is that older kids are safest when left in a five-point harness, versus a belt-positioning booster. According to sales data, the Marathon is the top-selling convertible seat at chain stores like Babies R Us.

While we like this seat, there are several flaws with the 65-pound pitch. First, when does the average child hit 65 pounds in weight? The answer: between ages nine and ten. If you think you can use this seat until your child is in the fourth grade, don't kid yourself. A child will not want to ride in a "baby seat" at that age.

There are more practical limits to the Britax Marathon. First the top harness slot is just 18", only two inches higher than the Roundabout. Odds are, your child may outgrow this seat by HEIGHT long before they hit anywhere near 65 pounds. In fact, Britax limits the Marathon's use to kids under 49 inches tall, which undercuts their own 65-pound pitch. (On average, kids hit 48 inches around age 7).

We suspect parents pick a Marathon based on the false perception of how fast their child will grow. Babies triple their birth weight in the first year—hence a seven-pound newborn should be a hefty 21 lbs. by their first birthday. By age two, that same child will be 28 lbs. You can forgive parents for thinking that a 40 lb. seat might be too restrictive for junior . . . yet the fear their child will continue to grow fast is misplaced. After age two, most kids' growth slows dramatically—most only gain four pounds a year after age two!

Bottom line: most kids will outgrow a 40 lb. convertible seat around age four; if you go for the Marathon, it is possible you will be able to squeeze another year or two of use out of the five-point harness. While we would agree that keeping your child in a five-point harness as long as possible is preferable, don't harbor any illusions that you will use this seat until your child is age ten.

So, who really needs a Marathon? If your child is above 50% on their growth curves, the Marathon may have value. But it still won't prevent you from having to buy a belt-positioning booster when your child outgrows it, as most states now require a booster seat up to age eight.

Another important consideration: you must have a vehicle that can fit the Marathon. It is bigger/wider (it's 19.5" wide and 28" tall) than the Roundabout and hence may not fit into some smaller cars (go to carseatdata.org to see which vehicles work and which ones don't).

And let's talk about the HUGS system, which appears on the Marathon. Britax says this harness system is designed to "better distribute webbing loads to reduce head movement and minimize the chance for webbing edge loading on the child's neck in the case of an impact. In addition, it is designed to reduce the chance of improper positioning of the chest clip."

The first version of HUGS generated many complaints from parents, who said it didn't fit larger children and was confusing to use. Britax has subsequently fixed HUGS by coming out with larger HUGS straps and clarifying its use in the seat's instructions.

The Marathon hasn't changed much in the past year so if you find last year's version (or a discontinued fabric) on sale, we'd say go for it. As for ease of use, parents give this seat top ratings, according to reviews posted to our web site. With the exception of this seat's large size and cost, most parents are happy with their Marathons.

As for crash tests, the Marathon earned lower marks than the Roundabout in *Consumer Reports*, notably scoring only a "good" when crash-tested with LATCH in rear-facing mode. The seat scored "excellent" when tested forward-facing with LATCH; and "very good" when tested with vehicle belts.

All in all, we recommend the Marathon—IF you have a vehicle in which it can fit! We are raising our rating of this seat, based on reader feedback.

Rating: A-

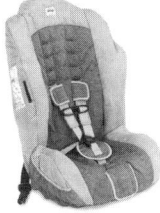

BRITAX REGENT
Type: Forward-facing seat.
Weight range: 22 to 80 pounds.
Price: $270.
Pros: One of the few seats that works with a five-point harness up to 80 pounds.
Cons: Very wide and heavy.

Comments: Ah, the power of YouTube.com—witness the case of the Britax Regent and its sudden popularity. In an emotional video posted to YouTube in 2006, a mother who lost her son in a car accident recounted the story of when their vehicle was broadsided and flipped upside down in a ditch. The child, who was sitting in a belt-positioning booster, died when he was ejected out of the car. The gist of the video: the parents believed the seat belt failed and their child would have survived if he was sitting in a harnessed seat, secured to the vehicle by LATCH. At the end of the video, the parents suggested the Britax Regent as just such a seat.

Well, a million views later, the video became legendary, sparking debate among car seat advocates as to its accuracy (we detail the debate on our blog). And faster than you can say YouTube, the sales of the Britax Regent zoomed into the stratosphere (selling out in some stores).

As it turns out, this isn't the first time the Regent has been in short supply. Debuting in 2001 as the Super Elite (and then dubbed, believe it or not, the Husky), the Regent has always been hard to find in stores—industry wags have openly speculated that Britax has intentionally kept production down on this seat to stoke demand.

Despite the hype, the Regent is a basic forward-facing seat (that's right—it can NOT be used rear-facing for kids under a year). It works from 22 to 80 pounds with a five-point harness . . . and that's the key feature that separates the Regent from other "toddler" seats. While "combo boosters" have a five-point harness, most can only use the harness up to 40 pounds. The Regent goes up to 80.

There is a catch to this, however: the Regent's instructions prohibit securing the seat with LATCH over 48 pounds. That means you have to use the vehicle's safety belt to secure the seat. And some vehicles have even lower limits on the weight of a child in a seat when secured with LATCH (Honda is 40 pounds). This sort of defeats the entire point of the YouTube hysteria, which speculated LATCH is a safer way to secure a seat like the Regent.

And beware that the Regent requires the *use of a tether beyond 50 pounds*. That means you won't be able to use it in some older vehicles, which lack tether anchors.

Finally, be aware that the Regent is a monster, size-wise—at 28 inches high, it is three inches taller than the Marathon. And it is 21.5 inches wide, among the biggest on the market. Therefore, you can forget about squeezing this in a smaller (or even mid-size) vehicle. Bottom line: while we do recommend this seat, we like two other competitors (the SafeGuard Go and Radian 80) as better (and more affordable) bets for toddlers. These seats are reviewed later in this chapter.

Rating: B

BRITAX ROUNDABOUT

Price: $220.

Type: Convertible, five-point harness.

Limits: 5 to 33 lbs. rear facing, 20 to 40 lbs. forward facing. 40" tall.

Pros: Excellent features—EPS foam, no-twist straps, can be tethered rear- or forward-facing, easy to adjust harness, double-strap LATCH, nice colors.

Cons: Harness slot a bit too high for smallest infants.

Comments: Here it is, folks—our pick once again as one of the best convertible seats. Yes, it is expensive, but you get a boatload of extras that make the seat easy to use . . . if the seat is easy to use and adjust, odds are folks will use it correctly.

Britax sells the Roundabout (and all its seats) on its safety record. Part of that safety advantage is rock-solid installation and this is where Britax excels—the lock-off clips provide snug belt install and Britax's double-strap LATCH connectors are among the best in the business. We also found Britax's harness to be easy to use and the straps don't twist. Finally, we should mention that you can tether the Roundabout either rear or forward facing, a key safety advantage. Crash tests bear that out—*Consumer Reports* recently rated this seat as first overall in their most recent report (2007) on convertible seats.

So, what are the downsides? These are mostly minor quibbles. The lowest harness slot (10") is too tall for the smallest infants, even though this seat is rated for use from five pounds and up. Other seats like the Evenflo Triumph (8.0") and the Graco ComfortSport (8.5") have lower harness slots and hence would be a better choice if you decide to forgo the infant seat and just buy one convertible. Another slight problem: the Roundabout is a bit wide—1" to 3" inches wider than other competing seats. Not a big deal . . . except if you try to take this seat on an airplane. While the FAA has approved the Roundabout for aircraft use, it may be a tight squeeze on some airlines. Finally, we should note that Roundabout uses a push-button harness adjustment, similar to the Decathlon. . . but for some reason, we don't get as many complaints about this for the Roundabout compared to the Decathlon (see earlier review).

One final caveat: the Roundabout has a 40 lb limit. As we discussed in the Marathon review above, parents of babies who at or above the 50th percentile of height/weight may want to consider a seat that goes to 65 pounds—that would mean a Marathon, not a Roundabout.

All in all, this is an excellent seat. Parents laud its comfort features and safety (EPS foam lines the child's head and torso area, while the seat has an extra layer of "comfort foam"). We give the Britax Roundabout our highest rating.

Rating: A

COMBI ZEUS

Type: Convertible
Weight range: 5 to 22 lbs. rear facing, 20 to 40 lbs. forward facing,
Price: $300
Pros: Base rotates from rear to forward facing without reinstallation.

Cons: 22 lbs. rear facing is too low.

Comments: Combi has retired its previous convertible models (the Avatar and Victoria) and plans to launch a new entry (the Zeus, $300) by the time you read this. The Zeus' most unique feature will be a turnable base—you will be able to flip the seat from rear to forward-facing without reinstallation. While that is nifty, we were dismayed to learn the Zeus will only be rear-facing to 22 pounds. Nearly every

convertible seats

convertible seat on the market works to 30 or 35 pounds rear-facing. That's important because safety advocates advise a baby should ride REAR-facing until one year of age—that 22 lb limit will force parents to turn around their babies long before a year in most cases. So despite the fact that this seat has some nice features (an anti-rebound bar, for example), the 22 lb rear-facing limit is a deal killer.

Rating: F

COMPASS TRUE FIT

Type: Convertible

Weight range: 5 to 35 lbs. rear facing, 20 to 65 lbs. forward facing,

Price: $190

Pros: Headrest pops off for easier rear-facing installation. EPP foam, easy-off pad for hand-washing, affordable price.

Cons: None.

Comments: The True Fit is Compass' first convertible seat and should be out by the time you read this. We saw a prototype and were impressed: the True Fit's most amazing feature is a headrest that pops off. That will make the True Fit easier to install rear-facing in smaller vehicles (you won't need the headrest for newborns riding rear-facing). We also like the automatic harness adjustments (no rethreading), side-impact wings, a seat entirely lined with EPP foam and three crotch positions to adjust for growing babies. Add in the 65 lb top weight and an affordable $179 list price and we have a winner!

Like the Sunshine Kids Radian seats, the True Fit will not have a base—this enables the seat to be deeper on the inside without increasing its overall dimensions.

Since this seat wasn't out yet as of press time, we don't have a rating yet.

Rating: Not yet.

COSCO ALPHA OMEGA *See Eddie Bauer Three in One.*

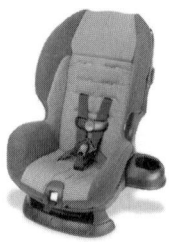

COSCO SCENERA

Price: $50

Type: Convertible, five-point harness.

Limits: 5 to 35 lbs. rear-facing, 22 to 40 lbs. front-facing.

Pros: Affordable car seat for a second car.

Cons: Avoid overhead bar shield

Comments: This simple seat is our top pick for that little-used car or Grandma's vehicle. The Scenera isn't fancy: you get a five-point harness with four height positions and three crotch slots. The padding is very simple and there isn't any EPS foam, side-impact protection or other goodies. But then again, this seat is just $50—perfect when you need an affordable seat that is easy to install and use. FYI: We do NOT recommend the bar-shield version of this seat (Scenera Versa), as we think it doesn't offer the best crash protection compared to the five-point harness.

Rating: B+

EDDIE BAUER DELUXE 3-IN-1

(a.k.a. Alpha Omega Elite, Safety 1st Alpha Omega Elite, Alpha Echelon)
Price: $160 to $180.
Type: Convertible, five-point harness.
Limits: 5 to 35 lbs. rear-facing, 22 to 40 lbs. front-facing, 30 to 100 lbs. as a booster.

Pros: It's an infant seat! It's a convertible! It's a booster!

Cons: Twisty straps. Poor recline. And much more!

Comments: This best-selling seat is sold under a zillion aliases, as you'd expect from Cosco. It is marketed under the Eddie Bauer, Safety 1st, Cosco and Alpha brands in a variety of price points and spin-offs. We've seen it in a stripped-down version for $100 at Costco . . . and deluxe version for $200 online. A typical offering is the tricked-out Eddie Bauer version sold for $170.

The pitch for this seat is simple: you can use it from birth to college. Ok, perhaps not college, but this seat aims for a triple play: rear-facing for infants up to 33 pounds, as a convertible with five-point harness up to 40 pounds . . . and then as a belt-positioning booster up to a whopping 100 pounds for toddlers and older kids.

The problem: it just doesn't live up to the hype. It is poorly designed, hard to use and expensive. Our reader feedback hasn't been kind to this seat: readers knock the instructions as "vague and confusing," the belts are hard to adjust in the rear-facing mode and the straps are so thin they constantly get twisted and snagged. Yet another problem: the highest harness slot in this seat (14.5") is a full inch lower than other seats like the Britax Roundabout. Why is this a problem? That low slot means some parents will be forced to convert this seat to booster mode too soon for larger children.

As for safety, this seat scored better in crash tests with LATCH than just with a safety belt. *Consumer Reports* latest tests pegged this seat as only "good" (most other seats in this price range scored "very good" or "excellent") for crash protection with a safety belt. And we're disappointed that this seat doesn't have EPS foam or side impact protection. Considering this seat is only $40 less than a Britax Roundabout, you clearly aren't getting the same value or ease of use.

FYI: Cosco makes two versions of this seat: the Alpha Omega

convertible seats

and the Alpha Omega Elite. While similar (both have EPP foam), the Elite goes to 100 pounds as a belt-positioning booster (the regular Omega is 80) and adds armrests and an adjustable headrest.

Bottom line: despite its pitch, this seat is too expensive and hard to use.

Rating: D

◆ *Other Cosco models:* The *Safety 1st Uptown* is a $100 convertible seat sold at Wal-Mart. This Uptown works up to 40 pounds and has EPP-type foam for seat padding and crash protection. EPP foam is more rubbery, while the better known EPS foam is rigid (as you see in bike helmets).

Also: the *Cosco Tote 'N Go*, a portable seat for taxis, is discussed on page 387.

EVENFLO TITAN

Price: $70 to $100

Type: Convertible; comes in five-point and bar-shield versions.

Limits: 5 to 30 lbs. rear-facing, 20 to 50 lbs. forward-facing.

Pros: Value, excellent crash tests.

Cons: Hard to clean cover and adjust straps.

Comments: Here's another seat to consider for grandma's car—the Evenflo Titan is a bare-bones seat where the price ($70) is right. Nothing fancy here: you get a five-point harness, four shoulder positions and simple padding. While we weren't wild about Evenflo's Triumph, the Titan shows how simpler is sometimes better.

FYI: Evenflo makes several versions of the Titan, including a Titan Deluxe (pictured) that adds more padding, a head pillow, cup holders and so on. But at $100, it is too pricey. If you plan to use this as a secondary car seat, save the $30 and just get the basic version.

Like the Cosco Scenera, the Evenflo Titan has no side-impact protection, fancy padding or EPS foam, but, hey, it's affordable. The big gripe we heard from parents on the Titan were the straps—some found the harness hard to adjust, especially when the seat is rear facing. So we will caveat our review: the Titan is probably best as a seat for kids over a year (and not riding rear-facing).

New for 2008, Evenflo plans to up the Titan's weight limit to 50 lbs.

Rating: B+

EVENFLO TRIUMPH ADVANCE

Price: $130 to $170.

Type: Convertible seat; five-point harness

Limits: 5 to 35 lbs. rear-facing, 20 to 50 lbs. forward-facing.

Pros: Special harness "remembers" last setting, EPS foam, up-front five-position recline and harness adjustment (no re-threading). Half the price of Britax.

Cons: Tension knob is hard to adjust when seat is in rear-facing mode. Wide base may not fit in smaller cars. Only can use the top harness slot when forward facing, making the seat difficult to use for larger (but young) infants. A litany of gripes from parents about this seat's usability.

Comments: We gave high marks to this Evenflo seat in our last edition, but a steady stream of complaints from parents has led us to revaluate our rating. Yes, it is feature-packed and a good value (it costs 50% less than a Britax Roundabout). This well-padded seat has several innovative features: among them, a cool "TensionRight" that lets you tighten the harness with a knob at the side of the seat. Also neat: the "Infinite Slide" harness system that lets you adjust the height of the harness without threading the belts. Yep, that is the same feature you see on the Britax Boulevard . . . for $150 less here.

So, what's not to like? While most parent reviews on the Triumph are positive, there is a sizeable minority that are not happy. First, this is a BIG seat—19.5" in width. That's 2-3" bigger than most other car seats and as wide as the Britax Marathon (but that seat can be used up to 65 lbs.; the Triumph stops at 50 lbs.). As a result, you may not be able to fit it in smaller vehicles. Another problem: the neat-o adjustment knobs that are placed up front. When the seat is in rear-facing mode, these neat-o knobs are impossible to access (as you might guess).

In fact, all this seat's whiz-bang features frustrate a good many parents, who find them hard to use or master. And the seat is quirky . . . when forward-facing, you can only use the top harness slot. Hence we received several complaints about this seat from parents of young (but big) babies, who didn't fit well in the Triumph. And removing the seat pad requires a screwdriver?! What is Evenflo thinking? So, this seat is hard to rate—on the upside, *when* it works for parents, it does well. Yet it is hard to ignore all the parent complaints about this seat posted to our web site. Our advice: if you buy it, keep the receipt and make sure the store has a good return policy.

New for 2008, Evenflo has debuted a new version of the Triumph: the Advance. Available in three trim levels (LX, DLX and Premier) the Advance now works to 50 pounds (older Triumphs only work to 40 pounds). Also new: EPP foam and improvements to harness adjustment system. While this seat just debuted as of press time, early reports indicate parents find it a bit easier to use then the older Triumph.

Rating: B

convertible seats

◆ *Other Evenflo models:* The Evenflo *Tribute I* ($60 to $75, rating: C-) is an overhead bar shield seat sold at chain stores like Sears and Baby Depot. We don't recommend bar shields (they aren't as safe as five-point harnesses, in our opinion), so we won't recommend this seat. We did notice that Wal-Mart and Target have a five-point version of the Tribute (Tribute 5) for $60.

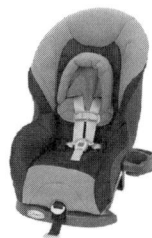

GRACO COMFORTSPORT

Price: $80 to $140.

Type: Convertible, five-point harness. (Wal-Mart has a version with an overhead bar shield, which we don't recommend).

Limits: up to 30 lbs. rear-facing, 20 to 40 lbs. forward-facing.

Pros: Front belt-adjuster, level adjuster, easy to use. EPS foam.

Cons: Cheaper versions have skimpy padding; average crash tests. Next to impossible to adjust straps in rear-facing mode.

Comments: In the last printing of our book, we picked the ComfortSport as a good convertible seat if you can't afford Britax. But given recent negative parent feedback, we've decided to give the simple seat crown to the Cosco Scenera, reviewed earlier.

Like most Graco products, the ComfortSport comes in a variety of configurations—from an $80 no-frills model in discount stores to a $140 deluxe version with fancy pad. The ComfortSport in most big-box baby stores is $80 to $100. (Be forewarned: there are three versions of this seat with a bar-shield, which we don't recommend).

Reader feedback on the ComfortSport has been mixed, trending negative in the past year. On the plus side, readers like the ComfortSport's smaller dimensions, which can fit easily into compact cars. And this seat is relatively easy to use when in forward-facing mode (yes, there is even a cup holder). But detractors say the harness is nearly impossible to adjust when the seat is rear facing. Others knock the skimpy padding, twisty straps and difficult harness adjustments. To top it off, the ComfortSport was recalled in 2007 for misrouted anchor belts.

Bottom line: this seat is showing its age—when even Evenflo ups the weight limit on their convertibles to 50 lbs. and competitors like Britax are busy adding side-impact protection, the ComfortSport now seems dated. And given the negative feedback from parents, we've decided to drop the ComfortSport's rating.

Rating: C+

GRACO TODDLER SAFESEAT (STEP 2)

Price: $130-190

Type: Forward-facing only, five-point harness.

Limits: 20 to 40 lbs. forward-facing.

Pros: EPS foam, five-position easy recline, deep side wings. EZ wash padding.

Cons: Can't use rear facing, so baby must be a year old. Only works to 40 lbs.

Comments: The Graco Toddler SafeSeat is part of the Graco's new three-step car seat program. With an infant seat (Step 1) that works up to 30 pounds, Graco's Step 2 seat is envisioned for toddlers older than a year of age who can ride forward facing. Hence the Toddler SafeSeat is NOT a convertible and won't work rear facing for infants.

We have been impressed with this seat and the feedback from parents—clearly, Graco has thought out the design features here and it shows. Example: you can remove the pad for cleaning WITHOUT removing the harness. The SafeSeat also includes items that are standard on more premium seats: EPS foam, deep side wings, plush padding and an easy-install belt path. We also like the seat's easy recline feature, which can be used even AFTER the seat is installed in your vehicle.

Compared to the ComfortSport, the Toddler SafeSeat Step 2 gets much better marks from readers for ease-of-use, installation and overall quality.

The only bummer: this seat just works to 40 lbs. (we wish Graco could have certified it to 55 or 65 lbs.). Yet Graco has priced the SafeSeat clearly for the middle part of the car seat market—$100 or so less than Britax. So we will give this seat our recommendation: the SafeSeat for Toddlers is a strong alternative to more expensive seats . . . if your child is over 20 lbs. and a year of age.

Rating: A

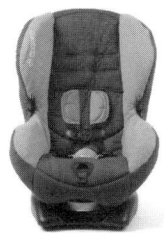

MAXI COSI PRIORI

Seat type: Convertible seat.

Weight range: 5 to 35 lbs. rear-facing, 22 to 40 lbs. forward facing.

Price: $200.

Pros: Five harness slots, padded buckle pads, EPP foam, upfront harness adjustment.

Cons: Only works to 40 lbs.

Comments: Maxi Cosi is Cosco/Dorel's European subsidiary—Cosco is bringing the Maxi Cosi brand to the U.S. as part of their strategy to give their brand a bit of Euro cache. It seems to be working: the Maxi Cosi Priori has earned good marks from readers in the short time it has been available stateside. Parents like the comfortable padding, easy LATCH installation and the four-position seat recline (nice for younger babies who are still napping). And yes, you can recline the seat while a baby is in it, a nice plus.

Bottom line: The Maxi Cosi is a decent alternative to the Britax Roundabout (both work to the same 40 pound limit) but the Priori is $20 less than the Roundabout.

Rating: A-

ORBIT TODDLER SEAT

Comments: Orbit plans to debut a convertible car seat in 2008—we saw a prototype of the seat, which will work up to 50 lbs. forward-facing (up to 35 lbs. rear-facing). The seat will also have EPP foam. Pricing has not been set, but it will be similar in price to Britax's offerings.

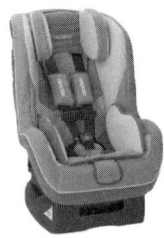

RECARO COMO

Seat type: Convertible.

Weight range: Rear facing 5-35 lbs., forward-facing 20-70 lbs.

Price: $250

Pros: Works to 70 lbs., adjustable headrest, EPP foam, side-impact protection wings. Higher harness slots than the Marathon.

Cons: May not fit rear-facing in smaller vehicles. Some kids may find the Como's head pillows too restrictive.

Comments: German car seat maker Recaro hopes to give Britax a run for its money with its new convertible, the Como. And yes, this is the first convertible seat to work to 70 lbs., five more pounds than Britax's convertibles.

Among the Como's unique features: side-impact protection wings made of cushy EPP foam. Similar to the Britax Boulevard, these wings provide both crash protection and head support for napping toddlers. The Como has many seat adjustments and the plush, microfiber fabric is impressive.

The negatives? Well, like the Britax Marathon, this is a big seat—it may not fit rear-facing into smaller vehicles. A few parents told us they found the Como's head pillows to be too restrictive for their older toddlers. And Recaro's thinner distribution (as of this writing, Recaro isn't in as many stores as Britax) means you may have to search for a local store that carries it to see the Como in person.

While this seat and parent feedback has been sparse, we will recommend it, given Recaro's track record for quality seats. With the initial positive reader reports, we think the Como will give Britax much needed competition at the high-end of the car seat market.

Rating: A-

RECARO SIGNO

Seat type: Convertible.
Weight range: Rear facing 5-35 lbs., forward-facing 20-70 lbs.
Price: $290
Pros: Similar to the Como, but adds infinite harness adjustment and additional head support.
Cons: No EPS foam lining the seat?
Comments: The seat is almost exactly the same as the Como, with two major differences: the Signo adds an infinite harness adjustment (like the Boulevard). And the headrest has additional support, plus infinite adjustments. We will give the Signo the same rating as the Como—the initial reader reports are positive and the features (including the 70 lb. limit) are impressive. The only negative: The Signo doesn't have EPS foam lining the seat, unlike the Como. Why Recaro omitted this is a mystery. (The Signo is much like the Britax Boulevard, which also omits EPS foam except in the headrest.) All in all, we would recommend the Signo.

Rating: A-

SAFEGUARD CHILD SEAT

Seat type: Forward-facing harnessed seat.
Weight range: 22 to 65 lbs. with harness.
Price: $400
Pros: Retractable harness, memory foam, special system to ensure tight LATCH fit.
Cons: Nope, that isn't a typo: the seat is $400.
Comments: Is the baby market ready for a $400 car seat? Well, folks didn't think Britax could sell seats for $200+ . . . but now Britax is the category leader as parents clearly voted with their dollars for more safety features. So, we imagine if folks will shell out $800+ for a Bugaboo stroller, perhaps a $400 car seat isn't that far-fetched.

Made by IMMI (see brand review of SafeGuard earlier in this chapter), the Safeguard Child Seat is impressive: its unique features include a retractable harness (like those in autos) and an impressive 65-pound weight limit WITH its five-point harness. Other Safeguard innovations include the "Posi-Latch" system that ensures a snug fit with LATCH. While some features of the SafeGuard are seen on Britax seats (the one-touch height adjuster for the harness is similar to the Boulevard/Decathlon), the overall impression here is quality and design detail. Note the memory foam, aircraft aluminum frame and color-coded knobs.

We were impressed with the SafeGuard's design—the generous 19" maximum harness height means kids will actually be able to use this seat up to 65 pounds.

Perhaps the biggest negative to the SafeGuard is its newness—it has not been independently crash-tested yet by *Consumer Reports*. Yet IMMI has two in-house crash test sleds (two more than most car seat makers), so we're sure this seat will perform well. We've also received little parent feedback on this seat's ease of use, again because it is so new. The few parents who have used it, however, have been impressed with the SafeGuard's incredible ease of installation. Yes, it costs a fortune, but the few parents who have used it say it is worth it.

Minor quibble: no one will accuse the SafeGuard of being the most fashionable seat on the market. Forget cutesy flowers or mod patterns—the SafeGuard has four rather dull color choices. And don't go looking for this seat in big chain stores—at the time of this writing, the SafeGuard was only available in a handful of indie stores as well as online (either direct from SafeGuardSeat.com or on EliteCarSeats.com).

Bottom line: based on the strength of its design alone and the track record of the parent company as a leader in car seat safety, we will give this seat our recommendation.

Rating: A

SAFETY 1ST ENSPIRA

(also known as Alpha 3-Phase, Eddie Bauer Deluxe Convertible)

Price: $100 to $120

Type: Convertible, comes in both bar shield and five-point harness versions. Converts to a belt-positioning booster.

Limits: 5 to 35 lbs. rear-facing, 22 to 40 lbs. forward-facing. 30 to 80 lbs. as a belt-positioning booster.

Pros: Two position recline. Converts to a belt-positioning booster for use up to 100 lbs.

Cons: Hard to install. Cosco's safety track record.

Comments: Similar to the Cosco/Eddie Bauer's Alpha Omega 3-in-1, the Enspira adds a two-position recline and extra padding. The Enspira comes both in a five-point harness and overhead bar-shield. You also get a few extras like a cup holder and removable harness pads plus a four-position adjustable headrest. Parent feedback on this seat is not very positive—many noted this seat's large size and (as a result) difficult installation; threading the belt in a rear-facing position vexed several parents. Again, Safety 1st/Cosco's poorly designed LATCH attachments make this seat difficult to install with LATCH. Yes, this seat converts to a belt-positioning booster, but as you read earlier in our review of the Eddie Bauer 3-in-1, we think this pitch is a bit overblown.

Rating: C

STROLEX SIT ´ N´ STROLL

Price: $200 to $220

Type: Holy convertible baby product, Batman! It's a car seat! And a stroller!

Limits: Birth to 40 pounds.

Pros: The only car seat that morphs into a stroller.

Cons: Doesn't function well either as a car seat or a stroller. Top harness slot is only 14″. Oddly, company recommends use for 20 pounds and up.

Comments: The Sit 'n' Stroll is made by Strolex Corporation (web: strolex.com), formerly known as Safeline, and has won a small but loyal fan base for its innovative car seat/stroller. With one flick of the hand, this convertible car seat morphs into a stroller. Like the Batmobile, a handle pops up from the back and wheels appear from the bottom. Presto! You've got a stroller without having to remove baby from the seat.

We've seen a few parents wheel this thing around, and though it looks somewhat strange, they told us they've been happy with its operation. We have some doubts, however. First, unlike the travel systems reviewed in the next chapter, the Sit 'n' Stroll's use as a stroller is quite limited—it doesn't have a full basket (only a small storage compartment) or a canopy (a "sunshade" is an option). We'd prefer a seat that reclines (it doesn't) and you've got to belt the seat in each time you use it in a car—even if you don't take it along as a stroller. Not only is installation a hassle, but the Sit 'n' Stroll's wide base (17.5″) may also not fit some vehicles with short safety belts or contoured seats. Plus, lifting the 14-pound car seat with a full-size child out of a car to put on the ground is quite a workout. Finally, we should note the seat's top harness slot is only 14″, much lower than other seats on the market today (that means baby will outgrow it that much quicker). And oddly, even though Strolex's web site says the car seat can be used from birth to 40 pounds, "we recommend 20-40 pounds." No word on why this is!

So, we're not sure we can wholeheartedly recommend this seat. Yes, we do hear from flight attendants who love their Sit 'n' Stroll—it wheels down those narrow plane aisles. So, it's a mixed bag for the Sit 'n' Stroll. For frequent fliers, the Sit 'n' Stroll is probably heaven-sent. Yet, like many hybrid products, it is not great at being either a car seat or a stroller.

FYI: As we were going to press, we noticed Strolex had just debuted the Strolex 2, which is like the Sit N Stroll but features an infant car seat that morphs into a stroller. The Strolex 2 is $188.

Rating: C+

SUNSHINE KIDS RADIAN 65 / RADIAN 80

Seat type: Convertible seat.

Weight range: 5 to 33 lbs. rear-facing, up to 65 or 80 lbs. forward facing. Maximum height: 49."

Price: $200 or $280

Pros: Folds up! Works to 80 lbs. with five-point harness. Great for airplane travel. EPS foam. Can use a tether rear facing.

Cons: Only works to 49" in height. Heavy weight. Biggest kids may find crotch strap too tight. Not as ideal for kids under one year of age riding rear-facing.

Comments: Sunshine Kids burst onto the car seat market a couple of years ago with their innovative Radian seat. It's unique feature: the Radian is the only car seat on the market that folds up! Yes, we can hear parents of kids in carpools applauding from miles around.

The Radian has another claim to fame: it is one of the few seats that can use a five-point harness up to 65 or 80 lbs. With all the interest in harnessed seats that work above the traditional 40 lb. limit, Sunshine Kids hit the market at just the right time.

FYI: The Radian comes in two versions—the Radian 65 ($200) works up to 65 lbs. And the Radian 80 ($280) works up to (you guessed it) 80 lbs. Both seats are quite similar: both Radians are lined with EPS foam, but lack the side impact protection wings you see in other models. This is a trade-off: the lack of head wings or side impact torso protection makes the Radian three inches wider in the shoulder area, again a plus for larger/older toddlers. Yet since the Radian's top height limit is 49", you'll probably have to buy at least a backless booster for the oldest kids to use before they can safely sit in the auto safety belt.

The Radian accomplishes its folding trick by omitting the base you see on so many convertible seats—the seat actually sits along the back of a vehicle's seat back. One plus to this: the Radian's narrow base allows for a three-across install in the back of a vehicle.

All in all, we are very impressed with this seat and think it gives Britax a run for its money (the Radian is about a $60-$80 less than Britax's 65 lb. limit models). Most of the parent feedback we've received on this model has been quite positive, however. The only complaint: the seat is quite heavy (at 20 lbs.)—so while it folds up for carpooling, it does require quite a bit of muscle to haul around. And the youngest babies (under a year, rear-facing) might not find the Radian as comfortable as other seats with side wings and more head support.

One major plus to the Radian: it is approved by the FAA for air-craft use, making it one of the few harnessed seats that can be used over 40 pounds on a plane. And the Radian can use a tether rear facing, which is rare in this market (Britax is one of the few other seats with this option).

FYI: The Radian 80 was a bit hard to find as we were going to press (EliteCarSeats.com carries it, among other sites). The Radian 65 seems to have a bit more distribution, including Target.com.

Rating: A

As you can imagine, the child safety seat world changes quickly—read our blog (BabyBargains.com) for the latest news, recalls and more with car seats.

Our Picks: Brand Recommendations

Here are our top picks for infant and convertible seats. Are these seats safer than others? No—all child safety seats sold in the U.S. and Canada must meet minimum safety standards. These seats are our top picks because they combine the best features, usability (including ease of installation) and value. Remember the safest and best seat for your baby is the one that best fits your child and vehicle. Finding the right car seat can be a bit of trial and error; you may find a seat CANNOT be installed safely in your vehicle because of the quirks of the seat or your vehicle's safety belt system. All seats do NOT fit all cars. Hence it is always wise to buy a seat from a store or web site with a good return policy.

FYI: See the chart on pages 424-425 for a comparison of features for both infant and convertible/front-facing car seats.

Best Bets: Infant car seats

Good. Let's be honest: if you're on a super-tight budget, consider not buying an infant car seat at all. A good five-point, convertible car seat (see below for recommendations) will work for both infants and children.

Better. The *Chicco KeyFit 30* is an excellent seat that works to 30 lbs. (fyi: the original KeyFit only worked to 22 lbs. and is still sold in stores). The KeyFit gets excellent scores from our readers on ease of use—installation is a snap and adjusting the harness is easy. The seat also features EPS foam and a newborn insert. The downsides? The seat is pricey at $170 and doesn't work with as many strollers as our top choice below.

Best. Tie: *Graco SnugRide* and *Graco SafeSeat.* Both of these seats are excellent, easy to use and install. Each features EPS foam. The key difference: weight limits. The SnugRide works only to 22 lbs., the SafeSeat is 30. So if you come from a family of six-foot tall folks, the SafeSeat is a better bet since you'll use it longer. The trade-off: the SafeSeat is heavier and bulkier (and $50 more expensive) than the SnugRide.

Dark Horses. Two other seats are also wroth considering: The *Compass 1410* (soon to the be the Via) and the *Peg Perego Primo Viaggio 30/30.* The Compass ($120) seat's wide and deep carrier, as well as the rock-solid design of the base impressed us. And if fashion is important, the Primo Viaggio is a very good seat that works up to 30 lbs. . . . and has the best selection of luxe fabrics, albeit at a steep price ($250).

Best Bets: Convertible & Forward-Facing car seats

Good. For a decent, no-frills car seat, we recommend the *Cosco Scenera*. Yes, we realize Cosco's safety track record has been rocky, but this seat is still worth considering for that little-used second car or Grandma's vehicle. The Scenera is a basic, bare-bones convertible that works to 40 lbs., is easy to install and costs $50—no, that's not a typo. With the prices of some car seats pushing $300, it's nice to know you can find a decent seat for just $50. Another good bet for Grandma: the *Evenflo Titan* ($70 to $100), which has a bit more padding than the Scenera.

Better. As its name implies. the *Sunshine Kids Radian 65* works up to 65 pounds and features EPS foam and a tether can work rear facing. At $200, the Radian 65 isn't cheap . . . but it also has another trick up its sleeve: it is the only car seat that can fold up. That's a plus for carpoolers. FYI: Sunshine Kids also makes a Radian 80 ($280) that works up to 80 pounds with a five-point harness, but is harder to find in stores or online. Bottom line: the Radian 65 is a winner.

Best. So, what is our top recommendation for convertible car seats? This year, we have a tie between two Britax seats: the *Britax Roundabout* and the *Britax Marathon*. Both seats feature an excellent five-point harness, EPS foam, no-twist traps, easy-to-adjust harness and a "double strap" LATCH system. Best of all, you can tether this seat either rear OR forward facing, for an extra measure of safety. The Roundabout ($220) works up to 40 pounds; the Marathon ($270) up to 65 pounds.

Since the Marathon is only about $50 more than Roundabout, should you just go for the Marathon? Well, before you buy a Marathon, consider the size of your car. The Marathon is three inches TALLER and 1.5 inches wider than the already big Roundabout—

that makes fitting in smaller vehicles a challenge (especially rear-facing). On the other hand, the Marathon is a good bet if you have a big baby (say, above 50% on their growth curves), as it will fit him or her longer with a five-point harness.

If Grandma is buying. What if money isn't an issue when buying a seat? One obvious seat that we'd suggest is the top-of-the-line *Britax Boulevard* ($300), which is much like the Marathon, but adds a height-adjuster knob (to better fit the harness to a growing child) and additional side-impact protection.

And then there is the ultimate in pricey but amazing car seats: the *SafeGuard Child Seat*. At $400, this seat is loaded with safety features such as a retractable harness and Posi-LATCH, which ensures a tight fit when installing with LATCH. Yes, it has the same 65 lb. limit as the high-end Britax seats, but adds memory foam, an aircraft-quality aluminum frame and more. The only negative: it isn't the most fashionable seat, available in four rather dull patterns. And the SafeGuard is hard to see in stores, as it is only sold in a handful of outlets as well as online.

Booster Seats

Now that your toddler has outgrown her convertible seat, what's the best booster? We'll review and rate the best option in this section, plus give you advice on how to get the best fit, the low down on seat belt adjusters and the new hybrid seats on the market.

Most parents know they have to put an infant or toddler into a car seat. What some folks don't realize, however, is that child passenger safety doesn't end when baby outgrows that convertible car seat—any child from 40 to 80 pounds and less than 4'9" (generally, kids age four to eight) should be restrained in a booster seat (or one of the new harnessed seats that work up to 80 pounds). And in some cases, booster seat use is mandated by law. Numerous states have passed laws requiring the use of booster seats. And more states are following their lead. Here's our look at the best and worst booster seats on the market today.

Getting Started: When do you need a booster?

Your child needs a booster seat when he outgrows his convertible seat. This happens when he exceeds the weight limit (typically

Continued on page 426

INFANT SEATS

The following is a selection of better known infant car seats and how they compare on features:

MAKER	MODEL	PRICE	WEIGHT/HEIGHT LIMITS
BABY TREND	FLEX-LOC ADJ. BACK	$80-$90	22 LBS./29"
BRITAX	COMPANION	$200	22 LBS./30"
CHICCO	KEYFIT 30	$170	30 LBS/30"
COMBI	CONNECTION/CENTRE	$110-180	22 LBS./29"
COMPASS	1410/VIA	$120	22 LBS./30"
EDDIE BAUER	DELUXE/DESIGNER 22	$100	22 LBS./29"
EVENFLO	DISCOVERY	$45-60	22 LBS./26"
	EMBRACE	$70-90	22 LBS./29"
GRACO	SAFESEAT	$115-170	30 LBS./32"
	SNUGRIDE	$72-$150	22 LBS./29"
MAXI COSI	MICO	$170	22 LBS./29"
PEG PEREGO	PRIMO VIAGGIO 30/30	$220	30 LBS./30"

CONVERTIBLE SEATS

The following is a selection of popular convertible car seats and how they compare on features:

MAKER	MODEL	PRICE	WEIGHT LIMITS (IN POUNDS)	
			REAR	FORWARD
BRITAX	BOULEVARD	$300	33 LBS.	65 LBS.
	DECATHLON	$285	33	65
	MARATHON	$270	33	65
	ROUNDABOUT	$220	33	40
EDDIE BAUER	DELUXE 3-IN-1	$160-180	35	100
EVENFLO	TITAN	$70-100	30	50
	TRIUMPH ADVANCE	$130-170	35	50
GRACO	COMFORTSPORT	$80-140	30	40
SAFETY 1ST	ENSPIRA	$100-120	35	40/80
SUNSHINE KIDS	RADIAN 65/80	$200-280	33	65/80

Infant seat chart:

SIDE IMPACT: Does the seat have side-impact protection?

HARNESS TYPE: Does the seat have a 3 or 5-point harness? "Both" means either type is available, depending on the model.

SIDE IMPACT	LEVEL IND.	HARNESS TYPE	BASE WIDTH	CARRIER WEIGHT	OUR RATING
YES	YES	5 POINT	16.5″	9 LBS.	B+
YES	NO	5 POINT	18.5	10	A-
YES	YES	5 POINT	15.25	9	A
NO	YES	5 POINT	17	8.6/9.9	C
YES	NO	5 POINT	16.5	7.6-9	A-
NO	NO	5-POINT	18	9	D+
NO	NO	3-POINT	17.5	5.5	D
NO	YES	5-POINT	18	N/A	D+
NO	YES	5-POINT	19	9.75	A
NO	YES	BOTH	17	8	A
NO	NO	5-POINT	17	8	B
YES	YES	5-POINT	17	10	A-

RATING	COMMENT
B	HARNESS HEIGHT ADJUSTER KNOB IS NICE, BUT THE PRICE.
B+	INCLUDES INFANT BODY PILLOW; AUTO HARNESS ADJUST.
A-	MUST RETHREAD BELTS TO ADJUST HARNESS HEIGHT.
A	EPS FOAM, NO-TWIST STRAPS, TETHER REAR OR FORWARD.
D	CONVERTS TO BOOSTER SEAT, BUT STRAPS ARE TWISTY.
B+	GOOD BARE-BONES SEAT, BUT HARNESS HARD TO ADJUST.
B	MEMORY HARNESS; CAN ADJUST BELTS WITHOUT RETHREAD.
C+	BEST BUY FOR BARE-BONES MODEL; GOOD FOR PLANES.
C	CONVERTS TO BOOSTER; HUGE SEAT CAN BE HARD TO INSTALL.
A	ONLY SEAT THAT FOLDS UP; CAN USE TETHER REAR-FACING.

LEVEL IND.: Does the seat have a level indicator for easier installation?

CARRIER WEIGHT: This is the weight of the carrier only (not the base).

Convertible seat chart: All of these seats have five-point harnesses.

40 pounds) or when he is too tall for the harness (his shoulders are taller than the top slots in the seat). For most children, this happens around ages three or four.

Parents in Cyberspace: What's on the Web?

We found several booster seat info resources online. Here are a couple to check out:

◆ **SafetyBeltSafeUSA** (www.carseat.org) has three good reports on booster seats (click on the button, Booster Seats) that explain proper installation and offer other tips. Another great site is CarSeatData.org.

◆ **The National Highway Traffic and Safety Administration** has an excellent online brochure on booster seats: "Boost 'em Before You Buckle 'Em." http://www.nhtsa.dot.gov/people/injury/childps/ Boosterseat/index.html. Also cool: the NHTSA now rates and reviews booster seats for ease of use and other factors. Go to: nhtsa.dot.gov/CPS/CSSRating/

Smart Shopping Tips

Smart Shopper Tip #1
Booster Laws

"My daughter just turned four, and my state doesn't require her to use a carseat anymore. She just uses the seat belt now."

A number of states have recently enacted stiffer car seat laws, usually requiring children to use "appropriate restraints" until age six or 60 pounds (some state laws are now up to age eight or nine and 80 lbs). But other states still only require car seat until a child turns four (some even just two) years old. So why should you continue to hassle with a car seat or booster after this time?

We like to remind parents that there is the law and then there is the law of physics. Car belts are made for adults, and children (as well as some short adults) just don't fit well, and don't get good protection from those belts. Lap belts used with four- to eight-year old children routinely cause such severe injuries and paralysis that the injuries even have their own name: "lap belt syndrome." Children using lap/shoulder belts often put the shoulder belt behind their back (since it is so darn uncomfortable), giving them no more protection than a lap belt alone. Ejections are another common problem with young children in adult belts, even if they are using both the lap and shoulder belt.

Booster seats (and of course regular car seats) work very simply to eliminate this problem. Boosters properly position the lap part of the belt on a child's strong hips, not their soft internal organs. They elevate the child and include a special adjuster so that the lap shoulder belt fits right on the strong shoulder bones. Booster seats should be used until a child fits the adult belts like an adult. Try out the 5 Step Test (later in this section) to see if your child is ready yet.

Smart Shopper Tip #2
Different seats, lots of confusion?

"When I was shopping for a booster seat, I was confused with all the types of seats out there. Why isn't there just one type of booster?"

Good question. We've noticed that buying a booster seat can be a bit more complex than buying another car seat. For example, an infant car seat is, well, an infant car seat. But a booster can come in several versions: high back boosters, backless boosters, combination seat/boosters, and more.

In this chapter, we'll try to simplify things a bit. Any time we refer to a *booster*, we mean a seat that uses the lap/shoulder belt to secure the child. Most other car seats (like convertible seats) use an internal harness to hold the child, while the seat itself is attached to the car with the seat belt or the new LATCH system.

What's made this so confusing is that car seat makers have blurred the lines between convertible seats and boosters in recent years by coming out with multi-purpose models—Cosco's Alpha Omega, for example, is a convertible seat that can be used for infants rear-facing 5 to 35 pounds, forward-facing harnessed from 20 to 40 pounds and THEN it becomes a booster to 80 pounds. Other makers, like Britax and Sunshine Kids, have debuted models that use a five-point harness for children up to 65 pounds—these seats are not boosters but new hybrid convertible seats, with top weight limits higher than the traditional 40-pound limit. And Britax has a forward-facing seat call the Regent that works to 80 pounds with a five-point harness

Confusing, yes we know. But we want this section to cover all the options for older children who've outgrown their traditional convertible seat . . . so you'll see a variety of options in this section. Let's break down what's out there:

◆ **Shield boosters:** These are what boosters USED to look like (see picture left). Most car seat companies stopped selling shield

boosters

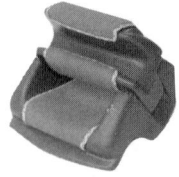

boosters in the mid 1990's when tougher crash standards were enacted. For some reason, however, we still see one shield booster (the Cosco Grand Explorer) sold online. Frankly, we think shield boosters are dangerous. "Cosco has been sued at least seven times because of injuries or deaths with its shield boosters, court documents show," reported *USA Today* way back in 2001. Yet Cosco says these shield boosters are needed for children who outgrow a convertible seat because of height but not weight (Cosco just recommends the shield booster for children between 30 and 40 pounds). Bottom line: we don't recommend shield boosters. If you have a child who is less than 40 pounds, keep him in a harnessed seat.

◆ **Hybrid/Combo seats:** These are probably the most confusing "booster" seats because sometimes they are a booster, and sometimes they aren't. They come with a five-point harness, which can generally be used up to 40 pounds. Then the harness comes off, and the seat can be used as a belt-positioning booster, usually to 80 or more pounds. They get the name "combination" or "combo" for short from the two jobs they do. What's great about these seats is that most of them have higher harness slots, so tall children can stay in a harness to a full 40 pounds even if they've outgrown their convertible height-wise. And then, after 40 pounds, the seat is still useful, converting to a booster that might be the last seat your child needs. Yes, there are a few combo seats with harnesses that can be used past 40 pounds, like the SafeGuard Go (more on this seat maker later) with a harness that goes to 60 pounds and then a backless booster after that to 100 pounds. The Britax Regent is a harnessed seat that works up to 80 pounds (with a five-point harness).

Combo boosters are great for children that have outgrown their convertible seats but aren't mature enough to sit in a belt-positioning booster (the types described below). The five-point harness provides that extra measure of safety and security while they are still young (typically, a child has to be three or older to be mature enough to handle the belt-positioners). Some combo seats start at just 20 pounds.

◆ **High back boosters (HBB):** These seats have often been called "small person's captain's chairs," which they kind of resemble. They are really simple, but provide vital safety features for children who've outgrown the harnessed seats. These boosters properly position the lap belt on

Harnessed seats that work beyond 40 lbs.

The following seats can be used with a five-point harness for kids who weigh up to 65 pounds (except as noted):

NAME	HARNESS HEIGHT IN INCHES	HIP WIDTH IN INCHES
Britax		
Boulevard	16.5"	11"
Decathlon	17	11
Marathon	17	11
Regent	20.5	13
Compass		
True Fit	**	**
Dorel/Cosco		
Apex	17	13.5
Graco		
Nautilus 3-in 1	**	**
Recaro		
Como (to 70 lbs)	19	**
Signo (to 70 lbs)	18.5	**
SafeGuard		
Child Seat	19	10
Go (harness to 60 lbs)	17.5	11
Sunshine Kids		
Radian 65	17.5	10.5

** *We don't have this dimension yet, as these seats were new as of press time.*

boosters

a child's strong hip bones, rather than letting it ride up on the soft internal organs. And they provide correct positioning of the shoulder belt, so the child can comfortably wear it and get critical upper body support. The high back also protects the child's head from whiplash if there are no head restraints in the vehicle, and the high back may also give some side sleeping support. ALL of these boosters require a lap and shoulder belt.

◆ **Backless boosters:** These work the same way as high back boosters—they just don't have a back. Safety-wise, these can be a bit better than a high back booster, since the child sits right against the vehicle seat. They do the same job positioning the lap belt, and usually include some sort of strap to adjust the shoulder belt. But they don't provide head support if you have low seat backs, and they don't give any side or sleeping support. On the other hand, they are often popular with older kids, since they can be quite inconspicuous. All of these also require a lap/shoulder belt.

◆ **Special Needs Seats:** There are a few seats on the market now that don't really fit into any category. One is the Britax Traveller Plus which is designed for special needs kids up to 105 lbs. (who can't sit in a regular seat). This seat has a five point harness.

Smart Shopper Tip #3
Avoid Seat Belt Adjusters
   "The shoulder belt was bugging my son's neck, so I bought a lit-tle adjuster thing. Is that as good as a booster?"

   Several companies make inexpensive adjusters ($10 or so), which help to properly position the shoulder belt on your child. Sounds good, right? Wrong. Look closely at the pictures on the box. In order to pull the shoulder belt down, and make it more comfortable for a short passenger, virtually all of these devices also pull the lap part of the belt UP, right back onto the tummy. Marketed to kids 50 pounds and up, these devices are also packed with statements that confuse even the most safety conscious parents, like "designed to meet FMVSS 213," a reference to a federal safety standard in crash testing. What's wrong with that picture? That federal standard doesn't even apply to items marketed for children 50 pounds and up! Worse yet, crash tests showed that a three-year-old dummy was less protected when using one of these adjusters compared to using the regular vehicle safety belt. When crash tested with a six-year-old dummy, the seat belt adjusters didn't improve crash protection either. So, bottom line, if your child doesn't fit that adult belt, get a booster.

Smart Shopper Tip #4
Cars with only lap belts
   "What if my car has only lap belts in the back seat?"

   While lap belts are just fine with infant and convertible seats, they are a no-no when it comes to boosters. If your vehicle doesn't have shoulder belts, check with your vehicle's manufacturer to see if they offer a retrofit kit. If that doesn't work, consider buying a newer vehicle with lap/shoulder belts in the back seat. In the meantime, there are a few seats that can be used with a lap belt for kids over

40 pounds. The Britax Regent, can be used up to 80 pounds, though it requires a tether after 50 pounds. The Britax Marathon and Wizard seats can be used to 65 pounds.

Smart Shopper Tip #5
LATCH system and boosters

"I have a car with the new LATCH attachments. Do booster seats work with this system?"

First, just what is LATCH? In a nutshell, LATCH is an easier way to attach a car seat to a vehicle—it is a series of buckles and hooks that latch onto metal loops installed in the seat back of all new vehicles. All car seats manufactured after September 1, 2002 must have LATCH attachments. So do booster seats work with LATCH? Yes and no. Basically, LATCH is only for seats using an internal harness. Some "combo" seats DO have LATCH attachments for you to use when using the internal harness; then you convert the seat to a booster (removing the internal harness) and secure your child with the vehicle lap/shoulder belt. Boosters without an internal harness (hence, most belt-positioning boosters) do NOT have LATCH—they don't need it. Check the seat's instructions before purchasing the seat to confirm LATCH compatibility.

Smart Shopper Tip #6
Back Harness Adjuster

"I loved our combo seat—until the day I discovered its fatal flaw. When it was cold, my daughter's thick coat required me to loosen the belts on her five-point harness. I discovered this could only be done from the BACK of the seat! What a pain!"

More and more booster seats are adding five-point harnesses so they can be used at younger ages/weights (some seats start at as little as 20 pounds). The problem? The cheapest combo boosters do NOT have up-front belt adjustments. You must adjust the belts from the back of the seat, which is a pain especially in cold weather. A word to the wise: if you get a combo seat, make sure the belt adjustments are UP FRONT and easy to access.

The question of coats/snowsuits and car seats comes up frequently—we should stress that most safety advocates suggest that a child in a safety seat wear a coat that is no thicker than a polar fleece (the Land's End Squall gets good reviews for this job). Big bulky coats are a hazard. Why? In the event of a crash, the coat will compress, creating a gap between the child and the restraint (and possibly ejecting the child from the seat).

Smart Shopper Tip #7
Shoulder belt guides

"I read in Consumer Reports *that some booster seats have dangerous belt guides. Which is best? My son is tall–do we need to use the belt guide at all?"*

This was an issue a few years ago: belt guides on some boosters that caused dangerous slack. But there is good news: nearly all booster seats on the market today have "open loop" guides that allow the belt to slide freely—and retract snugly against the child.

This is probably a good time to remind you not to buy/borrow a used booster seat. Older seats (some made as recently as 2002 or 2003) had these dangerous belt guides (called "locking glides"). So if you see a "pre-owned" booster seat at a garage sale, we say pass.

Smart Shopper Tip #8
Too Tall for a Convertible

"My daughter is too tall for her convertible car seat but is only 32 pounds. Now what?"

Many children outgrow their convertibles by height before weight. Most convertibles say that they are good to 40" tall, but a better measure is to make sure the child's shoulders are no higher than the top harness slot. If this happens well before a child is 40 pounds, the next step is a combo booster seat. Most have higher slots (17" or so inches, vs. about 15" for the convertibles). The exceptions are combo seats from Cosco. None of their combo booster seats have this feature, so unless you know you've got a very short torso child, skip the Cosco combos.

Smart Shopper Tip #9
Booster Testing—Do they Really Test it to 100 lbs?

"I just bought a booster rated to 100 pounds. What kind of testing is done to make sure that my booster really works for a child that heavy?"

Little notice has been given to the fact that current regulations only require booster seats to be tested with the three-year-old (33 pound) and six year old (47 pound) dummies. In fact, current regulations only apply to seats made for children smaller than 50 pounds. So how can so many seats have an upper limit of 80 or even 100 pounds? It all comes down to how the company thinks their product will perform. We contacted several companies that offer boosters rated up to 100 pounds. Britax, for example, told us they use "all dummies on the market appropriate for the rating of the restraint", including the 10-year-old, 4'6", 76-pound dummy. We didn't get any response from Cosco. So it appears that some companies are voluntarily using the appropriate weight of dummies to test their products, but we thought you should be aware that this is not required.

Frankly, this appears to be a case of where the market is outpacing safety regulations. More and more states are now requiring that children ride in safety seats (that is, boosters) until six years of age and manufacturers are quickly rolling out new seats to the meet the demand. While that's great, we urge the federal government to catch up with its safety regulations on this matter—if a booster claims to be effective to 80 pounds, we expect the federal government to REQUIRE that seat to be crash tested to 80 pounds! Having seat makers voluntarily test their seats and assign a weight limit based on what they "think" is the seat's limit sets a dangerous precedent.

Safe & Sound

1 **CHECK YOUR VEHICLE'S OWNERS MANUAL.** We're amazed at the detailed info on installing child safety seats you can find in your vehicle's owners manual, especially for newer vehicles. Car seats also include detailed installation instructions. Unfortunately, some parents don't read these manuals and attempt to "wing it" during installation.

2 **ALWAYS USE THE LAP/SHOULDER BELT WITH THE BOOSTER—** this provides crucial upper body protection in the case of an accident. NEVER use just the lap belt.

3 **DON'T EXPECT TO USE THAT BOOSTER ON AN AIRPLANE.** FAA rules prohibit the use of booster seats on airlines. Why? Booster seats must be used with a shoulder belt to be effective— and airplanes only have lap belts. Our advice: a child under 40 pounds should ride in a convertible or combo seat on a plane; over 40 pounds, just use the airplane seat belt (no booster). Just make sure to take the booster for the rides to and from the airport. Gate checking (or storing in an overhead bin) will insure that your boosters arrive at your destination with you.

4 **BE CAREFUL OF HAND-ME-DOWN AND SECOND-HAND BAR-GAINS.** Most old booster seats don't meet current safety standards. Older combo seats usually have the rear harness adjustment, which is a pain to use, as we discussed previously. If you do find a newer used booster, make sure you ask the original owner if it has been in a crash, and then check the seat for recalls (Safety Belt Safe has a great recall list at www.carseat.org). And if your seat has been in a crash, is over six years old or missing its proper labels, stick it in a black garbage bag and throw it away.

5 **ONLY USE CARDBOARD CUPS IN BOOSTER SEAT CUP HOLDERS.** You'll note that some seats now come with cup or juice box holders. These are a great convenience, but most manufacturers only recommend cardboard cups (like to-go cups) or juice boxes be put in such holders. Anything harder (plastic, etc.) is more likely to become a dangerous projectile in a crash.

6 **WHEN IS A CHILD BIG ENOUGH TO USE JUST THE AUTO'S SAFETY BELT?** When a child is over 4'9" and can sit with his or her back straight against the back seat cushion (with knees bent over the seat's edge), then he or she can go with just the auto's safety belt. Still have doubts? Try this 5 Step Test from Safety Belt Safe, USA:

◆ Does the child sit all the way back against the auto seat?
◆ Does the belt cross the shoulder between neck and arm?
◆ Is the lap belt as low as possible, touching the thighs?
◆ Can the child stay seated like this for the whole trip?
◆ Do the child's knees bend comfortably at the edge of the seat?

If you answered no to any of these questions, your child needs a booster seat, and will probably be more comfortable in one too.

Booster Car Seats (model by model reviews)

ALPHA
Comments: This Cosco/Dorel brand has its own version of the Safety 1st Apex 65 forward-facing seat (reviewed later in this section). Basically the same seat, just a Babies R Us exclusive fabric pattern.

BRITAX MONARCH
Booster type: High back booster.
Weight range: 30 to 100 lbs., 61"tall.
Price: $150
Comments: The Monarch is Britax's newest booster. Our verdict: good seat, but pricey. The Monarch's key feature: the back removes so you can use it as a backless booster. Great, but you could buy a Parkway (reviewed below) and a backless TurboBooster instead of a Monarch and still save $30! What else is different from the Parkway? The

Monarch has armrests that slide so the seat expands in width—from 9.5 to 11.5 inches, a plus for bigger toddlers. The armrests are a matter of debate—some parents/kids prefer the LACK of armrests (a la the Parkway), as it is easier for a toddler to buckle himself in without them.

Other than the armrests, adjustable seat and backless option, the Monarch is similar to the Parkway, including the same height (29″) and the narrow headrest (6″), which we will note in the Parkway review as a negative. Bottom line: the Monarch is a good booster, but too expensive.

Rating: A-

Dimensions: 16.5″ wide, 35″ high, 14.5″ deep.

BRITAX PARKWAY

Booster type: High back

Weight Range: 30 to 100 lbs., 38 to 60 inches tall.

Price: $100

Pros: Scaled down version of the Bodyguard is $30 cheaper; wider seat area plus cup holders.

Cons: No tether, so it can slide around a bit on leather seats.

Comments: The Parkway is Britax's excellent booster seat that boasts "true side impact protection." Britax pioneered side-impact protection in the car seat category—the Parkway has both torso and head protection with EPS protective foam. Yes, it costs $30 more than the Graco TurboBooster, but if your vehicle doesn't have side-curtain airbags in the back seat, the Parkway would be a wise investment.

So what's not to like with the Parkway? Well, some readers tell us the seat is a bit snug for larger toddlers. The Parkway's seat width is just ten inches, compared to 11.5 for the Graco TurboBooster and 12″ for the Compass boosters. We also hear complaints about the Parkway's headrest, which some kids find too confining (it is 8″ wide, compared to 12″ for the Graco seat). And what is with those dinky cup holders? They are too shallow to hold a juice box and not level when the seat is installed. We are also a bit disappointed that Britax ditched the lock-off clamps (seen on a previous model) that keep seats from flying around when empty. A final bummer: the back of the Parkway does NOT remove, so you can't use this model as a backless booster (that feature is common in competitors).

Despite all that, we'll give the Parkway a recommendation—with the caveat that if your toddler is over the 50th percentile on their growth chart, this may not be the best option.

Rating: A-

Dimensions: 17″ wide, 35″ high, 14.5″ deep.

Chicco KeyFit Booster

Booster type: High back
Weight Range: 40 to 100 lbs.
Price: $130
Comments: This seat will debut in 2008, the first booster offering from Chicco, a brand better known for its strollers and high chairs. We saw a prototype of the seat at a trade show and thought it was well-designed, if not a bit overpriced. The unique feature for this booster will be a "true recline," which most other boosters lack. This might be helpful for younger toddlers who are still napping in their boosters on long trips—the KeyFit will also have side impact protection and seat width adjustments. But the price? $130? If this seat was priced around $100, it would be a decent alternative to the Britax Parkway. But the KeyFit will need more than just a recline feature to justify that price premium.
Rating: Not yet.

Clek Olli Booster

Booster type: Backless booster
Weight Range: 40 to 100 lbs., 57" tall.
Price: $90
Pros: Only LATCH backless booster. Removable, washable seat cover.
Cons: No cup holders. High price.
Comments: Canadian car seat maker Magna's (magnaclek.com) backless booster is unique: it is the only backless booster that uses LATCH for a secure fit to the car. Your child then buckles in with the auto safety belt. We're not quite sure we see the point for the Clek—if your vehicle is in an accident, it is the auto safety belt (not the LACTCH connectors) that hold your child in place. So we guess the main advantage of the Clek is that the LATCH connectors hold the seat in place when it is unoccupied. Nice, but is it worth $90 when most other (LATCH-less) backless boosters run $20? The Clek is too new for us to assign a rating, given the lack of reader feedback to date.
Rating: Not yet.

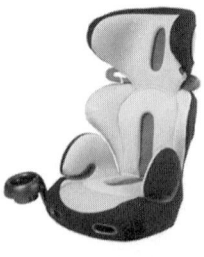

Combi Kobuck

Booster type: High back and backless booster.
Weight range: 33 to 100 lbs.; 33" to 57" in height.
Price: $80 to $100
Pros: Side impact protection; can be used as a backless booster.
Cons: Funky cup holder; high price.

Comments: Want side impact protection but turned off by the restrictive wings of the Britax Parkway? Combi's Kobuck aims to fill this niche with a protective headrest, minus the tight-fitting wings. We liked the padding of this seat (even the armrests are padded), but the cheesy cup holder and relatively high price ($20 to $40 more than the Graco TurboBooster) are a turn off. On the plus side, the entire seat is lined with EPS and "egg shock" (comfort) foam. Combi's pitch for the Kobuck includes a claim that its front air vents allow for "healthy ventilation." Well, given parent feedback, we don't think this seat is any cooler than other boosters, but it's hard to measure that claim. Bottom line: this seat scored well in *Consumer Reports* crash tests, but not as good as Britax. FYI: Combi sells a backless version of the Kobuck, dubbed the "Dakota" for $30.
Rating: B
Dimensions. 20" long, 18" wide, 27" high.

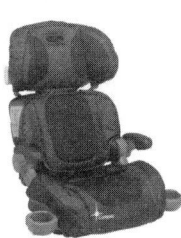
COMPASS B500
FOLDING BOOSTER SEAT
Booster type: belt-positioning booster
Weight range: 30-100 lbs.
Price: $60
Pros: Folds up, nicely padded, flip-up armrests, extra wide seat, good price.
Cons: None.
Comments: Compass was launched by several ex-Evenflo employees who bring their car seat expertise to a new company that aims to do more innovative products at the mid-price point level. Case in point: the Compass B500 LP Folding Booster car seat. This $60 belt-positioning booster features excellent padding and side impact protection (EPS foam) plus an extra bonus: it folds up for easy carrying. The low starting weight (30 lbs.) plus extras like two cup holders, flip-up armrests and six-position height adjustment make this a winner. We liked the quality construction and attention to detail with the Compass booster—it is apparent that the company has a passion for child passenger safety, rather than just producing the cheapest possible seat it can hawk in discount stores.
Rating: A

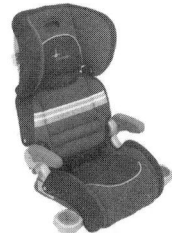
COMPASS B510
FOLDING BOOSTER SEAT
Booster type: belt-positioning booster
Weight range: 30-100 lbs.
Price: $80 to $100
Comments: The B510 is a premium version of their B500 folding car seat. The 510 is similar

to the 500, but is about 2" higher. The 510 also has wider headrest by a couple of inches and a more open belt path. Wal-Mart sells a version of this seat for $80, while other stores carry B510 seats with upgraded fabric for $100.

Rating: A

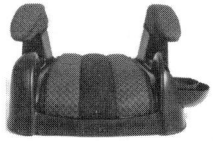

COSCO AMBASSADOR BOOSTER SEAT
AKA HIGH RISE AUTO BOOSTER SEAT

Booster type: Backless booster
Weight range: 30-100 lbs. Kids must be 52" or less.

Price: $15

Pros: Cheap backless booster. Cup holder. **Cons**: None.

Comments: These very simple and affordable seats are backless boosters. Both versions have padded armrests and a fold-down cup holder.

Rating: B

Dimensions: 16"D, 17"W, 9.5"H.

COSCO HIGH BACK BOOSTER

(aka Cosco Complete Voyager, Cosco Ventura)
Booster type: Combo
Weight range: 22-40 lbs. with harness, 30-80 as belt positioning booster. A newer version of this seat goes up to 100 lbs.
Price: Three different versions, $20 to $60.
Pros: Inexpensive, fits great in cars, five-point harness option from 22 to 40 lbs., headrest, armrests, storage bag, cup holder.

Cons: Straps twist, Cosco's abysmal safety record.

Comments: Cosco's High Back booster comes in several versions—the Complete Voyager ($20) is a belt-positioning booster (no five-point harness). The Cosco High Back Booster ($50) is a combo booster with a five-point harness from 22 to 40 lbs., then working as a booster from 30 to 80 lbs. But this seat has cut corners at every turn. First and foremost, the top harness slots on this seat are the same as Cosco's convertible, the Touriva, meaning that lots of kids get too tall for this seat before they reach 40 lbs. Second, the tether strap is also a total pain to adjust and get tight.

An upgraded version of this seat (the Ventura, $60), adds armrests and cup holders.

While this seat does fit well in cars, we don't give it high marks. The too-low harness heights are a deal killer. We also note that parent reviews of Cosco's boosters have been mixed. For every parent we interviewed who liked their Cosco booster, another gave it a thumbs down—some gripes were minor (Cosco's light tan fabric on some of the boosters stains too easily), while other frustrations were more serious (quality complaints, straps that twist and are hard to adjust, etc.). If you want a Cosco booster, we'd suggest the Summit (reviewed below) instead.

Rating: C

Dimensions. Top Harness Slot: 15.3", Back height: 25", Seat width: 17.3".

Cosco Pronto

Comments: This new booster should be on the market by the time you read this—the Pronto is an entry-level ($30) highback belt-positioning booster (that is, it won't have a five-point harness). We didn't see this seat before press time.

Cosco Protek

Booster type: High back

Weight range: 30 to 100 lbs.; up to 57" in height.

Price: $30.

Pros: Affordable price, padded armrests, removable pillow. Light weight (8 lbs).

Cons: Lacks side impact protection. Cup holders don't fold in; skimpy padding.

Comments: The Protek is Cosco's answer to the Graco TurboBooster; as usual, Cosco comes in at a great price with a few caveats. While we like the fact the seat is about $10 to $20 cheaper than the TurboBooster, we were a bit turned off with the skimpy padding. The molded-in cup holder in the base might be an issue if you have a tight squeeze in the backseat, as it sticks out on the side (the TurboBooster has cup holders that retract into the base). But perhaps our biggest beef is the lack of side impact protection—yes, the Protek has side wings but we think the Britax Parkway offers more side impact protection than the Protek. This may not be an issue if your car has side curtain air bags in the back seat, but for some that might be a deal breaker.

The Protek scored an "excellent" crash test rating in *Consumer Reports* latest tests—the best rated seat under $100. So we will give this one a thumbs-up. *FYI: As we were going to press, we heard Cosco plans to replace this booster with the Maxi Cosi Rodi (see review later in this section). So the Protek's days may be numbered.*

Rating: A-

Eddie Bauer Auto Booster

aka Disney Enroute

Weight: 30 to 100 lbs.

boosters

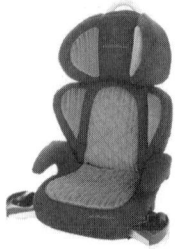

Booster type: High back belt-positioning booster

Pros: Affordable.

Cons: Not out as of press time, so no reader feedback yet.

Price: $70 (backless version is $30)

Comments: This new belt-positioning booster will be out by the time you read this—the Eddie Bauer Auto Booster (also known as the enRoute) will feature extra padding, double cup holders and it will convert to a backless booster. Or you can buy just the backless version for $30.

EDDIE BAUER COMFORT HIGH BACK BOOSTER
See Safety 1st Vantage

EDDIE BAUER ADJUSTABLE HIGH BACK BOOSTER
See Safety 1st Prospect

EDDIE BAUER DELUXE HIGH BACK BOOSTER
See Safety 1st Summit

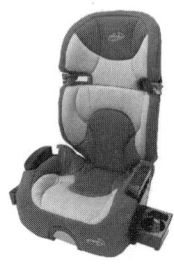

EVENFLO BIG KID / BIG KID CONFIDENCE

Weight: 30 to 100 lbs.

Booster type: Belt-positioning

Pros: Low price, extras like reading lights, EPS foam.

Cons: Skimpy padding in low-end version.

Price: $40-60; a backless version is $15 to $25. The Big Kid Confidence is $90.

Comments: Evenflo's answer to Graco's TurboBooster, the Big Kid adds a few bells and whistles that Graco doesn't have. Example: two reading lights for "evening activities." Also unique: The Big Kid is adjustable in both height and lap depth (most boosters are just height adjustable). The back removes as kids grow bigger, adding a discreet boost to older kids without having them look "uncool." On the plus side, the Big Kid is less expensive than the Graco Turbo Booster (a $40 version in Target is especially affordable). On the downside, the padding is a bit more skimpy than the Graco, making this seat less comfy for longer trips. And the Big Kid has less side impact protection than the Britax Monarch. As usual, it is the little things about the Evenflo seat that can drive you crazy: the reading lights are nice, but lack an auto shut-off feature (and hence, will consume batteries fast if left on).

Evenflo has rolled out a deluxe version of this seat, dubbed the Big Kid Confidence ($90). The Confidence offers "European Styling" (has anyone at Evenflo ever been to Europe?), retractable cup holders and armrests, as well as "visually accented" belt guides to help with correct installation. Nice upgrades, but at this price, you are better off with a Britax or Compass booster for the same price. The backless version of the Big Kid ($20 or so) is a good deal.

Rating: B

EVENFLO BOLERO

Comments: This seat is very similar to the Evenflo Generations, reviewed below. The Bolero has a bit less padding and omits the Generations slight recline feature.

EVENFLO CHASE DLX

Booster type: Combo
Weight: 20-100 lbs.; 20 to 40 lbs. with harness, belt-positioning booster for 30 to 100 lbs.
Price: $60 to $70
Comments: This older model combo seat comes in several versions: the DLX adds fancier padding (the Comfort Touch), armrests and a cup holder. For this, you pay an extra $20 than the LX. These seats are five years old and showing their age.

Rating: B

EVENFLO GENERATIONS

Booster type: Combo
Weight: 20-100 lbs.; 20 to 40 lbs. with harness, belt-positioning booster for 30 to 100 lbs.
Price: $100
Pros: Adjuster knob for belt harness; higher weight limit than other Evenflo combo seats.
Cons: Pricey.

Comments: This upgraded combo seat from Evenflo is similar to the Chase but features a fancier headrest, better padding and a 100 lb. weight limit. The knob, which adjusts the belts, gets better parent reviews than the harness adjuster on the Traditions. Flip-out cup holder is nice, especially if you have a small back seat. The Generation has a very slight recline feature.

Rating: B+

FISHER PRICE SAFE VOYAGE BOOSTER SEAT

This seat is now discontinued; an archive of the review is on our web page at BabyBargains.com (go to Bonus Material).

GRACO AIR BOOSTER *See Graco TurboBooster*

CHAPTER 8: CAR SEATS   **441**

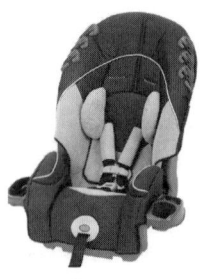

GRACO CARGO: TREASURED, ULTRA, AND PLATINUM

Booster type: Combo
Weight range: 20-40 lbs. with harness, 30 to 100 lbs. as high back booster.
Price: $70 to $100
Pros: Good price; starts at 20 lbs., up-front belt adjustment on some models, narrow.

Cons: Skimpy padding, mediocre shoulder belt adjusters.

Comments: Graco's first attempt at a booster, the Cherished CarGo, has given way to a whole line of CarGos: Treasured, Ultra and Platinum. The first Cherished CarGos felt flimsy, and the harness adjuster clip (paper-clip style) often broke. But these newer models all have the nice two-piece harness retainer clips and also handy cup holders. Graco really missed the boat with their Treasured CarGo—it has a rear harness adjuster that will prevent even the most diligent parent from tightening the straps every day. If your pre-schooler still naps in the car, the Platinum model is a good choice since they have the up-front adjuster and nice deep wings that gives some sleeping support. The top-of-the line Platinum CarGo adds a two-position recline, more plush padding and extra storage pockets—nice, but it runs a whopping $100. This version might be best for younger kids that are still napping in their car seats. The Graco CarGos are also the narrowest combos on the market . . . great if you've got two or three kids to squeeze next to each other. The biggest problem with all the CarGos is their mediocre shoulder belt adjuster. These clips tend to lock the belt into place, which might introduce dangerous slack in the belt. And they may make it difficult for your toddler to buckle himself into his seat, a major pain as we discussed earlier in this chapter. We'll give these seats separate grades since their different features make the Ultra and Platinum CarGos clearly superior to the Treasured CarGo.

Ratings: Treasured CarGo: C; Ultra Cargo: B, Platinum CarGo: B

Dimensions. Top Harness slot: 17", Back height: 26.5", Outside width: 16".

GRACO NAUTILUS 3-IN-1 MULTI-STAGE

Booster type: Combo
Weight range: 20-65 lbs. with harness, 30 to 100 lbs. as high back booster. Backless booster from 40 to 100 lbs.
Price: $150
Pros: Only combo booster that works to 65 lbs. with a five-point harness.

Cons: Not out as of press time.

Comments: Out by the time you read this, the Graco Nautilus is the first combo booster with a five-point harness that will work up to 65 lbs. (most stop at 40). That's a big plus if you have a toddler who has outgrown his convertible seat, but you wish to keep him in the harness for a while longer (the 65 lb. limit should fit most five year olds). The Nautilus will also convert to a belt-positioning, high back booster to 100 lbs.—and even becomes a backless booster to 100 lbs.

We saw a prototype of this seat and were impressed—we liked the over molded armrests (with side storage), three-position recline and decent padding. The seat is lined with EPS foam. Since it wasn't out as of press time, we don't have a rating yet . . . but the Nautilus should be a hot seller, even with the somewhat pricey $150 tag.

Rating: Not Yet.

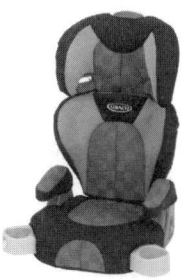

GRACO TURBOBOOSTER

(aka Graco Air Booster)

Booster type: Belt-positioner and backless

Weight range: 30 to 100 lbs. as high back booster (backless, it is 40 to 100 lbs).

Price: $50 to $80. Airbooster: $80. Backless version is $20.

Pros: Top choice in booster market—both affordable and well-designed.

Cons: Doesn't have as much side impact protection as Britax Parkway.

Comments: This is our top pick as a great, affordable booster seat. We love the sharp design and open loop belt adjuster, which is a major improvement over Graco's other booster seat (the CarGo). Graco did this one right: you get padded armrests that are height adjustable, EPS foam, hide-away cup holders and more. The seat pad removes for cleaning and there is an easy one-hand adjustment for the headrest. The TurboBooster converts into a backless booster for older kids. As usual, Graco makes the TurboBooster in a bazillion (yes, that is the technical term) colors and fabrics. Hence you'll see a bare-bones version for $50 at Target or Wal-Mart . . . and then "deluxe" models for up to $80. What's the difference? Just the fabric pad. More money, fancier pad.

New in the past year, Graco debuted a new version of this seat, dubbed the AirBooster. The AirBooster is basically the same shell and features of the TurboBooster, but with a mesh seat like you see in high-end office chairs. The AirBooster is $80 at Babies R Us.

So what are the drawbacks to the Graco TurboBooster? Well, Britax's Parkway offers more side impact protection and sleeping support than this seat; and some users say this seat can be complex for grandparents to use (you have to make sure you position the seat belt correctly with the arm rests, etc). But if your car already has side curtain air bags in the back and your child doesn't nap much in the car, the TurboBooster is a great choice.

And the feedback on the AirBooster has been very positive—most readers tell us their toddlers love the cushy mesh seat.

Dimensions. Back height: 27", seat width: 16".

Rating: A

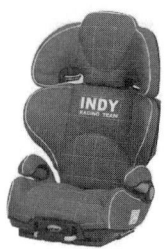

JANE INDY PLUS BOOSTER SEAT

Booster type: high back, belt-positioning booster

Weight Range: 30 to 80 lbs.

Price: $200

Pros: One of the few high back boosters that works with LATCH.

Cons: Price, not in many stores.

Comments: Spanish baby products maker Jane has been trying to crack the U.S. market with little success, first with expensive strollers and now with a pricey booster seat. The Indy Plus is a $200 high-back booster that has several unique features: it uses rigid LATCH, has a reinforced aluminum frame and many adjustment settings for the backrest and side wings. The seat is entirely lined with EPS foam and there is even a recline feature, unique in the booster seat world.

The rigid LATCH feature is perhaps this seat's Achilles heal—you won't be able to easily install the Indy Plus if your vehicle's LATCH connectors are deeply recessed. And remember that some vehicles limit LATCH use to as little as 40 lbs. (Honda, for example). That defeats one of this seat's key features.

Bottom line: this seat's high price, limited availability (Jane isn't in most stores) and LATCH quirkiness limit its appeal.

Rating: B-

MAXI COSI RODI

Booster type: high back, belt-positioning booster

Weight Range: 30 to 100 lbs.

Price: $100

Pros: Extra large side wings provide sleep support..

Cons: New—no reader feedback yet.

Comments: As we discussed earlier in this chapter, Cosco is bringing their sister European brand Maxi Cosi to the U.S. as part of the Quinny stroller launch. The Maxi Cosi Rodi is the booster seat entry—an attractive $100 seat with deep side wings for impact protection and sleeping support. We were impressed with the padding on the prototype we viewed—and the recline feature is unique. The only drawback: competitors like the Compass B510 have fully adjustable backrests, something the Rodi lacks. Since this seat was so new as of press time, we didn't have any reader feedback so no rating yet.

Rating: Not yet.

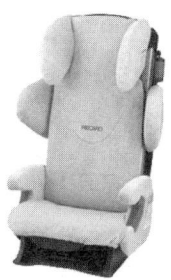

RECARO START

Booster type: high-back booster
Weight Range: 30 to 80 lbs.
Price: $350
Pros: Very comfortable, many adjustments.
Cons: $350?!! Shoulder belt lock off makes older children feel confined, adjustments hard to use.
Comments: Wow, a $350 booster? What is Recaro thinking? At least for all this money, you

do get a darn good seat. According to our child testers, the Recaro Start offers fantastic comfort. It also has more adjustments than most car seats, (height, shoulder width, and seat depth adjustments) and it has one of the highest high backs on the market. The deep side wings provide nice sleeping support and possibly side impact support. But the adjustments are cumbersome, so this is not a good seat to share between siblings. And it is a lousy choice for carpools at a hefty 26 lbs. The shoulder belt lock off MUST be used on this booster, for all ages, which can feel very confining for older children.

Rating: A-
Dimensions. Back height: 29", Outside width: 16.5"

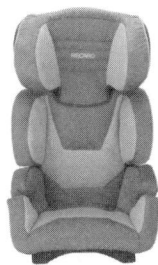

RECARO VIVO/ VIVO LITE

Booster type: high back booster
Weight Range: 30 to 100 lbs.
Price: $90 Vivo Lite, $100 Vivo.
Pros: Side wings provide impact protection and sleep support. Nice fabrics.
Cons: Just debuted as of press time, so no reader feedback yet.

Comments: Recaro's new Vivo high-back boosters are similar to the Britax Parkway, even down to the $100 price tag. The side wings provide side-impact protection and the seat is lined with EPS foam. The Vivo and Vivo Lite are identical, except for the fabric pad: the Vivo has a microfiber pad, while the Vivo Lite has a more breathable fabric with mesh inserts. These seats were so new as of press time that we haven't received any reader feedback yet.

Rating: Not Yet.

RECARO YOUNG STYLE

This seat is now discontinued; an archive of the review is on our web page at BabyBargains.com (go to Bonus Material).

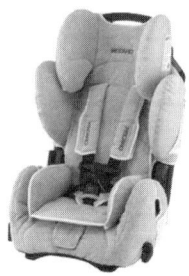

RECARO YOUNG SPORT

Booster type: Combo
Weight Range: 18 to 80 lbs.; five-point harness to 40 lbs. Up to 59".
Price: $250
Pros: Very comfortable, EPS foam, side impact protection.
Cons: Price. Five point harness only to 40 lbs.?
Comments: This is probably Recaro's best-selling seat—the Young Sport is a combo seat that combines a five-point harness up to 40 lbs. with a belt-positioning booster that works to 80 lbs. Feature-wise, it is quite similar to the Style with its EPS foam, side impact protection and adjustable headrest. The difference is a five-point harness and removable seat cushion for younger toddlers. As with the Start, kids give high marks to this seat's comfort . . . but, again, the adjustments could be more parent-friendly. Overall, quality (as for all Recaro seats) is high. But the price ($250) is way too high, especially compared with the new Graco Nautilus that will feature a five-point harness to 65 lbs. and cost $100 less.
Rating: A-
Dimensions. Width 18.1", Height 26" to 31.3".

SAFEGUARD GO

Seat type: Combo seat and backless booster.
Weight range: 30 to 100 lbs. To 60 lbs. with five-point harness. 34"-52" height for the five-point harness; 43"-57" for the backless booster.
Price: $165
Pros: Innovative hybrid seat that works up to 60 lbs. with five-point harness; great for taxis.
Cons: Requires a top tether when used with five point harness. No cup holder? Pricey. Check LATCH limit of your vehicle before ordering.
Comments: Now this seat is impressive—the SafeGuard Go features a five-point harness that can be used to 60 lbs. . . . and then the seat converts to a backless booster to 100 lbs. And it all folds into a travel bag, a boon for carpools or taxis (take note, New Yorkers). This hybrid is probably where the market for boosters is going in the future—a five-point harness for younger toddlers that works beyond 40 lbs. and then a backless booster for older kids up to 100 lbs.

One caveat to the Safeguard Go—it can only be used with its five-point harness in vehicles with LATCH and a top tether. That's not a problem if your car was made after 2003 . . . but if you are driving an older vehicle, it may not be compatible (some car makers added LATCH before 2003, but others did not). SafeGuard has a handy vehicle compatibility function on their web site so you can see if your vehicle would work.

And remember that your vehicle may have low LATCH limits—Honda is just 40 lbs., for example. Most are 48 lbs.; Subaru is 60. If your vehicle has a low limit, you won't be able to use the five-point harness—and hence you just bought yourself a $165 backless booster.

And just to add another layer of confusion: some vehicles have a different (lower) limit for tethers. Saturn has a 48 lb. LATCH limit, but a 40 lb. limit for a tether. In that case, the SafeGuard Go would be a poor choice.

Bottom line: this is a good seat IF your vehicle has high enough LATCH and tether limits to take advantage of its unique design.

Rating: B+

SAFETY 1ST APEX 65

(a.k.a. Safety 1st Apex 65, Alpha Elite Apex)
Type: Forward-facing seat and belt-positioning booster.
Weight range: 20 to 65 lbs. with internal harness; 40 to 100 lbs. as a belt-positioning booster. Kids must be 57" or less.

Price: $130

Pros: 65 lb. limit WITH a five point harness!

Cons: Limiting top harness slot and crotch strap means larger toddlers will outgrow the harness before 65 lbs. No EPS foam. Cosco's track record in this category is mixed.

Comments: The Apex is one of a handful of seats on the market that works to 65 lbs. with a five-point harness. Unlike the Britax Marathon/Boulevard/Decathlon seats, the Apex is NOT a convertible—that is, it can only be used forward-facing. You can use it forward facing with LATCH—check your vehicle's limits on this. The Apex also features an adjustable headrest, padded armrests, cup holder and padded insert to better fit smaller toddlers.

As a hybrid seat, the Apex morphs into a belt-positioning booster after a toddler has outgrown the harness. And that's the rub with this seat: the top harness slot is 17.5" (the same as the Britax seats that go to 65 lbs.). Given that harness slot, we'd guess that many toddlers will be too tall for the harness before they reach 65 lbs. And the lack of an adjustable crotch strap (it only has two positions) also limits the Apex's harness use. Other downsides to this seat: there's no EPS foam and the arm pads come off too easily, according to reader feedback.

Rating: B-

SAFETY 1ST SUMMIT

(aka the Safety 1st Summit and Eddie Bauer Deluxe High Back Booster)
Booster type: Combo
Weight range: 22-40 lbs. with harness, 40-100 lbs. as belt positioning booster.
Price: $100-$120
Pros: Top rated combo seat, armrests pivot, 100 lb. weight limit. EPP foam.

Cons: Top harness slots no higher than most convertibles, Cosco's abysmal safety record.

Comments: The Summit has a 100–lb. limit, a front harness adjuster, a two-piece harness retainer clip, armrests and cup holder. Sounds perfect, right? Well, not quite. The big disappointment with this seat is that top harness slots are no higher than an average convertible, about 15". So some kids can use this seat to a full 40 lbs., but many will outgrow it by height before weight. It also comes with the fussy Cosco tether adjuster, and Cosco's dubious safety record. But if you think that your child is average or short in the torso, then this might be the seat for you. FYI: There is an Eddie Bauer version of this seat (dubbed the Deluxe High Back Booster) for $120—same seat, just an upgraded fabric pad.

Rating: B+

Dimensions. Top Harness Slot: 15", Back height: 27", Seat width: 18".

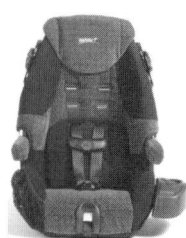

SAFETY 1ST VANTAGE

(aka the Safety 1st Surveyor, Eddie Bauer Comfort High Back, Alpha Vantage)
Booster type: Combo
Weight range: 22-40 lbs. with five-point harness, 40 to 100 lbs. belt-positioning booster. 52" height limit. EPP foam.
Price: $80.

Comments: A basic combo seat that is similar to the Cosco High Back Booster, but has a bigger seat area. While the seat now has EPP foam, the Vantage lacks side impact protection and other features you see on other seats in this price category. The shoulder belt guides can adjust to five positions. The Surveyor earned only a "C" in the government's ease of use ratings in the "securing a child" category. All in all, not very impressive. FYI: This seat is sold under the names Vantage, Surveyor, Eddie Bauer Comfort High Back booster and Alpha Vantage. The last is a Babies R Us exclusive.

Rating: C

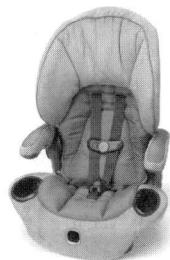

SAFETY 1ST PROSPECT BOOSTER

(aka the Eddie Bauer Adjustable High Back Booster)

Booster type: Combo and backless booster.
Weight range: 22 to 40 lbs. with five-point harness, 40 to 100 lbs. as a belt-positioning or backless booster.
Price: $80 to $90.
Comments: This seat's main advantage is its three uses: first as a combo seat, then as a belt-positioning booster and finally as a backless booster. We liked the wide, well-padded seat and two built-in cup holders. The side wings are lined with EPS. The Prospect is better designed than most Cosco offerings, but we wish the harness worked up to 65 lbs. (like the Apex). One downside: the Prospect earned only a "C" in the government's ease of use rating when it came to securing a child. FYI: A backless version of the Prospect ($25; 40 to 100 lbs.; pivoting armrests, extra wide seat) debuted in 2007.

Rating: B

SUNSHINE KIDS MONTEREY BOOSTER

Booster type: Belt-positioning booster.
Weight range: 30 to 100 lbs, 60" in height.
Price: $130
Comments: This seat should debut by the time you read this—the Monterey is Sunshine Kids first booster seat. A bit taller than the Britax Monarch, the Monterey features a dial-adjustable seat width, EPS foam, a deep seat, retractable cup holders, two recline positions and a cushy foam seat. The Monterey also will work with LATCH, among the few boosters on the market with this feature. While we did see a prototype of this seat and thought it was well-designed, we'll wait on a rating until it is released into the wild.

Rating: Not yet.

Our Picks: Booster Seat Recommendations

What's the best booster seat on the market? Before you can answer that question, you must look at your child—his/her weight, height and maturity (ability to sit in an auto safety belt) are the key factors to consider. In general, we recommend keeping your toddler in a harnessed seat as long as possible . . . whether that is a convertible that works to 65 lbs. or one of the new hybrid boosters that has a five-point harness up to 65 lbs. After that, we suggest a belt-positioning booster.

Here are our top picks for boosters. Detailed reviews of various brands follow this section.

◆ Best Bets: Harness Seats. Need a combo seat? The *Safety 1st Summit* ($100-$120) is a good choice if your child has outgrown their convertible seat, but isn't mature enough to sit in a belt-positioning booster like the Graco TurboBooster. This seat's best feature: a five point harness that can be used from 22 to 40 lbs. After that, the seat can be used as a belt-positioning booster to 100 lbs. This seat has an excellent shoulder belt adjuster—an open loop that allows the shoulder belt to pull out and retract smoothly. This model also has a front harness adjuster, a two-piece harness clip, armrests and cup holder.

Another seat to consider is the new *Graco Nautilus*—this combo seat has a five-point harness that can be used up to 65 lbs. The Nautilus also converts to a belt-positioning booster and even a backless booster to 100 lbs. At $150, the Nautilus should give the Safety 1st a run for its money. The only caveat: it wasn't out as of press time, so we have no real world feedback yet. But Graco's track record is solid, so we expect this seat to be a contender.

◆ Best Bets: Belt-Positioning Booster. We have two picks for the best booster: the *Graco TurboBooster/AirBooster* ($50 to $80) and the *Britax Parkway* ($100). Let's look at each:

The Graco TurboBooster packs a good number of features into an affordable package: height-adjustable headrest, open belt loop design, armrests, back recline, cup holders and more. Note it comes in two version: a high-back version and backless (the latter is about $20-$25). And the AirBooster version of this seat is excellent: its mesh seat wins praise from toddlers for comfort.

The Britax Parkway is an another great booster that adds one important feature over the TurboBooster: side-impact protection and head wings that provide more sleeping support. If your vehicle does NOT have side curtain air bags in the rear seat, then the Parkway is probably the better bet. The downside to the Parkway: it's narrow seat and headrest may be too confining for larger toddlers.

Runner-up: *Compass' Folding Booster B510*. This $80 belt-positioning booster features excellent padding and side impact protection (EPS foam) plus an extra bonus: it folds up for easy carrying. The Compass also has flip-up armrests and a wider seat than the Britax or Graco. Basically, as good as the Britax Parkway yet $20 cheaper.

◆ Best Bets: Backless Booster. Finally, we should mention the backless version of the *Graco TurboBooster*—at $20 to $25, this is the best value for a backless booster. A great choice for kids over 40 lbs. if you've got head rests and if your child doesn't nap anymore.

CHAPTER 9

Strollers, Diaper Bags, Carriers and Other Gear To Go

Inside this chapter

W hat are the best strollers? Which brands are the most durable AND affordable? We'll discuss this plus other tips on how to make your baby portable—from front carriers to diaper bags and more. And what do you put in that diaper bag anyway? We've got nine suggestions, plus advice on the best baby carriers.

Getting Started: When Do You Need This Stuff?

While you don't need a stroller, diaper bag or carrier immediately after baby is born, most parents purchase them before baby arrives anyway. Another point to remember: some stroller models have to be special-ordered with at least two to four weeks lead time. And some of the best deals for strollers and other to-go gear are found online, which necessitates leaving a week or more lead-time for shipping.

Sources to Find Strollers, Carriers

Strollers and carriers are found at similar sources as we mentioned for car seats in the previous chapter. Once again, the discounters like Target and Wal-Mart tend to specialize in just a handful of models from the mass-market companies like Cosco, Kolcraft, Graco and so on (lately, they've been adding premium brands to their web sites although they aren't available in their stores). The baby superstores like Babies R Us and Baby Depot have a wider selection and (sometimes) better brands like Peg Perego and Combi. Meanwhile, juvenile specialty stores almost always carry the more exclusive brands and other upscale options.

Yet perhaps the best deals for strollers, carriers and diaper bags are found online—for some reason, this seems to be one area the web covers very well. This is because strollers are relatively easy to ship (compared to other more bulky juvenile items). Of course, more competition often means lower prices, so you'll see many deals online. Another plus: the web may be the only way to find certain premium-brand strollers if you live in less-populous parts of the U.S. and Canada.

Beware of shipping costs when ordering online or from a catalog—many strollers may run 20 or 30 pounds, which can translate into hefty shipping fees. Use an online coupon (see Chapter 7 for coupon sites) to save and look for free shipping specials.

Parents in Cyberspace: What's on the Web?

Online info on strollers, diaper bags and carriers falls into two categories: manufacturer sites and discounters who sell online. Here's a brief overview:

◆ *Most manufacturers do not sell online, but you can find a wealth of info on their sites in some cases.* With stroller makers, you may find fabric swatches and technical info about different models. This is helpful since most stores don't carry every available fabric, accessory or model.

◆ *Discounters.* Besides previously mentioned web sites like BabyCatalog.com (which has excellent stroller deals), readers say they've had luck with smaller sites like TravelingTikes (travelingtikes.com). Another site to check out for stroller deals: BabyCenter (babycenter.com). This site's sale area often has deals with up to 20% off and free shipping. Readers also praise Net Kids Wear (netkidswear.com) for their stroller deals.

Of course, any mention of online bargains for strollers wouldn't be complete without discussion of eBay (eBay.com), the massive bargain bazaar. Go to eBay's baby section and choose both the "general" and "stroller" categories for deals. Sure, there are some dogs here (like Graco or Evenflo models that are virtually worthless at resale), but you'll also find new-in-the-box Perego models as well as jogging strollers by the score. Do your price research up front (know what things really sell for at retail) and you'll find many 50% off bargains.

Craigslist is yet another option for discounts on strollers. On the New York version of the site we found a Maclaren Twin Traveler stroller for a mere $90. New this would cost you $350. Now most of the strollers we saw on Craigslist were Graco, Evenflo, etc. So you'll need to be patient and quick! But the deals are there.

Strollers

Baby stores offer a bewildering array of strollers for parents. Do you want the model that converts from a car seat to a stroller? What about a stroller that would work for a quick trip to the mall? Or do you want a stroller for jogging? Hiking trails? The urban jungle of New York City or beaches near LA?

And what about all the different brand names? Will a basic brand found at a discount store work? Or do you need a higher-quality brand from Europe? What about strollers with anti-lock brakes and air bags? (Just kidding on that last one).

The $180 million dollar stroller industry is not dominated by one or two players, like you might see in car seats or high chairs. Instead, you'll find a couple *dozen* stroller makers offering just about anything on wheels, ranging from $30 for a bare-bones model to $900 for a Dutch-designed über stroller. A recent trend: tri-wheel strollers that are hybrids between joggers and traditional strollers.

We hope this section takes some of the mystery out of the stroller buying process. First, we'll look at the six different types of strollers on the market today. Next, we'll zero in on features and help you decided what's important and what's not. Then, it's brand ratings and our picks as the best recommendations for different lifestyles. Finally, we'll go over several safety tips, money saving hints, wastes of money and a couple of online sources that sell strollers.

Whew! Take a deep breath and let's go.

What Are You Buying?

There are six types of strollers you can buy:

◆ **Umbrella Strollers.** The name comes from the appearance of the stroller when it's folded, similar to an umbrella.

WHAT'S COOL: They're lightweight and generally cheap—that is, low in price (about $20 to $40). We should note that a handful of premium stroller makers (Maclaren and Peg Perego) also offer pricey umbrella strollers that sell for $150 to $300. Pictured above

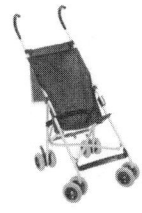

is a no-frills Kolcraft umbrella stroller.

WHAT'S NOT: They're cheap—that is, low in quality (well, with the exception of Maclaren and Peg Perego). You typically don't get any fancy features like canopies, storage baskets, reclining seats, and so on. Another problem: most umbrella strollers have hammock-style seats with little head support, so they won't work well for babies under six months of age.

◆ **Carriage Strollers.** A carriage (also called a pram) is like a bed on wheels—the seat lies flat and the leg rest pulls up to form a bassinet-like feature. Since this is most useful when a baby is young (and less helpful when baby is older), most companies make carriages that convert to strollers.

WHAT'S COOL: Full recline is great for newborns, which spend most of their time sleeping. Most combo carriage/strollers have lots of high-end features like plush seats, quilted canopies and other accessories to keep the weather out. The best carriage strollers and prams have a dreamy ride, with amazing suspensions and big wheels.

WHAT'S NOT: Hefty weight (not easy to transport or set up) and hefty price tags. Another negative: most Euro-style "prams" have fixed front wheels, which make maneuvering difficult on quick trips. Some carriage/stroller models can top $300 and $400. These strollers once dominated the market but have lost favor as more parents opt for "travel systems" that combine an infant seat and stroller (see below).

◆ **Lightweight Strollers.** These strollers are our top recommendation: they're basically souped-up umbrella strollers with many convenience features.

WHAT'S COOL: Most offer easy set-up and fold-down; some even fold up similar to umbrella strollers. Many models have a number of great features (canopies, storage baskets, high-quality wheels) at amazingly light weights (as little as eight pounds). Graco and Maclaren probably make the most popular lightweight strollers.

WHAT'S NOT: Can be expensive—most high-quality brands run $150 to $300. The smaller wheels on lightweight strollers make maneuvering in the mall or stores easy . . . but those same wheels don't perform well on uneven surfaces or on gravel trails. Skimpy baskets are another trade-off.

◆ **Jogging (or Sport) Strollers.** These strollers feature three big bicycle-tire wheels and lightweight frames—perfect for jogging or walking on rough roads.

WHAT'S COOL: How many other strollers can do 15 mph on a jogging trail? Some have plush features like padded seats and canopies—and the best fold up quickly for easy storage in the trunk. This category has boomed in recent years; now it seems like every stroller maker is rolling out a jogger model.

WHAT'S NOT: They can be darn expensive, topping $300. Jogging strollers are a single-purpose item—thanks to their sheer bulk and a lack of steering (joggers usually have fixed front wheels), you can't use one in a mall or other location. On the plus side, the flood of new models is helping lower prices. New, low-end jogging strollers run $100 to $150. The trade-offs to the new bargain price models: heavier steel frames and a lack of features.

◆ **All-terrain Strollers.** The baby equivalent of four-wheel drive sport-utility vehicles, these strollers are pitched to parents who want to go on hikes or other outdoor adventures.

WHAT'S COOL: Big air-filled tires and high clearances work better on gravel trails/roads than standard strollers. These strollers are great for neighborhoods with broken or rough sidewalks. All-terrain strollers have many convenience features (baskets, canopies, etc.) as well as one key advantage over jogging strollers: most all-terrains have swivel front wheels. That makes them easy to maneuver, whether on a trail or at the mall. Pictured here is the Valco Runabout TriMode

WHAT'S NOT: All-terrain strollers are wider than other strollers, which could make them troublesome in stores with narrow aisles. And air-filled tires are great for trails . . . but a pain in the neck if you get a flat. If you really want to run with a stroller, all-terrains with a swivel front wheel are not the best choice (a jogger with a fixed front wheel is better). And let's not forget the cost—most all-terrains are pricey, some topping $400.

◆ **Travel systems.** It's the current rage among stroller makers—models that combine infant car seats and strollers (also called "travel systems"). Century (now part of Graco) kicked off this craze way back in 1994 with its "4-in-1" model that featured four uses (infant carrier, infant car seat, car-

riage and toddler stroller). Since then, just about every major stroller maker has jumped into the travel system market. Travel systems have just about killed sales of carriage strollers; now even carriage stroller king Peg Perego has bowed to the travel system trend. Pictured on the previous page is the Graco MetroLite travel system.

WHAT'S COOL: Great convenience—you can take the infant car seat out of the car and then snap it into the stroller frame. Voila! Instant baby carriage, complete with canopy and basket. Later, you can use the stroller as, well, just a stroller.

WHAT'S NOT: The strollers are often junk—especially those by mass market makers Cosco and Evenflo. Quality problems plague this category, as does something we call "feature bloat." Popular travel systems from Graco, for example, are so loaded with features that they tip the scales at nearly 30 pounds! The result: many parents abandon their travel system strollers for lighter weight models after baby outgrows his infant seat. And considering these puppies can cost $150 to $250 (some even more), that's a big investment for such limited use. On the plus side, quality stroller makers Peg Perego, Maclaren and Combi have jumped into the travel system market, albeit with different solutions (see reviews later in this chapter).

Safe & Sound

Next to defective car seats, the most dangerous juvenile product on the market today is the stroller. That's according to the U.S. Consumer Product Safety Commission, which estimates that over 10,000 injuries a year occur from improper use or defects. The problems? Babies can slide out of the stroller (falling to the ground) and small parts can be a choking hazard. Seat belts have broken in some models, while other babies are injured when a stroller's brakes fail on a slope. Serious mishaps with strollers have involved entanglements and entrapments (where an unrestrained baby slides down and gets caught in a leg opening). Here are some safety tips:

1 **NEVER HANG BAGS FROM THE STROLLER HANDLE**—it's a tipping hazard.

2 **DON'T LEAVE YOUR BABY ASLEEP UNATTENDED IN A STROLLER.** Many injuries happen when infants who are lying down in a stroller roll or creep and then manage to get their head stuck in the stroller's leg openings. Be safe: take a sleeping baby out of a stroller and move them to a crib or bassinet.

3 **THE BRAKES SHOULDN'T BE TRUSTED.** The best stroller models have brakes on two wheels; cheaper ones just have one wheel that brakes. Even with the best brakes, don't leave the stroller unattended on an incline.

4 **FOLLOW THE WEIGHT LIMITS.** Most strollers shouldn't be used by children over 35 pounds.

5 **CHECK FOR THE JPMA CERTIFICATION.** The JPMA (the Juvenile Products Manufacturers Association) has a pretty good safety certification program for strollers. They require that strollers have a locking device to prevent accidental folding and meet other safety standards, such as those for brakes. You can contact the JPMA for a list of certified strollers at (856) 231-8500 or jpma.org.

6 **JOGGING STROLLERS ARE BEST FOR BABIES OVER ONE YEAR OF AGE.** Yes, some stroller makers tout their joggers for babies as young as six weeks (or six months) of age. But we think the neck muscles of such small infants can't take the shocks of jogging or walking on rough paths (or going over curbs). Ask your pediatrician if you need more advice on when it is safe to use a jogger.

Recalls: Where to Find Information

The U.S. Consumer Product Safety Commission's web site (cpsc. gov) and toll-free hotline at (800) 638-2772 (web: cpsc.gov) has the latest recall information on strollers and other juvenile products. It's easy to use—the hotline is a series of recorded voice mail messages that you access by following the prompts. The same info is online. You can also report any potential hazard you've discovered or an injury to your child caused by a product.

 **Smart Shopper Tips**

Smart Shopper Tip #1
Give it a Test Drive
"My friend was thinking of buying a stroller online, sight unseen. Should you really buy a stroller without trying it first?"

It's best to try before you buy. Most stores have at least one stroller set up as a floor model. Give it a whirl, practice folding it up, and check the steering. One smart tip: put some weight in the stroller seat (borrow a friend's toddler or use a backpack full of books that weighs about 15 pounds). The steering and maneuverability will feel different if the stroller is loaded than empty—obviously, that's a more real world test-drive.

Once you've tried it out, shop for price through 'net or mail order sources. Ask retailers if they will meet or beat prices quoted to you online (many quietly do so). What if you live in Kansas and the nearest dealer for a stroller you want is in, say, Texas? Then you may have no choice but to buy sight unseen—but just make sure the web site or catalog has a good return policy. Another tip: use message boards like those on our web site (BabyBargains.com) to quiz other parents about stroller models.

If you buy a stroller from a store, we strongly recommend open-

Guaranteed Frustration: Baby gear warranties can leave you fuming

It's a fact of life: sometimes you buy a product that breaks only days after purchase. So, you pick up the phone and call the manufacturer and ask about their warranty. "Sure, we'll help," says the customer service rep. In no time, you have a replacement product and a happy parent.

Fast forward to real life. Most parents find warranties only guarantee frustration—especially with baby products like strollers and other travel gear. Numerous hassles confront parents who find they have a defective product, from endless waits on hold to speak with a customer service rep (on a non-toll free line, naturally) to the process of returning a product.

First, consider the process of actually registering an item. Filling out a warranty card often requires information that you can only find on the product box or carton. Some parents find this out the hard way . . . after they've hauled all the boxes off to the trash. Even worse: some baby product makers like Peg Perego actually request a copy of the sales receipt for their warranty form. Hello? What about gifts?

Then, let's say something goes wrong. Your new stroller breaks a wheel. That brand new baby monitor goes on the fritz after one week. If it is a gift or you lost the receipt, the store you bought it from may say "tough luck"—call the manufacturer. With many warranties, you have to return the defective item to the manufacturer *at your expense*. And then you wait a few more weeks while they decide to fix or replace the item. Typically you have to pay for return shipping—and that can be expensive for a bulky item like a stroller. And then you must do without the product for weeks while they fix it.

Dealing with the customer service departments at some baby product makers can add insult to injury. It seems like some companies can count their customer service staff with one hand—or one finger, in some cases. The result: long waits on hold. Or it takes days to get responses to emails. The U.S. offices of foreign baby product companies seem to be the worst at customer service staffing (Chicco, Perego), while giant

ing the box and making sure everything is in there BEFORE you leave the store!

Smart Shopper Tip #2
What Features Really Matter?

"Let's cut through the clutter here. Do I really need a stroller that has deluxe shock absorbers and four-wheel drive? What features are really important?"

firms such as Graco and Evenflo have better customer service.

And customer service can go from good to bad in the blink of an eye. Combi was known for its good customer service until a meltdown back in 2001—then a large influx of calls from a recall and a staff shortage created long waits on hold, unreturned emails and frustrated consumers. Combi has long since the fixed the problem, but other companies (notably Fisher Price, Chicco, Peg Perego) continue to struggle with providing decent customer service.

The bottom line: it's no wonder that when something goes wrong, consumers just consider trashing the product and buying a new one. And let's be realistic: paying $20 in shipping to send back a broken $39 stroller doesn't make much sense. Here's our advice:

◆ **Keep your receipts.** It doesn't have to be fancy—a shoebox will do. That way you can prove you bought that defective product. If the item was a gift, keep the product manual and serial number.

◆ **If something goes wrong, call the manufacturer.** We're always surprised by how many consumers don't call the manufacturer FIRST when a problem arises. You might be surprised at how responsive some companies are at fixing an issue.

◆ **If the problem is a safety defect, immediately stop using the product** and file a complaint with the Consumer Product Safety Commission (www.cpsc.gov). Also contact the company.

◆ **Attack the problem multiple ways.** Don't just call; also send an email and perhaps a written letter. Be reasonable: allow the company one to two business days to reply to a phone call or email.

◆ **Let other parents know about your experiences.** The best way to fix lousy customer service? Shame companies into doing it better. Post your experiences to the message boards on our site (BabyBargains.com) and other parenting sites. Trust us, companies are sensitive to such criticism.

strollers

STROLLERS AND MORE

Walk into any baby store and you'll encounter a blizzard of strollers. Do you want a stroller with a full recline? Boot and retractable canopy? What the heck is a boot, anyway? Here's a look at the features in the stroller market today:

Features for baby:

◆ **Reclining seat.** Since babies less than six months of age sleep most of the time and can't hold their heads up, strollers that have reclining seats are a plus. Yet, the *extent* of a stroller's seat recline varies by model. Some have full reclines, a few recline part of the way (120 degrees) and some don't recline at all. FYI: just because a stroller has a "full recline" does NOT mean it reclines to 180 degrees. It may recline slightly less than that for safety reasons.

◆ **Front (or napper) bar.** As a safety precaution, many strollers have a front bar (also called a napper bar) that keeps baby secure (though you should always use the stroller's safety harness). Better strollers have a bar that's padded and removable. Why removable? Later, when your baby gets to toddler hood, you may need to remove the bar to make it easier for the older child to access the stroller. FYI: Some strollers have a kid snack tray, which serves much the same function as a napper bar.

◆ **Seat padding.** You'll find every possible padding option out there, from bare bones models with a single piece of fabric to strollers with deluxe-quilted padding made from fine fabrics hand woven by monks in Luxembourg. (Okay, just kidding—the monks actually live in Switzerland). For seating, some strollers have cardboard platforms (these can be uncomfortable for long rides) and other models have fabric that isn't removable or machine washable (see below for more on this).

◆ **Shock absorbers or suspension systems.** Yes, a few strollers do have wheels equipped with shock absorbers or suspension springs for a smoother ride. We're unsure how effective this feature really is— it's not like you could wheel baby over potholes without waking her up. On the other hand, if you live in a neighborhood with uneven or rough sidewalks, this feature might be worth considering.

◆ **Wheels.** In reality, how smooth a stroller rides is more related to the type of wheels. The general rule: the more the better. Strollers with double wheels on each leg ride smoother than single wheels. Most strollers have plastic wheels. In recent years, some stroller makers have rolled out models with "pneumatic" or inflated wheels. These offer a smoother ride.

◆ **Weather protection.** Yes you can buy a stroller that's outfitted for battle with a winter in New England, for example. The options include retractable hoods/canopies and "boots" (which protect a child's feet) to block out wind, rain or cold. Fabrics play a role here too—some strollers feature quilted hoods to keep baby warm and others claim they are water repellent. While a boot is an option some may not need, hoods/canopies are rather important, even if just to keep the sun out of baby's eyes. Some strollers only have a canopy (or "sunshade") that partially covers baby, while other models have a full hood that can completely cover the stroller. Look for canopies that have lots of adjustments (to block a setting sun) and have "peek-a-boo" windows that let you see baby even when closed.

What if the stroller you've fallen in love with only has a skimpy canopy? Or lacks a rain cover? Good news: you can buy after-market accessories for more strollers. See the box on this page for sources.

Features for parents:

◆ **Storage baskets.** Many strollers have deep, under-seat baskets for storage of coats, purses, bags, etc. Yet, the amount of storage can vary sharply from model to model. Inexpensive umbrella strollers may have no basket at all, while other models have tiny baskets. Mass-market strollers (Graco, etc.) typically have the most storage; other stroller makers have been playing catch-up in the basket game. Combi, for example, has added new models with bigger storage baskets. One tip: it's not just the *size* of the storage basket but the *access* to it that counts. Some strollers have big baskets but are practically inaccessible when the seat is reclined. A support bar blocks others. Tip: when stroller shopping, recline the seat and see if you can access the basket.

strollers

Handy stroller accessories

What if your stroller doesn't have a rain cover? One option is the Protect a Bub Rain & Wind Cover, which comes in both single ($23) and double versions ($29). Made by an Australian company (web:protect-a-bubusa. com).

What if you buy a stroller that is great, except for a skimpy canopy? You can fix that with a cool sunshade from Australia called the Pepeny (web: pepeny.com). This shade screens out the weather, sunlight and UV . . . and is all the rage in New York City. The Pepeny comes in several colors and fits most

stroller models. It's about $40 to $55 and available in stores and on web sites like BabySunProtection.com. This would also be a good idea for California parents to screen out low-angle sun.

◆ *Removable seat cushion for washing.* Let's be honest: strollers can get icky in a jiffy. Crushed-in cookies, spilt juice and the usual grime can make a stroller a mobile dirt-fest. Some strollers have removable seat cushions that are machine washable—other models let you remove *all* of the fabric for a washing. Watch out for those models with non-removable fabric/seat cushions—while you can clean these strollers in one of those manual car washes (with a high-pressure nozzle), it's definitely a hassle (especially in the winter).

◆ *Lockable wheels.* Some strollers have front wheels that can be locked in a forward position—this enables you to more quickly push the stroller in a straight line (nice for excising).

◆ *Wheel size.* You'll see just about every conceivable size wheel out there on strollers today. As you might guess, the smaller wheels are good for maneuverability in the mall, but larger wheels handle rough sidewalks (or gravel paths) much better.

◆ *Handle/Steering.* This is an important area to consider—most strollers have a single bar handle, which enables one-handed steering. Other strollers have two handles (example: Maclarens as well as Perego's Pliko line). Two handles require two hands to push, but enable a stroller to fold up compactly, like an umbrella. It's sort of a trade-off—steer ability versus easier fold. There are other handle issues to consider as well. A handful of strollers feature a "reversible" handle. Why would you want that? By reversing the handle, you can push the stroller while the baby faces you (better for small infants). Later, you can reverse the handle so an older child can look out while being pushed from behind. (Note: models with reversible handles seem increasingly rare in recent years; instead some strollers have reversible *seats*. We'll note which have this feature later).

Another important factor: consider the handle *height*. Some handles have adjustable heights to better accommodate taller parents (more on this later). However, just because a stroller touts this feature doesn't mean it adjusts to accommodate a seven-foot tall parent (at most, you get an extra inch or two of height). Finally, a few stroller makers offer "one-touch fold" handles. Hit a button on the stroller and it can be folded up with one motion. On our web site BabyBargains.com (click on Bonus Material), we have a chart that lists strollers with height-adjustable handles and one-touch folds.

◆ *Compact fold.* We call it the trunk factor—when a stroller is folded, will it fit in your trunk? Some strollers fold compactly and can fit in a narrow trunk. Other strollers are still quite bulky when folded—think about your trunk space before buying. Unfortunately, we are not aware of any web site that lists the size/footprint of strollers when folded. You are on your own to size up models when folded in a store, compared to your trunk (hint: take trunk measurements before you go stroller shopping). Not only should you consider how compactly a stroller folds, but also how it folds in general. The best strollers fold with just one or two quick motions; others require you to hit 17 levers and latches. The latest stroller fold fad: strollers that fold standing UP instead of down. Why is this better? Because strollers that fold down to the ground can get dirty/scratched in a parking lot.

◆ **Durability.** Should you go for a lower-price stroller or a premium brand? Let's be honest: the lower-priced strollers (say, under $100) have nowhere near the durability of the models that cost $200 to $400. Levers that break, reclining seats that stop reclining and other glitches can make you despise a cheap stroller mighty quick. Yet, some parents don't need a stroller that will make it through the next world war. If all you do is a couple of quick trips to the mall every week or so, then a less expensive stroller will probably be fine. However, if you plan to use the stroller for more than one child, live in an urban environment with rough sidewalks, or plan extensive outdoor adventures with baby, then invest in a better stroller. Later in this chapter, we'll go over specific models and give you brand recommendations for certain lifestyles.

◆ **Overall weight.** Yes, it's a dilemma: the more feature-laden the stroller, the more it weighs. And strollers are often priced via the Bikini Principle: the less it weighs, the more it costs. Yet it doesn't take lugging a 30-pound stroller in and out of a car trunk more than a few times to justify the expense of a lighter-weight design. Carefully consider a stroller's weight before purchase. Some parents end up with two strollers—a lightweight/umbrella-type stroller for quick trips (or air travel) and then a more feature-intensive model for extensive outdoor outings.

One factor to consider with weight: steel vs. aluminum frames. Steel is heavier than aluminum, but some parents prefer steel because it gives the stroller a stiffer feel. Along the same lines, sometimes we get complaints from parents who own aluminum strollers because they feel the stroller is too "wobbly"—while it's lightweight, one of aluminum's disadvantages is its flexibility. One tip for dealing with a wobbly stroller: lock the front wheels so you can push the stroller in a straight line. That helps to smooth the ride.

Smart Shopper Tip #3
The Cadillac Escalade or Ford Focus Dilemma

"This is nuts! I see cheap umbrella strollers that sell for $30 on one hand and then fancy designer brands for $300 on the other. Do I really need to spend a fortune on a stroller?"

Whether you drive a Cadillac Escalade or Ford Focus, you'll still get to your destination. And that fact pretty much applies to strollers too—most function well enough to get you and baby from point A to point B, not matter what the price.

So, should you buy the cheapest stroller you can find? Well, no. There *is* a significant difference in quality between a cheap $30 umbrella stroller and a name brand that costs $100, $200 or more. Unless you want the endless headaches of a cheap stroller (wheels that break, parts that fall off), it's important to invest in a stroller that will make it through the long haul.

The real question is: do you need a fancy stroller loaded with features or will a simple model do? To answer that, you need to consider *how* you will use the stroller. Do you live in the suburbs and just need the stroller once a week for a quick spin at the mall? Or do you live in an big city where a stroller is your primary vehicle, taking all the abuse that a big city can dish out? Climate plays another factor—in the Northeast, strollers have to be winterized to handle the cold and snow. Meanwhile, in Southern California, full canopies are helpful for shading baby's eyes from late afternoon sunshine.

Figuring out how different stroller options fit your lifestyle/climate is the key to stroller happiness. Later in this chapter, we'll recommend several specific strollers for certain lifestyles and climates.

One final note: name-brand strollers with cachet actually have resale value. You can sell that pricey stroller on eBay, at a second-hand store, or via Craigslist and recoup some of your investment. The better the brand name (say, Bugaboo), the more the resale value. Unfortunately, the cheap brands like Graco, Evenflo and Kolcraft are worth little or nothing on the second-hand market—there is a reason for that (beyond snob appeal). Take a quick look at eBay's stroller section to see what we mean.

Smart Shopper Tip #4
Too tall for their own good

"I love our stroller, but my husband hates it. He's six feet tall and has to stoop over to push it. Even worse, when he walks, he hits the back of the stroller with his feet."

Strollers are made for *women* of average height. What's that? About 5'6". If you (or your spouse) are taller than that, you'll find certain stroller models will be a pain to use.

This is probably one of the biggest complaints we get from parents about strollers. Unfortunately, just a few stroller models have height-adjustable handles that let a six-foot tall person comfortably push a stroller without stooping over or hitting the back of the stroller with his feet. One smart shopping tip: if you have a tall spouse, make sure you take him or her stroller shopping with you. Checking out handle heights in person is the only way to avoid this problem.

The best stroller brands for taller parents: Maclaren and Peg

Perego (particularly, the Pliko, which has height adjustable handles). The worst? Combi, a Japanese brand that has low-handle heights.

Smart Shopper Tip #5
The Myth of the Magic Bullet Stroller

"I'd like to buy just one stroller—a model that works with an infant car seat and then converts to full-featured pram and then finally a jogger for kids up to age 4. And I want it to weigh less than 10 pounds. And sell for just under $50. What model do you suggest?"

Boy, that sounds like our email some days! We hear from parents all the time looking for that one model that will do it all. We call it the Myth of the Magic Bullet Stroller—an affordable product that morphs into seven different uses for children from birth to college. Sorry, we haven't found one yet.

The reality: most parents own more than one stroller. A typical set-up: one stroller (or a stroller frame) that holds an infant car seat and then a lightweight stroller that folds compactly for the mall/travel. Of course, we hear from parents who own four, five or six strollers, including specialty models like joggers, tandem units for two kids and more. First-time parents wonder if these folks have lost their minds, investing the equivalent of the gross national product of Aruba on baby transportation. Alas, most parents realize that as their baby grows and their needs change, so must their stroller. Far be it from us to suggest you buy multiple strollers, but at the same time, it is hard to recommend just one model that works for everyone. That's why the recommendations later in this chapter are organized by lifestyle and use.

 *Wastes of Money*

GIVE THE "BOOT" THE BOOT. Some expensive strollers offer a "boot" or apron that fits over the baby's feet. This padded cover is supposed to keep the baby's feet dry and warm when it rains or snows. Sometimes you have to spend an extra $50 to $75 to get a stroller with this accessory. But do you really need this? We say save the extra cost and use a blanket instead. Or try a product like the Cozy Rosie or Bundle Me (mentioned later in this chapter), which are made of fleece and provide more warmth than a typical stroller boot. Or, if you decide you need a boot, buy a stroller model that includes this feature—several models now include a boot as standard equipment.

2 **SILLY ACCESSORIES.** Entrepreneurs have worked overtime to invent all kinds of silly accessories that you "must have" for your stroller. We've seen stroller "snack trays" ($15) for babies who like to eat on the run. Another company made a clip-on bug repellent, which allegedly used sound waves to scare away insects. Yet another money-waster: extra seat cushions or head supports for infants made in your stroller's matching fabric. You can find these same items in solid colors at discount stores for 40% less.

So which stroller accessories are worth the money? One accessory we do recommend is a toy bar (about $10 to $20), which attaches to the stroller. Why is this a good buy? If toys are not attached, your baby will probably punt them out the stroller. We also like Kelgar's Stroll'r Hold'r cup holder ($8, call 972-250-3838 or web: kelgar.com) for strollers that lack this feature.

What about stroller handle extensions? If you find yourself kicking the back of the stroller as you walk, you might want to invest in one of these $20 devices. An example: the Stroller Extension Extender Handle by Stroller Stretcher (strollerstrecher.com; sold on ComfortFirst.com for $15). Another option: the Stroller Handle Extender from MBS (mbsolutionsinc.com) for $23. It attaches to the stroller handle with Velcro and adds about eight inches.

3 **"NEW" OLD STOCK.** A reader alerted us to this online scam— the problem of "new" old stock. A stroller she ordered from a small web site was described as a "new Chicco stroller." Turns out, the stroller she got was seven years old. Yes, technically it was "new," as in "not previously used" and still in its original box. Unfortunately, since it was sitting in a warehouse for seven years, it had a cracked canopy, torn fabric and other problems. Apparently, there must be warehouses full of "new" old baby products out there for whatever reason. Our advice: request MODEL YEAR info on strollers or other products when that isn't clearly listed online. While previous year models can be a great deal, we wouldn't buy anything over three years old. . . even if a web site says it is "new."

 *Money-Saving Tips*

1 **STOP! DON'T BUY A FULL FEATURE STROLLER BEFORE THE BABY ARRIVES.** Here's a classic first-time parent mistake: buying an expensive, giant travel system stroller (a.k.a, the Baby Bus), thinking you need all those whiz-bang features. But the huge bulk and weight of those strollers will have you cursing the thing before your baby hits six months. A better bet: get a basic stroller frame for $50 (more details on these later), strap in an infant seat and viola! You have transport for an infant for up to six months. Trust us, after you've hung out with your baby for a few months, you'll have a much better idea what your stroller needs are. As your baby nears the limits on an infant car seat, THEN you buy a stroller.

2 **WHY NOT A BASIC UMBRELLA STROLLER?** If you only plan to use a stroller on infrequent trips to the mall, then a plain umbrella stroller for $30 to $40 will suffice. One caveat: make sure you get one that is JPMA certified (see the Safe & Sound section earlier). Second caveat: most plain umbrella strollers do NOT recline—you will not be able to use it until your baby is able to hold up his head (around six months).

3 **CONSIDER A CARRIER FOR NEWBORNS.** Yes, a simple baby carrier (sling, front carrier, etc) can be a much more affordable alternative to expensive strollers. The best carriers have padded straps and lumbar support to keep the strain off your back. Sure you will need a stroller at some point as your baby grows . . . but a carrier can be a cost-effective option to take your newborn or young infant to the store or mall.

4 **CHECK FOR SALES.** We're always amazed by the number of sales on strollers. We've seen frequent sales at the Burlington Coat Factory's Baby Depot, with good markdowns on even premium brand strollers (one caveat: read about Baby Depot's return policies in Chapter 2 before buying). Coupons are also common. Babies R Us offers occasional coupons in newspaper circulars as well as to parents on their mailing list. Another reason strollers go on sale: the manufacturers are constantly coming out with new models and have to clear out the old. Which leads us to the next tip.

5 **LOOK FOR LAST YEAR'S MODELS.** Every year, manufacturers roll out new models. In some cases, they add features; other times, they just change the fabric. What do they do with last year's stock? They discontinue it—and then it's sale time. You'll see these models on sale for as much as 50% off in stores and on the web. And it's not like stroller fabric fashion varies much from year to year—is there really much difference between "navy pin dot" and "navy with a raspberry diamond"? We say go for last year's fabric and save a bundle. See the Email from the Real World on the next page for a mom's story on her last year model deal.

6 **SCOPE OUT FACTORY SECONDS.** Believe it or not, some stroller manufacturers sell "factory seconds" at good discounts—these

E-Mail from The Real World
Last year's fashion, 50% off

A reader emailed her tip on how she saved over $100 on a stroller:

"When looking for strollers you can often get last year's version for a big discount. I purchased a previous year Maclaren model from babydealz.com for $190. That compares to the $300 price tag for the current year model from Babies R Us. As far as my research could tell, the models are identical except for the color pattern. A quick web search can turn up a number of sources that are selling last year's strollers; colors are limited (dmartstores.com had the widest selection) but it is a great way to save over $100 for a very nice stroller."

"cosmetically imperfect" models might have a few blemishes, but are otherwise fine. An example: one reader told us Peg Perego occasionally has factory sales from their Indiana headquarters. See Peg's contact info later in this chapter to find the latest schedule.

7 **DON'T FALL VICTIM TO STROLLER OVERKILL.** Seriously evaluate how you'll use the stroller and don't over buy. If a Toyota Camry will do, why buy a Lexus? You don't really need an all-terrain stroller or full-feature pram for mall trips. Flashy strollers can be status symbols for some parents—try to avoid "stroller envy" if at all possible.

8 **SELL YOUR STROLLER TO RECOUP YOUR INVESTMENT.** When you're done with the stroller, consign it at a second-hand store or sell it on Craigslist. You'd be surprised how much it can fetch. The best brands for resale are, not surprisingly, the better names we recommend in this chapter.

9 **WAREHOUSE CLUB DEALS.** Yes, Sam's and Costco periodically sell strollers, including joggers. At one point before going to press, Costco was selling Schwinn jogging strollers from their web site (Costco.com) at 45% under retail. Of course, these deals come and go—and like anything you see at the warehouse clubs, you have to snap it up quickly or it will be gone.

10 **EBAY/CRAIGSLIST**. It's highly addictive and for good reason—the site is more than just folks trying to unload a junky stroller they bought at K-Mart. Increasingly, baby gear retailers are using eBay to discreetly clear out overstock. Better to unload online the stuff that isn't moving than risk the wrath of local customers who bought the model for full price last week. An example: a reader scored a brand new Peg Perego for HALF the stroller's retail price through an eBay auction. Other readers regularly report saving $100 to $200 through eBay. Hint: many strollers sold online are last year's model or fashion. Be sure to confirm what you are buying (is it in an original box? No damage? Which model year?) before bidding.

And don't forget Craigslist either. Yes, this site has both junk and jewels. Be patient and search carefully to find worthwhile stroller buys.

The Name Game: Reviews of Selected Manufacturers

So, how to do we rate and review strollers? First, we do hands-on inspections in stores and trade shows. That involves giving the stroller a test spin, checking the fold and more. Next, we listen to you, the reader. The stroller message board on our web site is one of the most popular forums, brimming with over 1000 posts a month. As always, parent feedback is our secret sauce.

One key point to remember: the ratings in this section apply to the ENTIRE line of a company's strollers. No, we don't assign ratings to individual strollers, but we will comment on what we think are a company's best models. Following this section, we will give you several "lifestyle recommendations"—specific models of strollers to fit different parent lifestyles.

The prices quoted here are typical street prices—that is prices we saw in stores or on the 'net. In other cases, we used manufacturer's estimated retail prices.

The Ratings

A **EXCELLENT**—*our top pick!*

B **GOOD**— *above average quality, prices, and creativity.*

C **FAIR**—*could stand some improvement.*

D **POOR**—*yuck! Could stand some major improvement.*

Aprica *(310) 639-6387 or (201) 883-9800 web: apricausa.com.* Aprica has all but disappeared from the U.S. market in recent years, but you'll still see a few of their models in some stores. As a result, we've moved their former review to our web site (BabyBargains.com and click on Bonus Material).

Baby Jogger *Web: babyjogger.com.* Baby Jogger literally invented the jogging stroller category 20 years ago, but recently went through a bankruptcy and now has new owners. Their new emphasis: all-terrain models with swivel front wheels like the City Series (single, $350, double $550).

The models. The City Series has the easiest fold we've seen for such models: one-hand and zip! It's done. Baby Jogger seems to be moving away from its long-time emphasis on models for serious runners—now only one style features 20″ wheels while the others have 16″ wheels. Baby Jogger's running strollers now include the Performance series ($360 single, $460 double) and Q-series, the latter with a quick-fold feature ($230 to $350 for a single, $400 for a double). The Performance series has a one-step, quick-release seat recline, floating canopy for extra sun coverage, and a direct-pull brake.

Baby Jogger has made several improvements to the line over the past year—now, the company has a car seat adapter that works with Graco, Britax and Peg infant seats. And Baby Jogger has made the recline on the City Series even easier with just one central strap.

New for 2008, Baby Jogger has added two models to the City series: the City Mini ($200 single, $350 double) is Baby Jogger's first attempt to move into the regular stroller market (that is, strollers without air-filled wheels). The Mini (16.8 lbs. for the single, 23 lbs. for the double) is a tri-wheel model with 8″ quick-release wheels, an oversized canopy and full reclining seat. Also new: the City Elite ($400 single, $600 double) is similar to the Mini in terms of seat and canopy, but features 12″ air-filled tires and a parent console. Both the City Mini and Elite have Baby Jogger's quick-fold technology.

We were impressed with the City Mini's low weight—the double at 23 pounds makes it one of the lightest side-by-side strollers on the market. No, the fashion of the City Mini can't hold a candle to the Euro imports on the market today, but we thought it was well designed. If Baby Jogger adds a car seat adapter for the City Mini (unfortunately, it doesn't look like one will be available at launch), then these strollers could find a wide audience.

Also new for 2008: the ATS (All Terrain Swivel, $300, 21 lbs.). The ATS has 16″ rear wheels and a 12″ front wheel that can swivel or lock in place. Baby Jogger pitches this as a stroller that can be used both for walking and running. We're not so sure—runners tell us they find models like this vibrate even when the front wheel is locked (a better bet are true fixed wheel joggers). The ATS also features a parent console, suspension, large canopy and a 75 lbs. weight capacity.

Finally, Baby Jogger has also entered the hybrid jogging stroller/bike trailer segment with the Switchback ($580). It morphs back and forth between being a jogger and bike trailer without any special kit or tools.

Our view. How's the quality? Excellent, report our readers. Parents love the quick-fold and wide selection of accessories. We like how the company has tweaked models to add in features like parent consoles and better folding canopies. **Rating: A**

Baby Planet *630-790-3113, Web: Baby-Planet.com.* Baby Planet is the brainchild of former Kolcraft stroller designers who are aiming to inject a bit of high style into the stroller market. Their first results channel a bit of Maclaren and a touch of Stokke's Xplory.

The models. Baby Planet's most inno-vate model is the Max, a Stokke Xplory-like tri-wheel stroller that is sold in three versions: the Max Universal, Max Traveler and Max Pro (pictured). The Max Universal ($270) is a stroller frame that holds most major brand  car seats (Graco, Britax, Peg). The Max Traveler ($330, 21.2 lbs.) is a tri-wheel stroller with a lightweight aluminum frame, adjustable han-dle, parent tray with two cup holders, front swivel wheel and stor-age basket. Finally, the Max Pro ($400) includes both features: you get the stroller frame to hold an infant car seat AND the stroller seat.

Baby Planet's other stroller line is a riff on the Maclaren Volo . . . named the Solo. This lightweight model (15.4 lbs.) features a swoop-ing frame coated in a special metallic paint. Features include an oversized basket, adjustable footrest and compact fold. The Solo will be sold in two versions: Sport ($190) and Deluxe ($270). The Deluxe adds a napper bar, telescoping handle and child cup hold-er. A double version of the Solo, the Unity Sport (27.8 lbs.) is $320 and features a cool, foam-padded "Easy-Steer" handle, which is excellent for taller parents.

To add a bit of eco-cache to its brand, Baby Planet has rolled out an Endangered Species line of strollers–four versions of the Solo Sport that feature animal prints . . . the company will donate $5 per stroller to the Wildlife Conservancy Fund.

Our view. Baby Planet just began shipping its strollers about a month before we went to press, so feedback is limited. But what lit-tle we've heard so far is positive–the Max, while pricey, earns kudos for its ease of use. We think the Max Traveler or Max Pro are a bet-ter value than the Max Universal. Readers like the Unity Double and its clever handle. Parents also like Baby Planet's eco ethics: the com-pany even has a recycling program for used strollers, which are donated to charity or disassembled and sent to a recycling facility. So we'll give this brand an initial thumbs up. **Rating: A-**

Baby Trend *(800) 328-7363, (909) 902-5568, Web: babytrend.com.* Baby Trend's biggest selling stroller isn't really a stroller at all–it's a stroller *frame*. Here's an overview of the line:

The models. The Snap N Go is such a simple concept it's amaz-ing someone else didn't think of it years ago–basically it's a stroller frame that lets you snap in most major-brand infant car seats. Presto! Instant travel system at a fraction of the price. The original Snap N

strollers

Go was just a frame and wheels and sat low to the ground. Newer model Snap & Go's ($50) now have a big basket and sit higher. And memo to parents of twins: there's even a double version of the Snap N Go that holds two car seats ($90 on WalMart.com). Be aware that the Snap N Go doesn't work with ALL infant car seats (but most major brands will fit). Consult Baby Trend's web site (FAQ's) for a current list.

The Snap N Go has been so successful it has spawned knock-offs from several competitors, namely Kolcraft, Combi and Graco. We will review those options later. All in all, we think the Snap & Go is a winner.

Besides the stroller frame, Baby Trend also offers travel systems, double strollers and joggers.

Baby Trend's travel systems combine their Flex-Loc infant seat (see review in last chapter) with basic low-end strollers. Example: the Trendsport Traveler system for $110 (car seat and stroller). That's a great price, but the stroller (18 lbs.) is nothing fancy—steel frame, three-point harness and two-position recline. You do get a decent canopy, one-hand fold and big basket, but the recline is only to 145 degrees (not a full recline). Baby Trend sells more expensive travel systems with upgraded features and fabric for $150-$180. FYI: The company refers to its travel systems by the fabric name (the Zanzibar travel system, for example)—it's the same Trendsport stroller, just a different fabric.

Baby Trend is a big player in the jogging stroller market—their flagship model is the Expedition. This steel frame jogger is loaded with features (reclining seat, five-point harness, parent tray with cup holders and ratcheting canopy) and is sold as a travel system ($200) or separately ($100).

We should also note that Baby Trend markets their products under the name "Swan" for specialty stores. Basically, these are the same products/models as Baby Trend makes, albeit with a few cosmetic differences (fabric color, etc.).

FYI: Baby Trend still sells the Sit N Stand stroller, an innovative "pushcart" that combined a stroller with a jump seat for an older child. That has prompted a lawsuit from Joovy, a competitor that acquired the patent rights to the Sit N Stand. So you will see versions of this stroller both from Baby Trend (Sit N Stand) and Joovy (Caboose) on the market until a court sorts out the claims.

Our view. As we've noted in other parts of this book, the best word we can use to describe Baby Trend is flakey. The company clearly sells a large number of strollers and car seats . . . yet Baby Trend's marketing is at best inconsistent. It announces products that never ship and other hot-selling items often go out of stock. And since Baby Trend's distribution is often limited to chain stores, finding one of their products is hit or miss.

Different versions spark confusion

Here's a common question we get at the home office: readers go into a chain store like Babies R Us and see a major brand stroller they like. Then, they visit a specialty store and see a similar model, but with some cosmetic differences . . . and a higher price tag. What's up with that? Big stroller makers like Graco have to serve two masters—chain stores and specialty retailers. Here's a little trick of the baby biz: stroller makers often take the same basic model of stroller and make various versions for different retailers. Hence, you'll see a Graco stroller with basic fabric in Babies R Us—and then the same model sold as a Laura Ashley stroller with fancier fabric in specialty stores. So is there any real difference besides the fabric color to justify the increase in price? Yes, sometimes the fabrics are upgraded (or there is more padding). But overall, you are basically seeing the same stroller. Our advice: if you can live with the basic version, go for it.

Based on our reader feedback, parents seem to love some of their products (particularly the Snap N Go) and loathe others (basically, most of their other strollers). Sure, their basic jogging strollers are cheap ($100), but are designed more for walkers (the heavy steel frames make actually jogging with a Baby Trend quite a chore). All in all, Baby Trend has been dogged by numerous quality problems when it comes to their regular strollers. Parents say parts break, wheels fall off and worse—"bad engineering" was how one parent put it. Example, on the Baby Trend Shuttle stroller: you can't open the canopy and have a drink in the holder at the same time! Doh! And before you buy a Baby Trend travel system, be sure to read the caveats to their infant car seat in our last chapter. So, it's hard to assign a rating. If we were just looking at the Snap N Go, we'd give them an A. Yet, the other models would barely earn a C. So, we'll compromise. **Rating: B-**

BeBeLove USA *Web: BeBeLoveUSA.com.* These low-end jogging strollers are sold on discount websites for $150 to $180. We weren't that impressed with the stroller design or features; and this brand is so obscure that we haven't heard much feedback from parents. **Rating: Not yet.**

BOB Strollers *Web: bobgear.com.* BOB has won accolades for their innovative joggers—you can tell these were designed by runners for runners. (Trivia note: BOB stands for Beast of Burden trailers—they decided BOB was easier to spell . . . and would avoid a lawsuit from Mick Jagger). BOB's strollers are billed as "sport utility" strollers and that's an apt moniker, as their rugged design (poly-

strollers

mer wheels to prevent rust, for example) and plush ride make these strollers best sellers despite their $300+ price tags. The BOB Sport Utility stroller comes in regular ($280, 23 lbs.) and deluxe ($350, 22 lbs.) versions—the latter has aluminum alloy rims. In recent years, BOB has branched out into strollers with turnable front wheels (the Revolution, $360 single 23 lbs., $530 double). In the past year, BOB debuted the Revolution 12″ AW stroller ($380 single 22 lbs., $550 double), which has aluminum alloy rims. Also new in the past year: an infant car seat adapter for BOB's double (Duallie) strollers. Compared to previous years, current year models add a deeper seat recline and a rear foot brake.

If you are a serious runner, the BOB Ironman Stroller ($350, 21 lbs.) is probably the pick of the litter, with smooth tires, stiffer shocks, suspension wheels and more. Plus the bright yellow color gives it bit of pizzazz lacking in most other joggers.

Parents give BOB excellent marks on quality and durability. Yes, these joggers are expensive, but worth it. Minor quibbles: the handlebars are not height adjustable, frustrating some parents. And the baskets could be a bit bigger and easier to access, especially on the Revolution. Nonetheless, BOB gets our highest rating. ***Rating: A***

Britax *Web: britaxusa.com.* Best-known for its well-made car seats, Britax launched a stroller line in 2005 so it could compete in the travel system market.

The Models. Britax offers three stroller options: Preview, Vigour and Verve. Let's take a look at each.

The Preview ($140, 17 lbs.) is Britax's knock-off of the Peg Pliko, down to the two "ergonomic" handles. This stroller, one of the few on the market that works with the Britax Companion infant seat, features a removable hood with window, aluminum frame, five-point harness, four position recline, adjustable leg rest and parent bag with bottle holder (but no cup holder).

The Vigour ($350, 27.5 lbs.) is Britax's take on the Bugaboo—a four-wheel model with 12″ rear wheels and smaller front wheels, a la the Cameleon. Compatible with Britax's Companion infant seat, the Vigour features a seat that removes (to fit an infant car seat) or reverses (so you can face your baby), infinite seat recline, removable sun canopy and height adjustable handle. Again, no cup holder.

The Verve ($200, 17 lbs.) is the only Britax stroller that doesn't work with their Companion infant seat. This tri-wheel stroller features dinky wheels and basket, aluminum frame, one hand fold, small basket and multi-position seat recline.

As we were gong to press, we learned Britax has discontinued the Verve and is phasing out the Preview (the Vigour lives on to see another day). Yet the Verve and Preview were still sold online as we went to press, so you may still see them out there in 2008. Britax does plan to release new stroller models in 2008, but details were not available (see our blog for updates).

Our View. Britax's stroller line is basically a "do over"—the company's first attempt at strollers bombed. And no wonder. For a company that made its name on a slew of *innovative* car seats, Britax initial strollers strangely lacked in both design and features. Let's get real: who comes out with a stroller today WITHOUT a parent cup holder? Britax, apparently, as the Preview omits this key feature that is standard on just about every other stroller on the market.

Our readers give the Britax stroller line similarly mixed reviews. The best thing that can be said for the Preview is that it works with Britax's Companion infant seat. Tall parents gripe about the low handles . . and the fact that you need THREE hands to recline the stroller—two hands to squeeze the release buttons and another hand to actually push the seat down. When you recline the seat, you can't access the basket. While you might expect to see those flaws on a cheap-o $50 stroller sold at Wal-Mart, Britax owes its customers more at this price point. All in all, the durability and overall quality of the Preview is below average. It's no wonder Britax is discontinuing this model.

As for the Vigour and Verve, both of these strollers get somewhat better marks from parents—fans of the Vigour like its smooth glide and flat fold. But the skimpy sunshade and heavy weight (it is nearly 8 pounds heavier than the Bugaboo Cameleon) probably

E-Mail from The Real World
The Weight Game

"I saw the same stroller listed with two different weights online. How can the same model weigh five pounds less on one site?"

Good question—call it the weight shell game. We've noticed some web sites play fast and loose with the weights of strollers listed on their sites. Why? What parents' value most in a stroller is LIGHT overall weight—and online sellers know this. So, why not cheat and list a stroller's weight . . . minus a few items like a canopy, basket or other amenities? Another explanation: stroller manufacturers often tweak their models from year to year, adding new features. This can add additional ounces, but some web sites "forget" to update the weight. Yes, it is deceptive—but there are ways around the problem. First, this book lists the true weight for most models. If in doubt, check the manufacturer's web site, which almost always lists the correct weight.

explain the Vigour's anemic sales.

The take-home message: despite its strength in car seats, Britax has struck out so far in strollers. A lack of quality, design and innovation make Britax strollers not worthy of their namesake brand. If Britax expects to compete against the Maclarens and Bugaboos of the world, they need to try harder. *Rating: B-*

Shopping Cart Covers: Advice & Picks

Grocery store carts aren't exactly the cleanest form of transportation—yet once your baby outgrows her infant car seat, you will put likely baby in the little seat up front . . . and quickly realize that keeping the carts clean doesn't seem to be a high priority for most stores. Some stores have added in a wipes dispenser near the carts, but you can't get the gook off the fabric belts— that's just gross.

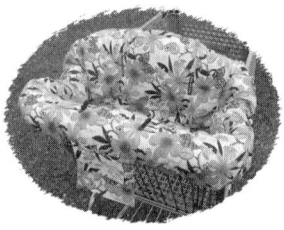

To the rescue comes the shopping cart cover, basically a fabric seat that provides a clean and safe space for baby while you shop. If you decide one is for you, there are surprisingly quite a few options to choose from in a variety of price ranges. Here's what to look for in a shopping cart cover:

◆ *Washability*. Well, that sounds like a no-brainer, but be sure to check the cover's washing instructions. Machine washable and dryable are key.

◆ *Side coverage*. Cheaper cart covers don't cover the entire cart seat—some leave the sides of the cart exposed, etc. Make sure the ENTIRE cart seat is covered.

◆ *Pockets and toy loops.* The best covers have pockets for toys, diapers, wipes, etc. Make sure the pockets have zipper or Velcro closures—and are located on the back of the cover, so they are out of baby's reach. Toy loops are great for attaching toys.

◆ *Flexibility*. Can the cover also work on restaurant high chairs? Will the cover work on those super-sized carts you see at Costco, BJ's or Sam's? Make sure the cover has large enough leg holes to accommodate a growing child.

Bugaboo *800-460-2922. Web: bugaboo.nl.* Bugaboo. It's Dutch for "priced as if from a hotel mini-bar."

The Models. Here's an unlikely recipe for success in the stroller biz. Take a Dutch-designed stroller, attach a $700 price tag and voila! Instant hit, right? Well, chalk this one up to some creative marketing (or at least, lucky timing).

Bugaboo's breakthrough success was the Frog, named as such

◆ **Safety**. Make sure the cover has enough padding for smaller infants. Seat belts are a must—the cover should have its own seat belt to secure baby AND securely attach the cover to the cart. Of course, the cover should be easy to install and remove.

Speaking of safety, that's another reason to have a cart cover—falls from shopping carts are the leading cause of head injuries to young children, according to the Consumer Products Safety Commission. Every year, 12,800 kids under age five are taken to the hospital emergency room after falling from shopping carts. A key reason: carts with broken or missing safety belts. Having a shopping cart cover with a secure belt is a smart way to avoid such injuries.

Here are our top picks for shopping cart covers:

◆ **SewCuteBoutique.com** is queen of the cart cover world, based on reader feedback from our message boards. Their $43 cover is all cotton with one-inch thick quilt batting, storage pocket, toy loops, matching pillow and adjustable safety belt. It fits all carts, including the ones at warehouse clubs.

◆ **ChubbySeats.com** is another great choice, with thick batting and customized fabric options. Their $45 cover includes two bungee bands for toys and cups, two pockets an attached tote bag and more.

◆ **The KozyPal** cart cover (kozypalcartcovers.com) is available in 250 different fabrics and wins kudos from our readers for quality. The company has three dozen styles of in-stock covers for $60 to $100 (most are under $70). Or have one made-to-order, with their fabric or yours. Options include diaper pouches, bottle holders and more.

Our readers also recommended the Kangaroodle.com cover ($50) with its matching storage bag, the BuggyBagg ($60), and the Clean Shopper ($35). The latter just has quilted cotton fabric, no batting— it is no frills, but does the job. Readers gave much lower marks to the cart covers from Infantino and Nojo, which we would avoid.

strollers

for its small wheels in front that give it a frog-like look. The Frog is a clever hybrid of an all-terrain and carriage stroller, pitched to parents for its multiple uses. The Frog comprises three parts: an aluminum frame and bassinet that can later be replaced by a stroller seat (included with canopy and basket). It weighs about 20 lbs., which is rather amazing.

Oh, and we forgot the fourth ingredient of the Bugaboo—hype.

The Bugaboo folks were at the right place at the right time. How did the Bugaboo become so hot? Sure, it was fashionable, but that doesn't quite explain it. Nope, the answer is Bugaboo had one of the great product placements of all time . . . it was the featured stroller on HBO's *Sex in the City*. The rest is stroller history. In no time, celebs like Gwyneth Paltrow were swishing their Bugaboos across the pages of *People* magazine. The Bugaboo was the first baby stroller to cross paths with the white-hot supernova that is celebrity culture these days.

Cleverly, Bugaboo played on its Dutch design roots . . . even though (shhh! don't tell anyone!) the Bugaboo is made in Taiwan, not Amsterdam.

Figuring a $700 stroller was a bit bourgeois, Bugaboo's sequel to the Frog—the aptly named Cameleon—now costs $900. The Cameleon adds a more springy suspension on the front wheels, plus a slightly larger seat frame and higher chassis. Unlike the Frog, the Cameleon is available in a wide range of color combinations—you can choose from four base colors and eight top colors, mix and match. Also new: a height adjustable handle.

If that is too much, the stripped down Gecko also joins the Bugaboo line. The Gecko omits the front suspension and is lighter (18 lbs. versus 20 lbs. for the Cameleon). It sells for $680. We suppose the Gecko is for B-list celebrities.

And for those with a three-picture movie deal with Dreamworks, Bugaboo has a limited edition Cameleon model sold at Neiman Marcus: $1200 for a stroller with metallic silver fabric. And, here's a shock, the special silver cup holder is included!

New in the past year, Bugaboo has debuted their first compact stroller: the Bee ($530, 22 lbs). The Bee is pitched to urban dwellers with its narrow width (20", about four inches narrower than other Bugaboos) oversized canopy, reversible seat, and four-position seat recline.

In other news, Bugaboo has brought back the Frog and is selling it at (gasp!) Babies R Us. Sure, BRU just has two colors (black, red), but that is a sure sign that Bugaboo is going mainstream.

FYI: Bugaboo also sells a raft of accessories for its strollers (what? you thought that would be included?). Add in these extras and you could be out $1000 or more. Example: a $45 car seat adapter lets you attach most major brand infant car seats to the frame. A cup holder is $25, parasol $40, foot muff $70 to $130.

Our view. In our last edition, we rated the Bugaboo an "Oh, please!" This apparently upset some readers, who thought we should have at least assigned a letter grade. So, let's look at this rationally. Parents who have bought a Bugaboo almost unanimously praise its quality and ease of use—fans love the smooth steering, cozy bassinet, reversible seat and so on.

The downsides to owning a Bugaboo, besides the price? Unlike other strollers that just pop out of your trunk and set up with one motion, the Bugaboo Cameleon, Frog and Gecko require a bit of fussing to assemble. Why? To fold a Bugaboo, you must first remove the seat—that's a major pain, especially for folks who live in the suburbs and plan to fold it up frequently to fit in a trunk (and you'll need a big trunk). So, setting up the Bugaboo requires re-attaching the seat to the frame. Sure, this takes 30 seconds or so, which isn't forever—but about 25 seconds longer than most strollers.

So, a Bugaboo is probably best for urban dwellers or folks who don't plan to break it down frequently. (The Bee is an exception—it is easy to fold and set-up).

But does ANYONE need a $1000 stroller? (Let's get real—after you add all those cute accessories, we are talking about spending a grand on a baby stroller). We realize this is a rhetorical question . . . and in a country where a pair of Manolo Blahniks are the same price as a Bugaboo stroller, we can see how some folks could do the mental gymnastics to convince themselves this stroller isn't THAT expensive.

On the other hand, we know readers of this book sometimes get a stroller as a gift—and if your relative has the bank roll, why not? So we will give Bugaboo a rating and our recommendation . . . if the funds are coming out of someone else's wallet! ***Rating: A—if someone else is paying for it.***

BumbleRide *800-530-3930. Web: bumbleride.com.* BumbleRide's mission is to inject a bit of fashion into a stroller market often marked by models that are dull and duller. Started by a husband and wife team in San Diego, BumbleRide's bright colors have set our message boards buzzing with parents who have been impressed with the brand.

The Models. The Flyer is a good place to start. This $325 carriage stroller weighs 19 lbs. and features a five-point harness, reversible handle (which is nice), four-position recline, adjustable footrest and mesh basket. Best of all, it is compatible with several major infant car seats. The only negative: it is quite bulky when folded, so you'll need a large trunk to haul it around. In a recent update, BumbleRide made the rear wheels of the Flyer unlock and swivel, which makes pushing easier when the handle is reversed. A detachable cup holder rounds out the features.

New this year is the Indie ($400, 20 lbs.), which replaces Bumbleride's most popular model, the Rocket. Much like the model it replaced, the Indie is a tri-wheel stroller with quick release 12" inflated tires, boot, adjustable handle, full recline and deep storage basket. The big difference: the Indie has a much more compact fold, weighs five pounds less . . . and costs about $70 more than the Rocket. Basically, the Indie is a more stylish version of the Mountain Buggy Urban Single.

BumbleRide's most expensive model is the Queen B ($430, 31 lbs.), a pram-style stroller with wire basket. Yes, it comes with plush padding, reclining seat, boot and more. Good news: the current Queen B has front swivel wheels, replacing the fixed wheels of previous models.

And now, from Europe . . .

Ah, you've got to love the web. Today you can zip over to European baby product web sites and ogle the latest strollers swishing down the streets of Milan or Paris. Many of these strollers are discussed on our message boards at BabyBargains.com, as parents scheme to find ways to import them to the U.S.

The biggest cross-ocean import in recent years was the Bugaboo, that legendary stroller designed in the Netherlands (but made in Taiwan). So why don't we see more European strollers here? And why are U.S. stores instead filled with cheap Chinese-made models, invariably in navy blue?

Let's take a look at the biggest trends for strollers in Europe . . . and why many of these strollers fail to make a splash here in North America (special thanks to "American Mama," a member of our message boards for sharing these insights after living and traveling extensively in Europe).

◆ **Pram madness.** Europeans live a much different lifestyle than your average American—they walk more places, take public transport and don't drive as much. Hence, strollers tend to be heavier since you aren't lifting the thing in and out of a trunk. European strollers feature big wheels, the better to ride over cobblestones and rough sidewalks. Prams are common—these combine a stroller and bassinet. Again, nice when walking from your flat to a café in Rome. Prices for prams run $450 to $700 in Europe—the bassinets alone can cost $170 or more! An odd contradiction: big strollers are popular in Europe, despite the fact that their apartments, elevators and shops are small. And public transport is so crowded.

Our view. We will give BumbleRide its due—they have helped brighten an otherwise navy blue world. And the company has tried to improve the line's initial shortcomings—we like the new, lower weight Indie, whose compact fold addressed a past gripe. Sure, the models have occasional hiccups (the cup holder on the new Indie gets in the way when you fold the stroller), but BumbleRide is quick to fix problems. All in all, quality is good and we will give BumbleRide our recommendation. **Rating: A-**

Carter's *These strollers are made by Kolcraft; see their review at the end of this section in "Other Brands."*

Chariot *Web: ChariotCarriers.com.* Canuck outdoor brand Chariot takes a different approach to the jogger market—Chariot makes bicycle trailers that covert into jogging strollers. If you are an

◆ *My stroller, my country.* Imagine if every state had its own stroller brand—Texas joggers, Utah umbrella strollers, etc. Europe is like that, with many countries boasting their own stroller brands (Emmaljunga in Sweden, Jane in Spain, Bebe Confort in France, etc). Europeans are often loyal to their own country's stroller maker (thanks to good distribution and marketing), but what sells in Portugal doesn't necessary translate across the border. Or the ocean.

◆ *Cup holder, what cup holder?* Here's one key reason many European strollers fail in the U.S.—no cup holders. Europeans don't understand why mom needs a place to put that Starbucks cup; or why baby would need to have a snack tray. When Europeans want coffee, they go to a café, sit down and drink coffee. The whole concept of toting a beverage is alien. As a result, many European stroller makers fail to include this crucial feature in their models.

◆ *Colors.* Europeans love bright colors—strollers come in bright orange, plaids, two contrasting (clashing?) colors and more. Larger prams let Europeans show off strollers with lots of chrome. Why are dull colors so common here in the U.S.? Hard to say, but we wonder if it has something to do with the chains, which dominate retailing here. There seems to be a mindset among chain store buyers that unless it is dull and blue, it won't sell in South Dakota. Chains must stock one model nationwide, so they play it safe. And stroller makers simply respond to what the chain store buyers say they want.

avid bicyclist who also wants to occasionally jog with baby, Chariot offers nine models of bike trailers with optional kits that turn the trailers into jogging strollers. Example: the Chariot Cougar 1 ($435), which features plush harness straps, padded seats and adjustable suspension. Add a $68 jogging kit and you've got a stroller. While this is very pricey, we've been impressed with Chariot's quality—no, they aren't cheap . . . but you'll be amazed with the ease of use and adjustments. The downside: these trailers/joggers are too wide to take into most stores, so this isn't a good solution for shopping. Obviously, if you aren't a serious biker or jogger, a Chariot is probably overkill. But if you want a quality bike trailer, this brand should be on the top of your shopping list. **Rating: A**

Chicco *(877) 4-CHICCO or (732) 805-9200. Web: chiccousa.com.* Chicco (pronounced Kee-ko) has a 50-year history as one of Europe's leading juvenile products makers. Along with Peg Perego, Chicco is Europe's biggest producer of strollers and other baby products and toys. On this side of the Atlantic, however, Chicco was always (until recently) an also-ran while Perego was a top-seller. Chicco's fortunes began to turn in the past year with the success of their KeyFit infant seat and new lightweight strollers. Here's an overview:

The models. Chicco's emphasis is on lightweight strollers designed for the mall—their entry-level Capri ($60, 11 lbs.) features a two-position seat recline, five-point harness and basic canopy . . . a bit like the Maclaren Volo, but almost half the price.

New this year, the Trevi ($130, 19 lbs.) is designed to work with the Chicco infant car seats (which we rate highly). The Trevi features a full recline, umbrella-style fold, two handles, cup holder and removable child tray.

You can also make a travel system out of Chicco's other full-feature model, the Cortina ($150, 23 lbs.). This stroller features a more traditional design with height-adjustable handles and decent size basket. We thought it was well designed—we liked the one-hand fold and fully reclining seat. The Cortina travel system (stroller and car seat) runs $280 to $300.

Chicco also sells a few other lightweight strollers—the entry-level Caddy ($50, 11 lbs.) has a five-point harness, two-position recline and a rather skimpy sunshade (but no basket). Parents love the included rain cover and bright colors—the quality is very good and the handle height is great for taller moms. The C6 ($60) is basically the same as the Caddy, but with an upgraded canopy.

The affordable C5 ($90, 13.7 lbs.) features a multi-position reclining seat, decent size basket and nice canopy. Combine this with a compact, umbrella-style fold and Chicco has a winner.

New in the past year, Chicco debuted its first tri-wheeled stroller, the S3 ($400, 23 lbs). This swivel wheel stroller will feature suspension, foot muff and quick release wheels.

If you are looking for a lightweight double stroller, Chicco offers two options: the Citta Twin ($140, 29 lbs.) and C5 twin ($190, 29 lbs.). While both are similar, the C5 has upgraded canopies, padded harness straps and a different handle design than the Citta. In spring 2008, Chicco will debut a Trevi Twin with fully reclining seat.

Our view. Despite the Italian pedigree, most Chicco strollers sold in the U.S. are made in China. So if you want a true Italian stroller, Peg Perego may be a better bet (all Peg strollers are still made in Italy, with the exception of the Chinese-made Aria).

That said, we like Chicco and think the brand finally has a winning line-up here in the States. So which Chicco strollers get the best marks? Readers give the full-featured Cortina and new Trevi very good reviews—fans cheer the easy steering, one-hand fold and padding (detractors point out both are a bit bulky).

How about the lightweight strollers? While readers love the design and fashion of most of Chicco's offerings, quality is hit or miss. The Capri gets mixed reviews—taller parents find the handles too low and the smallish basket irks some. The C5 get better marks for quality and ease of use.

Overall, we think Chicco is a good brand and the prices are a decent value. If you like the look of Maclaren but don't have a Maclaren bank account, Chicco is a good alternative. **Rating: B+**

Combi *(800) 992-6624, (803) 802-8416; Web: combi-intl.com.* Japanese-owned Combi came to the U.S. in the late 80's and staked out a claim as a leader in lightweight strollers. Their famous Savvy Z was a seven-pound wonder that was often imitated. But Combi has had its ups and downs in recent years; it has shifted strategies more often than Italy changes governments. Here's an overview of their current offerings.

The models. Combi's focus is on lightweight, compact strollers. The company's flagship model, the Cosmo, is a good starting point. The Cosmo ST ($60, 11.5 lbs.) is affordable, yet features a full recline and compact fold. The Cosmo DX/EX ($100, 13 lbs.) adds more plush padding and a fancier canopy. All of the Cosmo models can be paired with the Combi Centre infant car seat to make a travel system.

Stepping up in price is the Combi City Savvy LX ($180, 13.2 lbs.), which works with the Combi Connection infant seat. This stroller features larger wheels, a travel bag and a handle that is about an inch taller than other Combi strollers.

Combi also makes a couple more full-feature strollers that are a touch bigger/heavier than the Cosmo or City Savvy LX. These include the Torino DX ($160, 16.5 pounds), which works with the

Centre DX infant seat, and the Spoleto LX ($200, 16.5 lbs.), which works with the Connection infant seat. These two models are similar, but the Spoleto has upgraded fabric, removable diaper bag, reflective trim and other goodies. Both the Torino and Spoleto feature a taller adjustable handle, parent cup holder, telescoping canopy, kid tray and push button seat recline.

To hedge its bets in the travel system market, Combi has a stroller frame that holds other brand infant car seats. The Flash ($60) is much like the Baby Trend Snap & Go, but adds a stroller back with two bottle holders.

Got twins? Combi offers both side-by-side and tandem models for parents of multiples (or a toddler and infant). The Combi Twin Savvy is a side-by-side model that weighs 21 pounds and sports a removable napper bar, machine washable cushions, a 165-degree reclining seat, a separate canopy and a stroller pack with two insulated bottle holders. At 30" wide, this side by side should fit through most doors. The Twin Savvy EX will accommodate one infant car seat (the Combi Connection) on one side of the stroller, which is a plus. The price, however, is a bit steep: $300.

If the Twin Savvy is a bit much, Combi also sells a less-expensive double: the Twin Sport ($200, 21 lbs.), which has less fancy padding and omits goodies like the child cup holder.

Finally, the Combi Counterpart Tandem is the company's first front/back stroller in several years. This 25.6 lb. stroller includes a third set of wheels for easy turning, push-button recline and the ability to hold one infant seat. It sells for $230.

New for 2008, Combi is launching the Helio ($130, 13.4 lbs.) which is similar to the Cosmo but a bit wider and will feature a taller handle, removable napper bar, deep seat recline for infants and will work with the Combi Shuttle infant seat.

For fans of the movie *Office Space*, Combi will introduce the Flare in 2008 ($70, 11.7 lbs.). The Flare will replace the Cosmo ST as Combi's flagship model and will work with the Shuttle infant car seat. The Flare is very similar to the Cosmo (full recline, compact fold, etc).

Also new this year: the Flex ($190, 15 lbs.), which features micro fiber fabric, a stroller pack/tote and deep seat recline for infants. The Flex will work with Combi's more expensive infant car seat, the Connection.

Our view. Combi has slimmed down their line in the past year and that's a good thing—in the past, this company's myriad of overlapping offerings made Combi a tough sell. Also gone: many of the super expensive strollers. Again, a good thing, as Combi has decided to concentrate on what it does best: lightweight strollers in the affordable to middle price points.

As for parent feedback, we'd peg Combi's reputation as mixed.

Take the simple Combi Flash stroller frame—this $60 product should be a no-brainer. And while most parents praise the Flash's lightweight and easy fold, it has one fatal flaw: when you snap in a car seat, the storage basket is inaccessible. Doh! This is the kind of bone-headed design mistake Combi makes.

Other parents gripe about Combi's low handles, which can make their strollers a chore to push for anyone over 5'6". (You'd think the Japanese would have better adapted these model to America after being here for 20 years). And while parents universally like Combi for their lightweight and easy folds, there always seems to be some fatal flaw that pops up . . . a too small basket, difficult seat recline, handle design, etc.

So, we've dropped Combi's rating a bit this year to reflect the disappointing parent feedback. While the company is on the right track in focusing its line on what it does best, more attention to design, quality and ease of use needs to happen. ***Rating B***

Compass *(888) 899-2229, Web: CompassBaby.com.* Launched in 2004 by ex-Evenflo employees, Compass is probably better known for its booster and infant car seats than strollers. Compass founders envision the brand as a mid-price offering—better features and quality than mass-market competitors like Cosco and Graco, but prices still lower than the Britax's and Maclaren's of the juvenile world.

Compass follows this philosophy into the stroller market with their S330 Sedan Ride Carriage Stroller ($120, 14 lbs.). The S330 offers a full recline, one-hand standing fold, height adjustable handle and a storage basket that can be accessed from the rear or side. The S330 works with Compass 1400 infant seat.

Compass S350 Lightweight Tandem Stroller ($160, 22 lbs.) is a clever hybrid of an umbrella style stroller and a tandem double. Unlike other tandems that push 30 pounds, the Compass S350 combines a low weight with a smaller wheelbase, making it easier to maneuver.

New for 2008, the Compass S340 ($120, 14 lbs.) is an upgrade over the S330—it features a magnesium frame for light weight, height adjustable frame and full seat recline. The S340 will also be sold as a travel system with Compass' excellent infant seat for $240.

Our view. Compass strollers haven't exactly set the world on fire sales-wise and there is an obvious answer. Despite being well priced and designed, Compass has flubbed the marketing here. First, nobody names strollers with numbers like the S330—folks like prosaic monikers, even if they are silly. Second, Compass' fashion needs a major overhaul . . . in a market where bright colors/accents are the norm (and even Graco has limited edition designer models), Compass' dull fashions seem so 1995. Yes, Compass was smart to team with

Italian stroller maker Inglesina to market a travel system with their infant seat and Inglesina's Zippy stroller . . . but unfortunately, none of Inglesina's fashion smarts seems to have rubbed off on Compass.

So we will give Compass a mixed review—good quality, decent prices . . . but to be more than a niche player in the stroller market, Compass needs a pizzazz transplant. ***Rating: B***

Cosco (812) 372-0141. Web: djgusa.com. Dorel (the parent of Cosco), the baby products powerhouse, has struggled in the stroller market for years. Why? The key driver of stroller sales in discount stores are travel systems . . . yet, Dorel/Cosco's main offering for infant car seats (the Designer 22) has failed to win many fans. That has undercut their momentum in this category, forcing the company to come up with several alternatives. Key among these: licensed brand names. Dorel is probably better known for its alter egos, Eddie Bauer and Safety 1st.

The models. The biggest news at Cosco in the past year was their launch of Quinny strollers and Maxi Cosi car seats. These are both sister companies to Cosco (part of parent Dorel's global brands). We will review Quinny separately later in this section.

Meanwhile, Cosco is still churning out travel systems and basic strollers, mostly under the Eddie Bauer and Safety 1st nameplates.

A typical offering is the Eddie Bauer Adventurer Travel System ($200). Paired with the Eddie Bauer Comfort (Designer 22) car seat, you get a stroller that features a one-hand fold and stand feature, big storage basket, parent tray with two cup holders, full reclining seat and upgraded fabric. This is the design direction Dorel is going in for strollers . . . you can see similar features on their stand-alone models, like the Safety 1st Acella Alumilite for $90.

We will give Dorel its due—they are trying to innovate in the stroller market. Example: the Safety 1st Acella Sport Travel System. This hybrid jogger features a tri-wheel stroller with turnable front wheel and one-hand standing fold. Price: $150 at Baby Depot. That includes the Designer 22 car seat.

Cosco is a big player in the double stroller market—their Safety 1st Two Ways tandem ($150) has a reversible front seat so kids can face each other.

Our view. Cosco has seen improving parent feedback and design features in recent years and our rating reflects this.

That said, Cosco still has a way to go when it comes to quality and durability. We still get emails and message board posts from parents who fall for the cool Eddie Bauer colors . . . and then the regrets start. Complaints about wheels that squeak within the first month, hard-to-adjust harnesses, and other quality woes still dog these strollers. Spending a fortune on a tricked out Eddie Bauer

> ### *Stroller overload?*
>
> Whoa! Finding yourself overwhelmed with all this stroller stuff? Take a break for a minute. We realize making a stroller choice can seem daunting. Here's our advice: first, read our specific recommendations by lifestyle later in this chapter. We boil down all the options to our top picks, whether you live in Suburbia or in downtown Giant Metropolis. Second, realize that you don't have to make all these stroller decisions BEFORE baby is born. Most parents will buy an infant car seat—pair this with an inexpensive stroller frame from Kolcraft (Universal Car Seat Carrier, $55), Combi (Flash EX, $60), Maclaren (Easy Traveler Car Seat Carrier, $90) or Baby Trend (Snap N Go, $50) and you've got an affordable alternative to those pricey travel systems. One of these stroller frames will last you for your baby's first six months . . . or longer. That will give you plenty of time to think about/research your next stroller.

travel system is a mistake.

The take home message: Cosco's basic strollers are probably the best bet—and only when on sale or for a steal on Craigslist. A parent who snagged a Safety 1st Acella Alumilite stroller for $60 at Baby Depot complimented the stroller's easy steering and large basket. She felt she got her money's worth and we would agree—set your expectations appropriately and one of these strollers could be a good basic model for the mall or grandma's house. *Rating: C+*

Dreamer Design *(509) 574-8085; web: dreamerdesign.net.* Dreamer specializes in jogging strollers and is best known for their great bubble canopies that provide more coverage than most joggers.

The models. Most Dreamers have aluminum frames and run $200 to $300—that's about $100 less than competitors. Among the standouts here: the Manhattan Lite for $220, Dreamer's first design with a turnable front wheel and optional infant car seat adapter. The best Dreamer for jogging would probably be the Rebound ($250, 27 lbs.), a fixed front wheel jogger with one-step fold, reclining seat, aluminum frame and height adjustable handle.

FYI: Dreamer makes all of their models in both "lite" and "deluxe" versions—the latter feature upgraded fabric for an extra $100 or so. Dreamer also makes a line of double strollers that run $400 to $450.

New this year, Dreamer has debuted the Park Avenue ($300, 24.5 lbs.), a deluxe model with 12" wheels, front swivel wheel that can lock, height adjustable handle and an included car seat adapter. Oddly,

Dreamer leaves off its famous bubble canopy for this model, which also lacks a cup holder. The small, cramped seat would be a tight fit for any larger toddler (over two years of age). With an optional bassinet ($150), the Park Avenue is pitched as an alternative to the Bugaboo—but we found this model to be disappointing overall.

Our view. Dreamer combines the best of both worlds—above-average quality AND affordable prices. Dreamer's bubble canopy is the best on the market. With the exception of the Park Avenue, we found Dreamer's joggers and swivel wheel models to be excellent choices. **Rating: A-**

Easy Walker *Web: easywalker-usa.com.* Here's the story of two Dutch stroller companies: Easy Walker and Bugaboo. One has sold hundreds of thousands of strollers . . while the other has sold just dozens. Unfortunately, Easy Walker was the latter case. While the company's Sky model is a hit in the Netherlands, it was a flop here in the U.S. Why? The first version of Sky was an expensive model ($800) bundled with a carry cot—that's popular in Europe, but here in the U.S. a car seat adapter is more appropriate. And the Sky was hobbled by poor design: it featured a fixed wheel that could be swapped out for swivel wheels—that means you have to carry along those extra wheels if you want to switch modes.

So it was back to the drawing board for Easy Walker and there is good news: the latest version of the Sky fixes the model's early flaws. No longer bundled with a bassinet, the stroller is now $500 (we've seen it discounted online to $400). A car seat adapter (for the Maxi Cosi or Graco Snug Ride) is $40. The Sky's front wheel can either swivel or lock into place (no need to swap wheels). Also new: a mesh basket, which replaces the inferior metal basket on the old model. There's also a double version of the Sky for $600.

All in all, the Sky is now much more comparable with the Mountain Buggy Urban, although the Sky has a full recline. Also new: Easy Walker has an accessory fashion pack ($90) that let's you swap out pads to change the Sky's look.

The revised Sky is so new, we don't have much feedback—our initial impression is that the Sky doesn't push quite as smoothly as the Mountain Buggy. And the $500 retail makes it about 20% more expensive than competitors, without making a compelling case as to why should spend that premium. And, unfortunately, Easy Walker's few distributors (it is sold in about 30 stores nationwide) will make seeing it in person difficult.

Eddie Bauer *These strollers and travel systems are made by Cosco. See the above review for more info.*

Emmaljunga *Web: emmaljunga.com. This Swedish stroller brand withdrew from the U.S. market in 2001.*

Esprit *See Rock Star Baby.*

Evenflo *(800) 233-5921 or (937) 415-3300. In Canada: (519) 756-0210; Web: evenflo.com.* Evenflo's claim to fame, stroller-wise, is their one-hand steering. All of Evenflo's strollers and travel systems have this feature. Here is a breakdown:

The models. Evenflo's flagship stroller is the Aura, which is paired with Evenflo's Embrace infant seat in a travel system. The Aura has probably one of the most amazing parent trays on the market, complete with two cup holders with "automotive cup grippers" and a storage area with "privacy lid." If only Evenflo had put as much effort into the rest of the stroller as they did with the parent tray.

While the Aura has a one-hand fold feature, folding it is not easy or intuitive—and once folded, this thing is big and bulky, clocking in at nearly 30 lbs. and filling up most of just about any vehicle's trunk space. The Aura travel system comes in two flavors: the Select ($160) and the Elite ($180), which offers upgraded fabric and canopy.

Evenflo's other major stroller offering is the Journey. Similar in size and weight to the Aura, it lacks the one-hand fold, cool parent tray (the Journey's parent tray is much simpler) or retracting child tray (to keep it from getting scuffed when folded). The Journey travel system (paired with the Evenflo Embrace) is $120 to $140.

New for 2008, Evenflo plans to launch a new entry-level model, the Export ($40, 10 lbs.). This bare bones stroller will feature a basket, parent console and telescoping handle. A version without the adjustable handle will be $30.

Evenflo is a major player in the tandem stroller segment with their Take Me Too. This 29 lb. double stroller has a couple of unique features. First, a side entry step for toddlers lets them get in and out of the back seat better than other models. And they've included an extra large basket. Yes, this unit can hold TWO infant seats (including non-Evenflo seats) and the one-hand fold feature is good. Price: $90 for a stripped down version (the Express) in discount stores to $140 for an upgraded model (the Premier).

Our view. One-handed steering is Evenflo's strongest feature—why every other stroller maker hasn't copied this yet is a mystery. Fans of Evenflo love how these strollers push.

Quality and durability, however, is another story. If you've been reading our blog (BabyBargains.com), you'll recall our discussion of quality woes that dogged an Evenflo stroller line back in 2005. While Evenflo's more recent models (including the Aura) have faired a bit better, a litany of complaints is par for the course for this brand.

Like Cosco, Evenflo's weakness in the travel system market stems from their sub par infant car seat offering. And Evenflo's strollers are a prime example of what we mean when we complain about super-size travel systems—most parents like their Evenflo system when used with the car seat. But as a stroller, parents quickly realize how heavy, bulky and hard-to-use the stroller is. Parents fall in love with that amazing parent tray . . . but soon curse a reclining seat that won't recline, an easy "one-hand fold" that is anything but easy and so on.

So, it's a mixed bag for Evenflo. We give them bonus points for trying to freshen up the line with innovative models, especially the Take Me Too tandem. We also like their customer service department, which earns good marks from our readers for promptly taking care of problems. Yet, the bottom line for us is quality and durability. And on that score, Evenflo falls short. ***Rating: C+***

Fisher Price. *Web: fisher-price.com.* Fisher-Price is sort of like the Gilligan's Island of the stroller biz—the company has tried a million hare-brained schemes to crack the market, most of which have failed miserably. Initially, Fisher-Price made its own strollers (and car seats), but those bombed. Then the company teamed with low-end stroller maker J. Mason for an ill-fated run at the Wal-Mart crowd . . . again, a washout.

Finally, Fisher-Price teamed with partner Kuji Sports to launch a series of innovative models under the "Active Gear" moniker. Okay, most of the models bombed (including the odd Kid Utility Vehicle), but the partnership did produce one hit . . . the unglamorously named "Infant-to-Toddler Stroller," the best knock-off of the Bugaboo we've seen. This stroller ($150 on Wal-Mart.com) features a stroller seat that reverses and is a bit wider than the Bugaboo (no bassinet). It's very clever—and worthy of consideration if you don't have a wealthy relative offering to spend $1000 on a stroller as a shower gift. Yes, you do have to remove the seat to fold it (the same flaw as in the Bugaboo), but we still think this model is great. ***Rating: A***

GoGo Babyz *Web: GoGoBabyZ.com.* This brand is reviewed by on our web page, BabyBargains.com (click on Bonus Material).

Graco *(800) 345-4109, (610) 286-5951; Web: gracobaby.com.* Graco is a great example of what's right (and wrong) with the stroller biz today. The company (a division of Rubbermaid) is probably the market-leader in strollers, with affordable models that are packed with features like oversized baskets. What drives Graco's success? Well, it is NOT quality or design (Graco's efforts are no better than other mass market strollers). Graco's secret sauce is the runaway success of Graco's SnugRide infant car seat . . . and that feeds travel system sales, the heart of stroller sales at chain stores. You'll find Graco everywhere: discount stores, baby superstores, specialty shops and more.

Graco's primary target market is first-time parents, who want a SUV-like stroller (that is, one packed with tons of features and gizmos). Unlike years past, Graco is now more of a mid-priced brand. Gone are the super-cheap low-end strollers . . . Graco seems to have ceded this market to Cosco.

Graco's line is huge, so let's get to the highlights:

The models. Graco divides their stroller line into four areas: lightweight (Cleo, Ipo, MetroLite), full-size (Quattro, Vienna), travel systems and double models (mostly tandems like the DuoGlider).

In the lightweight category, Graco has three models: the Cleo, Ipo and MetroLite. The Cleo ($250, 18.5 lbs.) is Graco's riff on the Peg Perego Pliko—two handles, large basket, full spring suspension, two parent cup holders, one-hand fold and full recline. It works with both Graco infant car seats. In the past year, Graco has tweaked the Cleo to make the basket access better and added spring suspension.

The new Ipo ($80, 17 lbs.) is a budget version of the Cleo, but omits the napper bar and cup holder. Instead, you get a one-hand fold . . . but the Ipo doesn't work with a car seat.

The Mosaic is now discontinued but still sold online— it is an 18 lb. umbrella stroller with two handles, deep basket and partial recline. This stroller has a "three-dimensional" fold—that basically means it folds down to the ground but doesn't scrape or dirty the stroller in the process. The Mosaic sells for $100 to $130.

As for Graco's entry-level price point in the lightweight category, the LiteRider is a mid-size stroller that comes both as a $60 standalone model and a $140 travel system. Finally, the MetroLite is Graco's last lightweight offering—it runs $120 to $140 as a standalone model or $200 to $250 as a travel system. The MetroLite (18 lbs.) features rubber tires for a smooth ride, three-position reclining seat and plush padding. The MetroLite also has a full recline and height adjustable handle. We've heard very good feedback on both of Graco's lightweight strollers, which combine decent features and an affordable price.

The Quattro, a tank-like stroller that weighs nearly 30 lbs. empty, anchors Graco's "standard-size" strollers. The Quattro Tour runs $130 to $150 separately or $230 to $250 as a travel system. Graco throws just about everything into this model, including a fully enclosing hood, all weather boot, one-hand gravity fold, four-position full reclining seat, plush padding and more.

New this year, Graco is rolling out a Quattro Tour Sport ($150, 27 lbs.) with a sleek new look that riffs on the Quinny's elliptical tubing. The stroller features spring suspension, one-hand fold and a new rotating canopy.

Graco also makes a slew of other standard-size strollers: the Spree ($80), Alano ($90), Passage ($90), and Vienna ($100). Basically, these are all scaled-down versions of the Quattro, with somewhat less weight and bulk. All feature Graco's voluminous storage basket (which drops down for access when the seat is reclined) and the ability to hold a Graco infant seat.

Finally, double strollers are Graco's last major forte–the DuoRider ($120) is Graco's side-by-side model, while the DuoGlider ($130 to $150) is a front/back tandem. Graco's claim to fame in the tandem market is their "stadium seating," where the rear seat is elevated. Of course, you get all the standard features: huge storage baskets, removable canopies, etc. Graco also offers the DuoGlider in a travel system that will now accept two infant car seats (note to parents of twins) for $250, but that price just includes one infant seat.

New in the past year, the Graco Quattro Tour Duo (32 lbs., $205 to $230) features a curvy frame, fancy cup holders, stadium seating, one-hand "gravity" fold, large basket and a back seat with full recline. The Quattro Tour Duo is about 20% smaller than the DuoGlider.

Graco's entry in the stroller frame category, the Snug Rider, is a winner–this $60 frame holds the (what else?) Graco Snug Ride infant car seat with a secure lock-in feature and has a one-hand fold and basket. FYI: The Snug Rider also works with Graco's newer infant seat, the Safe Seat.

Graco also sells its strollers under the Laura Ashley banner–same models and features as Graco, just a fancier fabric (and higher price, naturally).

Our view. Graco has come a long way and now sits atop the mountain as the top-selling mass market brand for strollers.

We don't fault Graco for focusing on the lucrative first-time parent niche, but we can't help but point out to folks that NO, you do not need a 30 lb. stroller to push around baby. In fact, many parents end up cursing their Graco Hummers as impossible to wrestle in and out of a trunk, among other sins. Stick with the lighter-weight models (Cleo, MetroLite, Ipo) and you'll be happier here.

Other little annoyances frustrate Graco owners too. Look at how some Graco strollers fold up . . . when folded, the front tray hits the ground, inevitably damaging or scratching it in a parking lot. Parents complain canopies that break or reclining seats that stop reclining. Durability is one of Graco's key weaknesses–these strollers wear out way too quickly (wheels squeak, fabric rips, etc). Forget about a Graco stroller lasting for more than one kid . . . often they don't make it through one year.

The take-home message: stick to Graco's lightweight strollers, try to buy it on sale or used and set your expectations accordingly. ***Rating: B-***

Inglesina *(877) 486-5112 or (973) 746-5112; web: Inglesina.com.* Inglesina has always played second fiddle to its Italian cousins Peg Perego and Chicco in the stroller market. While other Italian players have had significant success peddling their wares to North American parents, Inglesina always seemed stuck in low gear.

Not any more. Inglesina hit a home run with the Zippy and followed this success with a slew of lightweight models that have earned kudos from readers. Here's an overview of Inglesina's models:

The models. So, what's cool about the Zippy? Check out the one-hand fold—you lift up on a lever on the back of the stroller and poof! Instant folded stroller. This 17 lb. model has all the great features most urban moms want—full recline, adjustable backrest, removable front bumper and storage basket. Best of all: the Zippy has a universal car seat adapter that lets you secure an infant car seat to the stroller (yes, the Graco SnugRide works well with it).

So what's not to love? Well, the Zippy is darn expensive: $340. Yes, the Zippy is much like the Peg Perego Pliko, but costs $50 to $100 more for that easier fold. Inglesina has made some nice improvements to the Zippy over the past couple of years, including an extended canopy and front snack tray. Also, Inglesina has teamed with Compass to do matching fabrics, so you can use the Compass infant seat as a travel system with the Zippy.

The Inglesina Urbe ($200 to $250, 17 lbs.) is similar to the Zippy, but omits the one-hand hold fold. The Urbe features a full recline, extendable leg support, extended canopy and rain/wind shield.

Inglesina has two other models: the Trip and Swift. The Trip ($180, 14.5 lbs.) is a scaled-down Urbe, with a less-fancy canopy but you still get a fully reclining seat and cup holder. A rain cover is optional. The Swift (11 lbs., $120) is a super-lightweight stroller with four-position reclining seat, detachable storage basket and two handle design (like the Peg Pliko). The downside? A rather skimpy canopy and no cup holder.

FYI: All of Inglesina's strollers bound for the American market are made in China (with the exception of the Zippy, which is made in Italy).

Parents of twins and triplets may want to give Inglesina's double and triple strollers a look-see. The Twin Swift is a side-by-side model weighing 28 lbs. and featuring dual-operating canopies for $250. Inglesina's Domino is a pram-like stroller that comes in both double and triple versions ($600 to $800).

Inglesina hasn't rolled out many new models in the past year—the company's U.S. distributor has concentrated on rolling out the

Mutsy line (reviewed below). That's too bad . . . if you stand still in this market, you'll liable to get run over. So we're hoping Inglesina has something new up its sleeve in the coming months.

Our view. The feedback on these strollers is very positive—reviews by parents on our web site give Inglesina good marks overall for quality, durability and function. While we'd like to see Inglesina beef up their dinky cup holder and make their strollers work with more infant car seats, the line is still a winner. **Rating: A**

InStep *is better known by their alter ego, Schwinn—see review on page 508.*

i'coo/Traxx *See Rock Star Baby.*

Jane (866) 355-2630. Web: janeusa.com. Spanish baby products maker Jane (pronounced HA-nay) traces its roots back to 1932 in Barcelona and now has decided to give the U.S. market a try.

Jane's PowerTwin is a good example of how European stroller companies just don't get this market. This innovative tri-wheel stroller (with a turnable front wheel) is impressive: it boasts two seats (the rear fully reclines), quick release wheels, hand break and cushy suspension. Cool, eh? Except the price is $540 and it weighs 41 lbs. And there are no cup holders. Whoops.

And there, in a nutshell, is why so many European stroller companies wash out here in the U.S. The fashion is right, but the price blows the deal. As for quality, readers tell us they have been mostly happy with the PowerTwin, but one parent reported her PowerTwin was defective, pulling to the right. The store replaced the unit, but the replacement had the same tracking problem.

While Jane may some day break through in America, its first effort is a disappointment. **Rating: C**

Jeep *These strollers are made by Kolcraft, reviewed on page 496.*

Joovy (214)761-1809. Web: joovy.com. Newcomer Joovy is headed by a former Baby Trend executive. In fact, Joovy scored its first big coup by winning the license to the English pushcart better known as the Baby Trend Sit N Stand. Joovy has re-christened this model the Caboose Stand-on Tandem ($150, 26 lbs.). Compared to the old Sit N Stand, Joovy's Caboose features a higher handle height, foam handle, improved car seat attachment and nicer canopy. The company also brightened up the fashion.

Joovy has made a few improvements to the Caboose—now the seat recline doesn't interfere with the space a toddler has to sit in back. And the infant car seat attachment sits higher than the previous model. FYI: the Joovy works with 13 infant seats, including the Graco SnugRide and Britax Companion.

In 2008, Joovy will launch the Caboose Ultralight, a $230 version of the Caboose that is 20% lighter (21 lbs.) and will feature a new canopy and neoprene parent organizer.

Joovy also makes a super-sized version of this stroller: the Big Caboose ($300, 37 lbs.) with two seats plus a toddler jump seat/standing area. This model also can handle two infant car seats—so if you have twins and an older toddler, this would be one of the few models out there to hold all three kids.

While the Caboose is Joovy's flagship model, the company has also launched three other models. The Groove ($200, 16 lbs.) is a high-end umbrella with aluminum frame, adjustable footrest, draw-string seat recline, extended canopy and two cup holders. It also comes in a twin version (Groove 2, $250, 26 lbs.). Joovy's Zoom ($250) is a jogger with no rear axle (so you can run without kicking the back), full canopy and parent tray. The Easy Rider also comes with a sun filter and rain/wind cover.

New for 2008, the Joovy Kooper is an umbrella fold lightweight stroller ($250, 15.5 lbs.) with compact fold and quick release wheels.

Our View. Joovy is so new, we don't have much parent feedback yet, but the initial word on the Caboose is positive. We liked the thoughtful design touches through out this line (a jogger with parent cup holders—what a concept!) and the bright yet simple fashion is a nice alternative to navy blue. Yet we thought the Groove was over-priced—if Joovy plans to compete with Maclaren in this segment, they better come up with something more innovative than this. So, we'll give them good marks for a good initial effort . . . but we'd like to see what they have planned for an encore. **Rating: B+**

J. Mason (818) 993-6800; web: jmason.com. This brand is reviewed on our web page (BabyBargains.com, click on Bonus Material).

Kelty (303) 530-7670, web: kelty.com. Kelty is best known for their backpacks, but they jumped into the jogger market back in 2001. Their re-designed jogger won kudos when it was launched in 2005 but it is now showing its age: the Speedster is $260. They also offer a "deluxe" version for $335 that adds an easier fold, height adjustable handle, hand break and reclining seat. A double version (Speedster Deuce 16) runs $410. Quality is very good, although the canopy coverage is a bit skimpy.

In 2008, Kelty plans to launch a slew of new models. The Speedster 08 ($260, 20 lbs.) will be an update to the Speedster with a bigger canopy and a weight of six to nine lbs. less than the original Speedster, depending on the version.

Kelty's other new models had us scratching our heads—the company is belatedly joining the rest of the market with a tri-wheel stroller with a turnable front wheel. The 3-Tech ($375, 33 lbs.) features full suspension, adjustable handle and reversible seat. But the basket is dinky and the 3-Tech is much heavier and more expensive than similar models on the market. A four-wheel version of this stroller will also debut in 2008—the Astro ($400, 26 lbs.) and a deluxe model, the Turbo ($450, 33 lbs.).

While we like the Speedster, the jury is out on Kelty's more experimental models. ***Rating: B+***

Kolcraft *(800) 453-7673. Web: kolcraft.com.* Kolcraft has always been an also-ran in the stroller market—that is, until their recent hot selling Jeep-branded strollers took off. Since Kolcraft exited the car seat business in 2001, the company has no travel systems to offer. That's a blessing in disguise: many Kolcraft models hold other major brands of car seats, giving parents more flexibility.

The models. Kolcraft sells strollers under four brands: Kolcraft, Sesame Beginnings, Jeep and Contours. Kolcraft and Sesame Beginnings are sold as entry-level models at chains stores like Wal-Mart. The real story here is the success of Kolcraft's Jeep line—Kolcraft has an entire line of Jeep strollers, complete with SUV-like knobby wheels, beefed up suspension, and sporty fabrics at affordable prices ($30 to $150). Clever touches like simulated lug nuts on the wheels and a toy steering wheel for baby have made these models quite popular.

The best-selling Jeep is the Liberty SE Terrain—a three-wheel stroller with turnable front wheel that can be locked in a forward position. This hybrid between jogging and sport strollers features one-hand fold, child snack tray with the aforementioned toy steering wheel and parent tray. At $120 at Wal-Mart, it's no surprise this one has been a hot seller. And surprise: parent reviews have been very positive on this model, albeit with a stray complaint that the handle is too low for very tall parents. In the past year, Kolcraft rolled out an upgraded version of the Liberty (dubbed the Limited), with extra storage (a bag on the side of the basket), fancier padding and an electronic toy steering wheel. It is $140 at Target.com.

Kolcraft also makes a raft of other Jeep models, including an umbrella style (Wrangler, 12 lbs., $30) and a more traditional lightweight model, the Cherokee ($70). There is also a tandem, the Jeep Wagoneer ($140 to $170, depending on the version). This affordable tandem has won kudos from readers for its basket, which is the size of Montana. It also holds any brand infant car seat, which is another nice plus. The Wrangler Twin Sport is a side-by-side model for $80.

Finally, we should mention Kolcraft's knock-off of the Baby Trend's

Snap & Go: the Universal Car Seat Carrier (13 lbs.) for $46 to $55. This stroller frame will accommodate most car seats and has a large basket and one-hand fold.

In the past year, Kolcraft has invaded the jogger category with their Jeep Overland Limited ($160), a 25 lb. aluminum jogger with one-hand fold, 16" wheels and height adjustable canopy.

Kolcraft's other major stroller label is Contours, which feature a bit more style than one would expect from Kolcraft (bright red fabrics, curved tubular frames, etc.). The Contours Option 3 Wheel Stroller ($130, 26 lbs.) has an infant car seat adapter and reversible seat, so you can see baby while pushing, while the Contours Options Tandem ($210, 32 lbs.) is a double stroller with Bugaboo-like front wheels. Speaking of the Bugaboo, Kolcraft will also debut an Options 4 Wheel ($140, 25 lbs.), a credible knock-off of the Dutch best seller.

New for 2008, the Contours Options Tandem will have seats that can face each other—and the stroller comes with a car seat adapter (a second one is available as an accessory). In mid 2008, Kolcraft will release new Jeep models—we'll post the news on our blog when we have the details.

Our view. Kolcraft has improved its quality in recent years and our rating reflects this. Dollar for dollar, these are the best affordable strollers on the market—the Jeep Liberty Urban Terrain is a great example and the pick of the litter. Also winners: Kolcraft's simple umbrella strollers and side-by-side models. Compared to other low-end brands (Graco, Cosco), Kolcraft shines. That said, you can't compare these to models to high end models like Mountain Buggy or Maclaren . . . Kolcraft still has a way to go to match their durability. But for suburbanites who need a sturdy stroller with lots of storage and decent looks for the mall and occasional outing, Kolcraft's Jeep line fits the bill. **Rating: B+**

Kool Stop (800)586-3332, 714-738-4973; koolstop.com. See our web page (BabyBargains.com, click on Bonus Material) for a review.

Laura Ashley These strollers are made by Graco, reviewed earlier.

Maclaren (877) 504-8809 or (203) 354-4400; Web: maclarenbaby. com. Maclaren is the brand with British roots that sells 500,000 strollers each year in 30 countries worldwide. Their specialty? High-quality umbrella strollers made from lightweight aluminum. Maclaren is most popular on the East Coast and the brand has many fans in New York City and Boston. You might wonder whether these parents (who fork over $200 to $300 for a Maclaren) have lost their minds—can't they just go down to a discount store and buy an umbrella stroller for $30? Well, unlike the cheap-o umbrella strollers you find at Toys R Us, Maclaren strollers are ultra lightweight and packed with urban-friendly features. Plus, they look oh so stylish, which is important when you're zipping around the Upper West Side.

The models. Okay, let's take a deep breath. Maclaren offers a DOZEN models, so there is much to cover. There will be a quiz at the end of this review.

Maclaren's entry-level model, the Volo ($100-130, 8.6 lbs.) is a super light, stripped down stroller (this year's version does have a canopy). You get a five-point harness and a mesh seat and basket but that's about it. A "Volo Accessory Pack" includes rain cover, seat liner and carry bag . . . for another $40. The Volo seat does not recline, so this stroller is best for babies six months and up.

A more full-featured model from Maclaren is their Triumph, ($175) which weighs 11 lbs. and features a fully enclosed protective hood and one-hand fold. This seat does have a two-position recline (it is designed for babies three months and up).

Next up is the Quest (12.2 lbs.), which adds more padding, a four-position partial seat recline and an extendable footrest. Price: $200. The Quest comes in three versions: the Quest Sport (basic colors), Quest Mod (fancy retro look with circular design fabric) or Kate Spade Quest (a designer fabric print, $300).

The Techno XT (14.2 lbs., $300) is the top of the line Maclaren—it features the most padding, a new flip-down sun visor and three-position adjusting handles that can be extended to a height of 42 inches. And yes, Maclaren throws in a cup holder for the Techno. The Techno also has upgraded wheels and reflective trim; there is also a Techno XLR ($350, 16.3 lbs.) which is an inch and a half wider than the Techno XT and will come with an infant car seat adapter. You can also use this stroller for a child who weights up to 64 pounds—the most of any Maclaren.

The Maclaren MX3 ($350, 21.6 lbs.) is Mac's first tri-wheel stroller, which features a removable/washable seat, rain cover, front swivel wheel that can lock, extendable leg rest and reflective trim.

Finally, we have to talk about Maclaren's top-selling side-by-side strollers, the Twin Triumph ($220, 21.6 lbs.) and the Twin Techno ($360, 25.7 lbs.). The basic difference between these models: the Twin Techno is more plush and comes with a boot, head support and upgraded canopy. Parents of twins rave about these strollers, which are among the best made side-by-side models on the market. Maclaren's doubles are good for older child/infant needs as well.

A bit late to the party, Maclaren has debuted their own stroller frame (a la the Snap N Go), dubbed the Easy Traveller ($70, 10.6 lbs). Mac's stroller frame features a large basket with an easy fold similar the Volo. This model works with most major infant car seats, including Britax, Combi, Peg Perego and the Graco Snug Ride or Safe Seat.

So, what's new for Maclaren this year? The company is now offering parents a chance to customize their stroller—you can build your own Volo with a frame color, seat fabric, liner and harness color. Price: $250.

Also new: a "Four Seasons" stroller ($500, based on the old Ryder frame) with four different/reversible seat liners to match the changing seasons. You also get a winter foot muff, blanket and carry bag. Maclaren is also offering reversible seat liners for the Twin Triumph.

And yes, designer Philippe Starck is still churning out special edition Maclarens ($300).

In the past year or two, Maclaren has been concentrating on beefing up its customizability and accessories rather than roll out new models. One key accessory: a $20 universal stroller organizer that fits on the back handles—it includes two bottle pockets that can hold drinks, a cell phone pocket and a mesh storage bag. This helps address parent complaints that Maclarens lack adequate storage.

One important caveat to this line: all Maclaren strollers lack napper or bumper bars on the front of the seat. Yes, these models all have five-point harnesses to keep baby securely inside the strollers, but the absence of a napper bar will turn off some parents.

Our view. While we still think Maclaren is one of the best quality stroller brands on the market, there are a couple of caveats. First, while this brand stakes its reputation on its British heritage, Maclaren switched all its production to China back in 2001. While there were some initial hiccups with this, the quality of the Chinese-made Maclarens is now excellent. We've also been impressed that Maclaren has been rolling out service centers (35 at last count) to address any problems.

Another issue: Maclaren's finicky fold. Retailers who sell many Macs tell us you must be careful to correctly fold up the stroller (you have to make sure the backrest is completely upright and the canopy is back before folding). You never want to force or jam the stroller, which can bend the frame.

The other perennial Maclaren complaint: skimpy canopies. We wish Maclaren offered an accessory canopy that would really screen out the sun.

Despite all these faults, we will still give Maclaren a good rating. If you understand the caveats and take care with the fragile fold, then this is still among the better brands on the stroller market.
Rating: A

Mia Moda *610-373-6888, Web: MiaModainc.com.* Former Graco and Maclaren veterans have joined forces to launch Mia

strollers

Moda. We're not sure where Mia Moda came up with the description of their strollers as "Euro-design"—the company is based in Pennsylvania and imports their strollers from China.

Nonetheless, we will give Mia Moda brownie points for creativity. The clever Cielo ($135-150, $15 lbs.) has the most amazing fold on the market—basically, the Cielo folds down into the size of a briefcase. (You have to see the video demo on their web site to believe it). While this stroller itself is nothing fancy (basic canopy, five-point harness, draw-string, partial seat recline), the ultra compact fold might be just the trick for air travelers who fear gate-checking a stroller. (FYI: The Cielo is best for babies over six months of age, as the seat does not fully recline. And there are no sides to this stroller, which makes it more appropriate for toddlers).

For 2008, Mia Moda will debut the Cielo Evolution (16 lbs., $180)—similar to the Cielo but with larger wheels, a cup holder, arm rests and a deeper recline.

We wish the rest of the Mia Moda line was that amazing—the company is launching a slew of mostly me-two models that duplicate what's already on the market. Perhaps the best offering is the sleek Energi ($270-$330, 23 lbs.), a tri-wheel model with full recline, front swivel wheel, child's tray, and height adjustable handle.

Mia Moda's other offerings include the Terra (basically a four wheel version of the Energi, $320, 24 lbs.), the Libero (a Peg Pliko clone, $200, 20 lbs.), and the Sprito (a Mac Volo clone, $89, 13 lbs.)

New for 2008, Mia Moda plans to add a knock-off of the Baby Trend Sit N Stand to the line: the Compagno will run $180. Also new: the Veloce ($100, 15 lbs.), a simple umbrella stroller with extended canopy and the Atmospherra ($280), a Bugaboo-like stroller with reversible seat and telescoping handle.

So, how's the quality? It's hard to get a reading on Mia Moda, since the company has sold so few strollers. As a result, we have little parent feedback. What little we've heard, however, has been positive—parents give the unique and clever Cielo good marks, for example.

Mia Moda has probably gained little traction due to its slew of me-too models—for a new brand to stand out in this market, you must be try something different. Simply knocking off Mac and Peg isn't going to cut it. Yes, Mia Moda's web site is excellent (we like the "folding demo" for each model, plus comparison matrices), but if that is the extent of Mia Moda's mojo, then we don't see the point. And as of press time, we noticed many Mia Moda models heavily discounted online (30% in some cases)—that's not a good sign.

FYI: Mia Moda plans to launch their own infant car seat (the Viva), which will work with four of Mia Moda's models. ***Rating: B-***

MicraLite Strollers *877-844-9575; Web: www.Euro-Baby.us.*
UK-import MicraLite debuted in the past year with their Fastfold
FTS stroller ($370, 15 lbs.), a lightweight model with a quick, stand-
ing fold that is pretty amazing. Despite the two air-filled 12" rear
tires (and small front swivel wheels), the Fastfold still comes in at 15
lbs. Other features include adjustable handle, suspension, and
included rain cover and storage pouch.

So, given the hefty price, is it worth it? Reviews are mixed.
Parents tell us they like the one-hand, stand-up fold, the head-turning good looks and hammock like seat, which is nice for older
babies. But, the slight recline makes this seat a poor choice for
infants—and the skimpy canopy and tiny basket are major negatives. Quality also isn't there—one mom reported to us that her
Fastfold's recline feature didn't work properly after a short while.
That's not good for a $370 stroller.

New for 2008, MicraLite has launched the Toro (18 lbs.), which is
similar to the Fastfold but adds a few Bugaboo-like tricks. The Toro
has a full, three-position recline, interchangeable seat pads and an
optional carrycot. Fortunately, MicraLite has added a more significant canopy and basket to the Toro, which also includes a rain
shield and foot muff. But the price: $600 (stroller) or $800 (with the
carry cot) is a whopper. And you have to adjust the handles with
an . . . allen wrench? For $800, we'd expect MicraLite to personal-
ly visit our home to adjust the handles, much less require a soon-
to-be-lost tool. The Toro was too new for any parent reviews.

So, a mixed review for MicraLite—the quality isn't there to justify
the price on the Fastfold. And while the Toro fixes the Fastfold's
flaws (better canopy, basket, recline), it is too new to judge.
Rating: C

Motobecane *Web: motobecane.com.* Motobecane is reviewed
on our web page (BabyBargains.com, click on Bonus Material).

Mountain Buggy *Web: mountainbuggy.com.* This little company
from New Zealand has a hot seller in its rugged, all-terrain strollers,
which have won fans in both urban areas and the 'burbs. These tri-
wheel strollers feature lightweight aluminum frames (19-22 lbs.
depending on the model), 12" air-filled wheels with polymer rims
(great for use near the beach), full reclining seats, height adjustable
handles, one step folds and large two-position sun canopies.

The models. Mountain Buggy's flagship model is the Urban
($430 single, $670 double), which has a front wheel that can swivel or be fixed. The result is great maneuverability, unlike other joggers with fixed wheels (which limits their appeal for more urban
uses). If you don't need the swivel front wheel, Mountain Buggy

offers a model with a fixed front wheel—the Terrain ($360 single, $530 double).

Does the size of these strollers concern you? Check out the Breeze, a mini-version of the Terrain with a fixed front wheel, wire basket and fully reclining seat. It features 10" tires and weighs just 14 lbs. Price: $330.

Got three kids? Mountain Buggy even sells triple versions of the Urban and Terrain that run just under $1000.

In the past year, Mountain Buggy debuted two upgraded versions of the Urban: the Urban Elite ($500 single, $800 double) and the Urban Designer ($450 single, $700 double). The Urban Elite has an upgraded canvas seat, padded straps, infant insert, diaper bag and bottle holder. The Urban Designer is a fashion upgrade: fancier colors compared to Mountain Buggy's typical red or navy palette.

Our view. Okay, those prices are high. BUT, Mountain Buggies have a weight limit of 100 pounds, so you can use this stroller for a LONG time. And parents love the slew of optional accessories, including a bug shield and full sun cover . . . AND a clip that lets you attach an infant car seat to their single stroller models. Too tall for most strollers? Mountain Buggy also sells a "handlebar extender" ($40) that adds 3" of height for taller parents.

But the Mountain Buggy's key advantage is its light weight: the Urban Single's 22 lbs. is 10% to 20% lighter than competitors. That makes the Urban easier to push and maneuver.

So, we'll give this brand our top rating despite the stiff prices. Positive parent reviews and added flexibility from all those accessories make these strollers worth the price. FYI: Mountain Buggy is so new to North America that these strollers are hard to see in person. Nonetheless, if you have a dealer near by, they are worth a look. **Rating: A**

Mutsy (973)243-0234, Web: Mutsy.com. Dutch-bred Mutsy hoped to follow in the footstep of that other Holland stroller company that made a splash in the U.S. Like Bugaboo, Mutsy offers a series of stroller frames that can fit an infant car seat, stroller frame or bassinet. And like Bugaboo, Mutsy imports its strollers from Asia. So is Mutsy a hit or a flop? Read on.

The models. Mutsy's Urban Rider ($700, 25.4 lbs.) comes complete with bassinet, stroller seat and two sets of wheels—that's right, you can swap out air-filled front tires for smaller, swivel wheels. And the rear wheels swivel, giving the Urban Rider even more maneuverability. Mutsy also sells an upgraded version of the Urban Rider as the Urban Rider Next ($760) with a leather handle, diaper bag and a few other extras.

The 4Rider ($700, 24 lbs.) lacks the Urban Rider's ability to swap front wheels, instead going with 10″ single spoke, swivel wheels. The 4Rider includes a car seat adapter, bassinet and stroller seat that is fully adjustable (adjustable leg rest, even seat depth). The 4Rider Light ($680, 19 lbs.) swaps the 4Rider's air-filled tires for rubber versions.

The Mutsy Spider ($250, 20 lbs.) is a funky tri-wheel model with telescoping handle, partial seat recline and a unique fold (the Spider folds back upon itself).

New for 2008, Mutsy debuts the Slider ($760, 22 lbs.), which features foam wheels (which provide the lighter overall weight), reversible handle, bassinet and stroller seat, micro fiber fabric and more.

Also new: Mutsy now has car seat adapters for the Maxi Cosi and infant seats.

Our view. Mutsy had a lot going for it when it landed last year—an experienced distributor (the same folks who run Inglesina here in the U.S) and a line that just oozed cool Euro chic. Unlike other strollers that tout a faux "European-inspired" patina, Mutsy is the real deal. These strollers are head turners.

Yet, so far, Mutsy has barely been a blip on the sales radar or baby stores. Why the washout? In a word: weight. Mutsy made the mistake of launching strollers that were too heavy for the U.S. market. The Urban Rider is 25% heavier than the Bugaboo Cameleon. Yes, that's works out to four pounds and you might say big deal? But four pounds in the stroller biz is indeed a big deal— it impacts maneuverability and how easy it is to haul in/out of a trunk or up a set of subway stairs.

Even Mutsy's "light weight" model, the Spider is 20 lbs.—17% heaver than the Bugaboo bee.

Hence it is no surprise that Mutsy's most successful model is the 4Rider Light, which is more in line weight-wise with the Dutch competition.

That doesn't mean Mutsy is a total washout. Fans of the strollers (especially taller parents) love the super-adjustable handles, plush fabrics and ease of use. And readers also tell us they love the head-turning ability of these strollers—you can't go to the park or mall without someone stopping you to ask about the stroller. Quality for Mutsy is high.

The take-home message: these strollers well designed, but too heavy. Mutsy should have launched its line with lighter-weight models like the new Slider or the 4Rider Light. By emphasizing the heavy Urban Rider with its awkward swap-able front wheels, the brand has so far failed to gain much traction. **Rating: B**

Orbit Web: orbitbaby.com. Orbit is the über expensive travel system that combines an infant car seat (reviewed in the last chapter) and stroller frame. Price: $900. And no, the Orbit doesn't come with a toddler stroller seat—that's an extra $180. At this price, you can imagine that the Orbit hasn't exactly been selling like hot cakes . . . we've only heard from a handful of parents who own one.

The verdict? Folks who have the Orbit love it—the unique car seat base makes for simple, rock solid installation, as we noted in the last chapter. The engineering on the Orbit is top notch: parents like the stroller frame's simple one-hand fold and ergonomic handles. And the frame lets you shift the car seat in a 360-degree range of motion.

Downsides? The Orbit car seat only works up to 22 lbs. (compared to other infant seats that work to 30). That means bigger babies will outgrow this travel system before six months—and that's a lot of money to spend for such brief usage. Yes, you can pony up another $180 for a toddler seat—but by now you've spent $1100.

As we noted in the Orbit car seat review, the carrier is heavy (nearly 10 lbs.) and bulky, making it a tight fit in smaller vehicles. Once your baby is nearly the weight limits of the seat, carrying the Orbit's 30 lb weight (baby plus car seat) will be a handy upper-body workout.

Other negatives: there are only two colors to the Orbit—brown and black. And the Orbit is only sold in a handful of boutiques mostly on the coasts, so forget about seeing an Orbit in person if you live in Denver or Atlanta.

The take-home message: if you are looking for a travel system that is a conversation starter, then Orbit is your brand. Parents love the Jetsons-like look . . . and having a stroller/car seat that no one on the block has. While we understand that appeal, we would be much more excited about the Orbit if it were half the price. **Rating: B**

Peg Perego (260) 482-8191. Web: perego.com. Perego is among the most popular stroller brands in America and that's no small feat. Most European stroller makers have either failed here (Emmaljunga, Teutonia) or moved their production to China (Maclaren, Inglesina) . . . Perego still makes most of its strollers in Italy. And sells them by the boatload here in America, despite premium prices.

Yet for all their success, Perego has stumbled in recent years and lost its momentum. The company has completely missed out on the all-terrain and tri-wheel stroller craze, only belatedly adding one such model to its line in the past year. Meanwhile, Perego has been content to rest on its laurels and occasionally roll out a novelty model that invariably never ships (exhibit number one: the Dinamico self-propelled stroller for $700).

No wonder all the buzz on our stroller message boards omits Perego. You can't stand still in this biz, or else the Bugaboos (and a host of smart competitors) will roll right over you. Perego has also lost a bit of its cache as it began selling strollers in chains stores like Babies R Us (closeouts too, at places like Marshall's), although many parents still think Perego's European pedigree and fashion are superior to strollers from China.

Let's take a look at Perego's current lineup.

The models. Perego's best-selling models are their lightweight strollers, including the Pliko P3 Classico and Aria OH. We'll discuss each in-depth in just a minute . . . but first, let's take a look at the big news from Perego: the Skate, Peg's Bugaboo-killer.

Yes, five years after the Bugaboo became a hit, Peg has finally answered with the Skate. Was it worth the wait? At first impression, the answer is yes. The Skate has that Bugaboo mojo—it starts as a bassinet and then morphs into a toddler stroller. But the Skate is a ONE-piece stroller and, yes, it folds with the seat on (the Bugaboo Cameleon/Frog is a two piece system and you can't fold it with the seat). The Skate's seat is also height adjustable, something not seen on the Bugaboo.

Peg has loaded the Skate with a gazillion adjustments—we don't have space here to detail it all (see the online video on Peg's web site for the low down—us.skate-pegperego.com). In short, the Skate features a height-adjustable handle, four wheel suspension, ball-bearing wheels for a smooth glide, three seat heights and (drum roll) a cup holder. All yours for $900.

So, what's not to like? Well, the included car seat adapter only works with Peg's own infant seat (sorry Graco or Chicco fans). And there is no storage basket: instead, you get an elastic shelf with bungee cord straps. Huh? Sure, the Skate has an accessory diaper bag that attaches to the back of the stroller, but the non-basket basket seems like a major oversight.

Finally, we have to reveal the Skate's biggest flaw: it weighs 33.7 pounds. Yes, that's 13.7 pounds (68%) more than the Bugaboo Cameleon. While we salute Peg for including many accessories in the package (rain cover, boot, car seat adapter), we still think that weight will be a deal killer. The Skate wasn't out as we went to press, so no parent feedback yet.

Meanwhile, the other mainstays of the Peg line—the Pliko and Aria—get minor makeovers for 2008.

The Pliko features a five-point safety harness, storage basket, 150 degree reclining seat (note: that is NOT a full recline), adjustable leg rest, adjustable height handle and removable/washable seat cushions. The 2008 version (the Pliko P3 Classico, $340, 18.7 lbs.) has changed little from last year's model, which features ergonomic handles, cup holder, removable tray and easier fold. One nice feature: a one-hand fold, which was sorely lacking in the previous Pliko. No, the Pliko is not as easy to fold up as the Zippy (it takes a few more motions), but at least they are moving in the right direction. For 2008, the Pliko P3 Classico adds a pocket in the canopy, an improved cup holder and improved brake.

FYI: You can often find previous year versions of the Pliko discounted under $300.

Perego's other major lightweight offering is the Aria ($150 to $200, 14.3 lbs.). It features a seat that reclines to 150 degrees (same as the Pliko), decent storage basket, canopy and a five-point restraint. This year's version, the Aria OH ($200) features a one-hand fold (hence the OH suffix), larger canopy that ratchets and adjustable cup holder. FYI: The Aria is the only Peg stroller that is NOT made in Italy (the Aria is imported from China).

Yes, the Aria does hold the Perego infant car seat and there is also a twin (side-by-side) version of the Aria that is 32" wide and sells for $330. New this year, the Aria Twin can hold an infant car seat—the new 60/40 seat configuration holds the seat in the larger space.

FYI: All Peg strollers can hold Perego's infant car seat, the Primo Viaggio. And you can find the same matching fabric for the car seat in the stroller line for most models. No, Peg doesn't sell them together as a "travel system" per se, but same difference; just buy them a la carte.

Will the Perego strollers work with other brand infant seats? No. In the past, Perego did offer an adapter bar, but it is now discontinued. Peg seems to change its mind on this issue frequently, so check their web site for the latest word.

Peg has de-emphasized its large carriage strollers in recent years and recently discontinued its flagship Venezia (18 lbs., $400), although you might see it for sale online. The Venezia featured a fully reclining seat, reversible handle, removable boot that snaps and folds back plus a height adjustable handle. Like all Pegs, the Venezia has a decent size storage basket and stylish fabrics.

In the past year, Peg is rolled out the Uno ($350) to replace the Venezia. The Uno looks a bit like the Bugaboo, with smaller wheels up front, larger ones in the back. It doesn't include a bassinet, however. Otherwise, the Uno is much like the Venezia with its reversible handle, boot and adjustable handle.

In the category "better late than never," the Perego GT3 (aka Grand Tourismo, 28.6 lbs.) is Peg's first tri-wheel stroller with inflated tires, a swivel front wheel with lock, big canopy, boot, rain cover and adjustable suspension. At $600, it is a hefty investment.

Got twins? Peg's Duette tandem (32 lbs., $790) has front wheels that can turn with the aid of a steering wheel mounted on the back handle bar. Nope, we are not making that up. The Duette can hold two infant seats (you remove the stroller seats to lock the infant seats into the chassis) and the seats can face in or out.

The Duette joins Peg's other tandem, the Tender CSR ($600) for parents of twins. The big difference between the Tender XL and the Duette is the Duette has seats that can face each other, while the Tender XL does not. And yes, Perego even has a Triplette stroller for a whopping $1060.

Our view. Which Perego is best? Our readers give the Pliko P3 the top honors, although folks wish there was a better cup holder and an easier fold. The Pliko's basket could also be bigger and easier to access. That said, most parents love their Pliko's . . . the same can't be said for the Aria, however. Clearly, Peg cut corners quality-wise on the Chinese-made Aria—parents complain about flimsy cup holders that fall off frequently, squeaking wheels and worse. Yes, the reviews for the Aria on our home page have ticked up a bit in the past year, indicating Peg is addressing some of the problems. But we'd still stay away from the Aria, given its history. The Pliko is a much better bet.

And what of the Skate? The jury is still out on that one. **Rating: B**

Phil & Ted Most Excellent Buggy Company Web: philandteds.com or regallager.com. Phil & Ted followed their fellow kiwis from Mountain Buggy to the U.S. stroller market in 2000, but it took a while for them to hit their stride. Then Phil & Ted hit a home run with the Sport ($400, 22 lbs.), which used to be known as the e3.

Like Mountain Buggy and Valco, Phil & Ted's flagship stroller is a tri-wheel with a swivel front wheel and air-filled tires. What sets Phil & Ted apart is their second-child seat ($90 extra; for kids six months and up), which can attach to the BACK of the stroller (for comparison, Valco's toddler seat attaches to the front). Yep, that's a funky configuration that turns off some parents (safety hint: the child in the backseat has to be removed first to prevent tipping). And if you put a larger toddler in the back seat, the access to the stroller's storage basket is limited. But that caveat aside, folks seem to love the Sport. Parents tell us the all-terrain 12" air-filled wheels are perfect for both the mall and hiking trails, plus the wide seat accommodates children for many years.

FYI: The second seat for the Sport can either attach to the *rear* or *front* of the stroller; and the second seat can be used for either a baby (over six months of age) or a toddler. See Phil & Ted's web site for pictures on how the Sport can be configured (yes, we realize this sounds confusing).

Phi & Ted also make an e3 twin ($550, 36 lbs.), a side-by-side stroller with a 29" width and a maximum capacity of 88 lbs.

For 2008, Phil & Ted plan to roll out several new spin-offs of the Sport. The Classic ($300) will be a stripped-down model, with only a two-position handle and no bumper bar. The Dash ($500, 24 lbs.)

strollers

is an upgraded Sport with fancier padding and canopy. Also new: the Vibe ($600, 21 lbs.), a version of the Sport with a Quinny-like aluminum frame. The Vibe's bumper bar has a snack tray and a larger adjustable canopy than the other models.

Our View. Readers give the Sport an enthusiastic thumbs up for its smooth ride and second-seat functionality. The height adjustable handle also wins raves. Sure, folks wish for a bigger canopy and cup holder (there isn't one), but overall the Sport is a winner.

We have to scratch our heads, however, when it comes to Phil & Ted's plans for the Sport spin-offs. We doubt there is much of a market for the $600 Vibe and we are disappointed in the sparse color choices for the Classic (red) or Dash (red or black). Only the Sport has a wide palette of colors.

That said, we still recommend the Sport and the Phil & Ted brand—their excellent customer service, wide range of accessories and good quality overall make this a good choice for parents who want an all-terrain at a decent price. ***Rating: A-***

Quinny *Web: quinny.com.* The big news in the stroller market last year was the launch of Quinny, a Dutch brand of strollers that was bought by Cosco's parent in 2001. Actually, Cosco tried to bring Quinny to the U.S. back in 2003 with an ill-conceived line of jogging strollers that soon disappeared. But this time, Cosco did things right, bringing to the U.S. domestic versions of Quinny's best sellers in Europe.

The Quinny Buzz (18 lbs.) is one of the line's key new strollers—this clever tri-wheel stroller has an innovative "automatic unfolding" feature plus a sleek look with a fully reclining seat that can face forward or back toward the parent. Like the Bugaboo, the Buzz is a modular system, albeit sold separately: $500 for a stroller, $190 for a carry cot (Dreami) and $170 for a matching Maxi Cosi Mico infant car seat. There is even a two-tone fashion option, like the Bugaboo Cameleon.

The Zapp ($200 to $240, 12 lbs.) is Quinny's ultra-lightweight stroller with compact fold. This model will also accommodate an infant car seat. Unlike the Zapp's European counterpart, the U.S. Zapp will have a basket. A cup holder, however, will be an extra $15.

Our View. Yes, we thought the day would never come when we could write the following words: Dorel/Cosco did something right. The Quinny launch has been a success, thanks in part to Dorel's smart adaptation of these models for the US market (example: Zapp's storage basket). Yet Dorel also kept the sharp Euro fashion for Quinny, which no doubt is driving sales.

Parent reviews of Quinny have been positive: the Buzz is a crowd-pleaser, with its automatic unfolding feature winning raves. Unfortunately, that feature is missing from the Zapp, but it also is half the price. Another caveat to the Zapp: it doesn't recline, so this probably isn't the best choice for newborns (although infants can ride in the Maxi Cosi car seat). And the ride on the Zapp isn't as smooth as a Bugaboo, readers tell us.

Despite these caveats, we recommend both the Buzz and Zapp, both of which are credible (and more affordable) alternatives to the Bugaboo. *Rating: A*

Rock Star Baby (Esprit) *Web: GTBaby.com.* German stroller maker Hauck launched the Rock Star Baby license in 2005, as a partnership with rocker Bon Jovi's drummer Tico Torres. Yes, this brings the number of rock star endorsed strollers to . . . one. Memo to Justin Timberlake: the diaper pail market is wide open.

Rock Star Baby's main offering is a Bugaboo knockoff, basically a repurposed Infinity stroller with bassinet, originally marketed in Europe. The Rock Star Baby stroller ($500, 24.2 lbs.) has a height-adjustable handle, air-filled rear tires, reversible seat and rain cover. But, unlike the Bugaboo, a baby can't lie in the bassinet when it is removed from the stroller. And the large Rock Star Baby logo on the front of the stroller is cheesy at this price point.

For 2008, the Rock Star will feature a bigger canopy, new wheels and universal car seat adapter that holds 14 different models. The price will be going up to $600—and surprise, the giant logo on the front of the stroller will be less prominent.

FYI: the same distributor that brought Rock Star Baby to the U.S. has launched another Hauck-licensed effort: Esprit strollers. Esprit offers three lightweight strollers: the Candy Classic ($140, 14 lbs.) features bright colors and riffs off Maclaren's umbrella models; the Sun Speed ($100, 13 lbs.) umbrella stroller with two handles and a full recline; the Sun Speed Duo ($200, 22 lbs.), a side by side version with full recline.

Honestly, we weren't that impressed with Esprit's offerings, which looked like a transparent effort to slap a well-known brand name on otherwise unremarkable designs.

Just to confuse you, there is a Rock Star version of the Candy as well (same stroller, different fabric).

New for 2008, Rock Star will roll out a model under the I'coo label—the Targo ($600, 21 lbs.), which is much like the Rock Star Baby: it features a reversible seat, car seat adapter and built-in boot.

What do parents think of the Rock Star Baby? Readers tell us they love this stroller's maneuverability and smooth steering. Negatives include a smallish canopy (which may be addressed by the 2008 version) and the weight—it is two pounds heavier than the Bugaboo. We were dismayed with the price increase, which diminishes some of the price advantage the stroller had over the Bugaboo.

As for the Esprit models, feedback on these models has been thin since they are such poor sellers (and generally hard to find, either in stores or online). One parent who did buy the Esprit Sun Speed Duo told us she loved the low price, light weight and deep seat recline. But there are no cup holders, boot or rain cover.

All in all, we will tick up the rating for Rock Star Baby this year, reflecting the positive reviews for their main offering. ***Rating: B-***

Safety 1st *These strollers and travel systems are made by Cosco. See the earlier review for more info.*

Schwinn *Web: instep.net.* Schwinn is made by InStep, which is in turn part of the Dorel/Cosco stroller empire. Basically, Schwinn models are the same as InStep, with upgraded fabric and additional accessories (insulated cooler bag, etc). A single Schwinn is $180, while a double is $270. New for 2008, Schwinn is redesigning their flagship Safari ($160 single, $250 double) swivel-wheel model with a new oval frame, added headrest, car seat adapter, one-hand fold, adjustable handle and bug screen. A double Safari omits the adjustable handle. These strollers are quite heavy—the single is 30 lbs. and the double is 37 lbs.

If you are looking for a fixed-wheel jogger for running, Schwinn offers the Free Runner, in either steel (ST $180) or aluminum (AL $220). Both feature an adjustable handle, suspension and wider tires.

Here's the take-home message: if you just want stroller for walks around the neighborhood, we'd stick with the less-expensive InStep versions. A fixed-wheel Instep Run Around jogger is $100 at Target. However, if you want to run with a stroller (or plan to spend over $200), we'd suggest going with a quality brand (BOB, Dreamer, Baby Jogger). Schwinn/InStep simply doesn't stack up quality wise with the competition. ***Rating: C (Schwinn); B (InStep)***

Silver Cross *Web: SilverCrossAmerica.com; (858) 587-4745.* Silver Cross has been star-crossed in the U.S., after their first distributor collapsed in 2005 amid poor sales. Then the British parent yanked the replacement distributor in 2007, leaving their Canadian sales arm to fill in as of press time. Basically, Silver Cross' specialty are light weight strollers, similar to Maclaren.

The models. The Micro V.2 ($125, 12.5 lbs.) is a lightweight cross between the Mac Volo and Peg Pliko—it includes a basket and carry bag. The Pop ($250, 15.4 lbs.) is an upgraded Micro, adding a fully reclining seat and upgraded canopy.

New this year, the Dazzle ($300, 15.4 lbs.) is a riff on the Maclaren Starck, with a curvy frame, two-position canopy and bright color palette. Also new: the Fizz ($130), which is similar to the Pop but has a wider seat. Gone this year are Silver Cross' bigger, pram-like strollers, the Classic Sleepe and Linear Freeway, now discontinued.

Our View. Simply copying a competitor is no business strategy, as Silver Cross has learned the hard way. The company has failed to gain traction here for a simple reason: there's nothing innovative or compelling about Silver Cross' strollers. And the Dazzle is such a blatant copy of the Mac Starck (down to the same price point and solid gray wheels) we're amazed Silver Cross didn't call it the Darck.

Given the turmoil in this brand's distribution, we'll pass on recommending it until things settle down. **Rating: D**

Stokke *For a dealer near you, call* (877) 978-6553. *Web: stokkeusa.com.* And now for something totally different: the Stokke Xplory, a stroller so bizarre we have to show you a picture just to explain it. Yeah, it looks like something George Jetson might have pushed Elroy around in, but it's more than a museum piece about what

strollers might look like in the year 2050. We will give Stokke bonus points for creativity (they've tried to push it as the next Bugaboo), but the $800 Xplory is a bit too funky for its own good. Like the Bugaboo, you get a modular system that includes a frame with rubber tires and a seat that can attach to the frame either forward or rear facing. The baby's seat can ride high on the frame, which gives the Xplory a weird mobile high chair look. The pitch, according to Stokke, is to keep baby higher off the ground so they are away from exhaust fumes, etc. (the target market is urban parents).

So why haven't you seen the über rich pushing the Stokke Xplory around Greenwich Village? That's because for the most part, the Xplory has been a bust sales-wise. First, most of the Xplory's frame and handle is injection-molded plastic, not something you'd expect from a $800+ stroller. The "plastic-y" feel turns off many, while the lack of a basket is another major negative. Instead the Xplory has a "shopping bag" that attaches to the frame . . . close, but no cigar.

In the past year, Stokke has rolled out a Complete Xplory for $1000 that includes a bassinet (a la the Bugaboo). Also new: a car seat adapter accessory for the Perego Primo Viaggio or Graco SnugRide, which addresses a key complaint about past versions. So while we still wouldn't recommend the Xplory (its high price alone is a deal killer), we will raise the rating a touch this year to reflect the new car seat adapter. **Rating: C-**

Stroll Air (519) 579-4534. *Web: stroll-air.com.* Polish-made Stroll Air is another European stroller company hoping to become the next Bugaboo. Stroll Air's modular stroller systems come with both bassinet and stroller seat, for use on an aluminum chassis. An example: the Driver 3XL, a tri-wheel stroller with two larger inflated tires and a double front wheel that can lock or swivel. You also get a decent basket, height adjustable handle and a nice series of extras (foot muff, wind cover, diaper bag, umbrella, mosquito net). Price: $600-$700. Okay, that's not cheap, but at least Stroll Air isn't charging you those big bucks for a stroller and then expecting you to shell out $40 for an umbrella or $120 for a foot muff (ahem, Bugaboo). The negatives: the weight (the Driver 3XL is 26-28 lbs., depending on how you configure it) and the drab fashion (three colors, red, blue or black—although a limited edition pink is popular). Stroll Air also makes a four-wheel version of the Driver (dubbed the 4XL, $600-$700) and a double stroller (the Spider Duo NV, $900-$1000).

New in the past year, Stroll Air rolled out the Driver NV—a tri-wheel stroller chassis that comes with both a bassinet and stroller seat. At $700, it clearly is aiming at the Bugaboo crowd, yet it is quite heavy (22 lbs. for the chassis alone; add another 8 lbs. for the bassinet or stroller seat). But like its other models, Stroll Air does pull out all the stops for this model: you get a reversible seat, multi-position foot and backrest, adjustable handle, plush padding, air tires, adjustable suspension, rain cover and more. And yes, the Driver NV includes a diaper bag and umbrella. We liked the Driver NV's mini-front wheel, which should give the model more maneuverability in the supermarket than the Driver 3XL or 4XL models.

Also new: a double version of the Driver called the Spider Duo NV2 ($900) with individual, reversible seats. Stroll Air also will debut the Solo (24 lbs.) in 2008, a $500 model with a bassinet, stroller seat, boot and diaper bag. Also included: rain cover, mosquito net, adjustable handle and flat fold.

Our View. Parent feedback on Stroll Air is limited, but the few reports we've received are positive. One reader loved her Driver 4XL, especially the reversible seats, smooth ride and numerous adjustments for the seat, handlebar and so on. The downside: the front wheels on that model only pivot, they don't rotate 360 degrees—that makes tight turns hard to do. Hence this model is best for outdoor walks and off-road trails, not the mall (the new Driver NV might be a better urban stroller).

As for the Spider Duo, the one review we received was quite positive, calling the stroller "the best stroller I have owned . . . and I have had almost every name brand double stroller that is of quality." Yet we also heard from a parent who bought a Stroll-Air Driver NV for $700 who was disappointed by the tires, which constantly went flat. Her email pleas to the company for help weren't returned. While that hopefully was an aberration, we expect more from a company that sells such pricey strollers. Another bummer: Stroll Air is only sold in a handful of stores and online sites.

So, it is a mixed review for Stroll Air—there is some decent value here with all the included extras. But the company must be more responsive to customers in fixing problems. **Rating: B**

Strolee *See Combi.*

Swan *See Baby Trend's review earlier in this section.*

Tike Tech *Web: xtechoutdoors.com.* Tike Tech's claim to fame is their Double T jogger—at $300, it is among the cheapest double joggers on the market. Of course, they do singles too: the ATX All Terrain with 16″ wheels ($200) has a height-adjustable handle and removable safety bar for kids (which is unique). New in the past year is the Tike Tech Trax360 ($270 single, $400 double), which features a front swivel wheel, deep recline seat and bright orange fabric.

All in all, these are mid-price joggers made of aluminum, sold online at BabiesRUs.com as well as other web sites. Parent feedback on this brand is mixed: some complain about quality glitches and most are unimpressed with the canopy, which doesn't offer as much coverage as the competition. Tike Tech strollers can be prone to tipping because the weight of the child is so far back in the stroller. Fans of Tike Tech like the mountain bike-like tires and over-all value—these strollers fill a niche between the ultra-cheap joggers you see in chain stores and pricey $300+ models. We're impressed with new features Tike Tech has rolled out in the past year, including a removable sun visor and a fully reclining seat. **Rating: B-**

Traxx *See i'coo review earlier in this section.*

UPPABaby *(800)760-2060, Web: UppaBaby.com.* Newcomer UPPABaby was started by Bostonians Bob and Lauren Monahan. Bob worked for First Years and Safety 1st in product development before striking out on his own; Lauren provides the PR and design mojo. Obviously, Bob and Lauren have kids, as you can tell from the well thought-out design of their first strollers.

UPPABaby has two strollers: the Vista and the G-lite. The Vista ($600, 25 lbs.) is UPPABaby's take on Bugaboo, albeit at a lower price. Made of an aircraft alloy frame, the VISTA stroller system includes a bassinet and stroller seat, telescoping handle and easy fold. We liked all the included extras, such as a rain shield, mesh sun shade and bug cover. Plus the Vista uses rubber-like foam wheels that give a smooth ride, but don't go flat. Unlike the Bugaboo, you can fold the Vista with the seat attached.

UPPABaby offers car seat adapters for the Graco SnugRide or

SafeSeat, as well as the Peg infant seat. While the Vista does include a weather shield, mesh sunshade and bug cover there are few other accessories (no cup holder, matching boot, etc). And the fashion (six colors) is a bit dull.

UPPABaby's second offering is the G-Lite ($99, 7.9 lbs.), a super lightweight umbrella stroller with a standing fold and mesh seat (like the Mac Volo) and seat pad. The G-lite doesn't recline, so it is best for babies six months and up.

Parent feedback on UPPABaby has been positive. Readers who like the Vista praise its quality, huge basket and high-riding seat and bassinet. The no-flat foam tires also win raves. The negatives include a basket that is a bit hard to reach with the bassinet attached—and the rear wheel base on the Vista is rather wide, making the stroller harder to maneuver in tight aisles at the mall.

The G-lite wins similar kudos, with fans citing its super light weight and included cushions (that's extra on the Mac Volo, for example).

So, we will recommend UPPABaby—no, the Vista isn't inexpensive. But at least for $600, you get decent value (the sun canopy is included for the Vista; a $40 add-on for Bugaboo Cameleon, which is $300 more than the Vista). ***Rating: A***

Valco *(800) 610-7850. Web: valcobaby.com.* Australian-based Valco has made a splash in the all-terrain stroller market with their Tri-Mode (formerly the Runabout), a tri-wheel stroller whose key selling point is its expandability. The basic Runabout comes in both a single ($425, 23 lbs.) and double ($660, 33 lbs.) version and features a five-position, fully reclining seat, large storage basket, aluminum frame, newborn insert and swivel front wheel that can be locked in a fixed position.

That's nice, but what really has parents jazzed are Valco's add-ons: a bassinet ($150) and toddler seat ($80) that extend the use of this stroller. The bassinet is fine, but the toddler seat is really cool, turning the Valco into a double stroller. Valco's other accessories include a car seat adapter ($40, which holds a Graco seat) and foot muff ($60).

How does the Valco stack up versus its main competitors in the swivel wheel, all terrain category? Well the Valco is a touch heavier than the Mountain Buggy Urban Single, although Valco has reduced its weight in the past year to be more comparable. And folks seem to like the Valco's toddler seat configuration better than Phil & Ted, although there is a split opinion here. Fashion wise, Valco is a bit dull, with mostly dark/black fabric options.

Valco does have two other models: the lightweight Buggster ($325, 15 lbs.) is like the Runabout on a diet—a bit like the Quinny Buzz in looks. The Buggster comes with a boot, rain shield, bug net and other goodies, which makes the somewhat steep $325 price a bit easier to swallow.

Valco's other offering is the Rad ($475, 29 lbs.), a Bugaboo knock-off. The Rad comes in a stroller only version or with a bassinet for $600 and features a telescoping handle, flat one-hand fold and reversible seat. Why Valco decided to charge an extra $15 for a cup holder is a mystery, however. It should be part of the package at this price! Another bummer: the seat doesn't fully recline.

For 2008, Valco plans to debut two new models: the Ion and Latitude. The Ion (single: $325, 14 lbs.; double: $550, 17 lbs.) is a tri-wheel model with a Quinny like curved frame, adjustable handle and full recline. The Latitude (single: $200, 16 lbs.; double: $450, 22 lbs.) is also a tri-wheel with telescoping handle, fully reclining seat and a rather amazing fold.

Both the Ion and Latitude will debut in mid 2008, as will a lighter version of the Tri-Mode (the Tri-Mode Lite), which will feature tube-less tires that will shave three to four pounds off the stroller's weight. If that weren't enough, Valco plans to revive its Rebel ($450) model and morph it into a four-wheel model that has a compact fold.

Our View. Parent feedback on the Tri-Mode has been positive, with folks lauding Valco's quality, maneuverability and sturdy ride. We've been impressed with how Valco has trimmed the weight on the Tri-Mode, as that was a previous major drawback. The Buggster also draws kudos for its maneuverability and light weight; but the fold takes practice, the handles don't extend and there isn't a cup holder. For 2008, Valco will tweak the fold to make it easier.

The new Ion and Latitude are unknowns, as we only saw proto-types of these new models. The super-lightweight Ion double might be one to watch.

All in all, Valco is a winner. **Rating: A**

Zooper *(503) 248-9469; Web: zooper.com.* Zooper is one of the brands that flies under the radar—you won't see it in chain stores (except perhaps their online outposts). The company sells a mix of mall strollers and all-terrain, tri-wheel models.

The models. The Boogie (26 lbs., $450) is Zooper's flagship tri-wheel stroller. No, it isn't cheap, but check the specs: it has a four-position full reclining plush seat that reverses so you can see baby when pushing it, full canopy, boot, rain cover, decent size basket and (drum roll) it holds an infant car seat. Note: all those features are usually pricey extras with other brands—that is Zooper's secret sauce. Best of all, the Boogie has a swivel front wheel that can be locked plus better access to its basket. FYI: We've seen the Boogie discounted to $360 online.

At first glance, you might think the Zooper Waltz (16 lbs., $290) was really a Peg Aria. But this stroller offers a napper bar, ergonomic handle and is compatible with most infant car seats—the Aria only works with its own infant seat. And Zooper again throws in all the extras (full boot, rain cover, basket) that make it a much better deal. The Zooper Waltz has a four position, full seat recline. For 2008, the Waltz adds a small snack tray.

While the Boogie and Waltz are Zooper's best sellers, the company offers a plethora of different models in three categories: Elite, Everyday and Escape.

The Boogie is in the Everyday category, along with the Waltz and three other models: the Twist, Hula, and Tango. The Twist ($160, 13.4 lbs.) is a bit like the Peg Perego Pliko, with two handles and a compact fold. The Hula (16 lbs., $270) is a plush version of the Twist, adding height adjustable handles, one-hand recline and an extra sunshade. Need a double? The Zooper Tango is a side-by-side stroller (26 lbs., $400) with a 30″ width and newborn-friendly reclining seats.

Zooper's most expensive strollers are the "Elite" models: the Bolero and Zydeco. The Bolero ($300, 20 lbs.) is a new model featuring a fully reclining seat, adjustable leg-rest and one-hand fold.

The top of the line Zooper is the Zydeco ($520, 29 lbs.). This funky three-wheel stroller looks like one of those concept cars you see at auto shows. It has a "magnesium encased multi-direction suspension system," a height adjustable handle and is infant car seat compatible. The Zydeco has a reversible seat, large basket and full recline. You also get a rain cover and (new this year) a "sleeping bag" (basically a souped-up boot).

If that weren't enough, Zooper also makes three bare bones models: the Salsa ($129), Stomp ($99) and Ska ($190). The Salsa is a super-lightweight mesh model that weighs nine lbs. It includes a canopy, basket and rain cover for $120. The Zooper Salsa is much like the Mac Volo (but Maclaren charges $40 extra for a rain cover in an accessory pack that also includes a seat liner). The Stomp is a scaled down Salsa; the Ska is an upgraded version with fancy padding and a napper bar.

Zooper told us they are discontinuing the Salsa, Stomp and Ska in 2008, so you might be able to pick up one at a discounted price online.

New this year, Zooper is debuting the Mambo (240, 17 lbs.), which features a telescoping handle and embossed fabric. Also new: the Bolero will have a $110 bassinet accessory and will add a one-hand fold. Zooper is also adding extended canopies to many of its strollers such as the Tango and Waltz.

Whew! Confusing, no? Good news: Zooper's web site has detailed descriptions of all models in case you need more info.

Our view. Judging from reader reviews posted to our web site, the Zooper Waltz is the company's most popular model. Folks love the Waltz's smooth ride, big canopy and overall ease of use. Detractors point out the Waltz lacks a cup holder and the fold requires two-hands. Otherwise, this is an excellent choice.

The Zydeco is probably #2 in popularity, with kudos for its all-terrain handling, plush seat, great canopy and nice storage. But . . . it is very heavy, so forget about any serious exercise with this model. The Boogie is a more affordable alternative to the Zydeco, although readers tell us the fold is a bit cumbersome. The weight on the Boogie (26 lbs.) is also a few pounds more than competitors like Mountain Buggy.

For 2008, Zooper seems to be going for the bling, fashion-wise. We liked the embossed, embroidered accents on the new models. But we were puzzled to see several white fabric strollers in the line-up—those won't look that pretty in the real world after a few moments with baby.

Zooper has been drifting design-wise in the last few years; the company also only tweaked existing models instead of innovating, which is a bit troublesome. That said, we still think Zooper has good value: all the included extras (rain cover, boot, etc) make these strollers standout when compared with competitors. **Rating: A-**

◆ **Other brands to consider.** Archived reviews of obscure and previous stroller brands are on our web site. Go to BabyBargains. com and click on Bonus Material.

Our Picks: Brand Recommendations by Lifestyle

Unlike other chapters, we've broken up our stroller recommendations into several "lifestyle" categories. Since many parents end up with two strollers (one that's full-featured and another that's lighter for quick trips), we'll recommend a primary stroller and a secondary option. For more specifics on the models mentioned below, read each manufacturer's review earlier in this chapter. Let's break it down:

Mall Crawler

You live in the suburbs and drive just about everywhere you go. A stroller needs to be packed with features, yet convenient enough to haul in and out of a trunk. Mostly the stroller is used for the mall or for quick trips around the block for fresh air.

In the past, we recommended buying a travel system that combined an infant seat and stroller. This time we have one word of advice when it comes to travel systems: DON'T. Don't waste your money on those huge, bulky systems from mass-market brands like

Graco, Eddie Bauer/Cosco, or Evenflo. Why? Parents repeatedly tell us the strollers in these travel systems are aggravating to use, thanks to low quality and hefty weight. Many readers tell us they usually chuck the stroller when their baby outgrows the infant seat.

Instead, consider one of the great new alternatives to the massive travel system—look at stroller frames like the *Baby Trend Snap & Go* $50 (pictured) or the *Graco Snug Rider* for $60. The Baby Trend works with most infant car seat brands; the Graco works just with the Graco SnugRide and SafeSeat.

FYI: When trying out different stroller frames, take a second and snap your favorite infant car seat into the various stroller frames in the store before purchasing. Check the instructions, as some stroller frames have bars that have to be adjusted into a certain position to accommodate different brands.

The bottom line: take a stroller frame, pop in a compatible infant seat and poof! Instant travel system . . . without the expense.

When baby outgrows the infant seat, then you go stroller shopping. This is smarter for two obvious reasons: a) you already have a baby and can see what best fits your infant. And b) you're more experienced as a parent, so you'll have an idea where you want to go with a stroller.

"But really, Denise and Alan, which travel system do you like?" No matter how much we editorialize against pre-packaged travel systems, we still get emails from parents who want to go this route. Okay, if you want to ignore the above advice, we'd suggest one of Graco's more affordable offerings, such as the *Graco MetroLite* travel system (about $200). At least then you are getting a decent infant seat (the Graco SnugRide). Another favorite: the *Chicco Cortina* travel system for $280.

Above all, stay away from the travel systems with heavy strollers—if the stroller is over 23 lbs., don't buy it.

Second stroller. The best stroller for a mall crawl is ultra lightweight and has a compact fold.

At the budget end, the *Chicco C5* ($90, 13.7 lbs.; pictured) is a best bet, combining a multi-position reclining seat, decent-size basket and a compact fold. We also recommend the *Maclaren Volo* ($100, 9.2 lbs.)—nothing fancy, but an easy fold and super-lightweight.

FYI: Both the Chicco C5 and Mac Volo are best for babies over six months of age, as they don't have fully reclining seats.

Flying on a plane and dreading gate-checking your stroller? Need something for just a quick mall run? Then we'd suggest an affordable Kolcraft umbrella stroller, starting at $20 to $30 in chain stores. Of all the low-end umbrellas you see in discount stores, these are the best bets.

For a mid-range mall crawler stroller, we recommend the *Quinny Zapp* ($200 to $240, 12 lbs.), a super lightweight model that fits a Maxi Cosi infant seat and features a compact fold. But the Zapp doesn't recline, so it is best for babies over six months.

Is Grandma paying for your second stroller? The best options at the top of the market for suburban parents are probably the *Inglesina Zippy* ($340, 17 lbs.), the *Maclaren Techno XT* ($300, 17 lbs.) or the *Peg Perego Pliko P3 Classico* ($240 to $270, 17 lbs.). If you would like to skip the stroller frame and just use a stroller, the new *Maclaren Techno XLR* ($350, 16.3) is expensive but includes a infant car seat adapter and a slightly wider seat then the XT. Again, nice if Grandma is paying.

A dark horse choice for the Mall Crawler: a tri-wheel all-terrain stroller with an air-filled front wheel that either swivels or locks. We'll review those strollers in the Green Acres section later because most of those strollers are pitched for hiking or gravel roads. You can use these strollers in the mall, but beware: they are heavier and some-what less maneuverable than the strollers discussed above.

Urban Jungle

When you live in a city like New York, Boston or Washington D.C., your stroller is more than just baby transportation—it's your primary vehicle. You stroll to the market, on outings to a park or longer trips on weekend getaways.

Weight is crucial for these parents as well. While you are not lug-ging a stroller in or out of a trunk like a suburbanite, you may find yourself climbing up subway stairs or trudging up to a fourth-floor walk-up apartment. It's a major trade-off here: full-featured strollers that are outfitted for the weather (full boot, rain cover) can weigh more than lightweight models designed for the mall. Basically, you want a rugged stroller that can take all the abuse a big city can dish out—giant potholes, uneven sidewalks, the winter from Hell . . . without the weight of a bulldozer.

In the past, carriage strollers or prams were the primary "urban jungle" stroller, but these have fallen out of favor for their bulky weight and other disadvantages (prams typically have front wheels that don't turn).

Our top pick is the *Valco Tri-Mode*. This tri-

strollers

wheel stroller ($425, 23 lbs.) has 12" inch air-filled wheels and all the comforts you need for the city: five-position fully reclining seat, decent size storage basket, five-point harness, cushy padding, reflective trim for nighttime visibility and more. The front wheel swivels . . . or can be locked for a little exercise in the park.

But here's the best part: Valco offers a variety of accessories to extend the use of the Tri-Mode. First is a bassinet ($150) that snaps into the aluminum frame. Second, check out the innovative toddler seat ($80) that turns the Tri-Mode into a double stroller. There's also a car seat adapter ($40), foot muff ($50) and full rain cover ($20). All in all, Valco is a great hybrid, combining the plushness of carriage strollers of the past with the flexibility of all-terrain models that can be used both for shopping and the park.

BUGABOO SMACKDOWN!

The Bugaboo Cameleon ($880, 20 lbs.) is the reining champ of ultra expensive, three component strollers (combining a bassinet, stroller frame and seat). Whether you think it is a cleverly designed

CONTENDER	PRICE	WEIGHT	BUGABOO-ISH?
BRITAX VIGOUR	$350	27.5 LBS.	🪵
FISHER PRICE INFANT-TO-TODDLER STROLLER	$150	21 LBS.	🪵🪵
KOLCRAFT OPTIONS 4 WHEEL	$140	25 LBS.	🪵
MUTSY URBAN RIDER	$700	25.4 LBS.	🪵🪵🪵
PEG PEREGO SKATE	$900	33.7 LBS.	🪵🪵
QUINNY BUZZ	$500	18 LBS.	🪵🪵🪵
ROCK STAR BABY	$600	24.2 LBS.	🪵
STROLL AIR DRIVER NV	$700	30 LBS.	🪵🪵
UPPA BABY VISTA	$600	25 LBS.	🪵🪵🪵
VALCO RAD	$600	29 LBS.	🪵🪵

Finally, let's talk about the 800-lb. gorilla in this category: the **Bugaboo Cameleon**. Dutch-designed (but made in Asia), the Bugaboo's claim to fame is its flexibility. You get an aluminum frame that can hold either a bassinet or stroller seat (both included). It pushes like a dream and most parents who have a Bugaboo absolutely adore it . . . but there is a catch. The price: $880. Add in accessories (you wanted a stroller with a sun canopy?) and you can easily see the total soar past $1100. Even a Valco with an added bassinet is 40% less than a Bugaboo. So unless you have a rich uncle, we say pass.

There is good news for folks who like the Bugaboo . . . but don't have the Bugaboo bankroll. A series of knock-offs (both credible and less so) have debuted in the past year. See the "Bugaboo Smackdown" box below for our look at the competitors. Our fave

---

stroller that embodies urban chic . . . or a sign of wretched yuppie excess, Bugaboo sure has been one thing: a hit. Now competitors are nipping at Bugaboo's wooden shoes. We rate the contenders on a scale of one to three klompen! (Google it.)

COMMENTS/VERDICT

While it **lacks design mojo**, reversible seat does remove to fit a Britax infant seat and features infinite recline, removable sun canopy and height adjustable handle. No cup holder. Heavy.

Best value. Three-position, reversible seat and height adjustable handle. Canopy has viewing window. But it is a bit wider than a Bugaboo; no separate bassinet. Doesn't fit an infant seat. Light weight.

Holds most infant car seats; reversible seat, child snack tray and yes, even a cup holder for parent. **But weighs 20% more** than Fisher-Price.

Best style. Comes with bassinet and swapable front wheels. 20% cheaper than Bugaboo . . . but 25% heaver. Euro fashion.

Folds with seat, **includes accessories like car seat adapter,** rain cover and boot. But it is 68% heavier than Bugaboo. Expensive.

Tri-wheel stroller, reversible seat; auto unfold; **carry cot and car seat are extra.** Fold isn't compact. Nice fashion.

Expensive, height adj handle, reversible seat, rain cover. Baby can't lie in bassinet when removed from stroller.

Includes bassinet, reversible seat, adj. handle, plush padding, rain cover, diaper bag, umbrella. **Tri-wheel.** But it's 10 lbs. heavier than Bugaboo.

Pricey, but includes bassinet, height adj. handle, rain shield, mesh sun shade, rubber-like foam wheels. But weighs 25% more than Bugaboo.

Includes bassinet, flat one-hand fold, reversible seat, light weight. **But an extra $15 for a cup holder?** And the seat doesn't fully recline.

strollers

Bugaboo competitor: the **UPPABaby Vista** ($600, 25 lbs). Yes, it is a five pounds heavier than the Cameleon, but you get decent value with all sorts of included accessories.

We also recommend the **Quinny Buzz** ($500, 18 lbs.) for urban dwellers looking for a Bugaboo without the hefty price. We like the Buzz's automatic unfolding feature and reversible seat—plus it holds a Maxi Cosi car seat.

Second stroller. While full-featured strollers are nice, they do have one disadvantage. They're heavy (many are 20 to 40 lbs.) and most don't fold compactly. Sometimes, all you need is a lightweight stroller that can withstand big-city abuse YET quickly folds like an umbrella so you can get in a taxi or down a set of subway stairs. (Just try lugging a 30-pound stroller up the stairs at a T stop in Boston). The solution: Maclaren—their strollers weigh just ten to 14 lbs. and fold compactly. The entry-level **Maclaren Triumph** ($175; pictured) has all the features you'd need (including a partially reclining seat) yet weighs a mere 11 lbs. For another $50 to $100, you can get a plusher seat and other upgrades with the Maclaren Quest, Ryder or Techno XT—with the caveat of added weight.

Another recommendation for a lightweight stroller for urban parents would be the **UPPABaby G-Lite** ($99, 7.9 lbs.). No, that's not a typo: the G-Lite weighs a mere 7.9 pounds yet features a standing

	STROLLER ROUND-UP		Here's our round-up of popular lightweight models by the major stroller manufacturers.		

MAKER	MODEL	WEIGHT	PRICE	RECLINE
CHICCO	C5	13.7 LBS.	$90	PARTIAL
COMBI	COSMO ST	11.5	$60	FULL
GRACO	IPO	17	$80	PARTIAL
INGLESINA	SWIFT	11	$120	PARTIAL
JEEP/KOLCRAFT	WRANGLER	12	$30	PARTIAL
MACLAREN	VOLO	8.6	$100	NONE
PEG PEREGO	PLIKO P3	18.7	$340	PARTIAL
QUINNY	ZAPP	12	$200-240	NO
SILVER CROSS	MICRO V.2	12.5	$125	PARTIAL
UPPA BABY	G-LITE	7.9	$99	NONE
VALCO	BUGGSTER	15	$325	PARTIAL
ZOOPER	TWIST	13.4	$160	PARTIAL

fold and mesh seat with included seat pad. FYI: The G-Lite doesn't recline, so this stroller is best for babies over six months of age.

If a stroller with a one-hand fold is a must, the *Inglesina Zippy* ($340) is pricey but the fold is amazing and quick.

While it's easy to spend less money on other models, don't be penny-wise and pound-foolish. Less-expensive strollers lack the durability and weatherproofing that living in an East Coast city requires. And since baby spends more time in the stroller than tots in the suburbs, weatherized fabrics and padding are more of a necessity than a luxury.

Green Acres

If you live on a dirt or gravel road or in a neighborhood with no sidewalks, you need a stroller to do double duty. First, it must handle rough surfaces without bouncing baby all over the place. Second, it must be able to "go to town," folding easily to fit into a trunk for a trip to a mall or other store.

This is a tough category to recommend a stroller for—there are many so-called "all-terrain" strollers on the market. Yet, we found those made by the big guys (Cosco, Evenflo) were just pretenders. Yeah, the box says "all-terrain" and they have larger wheels and shock absorbing suspensions, but we just don't think most of them really cut it. Like faux-SUV's that couldn't handle two inches of

strollers

COMMENTS

COMPACT UMBRELLA FOLD, NICE FASHION, DECENT-SIZE BASKET.

AFFORDABLE, COMPACT FOLD, CAN BE PAIRED WITH COMBI INFANT SEAT.

ONE-HAND FOLD, NO NAPPER BAR; DOESN'T WORK WITH INFANT SEAT.

SKIMPY CANOPY, NO CUP HOLDER, TWO HANDLE DESIGN.

AFFORDABLE, BUT BARE BONES (NO BASKET, CUP HOLDER).

MESH SEAT, CARRY STRAP—BUT NO SEAT RECLINE. GOOD QUALITY.

ERGONOMIC HANDLES, CUP HOLDER, EASY FOLD.

TRI-WHEEL, COMPACT FOLD, FIT AN INFANT CAR SEAT, BUT NO SEAT RECLINE.

CARRY BAG INCLUDED, FOAM WHEELS, ONE-HAND FOLD.

LIGHTEST WEIGHT. STANDING FOLD, MESH SEAT, MACHINE-WASHABLE PAD.

BOOT, RAIN SHIELD, BUG NET, TRI-WHEEL, BASSINET ACCESSORY.

RAIN/SUN COVERS, FOOT MUFF, SIMILAR TO PEG PLIKO IN LOOKS.

snow, these strollers are long on promise and short on delivery.

There is good news on the Green Acres front: in the past year, more "all terrain" models have debuted, providing parents with more choice. Now, the best options for this lifestyle would probably be the Phil & Ted e3 or Mountain Buggy Urban Single.

Phil & Ted's Sport ($400, 22 lbs.) is a tri-wheel stroller with swivel front wheel and air-filled tires. What's unique about the Sport: a toddler seat accessory ($90) that attaches to the BACK of the seat, giving you added flexibility if you have multiple kids.

For Green Acres parents, we'd also recommend the **Mountain Buggy Urban Single** (22 lbs.; pictured) from New Zealand. Nope, it isn't cheap at $430 but it is built to last with quality features like polymer wheels that won't rust (memo to parents who live near an ocean: avoid steel wheels).

Also recommended: **BOB Revolution** stroller ($360-$380, 22-23 lbs.), which comes in two versions—the regular Revolution has polymer wheels (better for the beach or salt air) or the AW model has aluminum wheels (a touch lighter and more stylish).

While we like Phil & Ted and Mountain Buggy, both strollers are rather plain vanilla, style-wise. If you are looking for a tri-wheel stroller with turnable front wheel with a little pizzazz, check out the **BumbleRide Indie** ($400, 20 lbs.). This stroller features a boot, adjustable handle and optional carrycot—plus a more compact fold.

All right, the above strollers are great, but what if you want a simpler all-terrain stroller with a swivel front wheel that costs less than $120? The **Jeep Liberty SE Terrain** is an excellent choice: it features a one-hand fold, child snack tray with a cute toy steering wheel, and parent tray. Target sells a slightly upgraded version of the Liberty for $140.

SPORT STROLLERS

How top sport/jogging strollers compare:

MODEL	CAPACITY	PRICE	BRAND RATING
BABY JOGGER PERFORMANCE	100 LBS.	$360	A
BABY TREND EXPEDITION	50	$100	B-
BOB SPORT UTILITY D'LUX	70	$350	A
DREAMER REBOUND GST	80	$250	A-
INSTEP ULTRA RUNNER	50	$180	B
KELTY SPEEDSTER 08	75	$260	B+
KOOL STRIDE SR 16"	85	$375	A
SCHWINN JOY RIDER	50	$300	C

Exercise This: Jogging and Sport Strollers

How times have changed. When the first edition of this book appeared in 1994, there were just a handful of jogging or "sport" strollers on the market, most of which cost $200 or more. Today, the number of offerings in this category has exploded—over 30 jogging strollers are offered on the market at last count, with prices as low as $100. And it's not just the small companies . . . the big boys are busy rolling out joggers and sport strollers as well.

So, what's all the fuss about? Most jogging or sport strollers have three wheels and are built like bicycles—they boast large rubber wheels with rugged tread that can handle any terrain, yet move smoothly along at a fast clip. Folks who like to jog or even walk for fitness favor joggers over regular strollers for that reason.

FYI: Jogging strollers have FIXED front wheels—this makes it easier to walk or run in a straight line. If you want an all-terrain stroller with a turnable front wheel, see the previous section (Green Acres) for ideas. Strollers with turnable front wheels are NOT recommended for folks who want to fast walk or run.

How young can you put a baby in a jogger? First, determine whether the seat reclines (not all models do). If it doesn't, wait until baby is at least six months old and can hold his or her head up. If you want to jog or run with the stroller, it might be best to wait until baby is at least a year old since all the jostling can be dangerous for a younger infant (their neck muscles can't handle the bumps). Ask your pediatrician for advice if you are unsure.

Before heading out to buy a jogging stroller, consider how you'll use it. Despite their name, few parents actually use a jogging stroller for jogging. If you just plan to use the stroller for walks in the neighborhood, a lower price model (we'll have specific recommendations below) with 12" wheels will do fine. If you really plan to run

strollers

Suspension	Adj. Handle	Cup holder	Pin-free folding
✔			✔
		✔	
✔			✔
✔	✔		✔
		✔	
✔			✔
✔			
✔			

with a jogger, go for 16" or 20" wheels for a smoother glide and a higher-quality brand name for durability.

Another decision area: the frame. The cheapest strollers (under $200) have steel frames—they're strong but also heavy (and that could be a drawback for serious runners). The most expensive models ($200 to $350) have aluminum frames, which are the lightest in weight. Once again, if you plan casual walks, a steel frame is fine. Runners should go for aluminum.

Check the seat fabric carefully. The best strollers use Dupont Cordura, which is also used in backpacks for its durability and strength. As for other features, go for a model that has a hand brake

Three mistakes to avoid when buying a jogging stroller

With jogging strollers available everywhere from Target to high-end bike stores, it is easy to get confused by all the options. Keep in mind these traps when shopping for a jogger:

◆ **Rust.** Warning: cheaper jogging strollers are made of steel—rust can turn your jogging stroller into junk in short order. This is especially a problem on the coasts, but can happen anywhere. Hint: the best joggers have ALUMINUM frames. And make sure the wheels rims are alloy, not steel. All-terrain strollers like Mountain Buggy use polymer wheels (in most models) to get around the rust problem.

◆ **Suspended animation.** The latest rage with joggers is cushiony suspensions, which smooth out bumps but can add to the price. But do you really need it? Most jogging strollers give a smooth ride by design, so no added suspension is necessary. And some kids actually LIKE small bumps or jostling—it helps them fall asleep in the stroller.

◆ **Too narrow seats.** Unlike other baby products, a good jogging stroller could last you until your child is five years old—that is, if you pick one with a wide enough seat to accommodate an older child. The problem: some joggers (specifically, Baby Jogger and Kelty) have rather narrow seats. Great for infants, not good for older kids. We noticed this issue after our neighbors stopped using their Baby Jogger when their child hit age 3, but our son kept riding in his until five and beyond. Brands with bigger seats include Dreamer Design and BOB. (As always, confirm seat dimensions before committing to a specific stroller; seats can vary from model to model).

on the handle (the cheapest models omit this). The brake is used to slow the stroller when you are going down a steep incline. And always check the folding feature: some are easier than others.

Finally, remember the Trunk Rule. Any jogger is a lousy choice if you can't get it easily in your trunk. Check the DEPTH of the jogger when it is folded—compared this to your vehicle's trunk. Many joggers are rather bulky even when folded. Yes, quick release wheels help reduce the bulk, so check for that option.

A good web site with detailed jogging stroller info: JoggingStroller.com. The site has user reviews and even editorial opinions from the owner about which stroller has the best fold, etc.

So, which jogging stroller do we recommend? Let's break that down into two categories: low-end and high-end. Note that all these strollers have fixed front wheels; if you want a stroller with a turnable front wheel (more suited to the mall or light duty outdoor activities), see the Green Acres section on page 523.

Low end (walks, hikes). Baby Trend's affordable joggers (see earlier review for more background on Baby Trend) are sold in Babies R Us and other chain stores. The entry-level **Baby Trend Expedition** ($100 stand alone, or $200 as a travel system with infant car seat) has a five-point harness, canopy and two-position seat recline. These steel frame strollers will do fine for occasional walks and other light-duty use.

Similarly, **InStep's Run Around LTD Jogger** ($100 at Target.com) is a good value. It is similar to the Baby Trend in features.

High end (serious runners). What if you really want to jog or run with a sport stroller? Or you plan to use it intensively for exercise (say more than two times a week)? Or go for true off-road adventures? Then we suggest investing in a top-quality stroller from BOB.

BOB this year captures the top spot in our jogger review. Our favorite model is the **BOB Ironman** stroller ($350). The Ironman has all the quality features of a regular BOB, but adds adjustable tracking, stainless steel wheel spokes, new smooth tires and bright yellow fabric. This jogger weighs just 20 pounds.

Looking for a quick-fold jogger? Check out the **Baby Jogger Q Series** 16″ single ($230 to $350). No, the canopy isn't as nice as a Dreamer Design, nor is it as plush—but the quick one-hand fold may outweigh the cons.

So, let's sum it up. For high-end joggers for serious runners, we suggest BOB or Baby Jogger. On the low end, Baby Trend or InStep should do the trick.

The same advice for brands applies to double joggers—the better brands for single joggers are the same as the ones for doubles.

Plan to take your jogger out in the cold weather? Instead of bundling up baby, consider a stroller blanket. One of our favorites is the **JJ Cole Bundle Me** (web: bundleme.com), which comes in several versions for $25 to $60.

Double The Fun: Strollers for two

There are two types of strollers that can transport two tikes: tandem models and side-by-side styles. For the uninitiated, a tandem stroller has a "front-back" configuration, where the younger child rides in back while the older child gets the view. These strollers are best for parents with a toddler and a new baby.

Side-by-side strollers, on the other hand, are best for parents of twins. In this case, there's never any competition for the view seat. The only downside: some of these strollers are so wide, they can't fit through narrow doorways or store aisles. (Hint: make sure the stroller is not wider than 30" to insure door compatibility). Another bummer: few have napper bars or fully reclining seats, making them impractical for infants.

So, what to buy—a tandem or side by side? Our reader feedback shows parents are much happier with their side-by-side models than tandems. Why? The tandems can get darn near impossible to push when weighted down with two kids, due to their length-wise design. Yes, side by sides may not be able to fit through some narrow shopping aisles, but they seem to work better overall.

Double strollers can be frustrating—your basic choices are low-price (and low-quality) duos from Graco, Cosco or Baby Trend or high-price doubles like those from Perego, Maclaren or Combi. There doesn't seem to be much in between the low-price (at $150) and the high-end ($300 and up).

Given the choices on the low end for tandems, we like the **Graco DuoGlider** best (37 lbs., $130-$150; pictured). Yes, this one accepts not one but TWO infant car seats, but probably most parents who buy this will have an older/younger child configuration. The DuoGlider has stadium seating (the rear seat is  higher than the front)) and the rear seat fully reclines for infants. Plus, you get a giant basket.

We also would recommend the **Compass S350 Lightweight Tandem Stroller** ($160, 22 lbs.), a clever hybrid between umbrella-style strollers and a tandem double. Note the weight difference between the Compass S350 and the Graco DuoGlider!

Another good bet on the low end: the **Joovy Caboose Stand-on Tandem** ($150, 26 lbs.). It really isn't a tandem, but a pushcart—

E-MAIL FROM THE REAL WORLD
Biting the bullet on a pricey twin stroller

Cheapo twin strollers sound like a good deal for parents of twins, but listen to this mother of multiples:

"Twins tend to ride in their strollers more often and longer, and having an unreliable, bulky or inconvenient stroller is a big mistake. As you suggest, it's a false economy to buy an inexpensive Graco or other model, as these most likely will break down before you're done with the stroller. My husband and I couldn't believe that we'd have to spend $400 on a stroller, but after talking to parents of multiples, we understand why it's best to just bite the bullet on this one. We've heard universally positive feedback about the Maclaren side-by-side for its maneuverability, durability and practicality. It fits through most doorways and the higher end model (Twin Techno) also has seats that fully recline for infants. We've heard much less positive things about front-back tandems for twins. These often are less versatile, as only one seat reclines, so you can't use them when both babies are small (or tired). And when the babies get bigger, they're more likely to get into mischief by pulling each others' hair and stuff."

the younger child sits in front while an older child *stands* in back (there is also a jump seat for the older child to sit on).

What about side-by-side strollers? For parents of twins on a tight budget, we suggest the *Jeep Twin All Weather Twin Sport Umbrella* (27 lbs., pictured.) for $80 at Wal-Mart. It's bare bones (no basket) but will get the job done with reclining seats and a compact fold. If you've got a bit more budget, the *Inglesina Twin Swift* ($250, 28 lbs.) gets rave reviews from our readers. We also would recommend the *Maclaren Twin Techno* ($360, 25 lbs.; pictured) with its fully reclining seats.

Finally, for outdoor treks with two kids, we'd suggest looking at our top-rated all-terrain stroller brands (Phil & Ted, Mountain Buggy)—most make swivel wheel doubles that, while pricey, feature great quality and comfort.

 *Do It By Mail*

THE BABY CATALOG OF AMERICA.

To Order Call: (800) PLAYPEN or (203) 931-7760; Fax (203) 933-1147
Web: www.babycatalog.com

This web site won't win any design awards (the main stroller section is just a few paragraphs of advice on buying strollers), but they've added more thumbnail graphics to each category. And the selection is still great. Baby Catalog has it all—over three-dozen models from such brand names as Peg Perego, Maclaren, Mountain Buggy and more. Prices are rock bottom, about 20% to 30% below retail. Once you click to each stroller's page, you'll find detailed pictures and fabric swatches that make shopping easy.

Baby Catalog has been in business since 1992, first as a printed catalog and now primarily a web site (don't waste your time with the printed catalog as it is only produced sporadically and the web site has more up-to-date stuff). The company has a good record when it comes to customer service. The site does offer a baby registry as well.

Of course, this site sells much more than strollers—they also discount Avent bottles, Dutailier gliders, designer bedding and more.

One tip: you can save an additional 10% off the site's prices by purchasing a membership, $25 for a year (or $49.95 for three years). Even more cool: if you're in the military, Baby Catalog offers a free membership. With each membership, you also get three "associate" memberships for friends/relatives to purchase items for you at the same discount. Interestingly, this is a clever way to get a premium brand that is rarely discounted online—for some reason, manufacturers who don't allow sites to discount their products don't seem to mind when Baby Catalog offers their members that 10% discount.

Top 6 Tips for Traveling with Baby

I **AIRLINE-PROOF YOUR STROLLER.** Even if you have a stroller that folds as compact as an umbrella, you may still find the airline will ask you to "gate check" it if the plane is full (read: 98% of the time). That means before you board the plane, you leave it outside the aircraft door . . . and pray you'll see it again in one piece. It's the ugly part of traveling with baby—having an airline baggage handler manhandle your stroller. We've heard numerous stories of strollers that disappeared into cargo holds, only to reappear damaged, trashed and worse. Our advice: take an affordable umbrella-type stroller on the road (prices start at $30 to $50), not that $200 model. That way, if the airline trashes it, you don't take that big of a financial hit.

If you insist on taking your $300 stroller on a plane, remove any child tray, hood or cup holder and put them in a suitcase (these items are mostly likely mangled). Get a stroller carry bag (some brands sell these as accessories.

2 **PACK FOOD AND DIAPERS, TIMES THREE.** Ever try to buy diapers at a major airport? While airports are great at catering to business travelers, families stuck with a three-hour delay are often out of luck when it comes to finding baby necessities. A word to the wise: calculate how many diapers and formula/snacks you need for a trip and then triple it to deal with delays. Yes, if you are breastfeeding, you have that part covered, but other supplies can be hard to track down (and very expensive) if you run out.

3 **PLAN AHEAD AND PACK SNACKS.** Airlines have cut most meal service, so it's up to you to be the snack cafeteria. Pack a snack lunch or pick up a snack at the airport. And if by some weird fate of chance, your airline still offers food, go ahead and order a child's meal (even if you are still breastfeeding). Why? You can always eat the meal if you are still hungry. And trust us, hauling all those diapers from tip #2 through the airport requires a significant amount of energy. Moment of irony: kid's meals often taste better than what airlines serve adults.

4 **THINK "SHERPA."** Those expert mountain guides in Nepal know how to pack smart and you should too. Always consider the WEIGHT of any item when you travel. Buy a lightweight, simple stroller and car seat. And a cheap stroller might also be a good idea since the airlines are well known for crunching strollers.

5 **USE A CARRIER.** The best way to move through an airport is with a front carrier like the Baby Bjorn, reviewed in this chapter. That way, you have two hands free to carry everything else. Yes, we still recommend buying a baby a separate seat and bringing/using a child safety seat. But if you use a carrier like the Bjorn, you won't need a stroller when shuttling between gates, etc.

6 **PACK YOUR OWN CRIB SHEETS.** Yes, most hotels have cribs, but some try to cheat when it comes to bedding—attempting to wrap a crib mattress with a twin sheet or worse. Be safe: pack your own crib sheets just in case.

Bike Trailers, Seats & Helmets

Bike Trailers. Yes, lots of companies make bike trailers, but the gold standard is **Burley** (866-248-5634; web: burley.com). Their trailers (sold in bicycle stores) are considered the best in the industry. A good example is the **Burley *"d'Lite."*** It features a
multi-point safety harness, built-in rear storage, 100 lb. carrying capacity and compact fold (to store in a trunk). Okay, it's expensive at $450 but check around for second-hand bargains. All Burley trailers have a conversion kit that enables you to turn a trailer into a jogging stroller (although we hear mixed reviews on the Burley as a jogging stroller for its wobbly steering).

A close runner-up to Burley in the bike trailer race is Canada's **Chariot** (chariotcarriers.com). "These are the best engineered bike trailers I've ever seen," opined a reader and we agree. Sold at REI, the basic Caddie runs $350, although they sell a pricey version that combines a stroller and bike trailer for an astounding $695.

Kool Stop (the jogger company reviewed earlier in this chapter) offers three child trailers, the Original, the Koolite and the Papoose Caboose. All three have the towing bar in the center rather than to the right or left as with Burley (Burley then bends the bar so the trailer stays centered behind the bike). Kool Stop claims the center bar helps "enhance towing, tracking, turning and control." These new trailers start at $270 and go up to $375.

Another jogging stroller manufacturer, **Baby Jogger**, has entered the bike trailer market this year. As we mentioned earlier, the Switchback is a hybrid jogging stroller/bike trailer. It morphs from one to the other without any special tools or kit. Cost: $580.

What about the "discount" bike trailers you see for $150 to $200? **InStep** makes a few of these models: the Quick N Lite ($140), the Rocket Aluminum ($240), Take 2 ($100), Ride N' Stride ($180) and Quick N EZ ($100). InStep also makes four Schwinn bike trailers, which are upgraded versions of their regular line. Cost: $165 to $210.

What do you give up for the price? In general, lower priced bike trailers have steel frames and are heavier than the Burleys (which are made of aluminum). And the cheaper bike trailers don't fold as easily or compactly as the Burleys, nor do they attach as easily to a bike.

The key feature to look for with any bike trailer is the ease (or lack thereof) of attaching the stroller to a bike. Quick, compact fold is important as well. Look for the total carrying capacity and the quality of the nylon fabric.

So, should you spring for an expensive bike trailer or one of the $150 ones? Like jogging strollers, consider how much you'll use it.

For an occasional (once a week?) bike trip, we'd recommend the cheaper models. Plan to do more serious cycling, say two or three times a week? Then go for a Burley, Schwinn or Kool Stop. Yes, they are expensive but worth it if you really plan to use the trailer extensively. Hint: this might be a great item to buy second-hand on eBay or Craigslist.

Safety information: you should wait on using a bike trailer until your child is OVER one year of age. Why? Infants under age one don't have neck muscles to withstand the jolts and bumps they'll hit with bike trailers, which don't have shock absorbers. Remember you might hit a pothole at 15+ mph—that's not something that is safe for an infant to ride out. Be sure your child is able to hold his head up while wearing a helmet as well. Your child should always wear a helmet while riding in a bike trailer—no exceptions. And, no, there is no bike trailer on the market that safely holds an infant car seat, which might cushion the bumps. Most trailers will accommodate children up to about age six. Check the instruction manual for individual trailers.

Bike seats. When shopping for a bike seat, consider how well padded the seat is and what type of safety harness the unit has (the best are five-points with bar shields; less expensive seats just have three-point harnesses). The more expensive models have seats that recline and adjust to make a child more comfortable.

One good model is the *CoPilot Limo Child Seat* ($110-$140) by CoPilot (formerly called Rhode Gear), which has a florescent orange safety bar, three-point harness and four-position reclining seat (sold by LL Bean and REI). A simpler version of this seat is called the CoPilot Taxi for $90, which lacks the reclining seat. Another option is the *Topeak*  *BabySitter*. It has a spring suspension system to cushion bumps. They also include dual safety latches to lock the seat to the rack, adjustable foot rests, a quick release padded safety bar, and four-way safety harness. Cost: $120 to $140.

We've not seen any safety problems with the cheaper bike seats sold in discount stores; they just tend to lack some of the fancier features (padding, reclining seats) that make riding more comfortable for a child.

Safety advice: as with a bike trailer, your child should be able to hold her head up easily while wearing a bike helmet to ride in a bike seat. We think it's best to use a bike seat for children two or over. They can accommodate children up to 40 pounds.

Bike helmets. *Consumer Reports* tested kids bike helmets in 2006 and recommended options from *Bell* (who also makes *Giro*).

bike trailers/seats

CR noted that all toddler models were a bit lacking in ventilation, but the Bell Boomerang ($30) did a very good job at impact absorption and scored best for ease of use. Although Bell makes other models of toddler bike helmets, they didn't all score the same. We would agree with *Consumer Reports*, as their research matches feedback from parents on Bell. We'd recommend avoiding the really cheap helmets under $20.

Safety advice: many states are requiring all children to wear bike helmets when riding in a bike seat or trailer. That makes sense, but it is sometimes hard to find a helmet to fit such small heads. One tip: add in thick pads (sold with some bike helmets) to give a better fit. Don't glue pads on top of pads, however—and adding a thick hat isn't a safety solution either. If your child cannot wear a bike helmet safely, put off those bike adventures until they are older. Be sure your child wears the helmet well forward on his head. If a helmet is pushed back and your child hits the ground face first, there is no protection for the forehead.

The Well-Stocked Diaper Bag

We consider ourselves experts at diaper bags—we got five of them as gifts. While you don't need five, this important piece of luggage may feel like an extra appendage after your baby's first year. And diaper bags are for more than just holding diapers—many include compartments for baby bottles, clothes, and changing pads. With that in mind, let's take a look at what separates great diaper bags from the rest of the pack. In addition, we'll give you our list of nine items for a well-stocked diaper bag.

Parents in Cyberspace: What's on the Web

Just because you have a new baby doesn't mean you have to lose all sense of style. And there is good news: an entire cottage industry of custom diaper-bag makers has sprung up to help fill the style gap. One good place to start: our message boards. Go to BabyBargains.com, click on the message boards and then to Places to Go (All Other Gear, Diaper Bags, etc). There you'll find dozens of moms swapping tips on the best and most fashionable diaper bags. Here's a round up of our readers' favorite custom diaper bag makers (most sell direct off their sites, but a few also sell on other sites):

Amy Michelle	amymichellebags.com
Chester Handbags	chesterhandbags.com
Ella	ella-bags.com
Fleurville	fleurville.com
Haiku Diaper Bags	haikubags.com
Holly Aiken	hollyaiken.com
I'm Still Me	imstillme.com
Kate Spade	katespade.com.
Kecci	kecci.com
Oi Oi	oioi.com.au
One Cool Chick	onecoolchick.com
Reese Li	reeseli.com
Skip Hop	skiphop.com
Timbuk2	timbuk2.com
Tumi	tumi.com
Vera Bradley	verabradley.com

No doubt there are dozens more, but that's a great starting point. You can expect prices to be commensurate with style. Kate Spade can cost over $300 a diaper bag. But there are some great looking options for under a $100 too. One caveat: many of these manufacturers are small boutique companies. Often it may be the owner who's taking the order. . . and also sewing the bag! While we admire the entrepreneurship of these companies, many are so small that a minor event can put them off kilter. All it takes is one hurricane or a deluge of orders to turn a reputable company into a customer service nightmare. Check the feedback on these companies on our message boards before ordering.

Smart Shopper Tips

Smart Shopper Tip #1
Diaper Bag Science

"I was in a store the other day, and they had about one zillion different diaper bags. Some had cute prints and others were plain. Should I buy the cheapest one or invest a little more money?"

The best diaper bags are made of tear-resistant fabric and have all sorts of useful pockets, features and gizmos. Contrast that with low-quality brands that lack many pockets and are made of cheap, thin vinyl—after a couple of uses, they start to split and crack. Yes, high-quality diaper bags will cost more ($30 to $100 versus $15 to $25), but you'll be much happier in the long run. High-end diaper bags (like those made by Kate Spade and other designers) can reach the $300 mark or more. Of course, many of our readers have found deals on these bags, so check out our message boards for shopping tips.

Here's our best piece of advice: buy a diaper bag that doesn't *look* like a diaper bag. Sure those bags with dinosaurs and pastel animal prints look cute now, but what are you going to do with it when your baby gets older? A well-made diaper bag that doesn't look like a diaper bag will make a great piece of carry-on luggage later in life. The best bets: Lands' End's or Eddie Bauer's high-quality diaper bags (see reviews later).

Smart Shopper Tip #2
Make your own

"Who needs a fancy diaper bag? I just put all the necessary changing items into my favorite backpack."

That's a good point. Most folks have a favorite bag or backpack that can double as a diaper bag. Besides the obvious (wipes and diapers), put in a large zip-lock bag as a holder for dirty/wet items. Add a couple of receiving blankets (as changing pads) plus the key items listed below, and you have a complete diaper bag.

Another idea: check out the "Diaper Bag Essentials" from Mommy's Helper (call 800-371-3509 or 316-684-2229 for a dealer near you; web: mommyshelperinc.com). This $20 to $30 kit is basically everything for a diaper bag but the bag—you get an insulated bottle holder, changing pad, dirty duds bag, toiletry kit, etc. That way you can transform your favorite bag or backpack into a diaper bag. We found it on Target.com for $20.

Top 9 Items for a Well-Stocked Diaper Bag

After much scientific experimentation, we believe we have perfected the exact mix of ingredients for the best-equipped diaper bag. Here's our recipe:

1 **GET TWO DIAPER BAGS**—one that is a full-size, all-option big hummer for longer trips (or overnight stays) and the other that is a mini-bag for a short hop to dinner or the shopping mall. Here's what each should have:

The full-size bag: This needs a waterproof changing pad that folds up, waterproof pouch or pocket for wet clothes, a couple compartments for diapers, blankets/clothes, etc. Super-deluxe brands have bottle compartments with Thinsulate to keep bottles warm or cold. Another plus: outside pockets for books and small toys. A zippered outside pocket is good for change or your wallet. A cell phone pockets is also a plus.

The small bag: This has enough room for a couple diapers, travel wipe package, keys, wallet and/or cell phone. Some models have a bottle pocket and room for one change of clothes. If money is tight, just go for the small bag. To be honest, the full-size bag is often just a security blanket for first-time parents—they think they need to lug around every possible item in case of a diaper catastrophe. But, in the real world, you'll quickly discover schlepping that big full-size bag everywhere isn't practical. While a big bag is nice for overnight or long trips, we'll bet you will be using the small bag much more often.

2 **EXTRA DIAPERS.** Put a dozen in the big bag, two or three in the small one. Why so many? Babies can go through quite a few in a very short time. Of course, when baby gets older (say over a year), you can cut back on the number of diapers you need for a trip. Another wise tip: put whole packages of diapers and wipes in your car(s). We did this after we forgot our diaper bag one too many times and needed an emergency diaper. (The only bummer: here in Colorado, the wipes we keep in the car sometimes freeze in the winter! As they say, you don't know cold . . .)

3 **A TRAVEL-SIZE WIPE PACKAGE.** A good idea: a plastic Tupperware container that holds a small stack of wipes. You can also use a Ziplock bag to hold wipes. Some wipe makers sell travel packs that are allegedly "re-sealable"; we found that they aren't. And they are expensive.

4 **BLANKET AND CHANGE OF CLOTHES.** Despite the reams of scientists who work on diapers, they still aren't leak-proof—plan for it. A change of clothes is most useful for babies under six months of age, when leaks are more common. After that point, this becomes less necessary.

5 **A HAT OR CAP.** We like the safari-type hats that have flaps to cover your baby's ears (about $10 to $20). Warmer caps are helpful to chase away a chill, since the head is where babies lose the most heat.

6 **BABY TOILETRIES.** Babies can't take much direct exposure to sunlight—sunscreen is a good bet for all infants. Besides sunscreen, other optional accessories include bottles of lotion and diaper rash cream. The best bet: buy these in small travel or trial sizes. Don't forget insect repellent as well. This can be applied to infants

diaper bags

two months of age and older.

7 **DON'T FORGET THE TOYS.** We like compact rattles, board books, teethers, etc.

8 **SNACKS.** When baby starts to eat solid foods, having a few snacks in the diaper bag (a bottle of water or milk, crackers, a small box of cereal) is a smart move. But don't bring them in plastic bags. Instead bring reusable plastic containers. Plastic bags are a suffocation hazard and should be kept far away from babies and toddlers.

9 **YOUR OWN PERSONAL STUFF.** Be careful putting your wallet or checkbook into the diaper bag—we advise against it. We left our diaper bag behind one too many times before we learned this lesson. Put your name and phone number in the bag in case it is lost.

Our Picks: Brand Recommendations

We've looked the world over and have come up with two top choices for diaper bags: Lands End and Eddie Bauer (plus a couple of other smaller brands worthy of consideration). They both meet our criteria for a great diaper bag—each offers both full-size and smaller bags, they don't look like diaper bags, each uses high-quality materials and, best of all, they are affordably priced. Let's take a look at each:

Lands End (800) 356-4444 (web: landsend.com) sells not one but four diaper bags: The Do-It-All Diaper bag ($30), the Backpack Diaper Bag ($40), the Little Tripper ($20) and a diaper bag tote for $35.

The Do-It-All features a wide mouth (like a doctor's bag) that lets you see the large main compartment for diapers and wipes. There is also a parent pocket for your stuff, extra long changing pad and exterior bottle pockets. Then there's another zippered compartment for a blanket or change of clothes and an expandable outside pocket for books and small toys. In the past we praised the bag's long carry straps but one parent pointed out that the new design leaves only about 17" of strap meaning the bag rides right under her armpit. Another parent complained that the design of the bag makes it very heavy too.

Beside those drawbacks, the bag does seem to hold a lot of stuff. After all these years of recommending the Do-It-All, it's still a winner with most parents. Readers have hauled this thing on cross-country airline trips, on major treks to the mountains, and more. At $30, it's a good buy considering the extra features and durability. How about those quick trips to the store? We bought the Little Tripper ($20) for this purpose and have been quite happy. It has a changing pad and two exterior pockets. With just enough room for a few diapers, wipes and other personal items, it's perfect for short outings.

This might be a good place to plug the "Overstocks" page on Lands End's web site (landsend.com). This regularly updated section has some fantastic bargains (up to 50% off) on all sorts of Lands End items, including their kids clothing, bedding, diaper bags and more. You can also sign up for their newsletter, which updates you on the site.

Not to be outdone, **Eddie Bauer** (800) 426-8020 (web: eddiebauer.com) offers five diaper bags—a backpack ($50), case bag ($55), messenger bag ($50), a Diaper Tote ($50) and a Diaper Small Daypouch ($35). Each is made of fabric that's easy to clean and contains a removable changing pad (except the Daypouch), bottle pockets, and a detachable wet/dry pouch for damp items. The *Wall Street Journal* called Bauer's offerings "the most manly diaper bag available" and we have to agree—the look does not scream baby.

Just to confuse you, we should note that Eddie Bauer has a SEPARATE line of diaper bags that are in Babies R Us: these options range from $18 to $35. Parents we interviewed gave these bags a thumbs up, but not as high as the ones Eddie Bauer sells from its web site and catalog (they come from different suppliers apparently).

Baby Bjorn also makes a couple types of diaper bags including the Diaper Bag Dynamic ($100), which converts from a tote to a

E-MAIL FROM THE REAL WORLD
Diaper Bag Find

This reader found a great diaper bag from California Innovations (web: www.ca-innovations.com) for $25. FYI: These bags are sold from time to time in Costco warehouse clubs.

"I got a fantastic diaper bag by a company called California Innovations. They have several different types but they all seem to be made from black or navy blue microfibre with insulated bottle compartments, plastic lined interiors, and lots of special pockets. The one I purchased has a removable plastic liner (for easy cleaning), a portable padded changing station, plastic "dirty bag", one insulated bottle pocket that holds two bottles, one outside bottle pocket, a separate insulated section that attaches to the bottom of the bag, a side zipper pocket for a wallet/keys/other small stuff, and snap on cell phone and pacifier holders on the outside. The straps are set up so it can be carried with a small handle like a shopping bag, used as a single or double strap backpack. A great find for $20!"

backpack. Included in the Dynamic is a removable changing case that will allow parents to take along just a few diapers for a short trip. The Baby Bjorn Diaper Bag is their more traditional over the shoulder style. This bag is designed to stay upright so you can use it one-handed when changing baby. It sells for $80 on Target.com.

A dark horse contender in the diaper bag wars is *Combi*, the stroller maker mentioned earlier in this chapter. Their main offering is the Urban Sling, a well-designed bag with nice features (cell phone pocket, insulated bottle pocket, etc) and fashionable colors (Pink Diva, Keylime). Price: $40.

If you're looking for more fashion forward, less utilitarian designs, check out our list above in the CyberSpace section for custom diaper bag makers. What about the fancy pants designers? Spade tops the list of designers that get the highest marks from our readers. But some of the more obscure options are worth checking out to.

In the end we recommend Lands End, Eddie Bauer or Combi as your best bets for the money. They may be basic in the fashion department but they do the job for a good price.

Carriers

Advocates of baby wearing from Dr. Sears to your next-door neighbor tout the benefits of closeness with your child (attachment parenting). But we like carriers for the convenience too. When you have a baby who just won't be put down and you've got dinner to get on the table, a hands free carrier is a godsend. Just to make it more confusing, thought, there are 437 different carriers makes and models on the market, from simple slings to fancy backpacks. And we've noticed over the years that every single one of those models has a fan. Some more than others, but almost all carriers are recommended by someone. The key is to find the right carrier for you. We highly recommend you consider buying an instructional DVD on baby wearing called Tummy 2 Tummy (tummy2tummy.com). The DVD covers different types of carriers and how to wear them.

Parents in Cyberspace: What's on the Web

The Baby Wearer
Web Site: thebabywearer.com
What It Is: A resource for parents interested in "baby wearing"
What's Cool: This site is extensive. You'll find articles, reviews, product listings, ads, you name it. The main emphasis seems to be on sling-type carriers, not so much front carriers. There are a couple of

great charts that offer detailed comparisons for carriers. In fact, there is so much here, you could spend days on the site. If you're a newbie to baby wearing, be sure to start with the basic articles as well as the glossary of terms. Then you can join chats and message boards or click on product links.

Needs Work: There's a lot of advertising here. And the site is very jumbled. You're probably smart to take their recommendations with a grain of salt and verify reviews with other sites before you buy.

What Are You Buying?

Carriers come in several flavors: slings, hip carriers, front carriers and frame or backpack carriers. Let's take a look at each type:

◆ **Slings.** Slings allow you to hold your baby horizontally or upright. Made of soft fabric with an adjustable strap, slings drape your baby across your body (see picture). The most famous sling, made with input from Dr. Sears (the father of "baby wearing"), is made by NoJo, but many other manufacturers have jumped into the sling market. Whichever brand you choose, devoted sling user Darien Wilson from Austin, Texas has a great tip for new moms: "The trick for avoiding backache when using a sling is to have the bulk of the baby's weight at the parent's waist or above."

Some parents complain that there isn't much between your baby's head and a collision with a wall, furniture, etc. It's true you have to watch where you're going and what you're doing, but sling aficionado's say once you get the hand of it, slings are simple to use.

Weight Limit: 20 pounds. *(Note: weight limits may vary by manufacturer. This is only an approximate weight limit. Please check the directions for each item you purchase.)*

Recommendations: While NoJo was the first, we don't really think they're the best slings out there. Readers complain that they hang too low and hurt their backs. Instead, our readers recommend the **Maya Wrap Sling** ($44-$75; mayawrap.com; pictured) citing its flexibility and comfort. Others praise the **Over the Shoulder Baby Holder** ($45-60; web: otsbh.net).

If you're looking for unusual fabrics so you can be a "stylish" baby wearer, go no further than the **ZoLo** sling (zolowear.com). The silk version (it's machine washable) will set you back a hefty $125 but wow, is it beautiful! And they'll send you fabric swatches if you have trouble deciding from one of their 20 fabrics (other fabrics start at

$70). Another parent recommended the ***Moms in Mind*** sarong carrier. (momsinmind.com, $42 to $50 with video) saying it had a simpler buckle and enough support to allow for hands free nursing. ***Mamma's Milk*** (mammasmilk.com) offers a streamlined sling with "invisibly adjustable pouches." These slings use Aplix (a stronger version of Velcro), to allow for adjustments without using zippers or snaps. Prices range from $45 to $85 depending on fabric.

New Native Baby carriers are yet another option in the sling department (newnativebaby.com, $44 to $138). They tout their streamline design, which allows you to stuff it into a diaper bag for on-the-go convenience, and their organic fabric.

Kangaroo Korner (kangarookorner.com) makes adjustable "pouches" in fleece, cotton, mesh and solarveil. They're the first we've seen to use a UV barrier fabric. And their unpadded pouches can be used in water as well. Cost: $60. Finally, we liked the ***Sling Baby*** from Walking Rock Farm (walkingrockfarm.com). The well-padded strap plus soft knit fabrics make this a great option for $64 to $67.

Where to buy: Most sites sell their slings directly, but ***Kangaroo Korner*** (kangarookorner.com) is a web site recommended by readers for their wide selection. They carry several brands and will even custom design a sling for you. Best of all, they offer tips and advice for using a sling.

◆ ***Hip Carriers.*** Hip carriers are a minimalist version of the sling. With less fabric to cradle baby, they generally work better for older babies (over six months). Baby is in a more upright position all the time, rather than lying horizontally. And like a sling, the hip carrier fits across your body with baby resting on your hip.

Weight/Age Limit: Manufacturers claim hip carriers can be used up to three years of age. *(Note: weight/age limits may vary by manufacturer. This is only an approximate limit. Please check the directions for each item you purchase.)*

Recommendations: A reader with back problems recommended the ***Hip Hammock*** ($48; web: hiphammock.com)—she said this was the most comfortable carrier for her. And the Hip Hammock (made by Playtex) can be used up to age three. FYI: As we went to press, the Hip Hammock was being recalled for a defective strap, which the company is  fixing. If you use a hand-me-down, make sure it was made after this was corrected.

Cuddle Karrier (cuddlekarrier.com), another hip carrier, claims to do everything but make toast. It converts from a carrier to a shopping cart restraint, high chair restraint, even a car seat carrier. Cost: $75

Walking Rock Farm makes a hip carrier appropriately named the

Hip Baby ($72 to $84). This carrier has a full seat and extra thick shoulder pad. We liked the numerous adjustments—this is one of the few hip carriers you can use hands-free. FYI: Walking Rock Farm also makes a baby sling (Sling Baby, $67).

◆ *Front (Soft) Carriers.* The most famous of all front carriers is the *Baby Bjorn*, that Scandinavian wonder worn by celeb moms among others. Front carriers like the Bjorn are basically a fabric bag worn on your chest. Your baby sort of dangles there either looking in at you (when they're very young) or out at the world (when they gain more head control).

Who Makes Them: Baby Bjorn (babybjorn.com), Ergo (ErgoBabyCarrier.com) Maclaren (maclarenusa.com), Baby Trekker (babytrekker.com), MaxiMom (4coolkids.com), Kelty Kangaroo (kelty.com), Water Tot (watertot.com), Evenflo Snugli (Evenflo.com), Infantino (infantino.com).

Weight Limit: 25 to 30 pounds. *(Note: weight limits may vary by manufacturer. This is only an approximate weight limit. Please check the directions for each item you purchase.)*

Recommendations: The Baby Bjorn was our top carrier pick in the last several editions of our book, but we have crowned a new winner this time out: the Ergo Baby Carrier.

Made by a small Hawaii company, the *Ergo* ($92; pictured; ErgoBabyCarrier.com; 888-416-4888) has won kudos on our boards for its ease of use (you can wear it in front or back) and less strain on the back. While most front carriers put the strain on your shoulders and back, the Ergo comes with a padded hip belt that takes the strain off your

upper back. Best of all, you can use from it birth (with a newborn insert, $25) up to an amazing 40 pounds (toddlers)—most front carriers can only be used for a short time (the Bjorn limit is 22 pounds).

Given the reader raves on the Ergo, we will give it our top recommendation. One caveat: your baby can't face outward in an Ergo—only towards you. If that bothers you (we don't see it as a major issue), consider one of the other carriers below. Also: the Ergo is just sold in specialty stores and online (BabyCenter.com and MyFavoriteBabyCarrier.com carry it). So it may be hard to see in person.

A similar carrier to the Ergo (in terms of positive feedback) is Eco Baby's *Beco Baby Carrier* ($110-140, becobabycarrier.com), designed by a mom who is also a rock climber. Yep, it is pricey—but seems to fit shorter parents a bit better than the Ergo.

The 800-pound gorilla in the carrier category is the *Baby Bjorn*, the Swedish import that comes in three flavors (Original $80, Air $100 and Active $120). The Original is easy to use and adjust (baby can ride facing forward or rear). Best of all, you can snap off the front of the Bjorn to put a sleeping baby down. The Active adds lumbar support for longer walks and the Air version features a mesh fabric to keep baby cooler in warmer climates.

Fans of the Bjorn like the easy adjustments and fashionable fabrics. But detractors point to the high price and limited use (babies outgrow it fast). Back/neck strain is a common complaint of Bjorn users (the Bjorn Active generates fewer complaints on this, thanks to the lumbar support). So while the Bjorn is ok for occasional use, this probably isn't the best choice if you plan to use it daily.

So, what else is out there?

Better known for its strollers, **Maclaren** also has a line of baby carriers (an outgrowth of its acquisition of Theodore Bean in 2004). These front carriers ($80 to $90) work from eight to 12 pounds with a "pod insert" and up to 25 pounds otherwise. We liked the one-hand, quick-release buckles and enclosed harness system.

Canadian parents write to us with kudos for the **Baby Trekker** (800-665-3957; web: babytrekker.com). This 100% washable cotton carrier has straps that wrap around the waist for support. Canucks like the fact a baby can be dressed in a snowsuit and still fit in the Baby Trekker. The carrier ($110) is available in baby stores in Canada or via the company's web site for folks in the U.S.

We've had several readers write to extol the virtues of the **MaxiMom** carrier (4coolkids.com). "It does everything short of making dinner. It can be used as a front carrier facing forward or backward, backpack facing forward or backward, emergency high chair, sling and can be used for a child up to 35 pounds. Here's the great part: MaxiMom is designed to also be used with multiples!" The cost: $55 to $125 depending on how many children you'll be using it for.

Asian-inspired carriers (called Mei Tai's) that tie instead of snap or buckle have increased in popularity in recent years. Fans love the ability to adjust and configure these carriers—plus they are very comfortable. Among the top Mei Tai-like carriers is the **Kozy Carrier** ($80-85, KozyCarrier.com), which can be can be worn on the front, rear or side. The reader feedback on the Kozy Carrier has been quite positive.

Finally, what about a carrier so you can get into a swimming pool with your older kids and not worry about baby? **WaterTot** makes a "water friendly baby carrier" which allows babies to face forward and play in the water (watertot.com, $40). Made of neoprene, the carrier can also be used on the hip.

What about those low-end carriers like **Snugli, Infantino, Eddie Bauer**? We don't recommend them. Let's be honest here: yes, you can spend $20 on a carrier at a discount store. And that is much less than an Ergo or the other aforementioned carriers. But take a second to read parent reviews of carriers, whether on our site or other baby message boards. Most parents quickly realize a bargain carrier can be a pain to use . . . literally. Cheap-o carriers are more complicated to put on and adjust as well as just being darn painful on the back.

Of all the cheaper carriers, Infantino's models are probably the most well-known. And we will give Infantino kudos for trying to innovate here: their *SmartRider Baby Carrier with Intelligel* ($50) has straps with gel cushions. Yet if you're going to spend $50 on an Infantino, you might as well pony up another $20 to $40 and get something that is even better designed. Your back will thank you later.

Bottom line: our top pick for a front (soft) carrier would be the Ergo or Beco. If an Asian-inspired (also called Mei-Tai) carrier intrigues you, the Kozy Carrier would be a great choice.

Where to buy: Chain stores only seem to carry the major brands like Bjorn or Snugli; the internet is your best bet for the more obscure brands. A bargain hint: many carriers are sold second-hand at low prices on boards like TheBabyWearer.com. And be sure to visit our boards (BabyBargains.com) to read the latest on our board dedicated to carriers.

◆ *Frame (or backpack) Carriers.* Need to get some fresh air? Just because you have a baby doesn't mean you can never go hiking again. Backpack manufacturers have responded to parents' wish to find a way to take their small children with them on hikes and long walks. The good news is that most of these frame carriers are made with lightweight aluminum, high quality fabrics and well-positioned straps. Accessories abound with some models including sunshades, diaper packs that Velcro on, and adjustable seating so Junior gets a good view.

Weight Limit: 45 to 50 pounds. *(Note: weight limits may vary by manufacturer. This is only an approximate weight limit. Please check the directions for each item you purchase.)*

Recommendations: Kelty (web: kelty.com) and *Sherpani Alpina* (sherpanipacks.com) have come to the rescue of parents with full lines of high-quality backpack carriers.

If you want a frame carrier, Kelty offers six models, including the Adventure ($240) that has all the bells and whistles. Kelty still offers its combo backpack stroller, the Convertible (basically a Tour pack with wheels) for $175 that weighs just nine lbs.

Sherpani offers frame carriers built specifically to accommodate women's bodies. The Rumba (pictured on the next page) is their flagship full feature carrier. This carrier ($230) has an aluminum frame and suspension system to take the strain off your back. It's

carriers

also the only backpack carrier that can be adjusted while on your back. It has a five-point safety
harness and padded chest plate among other
features. New this year is a "super light" version of
the Rumba for $166 (4.5 lbs.).

What most impressed us with Kelty and
Sherpani is their quality—these are real backpack
makers who don't skimp on details. Backpack carriers made by juvenile product companies are wimpy by comparison.

If those prices are a bit hard to swallow, check out the **Tough
Traveler Kid Carrier** ($176, toughtraveler.com). Adjustable for just
the right fit, the Tough Traveler features cushioned pads, tough
nylon cloth, and two-shoulder harnesses for baby. A comfortable
seat provides head and neck protection for smaller children—you
even get a zippered pouch for storage. Tough Traveler has several
other models that combine great quality and decent pricing. Check
out their web site recommendations regarding the best pack for
your height.

So, what's the best backpack among Kelty, Sherpani or Tough
Traveler? That's a tough one—each has great features. Readers give
the slight edge to the Tough Traveler for its quick and easy adjustments, lightweight and great storage. Sherpani, however, is technically amazing, made to fit a woman's body structure better.

Where to buy: A good source for outdoor baby gear is the
Campmor catalog (800) 226-7667 campmor.com). Also try outdoor retailers like REI. There are discounts on Tough Traveler's web
site if you don't mind last year's models or factory seconds.

So, how do you decide which carrier is best for you and your
baby? The best advice is to borrow different models from your
friends and give them a test drive. For most parents, a front carrier
is all one really needs, although some parents like slings.

The Bottom Line:
A Wrap-Up of Our Best Buy Picks

Whew! And you thought car seats were complex! Now that
we've covered strollers, diaper bags, and carriers, let's take a look
at an even bigger expense: child care.

CHAPTER 10 CHILDCARE

Childcare: Options, Costs and More

Inside this chapter

E ven stay-at-home parents agree there are days when you need a break. So whether you're a full time executive or a full time diaper changer, childcare will be an issue after your baby arrives. And your choices run from Mom's Day Out services at the local church to full time in-home care and everything in between. In this chapter we'll explain a few of the different options, scare you with the costs of day care and advise you where to look to find the best quality childcare in the best setting for your child.

Childcare

"It's expensive, hard to find and your need for it is constantly changing. Welcome to the world of child care," said a recent Wall Street Journal article—and we agree. There's nothing more difficult than trying to find the best childcare for your baby.

With 59% of moms with children under age one back in the workforce today, wrestling with the choices, costs and availability of childcare is a stark reality. Here's a brief overview of the different types of childcare available, questions to ask when hiring a provider and money saving tips.

What are you buying?

On average, parents pay 8% of their pre-tax income for childcare. And if you live in a high-cost city, expect to shell out even more. As you'll read below, some parents spend $20,000 or more per year.

Whatever your budget, there are three basic types of child care:

◆ **Family Daycare.** In this setting, one adult takes care of a small number of children in her home. Sometimes the children are of mixed ages. Parents who like this option prefer the lower ratio of children to providers and the consistent caregiver. About 27% of families place their children in family daycare. Of course, you'll want to make sure the facility is licensed and ask all the questions we outline later. One drawback to family daycare: if there is only one caregiver, you might have to scramble if that person becomes ill. How much does it cost? Family daycare typically runs $6000 to $15,000 per year—with bigger cities running closer to the top figure.

◆ **Center Care.** Most folks are familiar with this type of daycare—commercial facilities that offer a wide variety of childcare options. And they are by far the most common—66% of parents take their children to child care centers. Convenience is one major factor for center care; you can often find a center that is near your (or your spouse's) place of work. Other parents like the fact that their children are grouped with and exposed to more kids their own age. Centers usually give you a written report each day that details your baby's day (naps, diaper changes, mood). On the downside, turnover can be a problem—some centers lose 40% or more of their employees each year. A lack of consistency can upset your child. Yet center care offers parents the most flexibility: unlike nannies or family care, the day care center doesn't take sick or vacation days. Many centers offer drop-off care, in case you need help in a pinch. The cost: $3000 to $15,000 per year, yet some pricey centers can cost over $30,000 in the biggest cities. As with family daycare, the cost varies depending on how many days a week your baby needs care.

Sources For The Best Child Care Facilities. Which childcare centers have the highest standards? The National Association of Family Childcare (800) 359-3817 (web: www.nafcc.org) offers lists of such facilities to parents in every state.

◆ **Nanny Care.** No, you don't have to be super-rich to afford a nanny. Many "nanny-referral" services have popped up in most major cities, offering to refer you to a pre-screened nanny for $500 to $800 or so. Parents who prefer nannies like the one-to-one attention, plus baby is taken care of in your own home. The cost varies depending on whether you provide the nanny with room and board. Generally, most nannies who don't live-in run $10 to $19 per hour. Hence, the yearly cost would be $10,000 to $25,000. And the nanny's salary is just the beginning—you also must pay social security and Medicare taxes, federal unemployment insur-

ance, plus any state-mandated taxes like disability insurance or employment-training taxes. All this may increase the cost of your $20,000 nanny by another $4500 or more per year. And the paperwork hassle for all the tax reporting can be onerous. The other downside to nannies? You're dependent on one person for childcare. If she gets sick, needs time off or quits, you're on your own. Perhaps for these reasons, nanny care is the least popular option with only 7% of families utilizing this option.

Money Saving Tips

1 ASK YOUR EMPLOYER ABOUT DEPENDENT CARE ACCOUNTS. Many corporations offer this great benefit to employees. Basically, you can set aside pretax dollars to pay for child-care. The maximum set aside is $5000 (total per couple; single parents can put away $2500). Both parents can contribute to that amount. If you're in the 31% tax bracket, that means you'll save $1550 in taxes by paying for childcare with a dependent care account. Consult with your employer for the latest rules and limits to this option.

2 SHARE A NANNY. As we noted in the above example, a nanny can be expensive. But many parents find they can halve that cost by sharing a nanny with another family. While this might require some juggling of schedules to make everyone happy, it can work out beautifully.

3 GO FOR A CULTURAL EXCHANGE. The U.S. government authorizes a foreign nanny exchange program, referred to as "au pair." Through this program, you can hire a foreign-born young adult for up to 45 hours a week of childcare. Your kids get exposure to another language and culture, your au pair gets to hang out in the US to learn about our culture and language. What's the catch? See our box on Au Pairs for more information and costs.

4 TAKE A TAX CREDIT. The current tax code gives parents a tax credit for childcare expenses. The amount, which varies based on your income, equals about 20% to 30% of childcare costs up to a certain limit. The credit equals about $500 to $1500, depending on your income. Another tax break: some states also give credits or deductions for child care expenses. Consult your tax preparer to make sure you're taking the maximum allowable credit/deduction. New in recent years, the federal government expanded the adoption credit up to $10,630 for "qualified" expenses related to adoption.

childcare

Questions to Ask

Here are questions to ask a daycare provider:

◆ *What are the credentials of the provider(s)?* Obviously, a college degree in education and/or child development is preferred. Additional post-college training is also a plus.

◆ *What is the turnover?* High turnover is a concern since consistency of care is one of the keys to successful childcare. Any turnover approaching 40% is cause for concern.

◆ *What is the ratio of children to care providers?* The recommended national standard is one adult to three babies (age birth to 12 months). After that, the ratios vary depending on a child's age and state regulations. With some day care centers, there is one primary teacher and a couple of assistants (depending on the age of the children and size of class). Compare the ratio to that of other centers to gain an understanding of what's high and low.

◆ *Do you have a license?* All states (and many municipalities) require childcare providers to be licensed. Yet, that's no guarantee of quality—the standards vary so much from locale to locale that a license may be meaningless. Another point to remember: the standards for family daycare may be lower than those for center care. Educate yourself on the various rules and regulations by spending a few minutes on the phone with your state's child care regulatory body. Check with the state to make sure there are no complaints or violations on record for the provider. Many states are putting this info on the web.

◆ *May I visit you during business hours?* The only way you can truly evaluate a childcare provider is an on-site visit. Try to time your visit during the late morning, typically the time when the most children are being cared for. Trust your instincts—if the facility seems chaotic, disorganized or poorly run, take the hint. One sign of a good childcare center: facilities that allow unannounced drop-in visits.

◆ *Discuss your care philosophy.* Sit down for a half-hour interview with the care provider and make sure they clearly define their attitudes on breast-feeding, diapers, naps, feeding schedules, discipline and any other issues of importance to you. The center should have established, written procedures to deal with children who have certain allergies or other medical conditions. Let's be honest: child-rearing philosophies will vary from center to center. Make sure you see eye to eye on key issues.

◆ *Do you have liability insurance?* Don't just take their word on it—have them provide written documentation or the phone number of an insurance provider for you to call to confirm coverage.

◆ *Does the center conduct police background checks on employees?* It's naive to assume that just because employees have good references, they've never been in trouble with the law.

Au Pair Child Care

Au pairs have become more popular recently for one big reason: the federal government (which regulates au pair programs) changed its rules to allow au pairs, or nannies from other countries, to stay in the U.S. as long as two years. That's up from only one year in the past. So if you find just the right nanny, you won't have to send him or her home in just 12 months and look for another childcare provider.

But how does the au pair idea work? First, only six organizations are allowed by the U.S. government to place au pairs with American families. These agencies must provide the au pair 24 hours of child safety classes and training. Au pairs are also required to have at least 200 hours of infant care experience if they are caring for children under two, be able to speak English proficiently, have a secondary school education (plus six hours of pos-secondary education) and pass both reference and background checks. Whew! That's a lot of work you won't have to do as a parent. The age range of au pairs is 18 to 26 years.

If you're interested in hiring an au pair, you contact one of six agencies (see below for a list). There is typically an application fee (about $350) and a program fee. The program fee is about $7000 and includes all the screening and prep of the au pair, as well as airfare, medical and travel insurance, training materials and support from the agency itself for the period of employment. Families must pay an au pair a $140 per week stipend and an educational allowance of $500. All these fees work out to about $15,000 per year, comparable to the high end of the family care childcare option (discussed earlier), but less than the cost of a nanny.

So how do you decide if an au pair is for your family? *The Wall Street Journal*, in a 2005 article on au pairs, noted that you should "choose an au pair only if you: can limit her work week to 45 hours a week, 10 hours a day, have a private bedroom available, value cross cultural experiences, can care for the emotions of a teen or young adult, can help and train an inexperienced caregiver, will treat her like a member of the family, (and) don't mind changing caregivers after two years."

Here's a partial list of au pair agencies:

AuPairCare	aupaircare.com
Au Pair in America	aupairinamerica.com
Cultural Care Au Pair (EF au Pair)	culturalcare.com
EurAuPair	euraupair.com
InterExchange	interexchange.org
GoAuPair	goaupair.com

childcare

◆ **Is the center clean, home-like and cheerful?** While it's impossible to expect a childcare facility to be spotless, it is important to check for basic cleanliness. Diaper changing stations shouldn't be overflowing with dirty diapers, play areas shouldn't be strewn with a zillion toys, etc. Another tip: check their diaper changing procedures. The best centers should use rubber gloves when changing diapers and wipe down the diapering area with a disinfectant after each change. Finally, ask how often toys are cleaned. Is there a regular schedule for washing children's hands?

◆ **What type of adjustment period does the center offer?** Phasing in daycare isn't easy—your child may need time to adjust to the new situation. Experienced providers should have plans to ease the transition.

Bottom Line

Wow! We're almost done. You've learned about how to save on everything for baby—now let's sum up the savings in our next chapter!

Does your nanny have a past?

Yes, it sounds like the plot of a bad Hollywood thriller—the nanny WITH A PAST! Still, many parents want to feel secure that the person they trust to take care of their child hasn't had any run-ins with the police. In the past, this required laborious background checks with local police or numerous calls to past employers. Today, the web can help. Several web sites now let you screen a nanny's background with a simple point and click. Examples: MyBackgroundCheck.com offers a range of searches for $25 to $70. ChoiceTrust.com has a proprietary criminal records database and court records search for $25 to $100. Wonder if the background checking service you found online is legit? Ask the International Nanny Association (www.nanny.org), a non-profit group, which keeps tabs on such agencies.

Of course, you can hire someone else to do the checking—most high-quality nanny employment agencies do those background checks, but of course you pay . . . about 10% of the nanny's first year salary as a fee. One note: while criminal background checks are relatively easy, drivers' records are another story. You may need to contact your state motor vehicle's bureau and have the nanny ask for a copy of her own report.

One smart tip: when asking for references from a nanny, get a LANDLINE phone number to call. Why? Some dishonest nannies have faked their references by having friends pose as past employers. That's easier to do with a cell phone versus a landline.

CHAPTER 11

What Does it All Mean?

How much money can you save if you follow all the tips and suggestions in this book? Let's take a look at the average cost of having a baby from the introduction and compare it with our Baby Bargains budget.

Your Baby's First Year

ITEM	AVERAGE	BABY BARGAINS BUDGET
Crib, mattress, dresser, rocker	$1600	$1300
Bedding / Decor	$315	$154
Baby Clothes	$525	$335
Disposable Diapers	$630	$300
Maternity/Nursing Clothes	$1260	$540
Nursery items, high chair, toys	$425	$225
Baby Food/Formula	$950	$350
Stroller, Car Seats, Carrier	$425	$334
Miscellaneous	$525	$500
TOTAL	**$6655**	**$4038**
TOTAL SAVINGS:		***$2617***

WOW! YOU CAN SAVE OVER $2600! We hope the savings makes it worth the price of this book. We'd love to hear from you on how much you saved with our book—feel free to email, write or call us. See the "How to Reach Us" page at the back of this book.

What does it all mean?

At this point, we usually have something pithy to say as we end the book. But, as parents of two boys, we're just too tired. We're going to bed, so feel free to make up your own ending.

And thanks for reading *Baby Bargains*.

APPENDIX A
Canada

$21,400.

Yes, that's the average cost of raising a child to age two in Canada (see chart on the next page). With those costs, Canadian parents need bargains just as much as parents in the U.S.!

Here's an overview of our best bargains sources for Canada.

Recap of Canadian sources

Many of the brands reviewed earlier are based in Canada. For example, crib makers AP, Cara Mia, Morigeau and others are reviewed in Chapter 2. Glider-rockers brands Shermag and Dutailier also are Canadian brands, of course.

In this section, we will focus on Canada's best bargains, baby stores and outlets. But be sure to read earlier sections of this book to find general reviews of Canadian baby product brands.

Layette Items and Diapers

If you're looking for great shoes for your little one, reader Teri Dunsworth recommends Canadian-made **Robeez** (800) 929-2623 or (604) 929-6818; web: www.robeez.com. "They are the most AWESOME shoes—I highly recommend them," she said in an email. Robeez are made of leather, have soft skid-resistant soles and are machine washable. They start at $26 for a basic pair. "My baby wears nothing else! They have infant and toddler sizes and oh-so-cute patterns." Another reader recommended New Zealand made **Bobux** shoes ($26, bobuxusa.com). These cute leather soft soles "do the trick" by staying on extremely well according to our reader.

A Canadian clothing manufacturer to look for in stores near you is **Baby's Own** by St. Lawrence Textiles (613) 632-8565.

The Mercedes of the cloth diaper category is Canada-made **Mother-Ease** (www.mother-ease.com), a brand that has a fanatical following among cloth diaper devotees. Suffice it to say, they ain't cheap but the quality is excellent. Mother-Ease sells both fitted diapers and covers; the diapers run $9 to $10 a pop, while the covers are about $9.75. Before you invest up to $400 in one of Mother-Ease's special package deals, consider trying their "introductory offer" for a good deal.

Other parents like **Kushies** (800) 841-5330 (web: www.kushies. com), another Canadian product. This brand offers several models.

One note: both Kushies and Mother-Ease are sold via mail-order only. Yes, you can sometimes find these diapers at second-hand or thrift stores, but most parents buy them via a catalog or on the 'net. Kushies are trying to branch out into retail stores—check your local baby specialty shop.

My Lil' Miracle (mylilmiracle.com; 877-218-0112 is another Canadian catalog that sells "Indisposables" all-in-one cloth diapers and diaper covers. You can buy from the catalog or from their direct representative. The catalog also has nursing bras, blankets, bibs and more.

Maternity

Toronto-based **Breast is Best** catalog sells a wide variety of nursing tops, blouses and dresses as well as maternity wear. For a free catalog and fabric swatches, call (877) 837-5439 toll free or check out their web site at www.breastisbest.com.

Carriers

Mountain Equipment Co-operative (MEC; web: www.mec.ca) is a unique, not-for-profit member owned co-op that sells baby carriers (among other outdoor products). A reader in Ottawa emailed us a rave for their "excellent" backpack carriers that are "renown for their excellent quality." At C$109, the MEC Happy Trails backpack carrier "clearly beats Kelty Kids and other U.S.-made carriers" at a

---

CANADA COSTS

What does it cost to raise a child in Canada? These figures are from Manitoba, but are a good general guide for most Canadian parents. Costs of raising a child to age two (total cost for two years):

FOOD	$2,399
CLOTHING	2,200
HEATH CARE	292
PERSONAL CARE	116
RECREATION	592
CHILD CARE	11,180
SHELTER	4,621
TOTAL	**$21,400**

Source: "Cost of Raising a Child," Manitoba government report (2004). Adjusted to 2007 dollars, in Canadian currency.

canada

much lower price. MEC has stores in major cities in Canada; call 888-847-0770 for details.

Canadian parents also write to us with kudos for the **Baby Trekker** (800) 665-3957; web: www.babytrekker.com. This 100% washable cotton carrier has straps around the waist for support. Parents like the fact a baby can be dressed in a snowsuit and still fit in the Baby Trekker. The carrier ($100 US, $125 Canada) is available in baby stores in Canada.

Readers also praise the **Tatonka Baby Carrier** ($145 US) from another Canadian manufacturer, Sherpa Mountain (www.sherpa-mtn.com).

Web Resources

Canadian Parents Online (www.canadianparents.com) is a great resource, with advice columns, chat/discussion areas and recall info for Canadian parents. We liked their "Ask an Expert" areas, which included advice on childbirth, lactation and even fitness.

The **Childcare Resources and Research Unit** (childcarecanada.org) has great info and statistics on childcare costs in Canada.

Sears may not have a catalog any more in the U.S., but the Canadian version of **Sears** (www.sears.ca) has both a web site and printed catalog with baby products and clothes. A reader said the catalog has a nice selection of products and is a great resource for Canadian parents who might live outside the major metro areas.

Baby gear shopping in Canada

Toronto mom Rhonda Lewis scouted the best baby stores and bargain sources in Canada for us (and did a great job, we must say). Here's her report:

Toronto

Macklem's *416-531-7188, www.macklems.com.* Family run business in Downtown area. Well known for stroller/pram repairs. Friendly and knowledgeable staff. Good selection of strollers, including Zooper Zydeco, Jazz, Boogie ($550), Swing ($249), Waltz ($239), Tango, Rhumba, Maclaren (Triumph $260, Techno $425, Global $475 and other models), Peg (high chairs, double strollers, umbrellas, travel systems), Bertini. They also carry products by Baby Bjorn, Britax and Dutailier to name a few. Good selection of bedding (four, five, and six piece sets from $99) and cribs including: AP, EG, Morigeau Lepine. Parking is available on the street nearby.

Dearborn Baby Express *72 Doncaster Avenue, Thornhill 905-881-3334.* Small store, crammed with merchandise. Wide selection of strollers, car seats, gliders and furniture. Infant car seats range from $159 to $239 and toddler car seats (rear and front facing) range from $189 to $350. Brands include Peg, Graco, Kidco, Evenflo, Inglesina. For furniture, brands include Pali, Morigeau Lepine, Generations and Cara Mia. If you're looking for double strollers they do have a few Peg & Baby Trend. However, it is very hard to maneuver strollers around store as it is so full. Bargains are limited, usually on end of year models. Lots of toys, layette accessories. The parking lot does get very busy, but you can usually find a spot.

Nestings' Kids *418 Eglinton Avenue W, Toronto, 416-322-0511. 2835 W. Fourth Avenue, Vancouver, 604-734-5437. www.nestingskids.com.* If you want exceptional furnishings, bedding, furniture, look no further than Nestings. They carry Morigeau-Lepine, EP and AG cribs. Their windows are always gorgeous and they carry great, unique items, but at a steep price. Cribs range from $848 to $2695. Lamps can be purchased for up to $395. They have very cute, whimsical lampshade nightlights which are $40 and custom bedding is priced around $1000. Parking is available on the street, or at a lot just to the west of the building.

Baby's Room Warehouse *Hwy 400 & 89, in Cookstown Outlet Mall (705) 458- 8050* Specializing in baby bedding, accessories, cribs and furnishings at wholesale prices. Cribs range from $189 to $649. Brands include Little Angel, EG and Cara Mia. They also offer discount packages consisting of a crib, mattress and bedding. There are many kinds of fabric to choose from for bedding ($99-$289), or if you cannot find something you like, simply bring your fabric of choice to them, and they'll create the bedding, typically 5-6 piece sets. Mattresses are $50, $60 or $100. Store is open Monday-Friday 10-9, Saturday and Sunday from 9-6.

Wal-mart. Great place to stock up on accessories and toys Difficult to see car seats and strollers as they are tied down and above eye level for safety reasons. Good place to go if you've done your research elsewhere and are shopping for the lowest prices. Example: Diaper Genie ($35.95 at Wal-mart compared to $49.95 elsewhere, $42.95 at Toys R Us).

Costco often has excellent products at great prices. They have carried highchairs, jogging strollers, gliders and other products. The only problem is that you never know what they will have and once it is out of stock, they typically do not reorder. Check often and ask anyone you know who is going there to check too. Items tend to sell quickly as their prices are superb.

Some **Toys R Us** locations also have **Babies R Us** stores where you can register. Prices relatively competitive, watch for flyers for sales. You receive a free gift package just for registering which is great.

Sears has a wonderful registry program called "Waiting Game" where you can guess the date that your baby will be born. You can change that date twice before you are seven months pregnant. If you guess the correct date, you get gift certificates in the amount of money you and your friends spent on your registry. It is free to join and you also receive a gift package just for taking the time to register.

Toronto Outlets

Baby City Outlet Store

734 Kipling Avenue, Etobicoke (416) 503-0313; 90 Northline Rd, North York (416) 752-0222; 7 Stafford Dr., Brampton (905) 450-1955; Keel and Wilson, Toronto. (416) 638-8777.

Save up to 45% on baby supplies from cribs, car seats, strollers and playpens to smaller items such as bottles, creams and soothers. A Luna crib is $179. Brands for strollers and car seats include Evenflo, Graco and Eddie Bauer. There are great deals on bulk packages of diapers (generic brand) and baby wipes. Parents of twins can save an extra 10% on purchases. Call store for hours.

Roots Outlet Store

120 Orfus Rd., (416) 781-8729

Great savings on Roots fashions for babies and the whole family including pajamas, sweats, jeans, hats, jackets. Discounts vary, but items have been seen at 80% off. Call for store hours. Parking is available at the back of the store.

Snugabye Factory Outlet

188 Bentworth Ave. (416) 783-0300; snugabye.com

Save up to 50% on Canadian-made, brand-name baby clothing and sleepwear ranging in sizes from newborn to 6X. They have great prices on items like crib sheets ($5.99 to $9.99). Bedding choices change seasonally and they do sell the occasional mobile. Hours are 10-5, Monday to Saturday.

And more: Mattel Outlet *Mississauga Outlet 905-501-5147. www.matteltoyoutlet.ca* offers a range of discontinued, closeout and excess product stock for toys at value prices, 50% savings on many toy items. Check the web site for monthly specials on toys and baby baskets. In fact, the Cookstown Outlet Mall has many other stores, offering a wide selection of accessories, clothing, footwear, gifts for the whole family. It's worth it to drive up and spend a few hours, you can save hundreds off regular retail prices!

Toronto Maternity Clothing

There are many maternity shops in Toronto which are excellent.

Rhonda Maternity (416) 921-3116 www.rhondamaternity.com. offers a wide range of career wear. Prices are high ($100+ for pants), but quality and service are excellent and they have a wide selection of merchandise including bathing suits in season and evening dresses. Another store that recently opened, **Kick,** 454 Eglinton Avenue West (416) 488-0255 has the latest trends in maternity wear. Or, try **Modern Maternity** www.modernmaternity.com. for casual clothes (Bathing suits $75, long black skirt $105 and tank dresses for fancier outings at $189 plus wrap $49). The brand has a warehouse outlet at 12B Ossington Ave. in Toronto.

Secrets from your Sister 476 Bloor St. W. Telephone: 416-538-1234; secretsfromyoursister.com. Beautiful lingerie in realistic sizes for all women. Bra fitting experts can fit you in maternity, nursing, sports or everyday bras.

Old Navy has four stores in Canada that sell maternity wear, a few of which are in the Greater Toronto Area (Promenade Mall and Mississauga Square One Mall). They have a great return policy so if you stock up at the beginning of your pregnancy and don't end up needing some items, you can return them at any time with your receipt. Watch for great sales as their merchandise often goes on sale.

If you happen to be near Thunder Bay, there is a store called **Bambino Paradise Outlet** where they sell breast pumps, maternity clothes, strollers and bedding (800) 524-6973. bambinoparadise.ca

Thyme Maternity (maternity.ca) is the largest maternity chain in Canada and they have locations in every province. Their fabric choices are at times clingy, but their merchandise turnover is high and they receive new shipments often. The location at Yorkdale Mall probably has the best selection. The prices are a bit high, but often you can find merchandise on sale at the end of season and during promotions. Sweater prices are $30 to $50, pants were on sale at $25 to $60. They also sell bras, underwear, swimwear, pajamas and formal wear.

Bravado Designs *www.bravadodesigns.com,* a Toronto-based company, has an excellent selection of funky, great quality bras ($37) for both pregnancy and breast-feeding, and underwear ($15). This company encourages women to maintain their style during pregnancy with funky, unique prints.

Toronto Resources & More

Help! We've Got Kids *www.helpwevegotkids.com* is a unique Children's Reference Directory book for Toronto which was put together over 10 years ago by two young mothers. It is updated yearly. There are many coupons in the back, valued at over $4000.

Cuddle Karrier. *www.cuddlekarrier.com. 1-877-283-3535* A popular carrier from newborn to toddler. There are eight ways to use it. $63 US.

BabySteps Children's Fund *www.babystepsgiftshop.com or call 905-707-1030.* Personalized gifts for all. Puzzle stools, coat racks & more. Baby's 1st Year/School Frames for monthly baby/annual school photos. Funky hairbrushes and much more. All proceeds to Hospital for Sick Children. They offer a wonderful selection of great gifts at reasonable prices and the money supports the hospital.

Today's Parent Magazine *www.todaysparent.com* is available monthly at a price of $18 (savings of 65% off newsstand if you order for one-year). It's an excellent national magazine, offering insight into parenting issues, nutrition, holidays, activities, etc.

Mothering 'n more *www.motheringnmore.com* is a new organization dedicated to providing education, preparation and support to women in their mothering years. They offer pre- and post-natal courses designed women to come while pregnant and then after with their newborns. Topics include nutrition, CPR, strollers, baby massage, and more.

Vancouver

Crocodile 2156 West 4th Avenue, Vancouver, 604-730-0232 *www.crocodilebaby.com.* They carry a wide range of strollers, including the Peg Pliko ($319), Maclaren Techno ($489), Maclaren Triumph ($279), Mountain Buddy Urban Jogger ($499) and the Bugaboo Frog ($1050). They sell cribs (the number one seller is $439), change tables, gliders with ottomans ($529). Peg Perego high chairs are sold from $219-$239. They sell car seats too including Graco, Peg Perego and Britax. You can find toys, videos and other child-friendly items. Parking is available at the back of the store.

Baby's World *6-1300 Woolridge Street, Coquitlam, BC 604-515-0888 www.itsababysworld.com.* Furniture lines include AP and EG. They have a large selection of strollers including Inglesina and Peg Perego. Sample prices include: Peg Atlantico $449, Peg Pliko $369, Peg Pliko Pramette $519, Snap 'n Go $129, Inglesina Zippy $399 and Inglesina Swift $209. They also have a Chicco Caddy umbrella stroller with tall handles, a rain cover and carrying bag for sale at $129. Peg car seats are $239 and Graco infant car seats are $189. They have Baby Bjorns from $129.

Vancouver Maternity Clothing

Hazel & Company *3190 Cambie St 604-730-8689* They carry a wide selection of their own brands and other well-known brands. Offer casual and dressy clothes (mix & match two-piece set, tops run from $65 to $75 and skirts $59). Jean brands include Rebel, Tummyline, Duet and range from $50 to $95 (low-rise are more expensive). They do carry Bravado undergarments, maternity bras $37 and underwear $15. Open seven days a week. There are two parking spots behind the store, otherwise look for lot parking nearby.

Thyme Maternity *www.thymematernity.com* has several locations in British Columbia including: Burnaby, Richmond, Victoria, Surrey, Coquitlam, Abbotsford.

Kid Clothing & Consignment

Boomers & Echoes Kid's & Maternity, *1985 Lonsdale Ave. (at 20th) 604-984-6163; web: boomersandechoes.com.* Boomers and Echoes carries: new and consigned quality items; new maternity including Rebel, Ripe, Duet, Bravado & Gem (jeans from $15, tops from $9.95 including tanks, nursing tops); seasonal clothing such as capris, shorts, sweaters is always available. New kids' wear including Robeez, Kushies, Baby Byon, Jelly Beans, Vals Kids & more; consignment including maternity and kids wear (by appointment only); car seats, strollers, furniture. Boomers and Echoes takes great pride in re-merchandising the store with new and consignment and ensures stock reflects current fashions. Large turn-over of inventory but items such as a Chariot Jogger ($375) and Peg Perego Pliko ($149) have been seen there. Plenty of parking in back.

Little Critters Outfitters *5631-176A St., Cloverdale (604) 575-2500* is children's store carrying new and nearly new clothing, toys, furniture and accessories at a fraction of the original price. They offer the style and quality of brand names such as Gap, Oshkosh, Tommy, Gymboree, V-tech, Fisher Price, Little Tikes and Discovery Toys. Examples of prices include a Gap Fleece Hoody ($15), Girls Cardigan

($18-$20) and toys are for sale at approximately 50% off original prices. They also feature a great selection of new and consigned dance wear. Their Critter Card program gives you 10%-20% back on all your purchases and there is no fee to join.

Trendy Tots: *22344 Dewdney Trunk Rd, Maple Ridge, (604) 467-0330* Name-brand clothing, books, videos, toys and infant care items! Trendy Tots offers a great alternative to consignment. The store buys your items outright. All seasons of clothing from newborn to teen and maternity wear are accepted, as are baby equipment, furniture and toys. Trendy Tots only accepts items in excellent condition. No appointment is necessary.

Online Resources

◆ Don't want to leave the comfort of your home? Visit *www.canadaretail.ca/Babies.html* for Canadian baby products, priced in Canadian dollars. Tons of links and resources for local and national shopping.

◆ Here are some web sites that offer discounts for parents of multiples: *www.multiplebirthscanada.org*. Brand offerings include: Huggies, Pampers, Diaper Genie, Similac, Evenflo

◆ For you crafty people out there who are looking to document the first years of their babies lives, check out **Scrapbook Warehouse** *www.scrapbookwarehouse.com* for the latest in scrapbooks, accessories, cutters, stickers. They carry over 5000 products and have over 100 scrapbooks ranging from $12 to $60. They will teach you how to use the products you buy (i.e. cutters and scissors) so that you will have no problems when you get home. (604) 266-4433. They also offer classes. 8932 Oak St. @ Marine Dr. They are located about 5 minutes from the Vancouver Airport.

◆ *Local Guides to Pregnancy and Parenting Resources*. There are interesting articles/sections on topics including: coupons and freebies, classes for kids, summer camps, pregnancy, breastfeeding, vacation guide, etc. You can also track your pregnancy with a daily journal. *toronto.parentzone.com. vancouver.parentzone.com, montreal.parentzone.com.*

Additional resources for Vancouver and Montreal are on our web site, BabyBargains.com (click on Bonus Material).

APPENDIX B

Sample registry

Here's the coolest thing about registering for baby products at Babies R Us—that neato bar code scanner gun. You're supposed to walk (waddle?) around the store and zap the bar codes of products you want to add to the registry. This is cool for about 15 seconds, until you realize you have to make DECISIONS about WHAT to zap.

What to do? Yes, you could page through this book as you do the registry, but that's a bit of a pain, no? To help speed the process, here's a list of what stuff you need and what to avoid. Consider it *Baby Bargains* in a nutshell:

The order of these recommendations follows the Babies R Us Registry form:

Car Seats/Strollers/Carriers/Accessories

◆ *Full Size Convertible Car Seat.* Basically, we urge waiting on this one—most babies don't need to go into a full-size convertible seat until they outgrow an infant seat (that could be in four to six months or as much as a year). In the meantime, new models are always coming out with better safety features. Hence, don't register for this and wait to buy it later.

If want to ignore this advice, go for the **Britax Roundabout** ($220) or **Marathon** ($270). Two other good choices for less money: the **Cosco Scenera** ($50) or the **Sunshine Kids Radian 65** ($200).

◆ *Infant car seat.* Best bet: the **Graco SnugRide** ($72-$150).

◆ *Strollers.* There is no "one size fits all" recommendation in this section. Read the lifestyle recommendations in Chapter 8 to find a stroller that best fits your needs. In general, stay away from the pre-packaged "travel systems"—remember that many of the better stroller brands now can be used with infant seats.

◆ *Baby Carriers.* Ergo Baby Carrier ($92). You really don't need another carrier (like a backpack) unless you plan to do serious outdoor hikes. If that is the case, check Chapter 8 for suggestions.

◆ *Misc.* Yes, your infant car seat should come with an infant head support pillow, so if you buy one of these separately, use it in your stroller. There really isn't a specific brand preference in this category (all basically do the same thing). Any other stroller accessories are purely optional.

SAMPLE REGISTRY

Travel Yards/High Chairs/Exercisers/Accessories

◆ **Gates.** The best brand is *KidCo* (which makes the Gateway, Safeway and Elongate). But this is something you can do later—most babies aren't mobile until at least six months of age.

◆ **Travel Yard/Playard.** Graco's *Pack 'N Play* is the best bet. Go for one with a bassinet feature.

◆ **High Chair.** The best high chair is the Fisher Price Healthy Care ($90-$100)—go for the Aquarium or RainForest version.

◆ **Walker/Exerciser.** Skip the walker; an excerciser is optional. Good model: ExerSaucer Classic Activity Center. See Chapter 7 for details.

◆ **Swing.** We like Graco's swings ($100 or so) best.

◆ **Hook on high chair.** Graco's Travel Lite table chair is $35—affordable and easy to use.

◆ **Infant jumper.** Too many injuries with this product category; pass on it.

◆ **Bed rail.** Don't need this either.

◆ **Bouncer.** Fisher Price (fisher-price.com) makes the most popular one in the category—their basic bouncer is about $20.

Cribs/Furniture

◆ **Crib.** For cribs, you've got two basic choices: a simple model that is, well, just a crib or a "convertible" model that eventually morphs into a twin or full size bed. In the simple category for best buys, *Child Craft's Shaker Ridge* crib is a basic hardwood crib for just $200. Other features that are nice (but not necessary) for cribs include a double drop side, a quiet rail release and hidden hardware. If you fancy an imported crib, there are few bargains but we found that *Sorelle/C&T* has reasonable prices ($300 or so) for above average quality.

◆ **Bassinet.** Skip it. See Chapter 2 for details. If you buy a playpen with bassinet feature, you don't need a separate bassinet.

◆ **Dressing/changing table.** Skip it. Just use the top of your dresser as a changing area. (See dresser recommendation below.)

◆ **Glider/rocker and ottoman.** In a word: *Dutailier*. Whatever style/fabric you chose, you can't go wrong with that brand. Hint: this is a great product to buy online at a discount, so you might want to skip registering for one. **Shermag** is another great brand.

◆ **Dresser.** Dressers and other case pieces by **Munire** is our top pick—prices run about $600. Quality is excellent.

◆ **Misc.** Babies R Us recommends registering for all sorts of miscellaneous items like cradles, toy boxes and the like. Obviously, these are clearly optional.

Bedding/Room Décor/Crib Accessories

◆ **Crib set.** Don't—don't register for this waste of money. Instead, just get two or three good crib sheets and a nice cotton blanket or the Halo Sleep Sack. See Chapter 3 for brands.

◆ **Bumper pads, dust ruffle, diaper stacker.** Ditto—a waste.

◆ **Lamp, mobile.** These are optional, of course. We don't have any specific brand preferences.

◆ **Mattress.** We like the foam mattresses from **Colgate** ($100 for the Classica I). Or, for coil, go for **Simmons** Super Maxipedic 160 coil mattress for $100 at Babies R Us. Unfortunately, Babies R Us and other chains don't sell foam mattresses but you can find them online.

◆ **Misc.** Babies R Us has lots of miscellaneous items in this area like rugs, wallpaper border, bassinet skirts and so on. We have ideas for décor on the cheap in Chapter 3.

Infant Toys, Care & Feeding

◆ **Toys:** All of this (crib toys, bath toys, blocks) is truly optional. We have ideas for this in Chapter 6.

◆ **Nursery monitor.** In general, *Fisher Price* and *Sony* are the best bets but keep the receipt—many baby monitors don't work well because of electronic interference in the home. The **Graco imonitor** is the best bet among digital offerings.

◆ **Humidifier.** The *Holmes/Duracraft* line sold in Target is best. Avoid the "baby" humidifiers sold in baby stores, as they are overpriced.

◆ **Diaper pail.** The *Baby Trend Diaper Champ* is best.

◆ **Bathtub.** While not a necessity, a baby bath tub is a nice convenience—try to borrow one or buy it second hand to save. As a best bet, we suggest the *EuroBath by Primo*—it's a $30 bath tub that works well.

◆ ***Bottles.*** *Born Free* is the best bet, according to our readers.

◆ ***Bottle Warmer.*** Also optional—remember, baby doesn't need to have a warm bottle! But if you insist, go for the Avent's ***Express Bottle and Baby Food Warmer*** ($40). It can heat a bottle in four minutes.

◆ ***Sterilizer.*** Also optional, *Avent's* "*Microwave Steam Sterilizer*" ($30) is a good choice. It holds four bottles of any type and is easy to use—just put in water and nuke for eight minutes.

◆ ***Thermometer.*** Don't register for a fancy thermometer—the cheap options at the drug store work just as well. *First Years* has a high-speed digital thermometer ($10) that gives a rectal temp in 20 seconds and an underarm in 30 seconds. Ear thermometers are not recommended, as they are not accurate.

◆ ***Breast pump.*** There isn't a "one size fits all" recommendation here. Read Chapter 5 Maternity/Nursing for details.

◆ ***Misc.*** In this category, Babies R Us throws in items like bibs, hooded towels, washcloths, pacifiers and so on. See Chapter 4 "Reality Layette" for ideas in this category.

Diapers/Wipes

◆ ***Diapers.*** For disposables, the best deals are in warehouse clubs like *Sam's* and *Costco*. Generic diapers at *Wal-Mart* and *Target* are also good deals. We have a slew of deals on cloth diapers in Chapter 4.

◆ ***Wipes.*** Brands like *Pampers* and *Huggies* are the better bets, although some parents love the generic wipes that Costco stocks.

Clothing/Layette

◆ See the "Reality Layette" list (Ch. 4) for suggestions on quantities/brands.

APPENDIX C
Multiples advice

Yes, this year, one in 35 births in the US is to twins. As a parent-to-be of twins and that can mean double the fun when it comes to buying for baby. Here's our round-up of what products are best for parents of multiples:

Cribs

Since twins tend to be smaller than most infants, parents of multiples can use bassinets or cradles for an extended period of time. We discuss this category in depth in Chapter 2, but generally recommend looking at a portable playpen (Graco Pak N Play is one popular choice) with a bassinet feature as an alternative. A nice splurge if your budget allows it: the *Arm's Reach Co-Sleeper*.

Cool idea: a mom of twins emailed us about the Leachco Crib Divider for $25 that lets you use one crib for twins. Available on Baby Universe.com

Nursing help

Check out *EZ-2-NURSE's pillow* (800-584-TWIN; we saw it on www.doubleblessings.com). A mom told us this was the "absolute best" for her twins, adding "I could not successfully nurse my girls together without this pillow. It was wonderful." This pillow comes in both foam and inflatable versions (including a pump). Cost: $40 to $48.

Wal-Mart has a breastfeeding collection with *Lansinoh* products (including their amazing nipple cream). Check the special displays in the store or on their web site at walmart.com.

Yes, nursing one baby can be a challenge, but two? You might need some help. To the rescue comes *Mothering Multiples: Breastfeeding & Caring for Twins and More* by Karen Kerkoff Gromada ($14.95; out of print, but you can find used copies on Amazon). This book was recommend to us by more than one mother of twins for its clear and concise advice.

FYI: Skip buying a glider-rocker if you plan to nurse your twins. The large nursing pillows won't fit! Instead, go for a loveseat.

Car seats

Most multiples are born before their due date. The smallest infants may have to ride in special "car beds" that enable them to lie flat (instead of car seats that require an infant to be at least five or six pounds and ride in a sitting position). The car beds then rotate to become regular infant car seats so older infants can ride in a sitting position.

The **Cosco Dream Ride** ($70-$130, rating: A). Another option: **Graco** will debut a new travel bed for preemies in 2007. Also: EliteCarSeats.com sells the **Angel Guard AngelRide** infant car bed for $100—it can be used for premature infants up to nine pounds. . The key feature: a wrap-around harness to protect a preemie in an accident. FYI: ALL premature infants should be given a car seat test at the hospital to check for breathing problems—ask your pediatrician for details.

Another idea: check with your hospital to see if you can RENT a car bed until your baby is large enough to fit in a regular infant car seat.

Strollers

Our complete wrap-up of recommendations for double strollers is in Chapter 8 (see Double the Fun in the lifestyle recommendations). In brief, we should mention that the **Graco DuoGlider** accepts two infant seats ($125-$150). Evenflo sells a similar model with their Take Me Too tandem ($90-$160).

If Grandma is paying for a stroller as a gift, Perego's **Duette** double stroller ($790) allows parents of twins to attach TWO infant car seats (included) to the G-matic frame. (And there is also a *"Triplette"* version of this stroller).

Those strollers are great since they can handle two infant car seats, but most parents of twins find that side-by-side strollers do better for them than tandem (front/back) models. Why? Tandem strollers typically only have one seat that fully reclines (when parents of twins find they need two reclining seats). And the front/back configuration seems to invite more trouble when the twins get older—the back passenger pulling the front passenger's hair, etc.

Here are our picks for side by side strollers. For parents of twins on a tight budget, we suggest the **Jeep Twin All Weather Twin Sport Umbrella** (27 lbs.) for $80 at Wal-Mart. It's bare bones (no basket) but will get the job done with reclining seats and a compact fold. If you've got a bit more budget, the **Inglesina Double Swift** ($250, 28 lbs.) gets rave reviews from our readers, as does the **Maclaren Twin Techno** ($360, 25 lbs.) with its full reclining seats. Finally, for outdoor treks with twins, we like the **Mountain Buggy's** side-by-side double all-terrain strollers—very pricey at $520 to $660 but built to last.

In the dark horse category, consider the **Double Decker Stroller** (941-543-1582; www.doubledeckerstroller.com), a jogging stroller than can accommodate two infant car seats. It runs $265. The same company also sells a "Triple Decker," a model that will hold three babies!

As for other jogging strollers, the side-by-side versions of **Dreamer Design** and **Baby Jogger** are probably best if you really plan to exercise with a sport stroller.

Carrier

A mom of twins emailed us to rave about the **MaxiMom** carrier. She found it easier to use and adjust. The best feature: you adjust it to be a sling and nurse a baby in it. We saw this carrier on 4CoolKids (4coolkids.com) for $85 for twins; a triplet version is $125.

Deals/Freebies

◆ Chain stores like Babies R Us and Baby Depot offer a 10% discount if you buy multiples of identical items like cribs.

◆ Get a *$7 off coupon for the Diaper Genie from Playtex* when you send proof of multiple births to Playtex (800) 222-0453; www.playtex.com.

◆ *Kimberly Clark Twins Program:* Get a gift of "high-value coupons" for Huggies diapers by submitting birth certificates or published birth announcements. (800) 544-1847).

◆ *The First Years* offers free rattles for parents of multiples when you send in copies of birth certificates. Web: www.thefirstyears.com.

◆ *The National Mothers of Twins Clubs* (www.nomotc.org) has fantastic yard/garage sales. Check their web page for a club near you.

Source: Twins Magazine is a bi-monthly, full-color magazine published by The Business Word (800) 328-3211 or (303) 290-8500 (www.twinsmagazine.com). Remember that offers can change at any time. Check with the companies first before sending any info.

Miscellaneous

For clothes, make sure you get "preemie" sizes instead of the suggestions in our layette chapter—twins are smaller at birth than singleton babies.

As we discussed earlier in this book, we don't think fetal monitors are a necessary expense for most parents. But, we realize that parents-to-be of multiples are a bit more nervous than others! So, if you plan to get a monitor, **BabyBeat** is one to consider. The company lets you rent the device instead of buying—$18 to $50 per month depending on the model. You can also buy the unit at $450 to $600. For details, call 888-758-8822 or babybeat.com. Unlike cheaper ultrasound monitors that are low-quality, BabyBeat is similar to the Doppler instruments found in doctor's offices. FYI: You must have a prescription from your doctor before purchasing a fetal monitor; be sure to check with your OB before any purchase.

APPENDIX D
Phone/Web Sites

Contract Name	Toll-Free	Phone	Web Site

General Baby Product Manufacturers

Baby Trend	(800) 328-7363	(909) 773-0018	babytrend.com
Chicco	(877) 4-CHICCO		chiccousa.com
Cosco	(800) 457-5276	(812) 372-0141	djgusa.com
Evenflo	(800) 233-5921	(937) 415-3229	evenflo.com
First Years	(800) 225-0382	(508) 588-1220	thefirstyears.com
Fisher Price	(800) 828-4000	(716) 687-3000	fisher-price.com
Graco	(800) 345-4109	(610) 286-5951	gracobaby.com
Peg Perego		(260) 482-8191	perego.com
Safety 1st	(800) 962-7233	(781) 364-3100	safety1st.com

Introduction

Alan & Denise Fields (authors)		(303) 442-8792	babybargains.com

Chapter 2: Nursery Necessities

JCPenney	(800) 222-6161		jcpenney.com
CPSC	(800) 638-2772		cpsc.gov
Baby Furniture Plus			babyfurnitureplus.com
Baby News			babynewsstores.com
NINFRA			ninfra.com
USA Baby			usababy.com
EcoBaby			ecobaby.com
Hoot Judkins			hootjudkins.com
Crib N Carriage			cribncarriage.com
Baby Furniture Outlet	(800) 613-9280	(519) 649-2590	babyfurnitureoutlet.com
Buy Buy Baby			buybuybaby.com
Babies R Us	(888) BABYRUS		babiesrus.com
Baby Depot	(800) 444-COAT		coat.com
Room & Board			roomandboard.com
Baby Furniture Warehouse			babyfurniturewarehouse.com
Fun Rugs			funrugs.com
Decorate Today			decoratetoday.com
Rugs USA			rugsusa.com
NetKidsWear			netkidswear.com
Baby Bunk			babybunk.com
Kiddie Kastle (outlet)		(502) 499-9667	
Baby Boudoir (outlet)	(800) 272-2293	(508) 998-2166	
Pottery Barn (outlet)		(901) 763-1500	potterybarnkids.com
Baby Catalog America	(800) PLAY-PEN		babycatalog.com
Baby Style			babystyle.com
Pottery Barn Kids			PotteryBarnKids.com
Danny Foundation			dannyfoundation.org
Great Beginnings	(800) 886-9077	(301) 417-9702	childrensfurniture.com
Rocking Chair Outlet			rockingchairoutlet.com
Crib parts			productamerica.com
Amish Furniture Makers			SimplyAmish.com
AmishOak.com			StoneBarnFunishings.com
AmishOakInTexas.com			PureOak.com
AmishEtc.com			

Crib manufacturers

Amby Baby Bed			AmbyBaby.com
Angel Line	(800) 889-8158	(856) 863-8009	angelline.com
AP Industries	(800) 463-0145	(418) 728-2145	apindustries.com
Baby Appleseed			babyappleseed.com
Baby's Dream	(800) TEL-CRIB	(912) 649-4404	babysdream.com
Bassett		(540) 629-6000	bassettfurniture.com
Bellini	(800) 332-BABY	(516) 234-7716	bellini.com
Berg		(908) 354-5252	bergfurniture.com
Bonavita	(888) 266-2848	(732) 346-5150	bonavita-cribs.com
Bratt Déécor	(888) 24-BRATT	(410) 327-4600	brattedecor.com
Canalli		(973) 247-7222	canallifurniture.com
Cara Mia	(877) 728-0342	(705) 328-0342	caramiafurniture.com
Capretti Home			caprettihome.com
Chanderic	(800) 363-2635	(819) 566-1515	www.shermag.com
Child Craft		(812) 883-3111	childcraftind.com
Corsican Kids	(800) 421-6247	(323) 587-3101	corsican.com
Creations			creationsbaby.com
Generation 2	(800) 736-1140	(334) 792-1144	childdesigns.com
Delta		(718) 385-1000	deltaenterprise.com
Domusindo			domusindo.com
ducduc			ducducnyc.com
Dutailier			Dutailier.com
Eden			edenbaby.com
El Greco			elgrecofurniture.com
Ethan Allen	(888) EAHELP-1		ethanallen.com
LA Baby			lababyco.com
Land of Nod			landofnod.com
Litto			littokids.com
Million Dollar Baby		(323) 728-9988	milliondollarbaby.com
Morigeau/Lepine	(800) 326-2121	(724) 941-7475	morigeau.com
Mother Hubbard		(416) 661-8201	mhcfurniture.com
Munire	(973) 574-1040		MunireFurniture.com
Natart		(819) 364-2052	natartfurniture.com
Netto Collection			nettocollection.com
Newport Cottage			newportcottages.com
Nursery Smart			nurserysmart.com
Oeuf			oeufnyc.com
Pali	(877) 725-4772		paliltaly.com
Pottery Barn	(800) 430-7373		potterybarnkids.com
Ragazzi			ragazzi.com
Restore & Restyle			see target.com
Relics		(612) 374-0861	relicsfurniture.com
Romina			rominakidsfurniture.com
Room and Board			roomandboard.com
RT Furniture			rtfurnitureusa.com
Sauder			sauder.com
Simmons		(920) 982-2140	simmonsjp.com
Simplicity	(800) 448-4308		simplicityforchildren.com
Sorelle	(888) 470-1260	(201) 461-9444	sorellefurniture.com
Stanley	(888) 839-6822		stanleyfurniture.com
Stokke/Sleepi	(877) 978-6553		stokkeusa.com
Stork Craft		(604) 274-5121	storkcraft.com
Westwood Design			westwoodbaby.com
Young America by Stanley			stanleyfurniture.com
Babies Boutique			babiesboutique.com
IKEA		(610) 834-0180	ikea.com
JPMA		(856) 439-0500	jpma.org
Arm's Reach	(800) 954-9353		armsreach.com

web/phone directory

Colgate		(404) 681-2121	colgatekids.com
Halo Innovations	(888) 999-4256	(218) 525-5158	halosleep.com
SIDS Alliance			SidsAlliance.org

Moses Baskets:

Moses Baskets		mosesbaskets.com
Badger Baskets		badgerbaskets.com

Sleep Tight Soother	(800) NO-COLIC		colic.com
Burlington Basket Co.	(800) 553-2300	(319) 754-6508	burlingtonbasket.com
Container Store	(800) 733-3532		containerstore.com
Rumble Tuff	(800) 524-9607	(801) 226-2648	rumbletuff.com
Camelot Furniture		(714) 283-4194	
Dutailier	(800) 363-9817	(450) 772-2403	dutailier.com
Rocking Chairs 100%	(800) 4-ROCKER		rocking-chairs.com
Brooks	(800) 427-6657	(423) 626-1111	
Conant Ball	(800) 363-2635	(819) 566-1515	shermag.com
Towne Square	(800) 356-1663		gliderrocker.com
American Health	(800) 327-4382		foryourbaby.com
Lee Rowan	(800) 325-6150		leerowan.com
Hold Everything	(800) 421-2264		holdeverything.com
Closet Factory	(800) 692-5673		closetfactory.com
California Closets	(800) 274-6754		californiaclosets.com
Shades of Light	(800) 262-6612		shades-of-light.com

Mattresses

Moonlight Slumber		moonlightslumber.com
NaturePedic		naturepedic.com
NaturaWorld		naturaworld.com
Container Store		containerstore.com
Best Chair		bestchair.com
Rocky Chairs 100%		rocking-chairs.com
Little Castle		littlecastleinc.com
Plow & Hearth		plowhearth.com

Closet Organizers

Closet Maid		closetmaid.com
Closet Factory		closetfactory.com
Closet Maid	(800) 874-0008	closetmaid.com
Mills Pride	(800) 441-0337	millspride.com
Mommy Bee Happy		mommybeehappy.com
Itzbeen Baby Care Timer		itzbeen.com

Chapter 3: Bedding & Déécor

Baby Supermarket		babysupermarket.com
Overstock		overstock.com
Country Lane		countrylane.com
Basic Comfort	(800) 456-8687	basiccomfort.com
Kiddopotamus	(800) 772-8339	kiddopotamus.com
Clouds & Stars		cloudsandstars.com
Michaels Arts/Crafts	(800) MICHAELS	michaels.com
Stay Put safety sheet		babysheets.com
Baby-Be-Safe		baby-be-safe.com
Wall Nutz		wallnutz.com
Blik Re-Stik stickers		whatisblik.com
WallPops!		Wall-pops.com
Wallies		wallies.com
Creative Images artwork		crimages.com

Outlets

Garnet Hill	(802) 362-6198
The Interior Alternative	(413) 743-1986

Bedding Manufacturers

Amy Coe	(203) 221-3050	amycoe.com
Baby Guess	(714) 895-2250	crowncraftsinfantproducts.com
Bananafish	(800) 899-8689	(818) 727-1645 bananafishinc.com
Beautiful Baby	(903) 295-2229	bbaby.com
Blueberry Lane	(413) 528-9633	blueberrylanehome.com
Blue Moon Baby	(626) 455-0014	bluebaby.com
Brandee Danielle	(800) 720-5656	(714) 957-1240 brandeedanielle.com
California Kids	(800) 548-5214	(650) 637-9054 calkids.com
Carters	(800) 845-3251	(803) 275-2541 carters.com
Celebrations	(310) 532-2499	baby-celebrations.com
Cotton Tale	(800) 628-2621	(714) 435-9558 cottontaledesigns.com
CoCaLo	(714) 434-7200	cocalo.com
Crown Crafts	(714) 895-9200	crowncraftsinfantproducts.com
Dwell		dwellshop.com
Fleece Baby		fleecebaby.com
Gerber	(800) 4-GERBER	gerber.com
Glenna Jean	(800) 446-6018	(804) 561-0687 glennajean.com
Hoohobbers	(773) 890-1466	hoohobbers.com
KidsLine	(310) 660-0110	kidslineinc.com
Kimberly Grant	(714) 546-4411	kimberlygrant.com
JoJo Designs		amazon.com
Lambs & Ivy	(800) 345-2627	(310) 839-5155 lambsivy.com
Luv Stuff	(800) 825-BABY	(972) 278-BABY luvstuffbedding.com
Martha Stewart		kmart.com
Maddie Boo		maddieboobedding.com
Mr. Bobbles Blankets		MrBobblesBlankets.com
My Baby Sam		mybabysam.com
Nava's Design	(818) 988-9050	navasdesigns.com
Nojo	(800) 854-8760	(310) 763-8100 nojo.com
Nurseryworks		nurseryworks.net
Patchkraft	(800) 866-2229	(973) 340-3300 patchkraft.com
Picci		picci.it
Pine Creek	(503) 266-6275	pinecreekbedding.com
Quiltex	(800) 237-3636	(212) 594-2205 quiltex.com
Red Calliope	(800) 421-0526	(310) 763-8100 redcalliope.com
Sleeping Partners	(212) 254-1515	sleepingpartners.com
Springs	(212) 556-6300	springs.com
Sweet Kyla	(800) 265-2229	sweetkyla.com
Sumersault	(800) 232-3006	(201) 768-7890 sumersault.com
Sweet Pea	(626) 578-0866	
Trend Lab Baby		trend-lab.com
Wendy Bellissimo	(818) 348-3682	wendybellissimo.com
Creative Images	(800) 784-5415	(904) 825-6700 crimages.com
Eddie Bauer	(800) 426-8020	eddiebauer.com
The Company Store	(800) 323-8000	companykids.com
Garnet Hill	(800) 622-6216	garnethill.com
Graham Kracker	(800) 489-2820	grahamkracker.com
The Land of Nod	(800) 933-9904	landofnod.com
Lands' End	(800) 345-3696	landsend.com
Pottery Barn Kids	(800) 430-7373	potterybarnkids.com

Chapter 4: Reality Layette

Bella Kids	bellakids.com
One of a Kind Kid	oneofakindkid.com
Preemie.com	preemie.com
SuddenlyMommies	suddenlymommies.com
Kids Surplus	kidssurplus.com
Internet Resale Directory	secondhand.com

Nat'l Assoc. Resale & Thrift		narts.org
Minnetonka Moccasins	(718) 365-7033	minnetonka-by-mail.com
Robeez shoes	(800) 929-2623	(604) 435-9074	robeez.com
Bobux shoes		bobuxusa.com
Scootees		scootees.com
Once Upon a Child	(614) 791-0000	onceuponachild.com

Outlets

Carter's	(888) 782-9548	(770) 961-8722
Flapdoodles		(970) 262-9351
Hanna Andersson		(503) 697-1953
Hartstrings		(610) 687-6900
Health-Tex	(800) 772-8336	(914) 428-7551	vfc.com
JcPenney outlet	(800) 222-6161		jcpenney.com
Osh Kosh		(920) 231-8800	oshkoshbgosh.com
Talbot's Kids	(800) 543-7123	(781) 740-8888	talbots.com
Outlet Bound mag	(800) 336-8853		outletbound.com

Clothing Manufacturers

Baby Gap	(800) GAP-STYLE	babygap.com
Baby Lulu		babylulu.com
Carter's	(770) 961-8722	carters.com
Cozy Toes		cozytoes.com
Flap Happy	(800) 234-3527	flaphappy.com
Flapdoodles	(302) 731-9793	flapdoodles.com
Funtasia! Too	(214) 634-7770	funtasiatoo.com
H & M		hm.com
Hanna Andersson		hannaandersson.com
Hartstrings/Kitestrings	(212) 868-0950	hartstrings.com
Hedgehog		hedgehogusa.com
Jake and Me	(970) 352-8802	jakeandme.com
Janie and Jack		janieandjack.com
Little Lubbaloo		littlelubbaloo.com
Little Me	(800) 533-5497	littleme.com
LL Bean		llbean.com
MiniBoden		miniboden.com
MulberriBush (Tumbleweed too)		mulberribush.com
Naartjie		naartjie.com
OshKosh B'Gosh	(800) 692-4674	oshkoshbgosh.com
Patsy Aiken	(919) 872-8789	patsyaiken.com
Pingarama		pingorama.com
Sarah's Prints	(888) 477-4687	sarasprints.com
Sweet Potatoes/Spudz	(800) 634-2584	sweetpotatoesinc.com
Wes & Willy		wesandwilly.com
Zutano		zutano.com
Children's Place		childrensplace.com
Good Lad of Phila.	(215) 739-0200	goodlad.com
Gymboree	(877) 449-6932	gymboree.com
Lands End		landsend.com
Le Top	(800) 333-2257	letop-usa.com
Sprockets (Mervyn's)		mervyns.com
Target (Little Me, Classic Pooh, Halo, Tykes, Circo)		target.com
Wal-Mart (Faded Glory)		walmart.com

Catalogs

Childrens Wear	(800) 242-5437	cwdkids.com
Hanna Andersson	(800) 222-0544	hannaandersson.com
Lands End	(800) 963-4816	landsend.com
LL Kids	(800) 552-5437	llbean.com
Patagonia Kids	(800) 638-6464	patagonia.com
Talbot's Kids	(800) 543-7123	talbots.com
Wooden Soldier	(800) 375-6002	(603) 356-7041	woodensoldier.com

Disney Catalog	(800) 237-5751	disneystore.com
Fitigues	(800) 235-9005	fitigues.com
Campmor	(800) 226-7667	campmor.com
Sierra Trading Post	(800) 713-4534	sierratradingpost.com

Diapers

BioKleen		biokleen.com
All Together Diaper Company		clothdiaper.com
Baby Lane		thebabylane.com
Diapers 4 Less		diapers4less.com
Drug Emporium		drugemporium.com
CVS Pharmacy		cvspharmacy.com
Baby's Heaven		babysheaven.com
Diaper Site		diapersite.com
Costco		costco.com
Weebees		weebees.com
Baby J		babyj.com
BarefootBaby		Barefootbaby.com
Kelly's Closet		kellyscloset.com
Jardine Diapers		jardinediapers.com
Baby Bunz	(800) 676-4559	babybunz.com
Organic Bebe		organicbebe.com
Huggies		huggies.com
Luvs		luvs.com
Diaper Wraps		diaperaps.com
Tushies		tushies.com
Nature Boy & Girl		natureboyandgirl.com

Cloth Diaper Resources

Diaper Changes book	(800) 572-1826	homekeepers.com
Mother-Ease		motherease.com
Kushies	(800) 841-5330	kushies.com
DiaperDance		diaperdance.com
Daisy Diapers		diasydiapers.com
All Together	(801) 566-7579	clothdiaper.com
Bumkins	(800) 338-7581	bumkins.com
Indisposables	(800) 663-1730	
Baby J		babyj.com
Barefoot Baby		barefootbaby.com
		kellyscloset.com
		cottonbabies.com
		aunaturalbaby.com
		babybunz.com
Baby Because		babybecause.com
Seventh Generation		seventhgeneration.com
Sugar Plum Babies		monkeytoediapers.com/sugarplumbaby
Bizzy B Hive		hyenacart.com/bizzybhive
Bijou Baby Gear		bijoubabygear.com
Benjamuffins		benjamuffins.com
AngelDry		angeldrydiapers.com
Bummis		bummis.com
Luxe		Sluxebabydiapers.com
Bizzy B Hive		hyenacart.com/bizzybhive
Proraps		prodiaper.net

All-In –Ones:

Girl Woman Goddess		girlwomangoddess.com
Lullaby Diapers		lullabydiapers.com
Daisy Doodles		daisy-doodles.com
Cuddlebuns		cuddlebunsdiapers.com
DryBees		drybees.com

web/phone directory

Pockets:		
Happy Heiny's		happyheinys.com
Olive Branch Baby Marathon		olivebranchbaby.com
Sams Club		samsclub.com
BJ's		bjswholesale.com
Baby Works	(800) 422-2910	babyworks.com
Nurtured Baby	(888) 564-BABY	nurturedbaby.com

Chapter 5: Maternity/Nursing

Expressive		expressiva.com
Motherwear		Motherwear.com
eStyle		estyle.com
2 Chix		2chix.com
Maternity 4 Less		maternity4less.com
Fashion Bug		fashionbug.com
Mom Shop		momshop.com
One Hot Mama		onehotmama.com
Thyme Maternity		thymematernity.com
Birth and Baby		birthandbaby.com
Mommy Gear		mommygear.com
Fit Maternity		fitmaternity.com
Liz Lange Maternity		lizlange.com
Naissance Maternity		naissancematernity.com
Pumpkin Maternity		pumpkinmaternity.com
Twinkle Little Star		twinklelittlestar.com
Baby Becoming		babybecoming.com
Motherhood		maternitymall.com
Plus Maternity		plusmaternity.com
Jake and Me Clothing Company		jakeandme.com
Eva Lillian		evalillian.com
Isabella Oliver		isabellaoliver.com
Prenatal Cradle		prenatalcradle.com
Bella Band		bellaband.com
Bravado Bras		bravadodesigns.com
Playtex Bras		playtex.com
Danish Wool breast pads		danishwool.com
LilyPadz		lilypadz.com
Soothies		soothies.com
Elizabeth Lee		Elizabethlee.com
Majamas		Majamas.com
Wears The Baby		wearsthebaby.com
Yes Breastfeeding		yesbreastfeeding.com
iMaternity		Simaternity.com
Fit Maternity		fitmaternity.com
Due Maternity		duematernity.com
Decent Exposures		decentexposures.com
Birth and Baby		birthandbaby.com
One Hanes Place		onehanesplace.com
Simplicity Patterns		simplicity.com
McCall Patterns		mccall.com
Destination Maternity Superstore		destinationmaternity.com

Chapter 6: Feeding

Breastfeeding

La Leche League	(800) LALECHE		lalecheleague.org
Nursing Mothers' Council		(408) 272-1448	nursingmothers.org
Int'l Lactation Consultants Assoc		(703) 560-7330	iblce.org
Bosom Buddies	(888) 860-0041	(720) 482-0109	bosombuddies.com
Avent	(800) 542-8368		aventamerica.com

Medela	(800) 435-8316		medela.com
White River Concepts		(800) 824-6351	
Ameda Egnell	(800) 323-4060		hollister.com
My Brest Friend	(800) 555-5522		zenoffproducts.com
EZ-2-Nurse	(800) 584-TWIN		everythingmom.com
MedRino			breastpumps-breastfeeding.com
Nursing Mothers Supplies			nursingmotherssupplies.com
Baily Medical			bailymed.com
Affordable Medela Pumps			affordable-medela-pumps.com
Mother's Milk			mothersmilkbreastfeeding.com

Baby Formula

Baby's Only Organic		babyorganic.com
BabyMil	(800) 344-1358	storebrandformulas.com
Mothers Milk Mate	(800) 499-3506	mothersmilkmate.com
Bottle Burper	(800) 699-BURP	

Bottles

Dr Brown's			babyfree.com
Munchkin	(800) 344-2229	(818) 893-5000	munchkininc.com
BreastBottle			breastbottle.com

Baby Food

Beech-Nut	(800) BEECHNUT	beechnut.com
Earth's Best	(800) 442-4221	earthsbest.com
Gerber		gerber.com
Healthy Times		healthytimes.com
Natures Goodness		naturesgoodness.com
Super Baby Food book		superbabyfood.com

High chairs

Boon	(888) 376-4763	booninc.com
Calla Chair		callachair.com
Rochelle		rochellefurniture.com
Stokke		stokkeUSA.com
Svan of Sweden		scandinavianchild.com

Chapter 7: Around the House

Kel-Gar	(972) 250-3838	kelgar.com
EuroBath		primobaby.com
Comfy Kids	(888) 529-4934	comfykids.com
Nature Company		naturecompany.com
Container Store	(800) 733-3532	containerstore.com
Diaper Genie	(800) 843-6430	playtexbaby.com
Toy Portfolio		toyportfolio.com
Buffoodles		marymeyer.com
Infantino	(800) 365-8182	infantino.com
Gymini	(800) 843-6292	tinylove.com
EZ Bather Deluxe	(800) 546-1996	dexproducts.com

Coupon sites

Fat Wallet	fatwallet.com	Clever Moms	clevermoms.com
Mobicam			getmobi.com
Philips Baby Monitors			consumer.Philips.com
BeBe Sounds			unisar.com
Summer Infant Products			summerinfant.com

Chapter 8: Car Seats

NHTSA	(888) DASH2DOT	(202) 366-0123	nhtsa.dot.gov
American Academy of Pediatrics			aap.org
National Safe Kids Campaign			safekids.org
Safety Belt Safe USA			carseat.org
Car Seat Data			carseatdata.org
Fit for a Kid			fitforakid.org

web/phone directory

Safety Alerts			safetyalerts.com
ParentsPlace			parentsplace.com
Auto Safety Hotline	(800) 424-9393		
Might Tite	(888) 336-7909		might-tite.com
Fit for a Kid	(877) FIT4AKID		fit4akid.org
Britax	(888) 4-BRITAX	(704) 409-1700	childseat.com
Compass			compassbaby.com
Orbit			Orbitbaby.com
Recaro			Recaro-nao.com
SafeGuard			safeguardseat.com
Sunshine Kids			sunshinekidsjp.com
Strolex Sit N Stroll			Strolex.com
Kiddopotamus	(800) 772-8339		kiddopotamus.com

Chapter 9: Strollers & To-Go Gear

Traveling Tikes			travelingtikes.com
Lots4Tots			lots4tots.com
PePeny canopies			pepeny.com
Aprica		(310) 639-6387	apricausa.com
Baby Jogger			babyjogger.com
Baby Planet		630-790-3113	Baby-Planet.com
BeBeLove USA			BeBeLoveUSA.com
BOB Strollers			bobgear.com
Britax			britaxusa.com
BumbleRide	800-530-3930		bumbleride.com
Chariot			ChariotCarriers.com
Chicco	(877) 4-CHICCO	(732) 805-9200	chiccousa.com
Compass	888-899-2229		CompassBaby.com
Dreamer Design		509-574-8085	dreamerdesign.net.
GoGo Babyz			GoGoBabyZ.com
Inglesina	(877) 486-5112	(973) 746-5112	Inglesina.com
Jane	866-355-2630		janeusa.com
Joovy		214-761-1809	joovy.com
J. Mason		(818) 993-6800	jmason.com
Kelty		303-530-7670	kelty.com
Kool Stop	800-586-3332	714-738-497	koolstop.com
Maclaren	(877) 504-8809	(203) 354-4400	maclarenbaby.com
Mia Moda		610-373-6888	MiaModainc.com.
MicraLite Strollers	877-844-9575		Euro-Baby.com
Motobecane			motobecane.com
Mountain Buggy			mountainbuggy.com
Mutsy		973-243-0234	Mutsy.com
Phil & Ted Most			philandteds.com
Quinny			quinny.com
Silver Cross		858-587-4745	SilverCrossAmerica.com
Stokke	(877) 978-6553		stokkeusa.com
Stroll Air	(519) 579-4534		
Rock Star Baby (Esprit)			GTBaby.com
Tike Tech			xtechoutdoors.com
UPPABaby	800-760-2060		UppaBaby.com
Valco	(800) 610-7850.		valcobaby.com
Zooper		(503) 248-9469	zooper.com
Cozy Rosie	(877) 744-6367	(914) 244-6367	CozyRosie.com
			SewCuteBoutique.com
			ChubbySeats.com
SnazzySeat			SnazzyBaby.com
			Kangaroodle.com
Burley	(800) 311-5294		burley.com
Schwinn	(800) SCHWINN		schwinn.com

Tanjor		lodrag.com
Rhode Gear		rhodegear.com

Diaper Bags

Amy Michelle	amymichellebags.com
Chester Handbags	chesterhandbags.com
Ella	ella-bags.com
Fleurville	fleurville.com
Haiku Diaper Bags	haikubags.com
Holly Aiken	hollyaiken.com
I'm Still Me	imstillme.com
Kate Spade	katespade.com.
Kecci	kecci.com
Oi Oi	oioi.com.au
One Cool Chick	onecoolchick.com
Reese Li	reeseli.com
Skip Hop	skiphop.com
Timbuk2	timbuk2.com
Tumi	tumi.com
Vera Bradley	verabradley.com

Carriers

Maya Wrap			mayawrap.com
Over the Shoulder Baby Holder			otsbh.net
ZoloWear			zolowear.com
Walking Rock Farm			walkingrockfarm.com
Kangeroo Korner			kangerookorner.com
Cuddle Karrier			cuddlekarrier.com
Hip Hammock			hiphammock.com
Baby Bjorn	(800) 593-5522		babybjorn.com
Theodore Bean	(877) 68-TBEAN		theodorebean.com
Baby Trekker	(800) 665-3957		babytrekker.com
Kelty		(303) 530-7670	kelty.com
Tough Traveler	(800) GO-TOUGH	(518) 377-8526	toughtraveller.com
Sherpa Mountain			sherpa-mtn.com
Ergo			ErgoBabyCarrier.com
MaxiMom			4coolkids.com
Water Tot			watertot.com

Chapter 10: Childcare

Nat'l Parenting Ctr	(800) 753-6667	(818) 225-8990	tnpc.com
Au Pair in America	(800) 727-2437 x6188		aupairamerica.com
Cultural Care Au Pair (AKA EF au Pair)			culturalcare.com
EurAuPair			euraupair.com
InterExchange			interexchange.org
GoAuPair			goaupair.com

Nat'l Assoc Family Child Care (800) 359-3817		nafcc.org
Nat'l Assoc Educ Young Child. (800) 424-2460		naeyc.org
My Background Check		mybackgroundcheck.com
Choice Trust	choicetrust.com US Search	ussearch.com
International Nanny Association		nanny.org
National Association of Family Childcare		nafcc.org

Appendix A: Canada

Transport Canada	(613) 990-2309	tc.gc.ca
Canadian Auto. Assoc		caa.ca
British Columbia AAA	(604) 268-5000	bcaa.bc.ca
Canadian Parents Online (877) 325-8888		canadianparents.com

index

index

How to Reach the Authors

Have a question about

Baby Bargains?

Want to make a suggestion?

Discovered a great bargain
you'd like to share?

Contact the Authors, Denise & Alan Fields
in one of five flavorful ways:

1. By phone:
(303) 442-8792

2. By mail:
436 Pine Street, Suite 600,
Boulder, CO 80302

3. By fax:
(303) 442-3744

4. By email:
authors@BabyBargains.com

5. On our web page:
BabyBargains.com

If this address isn't active, try one of our other URL's:
www.DeniseAndAlan.com or www.WindsorPeak.com.
Or call our office at 1-800-888-0385
if you're having problems accessing the page.

What's on our web page?
◆ Parent product reviews.
◆ The latest updates on our BLOG.
◆ MESSAGE BOARDS with in-depth reader feedback.
◆ CORRECTIONS and clarifications.

If this book doesn't save you at least

$250

off your baby expenses, we'll give you a complete refund on the cost of this book!

NO QUESTIONS ASKED!

Just send the book and your mailing address to

Windsor Peak Press • 436 Pine Street, Suite T Boulder, CO, 80302.

If you have any questions, please call
(303) 442-8792.

Look at all those other baby books in the bookstore—no other author or publisher is willing to put their money where their mouth is! We are so confident that *Baby Bargains* will save you money that we guarantee it in writing!